CW01066527

From Barra to Berneray

Archaeological Survey and Excavation
in the Southern Isles of the Outer Hebrides

Sheffield Environmental and Archaeological
Research Campaign in the Hebrides

Volume 5

From Barra to Berneray

Archaeological Survey and Excavation in the Southern Isles of the Outer Hebrides

Keith Branigan and Patrick Foster

with

Colin Merrony and John Pouncett

Published by
Sheffield Academic Press Ltd
Mansion House
19 Kingfield Road
Sheffield S11 9AS
England
Tel: 44 (0)114 255 4433
Fax: 44 (0)114 255 4626

Copies of this volume and a catalogue of other archaeological
publications can be obtained from the above address or from our home page

World Wide Web - http://www.SheffieldAcademicPress.com

The publishers wish to acknowledge with gratitude a grant
from Historic Scotland in the preparation of this volume

Typeset by Aarontype Limited
and Printed on acid-free paper in Great Britain
by Bookcraft
Midsomer Norton, Somerset

British Library Cataloguing in Publication Data

A catalogue record for this book is available from the British Library

ISBN 1-84127-137-3

Contents

LIST OF FIGURES ix
LIST OF TABLES xv
CONTRIBUTORS xvii
ACKNOWLEDGMENTS xix

1. **Introduction: Search in the Southern Islands** 1
   Keith Branigan
   The Programme of Survey and Excavation 1
   The Content and Format of this Volume 2

2. **The Archaeological Survey of Barra and Vatersay** 4
   Keith Branigan
   A Brief Description of the Islands 4
   General Survey Strategy 5
   Survey Methods and Problems 6
   Site-Types 7
   The Catalogue of Sites 9

3. **An Archaeological Survey on the Southern Outer Hebridean Islands of Sandray, Pabbay, Mingulay and Berneray** 54
   Patrick Foster and Roman Krivanek with a contribution by Martin Kuna
   Introduction 54
   Geology and Vegetation 55
   Methodology for the Southern Islands Survey 56
   Site Categorization 57
   The Landscape Periods 59
   Conclusion 61
   Some Preliminary Results and Comments on the Digitization and Analysis
   of the Survey Date 61
   Martin Kuna
   Sandray Survey, 1990–1995 65
   Pabbay Survey, 1992–1998 81
   Mingulay Survey, 1991–1998 93
   Beneray or Barra Head Survey, 1992 128

4. **The Excavation of Iron Age and Later Structures at Alt Chrisal T17, Barra, 1996–1999** 147
   Patrick Foster and John Pouncett
   Introduction 147
   The Excavations, 1996–1999 149
   The Structural and Stratigraphic Sequences 150
   Coarseware 167
   Jane Timby, with Emma Gowans and John Pouncett
   Plant Remains 178
   Helen Smith
   Flaked Stone 181
   Caroline Wickham-Jones and John Pouncett
   Coarse Stone 183
   John Pouncett
   Metalwork 185
   Emma Gowans
   Early Modern Pottery 186
   Patrick Foster
   Glass 187
   Emma Gowans and John Pouncett
   Calcined Bone 187

Small Finds — 187
Emma Gowans
Discussion — 189

5. **Excavations on Barra and Vatersay** — 191
Keith Branigan and Colin Merrony
Excavation of B55 — 191
Colin Merrony
The Excavation of Kerbed Cairn VS7, South Vatersay — 192
Colin Merrony
The Excavation of Kerbed Cairn VS4B, South Vatersay — 204
Keith Branigan
A LBA/EIA Occupation Site in the Borve Valley: B54 — 216
Keith Branigan
Excavations Outside Scurrival Cave (E16), Eoligarry — 224
Keith Branigan
Cleaning of a Midden Section at Borve Broch (B5) — 230
Keith Branigan
Excavation of an Oval Enclosure, E11, on the North Coast of Barra — 231
Keith Branigan

6. **Excavations on Pabbay, 1996–1998: Dùnan Ruadh (PY10) and the Bàgh Bàn Earth-House (PY56)** — 234
Patrick Foster and John Pouncett
Dùnan Ruadh (PY10) — 234
The Bàgh Bàn Earth-House (PY56) Excavations 1997–1998 — 271

7. **Sampling Excavations on Sandray and Mingulay, 1995–1996** — 278
Patrick Foster and John Pouncett
Sheader, Sandray (SY14) — 278
Mingulay (MY384) — 291
The Faunal Remains (excluding birds) — 299
Jacqui Mulville (mammals) and C. Ingrem (fish)
Mingulay (MY10, 11 and 12) — 307
Mingulay (MY346) — 307
Mingulay (MY347) — 309

8. **The Vegetational History of Barra** — 310
Kevin Edwards and Barbara Brayshay
Abstract — 310
Introduction — 310
The Sites and Field Sampling — 310
Laboratory Methods and Presentation of Results — 311
The Early Holocene Vegetational Record — 316
The Mid to Late Holocene Vegetational Record — 316
Plant Macrofossil and Pollen Evidence from Archaeological Contexts — 317
Conclusions — 318
Acknowledgments — 318

9. **The Earlier Prehistory of Barra and Vatersay** — 319
Keith Branigan
A Mesolithic Colonization? — 319
Neolithic Settlement — 319
Neolithic Burials — 322
Neolithic Ritual — 325
Bronze Age Settlement — 327
Bronze Age Funerary Monuments: Cists — 328
Bronze Age Cairns — 330

Contents

10. **The Later Prehistory of Barra and Vatersay** 334
Keith Branigan
Thick-Walled Round and Oval Houses 334
The Smaller Roundhouses 336
Wheelhouses 337
Brochs, Duns and Forts 338
Other Iron Age Sites 343
A Crowded Iron Age Landscape? 344

11. **Barra and its Islands in the Prehistory of Northern Britain** 346
Keith Branigan
Variability and Island Identities 346
The Western Isles 348
The Atlantic Province 352

BIBLIOGRAPHY 355
ABBREVIATIONS 361

List of Figures

1.1   The Outer Hebrides south of the Sound of Barra.   2

2.1   The Isle of Barra.   5
2.2   Vatersay, showing places mentioned in the text   6
2.3   A typology of 'shelters' used by the field survey team.   8
2.4   Idealized profiles of kerbed and bordered cairns   9
2.5   A measured plan of the remains of Dun Scurrival (E15)   11
2.6   Field sketches of large roundhouses A102, G22, VN121.   15
2.7   Measure plan of a small roundhouse on Fuiay (AF7).   16
2.8   Field sketches of stone rings S25 and S26.   21
2.9   A field sketch of the kerbed cairn, Site B2.   27
2.10   The broch on Borve Headland (B5).   28
2.11   Field sketches of small oval 'roundhouses' in the Borve valley, B37 and B69.   29
2.12   Ruins of a large roundhouse damaged by later shielings and rabbits, Site B44.   30
2.13   A field sketch of the remains at Dun Clieff, G9.   37
2.14   Field sketches of small roundhouses at G12 and G26.   38
2.15   Measured plan of a paved cairn overlooking the sea at G35.   39
2.16   A selection of kerbed cairns on Vatersay.   44
2.17   Kerbed cairn no. 5 in the cemetery of nine such cairns at VN85.   45
2.18   The megalithic chamber of cairn VS157 looking north to Heaval.   48
2.19   The fortification wall of the promontory fort (BM7) on the Islet of Biruaslam.   49
2.20   The rim of a Neolithic bowl recovered from the eroding midden at BM8 on the Islet of Biruaslam.   50

3.1   A relief map of the four southern islands with newly generated contours.   61
3.2   A histogram of the altitudes of 'prehistoric' sites.   63
3.3   A histogram of the altitude of Megalithic tombs.   63
3.4   A histogram of the altitude of cairns and mounds.   63
3.5   A histogram of the altitude of peat dryers.   65
3.6   Sandray, showing topography, place names, and excavation sites.   65
3.7   A view of site SY13, the settlement mound at Sheader.   68
3.8   Site SY16, a stone cairn and possible burial chamber.   69
3.9   Site SY22, a collapsed stone roundhouse and later shelter.   70
3.10   Site SY70, the broch seen from the north-west.   74
3.11   Sandray, showing the location of modern and mediaeval monuments.   78
3.12   Sandray, showing the location of prehistoric monuments.   80
3.13   Pabbay, showing topography, place-names and excavation sites.   81
3.14   Pabbay, showing the location of modern and mediaeval monuments.   90
3.15   Pabbay, showing the location of prehistoric monuments.   91
3.16   Mingulay, showing topography, place-names and excavation sites.   93
3.17   Site MY16.   98
3.18   Site MY49.   100
3.19   Site MY75.   102
3.20   Site MY104.   105
3.21   Site MY144.   107
3.22   Site MY160.   108
3.23   Site MY171.   109
3.24   Site MY202.   110
3.25   Site MY217.   111
3.26   Site MY225.   112
3.27   A selection of peat dryers.   113
3.28   Site MY344.   118
3.29   Site MY344.   119
3.30   Site MY345.   119

3.31	Mingulay, showing the location of modern and mediaeval sites.	123
3.32	Mingulay, showing the location of prehistoric sites.	127
3.33	Berneray, showing topography and place-names.	128
3.34	Sites BY2, BY3, and BY4.	131
3.35	Site BY17, the Barra Head lighthouse and the Iron Age dun wall in the foreground.	132
3.36	Site BY17, a detail of the massive masonry of the dun.	133
3.37	Site BY20.	134
3.38	Site BY39.	135
3.39	Site BY43.	136
3.40	Site BY45.	136
3.41	Site BY62.	139
3.42	Site BY68.	140
3.43	Site BY69.	141
3.44	Site BY76.	142
3.45	Berneray, showing the location of modern and mediaeval monuments.	143
3.46	Berneray, showing the location of prehistoric monuments.	145
4.1	Location map showing relationship to other excavated sites.	148
4.2	The aisled roundhouse during the course of excavation, facing south.	149
4.3	The Atlantic roundhouse	150
4.4	The early Iron Age structure of the Ben Tangaval roundhouse.	150
4.5	The aisled roundhouse.	151
4.6	An upright stone inserted into the wall of the aisled roundhouse.	152
4.7	The 'dressed' inner face of pier 2.	153
4.8	Pier 4, facing north-east.	153
4.9	Displaced stonework in the vicinity of cell F.	154
4.10	The south-facing entrance to the aisled roundhouse.	154
4.11	The depositional sequences associated with the aisled roundhouse.	155
4.12	The ash deposits associated with the hearth box.	156
4.13	Hearth sequences associated with the central hearth.	157
4.14	The cobbled surface, context 129, within cell A.	157
4.15	The subcircular pit within cell C and the subcircular pit within cell D.	158
4.16	The modified aisled roundhouse.	159
4.17	The section excavated through the depositional sequence within cell E.	160
4.18	The rubble wall blocking the space between pier 6 and the wall circuit.	160
4.19	The circular hearth associated with the secondary occupation of the aisled roundhouse.	161
4.20	The stone structures postdating the abandonment of the Ben Tangaval roundhouse.	162
4.21	The formal hearth constructed upon the secondary depositional sequence.	163
4.22	The shieling inserted into the tertiary depositional sequence.	163
4.23	The west wall of the subrectangular building.	164
4.24	The east wall of the subrectangular building, facing south-east.	164
4.25	The revetted enclosure, facing north.	165
4.26	Section through the deposits associated with the stone revetment.	165
4.27	Sections through the deposits to the south and west of the aisled roundhouse.	166
4.28	The early modern barn and enclosure.	166
4.29	Coarseware: pottery from the Atlantic roundhouse.	168
4.30	Coarseware: pottery from the aisled roundhouse.	169
4.31	Coarseware: pottery from the primary depositional sequence.	170
4.32	Coarseware: pottery from the secondary depositional sequence.	171
4.33	Coarseware: pottery from after abandonment.	172
4.34	Coarseware: pottery from the tertiary depositional sequence.	175
4.35	Coarseware: pottery from the stone revetment.	176
4.36	Coarseware: pottery from the early modern structures.	177
4.37	Coarseware: pottery from unstratfiedor intrusive deposits.	177
4.38	Flaked stone.	182
4.39	The leaf-shaped spearhead.	187
4.40	The shale bangle.	188
4.41	The spindle whorls.	188

5.1   Measured plan of stone ring B55 and sampling excavation.   192
5.2   Plan of cairn VS7 after removal of turf and topsoil.   193
5.3   The south-west quadrant of cairn VS7 after removal of turf and topsoil.   194
5.4   The north-east quadrant of cairn VS7 after removal of turf.   194
5.5   The central structure of cairn VS7.   195
5.6   The central platform of cairn VS7.   196
5.7   Soil mixed with cremated bone fragments and pebbles on the central platform of cairn VS7.   197
5.8   The magnetic susceptibility plots at cairn VS7.   198
5.9   The locations from which pollen samples were recovered under cairn VS7.   200
5.10   Percentage pollen and spore diagram for the monolith from beneath the cairn boulders in VS7.   200
5.11   Percentage pollen and spore diagram for the spot samples from beneath the cairn boulders in VS7.   201
5.12   Graph plot of sample scores on the first two DECORANA axes for the soil pollen samples from cairns
        VS7 and VS4B.   202
5.13   A section through cairn VS7.   205
5.14   Plan of cairn VS4B after removal of turf and topsoil.   206
5.15   The south-west quadrant of cairn VS4B.   207
5.16   The inner revetment in the north-east quadrant of VS4B.   207
5.17   The 'standing stone' in the north-west quadrant of VS4B.   208
5.18   The oval central mound covering the pyre material, VS4B.   208
5.19   The pyre material in cairn VS4B.   208
5.20   Cobbles sealed beneath the pyre material of VS4B.   209
5.21   A section from west (left) to east (right) acrosss cairn VS4B.   210
5.22   A bronze cloak fastener found in the cairn material of VS4B.   211
5.23   Three heavy stone artifacts from cairn VS4B.   211
5.24   The size of regular blades and flakes from VS4B (in mm).   212
5.25   Percentage pollen and spore diagram for the monolith rom beneath the kerbstone of VS4B.   213
5.26   Site B54.   216
5.27   Phase 1 and 2 features at site B54.   218
5.28   The well-worn paving slabs of phase 1 at B54.   218
5.29   The damaged stone-lined drain of phase 2 overlying the phase 1 slabs, B54.   219
5.30   Phase 3 features at site B54.   219
5.31   The inner face of the stone-founded roundhouse of phase 3, B54.   220
5.32   Pottery from site B54.   222
5.33   A plan of site E16.   225
5.34   A section of the trench excavated down the platform at E16.   226
5.35   A plan of stone ring E11.   232
5.36   A plan of features in the excavated area of E11.   233
5.37   The stone 'Plinth' near the centre of stone ring E11.   233

6.1   PY10: Dùnan Ruadh.   234
6.2   PY10: the internal elevation of the wall circuit at the full extent of excavation.   235
6.3   PY10: the extant arc of the wall circuit.   236
6.4   PY10: the apertures within the inner face of the wall circuit.   237
6.5   PY10: the perforated plug incorporated into the fabric of the wall circuit.   237
6.6   PY10: section excavated through the interior depositional sequence.   238
6.7   PY10: excavated features and structural elements identified within the interior of the site.   238
6.8   PY10: the stone-lined drain associated with phase 1b.   239
6.9   PY10: the post hole associated with phase 2.   239
6.10   PY10: section excavated across the circular pit associated with phase 3.   240
6.11   PY10: the western extent of the gallery.   240
6.12   PY10: the stone lintel at the eastern extent of the gallery.   240
6.13   PY10: sections excavated through the depositional sequence within the gallery.   241
6.14   PY10: chamber A, facing north.   242
6.15   PY10: chamber B, facing east.   242
6.16   PY10: sections excavated throught the depositional sequences within chambers A and B.   242
6.17   PY10: the displaced stonework derived from the collapse of the corbelled roof of chamber A.   243
6.18   PY10: the midden material sealing the depositional sequence within chamber B.   243
6.19   PY10: the pottery.   244

6.20   PY10: the pottery. 245
6.21   PY10: the pottery. 246
6.22   PY10: sheep: percentage survival by anatomical element. 256
6.23   PY10: sheep: mandibular wear stages. 257
6.24   PY10: cattle: percentage survival by anatomical element. 258
6.25   PY10: the worked bone and antler. 266
6.26   PY10: worked stone. 269
6.27   PY10: the Pabbay pin. 270
6.28   PY10: the crucible. 270
6.29   PY56: the Bàgh Bàn earth-house. 272
6.30   PY56: stone structures within the limits of dune encroachment at Bàgh Bàn. 272
6.31   PY56: the Bàgh Bàn earth-house. 273
6.32   PY56: chamber A, facing south-east. 274
6.33   PY56: the stone arcade within chamber A. 275
6.34   PY56: displaced stone lintels within the rubble fill of chamber A. 275
6.35   PY56: north and south elevations of the passage. 276

7.1   SY14: Sheader, facing south. 278
7.2   SY14: plan of the structural elements identified within the excavated area. 279
7.3   SY14: section excavated through the depositional sequence at Sheader. 280
7.4   SY14: shell midden (context 17). 281
7.5   SY14: walls 21, 19 and 20 within the lower levels of context 18. 282
7.6   SY14: walls 9 and 11 within the upper levels of context 15. 282
7.7   SY14: the pottery. 283
7.8   MY384: the Iron Age midden at Mingulay Bay. 291
7.9   MY384: section excavated through the mound. 292
7.10   MY384: section excavated the depositional sequence at Mingulay Bay. 293
7.11   MY384: plough marks etched into the subsoil at the base of the mound. 294
7.12   MY384: the structural elements identified within the excavated area. 295
7.13   MY384: the pottery. 297
7.14   MY384: percentage survival by anatomical element for sheep and cattle bones. 299
7.15   MY384: a cobble tool. 306
7.16   Site MY10. 307
7.17   Site MY346. 307
7.18   MY346: elevation against internal wall of putative wheelhouse. 308
7.19   Site MY347. 308

8.1   The location of pollen sites on Barra (contours in metres). 311
8.2   Selected pollen and spore diagram from Port Caol. 312
8.3   Selected pollen and spore diagram from the Borve valley cairn. 313
8.4   Selected pollen and spore diagram from the Borve valley mire. 314
8.5   Selected pollen and spore diagram from Lochan Na Cartach. 315

9.1   Earlier prehistoric sites on Barra. 320
9.2   The Late Neolithic hut T19, at Alt Chrisal. 321
9.3   The beaker found in the cist at the back of hut T19. 322
9.4   Earlier prehistoric sites on Vatersay. 323
9.5   Measured plan of the passage grave at VN157, Ben Orosay, Vatersay. 324
9.6   A measured plan of the stone ring and related features at site S28, Brevig. 326
9.7   The elongated cist at T180 after excavation. 329
9.8   The location of the elongated cists on a ridge overlooking Bretadale. 329
9.9   Bronze Age kerbed cairns and Iron Age (?) roundhouses west of Tresivick, north Vatersay. 331
9.10   Measured plan of the kerbed cairn cemetery at VN85. 332

10.1   Later prehistoric sites on Barra. 335
10.2   Histogram showing the external diameters of roundhouses on Barra and Vatersay. 336
10.3   Later prehistoric sites on Vatersay. 338
10.4   The door in the base of the broch wall on Borve headland (B5). 339

10.5	A measured plan of the broch at Dun Caolis, Vatersay.	340
10.6	Dun Scurrival (E15) perched at 60m OD on the summit of a steep hill.	341
10.7	Dun Clieff (G9) on a tidal islet on the west coast of Barra.	342
10.8	Measured plan of an unfinished monumental roundhouse at VN25.	343
11.1	A measured field plan of the wheelhouse at K34.	351

List of Tables

3.1   Site types and their frequencies on southern Outer Hebridean Islands.   62

4.1   Alt Chrisal: identified plant remains by context.   179

5.1   Bone fragments from the cremation deposit in cairn VS7.   197
5.2   Magnetic susceptibility results from cairn VS7.   199
5.3   Flint artifacts from cairn VS7.   203
5.4   Breakdown of the flint assemblage from cairn VS4B by type and context.   212
5.5   The location of the flint assemblage in Cairn VS4B.   212
5.6   The pottery assemblage by fabric and context at site B54.   221
5.7   Breakdown of the flint assemblage by type at site B54.   223
5.8   The pottery assemblage by fabric and context at site E16.   227
5.9   Breakdown of the lithic assemblage by type and material at site E16.   227
5.10   The lithic assemblage by context and raw material at site E16.   228
5.11   The faunal sample from site E16.   229
5.12   The faunal assemblage recovered from the midden at site B5.   230

6.1   Site PY10: mammals: number of identified specimens.   251
6.2   Site PY10: mammals: minimum nunber of individuals.   251
6.3   Site PY10: fish: number of identified species.   252
6.4   Site PY10: abundance of elements: 1st–3rd century.   253
6.5   Site PY10: abundance of elements: 2nd–4th century.   254
6.6   Site PY10: abundance of elements: 6th–9th century.   255
6.7   Site PY10: sheep: fusion data.   256
6.8   Site PY10: sheep: mandibular wear stage.   257
6.9   Site PY10: sheep: butchery by element.   258
6.10   Site PY10: cattle: fusion data.   259
6.11   Site PY10: cattle: mandibular wear stage.   259
6.12   Site PY10: cattle: butchery by element.   260
6.13   Site PY10: pig: fusion data.   260
6.14   Gadidae: body part representation.   261
6.15   Red sea bream and ballan wrasse: body part representation.   262
6.16   Site PY10: contents containing significant quantities of fish bones.   263
6.17   Site PY10: saithe: approximate size and age calculated from dentaries.   263
6.18   Site PY10: pollack: approximate size and age calculated from all elements.   263
6.19   PY10: summary of the same species present within the environmental sample taken from context 52.   267
6.20   PY10: MY384 and SY14: identified bird bones.   268

7.1   Site SY14: number of identified specimens.   285
7.2   Site SY14: abundance of elements.   286
7.3   Site SY14: fusion data.   287
7.4   Site SY14: Gadidae: body part representation.   288
7.5   Site SY14: fish: distribution according to context.   288
7.6   Site SY14: saithe: estimated length and age.   288
7.7   SY14: distribution of worked stone.   290
7.8   Site MY384: mammals and fish present by species.   300
7.9   Site MY384: abundance of elements.   301
7.10   Site MY384: fusion data.   302
7.11   Site MY384: mandibular wear stage.   303
7.12   Site MY384: butchery by element.   303
7.13   Site MY384: Gadidae: body part representation.   304
7.14   Site MY384: Gadidae: approximate age and size.   304

9.1   Possible Bronze Age huts on Barra and Vatersay.   328

List of Contributors

Keith Branigan	Department of Archaeology and Prehistory, University of Sheffield, UK
Barbara Brayshay	Department of Archaeology and Prehistory, University of Sheffield, UK
Judith Cartledge	Freelance Archaeological Consultant, Sheffield, UK
Andrew Chamberlain	Department of Archaeology and Prehistory, University of Sheffield, UK
Robert Craigie	Department of Archaeology and Prehistory, University of Sheffield, UK
Christopher Cumberpatch	Freelance Archaeological Consultant, Sheffield, UK
Kevin Edwards	Department of Geography, University of Aberdeen, UK
Patrick Foster	Research Archaeologist, Institute of Archaeology, Prague, Czech Republic.
Derilyn Frusher	Department of Archaeology and Prehistory, University of Sheffield, UK
David Gilbertson	Nene Centre for Research, University College Northampton, UK
Emma Gowans	Archaeological Survey and Evaluation Ltd, Sheffield, UK
Andrew Hammon	Department of Archaeology and Prehistory, University of Sheffield, UK
C. Ingrem	Faunal Unit, Department of Archaeology, University of Southampton, UK
Andrew Jones	York Archaeological Trust, UK
Roman Krivanek	Institute of Archaeology, Prague, Czech Republic
Martin Kuna	Institute of Archaeology, Prague, Czech Republic
Colin Merrony	Department of Archaeology and Prehistory, University of Sheffield, UK
Catherine Mortimer	Freelance Archaeological Consultant, York, UK
Jaqui Mulville	English Heritage, Oxford, UK
John Pouncett	Archaeological Survey and Evaluation Ltd, Sheffield, UK
Elizabeth Rega	Keck Science Centre, Claremont Colleges, California, USA
Duncan Robertson	Department of Archaeology and Prehistory, University of Sheffield, UK
Helen Smith	Department of Conservation Studies, University of Bournemouth, UK
Jane Timby	Freelance Archaeological Consultant, Stroud, Gloucester, UK
Pat Wagner	Department of Archaeology and Prehistory, University of Sheffield, UK
Caroline Wickham-Jones	Freelance Archaeological Consultant, Edinburgh, UK

Acknowledgments

This programme of research could never have begun, let alone seen through to its conclusion, without the support of many people and institutions and to all of them we are deeply grateful. Permission to work on land in their ownership was willingly given by both Macneil of Barra and the Department of Agriculture and Fisheries. Equally, we have been indebted to all the grazing committees of the townships on Barra and Vatersay, and to the crofters and the Barra Head Sheepstock Co., for generously allowing us to explore the land they graze and farm. For helping us to travel to, and work on, some of the more inaccessible parts of the island group we are particularly grateful to John Allen MacNeil, who, over an eight-year period, always supplied us in time, and got us off on the right day, and to Sandy MacLean who provided a roof over our heads on Mingulay. We are also grateful to Calum MacNeil, not only for getting us on and off some of the nearer islands, but also for sharing with us his formidable knowledge of the genealogy of most of the families living in these islands. We thank also Alistair MacNeil for taking us to Fuiay.

Our researches and our fieldwork have been helped and informed by the information and advice offered by the members of the Barra Historical Society, the members of the Buaile-nam-Bodach Preservation Society, the staff of the new Heritage Centre, and the staff of the Social Services office. There are many, many other islanders who have helped us in a myriad of ways over the last 12 years—providing accommodation, repairing vehicles, loaning equipment, providing services, giving us the benefit of their intimate knowledge of the landscape in which they live, and above all making us feel welcome. To all of them we are very grateful and very indebted.

Our work has been made much easier by the superb support we have had from our research assistants and supervisors. On Barra and Vatersay we are particularly indebted to Colin Merrony and John Pouncett, but also (for more limited periods) Kevin Colls, Sarah Darnborough, Andy Hammon, Steve Marsden, Keith Scherewode, and Andy Wigley. We are also grateful to Professor David Gilbertson for sharing the burdens of supervising the student team, as well as undertaking much environmental research and bringing together a team of highly qualified specialists to produce a detailed study of the past and present environments of the islands (see Gilbertson, Kent and Grattan 1996). The student teams, comprising over two hundred Sheffield students over the 12-year period, have worked hard, sometimes in awful weather, and have been a pleasure to work with. We are pleased to acknowledge also the contribution by a small team from Brno University (Czech Republic) during the excavation of the wheelhouse at Alt Chrisal.

On the southern, uninhabited islands, we have been especially indebted to Dr Roman Krivanek, geophysicist for the Institute of Archaeology, Prague, who undertook a great part of the landscape survey, measured site drawing and post-survey data production. We express our thanks to the MA students of Charles University, Prague, for measured drawings on Mingulay and Eva Witzova of the drawing office at the Institute of Archaeology, Prague, for her work as excavator, illustrator and nutrionist.

We are grateful to the student team from Opova University (Czech Republic) for excavation assistance at site PY10, and to the students of Charles University, Prague, for excavations at PY56 and MY347, and particularly indebted to Linda Cihakova for her supervisory role at both sites. Additional survey work on Mingulay was undertaken by Martin Kuna, D. Dreslerova, M. Gojda, and J. Turek. We are deeply indebted to Dr Kuna and his staff at the Department of Landscape Studies at the Institute of Archaeology in Prague for their huge input of time, materials and expertise in preparing maps and survey data for publication.

Organizing both the student teams and the logistics of our 12 seasons work was made much easier by our trio of successive project officers—Cathy Coutts, Sarah Darnborogh and Angie Foster, and we are very grateful to them. We must also mention the support offered by the office and technical staff of the Department in Sheffield in making our preparations each year, and especially the work done by Dorothy Cruse in keeping the accounts for so many different projects in order for 12 years! Keith Branigan would also like to thank Nong for her constant support and interest over the 12 years' work represented by this volume.

We have also been encouraged and stimulated in our work by the support and helpful advice and comments of the staff of Historic Scotland, notably Patrick Ashmore, Olwyn Owen and Noel Fojut, and we are also pleased to acknowledge the support of Dianne Murray and the staff of the RCAHMS. Advice, comment, ideas and information have constantly flowed from all of our colleagues in the Department of Archaeology and Prehistory, and we are very grateful to them all. Special mention must be made of Mike Parker Pearson, Kevin Edwards, Jane Downes, Anna Badcock and James Symonds.

In writing this report we have relied, as always, on the support of various specialists, whose names appear alongside their contributions. We thank them for their help, and for meeting the various deadlines with which we confronted them. We are particularly grateful, however, to John Pouncett and James Wood for the major role they played in helping to collate so much material from so many authors and to produce the finished volume. Steve Barganski of Sheffield Academic Press is also to be thanked for his customary efficiency in ensuring that our mistakes and omissions were identified and corrected—any which remain are our responsibility.

All of this work, from the first spadeful of earth removed and the first sire identified in survey, to the final words of the last chapter, has only been possible due to the financial support of individuals and institutions over the 12-year period. We have to be especially grateful to the Robert Kiln Charitable Trust, who made a grant for the first year's work and thereby allowed the project to get off the ground. They sub-sequently supported work in several other seasons too. Other charitable trusts and societies who offered financial support include the Pilgrim Trust, the Hunter Archaeological Trust, the MacNeil of Barra Community Trust, the Society of Antiquaries of Scotland, and the Society of Antiquaries of London. Support for fieldwork and publication was also given by the British Academy. The most substantial grants came from Historic Scotland (formerly the Scottish Development Department) to support a coastal erosion survey of all the islands from Barra southwards, the excavation of a number of threatened sites and the publication of the survey and excavation reports. Underpinning the whole operation each year was a grant from the University of Sheffield. In addition to all these sources we are grateful to MacNeil of Barra and Ethel MacNeil of the USA for personal donations towards excavation costs. Finally, in the early years of the project we were grateful to Loganair for support in kind that enabled us not only to fit visits to Barra into an otherwise difficult schedule but also to see something of the island from the air.

1. Introduction: Search in the Southern Islands

Keith Branigan

The Sheffield Environmental and Archaeological Research Campaign in the Hebrides (SEARCH) began in the summer of 1988. The idea of a project in the southern islands was the brain-child of our colleague Richard Hodges. We had been discussing possibilities for a major long-term programme of integrated environmental and archaeological research in a marginal landscape for some time. Ideally, we wanted a region where little archaeological work had been done in recent times and the landscape was archaeologically unexplored. We also wanted the opportunity to study the development of human settlement and society in a marginal landscape over several millennia. When Richard suggested the southern islands of the Outer Hebrides we were immediately taken with the idea, since not only did they meet our requirements but several of us were also interested in the archaeology of islands. So it was that we planned an initial 'reconnaissance' season in 1988 to be followed by a five-year programme of survey, excavation and environmental research.

The Programme of Survey and Excavation

Work began on Barra and South Uist, but rapidly expanded to other islands, several of them uninhabited (Fig. 1.1). The final tally of islands on which SEARCH teams have worked includes (from the north southwards) Berneray (off North Uist), North Uist, Benbecula, Monach Islands, South Uist, Eriskay, Fuday, Fuiay, Barra, Muldoanich, Vatersay, Biruaslum, Sandray, Pabbay, Mingulay and Berneray. The richness of the archaeology and the environmental record rapidly became apparent and offered a bewildering choice of individual projects for the staff and the research students who were drawn into the SEARCH programme. So it is that 12 years later we have still not concluded our project, even though it is now drawing towards a close.

Although field survey has been undertaken on South Uist, the focus there has been on excavation. On Barra and the islands to the south, much greater emphasis has been given to field survey, and all but one of the ten islands covered in this report have now been completely surveyed. The field survey was conducted annually from 1988 to 1999, with survey on Barra completed only in 1999. The total number of

sites and monuments found and recorded is almost 2,000, in contrast to the 37 listed in the RCAHMS report in 1928. That report, of course, listed no site or monument of later than mediaeval date, whereas ours includes those of modern date up to the later nineteenth century. Indeed, the majority of our recorded sites and monuments are believed to belong within the last three centuries. But there are still hundreds of sites known or believed to be of prehistoric and mediaeval date in our catalogue, which emphasize the much greater database we now have for studying human settlement and society on the southern islands before the modern era.

One of the problems we faced when we first arrived on the islands in 1988 was how to ascribe a date to a site or monument with any degree of confidence. Although the dates of some types of monument are reasonably well known—chambered tombs, 'brochs', wheelhouses and blackhouses, for example—the vast majority of the sites in our catalogue could not be labelled as prehistoric, mediaeval or modern, let alone dated with greater precision. Although we learnt to take careful notes on indicators, such as the degree of embedding and degradation, the effects of robbing and the relationship between various monuments and other structures of known date (especially land boundaries), we realized that the only way in which we could hope to better establish the date of some types of monument was by a series of targeted excavations.

The choice of sites to excavate was therefore driven, particularly in the earlier years, by our need to understand and if possible date a variety of type-sites. Wherever possible we integrated this objective with the need to excavate threatened sites. Thus we excavated seven hut-circles and shielings, three 'shelters', six cairns, an 'earth-house', a boat-shaped setting, three 'activity enclosures', a stone ring, three cists, two kelp ovens, three clearance cairns and three middens. In addition, the requirements of rescue excavation enabled us to excavate two blackhouses and their outbuildings, a church, a wheelhouse, a broch, a heeled cairn and a Neolithic occupation site. In recent years we have been able to add further excavations designed to answer specific (non-chronological) questions. Altogether we have excavated or sampled 51 sites on five of the islands (Barra, Vatersay, Sandray, Pabbay, Mingulay). Twenty-five of those excavations were reported in our first volume (Branigan and Foster 1995), and 9 will appear in volume 6 which will also

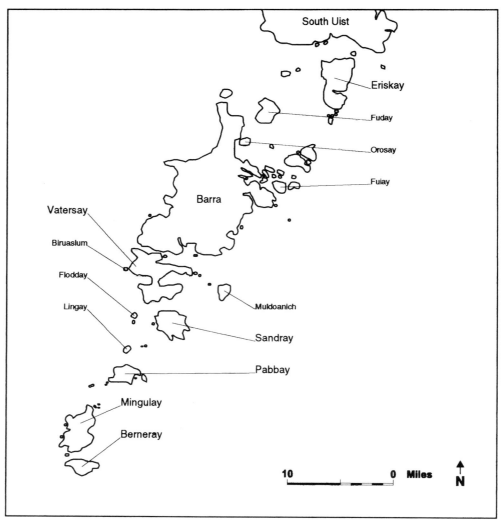

Figure 1.1 The Outer Hebrides south of the Sound of Barra, showing islands on which SEARCH has undertaken research.

include a discussion of the survey data on some type-sites such as the blackhouses, shielings, and boat-shaped settings. The remaining 17 excavations are recorded in this volume.

The two principal investigators involved in the survey and excavations recorded in this volume have had their own specific responsibilities. Keith Branigan (KB) was responsible for the survey of Barra and Vatersay, while Patrick Foster (PF) directed survey of Sandray, Pabbay, Mingulay and Berneray. Similarly, excavations on these most southerly islands have been the responsibility of PF, in addition to his long series of excavations on the important multi-period site at Alt Chrisal. KB's excavations have been focused mostly on small-scale and sampling excavations on Barra and Vatersay. These responsibilities are obviously reflected in the writing up in this volume, and the different quantities of excavation data for Barra and Vatersay (41 sites) and the islands to the south (10 sites) inevitably means that the interpretation of the evidence from the various islands has been treated somewhat differently the one from the other. Both in excavation and in writing up, KB and PF have

had the invaluable collaboration of their respective research assistants, Colin Merrony, Roman Krivanek and John Pouncett.

The Content and Format of this Volume

This publication, the fourth of six SEARCH volumes to go to press, draws a line under our research into the prehistory of the islands from Barra southwards. It presents all the results of our programme of field survey and the reports on our excavations on prehistoric sites.

The format of the volume is as follows. After the preliminaries we present, in the form of a gazetteer, the evidence we have collected for all the ancient sites and monuments of Barra and Vatersay, and four offshore islands. This chapter provides brief details of each site and illustrates a small representative sample by photographs, measured plans or measured field sketches. The following is devoted to the survey results from Sandray, Pabbay, Mingulay and Berneray, and the gazetteer of sites for each island is illustrated with plans and photos of selected sites.

Because there have been only a handful of excavations on these islands to enlighten the survey results, discussion of the evidence for the settlement history of each island follows its gazetteer.

Four chapters then present the results of excavations on five of the islands. First, the major excavations on the wheelhouse at Alt Chrisal on Barra are described. Chapter 5 is devoted to excavations at six other sites on Barra and Vatersay, Chapter 6 to the excavation of two house sites on Pabbay, and Chapter 7 to stratigraphic and sampling excavations on Sandray and Mingulay. The final four chapters offer an interpretation of the cumulative evidence provided by environmental research, field survey and excavation into the prehistoric settlement of Barra and Vatersay. Chapter 8 presents an outline reconstruction of the vegetational history of Barra. Chapters 9 and 10 provide an overview of the earlier and later prehistory of the two islands, and the final chapter attempts to put all our discoveries into their context both in the Western Isles and in northern Britain as a whole.

2. The Archaeological Survey of Barra and Vatersay

Keith Branigan

#This chapter records details of all the sites and monuments found during the field survey of the two islands of Barra and Vatersay, and of four offshore islands closely associated with them—Fuday, Fuiay, Muldoanich, and Biruaslum.

A Brief Description of the Islands

Barra (Fig. 2.1)

A roughly square island, about 8 km north–south and 7 km east–west, with a peninsula (Eoligarry) projecting some 4 km to the north, and projecting headlands in the north-east (Bruernish) and south-west (Tanagaval). The island is of heavily glaciated gneiss, which on some of the high ground—Heaval, Ben Tangaval and Ben Erival, for example—is exposed and bare. The highest point on the island is the peak of Heaval at 383 m, and the centre of the island is dominated by a series of peaks at around 200 m. Unlike the Uists to the north, the west coast is not a continuous belt of low-lying land but features a series of steep hillslopes and cliff faces, punctuated by small areas of machair at Tangusdale, Borve headland, Allasdale and Grean/Cleat. The only extensive area of machair is the Eoligarry peninsula. The east coast is rocky and generally bleak, but has three deep inlets at the north-east providing harbourage. The interior of the island is dominated by peat bog and moorland covered by heather. Apart from the restricted pockets of machair, the only lowland pasture areas of note are the Borve valley and the area behind Allasdale on the west of the island.

Vatersay (Fig. 2.2)

This island is separated from Barra by the Sound of Vatersay, which at its narrowest point is less than 200 m wide. In 1989–90 a causeway was built at this point to link the two islands. Vatersay is naturally divided into two unequal and rather different halves joined by a sandy isthmus. The northern part of the island, about 5.5 × 2 km at its greatest extent, is dominated by steep-sided Heishival, rising to almost 200 m, covered with peat soils and heather. To the north three low hills overlooking the Sound of Vatersay provide three different landscapes. Ben Orosay is a rounded hill with decent pasturage, Caolis is much more rugged, thin-soiled and covered with peat and heather, and Aird a'Chaolais is a glacially smoothed

headland with large areas of bare rock separated by patches of grassland, which on the south side develop into a small area of machair around Traigh Varlish. From the north-east corner of Heishival, a narrow peninsula projects eastwards, covered mostly by pasture but with pockets of peat-bog.

Across Vatersay Bay, a superb natural harbour, lies south Vatersay, only 3.5 × 1 km. Its eastern and western extremities form its highest points, Am Meall and Ben Rulibreck, but neither reaches 100 m OD, and south Vatersay is a more gentle landscape with only limited areas of peat and heather, and considerable stretches of machair and good pastureland.

Fuday

The largest of the four offshore islands surveyed, about 2 × 1 km, with an area of 570 acres (230 ha) and a high point at 90 m OD. Its gentle contours on the west, and offshore sand-based shelf, have created a band of machair where the grass now grows up to a metre in height. The island is unpopulated.

Fuiay

Off the coast of Bruernish, this island is 1 × 0.75 km, roughly oval and about 200 acres (84 ha) in extent. It is dominated by a central peak at just over 100 m OD, from which steep slopes descend in all directions, in most cases directly to the sea. Only at the north-west is there a reasonably flat area of land, behind a small enclosed tidal harbourage, and even here there are only peat soils and heather. The island is unpopulated.

Biruaslum

This is separated from the mainland of north Vatersay only by a narrow vertical-sided sea dyke. It is only 0.5 × 0.4 km, a mere 50 acres (20 ha) in size, but perhaps because of its highly defensible position has attracted significant occupation in at least three previous epochs. On the south side its cliffs are precipitous, but on the west the slopes are gentler and a thin soil supports grassland, although this area is totally exposed to the worst of the Atlantic storms. The island is unpopulated.

Muldoanich

The bleakest of the four islands visited, and stands a stern sentinel over the east approach to the Sound

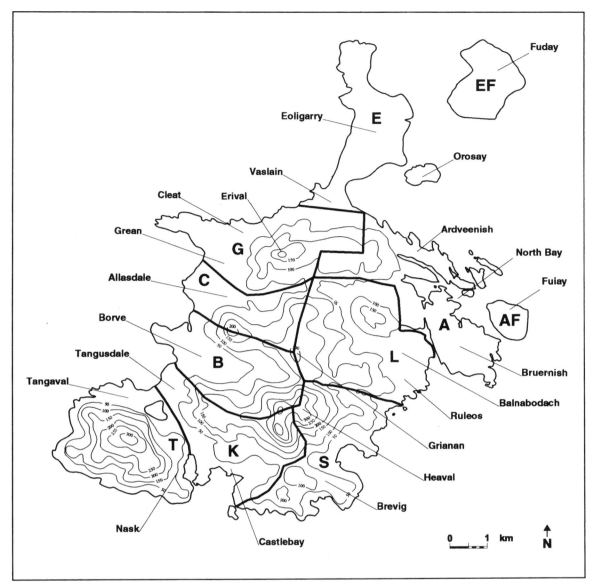

Figure 2.1 The Isle of Barra, showing places mentioned in the text, and survey zone boundaries.

of Vatersay and Castlebay. It is essentially a mass of gneiss, about 1.5 × 1 km, rising steeply out of the sea to a height of about 150 m. Its thin soil supports rough grassland, mostly on the only shallow slopes at the south end of the island. It is unpopulated.

General Survey Strategy

Archaeological survey has taken place on Barra and/or Vatersay every season since 1988, when the first area surveyed was the upper Borve valley. The survey of Barra was finally completed in June 1999. Survey for purely research purposes has been concentrated on blocks of landscape, such as the Borve valley, the Eoligarry peninsula and the Ben Erival massif. Coastal erosion survey on the other hand, funded by Historic Scotland, has by definition been concerned with the coastal corridor. This has been defined as a 50 m-wide corridor from the high-water mark, extended to 100 m

in areas of steep and precipitous cliffs. Coastal erosion survey has been undertaken around the entire coastline of all six main islands, on the tidal islets around the coast and on the offshore islands of Fuday, Fuiay and Biruaslam. In terms of publishing and interpreting the results of field survey, it would be nonsensical to separate sites and monuments found in the coastal corridor from those found outside it. The 50 m line is a purely arbitrary one that runs through the middle of some sites, separates clearly related sites from each other and takes no note of important social and economic relationships between coastal settlements and inland and upland areas. This report therefore includes sites and monuments found in both coastal erosion and research survey. Those sites included in the coastal erosion survey are indicated by an asterisk following their site number in the catalogue.

In order to facilitate the on-going handling of an expanding database of sites and monuments that was

5

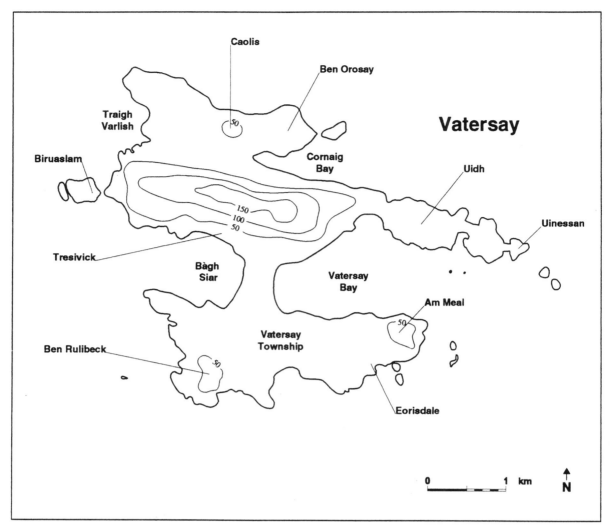

Figure 2.2 Vatersay, showing places mentioned in the text.

clearly going to run into many hundreds of entries, it was decided from the first that the Isle of Barra should be divided into a number of zones, within each of which the sites would be numbered consecutively from 1 upwards. The borders of each zone were established mainly for easy recognition in the field, utilizing roads and major land boundaries when available, but otherwise using significant topographical features, such as watersheds and streams. Nine zones were created on Barra, and each was given a single letter prefix to be used in the catalogue of sites. The nine areas, their prefixes, and their boundaries are shown in Fig. 2.1. In addition the islands of Fuday and Fuiay were given the prefixes EF and AF. In the case of Vatersay, it was decided to separate the island into northern and southern zones, which corresponded with the two townships of Caolis and Vatersay, the border between them running along the northern edge of the sandy isthmus that joins the two parts of the island together. These zones were given the prefixes VN and VS respectively, and prefixes BM and M were used for sites on the islands of Biruaslam and Muldoanich.

The entire land surface of all of these islands has been surveyed by the SEARCH team, in so far as that is practical, with the exception of Fuday, which was visited for a few hours on an opportunistic basis by P. Foster and D. Gilbertson. Otherwise, the only areas not surveyed have been excessively steep cliffs and in some cases the immediate environs (front and back gardens) of crofters' houses.

Survey Methods and Problems

Coastal erosion survey methods involved both geomorphologists and archaeological surveyors. The method of assessment of potential coastal erosion threats has been described by Gilbertson, Grattan and Pyatt in the second volume of the SEARCH monographs (Gilbertson, Kent and Grattan 1996: 103–109). To the assessments made by the geomorphologists was added the identification and recording of archaeological sites and monuments within the coastal corridor. This was undertaken by a team of four surveyors and a supervisor, walking at 12 m intervals. In the Hebridean landscape, where the ground surface is usually turf, heather, blanket peat or bare rock, there is no portable material culture to collect. Survey is largely a matter of identifying the remains of structures and making records of them. In most cases this meant measured field sketches and accompanying notes, but in some cases fully surveyed drawings were made. Within the coastal corridor all sites and monuments, including relict walls, were recorded. A full archive report on the coastal erosion survey of Barra and Vatersay was prepared (Branigan and Gratan 1998) and copies are lodged with Historic Scotland.

Away from the coastal corridor a team of surveyors varying in number between six and ten surveyed segments of landscape, walking at intervals that ranged from 20 m to 75 m, according to the precise nature of the ground surface and the topography. One supervisor was attached to each four surveyors and was responsible for overseeing the recording, taking photographs and making an assessment of the site or monument.

Outside of the coastal corridor relict walls were not recorded. Although we fully recognize the importance of the wall systems, there are so many fragmentary walls, often running for considerable distances, that their recording would have totally dominated the survey process. Furthermore these walls vary greatly and frequently in their method and materials of construction, partly due to immediate availability of materials, partly to constant destruction, rebuilding and robbing. The majority of these walls appear to belong within the modern era, but we have undertaken detailed study of wall systems in the Borve valley and on Ben Orosay on Vatersay in an attempt to unravel their history. These studies revealed many problems in the interpretation and understanding of the wall systems, but failed to provide many of the solutions. A study of the different types of boundary constructions is clearly an important topic for further study, but it will require a substantial investment of time and labour with no certainty of significant progress.

Site visibility is a problem that has to be taken account of both in the field and at the interpretative stage. Vegetation growth, which has hampered the discovery of sites and made their comprehension particularly difficult, includes dense heather and thick bracken. But we also have to cope with those areas where archaeological sites and monuments have been made all but invisible. This applies to the dune systems and the machair, mostly found in only small areas on Barra and Vatersay, where occasional exposures—mostly by rabbit action but also by wind erosion and dune deflation—indicate the existence of buried landscapes. It also applies of course to the upland areas covered with blankets of peat, often to such a depth that few sites and monuments have any

chance of offering even a glimpse of their existence. Finally, and perhaps most perversely, it applies to those favoured areas where there has been prolonged and intensive occupation associated with arable farming. Here, the repeated cultivation and clearance of land has long since removed traces of all but the most monumental ancient structures, so that areas that may have been particularly well occupied in the past may now reveal few if any remains more than a century old. A good example is Tangusdale on the west side of Barra, a small sheltered valley with an excellent water supply, an area of decent arable land, fronted by the machair which reaches into Halaman Bay. It should be a preferred site, and it has certainly been carefully and intensively used over the past two centuries. There is no trace of earlier occupation, but the quantity of large stone blocks built into modern walls and outbuildings and seen on clearance cairns suggests that there was earlier settlement here. It is precisely the attractions of the location for early settlers that have led to the repeated use and reworking of this small area of landscape and led to the total eradication (at least on the surface) of any trace of prehistoric or mediaeval occupation.

Another problem has been the constant reuse not only of specific locations but of building materials—which means stone—over the last five millennia. Sites have been repeatedly robbed, reused, modified or overlain, so that what survives as a visible field monument is often a miniature palimpsest, difficult to untangle and interpret without excavation.

Finally, we have had the difficulty, referred to in the Introduction, of ascribing even broad dates to many of our sites and monuments, particularly those we believe belong to the premodern era. The stone-walled circular hut or house, for example, seems to be in use in Barra at least as late as the early modern period, having made its debut in the Neolithic. We believe that 12 years' experience and the insights offered by excavation of some sites allows us to ascribe many of these circular structures to a broad date range with a degree of confidence, but some sites are hard to pin down, and in some cases we may be wrong.

Site-Types

In order to simplify the description of commonplace sites and avoid unnecessary repetition we have identified a series of site-types. In the first volume of the SEARCH reports we briefly described four site-types. To those original site-types we now add six further examples.

Shelters

As on the Tangaval peninsula (zone T) so on the rest of Barra and Vatersay these simple monuments are the most prolific. They come in circular, oval and rectangular (usually square) forms and mostly have an internal diameter or width under 2.5 m. We continue to identify six basic forms, illustrated in Figure 2.3. Many of types A and B can never have had a built superstructure of any sort, and we believe the stone blocks of which they are comprised were used to peg down a blanket or other cover that the shepherd carried with him. This may also explain why types A and B are always circular or oval rather than rectangular. Some examples of types A and B with a continuous ring of stone rather than spaced blocks, might have had a low turf-built wall constructed on the stone base. The other types (C–F) appear to have had low walls although few examples survive more than about 0.5 m high.

Three examples of shelters have been excavated and will be reported on in volume 6 of the SEARCH series.

Small circular huts

These differ from shelters of type C and D in being larger (4–7 m diam.) and having thicker and higher walls which, even when the structures have weathered and collapsed, leave noticeably more debris than the shelters. They are found both close to the sea and in the uplands and presumably acted both as storeplaces and

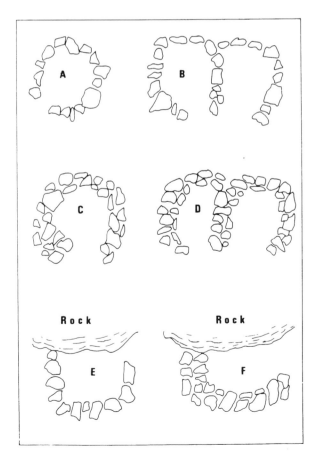

Figure 2.3 A typology of 'shelters' used by the field survey team.

shelters on a medium- to long-term basis. Some are clearly associated with shieling sites. One example, B54, has been excavated and is reported below (p. 216).

Oval huts

These are oval structures, around 5–6 m long and 3–4 m wide, with double-width walls of stone and earth or turf that clearly stood to a height of at least 0.5 m and possibly higher. They are invariably well-embedded and long-abandoned. Their size and construction suggest that they were more than temporary shelters but provided living space, perhaps on a seasonal basis.

Roundhouses

These monuments are marked by low heaps or mounds of stone blocks, often of a reasonably regular shape and size—as if they have been carefully selected for the purpose. Careful inspection reveals traces of a thick circuit wall around 0.8–1 m wide, which was probably the foundation for a wall the upper parts of which were built of turf. The diameter varies between about 8 and 12 m and some houses are in fact oval. Two examples, T134 and T166, were sampled by excavation and the results reported in Branigan and Foster (1995: 168–70), and remains of a third were found beneath the excavated wheelhouse at T17 (p. 150).

Wheelhouses

We distinguish some 'roundhouse' sites from others by reason of the notably larger quantity of stone debris that makes a very substantial mound. They are normally at the top end of the size range, the mounds being 10–14 m in diameter. The traces of the circuit wall can sometimes be seen to still stand up to 1 m in height and these buildings appear to have been built in stone rather than in turf on a stone foundation. On some sites potential lintel stones are to be seen. Excavation of such a site at T17 confirmed its identify as a free-standing wheelhouse, with a full stone wall.

Boat-shaped stone settings

These have been elevated to the status of a site-type because a considerable number were discovered on south Vatersay. They consist of blocks of stone set in a boat-shape with a pointed prow and a blunt or rounded stern. Their widest part may be amidships or towards the aft. There is no trace of a cairn or mound within the setting, although the ground surface inside the stones is usually slightly higher than that outside it. They vary in length from about 4 m to 10 m. One example has been excavated (VS42, see volume 6) but the excavation threw no light on either the date or function of the type.

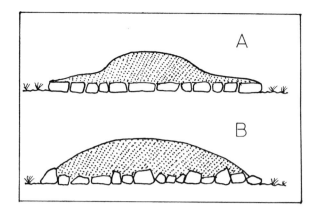

Figure 2.4 Idealized profiles of A, kerbed and B, bordered cairns.

Kerbed cairns

These monuments have been identified as a site-type following the discovery of about two dozen of them on Vatersay. They are low stone cairns, sometimes with a noticeable stepped or inverted bowl profile, with a well-constructed kerb of stone blocks set around the perimeter. The tops of the kerbstones are usually carefully laid to form a more or less continuous level surface (Fig. 2.4A). The long axis of the stones is usually set along the perimeter of the cairn rather than towards the centre. The smallest examples are only about 3 m in diameter and the largest around 10 m. Two examples (VS4b and VS7) have been excavated on Vatersay (see the reports in Chapter 5).

Bordered cairns

This is a term used for stone cairns that have a perimeter ring of stones that are not laid end to end to form a carefully constructed kerb but often have their long axis pointing along the radius of the cairn rather than along the circumference. The perimeter stones seem to vary more in shape than in the kerbed cairns; they are not laid to form a continuously level surface but undulate, and the cairns themselves do not show the stepped profile common amongst the kerbed cairns (Fig. 2.4B). Elsewhere such cairns are often called kerb cairns. Their relationship to the kerbed cairns is obviously of interest. There may be no cultural or chronological relationship at all, but if they are part of a single cultural tradition, then there are three possible chronological relationships. They may be an early form of the kerbed cairn before it became formalized; they may be a contemporary monument emulating but not matching the carefully constructed kerbed cairns; or they may be a late degenerate form when less importance was attached to the construction of the kerb and cairn. We shall return to these monuments in Chapter 9.

Stone rings

We have so far found no examples of stone circles on any of our southern islands, but we have found a number of monuments in which moderately sized stone blocks or boulders are set in a spaced ring that is often near-circular or oval. They range in size from 6 to 23 m diameter with the estimated number of original stones ranging from 8 to 25. The stones themselves range from 0.5 to 1.5 m in height. They have suffered from both stone robbing and modification, but they are still clearly recognizable as a type and they are quite different to the oval or sub-circular enclosures formed by a more or less continuous setting of small stone blocks. These monuments too are discussed further in Chapter 9.

Blackhouses

Much has been written about blackhouses, mostly on the basis of the standing evidence of such houses as those at Sollas on North Uist and Arnol on Lewis. In the field, we identify as a blackhouse any oblong building with thick, stone-faced and earth-filled walls, rounded exterior corners and doors only in one or both of its long walls. As built, the house will have no fireplaces and chimneys in its end walls, although it may have been modified in this respect later in its history. Similarly, doors may have been inserted into other than the original front wall at a time when the building changed use, usually from a house to an outbuilding of some sort.

The Catalogue of Sites

Given that over 80% of the sites and monuments recorded are thought to be the products of human activity in the period c. AD 1600–1900, and that many of these sites are simple structures with only very temporary usage (e.g. the shelters), we keep description and illustration to a minimum.

Lengthier descriptions are provided where we believe a site or monument justifies it. Certain terms are used repeatedly and six of these need brief definition here.

Stone setting: a deliberate arrangement of individual blocks of stone.
Stone structure: a deliberately built feature incorporating either blocks of stone or stone and turf/soil to make a structure that could, and often clearly did, stand two or more stones high.
Orthostat: a stone set upright on its long axis.
Heavily embedded: stones that are almost completely overgrown by turf or other vegetation.
Well-embedded: stones that are very firmly set in the soil or turf and partially covered by them.
Embedded: stones that are firmly set in the soil or turf but of which the surface is still mostly visible.

All sites and monuments are presumed to belong within the period c. AD 1600–1900 unless otherwise stated. Where a prehistoric or mediaeval date is suggested this is based on a combination of factors, including evidence from similar sites that we have excavated, similar sites elsewhere in Scotland and Ireland, and the degree of embedding. Although some of the more complex or unusual sites are discussed at some length here, significant sites are discussed at greater length and put into context in Chapters 9 and 10. This chapter is regarded as essentially a summary of the database generated by the field survey.

The total number of sites and monuments recorded on each of the islands is as follows:

Barra

Zone	EF	6
	E	26
	A	128
	AF	17
	L	36
	S	64
	K	153
	T	236
	B	164
	C	60
	G	93
Total		983

Vatersay

Zone	VN	157
	VS	65
Biruaslum Zone	BM	8
Muldoanich Zone	M	7
Total		237

The total number of sites and monuments recorded on these islands by the SEARCH survey was 1220. The two catalogues that follow record brief details of all of these sites and monuments with the exception of the 233 found in Zone T which were published in the first SEARCH volume. An asterisk after the site number denotes a site in the coastal erosion zone.

Zone EF (Fuday)

(Note: Fuday was not systematically surveyed by a team. We recorded six sites noted by P. Foster during a one-day visit in 1992.)

EF1* (NL733095) Stone cairn, 1 m high and 3.6 diam., with about ten kerbstones visible *in situ*. Kerbed cairn.
EF2 (NL732094) Stone cairn, 2 m high approx. 11 m diam., with its kerbstones visible around almost its entire circumference. An upright stone 0.6 m high as visible, is set in the kerb on the south side. Kerbed cairn.
EF3 (NL733092) A sand dune with a stone-clad facing around east–west quadrant on a diam. of c. 25 m. Purpose unknown.

EF4 (NL733091) An elongated dune, 14×3 m, covered by a thick scatter of stone blocks. Purpose unknown.
EF5 (NL732090) A 10 m diam. dune covered with a scatter of stone blocks. Purpose unknown.
EF6 (NL727079) An arc of 11 stone blocks well-embedded and, to judge from surface indications, part of a complete circle about 5.5 m diam. There is no trace of either stones or a mound inside the kerb, however, so that it does not appear to be a kerbed cairn like EF1 and EF2. It may be similar to the flat cairn excavated at T214 on Barra (Branigan 1995: 184–8), although the kerb at EF6 is far better constructed and much more akin to those found around the kerbed cairns.

Zone E (Eoligarry)

E1 (NF713062) Small grassed-over cairn, 3 m diam. This is probably but not certainly a clearance cairn.
E2* (NF715060) Stone setting against a rock face; 3–4 m long. Shelter type E.
E3* (NF717061) A cairn, c. 5 m diameter comprised largely of peat and other superficial material with traces of a rough kerb of boulders. Located on low ridge, 30 m from sea. Date uncertain but probably prehistoric.
E4* (NF712063) A huge midden and associated stone-built structures on a small promontory on the Sound of Orosay. The midden is represented by a grassed-over mound about 1 m high, but at its edge the sea-cut section shows a midden and various sand-blow deposits with a depth of 1.8 m, so that the total depth of the midden is probably between 2 and 3 m at its greatest. It is between 30 and 40 m across and seems to occupy the entire peninsula. In the section, a peat deposit at the base is overlain by traces of stone structures, with five stones laid horizontally at one point; two further stones appear to be set upright. A flint pebble was recovered at this level. The deposit above is several layers of midden separated by sand deposits; one midden deposit includes a lens of burnt material and shells. From a little below this deposit we recovered six pieces of a thin-walled, rather fragile reddish-orange pottery in a very sandy fabric, best paralleled on Barra by some Beaker sherds from Alt Chrisal. No other artifact material was seen, but a sampling of the shell content showed that cockles dominated the sample (as expected at the north end of one of the world's great cockle beaches). Other shell-fish were noted, however, including (in descending numbers) limpets, dog whelks, periwinkles, mussels, pecteus and razor shells. There were traces of further midden deposits, and possible stone structures, in the sea-cut section further north-east from the site, and the impression is that at some time in the prehistoric period this piece of coastline on Orosay saw a lot of activity. This is clearly a substantial site, probably of prehistoric date.

E5* (NF707064) A shell midden above a fossil soil and alongside an old track way. Its stratigraphic position suggests it may be relatively recent in date.

E6 (NF705066) A low but substantial mound c. 50 m east–west and 40 m north–south, on which rabbit disturbance has produced 20 sherds of reddish-brown gritty handmade pottery, similar to that found on midden site E17.

E7* (NF709065) Three upright stones about 3 m apart; with a cist-like stone setting immediately adjacent. We were informed by a local resident that this was a recent dog burial.

E8* (NF709066) Shepherd's shelter formed of a rock face, two large boulders and three stones infilling spaces, 3 × 2 m.

E9* (NF709068) Extensive but patchy shell midden over 200 m of coast, with five or six separated layers of shell debris and occasional charcoal and a few small sherds of coarse handmade pottery from the lower levels. Glazed 19th century ware was found in the topmost midden level.

E10* (NF698096) Temporary shelter standing? A slight depression, with traces of a stone surround of flat slabs, 4 × 2 m.

E11* (NF695096) A stone ring of about 70 stones, forming an oval about 14.5 × 12 m. The largest stone is about 1 m wide, and two stones are set upright with a narrow gap between them on the west side. The area inside the ring is slightly hollowed, and there are just two large stones lying within it. The site invites comparison with site G1 in a similarly exposed position, and with site T169 sample-excavated by us in 1992 (this proved to be an activity site with a lithic assemblage C14 dated to the period around 700–800 BC). Excavation report, Chapter 5.

E12* (NF693090) A rock shelter using a natural rock and a large boulder together with a built wall to create a shelter 1.9 × 1.8 m.

E13* (NF695089) A shepherd's shelter, about 2.5 m square, formed by an arc of boulders and an upright slab set against a right-angled rock face.

E14* (NF695082) Three small temporary shelters built against a rock face on a narrow shelf, looking north-west.

E15* (NF695081) Dun Scurrival. Oval stone-walled structure, 24 × 16 m overall, with internal area measuring 13 × 8 m. Masses of fallen masonry on slopes around the structure and inside the wall (Fig. 2.5). The wall structure is partly visible at the north-west and west and appears to comprise a thick outer wall, an irregular but narrow gallery and a narrow inner wall. The outer wall is 2.5–3.5 m wide, the gallery 0.5–1 m and the inner wall about 1 m wide. There are suggestions of an entrance at the east end of the structure. A trench has been dug at some time in the past towards the east end of the internal area and revealed remains of a wall three courses high, which must belong to a structural feature within the central 'courtyard'. The

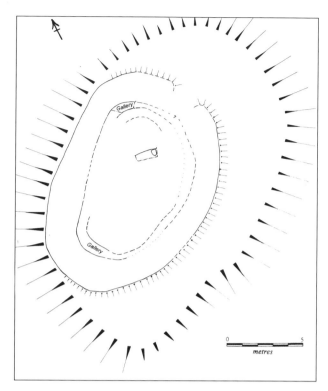

Figure 2.5 A measured plan of the remains of Dun Scurrival (E15).

NMS has a collection of c. 70 sherds, flints, a bone pin and a bone bobbin from the site. Iron Age 'dun'.

E16* (NF696079) Cave. A narrow cave, entrance c. 3 m wide but about 16 m deep. Too small for occupation, but we have been shown a human skull recovered from it some years ago. A platform in front of the cave is fronted by a crude revetment of fallen boulders and placed blocks. A trench was excavated down one side of this platform in 1998 and yielded evidence of prehistoric occupation (report Chapter 5).

E17* (NF695068) Midden, with mainly shells and some small coarse sherds of pottery. Probably prehistoric.

E18* (NF695067) A rather diffuse midden with shell and a few scraps of coarse pottery. Probably prehistoric.

E19 (NF695068) Buried soil or deposit on rammed crushed-shell surface seen in eroded dune section. Behind the section some large rectangular blocks of worked stone protrude above the sand. A significant building, though apparently heavily robbed. Excavated in 1990; report in SEARCH volume 6.

E20 (NF705074) The standing remains of the church of Cille Bharra (RCAHMS 1928: 123–25). The remains of three chapels, together with some mediaeval grave slabs. The runic stone found here is now in the National Museum, Edinburgh.

E21 (NF695091) A circular structure 4 × 3.8 m with a perimeter ring of stone blocks and remains of a stone cairn within. The perimeter stones are of irregular size and orientation and we identify this as a burial cairn. Probably prehistoric.

E22 (NF697093) Embedded traces of an oval stone setting 2.5 × 1.75 m. Shelter type A.

E23 (NF696095) An overhanging rock with a line of stone blocks set to enclose an area 2 × 0.75 m. Shelter type E.

E24 (NF704071) A midden deposit yielding shell, several sherds of a hard gritty handmade fabric and pieces of glazed tile.

E25 (NF696094) An oval stone setting, 3.5 × 2.5 m, with about 15 stones. Shelter type A.

E26* (NF692061) Remains of a wooden sailing ship with roofing slates and coal. The boat appears to be c. 30 m long, with remains of a mast. Seen in 1991/92 following movement and erosion at the edge of the dune system.

Zone A (Ardveenish)

A1* (NF717020) Shelter comprised of two walls at right angles built against a rock cleft, enclosing an area 4.3 × 3.3 m; probably a fisherman's store.

A2* (NF716423) Turf and stone blackhouse, 8 × 6 m, doorway in north-west corner.

A3* (NF716423) Partly demolished blackhouse, 9 × 6.6 m, the remaining south and west walls standing over 1 m high.

A4* (NF717019) Small shepherd or fisherman's shelter, 3 × 1.8 m, with stone and turf wall built against 10 m rock face.

A5* (NF728008) D-shaped hut(?) foundation (2.7 × 2.3 m) and boat-shaped enclosure (2.6 × 1.9m), both with a single line of stones demarcating them; considerable quantity of stone collapsed around them.

A6* (NF 733006) Incomplete foundations of a house 8.4 × 4.7 m; either robbed or never finished?

A7* (NF733006) Much ruined and overgrown blackhouse 8.2 × 5 m.

A8* (NF733009) Incomplete foundations of a house 7.8 × 4.1 m, inner facing stones only visible.

A9* (NF731012) Two-roomed blackhouse, 10 × 4 m, with door in centre of north wall. Only 3 m from the high tide point, but no threat visible.

A10* (NF732014) Two adjacent blackhouses. The smaller, 9.4 × 6.7 m, has a partition wall and is the more grassed over and robbed out. The larger, 10.7 × 6.2 m, has one room and apparently replaced the smaller building. Only 1 m above high tide and could be threatened by storm waves from the east.

A11* (NF734012) Two adjacent buildings. A is 6.5 × 5.5 m, with heavily grassed over turf and stone walls. B is 9 × 5 m, apparently built entirely of turf, and with the doorway in the narrow southern end.

A12* (NF733014) An unusual building, 9 × 4.3 m, the stone walls lining a 1 m deep cutting in the top of a 10 m mound. Possible internal cross-wall. Excavated 1999, report SEARCH volume 6.

A13* (NF730019) Much-destroyed traces of a small rectangular hut, 3 × 1.75 m, with stone and turf walls.

A14* (NF730019) Simple platform, 3.5 × 2 m, with partial stone revetment set against a small rock face.

A15* (NF725021) Turf and stone wall, c. 90 m long, running parallel to edge of sea inlet.

A16* (NF726019) Stone setting of uncertain form, with eight large stone blocks, the largest set upright over 1 m tall.

A17* (NF724021) Two adjacent blackhouses, 10 × 6 m and 6.5 × 5 m, doorways looking east to sea inlet.

A18* (NF723022) A small stone building 4 × 3 m, walls standing 0.3 m high, and a doorway at one corner.

A19* (NF722022) Well-preserved house, 8.5 × 5 m, with fireplaces at each end and several windows. Whitehouse.

A20* (NF721023) Blackhouse, 6 × 3 m, doorway in centre of long wall.

A21* (NF722024) Blackhouse, 8 × 5 m, rounded corners, much robbed.

A22* (NF723024) Blackhouse, 10 × 5 m, large boulder walls.

A23* (NF723024) House, 8 × 5 m, with doors in south and west walls.

A24* (NF723025) Blackhouse, 8.5 × 5 m, door in centre of south wall and small 'cupboard' built into the south-west corner.

A25* (NF723025) Boathouse? next to jetty, 3 × 5 m, largely destroyed.

A28* (NF724026) House with collapsed timber front and rear walls; end walls of stone, one with chimney.

A27* (NF722027) House, 5 × 4 m, reduced to stone foundations.

A28* (NF722026) House, 6 × 5 m, with central doorway and small lean-to shed to one side of doorway.

A29* (NF722026) Enclosure?, 6 × 5 m, comprised of stone wall and rock outcrop, the angle enclosed by an L-shaped turf wall.

A30* (NF721027) Small house, 6 × 3 m, walls 0.4 m high, door at corner.

A31* (NF720027) L-shaped house, 14 × 5 m, divided into two rooms with separate entrances. Walls stand to window height.

A32* (NF721028) Two-roomed building, 9 × 5 m, with two separate doorways and smaller room slightly set back from front wall line.

A33* (NF718029) Cluster of four buildings, oval enclosure and turf wall. Building 1, 11 × 5.5 m, is overlain by building 3, 12 × 7 m, which is divided into three rooms. Building 2, 10 × 6.5 m, has minor internal partitions, and building 4, 12 × 7 m, has no partitions. The oval enclosure to the east is 20 m along its axis. House walls of 2, 3 and 4 survive to a maximum height of 2 m.

A34* (NF717027) A substantial stone boulder wall, 15 m long.

A35* (NF717025) Blackhouse, 7.5 × 5.5 m, single-roomed with entrance in centre of west wall; walls stand to 1 m.

A36* (NF716025) Six well-embedded circular stone platforms, from 2 m to 2.5 m diameter. Rick stands?

A37* (NF715026) A stone-built causeway up to 4 m wide and 20 m long, linking the mainland to a small offshore islet. At high tide it is submerged to about 1 m.

A38* (NF715027) A slightly oval walled structure occupying most of a small islet approached at low tide by the causeway A37. Traces of an inner and outer wall can be followed around the circumference, although few traces are visible on the east and west sides. The overall dimensions are 19.8 × 17.1 m, and the interior space is 11.2 × 9.3 m. The inner wall was 1.2 m wide, separated from the outer by a space (on the east side) of 0.6 m. At the north end of the islet, a flat area about 11 × 8 m forms a yard-like feature outside the structure. Iron Age 'broch'.

A39* (NF725025) Blackhouse of turf and stone, 9 × 5 m, entrance in centre of north wall; no trace of internal partition. Used as a dump.

A40* (NF724025) Stone-built hut, 7.5 × 5 m, doorway in north-west corner.

A41* (NF724025) Stone-built hut, 6 × 4 m, door in centre of east wall. Small internal partitions in south-east and north-west corners.

A42* (NF723027) Blackhouse, 13 × 7 m, with circular hearth near centre; door in centre of west wall.

A43 (NF712025) Stone-built hut, 7.5 × 5 m with door at north-east corner, no internal partitions. Walls stand to 0.5 m.

A44 (NF713026) Small stone house, 7 × 5 m, heavily robbed on east and south sides; door at north-east corner. Three small stone cairns approx. 2.5 m diam. immediately to rear, west, of building.

A45* (NF712027) Small blackhouse, 5.5 × 4.5 m, with doorway in the centre of the east wall. No internal partitions.

A46* (NF710029) Blackhouse, thick-walled with earth core, measuring 11.5 × 6 m externally, oriented north–south with a door in the east side.

A47* (NF711029) Two clearance cairns, heavily overgrown, c. 1 m and 0.7 m diam. respectively.

A48* (NF712030) Causeway of large boulders, 6 m long, joining two small islands. No structures on islands.

A49* (NF713029) Stone setting, which could either be boat-shaped (4 m × 1.5m) or two separate but related features—a circle c. 1.5 m diameter and a V-shaped setting. Situated on headland of small island. Uncertain purpose and date.

A50* (NF713029) Circular stone setting 1 m diam., with one large stone (0.7 m long) and nettle growth in centre. Fireplace or animal burial?

A51* (NF710031) Causeway formed of boulders on bedrock, 1 m wide and 4 m long, joining a small islet to a larger island. No structures visible on either.

A52* (NF709031) A simple rectangular building platform, 5 × 4 m, entrance to east? Wall line marked by stone blocks set into edge of platform.

A53* (NF706030) Rectangular building, 11 × 5 m, oriented north-east to south-west with door in the south-east wall, and wall standing to maximum of 4 m.

A54* (NF705031) Outbuilding, 4 × 3 m, thick-walled with earth core, door in east end.

A55* (NF704033) Outline of rectangular building, 8 × 3 m, marked by stone blocks and turf wall, oriented north–south. Much robbed.

A56* (NF704033) A small hut, 3 m square, built of large boulders and only 2 m from corner of building A55. Shelter type A.

A57* (NF705034) Blackhouse, 8 × 4 m, oriented east–west with door in north wall. Walls stand to 1 m.

A58* (NF708033) Stone setting of three small stones in arc around base of 1 m high upright block. Fisherman's shelter type A.

A59* (NF708033) Boulder-built outbuilding, 4 m square with door in east wall.

A60* (NF709035) Two single-orthostat walls, meeting a T-junction, with a small 1 m diam. setting of six stone blocks at the wall junction. Shelter type A.

A61* (NF709036) Temporary shelter, 2 × 1 m, built of stone blocks against a large boulder. Shelter type E.

A62* (NF711036) Boat noost? Oval dug-out pit, 4 × 2 m, with gully downslope; under 10 m from water's edge.

A63* (NF712033) Small hut, 3 m square, stone footings almost totally grassed over, and possibly robbed in places.

A64* (NF710030) Small blackhouse, c. 7 × 5 m, with door in centre of east wall. Partly robbed-out and heavily grassed over.

A65* (NF707040) Complex of three small rectangular buildings adjacent to a sea loch and protected from the west by a rock outcrop. The central thick-walled building, 8.8 × 4.7 m, is divided into two rooms, each with its own external door but no connecting internal door. The larger room measures 5 × 2.8 m, and the smaller 1.6 × 2.8 m. In front of this building a second subrectangular structure 9.2 × 8.1 m is thinner-walled and mostly destroyed. Some 35 m to the rear of the central building a thick-walled building 7.2 × 4.1 m has a door at its eastern corner and an annexe 4.2 × 4.1 m with a door on the opposite (west) side. The central building appears to be a small blackhouse with a separate byre, and the other thick-walled building may also have originally been a blackhouse.

A66* (NF707040) Blackhouse, 9 × 7 m, with door and two flanking windows in east wall. The walls stand to over 1 m in height.

A67* (NF708042) Rectangular shed, 4.3 × 3 m internally, door facing east. Rectangular stone setting in north-east corner.

A68* (NF718041) Oblong stone setting, 3 × 1.7 m, with infill of stone rubble, at water's edge. Kelp oven?

A69* (NF701039) A small rectangular pen, 6.7 × 5.6 m, built against a rock face with grassed-over narrow stone footings.

A70* (NF723033) A rectangular hut or small house, 4.5 × 3.9 m, with embedded grassed-over stone foundations. Line of nine spaced orthostats runs 50 m north-west to south-east across neck of headland nearby.

A71* (NF723035) A rectangular building, 12 × 5.5 m, with stone-faced walls 1.2 m wide. A partition wall at the south-east end may be original and creates a room 3.2 × 2.1 m with no external doorway. The main doorway appears to be in the north-east wall. There are secondary rubble-built walls in the north-west end of the building, possibly lambing pens. To the front of the building a circular stone setting 1.7 m diam. is to one side of the door, and a wall 5 m long projects northwards on the other side to create a small yard area. Blackhouse.

A72* (NF721037) A rectangular thick-walled building, 12 × 7.5 m, with walls 1.6 m at their widest. There is the stump of a possible original partition wall to the left of the door in the east wall. Later rubble-built walls forming lambing pens are in the north-east and south-west corners. A byre, 6.5 × 4.5 m overall, has been added to the south end of the building, with a door at its north-east corner. Blackhouse.

A73 (NF719039) Oblong setting of stones, 3.7 × 1.4 m; some stones burnt, and pile of burnt stone close by. Kelp oven?

A74 (NF718039) Clearance cairn, 2.4 × 1.5 m, medium-small stones from secondary clearance?

A75 (NF718038) Substantial thick-walled building, 8 × 6.5 m, with no trace of internal partition or features; probably not a dwelling house. It may overlie an earlier structure; traces of a wall were noted below the north-west corner.

A76 (NF714042) Small circular hut, 4.6 m diam., with turf walls and stone walls; slightly inturned door on west.

A77 (NF713043) A low green mound 0.6 m high with traces of a kerb of stone blocks showing around the southern side. Prehistoric kerbed cairn, c. 5 m diam.?

A78 (NF713043) Immediately adjacent to A77, a prominent 2–3 m high grassed-over mound with a few blocks of stone showing through the sides. 9 × 7.5 m. This appears to be a similar monument to examples found on the Tanagaval peninsula and in the Borve valley, though with less stone visible. A large oval or round house of IA date?

A79 (NF712042) Setting of small boulders, 5 × 3.7 m. Shelter type A.

A80* (NF711042) Rectangular thick-walled building, 8.5 × 4.8 m, its walls varying between 1 m and 1.3 m in width. It has a door in its east wall, and may have had a second in the west wall. There is a secondary wall projecting into the main room from immediately alongside the door, and a rubble lambing pen built into the south-west corner. A modified blackhouse?

A81 (NF711042) Rectangular stone setting, 3.4 × 1.4 m, just 2 m from high-water mark. Kelp oven?

A82* (NF710042) Rectangular thick-walled building, 9.1 × 6 m, with door to the north. The wall is 1 m wide with an earth core. No partitions or secondary features at all. Blackhouse.

A83 (NF708045) Rectangular foundation 0.8 m wide, 9.7 × 7.3 m, against rock face with entrance to north. Lean-to shed.

A84 (NF708045) Substantial rectangular hut, 6 × 5.1 m, thick-walled and built against a rock face, entrance to north.

A85 (NF703045) Circular stone setting, 2.5 m diam., entrance to south. Shelter type A.

A86 (NF702045) Oblong building, 10.5 × 6.5 m, walls 1 m wide, door off-centre in north wall. Secondary stone setting in SE corner. Blackhouse with secondary lambing pen?

A87 (NF701045) Two conjoined oval stone settings, each 3 × 2 m. Shelter type B.

A88 (NF702044) Circular stone setting 3 m diam. Shelter type A.

A89 (NF704042) Right-angled stone structure built into relict field wall junction to form a trapezoidal enclosure 10 × 10 × 6 m.

A90 (NF702042) Circular stone setting 3 m diam. Shelter type A.

A91 (NF704040) Rectangular turf and stone structure, 4.8 × 3.5 m, with remains of circular stone setting 2.5 m diam. at SW corner. Small pen and shelter type A.

A92 (NF705039) Oblong stone structure, 11 × 8 m, with broad door in east wall, reduced walls of two earlier structures 11 × 7 m and 10.7 × 8 m attached to south. Recent outbuildings.

A93 (NF703038) Well-embedded and complex remains of stone structures covering an area c. 14 × 11.5 m, on a raised hillock. The only structures of which the form can be recognized are two small rectangular buildings 3.7 × 3 m and 3.2 × 2.6 m on the summit of the mound. There are suggestions of a substantial circular structure beneath the debris but no clear wall face. Prehistoric house and secondary structures including two shelters type B?

A94 (NF703038) Almost a twin of site A93, just 50 m to the north and standing on a second hillock. A mass of building debris much of it completely embedded, covering an area c. 16 × 11 m. Fragments of straight wall facing can be traced on a north–south axis and we suspect there may be a blackhouse here. It is unusual, however, for a blackhouse to be so ruined that it is not recognizable as such. The uppermost structure, whatever it may have been, appears to overlie remains of earlier stone structures. Possibly a prehistoric occupation site with a blackhouse superimposed.

A95 (NF703040) Subrectangular stone structure 5.5 × 4.5 m, door in east wall. Walls stand to a max. height of 1.5 m. Recent outbuilding.

A96 (NF703040) Circular stone setting 3 m diam. with traces of inner setting of smaller stones 1 m diam. Shelter type A and hearth?

A97 (NF702040) Oval stone structure 5 × 4 m, collapsed but not much embedded; door to south? Oval shieling hut?

A98 (NF701040) Heavily embedded remains of circular structure 2 m diam. with scattered stone blocks. Shelter type C.

A99 (NF702040) Sub-rectangular embedded stone structure, 4 × 3 m, door possibly to south. Shieling hut?

A100 (NF701040) Oval stone setting 3.5 × 2.5 m. Shelter type A.

A101 (NF701041) Oblong stone structure 2.5 × 1.5 m built against rock face. Shelter type F.

A102 (NF701040) Heavily embedded and robbed remains of a circular structure 7.3 × 6.8 m with stone faced wall 1 m wide, overlain by circular stone setting 2.5 m diam. The site sits on a steep sided knoll. Prehistoric roundhouse with superimposed shelter type A (Fig. 2.6).

A103 (NF699042) Subrectangular stone setting 5.1 × 2.5, some stones set on edge, and with offset in south wall to protect entrance? Shelter type A.

A104 (NF699042) Circular millstone, 1.2 m diam., 0.2 m thick.

A105 (NF696043) Circular stone setting 4.5 m diam. Shelter type A.

A106 (NF696037) Circular stone setting 2 m diam. within a larger arc of stone blocks. Shelter type A.

A107 (NF691038) Circular stone setting 2.7 m diam. with entrance to north. Shelter type A.

A108 (NF690040) Two adjacent circular stone structures 3.5 m diam. Shelter type C.

A109 (NF723016) A substantial grassed mound 23 × 20 m, on top of which are the remains of two stone structures. A a thick-walled building 6.3 × 5.5 m, with possible semicircular annexe at one end. B thick-walled building 8.4 × 6.7 m, with partition wall. Blackhouse and byre? but possibly a preferred site with earlier occupation.

A110 (NF725015) Heavily embedded remains of a circular stone structure on a local high spot. Overall diam. 6.3 m, wall 0.75 m wide, with entrance at east. Later shelter type A 3.4 m diam., built inside. Prehistoric hut and modern shelter.

A111 (NF733015) A cairn, 3 × 2.5 m, with some heavily embedded stone at the base. Probably modern.

A112 (NF723020) Partly robbed-out blackhouse, 11 × 6.4 m, with door to south and partition at east end.

A113 (NF724021) Entirely grassed-over foundations of a building approx. 8.5 × 6 m, possibly a demolished blackhouse.

A114 (NF722021) Stone setting, 3.7 × 2.8 m, of five large stones set on edge against a low rock face. Shelter type E.

A115 (NF713040) A prominent grassed-over mound, diam. 11.5 m and about 1 m high, on the top of which is a stone and turf, well-embedded oval hut 5 × 4.5 m, with a probable door at the south-east corner. Early modern shieling hut overlying an earlier shieling?

A116 (NF718026) Entirely grassed-over foundations of a building 7 × 6.8 m, with three clearance cairns nearby. Demolished outbuilding?

A117 (NF720025) Standing stone-walled building, 8.5 × 5.4 m, loosely built, with a 1 m door in the south wall. Outbuilding.

A118 (NF711035) 4 m square stone building, walls standing to two courses, with 0.9 m door in the east corner.

A119 (NF710037) Heavily embedded stone building, 9.3 × 7.3 m, walls 1.3 m wide, with door in middle of east wall. There is an annexe, 4.3 × 2.8 m, on the back wall. Blackhouse.

A120 (NF708037) Rectangular structure, 2.3 × 2.1 m, built against a low rock face with door at north-east corner.

A121 (NF708034) Partly robbed stone ring, 23.5 × 22.5 m, with ten stones mostly around western half,

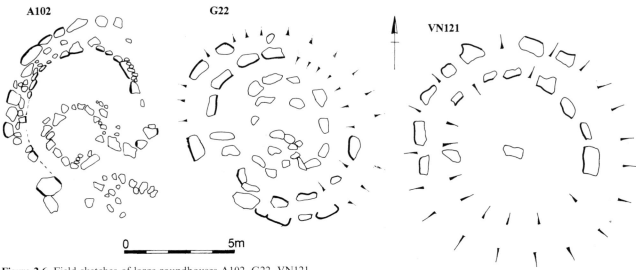

Figure 2.6 Field sketches of large roundhouses A102, G22, VN121.

not necessarily all *in situ*. Only two are upright. Prehistoric?

A122 (NF719036) Heavily embedded semicircular setting of stones, diam. 3.1 m, on low hillock at edge of bog. Shelter type A, part of hut-circle? Pre-modern?

A123 (NF708045) Oblong stone building 6.4 × 5.2 m, 1.15 m door towards the north-west corner, and wall standing to a maximum height of 0.75 m. The robbed remains of a totally embedded (turf-walled?) structure at least 5 × 3.5 m is immediately to the east, and to south is a turf-walled enclosure 5 × 4 m, butted to the rear wall of the main building. North of the building is a mound about 8 m diam. and 0.8 m high with traces of low embankment along its north edge, and an exposed shell-midden at its eastern edge. Blackhouse and garden plot; earlier building, and a possibly prehistoric occupation site.

A124 (NF706045) Three small embedded structures, represented by depressions, mostly full of nettles, with traces of wall or bank around each. A 3.5 × 2.9 m. B 4.5 × 3.8 m. C 3.2 × 2.8 m. Some modern rubbish apparently dumped into C. Their position, on a high rocky outcrop overlooking Traigh Mhor airfield, and their subterranean nature, is suggestive of a possibly military purpose, but they could be much older.

A125 (NF708031) The site of MacNeil's kelp factory, built c. 1832, now occupied by the Presbytery. The enclosure wall with several blocked arched gateways survives.

A126 (NF726014) An embedded ring of seven visible stone blocks forming a kerb around a low turfed mound 4.5 m in diameter. The regularity of the ring, its size and the apparent care with which the blocks are laid suggest this might be a kerbed cairn, but the area inside the kerb is almost flat and this perhaps points to nothing more than a platform, possibly as the stand for a hay rick.

A127 (NF707022) Two small circular stone structures 5 m apart. A is 2.5 m external diam., the wall 0.7 wide, with a door on the east. B is 3 m external diam., 0.7 m wide, with a door at the south-east. Both structures are very well-embedded, despite surface disturbance by sheep. They are only about 200 m from the end of Loch Obe and unlikely to be shieling huts. Possibly prehistoric round huts (see SEARCH volume 6)?

A128 (NF700028) Almost totally embedded stone-walled oblong building, 11.4 × 5.7 m. Damaged by erection of modern fence. No visible sign of internal partition, or of a doorway. Blackhouse.

Zone AF (Ardveenish, Isle of Fuiay)

AF1 (NF738023) Oval stone setting, 3 × 2.6 m. Shelter type A.

AF2 (NF738023) Semi-circular stone setting, 1 × 0.6 m. Shelter type A.

AF3 (NF738023) Stone structure, 3.7 × 2.5 m, partly overgrown but not embedded, with entrance to the south? Shelter type C.

AF4 (NF737023) Stone setting, 3 × 2 m, against a large boulder. Shelter type E.

AF5 (NF739024) Well-embedded stone and turf structure, 2.4 × 2.2 m, entrance to the south-west. Shelter type C.

AF6 (NF738025) Circular stone structure, 4.2 m diam., with wall 0.7 m wide. A door flanked by an upright stone is on the east, and on the north there is a small semicircular annexe. The foundations are well-embedded but the upper stonework is loosely built and may be a rebuild. Mediaeval hut?

AF7* (NF739025) Circular stone structure, 6.1 m diam., with well-embedded wall about 1 m wide. An entrance may be at the south-west. Prehistoric or mediaeval hut (Fig. 2.7)?

AF8* (NF737027) A heavily embedded and robbed rectangular stone structure, 6.5 × 3 m, with a wall 0.65 m wide. A door must have been located in the south wall. Small blackhouse, preceding main settlement (AF9)?

AF9* (NF737026) Settlement of blackhouses by small harbour. Nine structures were recorded, one of which (F) was reduced to grassed-over low banks and overlain by a standing structure (H), and is thought to predate the rest of the settlement. The buildings are set in a line along a low north–south ridge, and are recorded as structures A–H from north to south. Buildings A and B adjoined each other and measured 10.2 × 6.1 m and 8.7 × 5.9 m respectively. Each had a door in the east wall. There was no trace of internal partitions, but a lambing pen had been inserted into building A. Building C was oriented east–west, measured 11.8 × 7.2 m, and had a south-facing door. There was a secondary partition wall to the left of the door, and this may be contemporary with a second door that appears to have been inserted into the north wall, opposite the original door. Buildings D and E

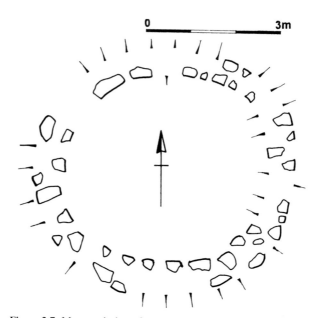

Figure 2.7 Measured plan of a small roundhouse on Fuiay (AF7).

were adjoined at right angles. Building D oriented east–west was 10.4 × 6.2 m, with a door facing north while building E was 10 × 6.7 m, and had an east-facing door. At some point in their history the two buildings became one with the insertion of a broad doorway through the conjoining wall. Building F surviving only as grassed-over banks, appears to have been 16 m long and was 7.5 m wide, with a doorway almost certainly in the east wall. It was overlain by building H 7.2 × 4.9 m, with an east-facing door and a internal pier or buttress on its west wall. A sheep dip was constructed outside its door. Attached to building H was a fenced pen 12.8 × 5 m that was constructed on the remains of a walled pen of the same size. Building G stood out of alignment with the other buildings, on a tiny promontory, and measured 11.3 × 6.9 m. Its door faced north, towards the other houses, and to the remains of a roughly built quay wall. This blackhouse settlement appears to have begun with one or two buildings (F and AF8), to have gone through a period of enlargement when eight houses were probably all in occupation together, and then to have been abandoned for permanent occupation and its buildings reused for lambing, storage of fishing tackle and other seasonal purposes.

AF10 (NF736026) Setting of stone blocks, 1.7 × 1.4 m, against a rock face. Shelter type E.

AF11 (NF734026) A stone-edged platform, 5.9 × 3.2 m, at the head of a small dyke. At the north end of the platform are the remains of a circular structure with a turf and stone wall 0.75 m wide, and about 2.8 m diam. Externally. All the structural remains are heavily embedded. Shelter type C or prehistoric/mediaeval circular hut?

AF12 (NF741029) A well-built rectangular stone structure 3.2 × 2.7 m, door to east, set in a sheltered gully high on the hillside. Shepherd's bothy?

AF13* (NF738025) Arc of stone and turf walling, enclosing an area 5 × 4.5 m against a rock face. Shelter type F or small pen.

AF14 (NF731027) Oval stone setting about 4 × 3 m, with two upright stones at the east end. Shelter type A?

AF15 (NF740023) A stone cairn with traces of kerbstones around the north side, but the southern half almost totally destroyed. The cairn, diam. c. 6 m, stands on the highest point on the island. The cairn material and kerbstones appear to have been demolished recently to build an arc of stone around the trig. point. Prehistoric kerbed cairn.

AF16 (NF740023) A stone cairn with a continuous kerb of large stone blocks. The cairn is 7 m diam. and survives to a height of c. 70 cm. The kerbstones are mostly 45–85 cm in length, but the largest is 1.2 m. AF16 stands 10 m from AF15. Prehistoric kerbed cairn.

AF17 (NF740022) Rough stone structure 2.1 × 1.8 m, built against a rock face, with entrance to west. Shelter type F.

Zone L (Loch Obe)

L1* (NF708003) Small rectangular hut, 4.6 × 2.1 m, constructed of three stone walls against a large rock; probably a fisherman's store.

L2* (NF708003) Remains of small blackhouse, 7 × 3 m, with last surviving course of 1 m wide wall.

L3* (NF710004) Turf-built house, 8.7 × 5.7 m, with stone-framed doorway at one end of long side, facing the sea 20 m to the south.

L4* (NF711004) Stone-built house, 7.65 × 5.5 m, with 1 m wide entrance at south-east corner, facing the sea. Two small secondary stone structures built into the north-east and south-west corners.

L5* (NF714003) Two turf walls forming a right angle, with traces of a ditch inside the angle. The walls partly enclose an area 20 × 14 m above the edge of the coast.

L6* (NF717004) A somewhat unusual blackhouse, 8.3 × 5.1 m, with two opposing doorways in the long (east and west) walls, and a narrow second room at the south end entered by a door midway along the partition wall.

L7* (NF716006) A substantial blackhouse, 10.3 × 5 m, with clear traces of internal stone-lined partitions. There is an interesting complex of lazy-bedded cultivation plots and remains of a small outbuilding to the west.

L8* (NF715017) A hamlet of seven houses, all reduced to little more than grassy humps, lying to the east of a small stream on a slope by Loch Obe. The houses range from 5.2 to 12 m in length, the biggest standing on an elevation a little above the others. Excavation report in SEARCH volume 6.

L9* (NF715017) A hamlet of eight structures, all with stone walls still standing to a metre or more, lying to the west of a stream on flat ground by Loch Obe. The structures include three or four houses (ranging from 7.15 to 14.3m), and two pens or sheds. Immediately west of the stream is an extensive midden, preserved in silt, producing 19th-century ceramics. There is a clear impression that L9 replaced L8 at some point in time. Excavation report and further discussion in SEARCH volume 6.

L10* (NF912019) Stone building, 4.5 × 3.85 m, door in centre of north wall. Outbuilding.

L11* (NF712018) Blackhouse, 9.6 × 5.5 m, with standing walls.

L12* (NF711018) Stone building, 16.6 × 6.1 m, wall width 1.2 m, with door near centre of east wall, and partition wall at north end. Blackhouse.

L13 (NF692003) A rather amorphous heap of stone blocks, heavily grassed over and disturbed, with possible traces of a wall alignment 2 m long and 0.6 m wide at one point. The site is located on a low rise between two streams on a steep hillside. There was undoubtedly a structure of some sort here, most probably one or more shepherd's shelters.

L14 (NF697007) Oval arrangement of large (40–50 cm) stones, 3.5 × 3 m, well embedded. Probably a shelter type A.

L15 (NF697007) Oval stone structure with a small rectangular annexe and an appended circular structure to the west. The site stands on a small knoll at the foot of a steep south-facing slope. The oval structure has a wall 0.75 m wide, stone-faced with an earth core, and measures 4.5 × 3.8 m overall. The entrance appears to be at the north-east corner. To the south is a rectangular annexe, 3 × 1.3 m, entered by a narrow door. This hut is very well embedded, and has been partly robbed and built over by a circular structure to the west. This is about 1.8 m diam. and has a wall of loose stone blocks. It clearly sits on an earlier heavily embedded foundation 3.8 m diam., the construction of which is similar to that of the oval structure. The upper of the two circular structures is a shelter type C. The lower and the adjoining oval hut are clearly considerably older. Excavated. Report in SEARCH volume 6.

L16 (NL695020) A difficult site to interpret due to heavy heather cover. A round or slightly oval knoll or mound has a series of large stone blocks embedded in it around its circumference and near its base. On top there is an oblong or oval depression with some stone blocks embedded within it and traces of horizontally bedded stone around the edge of the depression and further out at the edge of the knoll or mound's flat summit. We interpret the remains on the top of the knoll or mound as the ruins of an oval house, 10 × 7.5 m overall, with a wall about 0.8 m wide. We are uncertain whether this structure stands on a natural knoll or a man-made mound or cairn with a kerb around it. This cairn would be almost 15 m in diameter. On balance we reject the kerbed cairn hypothesis. Kerbed cairns are rare on Barra, and those so far discovered are small structures (up to 8 m diam.). Even on Vatersay, where there are many kerbed cairns, we know of none as large as this site. Finally, the configuration of the knoll itself, and what we can see of its character beneath the heather, suggests it is natural rather than a man-made cairn. It is possible that the stone blocks embedded at various points around the circumference are, nevertheless, traces of a deliberate structural feature, possibly associated with the house on the summit. We believe the house is probably of Iron Age date; a recent shelter of type C built of stone robbed from the summit structure stands to the east.

L18 (NF709009) Square stone and earth structure, 2.7 m external, with earth/turf bank faced inside with stone blocks. Entrance to west. Shelter type C.

L19 (NF709010) Almost circular raised turf bank, 7 × 6.3 m, with possible entrance 1.5 m wide on east north-east. Slight ditch around outside, and interior area appears sunken. The bank is about 1.2 m wide and survives 0.4 m high at its maximum. Its size

suggests comparison with stone-founded huts of IA date, the superstructures of which were perhaps built of turf or peat blocks.

L20 (NF706004) Rectangular building 11.25 × 6.5 m with rounded corners and a wall 1.1 m wide. There is a door in the centre of one long wall, facing north-east and 0.9 m wide. There is no trace of a partition but a lambing pen has been built into the east corner at a late date, and there may be a similar pen built against the rear, west, wall. Blackhouse.

L21 (NF707006) Two-period rectangular structure, the uppermost 3.3 m square with loosely set stone blocks and infilled with rather loose debris. There may be a small doorway at the north-east corner. This structure is built over and inside the well-embedded remains of a building 5.2 × 5.5 m. Both structures are probably outbuildings for the adjacent blackhouse (L20).

L22 (NF706004) A small building 5.6 × 4.8 m with a door in the north corner, butting on to a stone-and-turf enclosure 9.6 × 8.7 m. The hut is too small for a living house (4.2 × 3 m internal) and it is probably a lambing hut or temporary shelter associated with seasonal use of the pen.

L23 (NF706004) Semi-circular setting of four stone blocks, 2.3 m wide and a metre deep. The tallest block is 0.7 m, and the open side faces south. Probably a shelter type A.

L24 (NF707003) Much robbed and damaged remains of a rectangular building with rounded corners, 10.6 × 8.5 m. No visible remains of door or partitions. Blackhouse.

L25 (NF683020) A very overgrown heap of loose blocks of stone at the edge of a slab of bedrock, with suggestions of rough kerbstones on south side. Diam. approx. 2.5 m. A cairn of indeterminate date.

L26 (NF696032) Partly standing building and associated structures. Mill building, with east wall standing to full height. Internal 9 × 4.6 m. Walls of large boulders form two conduits approaching building from the south (upslope and loch). To the west of the mill building is an oblong structure 12.5 × 6.1 m, apparently divided into two rooms, the smaller of which at the north end is only 2.5 m wide. Each room has its own, east-facing doorway. West of this building is a small rectangular thick-walled structure 2.3 × 2.8 m seemingly open on the north side.

L27 (NF691021) Bank 16 m long, 4 m wide, and 1 m high, of earth and stone. This appears to be debris and upcast from stone quarrying immediately alongside the bank. Quarry.

L28 (NF714015) Two platforms, each about 2 m square, of small, heavily embedded stones. Rick-bases.

L29 (NF712018) Low flat-topped mound, 26 × 14 m, with marked edge around north and west sides. Set 25 m back from edge of Loch Obe close to a high rock face. Covered in ferns. Premodern occupation site and platform?

L30 (NF715016) Sub-rectangular revetted platform, 4.1 × 3.4 m, 1 m high on north side. Rick-base?

L31 (NF714018) Four clearance cairns, each 1–1.5 m diam.

L32 (NF702019) Remains of stone building on small islet in Loch na Ruaidhe. Collapsed masonry with five courses to 2 m high at west end. Two concentric walls, each c. 1 m wide separated by a 'gallery' about 50–60 cm wide, can be traced around the west end. The overall dimensions of the structure are c. 15 × 13 m. A submerged causeway 22 m long and 2 m wide joins the islet to the shore on its northern side, and there may be some sort of outwork between the causeway and the main structure. The causeway is up to 2 m below the present water level. The quantity of stone collapse, including that observed under water, suggest this structure may never have been carried up into a full 'tower'. Visited by L. Davison in 1999. (RCAHMS 1928: 134, No. 454). ARH.

L33 (NF694032) Remains of thick-walled circular building, c. 15 m diam., wall standing to three or four courses on north-west, with submerged causeway to shore. Broch? Now submerged in Loch an Duin reservoir, recorded by RCHAMS (1928: 131, No. 445)

L34 (NF718008) Rectangular structure apparently entirely of turf walling except for door framed in stone blocks in the north wall. Overall dimensions 10 × 6 m, walls 1.1–1.4 m thick. The door was probably about 1 m wide, but the stones on its lefthand side have been removed. Turf-built blackhouse. There are possible traces of a similar structure 30 m to the east.

L35 (NF702001) Well-embedded cairn about 1.3 m high, with ten stones visible forming a kerb around its periphery. Small stones embedded in turf on the top of the mound may be secondary clearance, but the regularity of the cairn, its profile and its neat kerb point to a primary kerbed cairn.

L36 (NF701001) An oval cairn, 4.5 × 3 m, with large blocks set mostly around its eastern arc and smaller stones loosely embedded on top. Primary and secondary clearance cairn.

Zone S (Skallary)

S1* (NL696982) Short length (9m) of rough boulder retaining wall, two clearance areas for cultivation (each c. 9 × 15m) and semicircular stone setting (2.5 m diam.) against a large rock. Shelter type E.

S2* (NL697982) Turf and stone wall enclosing a small headland, with stone facing on outer side. Within the enclosed area (75 × 35m) there are clear traces of lazy-beds; the wall is intended to keep sheep out of the enclosure.

S3* (NL691977) Roughly built turf and stone wall, no clear structure, 16 m long and 0.8 m wide, built between two rock faces on a steep slope c. 50 m from the sea.

S4* (NL689976) Rough boulder wall that shuts off a small headland on which there is a fern-covered mound with no sign of building stone and apparently little depth of soil. The wall is c.12 m long, 1 m wide, and is roughly faced on the mainland side, backed with an earth bank and traces of a ditch on the headland side. Too insubstantial to have a defensive purpose.

S5* (NL686975) Stone-built wall fronting a small hill flanked by two streams. The wall is roughly coursed but also incorporates large natural boulders/rock outcrops into its line. Its total length is c. 28 m and its width 1m; at its highest it stands 1.25 m high. It appears to have been built to protect the lower slope of the hill from the sea. To the north, about 50 m from the sea, on a fern-covered hillock, there is a pronounced rectangular platform 7 × 5 m, which is almost certainly the site of a small building.

S6* (NL686975) Three, possibly four, raised platforms covered in ferns. The largest (A) appears to be either trapezoidal or irregular in shape and measures 17 × 8 m (at its broadest, seaward end). At its broad end at least two courses of stone walling are visible for a length of c. 5 m, overlain by a deposit of dryish, slow-growing peat c. 20 cm deep. Platform B measures c. 9 × 3 m, and platform C c. 16 × 5 m. Along the south side of platform C there are traces of stones and rock outcrops. These appear to be the sites of three buildings forming a complex, and possibly of considerable antiquity to judge from the peat formation over the wall of building A. Mediaeval or earlier?

S7* (NL677976) A grassed-over heap of building blocks with traces of a rectangular structure c. 7 × 5 m, with a curving enclosure wall on uphill side. Shieling with hut?

S8* (NL675972) A 10 m roughly built wall shutting off a very small headland. The wall is 1.6 m long and 0.7 m wide; the headland is today only 1.6 m wide and 5.9 m long and it can never have been more than twice this size to judge from the rock formation below it. The 'enclosure' could have been used to pen a few sheep.

S9* (NL675973) Rectangular house foundation and an adjacent stone-built pen. The house foundations are relatively narrow (c.0.75 m) and measure 8.6 × 5.3 m; there is no trace of a chimney. The pen is 6 × 3.5 m. There may be a third rectangular structure north of the house beneath ferns, and there is a buttressed platform on a small headland south of the house. A stream runs close to the house on the west, and beyond the stream is a major 'sheep' wall of turf and stone that runs for almost a kilometre up the valley and over into Garygall. Local oral tradition claims that the house was built by Dermot O'Neil from Co. Sligo, shipwrecked on Barra c. 1780–90 and given this land by McNeil of Barra. When O'Neil subsequently married a local woman some years later he abandoned this house.

S10* (NL698989) Two short sections of stone and turf wall, each c. 6 m long, flanked by lazy-bedding, on south-facing slope.

S11* (NL699988) Stone and turf wall with terminal shepherd's shelter of large boulders (approx. 2.5 m square).

S12* (NL700988) Earth bank, c. 2 m wide at base and 1 m high, with large boulders embedded irregularly into it. It runs over crest of hill but does not completely cut off the headland.

S13* (NL702987) A complex of three banks forming part of two enclosed areas. The earthen bank (B), 1.6 m wide, extends across the headland, while banks A and C flank the east side of a shallow but soggy gully. The enclosed areas show signs of previous lazy-bedding.

S14* (NL703988) A rectangular blackhouse 10.3 × 5.5 m overall, with walls up to 1.5 m wide at base. The door is on the east side, and opposite the door is a partition wall that divides the house into two rooms. The walls survive up to four courses high in places.

S15* (NL701991) A rectangular house, 10.7 × 4 m, with a byre(?) attached to rear (6.5 × 4.1 m) and a small square outbuilding. The walls are of boulders and survive to a height of 1 m.

S16* (NL707991) A wall of single large blocks, running between two rock outcrops, on the small tidal islet of Orosay.

S17* (NL706992) Four small oval or oblong cairns, each c. 1.5 m long, on the tidal islet of Orosay. They appear to be clearance cairns.

S18 (NL689987) Semi-circular enclosure, 7.2 × 6.9 m, built against a rock face. The rough boulder-built wall has an entrance gap at the north-west corner flanked by an external shelter 2.1 × 1.3 m built against the rock. In the centre of the enclosure there is low round heap of stone blocks and some sort of structure seems to have stood there. A sheep-pen with shepherd's shelter, but the function of the central structure is unclear.

S19 (NL689990) Standing stone and broken second stone lying nearby. This is one of the few monuments recorded on the OS Map and by the RCAHMS on Barra. The standing stone is 2.74 m high above ground level, and has a maximum width of 0.86 m and thickness of 0.5 m. The second stone is broken into two pieces, the larger measuring 1.35 m and the smaller 0.9 m in length. From the angle at which the smaller stone is narrowing, we estimate it has lost about 0.35–0.45 m from its tip, so that the original height of the entire stone would have been 2.6–2.7 m, almost exactly matching that of the standing stone. At its widest it was 0.94 m across. We think that the fallen stone tapered to a central rounded tip, while the standing stone tapered asymmetrically from one side only. The two stones stand in a flat shelf approached through a shallow defile at the top of a steep slope from the low pasture immediately behind Brevig Bay. The stones overlook this area rather than Brevig Bay itself which is largely masked from the view of the stones by a low rise immediately south-east of the stones. Prehistoric ritual site.

S20 (NL688993) A stone ring comprised of six stones *in situ*, three apparently shifted a few metres, and three perhaps moved into a heap 15 m to the east. The ring stands on a slightly raised shelf flanked to the east by a shallow stream bed. On the east side the ring has been disturbed by peat cutting, and it is thought that the three stones just across the stream bed may have been moved from this segment. The diameter* of the ring is 11.3 m. None of the stones are large (the largest is about 0.75 m long), and it cannot be described as a 'megalithic' monument. Its function is uncertain. The stones have been deliberately placed, but unless each stone was used to support a fence post they could not indicate an enclosure except in a purely conceptual sense. We think a fenced enclosure on this high and exposed area is not only unlikely but also without a parallel in our experience in the southern isles. We therefore incline to the view that this is most likely to be a ritual site of some sort and associated, though not necessarily contemporary, with the two standing stones 300 m downslope.

S21 (NL688993) Rectangular structure, 3 × 1.5 m, built against rock face and heavily embedded. Shelter type F.

S22 (NL700994) Rectangular stone setting 2.4 × 2 m built against rock face. Shelter type E.

S23 (NL690995) Semi-circular stone structure 2.7 × 1.6 m built against rock face. Shelter type F. There are two small areas of lazy-bedding immediately alongside.

S24 (NL696992) Semi-circular stone structure 2.7 × 1.5 m built against a huge boulder. Shelter type F.

S25 (NL692989) Oval stone setting 21 x 10 m on a low-lying flat shelf 150 m from the sea. Eleven stones *in situ*; we estimate a similar number have been robbed out. The stones are not large (the largest is 0.7 m long). The function and date are unclear (Fig. 2.8).

S26 (NL693989) Circular stone setting 12 × 9 m on low-lying flat shelf 200 m from the sea. Nine stones *in situ*; we estimate two more have been robbed out and some stones lie near. The stones are 0.5–0.7 m in height. The function and date are unclear, but it has the appearance of an ancient setting (Fig. 2.8).

S27 (NL693992) A crude arc of stone and turf wall enclosing an area 2 × 1 m. Remains of shelter type C.

S28 (NL694991) An apparently oval setting of small megaliths, 16.5 × 14.6 m, with perhaps six stones thought to be *in situ* and another eight to nine moved but on site. It is possible that the setting was originally circular, as indicated by the five remaining standing stones on the north side of the setting, with a diameter of c. 14 m. The tallest standing stone is 1.5 m, and there is a recumbent stone 1.4 m opposite to it. Seven further stones are between 0.7 and 1 m in height. The straight alignment of stones on the west side appears to be part of a relatively recent rearrangement of stones that included a low wall to the south and a further straggly alignment to the south-east. North and north-east of

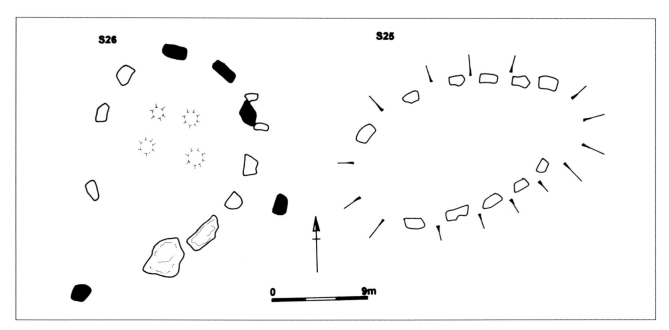

Figure 2.8 Field sketches of stone rings S25 and S26.

the standing arc of stones there is also a cluster of about 20 small cairns. These are not heavily embedded and presumably of relatively recent date. They are of interest, however, for two reasons. First, because, while neighbouring areas have traces of lazy-bed cultivation, the raised knoll on which this monument stands does not. While they may have been intended as clearance cairns, the knoll was not finally cleared, and nor was it cultivated. Second, several of the cairns include large stones, similar to those in the ring. At least a dozen were counted that were over 0.8 m in length. We conclude that the surviving ring was perhaps part of a rather more complex monument at some time in the past, that it was partly demolished with an intention to cultivate the land in relatively recent times, but that the clearance was never completed. We believe the monument is most likely to have originated as a ritual structure in the prehistoric period (Fig. 9.6).

S29 (NL697991) Three adjoining stone-built structures. At the southern end a poorly built blackhouse 9 × 5.5 m, central door 0.9 m wide, and no internal partition. At the north end a drying shed, 9.8 × 4.6 m, set at right angles to the house and with a raised platform with angled flue at one end. These two buildings were linked by the insertion of a shed or byre with internal measurements of 3.4 × 2.7 m.

S30 (NL 696996) U-shaped stone setting, 3 × 2.7 m, with six stones around the periphery and a gap on the south-east side. Probably a shelter type A but a mounding in the central area rather than the usual depression might possibly indicate a cairn.

S31 (NL692998) A roughly built three-quarter circle of stone wall, diam. 3 m, completed by two blocks of bedrock. Shelter type C.

S32 (NL693998) A very heavily embedded circular or oval stone structure, 6.5 × 5 m, wall c. 0.6 m wide and with a depressed central area. Much robbed but apparently an oval hut rather than a shelter.

S33 (NL696100) A rectangular built structure 2.5 × 1.6 m, on the end of a sheep wall. Shelter type C.

S34 (NL697997) Complex of three stone buildings. A house 12.5 × 6 m has a central door, no internal partitions, but a fireplace and chimney in one end wall. Behind the house stands a drying shed 9 × 6.3 m with a platform and diagonal flue at one end. Built against the shed is a byre 8.3 × 4 m with a drainage gully running out through the door, which is in an end wall. Immediately alongside is a stream, and on the far side is a walled cultivation area 23 × 7 m.

S35 (NL698996) Complex of three stone structures. A house 13 × 6.5 m has a central door that is divided in two by a partition wall. The room to the right has a fireplace and chimney, the room to the left is slightly larger and has a slightly wider door. Behind the house is an L-shaped wall that, together with a rock outcrop, may have formed the foundation of an open-sided shed. Immediately next to it is the third building, 6.1 × 5.1 m, with a single central door 0.8 m wide facing the shed.

S36 (NL698996) Two adjacent blackhouses. One is 11 × 7 m and divided into two rooms each accessed by its own door (0.5 and 0.6 m wide). The other is 11 × 6 m with a central door 1 m wide and no partition. A stream runs behind the houses.

S37 (NL698996) Outbuilding, 8.8 × 5.5 m with door in one corner of an end wall. This is a notably thin-walled building for its size-wall width 0.7 m.

S38 (NL699995) A flat-topped platform on a rock outcrop, little trace of any stone revetment. 12 × 8.8 m.

Possible emplacement for a timber building, or a stack.

S39 (NL700994) A circular stone structure on a small natural knoll in the centre of a well-sheltered hollow. Diam. 4 m. On the north side two courses of walling are visible although the structure is very deeply embedded in the grass. Possibly a prehistoric hut.

S40 (NL700996) A rectangular platform 3.5 × 2 m with large flat edging stones at one end, three at one edge, and one (1.2m) at the other. Well embedded. Purpose and date unknown.

S41 (NL700997) A large grassed-over mound of stone blocks, 17.5 × 12.6 m overall. It appears to be a multi-period monument, with several small oval and sub-rectangular hut-like structures built into and from the rubble of a lower building. This appears to have been a circular building of about 12–13 m diam. We interpret this lower structure as most probably a free-standing Iron Age wheelhouse, or possibly a large circular house without radial partitions.

S42 (NL700997) A curving stone and turf wall built against an outcrop of bedrock; internal diam. 1.5 m. Shelter type F.

S43 (NL696996) Blackhouse, 9 × 6 m, with central door and no internal partition, apparently used as an outbuilding for a whitehouse with chimney and three windows that replaced it on the other side of a small stream.

S44 (NL695997) Blackhouse, 11 × 7 m, with central door and no partition. To the rear is a second building 9 × 7 m with a partition wall and separate access to each room.

S45 (NL694981) Built structure, 2.5 m square, door at west corner; partially overlying a 1.5 m diam. shelter type A. Shelter type C.

S46 (NL697978) Rectangular stone structure 2.4 × 1.6 m, built against a south-facing rock face. Shelter type F.

S47 (NL676973) Oblong stone and earth structure, heavily embedded and partly robbed, with well-rounded end walls. Overall 7 × 4.75 m, door probably in east wall. Blackhouse.

S48 (NL671974) Mound, 3 m diam., of mainly largish stone blocks (about 50 cm length); a smaller mound of small stones is 30 m to the east. Primary and secondary clearance cairns.

S49 (NL677984) Two adjacent stone and earth structures. The larger is 13.6 × 7.6 m overall, with a 0.8 m door slightly off centre in the east wall. A secondary pen/shelter is built into one corner. On the same alignment, immediately alongside, the second building is 8 × 7.4 m, with a door in the south-west corner. The complex sits at the confluence of four linear boundaries. There appears to be an earlier rectangular structure 6.2 × 4.4 m partly overlain by the north-west corner of the larger building. Blackhouse and byre.

S50 (NL677984) Rectangular stone and earth building, 6 × 5 m, with 1 m door in the south-east corner.

The interior is divided into two almost equal halves by a stone partition wall. Byre?

S51 (NL676984) Four embedded heaps of small stones, 1.5–2 m diam. Secondary clearance cairns.

S52 (NL679984) Rectangular structure, 2.1 × 1.9 m, built against a boundary wall. Shelter type F.

S53 (NL678985) Oblong stone-walled sheep pen, 12 × 10.5 m, overlying an earlier thick-walled structure 11 m long and possibly 6 m wide. Apparently a blackhouse.

S54 (NL679985) Stone setting, 1.2 × 1 m, shelter type A.

S55 (NL677987) Circular stone and turf structure, badly damaged by cultivation and robbing. External dimensions 5 × 4.5 m, door to west. Prehistoric hut?

S56 (NL687986) Corner of a rectangular stone structure, 2 × 1 m. Wall width, 0.6 m, suggests a small outbuilding.

S57 (NL687986) Three small irregular piles of embedded field stones, and three dumps of similar stones against a low rock face. Secondary clearance cairns.

S58 (NL689984) Regularly shaped stone, 0.7 × 0.3 m, set upright with propping stones at base. Height 1.2 m. A few metres upslope two large stones set on edge and three smaller blocks appear to mark out a cist-like feature 2 × 0.8 m. If too small to be called a standing stone, the upright stone appears to be a positional marker of some sort.

S59 (NL689984) Strongly built stone rectangular structure 4 m square, with additional room 4 × 1.8 m at the west end. The door is in the east end and there appears to be a bench-like feature 0.6 m wide running along the inside of the south wall. The north wall of the building utilizes the line of an earlier boundary wall. At this point, for a distance of about 15 m, the boundary wall retains its stone, but beyond this in both directions there is only a low earth hump to mark its line. Presumably the building (a bothy?), was built after the wall had gone out of use and utilized its stone. To the north of the old boundary wall a raised semicircular area with stone blocks beneath the turf might mark the position of an earlier circular hut of about 4 m diam.

S60 (NL687988) Upstanding remains of a stone and earth walled oblong building, 13.4 × 6.6 m, with a 1.1 m door in the centre of the east wall. Blackhouse. 15 m south is a second thick-walled building 6.3 × 5 m, with a 0.8 m door in the north-east corner. This appears to be a byre.

S61 (NL687989) Well-embedded stone and earth wall of an oblong building 10.1 × 5.9 m, with a door near centre in the east wall. Blackhouse. Immediately alongside is a second thick-walled building, 7 × 6.8 m, with a door in the short north wall. No trace of a platform or flue; probably a byre.

S62 (NL687989) Heavily embedded and much robbed remains of an oblong stone and earth walled building, 8.85 × 5.7 m overall. A 1 m door is almost central in the southern wall. Blackhouse immediately alongside and on the same axis is a second thick-walled structure 6.1 × 4.9 m, with a door in the south-east corner. This is probably a byre, and appears to partly overlie an earlier thick-walled structure 6.7 m long.

S63 (NL683996) Roughly built rectangular stone structure 2.7 × 1.8 m, built against a west-facing rock face. Shelter type F.

S64 (NL683996) Two crudely built, irregular, conjoined structures, 2.2 × 1.5 m and 2.3 × 1.7 m. Shelter type D.

Zone K (Kiessimul)

K1 (NL665974) Extensive traces of docksides and foundations associated with herring fisheries, late 19th–early 20th century.

K2 (NL668980) Alleged site of totally destroyed 'dun'. A small flat-topped rocky hill. No traces of any structure were visible on it. Observation of a pipe trench cut alongside the east side of the hill revealed no archaeology at all.

K3 (NL656978) Further docksides and foundations connected with the late 19th–early 20th-century herring fisheries.

K4 (NL667980) Kiessimul Castle. RCAHMS (1928: 126–28) have a description and plan of the castle, the foundation of which they place in the later 15th century.

K5 (NL681988) Well-embedded thick-walled oblong building 11.2 × 8.6 m, 0.95 m door off centre in east wall. Against the inside face of the west wall, equidistant from the corners, is a rectangular structure 1.7 × 1 m (internal) with walls about 0.5 m wide. This appears to be as well-embedded as the rest of the main structure. A later semicircular shelter or pen of stone blocks is built against it. Blackhouse with built bed-box?

K6 (NL679992) Simple stone setting 1.2 × 1 m incorporating two rocks and four stone blocks. Shelter type A.

K7 (NL677989) Heavily embedded turf-walled oblong structure 4 × 2.2 m, oriented north–south, with a curving north wall and straight south one. East wall disturbed, door in south-west corner. Bothy?

K8 (NL676989) Much disturbed and robbed complex stone and earth structure, possibly L-shaped, 11.8 × 5.4 m max. diam. Possibly remains of a pen overlain by lazy-bedding.

K9 (NL676989) Heavily embedded and robbed remains of an oval stone structure approx. 11 × 8 m, overlain by (and robbed for?) a substantial sheep wall. Prehistoric roundhouse?

K10 (NL676986) Heavily embedded and robbed thick-walled oblong building 7.5 × 5.5 m, with 0.75 m door in centre of south wall and a possible second facing it in the north wall. Three linear boundaries, one a sheep wall, run up to the building. Blackhouse?

K11 (NL676986) Linear stone boundary overlying an oval platform 7.5 × 5 m, with a kerb of stone blocks surviving around eastern arc. Possible oval hut?

K12 (NL675986) Heavily embedded and much-robbed traces of a stone and earth structure 9 × 4.5 m. It does not appear to be a thick-walled structure. Mediaeval/early modern house?

K13 (NL676986) Embedded oval cairn 2 × 1 m of mostly smaller stones, 15 m from a second larger cairn 5 × 2 m, partly set on rock, with both large and small stones. Primary and secondary clearance cairns.

K14 (NL675986) Two stone cairns 9 m apart. The larger, 2.8 m diam., has many large and some smaller stones; the smaller 1.9 m diam., is entirely of small stones. Primary and secondary clearance cairns.

K15 (NL673988) Heavily embedded and reduced oval or subrectangular turf structure 6.9 × 4.3 m, largely destroyed on south and east sides. Oval hut?

K16 (NL673988) Much-disturbed stone setting with five stones set upright (0.5–0.7 m tall) in arc and others lying nearby or visible under turf. Original setting estimated 6 × 4.5 m with possibly 12 stones? Stone ring.

K17 (NL672987) Three adjacent stone cairns, 1.5–2.5 m diam., all incorporating small to medium stones. Clearance cairns.

K18 (NL672985) Thick-walled oblong building, 9 × 5.2 m, with door almost central in north wall. A paved pen, 2 × 1 m, has been inserted into the north-east corner. Blackhouse.

K19 (NL672985) Much-damaged and robbed stone structure, possibly L-shaped, c. 8 × 6 m. Outbuilding?

K20 (NL671986) Two heaps of stone, 3 m diam. and 3 × 1.3 m, on rock slabs. Primary and secondary clearance cairns.

K21 (NL671987) Lean-to stone building 5.7 × 4.3 m, against west-facing rock face. Outbuilding.

K22 (NL670987) Four heaps of stone, one of large and three of small stones against low rock face. Primary and secondary clearance cairns.

K23 (NL671988) Clearance cairn, 2 m diam., of small stones.

K24 (NL674992) Completely embedded remains of circular? stone structure forming mound about 1 m high. Rabbit infested. Visible stone blocks mostly 30–50 cm length. Original diam. c. 6 m. Prehistoric roundhouse?

K25 (NL674993) Oval stone setting, 3.5 × 2.5 m. Shelter type A.

K26 (NL671992) Roughly built stone and earth structure 3.5 × 2.3 m, entrance to S. Shelter type C.

K27 (NL670992) Heavily embedded stone setting 2 m diam. Shelter type A.

K28 (NL670993) Triangular stone setting 1.9 × 1.5 m. Shelter type A.

K29 (NL670994) Stone setting, 2.4 m diam. Shelter type A.

K30 (NL669995) Stone setting, 2.6 m diam. Shelter type A.

K31 (NL671995) Oval stone and earth structure, 6 × 5 m, with wall 0.75 m wide and entrance to south prehistoric roundhouse?

K32 (NL670995) Stone setting, 3.5 × 2.3 m. Shelter type A.

K33 (NL670996) Substantial spread of stone blocks on hillslope with remains of a 1 m wide circular wall surviving upslope. The structure was c. 7.2 × 6.2 m overall. In the centre of the surviving arc there is a large upright slab, separated by a gap from a similar slab tipped at 45°. Both slabs are covered by large block 1.4 m long. This has the appearance of an original stone-framed door, about 0.9 m wide. Prehistoric roundhouse.

K34 (NL671997) On a shelf at c. 200 m OD, a well-preserved circular stone and earth structure 11.75 m diam. The wall circuit can be clearly traced around its perimeter, and a door 0.8 m wide is at the north protected by a high rock face. A possible pier is identified to the north-east of the door, and several rock slabs up to 1.5 m long were noted, which may have been lintel slabs. Iron Age wheelhouse (Fig. 11.1).

K35 (NL670997) Much-destroyed and well-embedded complex stone structure, mainly identified by slabs set on edge forming between three and five rectangular conjoined cells. Overall area c. 8m × 8 m. Prehistoric?

K36 (NL669997) Substantial spread of stone blocks on small shelf above steep slope. Around south (downslope) side five successive substantial blocks can be seen firmly embedded in an arc. On the north side, the outline of a curving structure is marked partly by stone blocks and partly by a shallow cutting into the hillslope. A substantial circular structure stood here, about 8 m in diameter. Prehistoric roundhouse. A much later shepherd's shelter 1.7 × 1.3 m is built over one corner of the structure.

K37 (NL669997) Badly robbed and damaged circular stone structure, diam. 10 m. The structure lies on a slope and the bottom end is 2 m below the top end, and in a boggy hollow. The structure is represented by the remains of a roughly built wall 0.8 m wide around the upper western arc, but is reduced to a scatter of stone blocks, still on the circuit line, on the east. We believe it was robbed out to build a substantial sheep wall that runs about 10 m to the east of the structure. Mediaeval or early modern pen.

K38 (NL669996) Embedded stone structure 2.2 m diam. on low mound. Shelter type C.

K39 (NL669996) Three small stone settings on two adjoined hillocks, 2 m, 1.5 m and 1.5 m diam. Shelters type A.

K40 (NL669995) Oval stone setting 2.6 × 2.2 m, on low mound. Shelter type A. There is probably another, robbed, 10 m east.

K41 (NL668995) Stone setting, 2.5 m diam. Shelter type A.

K42 (NL668995) Scattered stone setting 3 × 2.3 m. Shelter type A.

K43 (NL668997) Stone setting 2.1 × 1.9 m. Shelter type A.

K44 (NL668996) Two conjoined circular stone and earth structures, each 4 × 3 m. Shieling huts?

K45 (NL668995) Oval stone and earth structure, 4 × 3 m, door at north? Shieling hut?

K46 (NL668996) Circular stone structure 2.3 m diam. Shelter type C.

K47 (NL666996) Oval embedded stone setting 3.5 × 2 m. Shelter type A.

K48 (NL668997) Heavily embedded stone structure, 2.2 m diam. Shelter type C. Second, much destroyed, example 10 m south. Shelter type C.

K49 (NL667996) Well-embedded oval structure 3 × 2.1 m. Shelter type C.

K50 (NL668996) Scattered stone setting, 2.5 m diam. Shelter type A.

K51 (NL666996) Scattered stone blocks 1.6 m diam. on larger mound 3 m diam. with five visible blocks set around perimeter. The soup-bowl profile is reminiscent of kerbed cairns. Prehistoric cairn, possibly kerbed.

K52 (NL666997) Sparse stone setting 3.3 × 2.2 m on low hillock. Shelter type A.

K53 (NL666997) Stone setting 2.5 m diam. Shelter type A.

K54 (NL667996) Stone setting 2.5 m diam. Shelter type A.

K55 (NL667996) Remains of stone structure 3 × 2 m, overlain by stone setting 1.3 m diam. Shelter type C overlain by shelter type A.

K56 (NL667996) Stone setting 1.8 m diam. Shelter type A.

K57 (NL667996) Stone setting 3.3 m diam. Shelter type A.

K58 (NL666996) Stone setting 1.8 m diam. Shelter type A.

K59 (NL666995) Stone setting 1.8 m diam. Shelter type A.

K60 (NL666997) Stone setting 2 m diam. Shelter type A.

K61 (NL666997) Stone structure 3.8 × 3 m. Shelter type C.

K62 (NL667997) Stone setting 1.9 × 1.5 m. Shelter type A.

K63 (NL664996) Stone setting 1.9 × 1.7 m. Shelter type A.

K64 (NL664996) Stone setting 2 m diam. Shelter type A.

K65 (NL664996) Stone setting 2 m diam. Shelter type A.

K66 (NL664997) Stone structure, 3 m diam. door to south-east. Shelter type C.

K67 (NL664997) Stone setting 2 m diam. Shelter type A.

K68 (NL664997) Stone setting 2.3 m diam. Shelter type A.

K69 (NL666999) Stone setting 2 m diam. Shelter type A.

K70 (NL664996) Stone setting 2 m diam. Shelter type A.

K71 (NL664995) Stone setting 2 m diam. Shelter type A.

K72 (NL664995) Grassy mound 0.7 m high, 6 m diam., with about ten stone blocks visible around perimeter, and a smaller central mound about 2 m diam. with stone visible in turf. Prehistoric bordered cairn?

K73 (NL663996) Stone setting 2 m diam. Shelter type A.

K74 (NL663996) Two stone settings, 2 m and 1.5 m diam. and 9 m apart. Shelters type A.

K75 (NL662996) Stone setting 2.5 m diam. Shelter type A.

K76 (NL661996) Rectangular stone structure 2 × 1.3 m against south-facing rock face. Shelter type F.

K77 (NL662996) Stone setting 2.6 m diam. Shelter type A.

K78 (NL662996) Stone setting 2.3 m diam. with two stones set upright suggesting 0.4 m entrance on south. Shelter type A.

K79 (NL662995) Stone setting 2 m diam. Shelter type A.

K80 (NL662995) Stone setting 2.3 m diam. Shelter type A.

K81 (NL661996) Stone structure 3 m diam. Shelter type C.

K82 (NL661996) Stone setting 2.6 m diam. overlying circular stone structure 3.5 m diam. Shelter type A and shieling hut?

K83 (NL663996) Stone structure 3 m diam., door to north protected by wall extension on west side. Shelter type C.

K84 (NL662995) Stone and earth structure 3.5 m diam. Shieling hut.

K85 (NL662995) Stone and earth structure 3.5 m diam. Shieling hut.

K86 (NL663995) Stone structure 3.5 × 3 m. Shieling hut.

K87 (NL663995) Stone setting 2 × 1.3 m. Shelter type A.

K88 (NL663994) Stone structure 2.6 m diam. Shelter type C.

K89 (NL664994) Stone structure 4 × 3.75 m. Shieling hut?

K90 (NL664994) Stone setting 2 m diam. Shelter type A.

K91 (NL664994) Stone and earth structure 3 × 2.6 m. Shelter type C.

K92 (NL664994) Stone setting 2.7 × 2 m. Shelter type A.

K93 (NL665993) Stone setting 2.8 × 2 m. Shelter type A.

K94 (NL663993) Stone setting 2.3 m diam. Shelter type A.

K95 (NL663993) Stone setting 2.1 m diam. Shelter type A.

K96 (NL663993) Stone structure 1.4 × 0.9 m, set against a very large boulder. Shelter type F.

K97 (NL663992) Stone and earth structure 4.2 m diam., entrance at west. Shieling hut.

K98 (NL663992) Stone setting, 2.5 m diam. Shelter type A.

K99 (NL663996) Stone and earth structure 3.6 × 3.2 m. Shieling hut.

K100 (NL663993) Stone setting 3 × 2 m. Shelter type A.

K101 (NL663993) Oblong stone and earth structure 3 × 2.75 m. Shelter type C.

K102 (NL663993) Stone setting 2.5 m diam. Shelter type A.

K103 (NL663993) Heavily embedded stone and earth structure 3 m diam. Shelter type C.

K104 (NL663993) Stone setting 2.1 × 1.7 m. Shelter type A.

K105 (NL662993) Stone and earth structure 2.5 m diam. Shelter type C.

K106 (NL662993) Stone and earth structure 2.3 m diam. Shelter type C.

K107 (NL662994) Stone setting 2 m diam. Shelter type A.

K108 (NL662994) Stone setting 1.5 m diam. Shelter type A.

K109 (NL660995) Oblong stone setting 3 × 2 m. Shelter type A.

K110 (NL660994) Stone and earth structure 3 m diam. Shelter type C.

K111 (NL659995) Setting of four large blocks to form rectangle 2 × 1.5 m against large boulder. Shelter type E.

K112 (NL659996) Stone setting 1.75 × 1.3 m against south-facing rock face. Shelter type E.

K113 (NL660996) Stone setting 2.1 m diam. Shelter type A.

K114 (NL661996) Stone setting 2.3 m diam. Shelter type A.

K115 (NL661997) Stone setting 2.1 × 1.4 m, against east-facing rock face. Shelter type E.

K116 (NL658997) Stone setting 3.5 m diam. Shelter type A.

K117 (NL657996) Stone setting 3 × 2.3 m. Shelter type A.

K118 (NL657996) Stone setting 3 × 2 m against a north-facing rock face. Shelter type E.

K119 (NL657997) Stone setting 2.8 m diam. Shelter type A.

K120 (NL666997) Collapsed stone structure 3.3 × 1.9 m against west-facing rock face. Shelter type F.

K121 (NF655000) Oval stone setting 3.5 × 2.2 m. Shelter type A.

K122 (NF655001) Three large stones set to form rectangle 2 × 1.5 m against north-facing rock face. Shelter type E.

K123 (NF655002) Embedded and robbed stone setting 4.5 m diam. Shelter type A?

K124 (NF654000) Stone setting 3 × 2 m, set against north-facing rock face. Shelter type E.

K125 (NF655002) Pile of small stones 2 × 1.5 m on rock outcrop. Secondary clearance cairn.

K126 (NF656000) Heavily embedded and robbed oval stone structure, 6 × 4.5 m. Entrance probably at south end. Prehistoric or mediaeval hut?

K127 (NL657999) Stone setting 2.5 m diam. Shelter type A.

K128 (NF658000) Stone and earth structure 3 m diam. Entrance at NW. Shelter type C.

K129 (NF660001) Stone setting forming two conjoined rings, one 1.7 m diam., the other 2 × 1.75 m. Shelter type B.

K130 (NF657002) Five stones forming a square setting against a rock face. Shelter type E.

K131 (NF654000) Much damaged and partly embedded oval stone structure 4.5 × 3 m. Shieling hut?

K132 (NF652001) Thick-walled stone and earth structure, 3.6 × 3.2 m, walls stand 0.6 m high. Shelter type C.

K133 (NL654998) Damaged and crudely built stone rectangular structure 3 × 2 m, door possibly at southwest. Bothy?

K134 (NL654996) Green mound, heavily damaged by rabbits, with medium-sized stone blocks protruding from turf and rabbit holes. About five blocks apparently *in situ* on north-west arc. Remains of a circular structure about 5 m diam. Prehistoric hut?

K135 (NL654995) Pile of largish stone blocks 1.7 × 1 m. Primary clearance cairn.

K136 (NL658992) Prominent green mound 1.3 m high, with many blocks of embedded stone and much rabbit disturbance, showing considerable soil depth and buried stonework. A relict boundary on the west kinks to follow the west edge of the mound, perhaps to utilize remains of existing wall. Appears to be the remains of a sizeable circular stone structure. Prehistoric roundhouse?

K137 (NL658993) Stone setting 2 m diam. Shelter type A.

K138 (NL658993) Heavily embedded stone setting 3.5 m diam. Shelter type A.

K139 (NL660992) Rectangular stone and earth structure, 3.5 × 2.5 m against an east-facing rock face. Shelter type F.

K140 (NL661992) Oval stone setting 3 × 2.3 m. Shelter type A.

K141 (NL661992) Two large blocks, 1.2 m and 1 m long, set parallel to each other 0.5 m apart. Two smaller blocks are set in line with the 1 m block and one with the 1.2 m block. Other scattered large blocks nearby. Largely destroyed semi-megalithic structure. Unknown function and date.

K142 (NL661992) Complex site with two pairs of conjoined stone settings overlying an earlier structure. Pair 1 are 3 m and 2 m diam. and pair 2 are 2 m and 1.5 m diam. Shelters type C. Pair 2 sit on top of an embedded, much disturbed and robbed oval stone and earth structure with some rabbit disturbance. The structure measures approx. 7 × 4.5 m. Prehistoric oval house?

K143 (NL662993) Stone structure 3 × 2.3 m built against a large boulder. Shelter type F.

K144 (NL662992) Spread of stone debris from a circular structure approx. 3.5 m diam. Shieling hut?

K145 (NL661991) Stone setting 2 m diam., and remains of an identical setting 15 m to north. Two type A shelters.

K146 (NL661990) Rectangular stone structure 2.6 × 2.1 m. Shelter type C.

K147 (NL663991) Stone and earth structure 2 × 1.5 m built against south-facing vertical face. Shelter type F.

K148 (NL664991) Collapsed stone structure 2 × 2.5 m built against a south-facing rock face. Shelter type F.

K149 (NL663990) Stone setting 4 m diam. Shelter type A?

K150 (NL662986) Thick-walled stone and earth structure 5.6 × 4.5 m, with curved north wall. Door in south-east corner. Byre?

K151 (NL664985) Stone setting 2.9 m diam. Shelter type A.

K152 (NL666984) Four piles of small stones 1 m to 2 m in diameter. Secondary clearance cairns.

K153 (NL667985) Two piles of small stones each 1.2 m diam. Secondary clearance cairns.

Zone T (Tangaval)

Sites T1–233 were published in the first SEARCH volume (Branigan and Foster 1995: 31–48). In 1998 two additional sites were recorded by P. Foster, and site T233 was visited for the first time in 1999 and is now identified as two separate monuments.

T233 (NL647996) On the larger part of a figure-of-eight islet in Loch Tangusdale, a tumble of stone masonry, heavily overgrown, marks the position of a probably circular stone structure about 8 m in diameter. The walls survive to about 0.7 m as visible. There is not a massive amount of masonry, nor is there any trace of a double wall, and together with the small overall diameter this suggests that this is not the site of a broch or ARH. Probably a prehistoric roundhouse, but possibly much later.

T234 (NL649987) Heavily grassed-over cairn, 3.5 m diam. and 0.8 m high, with a few perimeter stones visible and others on top of cairn. Location and structure confirm this is not a clearance cairn. Prehistoric funerary cairn, possibly kerbed.

T235 (NL651987) Heather-covered cairn, 3.5 m diam. and 0.6 m high, with some perimeter stones on south side. Close to T234 and also a prehistoric funerary cairn, possibly kerbed.

T236 (NL647996) Dun Mhic Leoid. A tower about 5.5 m square, originally of three stories, the upper of which has gone. The tower was entered at first floor level (RCAHMS 1928: 129, No. 440).

Zone B (Borve Valley)

B1 (NF672019) Dun Bharpa, chambered cairn (RCAHMS 1928:135, No.457; Henshall 1972:513). The cairn is c. 30 m in diameter and is still 5 m high, although stones have clearly been removed from the top exposing one of the huge cover slabs of the burial chamber. The tops of megaliths forming the passage can be seen protruding through the cairn to the east. Set within the periphery of the cairn are a series of upright stones, the largest of them apparently 3–4 m in height, and around a metre in width. Fifteen such stones survive, mostly around the western side, but whether there were once more and, if so, how many, is uncertain.

B2 (NF672017) A low cairn, 6 m diam., with clear traces of an edging kerb on the southern, downslope, side. Much of the cairn material has been robbed. Prehistoric kerbed cairn (Fig. 2.9).

B3 (NF676012) Balnacraig, chambered cairn (RCAHMS 1928:135, No.458; Henshall 1972:498). Henshall identifies this as a long cairn, but our examination of the site suggested that the cairn is circular, an interpretation shared by the RCAHMS. The cairn has been heavily robbed in prehistoric and later times, and its original dimensions are unclear. It may have been about 25 m in diameter. Its chamber is still marked by a group of disturbed megalithic slabs ranging from about 1 m to 1.8 m in length. Immediately north of the cairn a mound of stone blocks marks the site of what appears to be a circular stone-founded structure about 12 m in diameter, with a wall

up to 1.5 m in width. This too was noted by the RCAHMS and Armit (1992:162). The quantity and size of the stone blocks, and the dimensions of the structure and its wall, all suggest that this is most likely to be a free-standing wheelhouse rather than a thick-walled broch-like structure. Both this structure and the earlier cairn have small subrectangular and oval cabins or shelters built into them and around them. Some of these huts, particularly at the south end of the cairn, are very heavily embedded and are probably of considerable antiquity. One such hut is 2.1 m wide, with two rooms 2.3 m and 3 m long, each with its own door facing south-south-west. It overlies one end of a similar slightly larger two-roomed hut immediately to the west of it. Other huts are single-roomed structures between 2 m and 3 m 'square'. The least embedded sits on the large circular house, and a second loosely built and relatively recent oval hut lies west of the circular house. The impression is that after the circular house went out of use there was a long sequence of probably intermittent occupation on the site, the latest phases of which were probably no more than shieling huts. The date and purpose of the earliest subrectangular structures, however, is uncertain; we suspect they may be of late 1st or early 2nd millennium AD date.

B4 (NF653014) A standing stone (RCAHMS 1928: 136, No. 461). It now survives little more than 1 m in height, but was 1.7 m when recorded by the RCAHMS in 1915. Sunk into the sandy machair of Borve headland it may well be taller and better preserved than it appears. A second, fallen, stone almost 3 m long was noted by the RCAHMS but is now represented (if at all) only by a short block of gneiss, lying a few metres from the upright stone.

B5* (NF647017) A battered, well-constructed stone wall swings in an arc of about 16 m diam. below the wall of the modern cemetery, which actually follows the line of this earlier wall and uses it as a foundation (Figs. 2.10, 10.4). Inside the cemetery at this point there is a substantial mound, on top of which stands site B163. We identify the wall and mound as the buried remains of a broch, situated immediately overlooking the natural dyke that forms a protected harbourage at this point on the headland. Between the broch and the edge of the dyke are the remains of a bank that curves westwards and makes an enclosure around the broch on this side, with a possible entrance to the west. To the north of the broch, exposed in the steep and eroding edge of the machair, is a midden. We recovered 15 reddish-brown gritty handmade sherds, one with an applied and impressed cordon, probably of the early first millennium AD. We also found limpet shells, fragments of animal bone, teeth of sheep and fish-vertebra (see p. 230).

B6 (NF672017) A cairn, diam. c. 8 m, with possible traces of a kerb on the south side. It is close to site B2 and may be a second kerbed cairn.

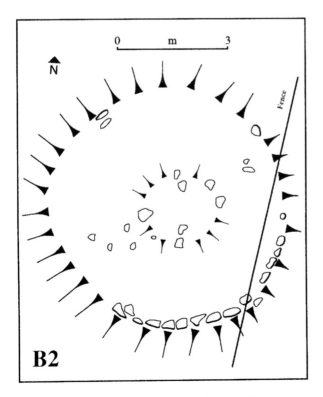

Figure 2.9 A field sketch of the kerbed cairn, Site B2.

Figure 2.10 The broch on Borve Headland (B5), showing the cemetery wall curving out to utilize the remains of the broch's wall, and inside the cemetery the prominent mound of the broch's collapsed superstructure.

B7 (NF672016) A cairn, diam. c. 9 m, with no clear trace of a kerb. Its size and proximity to B6 and B2 suggest it might be a kerbed cairn, but this is quite uncertain.

B8 (NF673018) A much-robbed subrectangular enclosure, 20 × 12 m, marked out by large boulders and apparently anchored by a huge boulder at its north-east corner. It underlies a later wall system that is itself at least two removes from the croft boundaries of the early 20th century.

B9 (NF672016) Apparently unfinished blackhouse, 10 × 4 m. There are no traces of the north and east walls or of any robber debris from them.

B10 (NF671017) Three small secondary clearance cairns, each c. 2 m diam., lying just to the east of a lazy-bed plot.

B11 (NF670017) A wall? of large blocks, up to three stones high and 1 m wide, buried under 40 cm of peat, exposed by a modern drainage cut, and running across the slope.

B12 (NF670017) Foundations of a wall?, 20 m from B11 but running downslope. Four blocks of stone with smaller stones on top appear to make a foundation 1.2 m wide, cut through by a modern drainage ditch.

B13 (NF672019) A D-shaped enclosure marked out by two banks that run in an arc from the west side of Dun Bharpa (site B1) to meet a major north–south land boundary which passes just to the east of the cairn. This enclosure is just visible on aerial photos of the area. Its purpose and date are uncertain.

B14 (NF672018) Small cairn 2 m diam., situated just outside enclosure B13. Despite its location, it is most likely a clearance cairn.

B15 (NF667017) A subrectangular enclosure, c. 12 m square, west of Dun Bharpa and enclosure B13, marked out by a slight bank of earth and stone. A small cairn, probably clearance, is located in the south-east corner of the enclosure.

B16 (NF666018) A subrectangular enclosure, c. 65 × 25 m, with a roughly built wall of turf and stone, except on the north where a rock outcrop is utilized. One, possibly two, circular stone structures are built against the rock face; shelters type E. Just inside the enclosure on the south, downslope, side there is a natural mound formed on a rock outcrop; a scatter of more than a dozen stone blocks here suggest it may have once had a structure on it.

B17 (NF669016) A small rectangular structure, 2 m square, built against a field boundary. Shelter type F.

B18 (NF658024) Small oblong house, 6.7 × 4.7 m, with a door to the north. A second building, 6.3 × 5.8 m, with a door in the north-west corner has traces of a raised platform at its east end. Blackhouse, and drying shed.

B19 (NF662018) Stone setting c. 3 m diam. Shelter type A.

B20 (NF663018) Stone setting c. 4 m diam., with arc of stones anchored on two large boulders. Shelter type A.

B21 (NF661018) Stone setting, c. 2.5 m diam. Shelter type A.

B22 (NF661018) Small cairn 2 m diam. Topography and soil suggest this is unlikely to be a clearance cairn; possibly a collapsed shelter type C.

B23 (NF659019) Foundations of a blackhouse, 11 × 6 m, with internal partition, and an outbuilding, 4 × 3 m, animal pen, field walls, and small lazy-bed plots.

B24 (NF657021) Stone setting, 2 m diam. Shelter type A.

B25 (NF661021) Two small structures of stone and turf, each 2 m square, built against a rock outcrop. Shelters type F.

B26 (NF661021) Foundations of a rectangular stone building, 6.5 × 4.5 m.

B27 (NF662017) Rectangular stone setting, 3 × 1.5 m, built against a rock outcrop. Shelter type E.

B28 (NF666024) Circular stone and turf structure, 3 m diam., entrance to south. Shelter type C.

B29 (NF658019) A stone-walled oval enclosure, 20 × 12 m, with entrance at the west end.

B30 (NF661016) Sub-rectangular 3 × 2 m setting of eight stones against a rock outcrop. Shelter type E.

B31 (NF673020) Fallen monolith, 3 m long and 0.6 m wide. It stands on the watershed between the Borve valley and Allasdale and is only 100 m from Dun Bharpa (B1). Although it could possibly have been removed from the ring of monoliths set into the cairn at Dun Bharpa, this seems unlikely. The monoliths at Dun Bharpa are all notably broader than this stone.

B32 (NF674015) Two circular structures with turf walls? The larger, 4.3 m diam., has an entrance to the west; the smaller, 3.1 m diam., may have had an entrance to the east. Shieling huts?

B33 (NF679014) A rectangular enclosure, 8.4 × 6.6 m, roughly built of boulders against a rock outcrop.

B34 (NF680013) A rectangular stone setting, 4.6 × 3.2 m, enclosing a large boulder. Purpose uncertain.

B35 (NF680012) Rectangular stone structure, 3.7 × 2.4 m, built against a field boundary. Shelter type B.

B36 (NF680012) Two heavily embedded circular turf and stone structures. The better preserved, 3.7 m diam., has an entrance to the north-west and its wall stands 0.6 m high. The second, 3 m diam., is badly damaged. Mediaeval shieling huts?

B37 (NF680012) An oval stone structure, 5 × 3.5 m, wall c. 70 cm wide, entrance possibly at the east. Prehistoric or mediaeval shieling hut (Fig. 2.11)?

B38 (NF680014) Two conjoined stone settings. The larger, 4 × 2.5 m, utilizes two large boulders for its east wall; the smaller is 1.8 m diam. Shelter type B.

B39 (NF684009) A fallen standing stone almost on the saddle at Beul a Bhealaich (the Pass of the Mouth). The stone was noted by Thom, who recorded it as 16 ft long. In fact, when we cleared the stone to its full extent, it was found to be 5.8 m long, and 1 m wide. Its tip appears to have been deliberately narrowed, since the edges of the stone are slightly 'scalloped', perhaps caused by dropping large stones on to the edge of the monolith at this end. When erect it would certainly have been an eye-catching feature at the head of the valley.

B40 (NF681008) Two adjacent stone settings, each 2.5 m square. Shelters type A.

B41 (NF679005) An arc of turf walling?, diam. 6 m, with an adjacent rectangular platform cut into the hillslope. Mediaeval shieling hut?

B42 (NF675999) Two adjacent square stone and turf structures, 4 m and 3 m square, with traces of a small enclosing wall to south. Mediaeval or early modern shieling huts?

B43 (NF675999) A prominent grassed-over mound 2.5 m high and c. 8 m diam., with traces of a heavily embedded stone structure within it. Prehistoric hut?

B44 (NF672003) An oval mound of stone blocks, 13 × 11 m, much disturbed both by rabbit infestation

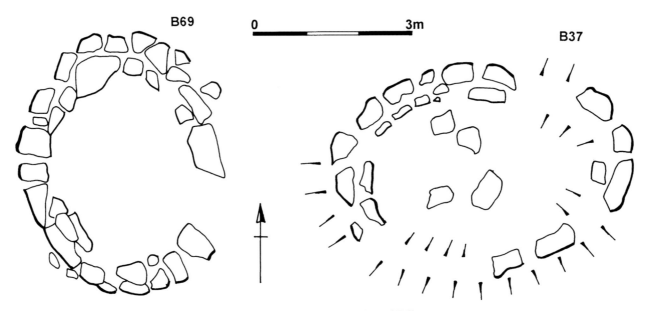

Figure 2.11 Field sketches of small oval 'roundhouses' in the Borve Valley, B37 and B69.

Figure 2.12 Ruins of a large roundhouse, damaged by later shielings and rabbits, Site B44.

and small secondary structures built from and within the debris. Large prehistoric house, possibly a free-standing wheelhouse, with later (mediaeval) shieling huts (Fig. 2.12)?

B45 (NF672003) Heavily embedded and partly destroyed stone structure of uncertain shape occupying an area about 9 × 6 m.

B46 (NF678009) Circular stone setting, 4 m diam. Shelter type A.

B47 (NF672004) Circular stone and turf structure, 4 m diam., adjacent to traces of an erased field boundary. Prehistoric or mediaeval circular hut?

B48 (NF670003) Three small clearance cairns, two c. 2 m diam., the third c. 3.5 m diam., against a field boundary.

B49 (NF670003) Complex of three small clearance cairns, an oval enclosure marked out by large boulders and remains of a stone and earth bank, and a fourth cairn or possibly circular hut site.

B50 (NF670003) Four lynchets on a steep lower slope, each about 20 m long, and 18 m apart. The uppermost terrace has lazy-bedding.

B51 (NF667013) Abandoned croft complex. Blackhouse 7 × 3.5 m, house with chimney 9 × 4 m, 3 × 2 m outbuilding, circular sheep pen, and traces of other pens, paths and plots.

B52 (NF676008) Collapsed circular stone structure, 2 m diam. Shelter type C.

B53 (NF667007) Abandoned croft complex. Blackhouse 6 × 4 m with one room, and door to north a small enclosed yard to the front with very lush vegetation (midden site?), two small enclosed garden plots to rear, and traces of three small fields to the east, west

and south. That on the west has a gateway to the stream, and to the north is an area of lazy-bedding.

B54 (NF670009) A low oval green mound, at the south end of which is a pile of large stone blocks. The mound has pronounced lazy-beds on it. Around the mound is a spaced kerb of stone blocks, enclosing an area 35 × 20 m. The area around the mound is rather boggy, but there is an outer spaced kerb that encloses an oval area c. 70 × 57 m. This site was sampled by excavation, see Chapter 5.

B55 (NF669008) On a knoll overlooking site B54, an irregular ring of large stones, forming an ovoid 14 × 12 m. Eleven stones are probably *in situ* and at least nine are moved or missing. On the north side, an arc of five large stones forms a 'cove' on the outside of the ring. This site was sampled by excavation, see Chapter 5.

B56 (NF673007) Well-embedded circular stone structure 4 m diam. on raised mound with rich grass growth. Mediaeval and later shieling.

B57 (NF672007) Very similar and adjacent to site B56, diam. 5 m. Mediaeval and later shieling.

B58 (NF672007) Very similar and adjacent to site B57, diam. 4 m. Excavated, to be published in SEARCH volume 6. The excavations revealed two separate structural phases, one in the mediaeval period and one early modern.

B59 (NF671007) Very similar to sites B56–58, but lying to the west of them. Diam. 3 m. Mediaeval and later shieling.

B60 (NF671006) Circular structure, 3 m diam., of stone and turf, abutting relict field boundary on the north, entrance on south. Excavated, to be published in SEARCH volume 6. Excavations revealed a D-shaped hut built against an already relict bank, probably in the later 17th century AD.

B61 (NF670004) Circular stone and turf structure, 2.5 m diam., built against a large boulder. Mediaeval shieling hut?

B62 (NF671003) Circular stone structure, 6 m diam., very heavily embedded. Prehistoric hut?

B63 (NF709001) Arc-shaped stone setting, 3.5 m diam. Shelter type A.

B64 (NF669001) Much-destroyed remains of an oval structure marked by a platform fronted by an earth and stone bank 25 cm high. Length c. 7 m, Width 4 m. Prehistoric or mediaeval hut?

B65 (NF665004) Heavily embedded remains of a circular stone structure, internal diam. c. 3 m, on a flat platform immediately above a stream. Prehistoric hut?

B66 (NF665004) Foundations of a 4 m square building with possible doorway at the north-west corner.

B67 (NF668006) Robbed foundations of a blackhouse, 11 × 6 m. Much of the east wall has been completely removed.

B68 (NL662998) Heavily embedded circular structure, 2.5 m diam., against the end of a rough boulder-built wall. A second less well-preserved structure lies 10 m to the north. Shelter type C.

B69 (NF664002) Oval stone structure, 5 × 4 m diam., entrance on the east side. Oval hut (Fig. 2.11).

B70 (NF665005) Heavily embedded circular stone structure, 7 m diam., with some tumble within. Prehistoric hut?

B71 (NL661997) Rectangular stone-setting, 2 × 1 m, against a rock face. Shelter type E.

B72 (NF664006) Well-defined but heavily embedded circular stone and turf structure, 6 m diam., with entrance to north. Prehistoric or mediaeval hut?

B73 (NF664006) Strongly built circular stone structure with some stone blocks entirely grassed over. Internal diam. 2.2 × 1.7 m, with entrance to south, and possibly a small annexe attached to the rear (north) side. Mediaeval or prehistoric hut circle?

B74 (NF668002) Circular stone setting, 3.5 m diam., well-embedded. Shelter type A.

B75 (NF668003) Complex consisting of heavily embedded foundations of a two-roomed building, 4.5 × 3 m, two small huts each 1.5 m square built either side of a nearby land boundary, and traces of a small rectangular stone setting. The three shelters are presumably of a different period to the small rectangular building, and in our view are probably the later of the two phases.

B76 (NF664005) Low grassy mound, 4 m diam., with arc of stones embedded around north side. Shelter type A?

B77 (NF663005) Eroded and heavily embedded circular stone structure, 3 m diam. Prehistoric or mediaeval shieling hut?

B78 (NF664002) Circular stone setting, 3 m diam. Shelter type A.

B79 (NF662005) D-shaped platform with very embedded stone structure, 3.5 × 2.5 m. Shieling hut?

B80 (NF662005) Circular stone setting, 6 m diam., covered by mossy vegetation around north circumference. Shelter type A.

B81 (NF664006) Circular stone and turf structure, 2.5 m diam. Shelter type C.

B82 (NF664007) Circular structure of turf and stone, 3 m diam. Shelter type C.

B83 (NF664006) Remains of a heavily embedded circular stone structure, 4.5 m diam., around a grassy mound? Prehistoric hut.

B84 (NF664006) Rectangular earth and stone enclosure, with a stone setting 1.5 m square. Pen and shelter type A.

B85 (NF646017) A sub-triangular enclosure, 32 × 29 × 26.5 m, attached to an old land boundary at the south-west tip of Borve headland. The enclosure is marked by a low bank on which a number of upright stones stand at irregular intervals; the south-east bank has nine stones still standing *in situ*. The land boundary, marked by a low bank, runs from the enclosure and disappears under the west wall of the modern cemetery 100 m away. It appears to be heading towards the mound in the far south-east corner of the cemetery, site B5. One further bank can be seen to run southwards from this boundary towards the water's edge. We believe this enclosure is ancient and may be broadly contemporary with site B5.

B86 (NF677008) A much-robbed blackhouse, estimated size 11 × 4 m, of which only the north-west corner is clearly visible.

B87 (NF673067) Stone and turf structure, 2 m square, built on the end of a cross-slope wall of similar construction. Shelter type C. Excavated, to be published in SEARCH volume 6.

B88 (NF673007) Steep-sided grassy mound 2.5 m high and 5 m diam. with traces of stone structure on summit. Mediaeval shieling hut. Excavated, to be published in SEARCH volume 6.

B89 (NF670017) Oval mound, 12 × 9 m, and c. 2 m high on the downslope side, with large stone blocks projecting through the turf. Some of the stones seem to have been robbed to build or rebuild the boundary wall just south of the mound. Prehistoric house?

B90 (NF663007) Rectangular stone setting, 3 × 2 m, set against a large boulder. Shelter type E.

B91 (NF663007) Upright monolith, apparently set upright with stones around its base. Surviving height 0.7 m; width 0.8 m and thickness 0.3 m. Base of standing stone?

B92 (NF660005) Grassy platform enclosed by oval turf and stone bank 3.5 × 3 m, possible entrance to east. Oval hut or shelter type C?

B93 (NF659004) Oval stone setting 4.4 × 3.6 m. Shelter type A.

B94 (NF663008) Four clearance cairns, all apparently secondary clearance; two well grassed-over.

B95 (NF662009) Three clearance cairns, two primary and one secondary.

B96 (NF660004) Protected hollow enclosed by an irregular oval kerb of stones, 35 × 20 m, joining up rock outcrops. A small rectangular shelter, type F is built against a low rock face on the south side.

B97 (NF659004) A roughly circular setting of stones, set partly on edge, forming an almost continuous kerb 25 m diam., enclosing a central rock outcrop. Enclosure of uncertain date.

B98 (NF658005) Low grassy mound with heavily embedded stone setting, 3.5 m diam. Shelter type A.

B99 (NF658005) Two rectangular stone settings, 5 m apart, against the west face of a rock outcrop. A 2 × 1.5 m, B 1.5 × 1.3 m. Shelters type E.

B100 (NF660006) Rectangular stone structure, 4 × 2.5 m, including collapsed stone. Shelter type C.

B101 (NF 660007) Arc of turf bank with a large stone set at each end, 3 m diam., gap to east. Shelter type C?

B102 (NF662009) Grassed-over secondary clearance cairn, 2 × 2.5 m, against a boulder.

B103 (NF670008) D-shaped stone and turf walled enclosure built into junction of two relict turf and stone walls.

B104 (NF666018) Enclosure, 50 × 30 m, formed by curving alignment of boulders against a rock face. Five stone settings are built against the rock face in two pairs, with the fifth between them, and three further settings are close to the enclosing alignment. Major pen with eight shelters of types A and E.

B105 (NF664018) Stone setting, 2.7 m square, built against a large boulder. Shelter type E.

B106 (NF664018) Curvilinear stone settings around a large boulder forming a pen 6 × 5.6 m, and a shelter type E.

B107 (NF663018) Pair of stone settings, each 2.5 m diam. Shelters type A.

B108 (NF662018) Arc-shaped stone setting, 3 × 2.2 m, against a rock face. Shelter type E.

B109 (NF670009) Rectangular stone and turf structure, 2.5 × 1.4 m, built against the outside face of a sheep wall. Shelter type F. Excavated, to be published in SEARCH volume 6.

B110 (NF661019) Structure of turf and stone, 2 m square, possible entrance at south-east, built against a relict boundary wall. Shelter type E.

B111 (NF661019) Two well-preserved turf and stone structures built against a south-facing rock face, within a semicircular enclosure 9 m diam. formed by a rough boulder and turf wall. Pen with shelters type F.

B112 (NF661019) Embedded stone setting 1.8 m square. Shelter type A.

B113 (NF656010) Blackhouse, 12.5 × 4 m, with no trace of internal partition, door on west.

B114 (NF657010) Low rectangular grassy platform 10 × 7 m, stones set around three edges, fourth cut by fence. Remains of a fenced enclosure?

B115 (NF658022) Stone setting, 3 m diam. Shelter type A.

B116 (NF658024) Two rectangular stone settings, 3 × 1 m and 3 × 2 m, against two adjacent rock outcrops. Shelters type E.

B117 (NF664008) Overgrown blackhouse, 11 × 6.5 m, door probably on west, no trace of internal partitions.

B118 (NF663009) Overgrown blackhouse, 12 × 7 m, with two rooms, the larger to the north. Door in the west wall.

B119 (NF663010) Remains of a much-robbed stone building, 12 × 6.5 m, with two rooms. The east wall of the southern rooms is exceptionally wide (1.5m) and projects beyond the line of the north room's east wall to give protection to the doors to each room, which are adjacent to each other.

B120 (NF663010) Foundations of a blackhouse, 12 × 6.5 m, no trace of internal partitions, door on the north.

B121 (NF658003) Incomplete circular structure of stones, 2.5 m diam., on bare rock close to relict land boundary on watershed along the crest of Benn na Moine. The wall still stands two stones high on the south and west sides. This is unlikely to be a shelter in this location, but a more permanent hut here is also difficult to understand.

B122 (NF658004) Circular stone setting, 2.5 m diam., around grassy platform. Shelter type A.

B123 (NF654004) Oval enclosure, 26 × 20 m, demarcated by setting of large stones, with a 2 m long arc of stones set against rock face at rear of enclosure. Pen with shelter type E.

B124 (NF654005) Small wall of turf with large anchor stones built against a right-angled rock face to form a shelter type E 1.5 × 1 m.

B125 (NF655006) Rectangular structure of stone slabs and blocks, 2 × 1 m, built against rock face. Shelter type F.

B126 (NF656005) Two walls of stone blocks, built against a rock face to form a triangular shelter type F 3 × 2 m.

B127 (NF654005) Well-embedded stone setting, 1 m diam. Shelter type A.

B128 (NF666012) Circular setting of stones, 16 m diam., around a large boulder. Uncertain purpose.

B129 (NF666012) Stone setting against a rock face, forming a shelter type E, 4 × 1 m.

B130 (NF666013) Tigh Talamhanta (RCAHMS 1928: 138, No. 473) identified as 'only a site, all traces of a structure having disappeared'. The name implies the former existence of an 'earth-house', and a similarly named site in Allasdale proved to be a free-standing wheelhouse on excavation (site C2). There is in fact a well-embedded mound of medium-sized stone blocks, about 1.5 m high and about 14 × 12 m in size. The impression is of a substantial structure buried here, and a free-standing wheelhouse would be of about the right size.

B131 (NF663011) Seven clearance cairns, four probably secondary, two primary, and two both.

B132 (NF658022) Setting of two large boulders and an arc of small stones forming a shelter type A 2.5 × 1.5 m.

B133 (NF655010) Rectangular stone setting, 1.3 × 1.1 m, at end of a relict stone and turf boundary. Shelter type A.

B134 (NF663011) Circular setting of nine large stones, 10 m diam., on low green platform, with a 1.5 m diam. stone setting on the east side. The latter is a shelter type A but the purpose of the larger setting is uncertain.

B135 (NF657006) Setting of stone blocks, 3 m diam., against rock face. Shelter type E.

B136 (NF660012) Dun an t'Sleibh (RCAHMS 1928: 138, No. 471) is said by RCAHMS to have been completely removed. However, Scott (1947: 4) reported traces of a thick wall on this raised rocky hillock and we found remains of the same. The wall foundation is about 3 m wide, and we tentatively traced the remains of an oval structure about 18m × 13 m, with an arc of smaller (later?) wall built against the outside of the thick wall at the west end. Thick-walled prehistoric structure, dun or broch.

B137 (NF664015) Ruined blackhouse, 15 × 6 m, with two doors on the east side but no trace of internal partitions.

B138 (NF662015) Three grassed-over clearance cairns, two primary (4.5 and 1.7 m diam.) and one secondary (1.7 m diam.).

B139 (NF662015) Much-ruined, modified and robbed blackhouse, 11.5 × 7 m, door on south.

B140 (NF661015) Complex of two blackhouses, enclosure and pen. A 11.5 × 5.8 m, door on north. B 7.2 × 5.4 m, door on north. Enclosure 16 × 13.4 m attached to west end of houses, making yard between. Pen 10 × 5 m to north of house A.

B141 (NF660016) Ruined and robbed two-roomed building, 14.8 × 5.8 m, doors on north side, with fireplace and chimney in west room.

B142 (NF660015) Complex of three rectangular buildings with wall enclosing yard to north-west. A 11 × 6.4 m, door on east. B 10.25 × 4.7 m, two rooms, each with door on north. C 4.3 m square, door to south; annexe, 3.2 × 4.3 m built on north door to east.

B143 (NF655004) Stone setting, 2 × 1 m, against rock outcrop. Shelter type E.

B144 (NF659021) Curving turf and stone wall against south-facing rock outcrop. Shelter type E 3.1 × 2.1 m.

B145 (NF659021) Curving turf and stone wall against rock outcrop. Shelter type E, 2 × 1.3 m.

B146 (NF659002) Stone setting, 2.5 m square. Shelter type A.

B147 (NF658024) Stone setting, 3.3 × 3 m, entrance to N. Shelter type A.

B148 (NF658023) Heavily embedded stone structure comprising two adjoining circles, each 3 m diam. Shelter type D.

B149 (NF657019) Semi-circular enclosure, 62 × 30 m, divided in half by stone-founded cross wall. In the northern half are traces of a two-celled stone setting, 7 × 3m; shelter type B. In the southern half are remains of a turf-walled structure 4 × 2 m, most probably a shelter type C.

B150 (NF656019) Heavily embedded and damaged stone structure, 2 m diam. Shelter type C.

B151 (NF658019) Stone setting, 2 × 1.5 m, against a rock outcrop. Shelter type E.

B152 (NF658019) Somewhat irregular stone setting, 4.1 × 1.5 m, divided into two unequal halves, and set against a rock face. Shelter type E.

B153 (NF658019) Irregular stone setting, 1.75 × 1 m, against rock outcrops. Shelter type E.

B154 (NF658018) Setting of large stone blocks, 2.4 × 2 m, against rock outcrop. Shelter type E.

B155 (NF664013) Three grassed-over clearance cairns. The largest, 10.7 × 5.8 m, is primary, the others (5.5 × 2.6 m and 4 × 3.7m) secondary.

B156 (NF664014) Five grassed-over clearance cairns, all probably primary. A 3 × 2.7 m, B 3.5 × 5 m, C 2.7 × 2.2 m, D 2 × 1 m, E 3 × 1.5 m.

B157 (NF658018) Two adjacent buildings. A Blackhouse, 9 × 5 m, with door to north and no internal partitions. B Building 10 × 5 m with no visible door, but north-west and south-west corners destroyed.

B158 (NF667009) Much overgrown blackhouse and byre. Blackhouse, 9.9 × 6.1 m, door to west and internal partition on left as entering. Byre, 5.7 × 4.6 m, with door in angle of north-east corner.

B159 (NF666008) Three ruined outbuildings in close proximity. A 6.2 × 4.7, door at south-west corner. B built against enclosure wall, 7.8 × 5.8 m, door in centre of west wall. C Built against enclosure wall, 5.2 × 4.6 m, door in centre of south wall.

B160 (NF665009) Heavily overgrown blackhouse, 7 × 5.5 m, door to east and no internal partitions. Annexe 5.5 × 3 m added to north end.

B161 (NF660012) Foundations of robbed blackhouse, 9 × 5 m, wall base 2 m thick, no trace of door. The building sits on a rectangular platform.

B162 (NF658008) Stone setting, 4 m diam. Shelter type A.

B163* (NF647017) Fragments of walling and a pile of stone debris, from St Brendan's chapel, standing in the corner of the modern cemetery on Borve headland and on top of site B5 (RCAHMS 1928: 125, No. 437).

B164 (NF647008) Pronounced mound against a south-west-facing rock face at the edge of the machair. Disturbed soil produced a few scraps of bone, iron slag and handmade pottery. A sample area of this site was excavated, to be published in SEARCH volume 6.

Zone C (Cueir)

C1 (NF680019) Heavily embedded stone structure, 3.6 × 2.9 m, on steep slope. The northern, downslope, wall was two/three stones wide, but other walls are marked by blocks laid flat or by large angular boulders. The walls were probably of turf on a stone foundation. Narrow door at south-east corner. Shieling hut.

C2 (NF677022) The wheelhouse, Tigh Talamhanta, excavated and published by Young (1952).

C3 (NF678022) Oblong building, 10.6 × 7.2 m, door in centre of north-east wall. Wall width 1.2 m. There is a secondary pen or shelter built into the west corner, and an enclosure wall runs east and west from the north-east and north-west corners of the building. Blackhouse.

C4 (NF677029) A 2 m high grassed mound, 12.8 × 11.5 m, with heavily embedded remains of an oval stone and turf hut, 3.3 × 3 m, with an annexe on the south side, 3 × 2.6 m. Mediaeval shieling hut overlying an earlier site?

C5 (NF676029) A 2.5 m high grassed mound, 12 × 9.5 m, with heavily embedded remains of a stone and turf hut 3.5 m square. At the south-east corner of the mound, and halfway down its slope, a shell midden has been exposed by sheep and yielded two small reddish-brown gritty sherds and a flint blade. Mediaeval shieling hut, overlying a Later prehistoric site.

C6 (NF677029) Robbed and disturbed oblong building, 9 × 6.5 m, no door visible. There appears to be a grassed-over partition towards the south end, and there are suggestions of a small rectangular annexe outside the north wall and semicircular structure built against the outside of the south wall. Blackhouse.

C7 (NF675029) Oval grassed mound 11.2 × 9.7 m, 0.8 m high, with scattered but embedded groups of stone blocks from a destroyed structure. Mediaeval or early modern shieling?

C8 (NF675031) Oval stone setting 5.2 × 3.8 m, heavily embedded and damaged. Shelter type A or shieling hut?

C9 (NF674030) Prominent grassed mound, 17.2 × 13.5 m, 2 m high, with complex and damaged, heavily embedded stone structure on the summit, 11 × 7.6 m. It appears to comprise at least three rooms or cells, but they may not all be contemporary. On the south side, a shell midden is exposed underlying the wall foundation. Shieling huts overlying earlier prehistoric? site.

C10 (NF673026) Rectangular stone structure, 3 × 1.5 m, built against a relict wall. Shelter type F.

C11 (NF674025) Recent sheep pen overlying and incorporating earlier structures. Two of these are reasonably clear. A Blackhouse 12 × 5 m, with door on east side. B Blackhouse 13 m × 7 m minimum, door on north side. These two buildings are set at right angles with traces of an enclosure wall joining them. There are suggestions of further foundations beneath the sheep pen.

C12 (NF670025) Irregular stone setting, 5.7 × 3 m, around raised platform. Remains of destroyed shieling hut?

C13 (NF670026) Stone and turf structure, 4.2 × 2.9 m, built against rock face. Shelter type F.

C14 (NF670026) Oblong building, 10.9 × 6.4, with 0.8 m wide door in east wall. Wall width 1.25 m. A line of single stone blocks across the interior just to the south of the door suggests late secondary usage. Blackhouse.

C15 (NF671026) Heavily robbed oblong building, 15.6 × 7.6 m, of which the north and east walls have been totally demolished. There is a secondary built stone structure 4.2 m wide against the inside face of the south wall. The thick (1.3 m wide) walls and rounded corners identify this as a blackhouse, with a late shelter type F built within it.

C16 (NF672026) Oblong building, 10.6 × 5.6 m, with 0.8 m wide door in north wall. Wall width 1.2 m. Blackhouse.

C17 (NF676026) A complex group of up to nine oblong structures of varying size and shape. Some appear to be in a demolished state when others were built. Buildings A–D are conjoined and may originally have been two buildings, A and C, set at right angles to each other. B appears to have been built to join A and C together, and D was perhaps built onto the rear of C. East of this group stands the largest building, E, which, to judge from the degree of survival, appears broadly contemporary to A–D. A small outlying building to the north, G also appears to belong with A–D. In front of E there are traces of a demolished earlier building, F and in front of A–C a second apparently earlier structure. Finally, to the north are the remains of another demolished building, I. Main measurements are as follows: A 9.2 × 5.4m; B 6 × 5.4m; C 10 × 5.4m; D 8.5 × 5.4m; E 11.1 × 5.8m; F 6.5 × 5m; G 4 × 2.5m; H 4 × 4m; I 5 × 3.5 m (F, H, I are minimal, surviving measurements). A E and probably C are blackhouses, B D and G are outbuildings. The original form and purpose of F H and I cannot be identified from the surviving fragments.

C18 (NF672032) Clearance cairn, 2.5 × 2.2 m, from both primary and secondary clearance.

C19 (NF672029) Partly robbed stone setting, 3 × 1.3 m, nine stones surviving on perimeter, with one stone set upright (0.6m) inside west end. Shelter type A?

C20 (NF665027) Oval stone setting, 5.4 × 4.9 m, incorporating large block of rock on the south side, adjacent to which a gap in the setting suggests an entrance. Heavily embedded. Size of setting and of individual stones suggests this is not a simple shelter type A; it may be the stone foundation for a turf superstructure. Prehistoric/mediaeval hut?

C21 (NF667029) Oblong building, 9.1 × 5.1 m, door towards west end of north wall, partition immediately west of door. Wall width 0.6 m. The narrow wall and loose build of smallish stones identify an outbuilding rather than a blackhouse.

C22 (NF667029) Arc-shaped setting of ten stones, three of which are upright, the rest lying flat. The tallest stone is 0.9 m high, and the chord of the arc is about 8 m. Despite its 'megalithic' appearance, this setting may be of relatively recent date.

C23 (NF669030) Stone structure, 1.6 × 1.3 m, against a rock face. Shelter type F.

C24 (NF669035) A whitehouse with remains of an earlier thick-walled building (wall width 1.2m) projecting eastwards from beneath the foundations. The earlier structure was 6.6 m wide, and its length can be traced for 5.7 m. Blackhouse.

C25 (NF677025) Stone structure, 2.6 × 2 m, built against a rock face. Shelter type F.

C26 (NF667027) Grassed-over mound, 12 × 9.6 m, with displaced blocks of stone around west and south quadrants. Possible house site?

C27 (NF665032) Five clearance cairns in plot between sheep wall and rock outcrop.

C28 (NF666031) Primary clearance cairn, 2.5 × 2 m.

C29 (NF669028) Group of three stone buildings. A 9.3 × 6.3 door in north wall, possible partition wall. B 7.2 × 5.8 m, door in north-east corner. To the north is C 6.2 × 5 m, with indications of a platform in the south-west corner. Door in south wall. A Blackhouse, B byre?, C drying shed.

C30 (NF668028) Complex of at least 23 and possibly up to 30 stone cairns with 2–3 m diam. Clearance cairns.

C31 (NF667029) Much-robbed remains of oblong stone building, 6.3 × 4.8 m, with a triangular pen 11.3 × 4 m, built against a nearby boundary wall. Outbuilding.

C32 (NF676030) Grassed-over mound 10 m diam., height 2 m. On the top a heavily embedded subrectangular stone and turf hut 3.8 × 3 m, with door in north side. Mediaeval? shieling hut, overlying earlier site.

C33 (NF670032) Totally embedded remains of robbed-out oblong building, 15.5 × 7.5 m. Its south wall was incorporated into a later boundary wall, and is 1.2 m wide, preserved to 1 m high. There are possible traces of a partition wall. Blackhouse.

C34 (NF669028) Oblong building, 12.3 × 6.4 m, door towards north-west corner. An annexe 4.5 × 2.8 m is built on to the north end. Blackhouse and byre.

C35 (NF665031) Oblong building with an apparently complex history. Overall the structure measures 19.1 × 6.7 m, but examination of the visible foundations suggest that it may originally have been 12 × 6.7 m, with a door in the middle of the south-west wall. It may then have been extended, with the demolition of the north-west wall, the extension wall footings being narrower than those of the original building. A door was created in the north-east wall at the junction of the original wall and the extension. There is no trace of an internal partition between the original room and the extension. The house stands in a walled enclosure, in the corner of which are traces of an inner enclosure marked out by a stone alignment. Against the west side of the large enclosure is a raised semicircular platform 6 × 3.2 m. There is a small clearance cairn close to the house. Blackhouse, pen and rick stand?

C36 (NF665031) Oval structure, 9 × 5 m, wall foundations showing as double line of stone blocks, presumably facing an earth core. Prehistoric house?

C37 (NF665031) Much-robbed and totally embedded stone oblong building, 9.1 × 5.1 m, walls 1 m wide. Possibly a small blackhouse.

C38 (NF663031) Robbed and heavily embedded foundations of an oblong stone building, 10 × 6.5 m, door in centre of south-east wall. There are the abutments of a small bridge over the stream 20 m to the north-east. Blackhouse.

C39 (NF664032) Oblong stone building, 12.6 × 8.6 m, with annexe (possibly a contemporary build) on the south end, 7 × 8.6 m. The main building has a door in the east wall, and there is secondary pen built into the south-east corner. The annexe has a platform with traces of a 'flue' against its south wall, and a door in its west wall. There is a semicircular platform against the west wall of the main building, and a third structure 7 m square 5 m to the west, with a narrow door in its south-east corner. A curving wall runs from the north-west corner of this building round to meet the north-west corner of the main building, thus creating a small yard or possibly garden plot. Blackhouse, drying shed, and byre.

C40 (NF665032) Well-built stone and turf rectangular enclosure, 20 × 15 m, with a rectangular annexe 2 × 1.6 m at its south corner. A turf and stone wall curves in from a major sheep wall upslope to meet the north corner of the enclosure. Immediately upslope to the east are three clearance cairns, and along slope to the north-west are five further cairns and traces of a cultivation plot. Pen and shepherd's shelter (type B).

C41 (NF661029) Heavily embedded and robbed foundations of oblong building 4.8 m wide and 6.1 m minimum length. Blackhouse.

C42 (NF664028) Circular stone setting 2 m diam. Shelter type A.

C43 (NF664026) Oval grassed-over mound 11.5 × 10 m, with complex remains of several successive stone structures. The latest appear to be two subrectangular structures 1.6 m and 1.8 m square respectively. The larger survives three courses (0.8m) high in one place. Lower on the slope, and apparently earlier, are less clearly defined traces of two small circular structures about 1.5 m internal diam. All of these appear later than a very heavily embedded and robbed oval structure, approx. 9.5 × 8 m, surviving only on the south side. Prehistoric house, overlain by mediaeval/early modern shieling huts?

C44 (NF666026) Oval stone setting, 2.1 × 1.9 m. Shelter type A.

C45 (NF663026) Totally embedded oval foundations, 4.7 × 3.8 m internal, with two large blocks 0.7 m apart, apparently flanking south-west facing entrance. Prehistoric hut.

C46 (NF662026) Circular stone structure, 4.9 m diam., with earth core. Partly robbed out around east side. Prehistoric hut?

C47 (NF662026) Stone structure, 2.3 m square, with loose tumble inside. Shelter type B.

C48 (NF662026) Stone setting 1.3 m wide, minimum length 1.6 m, of well-embedded stones set on edge. Similar to kelp-ovens but in high location. Animal burial?

C49 (NF663025) Oval stone setting, 2.5 × 2.2 m. Shelter type A.

C50 (NF660024) Oblong building, 5.5 × 5 m, walls 1–1.3 m wide, with door in south-west corner. Rough walling to the rear may create an annexe between this building and vertical rock face to the north. Outbuilding.

C51 (NF659024) Three cairns, 1–1.7 m diam. Clearance cairns.

C52* (NF655029) OS records IA pottery, bone and bronze objects found in dunes at this approx. NGR in 1959. Nothing seen in 1998.

C53 (NF659031) OS records pottery and shells etc. found in dunes at this approx. NGR in 1959. A few small sherds of reddish-brown gritty ware found here in 1992; nothing seen in 1998.

C54 (NF684033) Oval structure, 3.2 × 2.6 m, with thin earth and stone wall; well-embedded. Shelter type C.

C55 (NF681033) Rectangular thick-walled building, 10.2 × 6.5 m, with door in north wall, looking into valley. Wall 0.9–1.1 m wide. No trace of internal partitions, but secondary lambing pen built into north-east corner.

C56 (NF680030) Rectangular building, 12.4 × 6.1 m, with two doors in south wall giving access into two rooms with no interconnecting internal door. The easterly room is 4 m square, and the westerly 4.6 × 4 m. There are traces of a small rectangular pen (?) in the west corner of one room. The building stands at the back of an oval enclosure or pen, 17.5 × 15 m, and its doors open into the enclosure. Outbuilding.

C57 (NF679033) Rectangular thick-walled building, 9.4 × 6.3, with walls 1 m wide, door probably in north wall. Walls embedded and heavily robbed. Blackhouse.

C58 (NF677032) Rectangular thick-walled building, 12.5 × 7.1 m, with walls c. 1 m wide, door to north. There are no internal partitions, but traces of secondary lambing pens are found in the north-east and south-west corners.

C59 (NF671035) Dun Cuier, excavated by Young (1955). The structure stands on a steep rocky hill commanding good views in all directions. It consists of a double-walled circular building about 19 m diam.,

with a narrow intramural galley, and a central living area about 9 m diam. Armit (1992: 34–38) has offered a plausible reinterpretation of the structure's history, which began as an ARH and had a much flimsier cellular structure inserted into its centre in the 6th or 7th century AD.

C60* (NF 656029) An arc of stone walling observed by OS close to find-spot of Iron Age pottery and bronze (C52); possible wheelhouse?

Zone G (Greian)

G1* (NF652046) Heavily grassed over remains of a circular stone-built structure, 7.5 × 6.6 m. Extent of reduction and overgrowth suggests possibly ancient activity site?

G2* (NF652047) Grassed-over traces of semicircular shepherd's shelter, 2.8 × 1.6 m, built against south-facing outcrop.

G3* (NF651046) Oblong stone setting, 1 × 2.2 m; kelp oven?

G4* (NF650047) Grassed-over traces of small 4 × 3.5 m stone-built hut with part of a kelp oven to the south-east. Kelp-burners shelter?

G5* (NF648047) Scattered traces of a stone structure of substantial boulders and slabs, including two pairs of stones set upright. Possibly the remains of a megalithic structure of some sort.

G6* (NF651049) Semicircular shepherd's shelter, 4.2 × 3.7 m, built against a rock-face.

G7* (NF651049) Rectangular shepherd's shelter, 2.9 × 2 m.

G8* (NF655050) Shepherd's shelter of 10 m semicircular wall against a large boulder: 3 m across.

G9* (NF682053) Dun Clieff, on a small tidal islet. On the summit is a roughly built wall of small rocks and boulders enclosing an area 12 × 7 m, within which is much tumbled stone. This appears to be a late reduction of an earlier, more impressive monument measuring 20 × 10 m, the enclosure wall of which is set further downslope from the summit (Fig. 2.13). Where it survives and is visible this wall is built of selected roughly rectangular stone blocks set in courses. At the south end (nearest the mainland) the inturned entrance survives four courses high. Here, and elsewhere, there are traces of midden from which were recovered six sherds of coarse handmade pottery. Similar sherds from the site are in the NMS collections.

G10* (NF683053) Much-disturbed remains of a setting of large blocks, 9 × 1.5 m, possibly a kelp oven.

G11* (N 683053) Disturbed remains of a structure of large stone blocks set on exposed headland east of Dun Clieff, 4 × 2.5 m, three large blocks across north end. Not a hut or shelter; possibly some sort of ritual monument?

G12* (NF685065) Robbed and grassed over remains of a circular stone hut, 6 × 5.5 m, with traces of a small circular structure inside (Fig. 2.14).

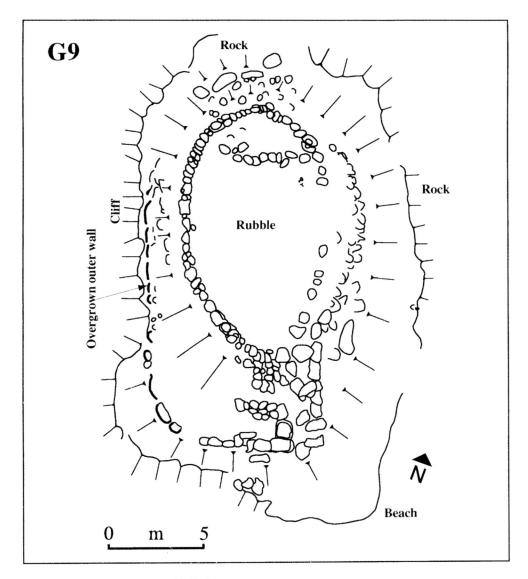

G9

Rock

Rock

Rubble

Cliff

Overgrown outer wall

N

Beach

0   m   5

Figure 2.13 A field sketch of the remains at Dun Clieff, G9.

G13* (NF688055) A much-reduced and grassed-over building, apparently with an apsidal enclosure at the east end. The building measures perhaps 13 × 5 m, with the enclosure extending a further 9 m. This appears to be the earliest of four buildings found along the northern foot of the hill at Suiachan and Vaslain.

G14* (NF687055) Oval cairn, well-bedded and grassed-over, 5 × 3.2 m and about 0.5 m high. Clear traces of edging on the west side.

G15* (NF687055) Remains of foundation course of oblong house, c. 7 × 4 m.

G16* (NF687056) A stone setting, 2 × 0.8 m. Kelp oven.

G17* (NF688055) Blackhouse, 8 × 5 m, grassed-over but well-preserved foundations.

G18* (NF69504) Foundations of oblong stone building, 19.3 × 6.1 m, door in centre of south wall, and another at west end of south wall. Interior divided in three by two partition walls. East room 4.3 × 3.5 m

with 1.8 m 'doorway' from main room. Main central room 4.3 × 6.5 m, with possible low platform, dresser setting or bed box in rear left corner. West room 4.3 × 4.8 m, with doorway 1.5 m from central room, as well as external door. The external wall is c. 1.2 m wide. Blackhouse.

G19 (NF690054) Foundations of a rectangular building 14.5 × 6.8 m, with 1 m wide door in north wall, on low rock platform. Wall c. 1.3 m wide. An annexe 9.9 × 7.35 m, probably a byre, has been added to the east end of the building, with a door facing east. Blackhouse. A triangular sheep pen, 15 × 11 m, stands 15 m east of the house.

G20 (NF690053) Foundations of two adjacent oblong buildings on identical north–south orientation, each with an east-facing door offset towards the north end of the east wall. Building A is 11 × 6.2 m and building B is 11.5 × 6.5 m. Neither has any trace of partitions, chimneys or windows. Blackhouses.

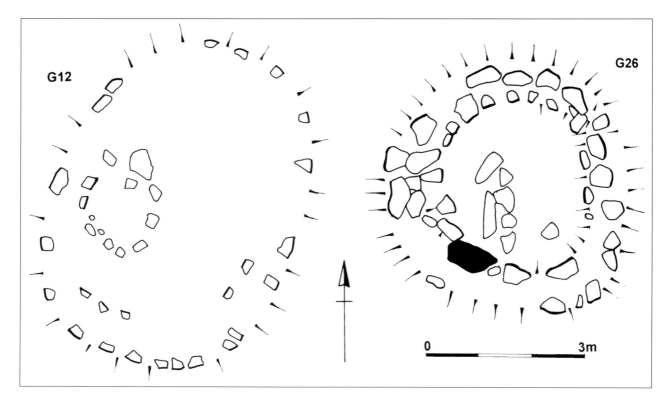

Figure 2.14 Field sketches of small roundhouses at G12 and G26.

G21 (NF690052) Collapsed and heavily embedded remains of an oval stone structure, 4.3 × 3.7 m, forming a pronounced mound. Entrance possibly to the north, into a semi-circular annexe. Prehistoric or mediaeval hut?

G22 (NF690052) Prominent grassed mound 1.6 m high. On the summit traces of a circular stone structure 3.5 m diam., overlying remains of more substantial oval building c. 9 × 7.5 m with a wall a metre wide. Shelter type C overlying a prehistoric oval house (Fig. 2.6).

G23 (NF690051) An earth and stone bank around an area of lazy-bedding broadens into a substantial stone-revetted platform. Two streams are diverted around the end of the platform to pass between two well-built stone walls 0.7 m apart. One large capping stone joining the two walls together is in place. Downstream of this structure is a built conduit, which leads to a natural ravine. Watermill?

G24 (NF688049) Oval stone setting, 2.5 × 2 m, incorporating a large boulder. Entrance to north. Shelter type A.

G25 (NF691049) Irregular alignment of upright stones, enclosing a space 22 × 10 m against a rock face. Midway along the rock face is a stone setting 1.2 × 1 m, and on the southern edge of the area an oval setting 1.5 m × 1.2 m. 15 m south of this complex is a small built stone structure 2.3 × 1.3 m against the continuing rock face. An enclosure with internal shelters type E and A and external shelter type F.

G26 (NF693051) Heavily embedded stone structure 7.5 × 6 m with wall 1 m wide. Orthostat marks one side of door on north-east. An apparent internal partition is a relatively recent insert. 3 m north-east of door are very embedded and robbed remains of a second structure approx. 5.5 × 4 m. Prehistoric oval hut (Fig. 2.14).

G27 (NF695049) Rectangular? stone structure 5 × 4 m, heavily embedded, with door to west. Possible remains of a secondary shelter at south-west corner. Hut of uncertain date.

G28 (NF696048) Remains of a stone setting, 2.5 m square as surviving, with stone set on edge. Possible remains of a second similar 10 m to east. Shelter type A.

G29 (NF696050) Foundations of two oblong buildings on same east–west orientation. A 10 × 6.5 m is the more northerly and has a door in centre of the north wall, overlooking Traigh Mhor. B 7.5 × 5.5 m is slightly to the south and east and also has a north-facing door. Its rear wall is on the alignment of a sheep wall that runs up to the building from both east and west but stops just short of it. Neither building has traces of internal partitions, chimneys or windows. Blackhouses.

G30 (NF696048) Embedded foundations of a small rectangular thick-walled structure 6 × 4 m oriented norh-east–south-west, with door in south-east wall. A small blackhouse or outbuilding?

G31 (NF688048) Much-disturbed remains of an oval stone structure 4 × 2.5 m. Shelter type C.

G32 (NF686049) Heavily embedded remains of a circular? stone structure 8 × 6 m, door possibly to the south-west, and adjoining subrectangular structure 4 × 2.5 m, door possibly to south. Possibly mediaeval shieling huts.

G33 (NF682049) Two embedded stone structures 30 m apart, both c. 2.5 m diam. Shelters type C.

G34 (NF681052) Oval stone setting 4 × 3 m. Shelter type A.

G35 (NF676050) Circular stone structure 4.3 m diam. with stones set and embedded as a kerb around the periphery. On the south side two upright stones, 0.86 and 0.77 m high respectively and each a little over 1 m long, flank a gap of 0.75 m in the stone kerb. Within the circle at this point is a recumbent regular stone block 0.85 m long and 0.4 m wide. The impression is that the two megaliths flanked an entrance into the circle, and that an upright stone stood in the entrance. The interior of the structure has many stone blocks within it, but these are not heavily embedded and appear to be much more recent than the circular structure itself. There is no suggestion of any cairn inside the kerb, and given that the kerb is still in place, it is unlikely that cairn material has been totally robbed out. Possibly a prehistoric burial/ritual monument in the Bronze Age tradition with some much later reuse and/or reworking (Fig. 2.15).

G36 (NF677049) Embedded circular stone structure 3 m diam. Shelter type C.

G37 (NF677049) Small 1.7 m square stone structure, not well embedded. Shelter type C or lambing pen.

G38 (NF678049) Well-embedded oval stone structure 5 × 3.5 m with annexe or earlier circular structure 1.3 m internal diam. at east end. Prehistoric or mediaeval shieling hut?

G39 (NF678049) Heavily embedded foundations of a circular stone structure 9 × 8 m with a recent rectangular built structure 3.3 × 2.3 m superimposed on centre. Prehistoric roundhouse and recent shelter type C.

G40 (NF678049) Circular stone setting 4 m diam. Shelter type A.

G41 (NF678487) Oval stone setting 2.8 × 1.7 m. Shelter type A.

G42 (NF678049) Cluster of at least two, probably four, small oval/circular stone structures. A is 2.8 m diam. B is oval, 1.9 m wide and least 2.8 m long but destroyed at south-east end. C and D are two circular depressions, 2.6 m and 1.7 m diam., with no stone visible. They appear to be remains of earlier structures, probably robbed out to build A and B. Mediaeval and modern shelters type C.

G43 (NF678049) Embedded remains of circular stone structure 7 m diam. Prehistoric or mediaeval shieling hut?

G44 (NF679049) Almost circular stone setting 2.5 m diam. against a low rock face. Immediately west of it, an embedded and partly robbed oblong structure 3.7 × 2.3 m built against same rock face. Two successive shelters of types F and E.

G45 (NF679049) Embedded remains of circular stone structure 5 m diam. Prehistoric or mediaeval shieling hut.

G46 (NF681046) Oval stone setting 2 × 1.5 m. Shelter type A.

G47 (NF681046) Oblong stone setting 1.5 × 1.2 m. Shelter type A

G48 (NF685040) A remarkable standing structure, 46 × 8 m! It is divided into seven sections, the largest 10.5 × 7 m. The northernmost section is quadrant shaped and the southern is D-shaped. The walls are relatively narrow and entirely of stone (i.e. no earth packing). The whole complex may be a series of pens. The building stands alongside the stream, Allt Loch an Duin.

G49 (NF685041) A rectangular structure 10 × 5 m, walls 0.7 m high, with partition wall towards the south end. House related to the use of structure G48?

G50 (NF686038) Two circular stone settings, 3 m and 1 m diam. Shelters type A.

G51 (NF687038) Irregular enclosure 19 × 10 m formed by earth and stone bank and incorporating a group of large rocks and a protruding rock face. Animal pen.

G52 (NF688035) Heavily embedded rectangular stone structure 5 × 4.1 m with walls 1–1.2 m thick. The door appears to be in the south-west corner, giving access to the single room measuring 2.8 × 1.9 m. Shieling hut?

G53 (NF684036) Semicircular stone and earth wall forming an enclosure 11.5 × 9 m against a rock face. On the south side the enclosure wall is interrupted by a rectangular building 6 × 3.5 m. Pen and associated hut or byre.

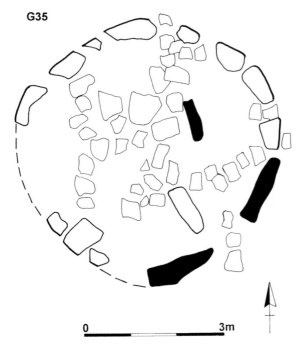

G35

0 _____ 3m

Figure 2.15 Measured plan of a paved cairn? overlooking the sea at G35 (upright stones shaded black).

G54 (NF684037) 4 m square stone structure with semicircular wall attached to the east end. Shieling hut and pen?

G55 (NF681037) Earth and stone semicircular wall built against a sheep wall, forming a pen 9 × 7 m.

G56 (NF678039) Rectangular stone setting 18 × 13 m of large blocks and boulders, many c. 1 m high, built against a high rock face. Enclosure.

G57 (NF678039) Semicircular stone setting 2.5 × 0.7 m against a large boulder. Shelter type E.

G58 (NF678040) Heavily embedded oval stone structure 8 × 5 m, door at south-east?, robbed to build oval stone setting 2.5 × 1.3 m. Prehistoric hut overlain by shelter type A.

G59 (NF672040) Sub-rectangular? built structure, 6.2 × 3.7 m, with a wall 0.75 m wide, and a door to the west. There is possibly a spur of walling forming a 'porch' in front of the door, and behind the structure is a less embedded almost square setting of stone blocks, 2.9 × 2.4 m. This appears to be a small (shieling?) hut with a type A shelter built adjacent to it.

G60 (NF677041) Rectangular stone enclosure marked by a continuous alignment of large blocks and boulders, built up to a rock face. Midway along the south-east side an oval structure 5 × 4 m incorporated into the alignment. Animal pen with shepherd's hut.

G61 (NF678042) Circular stone structure 5 m diam. built close to a high rock face. Prehistoric or Mediaeval hut?

G62 (NF676039) Partly destroyed circular stone setting 3.1 m diam. Shelter type A.

G63 (NF676044) Pronounced mound incorporating many embedded stone blocks on raised knoll. Possible traces of a circuit wall enclosing area 10.6 × 9.1 m, but much robbing has disturbed and obscured the structure. The overall size and character of the stone blocks is similar to prehistoric roundhouses and we tentatively identify this site as such.

G64 (NF676044) Rectangular enclosure, 24 m square, of stone blocks and boulders, built against a rock face. There is an inturned entrance 1.7 m wide in the west wall, and two built structures against the rock face. One is 2.4 m diam. and the other 3.2 × 1.8 m. Animal enclosure and two shelters type F.

G65 (NF674045) Oblong building 9 × 5 m, with door in centre of the north wall; no partitions or chimney. Blackhouse.

G66 (NF673047) Oblong building 10.2 × 5.8 m, door in centre of west wall. No partitions or chimney. Traces of fence alignment and small oblong platform nearby. Blackhouse.

G67 (NF675048) Scattered remains of stone structure 4 × 1.7 m against a low rock face. Shelter type F.

G68 (NF673048) Semicircular stone setting 7 m across against rock face with 2 m diam. circular setting in corner. Shelter type E inside small pen.

G69 (NF683035) Oblong thick-walled building, 11.7 × 5.8 m, door at south-west corner 1 m wide.

No trace of internal partition or secondary features. Immediately south-west of the building is a smaller structure, 5.5 × 4.2 m, with a door in one corner. Blackhouse and byre.

G70 (NF683035) Three somewhat irregular, grassed-over cairns, 2–3 m max. Length, in line below a rock face. Clearance cairns.

G71 (NF682035) Oblong building, 5.1 × 3.6 m, door in south-west corner and walls standing to six courses. An irregular pen is attached on the south side. Byre? and pen.

G72 (NF681035) Raised platform, 21.1 × 10.5 m, enclosed by stone and turf wall. No 'entrance' visible. Garden plot.

G73 (NF680035) Oblong thick-walled building, 8.4 × 5.7 m, door in centre of north wall. Blackhouse.

G74 (NF680035) Much-robbed and totally embedded oval structure, 8 × 5 m. Prehistoric house?

G75 (NF680035) Complex of structures on rocky shelf surrounding site G74. East of G74 are two adjoining buildings, 8.9 × 5.7 m and 5.6 × 5.9 m, the larger with a door to the north and the smaller with a door to the south. Blackhouse and byre. West of G74 are two further adjoining structures, 9.2 × 5.2 m and 4.7 × 4 m. The larger building may have an internal partition, and the smaller a raised platform at one end. No doors are visible. Blackhouse and drying shed. A fifth building, 5.3 m square, is immediately south of G74. This is very embedded and robbed, and could be contemporary with G74; it certainly appears earlier than the other buildings of G75. To the west of the site a pen or possibly a raised garden platform is built against a rock outcrop, and a much smaller platform, 8 × 7 m, is located to the east on a south-facing slope.

G76 (NF678035) Three cairns between 2 and 3 m diam., on 20 m wide shelf above low rock face. Clearance cairns.

G77 (NF675039) Heavily robbed and totally embedded foundations of an oblong building, 10.1 × 5.8 m, with an annexe at the west end, 6.5 × 5 m. The door may have been in the south wall. Blackhouse.

G78 (NF675037) Two cairns, 2 m diam., of mostly large stones. Primary clearance cairns.

G79 (NF674039) Much-robbed oblong building, 9.1 × 5.9 m, door in middle of west side. There is an annexe, 6.6 × 4.8 m, attached to the north end, with its own door in the north wall. Blackhouse and byre?

G80 (NF674039) Curving platform with kerb of large blocks of stone, overlain by modern road. If the curve of the kerb formed a complete circle it would be 9–10 m in diameter. In a different location we would identify this as a kerbed cairn, but here on a bend in the road it seems more likely to be a recent structure built to support the road itself.

G81 (NF672039) Oblong building, 7.25 × 5.3 m, door in the centre of the north wall, no internal partition. Immediately to the south is a second building,

8 × 4.8 m, with a door in the north-east corner. To the east is a raised and embanked platform 11.6 × 10.8 m. Blackhouse, byre? and garden plot.

G82 (NF672038) Cairn, 4.7 × 3.3 m, of large blocks of stone. Primary clearance cairn.

G83 (NF672038) Cluster of four irregular cairns, two mostly of large stones, and two of smaller field stones. Primary and secondary clearance cairns.

G84 (NF672039) Earth and stone wall, forming a right angle 5 × 4.1 m, with a line of boulders across the hypotenuse, forming a shelter or pen. It is unclear whether the earth and stone wall are the remains of an otherwise destroyed structure.

G85 (NF672040) Oblong building, 11.3 × 5.7 m, door towards southern end of east wall; concentration of rubble at north end could obscure partition. To the east is a second building, 10.9 × 6.2 m, with a door in the north wall, and an annexe 5.7 m square on the east end. Blackhouse, byre and outbuilding.

G86 (NF671040) Two raised and embanked platforms, 20 m apart. They are both 12 × 8 m. Garden plots.

G87 (NF671041) Oblong building, 12.9 × 6.1 m, door near centre of south wall, with possible short interior wall to left of door. There is a small open-ended annexe (shed?) on the east end. To the west is a second building, 9.2 × 5.7 m, with a door in the north-east corner. The two buildings are joined together by loosely built walls, forming a pen between them. Blackhouse and byre.

G88 (NF671041) Complex of buildings and pen. Oblong building, 9.6 × 6.5 m, door in middle of west wall. To the east is a second building, 11.27 × 6.35 m. The door is in the centre of east wall, with a platform built into the north end and traces of a partition at the south end. Nearby a large pen or enclosure, 34 × 9 m, has a small thick-walled building 5.7 × 4.1 m on a raised platform at its north-east corner. Blackhouse, drying shed, and byre?.

G89 (NF669041) Cluster of cairns. Four are oval and made up of small field stones, two (20 m distant) are more circular and comprised only of large blocks of stones. Primary and secondary clearance cairns.

G90 (NF669042) Five small cairns, three comprising field stones and two larger blocks, plus a circular platform with a cobbled base 2.3 m diam. Primary and secondary clearance cairns and rick-base.

G91 (NF673039) Stone structure, 3.4 × 1.1 m, built against 6 m rock face. Shelter type F.

G92 (NF673039) Slightly oval stone structure, 8.6 × 8 m, much-robbed and modified. There are several heaps of stone nearby that may have come from this structure. Around the east side there is a run of eight or nine stones *in situ* and a suggestion of a double-faced wall structure. Prehistoric house.

G93 (NF671040) Megalithic structure on rocky knoll. Seven large stones are set on edge, and there are other smaller blocks embedded nearby. The stones are set in the much-reduced remains of a cairn that appears to be D-shaped rather than circular, with the two largest blocks set along the eastern, straight side of the D. This appears to be a heeled-cairn of Shetland type.

Zone VN (North Vatersay)

VN1 (NL624976) Almost square stone-walled building, 4.9 × 4.7 m externally. Wall 1 m wide, doorway 1.3 m wide in north-east corner. Survives to one course.

VN2 (NL621977) Oval stone setting 2.5 × 1.5 m, well-embedded. Shelter type A.

VN3 (NL621977) Arc of stone set against two large blocks in an orthostat boundary. Shelter type E.

VN4 (NL621976) Two adjacent roughly semicircular (diam. 4.0m) stone settings against an orthostat boundary. Shelters type E.

VN5 (NL619977) Oval or possibly boat-shaped stone setting, 200 m from seashore. Oriented north–south, 6 m long, 2.8 m wide at 'stern'. Most stones lie flat but four are set upright. Purpose and date uncertain.

VN6 (NL616979) Curving embedded stone wall built up to a large rock, enclosing space 4.5 × 3 m. Shelter type F.

VN7 (NL617976) Embedded and damaged rectangular stone setting 3 × 2 m against a rock outcrop. Shelter type E.

VN8 (NL624974) Rectangular stone setting 5.4 × 4.2 m overall with possible partition. Shelter type B.

VN9 (NL624973) Arc-shaped stone setting, 11.4 × 8.6 m, against a rock outcrop, with roughly built wall linking the arc to a second rock face, thus forming an enclosure 25 × 8 m. The arc-shaped setting is too large to be a shelter type E and is presumed to be part of the enclosure system.

VN10 (NL624975) Roughly semicircular enclosure 22 m diam., with a (now) discontinuous stone wall and a straight earth and stone bank completing the circuit. There is a raised mound in the centre about 5 × 3 m with two stone blocks set on one edge. This appears to be a robbed and grassed-over shelter, probably of type C.

VN11 (NL621968) Sub-angular stone structure, 4 × 3 m, very heavily embedded and robbed, built against a relict stone and turf wall. Shelter type F.

VN12 (NL620968) A robbed rectangular stone structure, 2.4 × 2 m, probably a shelter type C.

VN13 (NL619969) Oval stone structure, 7 × 5.5 m, very heavily embedded, on a small hillock. The wall is about 0.7 m wide and on the side curve ten stones are set upright. An entrance is most likely on the north or east. Oval hut, possibly prehistoric.

VN14 (NL618969) Stone setting 3.5 × 2.5 m including three stones set upright, with traces of earlier underlying oval structure 3.5 × ?7 m with wall 1 m wide. Shelter type A and underlying oval hut?

VN15 (NL617968) Circular stone setting 4.1 × 3.6 m, with annexe 2.1 × 2 m to one side. Two stones lie at the centre of the annexe. Shelter type A with possible 'porch' entrance?

VN16 (NL616966) Circular stone structure 4.3 m diam., with 0.9 m wide door on west. The wall is 1.1 m wide, and adjoins a boundary wall that runs across the slope. Shelter type C?

VN17 (NL616965) Rectangular stone setting 3 × 2.5 m. Shelter type A.

VN18 (NL617966) Oval or subrectangular stone structure, 5.5 × 4.4 m, much disturbed and robbed. Probably a shelter type C with entrance to south.

VN19 (NL618967) Oval/subrectangular stone and earth structure 6 × 3.9 m, and stone wall 1 m wide. Heavily embedded. Oval hut, possibly prehistoric.

VN20 (NL618967) Circular stone setting, diam. 2.5 m. Shelter type A.

VN21 (NL620964) Sub-circular stone setting, diam. 2 m, with four stones set upright. Shelter type A.

VN22 (NL624969) Slightly oval stone setting, 4 × 3.7 m, with scatter of displaced stones. Shelter type A.

VN23 (NL625969) Circular stone setting, 2.5 m diam., nine stones of which six are set upright. Shelter type A.

VN24 (NL627970) Heavily embedded stone structure, apparently oval, 7.5 × 4.2 m overall. Possibly a prehistoric oval hut.

VN25 (NL627972) Heavily embedded and incomplete oval stone structure 9 × 7.5 m internally, with wall 1.9 m wide; overall dimensions 13.8 × 11.3 m. The largest blocks of stone *in situ* measure between 1.5 and 2 m in length. On the west side there is a pile of discarded or unused blocks that includes further stone of similar size. Nowhere is the structure above foundation level, and even this is only well preserved in the south-west quadrant. This is clearly the remains of a monumental structure of considerable interest and we discuss it further in Chapter 10 (Fig. 10.8). We identify this structure as an unfinished 'broch'.

VN26 (NL627972) Subrectangular or oval stone structure, 7.6 × 5.7 m, loosely built of small boulders, with gap 2.5 m wide at north end at foot of rock face. Small sheep pen.

VN27 (NL627969) Small grassed hillock with many stone blocks well embedded. Overall c. 7 × 4.6 m, but shape and nature of original structure unclear. Either a subcircular/oval hut or an amorphous shieling structure.

VN28 (NL625968) Small grassed hillock with scatter of embedded stone blocks over an area about 7 × 5.2 m. No clear trace of structure. Hut site or shieling.

VN29 (NL625968) A prominent grassed-over knoll, 15 × 14 m, with well-embedded stone blocks scattered on its summit. Rabbit burrowing suggests a good depth of soil on the knoll. Four sherds were found in rabbit spoil, three of which were small and featureless. The fourth was a flat-topped rim of possible LBA date. The blocks on the summit form an amorphous group about 6 × 4 m. Prehistoric site, possibly with later shieling structure.

VN30 (NL627969) Heavily embedded traces of a stone structure over an area 6.7 × 3.6 m. No clear indications of shape or wall structure. Hut or shieling?

VN31 (NL629968) Small grassed hillock with well-embedded stone blocks suggestive of a circular structure 4.5 m diam. Shieling hut?

VN32 (NL629968) Grassed hillock with area of much well-embedded stone, c. 6 × 4.5 m, on a slight platform c. 7 m diam. Rabbit burrowing suggests a depth of soil; it also yielded a small flint blade and three handmade sherds, one with traces of impressed decoration. Prehistoric oval hut?

VN33 (NL628968) Semi-circular stone structure, 2 m across inside, built against a sheepwall. Shelter type F.

VN34 (NL623968) Circular stone setting, c. 4 m diam., with 0.7 m diam. annexe on north side. Shelter type A.

VN35 (NL628967) Heavily embedded and amorphous scatter of stone blocks, c. 5 × 4 m, on small hillock. Shieling?

VN36 (NL630968) Collapsed circular? stone structure 4 m diam. Shelter type C.

VN37 (NL630968) Stone structure, much overgrown by heather, with alignment c. 5 m long and two possible 'returns'. Shelter type D?

VN38* (NL632967) Thick-walled circular hut with a second slightly smaller oval structure appended to the east. The larger hut is 4.9 m diam. overall, but only 2.3 m internally; the second structure, which seems to succeed the first, is 4.2 × 3.6 m overall and 2.2 × 1.6 m internally with a door to the east. Within the larger structure is a small recent shelter, while there are traces of an earlier circular structure showing around the outside of the wall on the north side. The site may thus have four phases, the last of which is recent.

VN39* (NL636966) A small oval mound, 3.7 × 3.2 m, with some stones embedded around the periphery. Location suggests it is unlikely to be a clearance cairn; most probably the collapsed and embedded remains of a small shelter.

VN40* (NL634966) A boulder-built almost square building, 13.8 × 12 m, standing to a max. height of 1.75 m. There is a door at the east, and the rear of the single room is divided into two 'stalls', 6.5 m and 3.5 m wide respectively, by a wall projecting from the back wall.

VN41* (NL635966) Oval shelter type A 4.1 × 3.55 m, indicated by a much-embedded and partly destroyed oval of single stone blocks. Only 2 m from high water and in danger of destruction in the medium term.

VN42* (NL634967) Heavily embedded and partly destroyed oval hut or shelter, 3.5 × 3.1 m, marked out by a single discontinuous row of stone blocks and a low grassed bank.

VN43* (NL 681972) A midden and buried land surface; the midden up to 0.5 m deep and with traces of simple stone structures within it. A local crofter, John Allen Macneil, records seeing buried stone structures c.15 m back from the edge of the sand cliff, at a point where there is a depression. Small scraps of pottery and two pieces of flint, including a small thumbnail scraper, were seen by us in the midden. The midden is exposed in a low sand cliff face that is on the south side of the west-facing Traigh Varlish and is hence subject to considerable erosion each winter.

VN44* (NL637966) A heavily embedded and collapsed oval stone and turf shelter type C 4.2 × 3.4 m, less than 0.5 m from the high-water mark.

VN45* (NL618971) Cist-like structure, 1 m wide, at least 1.7 m and probably over 4 m long, formed of small stone blocks set on edge. It seems likely to be a kelp oven, particularly in view of its location by a seaweed-rich bay.

VN46 (NL617961) Irregular stone setting, 5.4 × 2.7 m, possibly boat-shaped before some stone displacement. Heavily embedded. Possibly a shelter type A or a boat-shaped stone setting of a type common in south-east Vatersay.

VN47 (NL619963) Roughly rectangular stone setting, 4.5 × 2.85 m. Three stones set upright. Shelter type A.

VN48 (NL619963) Small rectangular stone setting with west end open, 2.45 × 1.8 m. Shelter type A.

VN49 (NL619963) Well-embedded subrectangular stone setting 3.5 × 1.3 m with open north end. Shelter type A.

VN50 (NL617963) Subcircular stone setting, diam. 1.7 m with two upright stones. Shelter type A.

VN51 (NL627961) Oval grassed hillock 10.3 × 9 m, with embedded stone blocks. No clear structure. Prehistoric roundhouse?

VN52 (NL626961) Oval stone setting, 3.5 × 2 m, with three stones set upright. Shelter type A.

VN53 (NL625962) Oval stone setting, 1.9 × 1.2 m. Shelter type A.

VN54 (NL630958) Arc of large stone blocks set against bedrock, enclosing area 1.9 × 1.8 m. Shelter type E.

VN55 (NL625962) Circular stone setting, 3.1 m diam., open to north. Shelter type A.

VN56 (NL622960) Well-embedded circular stone setting 6.5 m diam. immediately alongside rock face. There are suggestions of a small oblong setting inside the ring. Possibly an unusually large shelter type A but as likely to be an overgrown circular hut, possibly prehistoric.

VN57 (NL622960) A grassed mound 5.8 m diam., enclosed within an egg-shaped spaced kerb comprised on the east side and two ends of stone blocks and on the south by a curving line of bedrock. The kerb enclosed area is 26.4 m north–south, and 6.7 m across its broad north end. Possibly a prehistoric cairn.

VN58 (NL622965) A boat-shaped setting 8.3 × 3.4 m, including eight upright stones. Attached to 'enclosure' 23 × 15 m marked by a spaced line of stones built against a rock face.

VN59 (NL624964) Oblong stone setting 4.4 × 3.8 m, well-embedded, robbed. Shelter type A.

VN60 (NL631967) Oval stone setting, 6 × 3.5 m, heavily embedded. Probably shelter type A.

VN61 (NL631964) Heavily embedded oval or boat-shaped setting 7 × 4 m alongside shallow rock pool on high ground c.180 m OD.

VN62 (NL633957) A very pronounced grassed mound 12.2 × 11.9 m with heavily embedded stone blocks, average 0.7 m length. On the east-south-east side there are traces of wall facing. One small sherd of handmade pottery in a reddish-brown gritty fabric was found in rabbit spoil. Prehistoric roundhouse.

VN63 (NL632957) A boat-shaped stone setting 7 × 3.6 m with eight upright and three fallen stones; the 'stern' is marked by three smaller blocks lying flat. Oriented with 'prow' to the east. Uncertain purpose and age.

VN64 (NL632957) Oval stone setting 2.5 × 2 m, with rectangular annexe 2.5 × 1.7 m formed of three upright and two flat blocks. Shelter type A.

VN65 (NL627958) Oval stone setting 3.1 × 1.9 m, with annexe attached to south, 2 × 1.5 m. Shelter type A.

VN66 (NL627958) Three-sided 1.5 m square stone setting of three stone slabs set on edge; no trace of a fourth stone/side. Cist/box apparently associated with adjacent VN65.

VN67 (NL632957) Oval, very heavily embedded stone structure 7.4 × 4.1 m. Prehistoric hut?

VN68 (NL628958) An extremely complex site focused on a large, high mound (A) with masses of large stone blocks, but nothing one could designate a 'megalith'. Mound A is 36 × 25 m overall. Clustered around it are at least four oval or circular structures marked by smaller mounds with heavily embedded stone. B is 9 × 7 m, F is a similar size, G is 4.5 × 3 m, and H is 5 × 3 m. To the north are four further structures equally well-embedded, standing on the edge of small stream course and alongside a discontinuous and meandering wall. D which is an oblong structure 15 × 5 m, appears to be earlier than the wall and we believe the wall was built from one existing structure (or ruin) to another. C is a rectangular hut 10 × 5 m, I is a more oval structure 4 × 2 m, and E is a circular hut 3 m diam. It has been suggested to us that the underlying mound A might be a Neolithic funerary cairn. We are not convinced that the mound is entirely or mostly a stone cairn, and there are no visible megalithic slabs that may have formed a chamber. The alternative, in our view, is a major prehistoric stone structure, such as a broch. Mounds B and F are large enough to be round or oval houses, presumably later than the structure from which they appear likely to have derived their building materials, in mound A. Oval huts like G H and I are thought to be mostly IA but not yet well located within that long era. But some may be mediaeval or early modern. Buildings C and D are thought to be modern, but if they predate the relict wall alongside them, as we believe, they might well have been constructed no later than the early 19th century.

VN69 (NL633962) A low oval cairn, 6.5 × 3.5 m, with a rough kerb of stone blocks, the largest of which are on opposing ends of the north–south axis. Heavily eroded by wind and rain due to its exposed position on the high saddle between Heishival More and Heishival Beg. Prehistoric?

VN70 (NL628958) A rock shelter formed by three large boulders and overhanging rocks. Length 3.6 m, depth 2.5 m. No visible trace of cultural debris, but grassed over.

VN71 (NL625972) Rectangular stone setting 7 × 3.3 m against a rock face. Shelter type E.

VN72 (NL628972) Subrectangular stone setting 5.6 × 2.6 m. Shelter type A.

VN73 (NL628962) Oval stone setting 5.7 × 5 m. Shelter type A.

VN74 (NL628962) Two adjoining circular/oval stone settings, 2.6 m diam. and 2.6 × 1.4 m. Shelter type B.

VN75 (NL628961) A low boat-shaped mound, 9.2 × 4 m, the perimeter partly marked by natural rock but mostly by stone blocks. Some of the perimeter blocks have been robbed to build a circular stone setting about 1.5 m diam. on the centre of the mound. Purpose and date of mound uncertain; secondary shelter type A.

VN76 (NL630956) Prominent grassed mound, c. 7.5 m diam., with heavily embedded stone blocks and at least three stones set upright around northern perimeter.

Protected by a low rock face to the east, flanked by a stream to the west. Possibly a prehistoric cairn.

VN77 (NL628957) Complex of three stone buildings. A is 11.7 × 5.9 m with south-facing door to one end of long wall. B is to the west of A and at right angles to it; it is 11.5 × 7 m and partitioned into two almost equal rooms. C abuts B at right angles and is 11 × 6.5 m with a partition dividing the interior into one broad and one narrow room (2 m wide). On the slope behind the buildings are lazy-beds. Blackhouses and byre?

VN78 (NL626957) Oblong stone building 11.2 × 6.5 m with central south-east facing door 0.8 m wide. No partition to single room 8.2 × 3.5 m. Blackhouse.

VN79 (NL626958) Oblong stone building 10 × 6 m with central south-east-facing door protected by thickening of front wall to the west. There appears to be a low stone-built bench along the inside face of the east wall. Blackhouse. VN78 and 79 are both well-embedded and robbed and we are tempted to suggest that they were abandoned and replaced by the two houses at VN77, in a much more sheltered location immediately below.

VN80* (NL624958) Low, heavily grassed-over cairn, 8 m diam., with four stone blocks showing in its circumference. Probably a prehistoric kerbed cairn. Situated 5 m from the cliff edge.

VN81* (NL623958) A kerbed cairn, c. 7.3 m diam. and standing to c. 1.5 m high, with kerbstones clearly

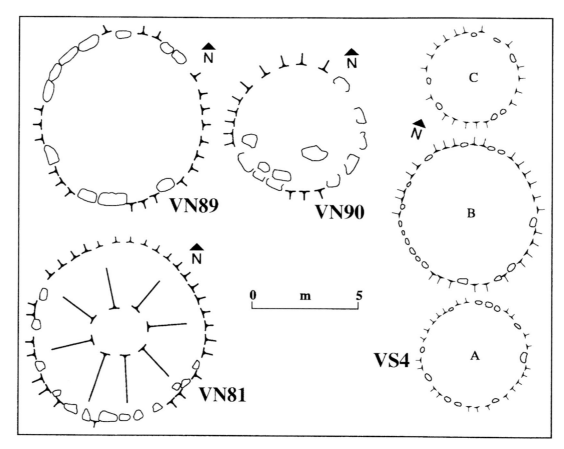

Figure 2.16 A selection of kerbed cairns on Vatersay (field sketches).

visible around the southern half of its circumference. Probably Bronze Age (Fig. 2.16).

VN82* (NL624959) Two-phase monument with a heavily robbed kerbed cairn overlain by an oval hut. The cairn is about 8 m in diameter, the kerb partly surviving on the south, east and north sides. The stone and turf hut is c. 6.5 × 5.5 m, with a possible entrance on the north.

VN83 (NL624959) Grassed mound 6 m diam. with embedded stone and traces of a perimeter kerb. Traces of secondary use and modification or robbing. Prehistoric kerbed cairn.

VN84 (NL624959) Two adjacent grassed mounds. A is 5.9 m diam. and has a well-preserved stone kerb around half its circumference and survives to a height of 0.9 m. B is almost totally destroyed but there are traces of a kerb on the north-west, diam. 4m? Prehistoric kerbed cairns.

VN85 (NL623960) A low hillock c. 40 m × 20 m with the remains of nine circular kerbed mounds in varying states of preservation (Fig. 9.9). (1) Diam. 8.8 m, robbed on north-east and disturbed at centre. Largest surviving kerbstones 1 m. (2) Diam. 6 m. Largest surviving kerbstone 0.9 m. (3) Diam. 7 m. Largest surviving kerbstone 0.6 m. (4) Diam. 5.6 m. Largest surviving kerbstone 0.6 m. (5) Diam. 6.6 m. Largest surviving kerbstone 0.6 m (Fig. 2.17). (6) Diam. 8 m. Largest surviving kerbstone 1 m. (7) Diam. 2.8 m. Largest surviving kerbstone 0.6 m. (8) Diam. 7 m. Largest surviving kerbstone 1.2 m. (9) Diam. 4.4 m. Largest surviving kerbstone 0.8 m. This remarkable cemetery of kerbed cairns is fully discussed, along with the other cairns in this area, in Chapter 9 of this volume (Fig. 9.10).

VN86 (NL623960) Oblong house 8.5 × 4 m with central door in south wall. Built against edge of cairn VN85A and of robbed cairn material. Blackhouse.

VN87 (NL624960) Low cairn 5.5 m diam. Eroded away around south perimeter, some kerbstones visible on north-east. Prehistoric kerbed cairn.

VN88 (NL623961) Cairn diam. 6.8 m with a dozen kerbstones visible around northern half of perimeter. Partly robbed out for adjacent sheep wall. Prehistoric kerbed cairn.

VN89 (NL623961) Cairn, 8 m diam., with eleven kerbstones visible. Prehistoric kerbed cairn (Fig. 2.16).

VN90 (NL623961) Circular stone structure 6.3 m diam. There are clear traces of a raised mound and the perimeter stones look more like building blocks than oblong kerbstones. However, the site has been robbed and badly damaged by rabbit burrows so its original appearance is not clear. We believe this is probably a prehistoric hut but it could be another kerbed cairn (Fig. 2.16).

VN91 (NL623961) A prominent grassed mound 30 × 20 m, with a mass of stone blocks heavily embedded in it, immediately below a high protective rock face. No discernible pattern to stone debris, but almost certainly a major building. The degree of embedding suggests to us a prehistoric structure rather than a modern one; possibly an Iron Age roundhouse to judge from the size of mound and amount of stonework.

VN92 (NL622960) A flat platform 2.5 m diam. Enclosed by a kerb of stones set on edge. This is not identical to the kerbed cairns in this area in that there is no suggestion of a mound, and the 'kerb' is orthostatic. A sheep wall runs up to it from the west and we

Figure 2.17 Kerbed cairn No.5 in the cemetery of nine such cairns at VN85. The kerbstones are to the left, and the mound of the inner cairn to the right.

believe that the wall and the circular platform are probably broadly contemporary. Unknown purpose.

VN93 (NL622958) Low mound c. 8 m diam. with kerb of large blocks and incorporating rock outcrop. Apparently another kerbed cairn but it stands in isolation from the others in this area and it is possibly a house site rather than a cairn.

VN94* (NL623958) An earth and stone mound, 12 × 8 m, standing to a maximum height of 2 m, attached to a low weathered bank that runs from the present shoreline to an outcrop. It may be the embedded remains of a circular house.

VN95* (NL623958) Five small mounds composed mainly of beach cobbles and c. 1.5–2 m in diameter. Their purpose is unclear but they appear to be relatively recent to judge from their condition.

VN96* (NL621958) Four circular huts, each c. 3 m diameter, and one rectangular hut, c. 4 × 3.5 m, built from large beach cobbles. They appear to be relatively recent fishermen's shelters or stores.

VN97 (NL622957) Semi-circular stone structure, 5.7 × 4.5 m, butted up to standing stone wall of large 80 × 80 m enclosure. Sheep pen and attached lambing pen?

VN98 (NL622959) A high, steep-sided grassed mound 15 × 12 m with embedded stone blocks in many areas and heaps of stones, probably disturbed/robbed for wall building but unused. We believe a mound of this size, 3–4 m high, must cover a very substantial structure, possibly an Iron Age 'broch', although a Mediaeval structure is also possible.

VN99 (NL621959) Low oval mound 11 × 7 m with embedded stone blocks. Robbed for wall building. Prehistoric oval house?

VN100 (NL621959) Slightly more prominent oval mound than VN99, 14 × 10 m, with only a few embedded blocks visible. On the south side sheep disturbance has exposed what appears to be a circular stone structure built into the edge of the mound. Prehistoric oval house with mediaeval shieling hut?

VN101 (NL621959) A low grassed mound 7 m diam. with embedded stone blocks. Prehistoric roundhouse? Sites VN98–101 form an important complex that is discussed further in Chapter 8.

VN102 (NL623962) Oval stone setting 5 × 4.5 m. Shelter type A.

VN103 (NL621962) Rectangular stone setting 2.5 × 1.2 m abutting a large boulder. Shelter type E.

VN104 (NL620960) Circular grassed mound, 10 m diam., much damaged by rabbit activity but with many embedded stone blocks. There is a low bank immediately to the south of it that may well be contemporary. Prehistoric round hut?

VN105* (NL620958) Oval stone setting, 8.2 × 4.5 m, including some stones set upright, with a possible entrance at the south-west corner and a small oval shelter, 3 × 1.7 m, built into the southern end. Purpose uncertain; its location on an exposed low cliff-top suggests it is unlikely to be a shepherd's shelter and pen.

VN106* (NL619959) Semi-oval setting of boulders, 3.6 × 2 m, similar to the type of shelter commonly found in the southern isles but here in an exposed position.

VN107* (NL619959) Irregular setting of stone boulders and blocks, outlining an oval area 5 × 4 m. This is too flimsy for the base of a hut, and perhaps too large for a shelter. Its location and nature suggest it may be broadly similar to site T169 on Barra which proved to be an activity site producing lithic material dated by C14 to c. 700 BC.

VN108 (NL619960) Small cairn of cobbles and boulders, 1.2 m diam., on end of turf and stone wall spur. Clearance cairn.

VN109 (NL619961) Rectangular stone setting, 3.9 × 2.1 m. Shelter type A.

VN110 (NL618961) Circular stone setting, 3.6 m diam., with traces of internal partition. Shelter type A.

VN111 (NL618960) Low peat-covered cairn, 2 m diam., with some small boulders around east side. Prehistoric?

VN112 (NL618962) Mound, 10.5 m diam., with embedded stone blocks, including possible arc of wall face around north side. Prehistoric house?

VN113 (NL618960) Circular stone structure, 3.6 m diam. Stones around perimeter but may be wall stones rather than kerb. Small hut or kerbed cairn?

VN114 (NL617920) Stone ring, 6 m diam., of stones mostly 0.5–0.7 m in size. Set into peat and probably relatively recent.

VN115 (NL617961) Oblong stone setting, 6 × 3 m. Stones continuous along west side but only 3–4 *in situ* along the east. Robbed shelter.

VN116 (NL616958) Oval stone setting, 3 × 1.7 m. Shelter type A.

VN117 (NL616959) Low oval grassed cairn, 4.5 × 3.5 m. Possibly a burial cairn.

VN118 (NL637955) A much-embedded oblong stone building, 8 × 5 m, with central door in south wall; back wall partly robbed. The building sits on a prominent grassed mound 14 × 12 m with traces of embedded blocks. Blackhouse built over prehistoric roundhouse?

VN119 (NL636955) Grassed mound, 12 m diam., rabbit-infested with stone blocks revealed in burrows and at edges. Prehistoric house site?

VN120 (NL636956) Heavily embedded and much-destroyed oval stone structure, 5 × 4 m. Entrance possibly on east. Prehistoric hut?

VN121 (NL634955) Partly destroyed stone structure, 10 m diam., with stone-faced wall 1–1.2 m wide. Prehistoric thick-walled roundhouse. (Fig. 2.6).

VN122 (NL639956) Circular stone structure, 5 m diam., heavily embedded with traces of superimposed subrectangular shelter in western half. Prehistoric/mediaeval hut?

VN123 (NL639956) Prominent grassed mound, 1.5 m high and 7 m diam., with many stone blocks embedded within it. An orthostat boundary is attached to it on the north side and there are traces of a similar boundary to the south-west. Prehistoric hut?

VN124 (NL640958) Rectangular stone structure, 6 × 3 m, incorporating a large rock, with a short partition wall inside south-facing door. Outside the door a revetted platform about 1.5 m wide has been built the length of the structure. Sophisticated version of shelter type D?

VN125 (NL642959) Grassed rabbit-disturbed mound, 15 × 8 m, against a rock outcrop, with a subcircular 4 m diam. stone and earth structure built against the edge of the mound. Possible prehistoric house site with shelter type C abutting.

VN126 (NL613614) Semicircular, 3.4 m diam., stone setting against a low rock face. Shelter type E.

VN127 (NL630955) Stone revetted rectangular platform c. 9 m along hillside, just inside low earth bank. It looks like a building platform but there is no trace of a structure to be seen.

VN128* (NL648952) Two large blackhouses, each c. 13 × 8 m, reduced to their foundations, with doors facing east into a small bay.

VN129* (NL648952) A D-shaped enclosure, the arc formed by an earth and stone bank, the straight side by the low sea-cliff. Although erosion here is not severe it is possible that the enclosure once extended further north and may even have been more oval than D-shaped. However, our impression is of a relatively recent monument.

VN130* (NL652962) A boat-shaped structure, c. 9 × 4.5 m, with stone walls c. 0.5 m wide. A single block forms the east-facing prow. At the stern is a rectangular 'cabin' 4 × 2 m. Bits and pieces of fishing tackle lie in the 'cabin'. The front end of the structure is quite well embedded but the stern end and 'cabin' are more upstanding and could be late additions or renovation. A boat noost. It is only 10 m from the sea, above a 2 m high cliff and a pebble beach.

VN131* (NL657961) Small single-roomed building, 6 × 4 m, with a door to the north north-west and walls 0.8 m wide. It stands on a ledge only 5 m from the sea, and about 4 m above it. Almost certainly associated with the nearby VN132.

VN132* (NL657962) Two adjacent stone buildings, each with walls 0.6 m wide. A 4 × 3.5 m with door in south-east corner. B 5 × 4 m, no doorway seen in remaining portion but badly damaged at the south end.

VN133* (NL665957) The slight remains of Cille Bhrianian. The mediaeval chapel, 11 × 5 m, sits on a mound from which rabbit infestation produces midden material including reddish-brown gritty handmade pottery, probably of Iron Age type.

VN134* (NL665956) A rough circle of stones, c. 2 m diam., with a line of four further stone blocks that link

the circle to the sea edge only 2 m to the west. Traces of fisherman's activity suggest a fisherman's shelter/store.

VN135* (NL665957) A revetted platform, partly natural?, 11 × 5 m, with grassed mound through which stones protrude, forming an arc c. 4 × 5 m. Very deeply embedded. Prehistoric hut circle?

VN136* (NL645957) Hut and pen. Thick-walled hut, 3.5 m square built against a 4 m high rock face and surrounded by a kerb of large upright blocks, forming an arc 6.5 × 5.3 m.

VN137* (NL653956) Stone setting, 2 × 2.5 m, of stone blocks set in an arc against south face of a large rock. Shelter type E.

VN138* (NL653956) Stone setting on a slight earth bank, 1.2 × 1.1 m, set against south face of a 7 m rock face with a slight overhang. Shelter type E.

VN139* (NL653957) Stone setting in an arc, 1 m diam., set against south face of a 5 m high rock face. Shelter type E.

VN140* (NL644948) A thin, straight-edged monolith, 1.7 × 0.55 m, lying on a slope about 15 m from the sea edge. Fallen standing stone?

VN141* (NL644948) A grassed-over mound with embedded stone blocks; c. 4 m diam. and standing to c. 1.5 m. Possibly a prehistoric hut site.

VN142* (NL644948) A thick-walled house, 15 × 6 m externally, with a door in the middle of the south-east wall facing into Vatersay Bay. No trace of subdivision, and no chimney. Blackhouse.

VN143* (NL644948) Adjacent to VN142. A thick-walled, one-roomed building, 8 × 4.5 m, with a door in the centre of the southeast wall. A 2 m square annexe is built on to the north wall.

VN144* (NL643948) A thick-walled house, 7 × 5 m externally, a door to the south-east and no visible partitions. A pen, 10 × 7 m, is appended to the back of the house. Blackhouse.

VN145* (NL643948) A rectangular stone-built hut, 6 × 3 m, very embedded but also very badly disturbed and destroyed by rabbit action. Probably an outbuilding of VN144.

VN146* (NL643947) A complex of three circular huts. A diam. c. 3 m with door to south walls at least two courses high; B diam. c. 4 m, foundations only and heavily grassed over; C diam. c. 3 m, foundations only, heavily grassed over. Possibly prehistoric to judge from embedding but could be post-mediaeval shelters.

VN147* (NL642947) Wreck of a Catalina flying boat which crashed on the east slope of Heishival Beg in 1944. Main parts of wreckage brought down and deposited in stream bed.

VN148* (NL642947) Rectangular pen, 14 × 12 m, formed of large blocks set against a north-facing rock face. Entrance on north side with a small shepherd's shelter immediately alongside.

VN149* (NL6379554) A complex of five buildings built on ledges and slope immediately above the road. The two nearest the sea appear to be more recent than the others with considerable stone still showing; the others are heavily embedded. Building A is c. 10×8 m externally, with a south-east-facing door and an appended wall running to a small square outbuilding to the south-west. Building B next to A is c. 7×5 m externally with a south-east-facing door. Building C is situated up-slope from B and is about 8×5 m with traces of a central partition or structure and a south-east-facing door. Building D is further up-slope behind C and is about 9 m square, with a south-east-facing door. Building E abuts building C to the south-west and is 6×5 m with some sort of platform or structure to the left of its doorway in the south-east wall. A wall runs south-westwards from one corner of building E along the back of building B to enclose a 'yard'. This is a most interesting complex. Buildings A B and C are blackhouses, D and E are outbuildings, but we believe not all the buildings were contemporary.

VN150 (NL629971) Dun Caolis, scheduled monument. The Dun stands on a rocky hill at about 30 m OD. Although the exterior face of the wall can be seen to a height of only a little over a metre, it is clear from a scarcement seen on the south-west interior arc and from the gallery slabs around the south and west side that if the interior were excavated the wall would probably stand 3 m or 4 m high. The overall wall thickness varies from about 3.2 to 3.6 m, a gallery around 0.9 m wide separating the 0.9–1.3 m wide inner and outer wall structures. There are suggestions of oval or circular cells within the wall around the south-east quadrant and the entrance was also probably here. The interior diameter is around 9 m. Outside the structure, to the west, is a semicircular platform area, partly supported by a rock formation and partly by built walling. This appears to be contemporary with the main structure, but a series of three subrectangular buildings clustered against the east and south sides of the main structure are clearly later and almost certainly built of stone robbed from its collapsed superstructure. Some of these buildings are quite substantial and they appear to be more significant than shieling huts or temporary shelters. Nine sherds of reddish-brown to dark-brown gritty pottery have been brought to the surface by rabbits. All are featureless but they are similar to material from the other broch and wheelhouse sites in the southern isles. Iron Age with later mediaeval? buildings (Fig. 10.5). The wall systems around this monument are complex.

VN151* (NL636969) Grassed-over stone structure, 2.6×2.1 m, built on end of boundary wall. Shelter type B.

VN152* (NL635969) Low platform, 3×2.2 m, revetted on south side by a curving row of large stones. Rick stand?

VN153* (NL635969) Low platform, 3.5×2.4 m, revetted on south side by a shallow arc of large stone blocks. Rick stand?

Figure 2.18 The megalithic chamber of cairn VN157 looking north to Heaval. The low remains of the cairn can still be seen.

VN154* (NL632969 to 632967) Curving stone wall, 1.5 m wide, barely structured, running across the head of Cornaig Bay. Tidal fish trap.

VN155* (NL621979) A very roughly built stone wall making an enclosure, about 11×7 m, on a small headland formed by a storm beach. A shelter is attached on the east side. An adjacent shelter type A 2 m diam., lies to the east.

VN156* (NL634974) Remains of the blackhouses of Caolis township, together with white houses and later buildings.

VN157 (NL63509694) A low cairn, probably about 13 m diam. originally but much robbed out on the north and west sides, in the centre of which 12 upright blocks of stone form an elongated structure that runs from the centre to the eastern edge of the cairn (Fig. 2.18). This is a reasonably well-preserved but previously overlooked passage grave. The chamber is about 3.4×2.8 m, approached by a passage about 4 m long, which broadens as it approaches the edge of the cairn to make a small triangular courtyard 4 m wide. (Fig. 9.5.)

Zone BM (Biruaslum)

BM1* (NL609962) Oval stone setting, 7×5.5 m, perched near the cliff edge. The northern segment is comprised of three large blocks 0.8–1 m in size, whilst the southern arc is a line of smaller blocks. Between the northern and southern segments, at the east and west ends, there are no stones at all. This does not appear to be a shelter: neither its form or location support that interpretation. Function and date unknown.

BM2* (NL609962) One circular and one oval stone setting with projecting spurs that link them to a rock face and create a small enclosure. The circular setting is 2.7 m diam., and the oval measures 4.5×3 m;

the enclosure is 9 × 3.5 m. Two shelters type A and small pen.

BM3* (NL607964) Semi-circular stone setting, 3.5 m diam., against rock face. Shelter type E.

BM4* (NL607963) Remains of semicircular stone setting, 5 m diam., against rock face. Shelter type E.

BM5* (NL607963) Rectangular stone setting, 5.5 × 2.5 m. Three stones on edge form a right angle at one end, with a fourth upright stone making a short return. The rest of the structure is of flat stones, but for a 1 m high stone in the south side. The overall impression is of a shelter, 3.5 × 2.5 m, with a porch or annexe, 2 × 2.5 m, but the location, on an open shelf totally exposed to westerly gales, must raise a query over this interpretation.

BM6* (NL611962) A remarkable linear arrangement of probably 12 circular structures strung out over c. 130 m near the cliff edge. They form two groups separated by a huge boulder. The north-eastern group appears to comprise 6 circular or oval structures, the largest c. 8 m diam. and the smallest c. 3.5 m. The latter is on the end of a spur wall that runs out from the end of the cluster of 5 structures. In addition, walls link some of the structures to form two irregular enclosures or yards. The south-western group comprises 4 linked structures, the largest c. 8 m diam., with a fifth standing slightly apart with a short stretch of straight wall attached to it. A sixth oval structure, 10 × 5 m, stands to the north, the only one of the 12 not on the main alignment. This appears to be a cluster of 11 huts with the largest oval structure more probably a pen. They are well-embedded and probably of considerable antiquity. Immediately to the north-east is the large defensive stone wall (BM7) usually, and probably rightly, attributed to the Iron Age. This wall clearly defends the eastern tip of Biruaslam from attack from the west (the east is defended by the sea dyke that separates Vatersay from Biruaslam). If the huts were Iron Age we would expect them to be within the defended area. Equally, if they were earlier than the defensive wall (and there is Neolithic occupation on Biruaslam, see BM8) then one might expect them to have been robbed out for building the wall. On balance, therefore, we incline to the view that this interesting settlement is post-Iron Age and probably mediaeval or early modern.

BM7* (NL611963) An impressive wall approx. 100 m long running in an arc from the southern cliff edge towards the eastern edge of the island north of the sea dyke (Fig. 2.19). The wall stands to a height of 3 m and is 2 m wide. At the highest point of its line across the hillside there appears to be an original entrance about 2.5 m wide. The wall runs to an area of large rock outcrops that continue its curving line, but it does not appear to continue beyond the rock to meet the cliff on the east side (pace RCAHMS, 134). Although it is possible that it has been completely robbed out, there is no structure on the island that

Figure 2.19 The fortification wall of the promontory fort (BM7) on the Islet of Biruaslam off the west coast of Vatersay.

would appear to have been built with its rather regular blocks of stone. The huts at BM6 not only appear to be built of different material but are also much closer to the south-west end of the wall that would have provided a nearer source of building stone. We conclude, therefore, that this wall, surely too massive to have been built for any reason other than defence, was never completed. Its closest parallels seem to be cliff-forts like Cahercommaun, Co. Clare and Dun Aongusa, Galway, dated broadly to the first millennium AD. Cultural material recovered from a midden (BM8) within the area enclosed by the wall includes five pieces of flint and five sherds. One of the sherds is Neolithic, and a second probably so. The remaining three sherds are undiagnostic but they are not in the typical reddish brown fabric associated with such sites as the broch on Borve headland, Dun Clieff and Dun Caolis. A final decision on the dating of this monumental structure should perhaps be deferred.

BM8* (NL611963) A midden deposit up to 1.5 m deep, eroding from the cliff edge at the south-east corner of the island. The deposit appears homogenous/ continuous throughout. At a depth of 1.38 m in the midden face a decorated bowl rim of Neolithic date was found (Fig. 2.20). An undecorated sherd in identical fabric was found at 0.48 m, and a third sherd in the same fabric with a small raised but undecorated cordon or lug was found lying in eroded debris at the base of the midden. From the same debris came two further small sherds, two chunks of flint pebbles and three flakes. The midden appears to be of Neolithic date.

Zone VS (South Vatersay)

VS1 (NL627945) Dun Vatersay, on a rocky hill overlooking both West Bay and East Bay, and dominating the land approach across the machair to southern

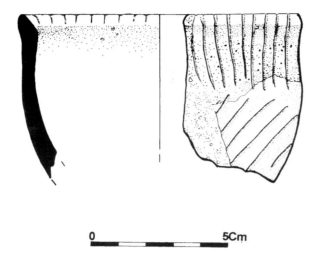

0   5Cm

Figure 2.20 The rim of a Neolithic bowl recovered from the eroding midden at BM8 on the Islet of Biruaslam.

Vatersay. The site has been very extensively robbed for stone but traces of the main oval circuit wall survive and indicate a structure 13 × 10.3 m overall, with an outer wall about 0.8 m wide. The largest stones used in this structure are over 1 m long. There is no visible evidence for an inner wall running parallel to the outer one. We concur with the RCAHMS (1928: 138) that there are suggestions of an enclosed yard to the east, which measures 10m × 9m. A few small sherds of reddish-brown gritty pottery have been seen in disturbed soil and match those from other broch/dun sites on Barra and Vatersay and from middens at Eoligarry and on South Uist. Two dozen similar sherds from the site are in the NMS collections. Iron Age 'dun'.

VS2 (NL627945) Small oval stone setting, 2 × 1.3 m, with small stones inside, grassed over. Very exposed location for a shelter, but both a clearance cairn and a burial cairn also seem unlikely. Probably modern, purpose uncertain.

VS3 (NL626947) Group of three small unstructured cairns. One appears to be primary clearance and the others both primary and secondary.

VS4 (NL626946) A group of four, possibly five, circular cairns with substantial kerbs. A is 5.5 m diam. with kerbstones visible around the western perimeter. B is 7.7 m diam. with kerbstones visible around the entire western arc. C is 5 m diam. with occasional kerbstones visible around most of the circumference (Fig. 2.16). D is c. 4 m diam. with only three or four kerbstones visible and appears to have been extensively robbed. E is uncertain. Unlike A–D, which form a more or less straight alignment on a north–south axis, E is located west of A and B and is either much damaged and robbed or else perhaps disturbed and moved stone from the other cairns. If it is the remains of a cairn it would be c. 4 m diam. Cairn B was excavated in 1995 and a report appears in Chapter 5.

VS5 (NL626946) Irregular unstructured cairn, 3 m across. Primary clearance cairn.

VS6 (NL625946) Low cairn, 6.5 × 5 m, with six large stones set around perimeter, four perhaps in original kerb position. This appears to be a further kerbed cairn but one that has been robbed and modified.

VS7 (NL625945) A cairn, diam. 8.4 m, with kerbstones showing around much of the perimeter. Kerbed cairn. Excavated in 1995, and a report appears in Chapter 5.

VS8 (NL624946) A low mound, 8 × 6 m, with nine stone blocks scattered across it and around its perimeter, all probably moved. Possibly an ancient cairn but more probably a recent temporary shelter or lambing pen.

VS9 (NL622947) Oblong low mound, 4 × 2 m, with stones set at one end and two on perimeter. Shelter type A.

VS10 (NL622946) Oval mound, 4 × 2 m, with some stone blocks embedded around southern half. Possibly a natural feature or remains of a shelter.

VS11 (NL623946) Subrectangular enclosure, 40 × 28 m, formed partly by rock outcrops and steep hillside and partly by a line of orthostats. There are traces of lazy bedding inside the enclosure, so this is presumably an enclosed cultivation plot.

VS12 (NL622943) Stone setting, 1.2 × 0.7 m, comprising two upright stones fronted by an arc of flat blocks. Shelter type A.

VS13 (NL623943) Cairn, 4.5 m diam., with eight or nine stone blocks well-embedded. No clear trace of a kerb. Probably a prehistoric cairn.

VS14 (NL622942) Oval- or boat-shaped cairn, 4 × 2.7 m, disturbed, but suggestion of a rough kerb of small blocks along the two long sides. Oriented north–south. Ancient cairn possibly adapted for a shelter in recent times.

VS15 (NL623942) Roughly circular cairn, 2.6 × 2.3 m diam., with nine perimeter stones *in situ*. This appears to be a small kerbed cairn but the kerbstones are not set lengthways as on the best examples of the type on Vatersay, rather they are either set into the mound on their long axis or are small squarish blocks.

VS16 (NL623940) Low mound, 6.5 m diam., with four stone blocks embedded inside perimeter. Prehistoric cairn.

VS17* (NL623938) Semicircular enclosure, 60 × 40 m, constructed of a turf wall to the west, large orthostats to the south and east, and a steep hillside and rock face to the north. A shepherd's shelter, type F is constructed against a large rock on the south side.

VS18 (NL624938) Small semicircular stone setting, 1.9 × 1 m, against rock face. Shelter type E.

VS19 (NL624936) Low grassed mound, 6.4 × 4.3 m, with seven stone blocks embedded but no apparent structure. Possibly a cairn or collapsed and robbed oval hut.

VS20 (NL635943) Two blocks of stone, each 0.5 m high, one 0.26 × 0.17 m in section and the other 0.28 × 0.24 m. They stand in machair and it is possible but unlikely that they are much taller than they appear. They appear on the OS map as 'standing stones' but on present evidence this is difficult to justify. Their location is insignificant in terms of the landscape.

VS21 (NL644941) Two low cairns, c. 4.8 m and 4.3 m diam. Both have a few large stones on the perimeter but they do not look like kerbstones. Probably clearance cairns connected with cultivation plots at Eorisdale.

VS22* (NL646940) Rectangular building platform, 10 × 4 m, with traces of stone alignment around edges, and with a 2 m wide raised area across the middle. The prepared base of a demolished and removed timber building; probably an outbuilding for the Eorisdale settlement.

VS23 (NL646940) An unstructured heap of large stone blocks at the foot of a rock face. Apparently a quarry site, most probably for the building of Eorisdale.

VS24 (NL646941) Two collapsed rectangular stone buildings, 9.3 × 5.4 m and 5 × 4.6 m. Originally two outbuildings, probably used as pens in their last phase.

VS25 (NL650943) A small natural rock shelter with traces of stones set between rock face and boulders to form a shelter type E.

VS26* (NL647946) Foundations of a rectangular building, 8.5 × 6 m, with possible entrance in north (long) wall facing sea. Traces of an enclosure (possibly no more than a fence line) around the house. Small jetty to the north-west.

VS27* (NL637–640/946) At least 12 rectangular building platforms cut into the hillside, some with traces of stone slabs forming base for timber structures. The longest platforms are up to 25 m, the smallest 4 m. The site of the herring fishing settlement.

VS28 (NL625939) Subrectangular stone setting, 1.7 × 1.2 m, against an overhanging rock face. Shelter type E.

VS29 (NL626944) Low cairn, 6 m diam., with at least six stones horizontally bedded around perimeter. Partly dug away and stone robbed on east. Prehistoric kerbed cairn.

VS30 (NL626943) Small circular stone setting, 1 m diam. Too small for shelter; possibly a temporary fireplace.

VS31 (NL626941) Two stone and turf walls built between a rock face and steep slope to form an enclosure 24 × 8 m, with a rectangular stone structure built into a corner against the rock face. Pen and shepherd's shelter type F.

VS32 (NL628939) Monolith, 1.8 m high, standing by the entrance to enclosure VS33. The stone is recorded by the RCAHMS as a standing stone, but it may not be prehistoric, at least in its present location, since it flanks one side of the entrance into enclosure VS33.

Whether the enclosure was built around an existing monument or the stone was brought here to incorporate into the enclosure is uncertain, but the enclosure itself looks relatively recent.

VS33 (NL628939) Roughly semicircular earth and stone bank, c. 35 m diam., built up to a rock face. On the south side there is a gap in the bank, flanked on the west by the standing stone VS32. West of the stone is a smaller banked structure, c. 8 × 4 m, built up to the main bank. A sheep pen with an internal lambing pen?

VS34 (NL629941) An almost circular grassed cairn, 5.7 × 5.3 m diam., with nine stones visible set around the perimeter. These appear to be well-embedded and *in situ*. In the west quadrant a stone set upright protrudes from the cairn; in view of the results of the excavation of cairn VS4B (see Chapter 5) this stone may also be *in situ*. Prehistoric kerbed cairn.

VS35 (NL629942) A boat-shaped stone setting, 11 × 3.9 m, oriented east–west. Eighteen stones mark its outline, an estimated five or six missing, mostly from the prow although the prow itself is marked by the biggest stone of the group. A very low relict stone and earth bank runs on roughly the same alignment and the stone setting was at first thought to sit over the bank. Careful study reveals that the bank curves to avoid the setting, and then resumes its original alignment. The purpose of the structure is uncertain; this example appears to be of some antiquity.

VS36 (NL643943) A circular earth and stone bank, 23 m diam., and preserved up to 1 m high. If there was an original break in the circuit it must have been in the south-east–south-west quadrant. This quadrant has the most stone in the bank construction and may have been rebuilt or strengthened at some time. Three blocks of stone lie across the central area but are probably not *in situ* since the area has also been lazy-bedded. The enclosure has clearly been used for cultivation but it seems unlikely to have been constructed initially as a garden plot. There is no good reason to make such a plot circular, nor do we know of any parallels elsewhere in the southern isles. It is possible that it was first built as a cattle pen (there is good machair grazing to both the west and down by Eorisdale to the east) and that the manure-enriched area was then used for cultivation. There is also the possibility of a prehistoric enclosure but the good preservation of the bank suggests a more recent date.

VS37 (NL643944) Remains of a roughly oblong stone setting, 5 × 3 m, against a rock face. Shelter type E.

VS38 (NL632944) Irregular walled enclosure with gravestones. The cemetery for Vatersay township and estate.

VS39 (NL629944) The standing ruins of the Vatersay estate house.

VS40 (centred on NL631945) The foundations of blackhouses in Vatersay settlement, some of which served as outbuildings and workshops until recently.

VS41 (NL641945) A stone-rich mound very heavily embedded, and infested by rabbits, built on a steep slope overlooking East Bay. On the downslope side much stonework is exposed and the mound stands 1.7 m high! On the top of the mound, which is 7 × 6 m, further embedded stones, almost certainly disturbed by rabbits, are visible. Possibly a prehistoric house or kerbed cairn. The lack of any visible kerbstones inclines us to the former.

VS42 (NL646945) Boat-shaped stone setting, 8.3 × 2.5 m, oriented north–south, with 16 stones visible around perimeter. The west side appears to be incorporated into a later, but relict, boundary structure. Excavated in 1995; a report will appear in SEARCH volume 6.

VS43 (NL646944) Boat-shaped setting, 4.2 × 1.7 m, oriented east–west with ten stones visible on the perimeter. A relict boundary bank runs alongside the structure. Date and purpose uncertain. All of these structures (VS42–56) will be discussed in SEARCH volume 6.

VS44 (NL646944) Boat-shaped setting, 4.7 × 2.4 m, oriented south–north, with eight stones visible on perimeter, mostly at the prow, but the outline marked by a slight mounding. Date and purpose uncertain.

VS45 (NL646944) Boat-shaped stone setting, 3 × 2.4 m as surviving, but the prow has been robbed out and the whole structure is badly damaged and heavily embedded. Only four stones visible on the perimeter but a slight mounding and differential vegetation marks the outline. Oriented west–east. Date and purpose uncertain.

VS46 (NL645945) Boat-shaped stone setting?, 3 × 2.1 m as preserved, but if it is a boat-shaped setting only the stern survives, marked by six stones. Oriented north north-east–south south-west. Date and purpose uncertain.

VS47 (NL645944) Boat-shaped stone setting, 5 × 2.5 m, oriented east–west, with 12 stones on perimeter, including 6 set upright. A relict boundary bank runs to meet the prow from the north-west. Date and purpose uncertain.

VS48 (NL645943) Boat-shaped stone setting, 4.5m × 2 m, oriented north north-east–south south-west, with eight stones on perimeter. It has been modified to form a small 2 m diameter shelter in the stern and this seems to have a fill of 'cobbles'. Date and purpose uncertain.

VS49 (NL645943) Boat-shaped stone setting?, 6 × 3.5 m, oriented south–north, almost entirely grassed over but with two stones visible at the prow and a third on the east side. However, the outline is clearly marked by vegetation change and a slight mounding. Date and purpose uncertain.

VS50 (NL646945) Boat-shaped stone setting, 5.3 × 2.5 m, oriented north–south, with nine stones on the perimeter and a slight mounding. Date and purpose uncertain.

VS51 (NL646946) Boat-shaped stone setting, 6.7 × 3.2 m, oriented north-east–south-west, with only four perimeter stones visible but its outline marked at the prow, stern, and one long side by slight mounding and vegetation change. The east side appears to have been completely robbed out, almost certainly to build a now relict earth and stone boundary bank which runs past a few metres to the east. Date and purpose uncertain.

VS52 (NL647946) Boat-shaped stone setting, 5.4 × 2.5 m, oriented north north-west–south south-east, with 16 perimeter stones visible. Date and purpose uncertain.

VS53 (NL647946) Boat-shaped stone setting, 5.5 × 2.5 m, oriented north north-west–south south-east, with nine perimeter stones *in situ* and two tumbled/pulled from line. The prow and stern have both been largely robbed out. Date and purpose uncertain.

VS54 (NL647946) Boat-shaped stone setting, 6 × 3 m, oriented north–south with only three perimeter stones visible. Heavily grassed and embedded, but the outline is clearly visible from a slight mounding. Date and purpose uncertain.

VS55 (NL648946) Boat-shaped stone setting, 7 × 2.9 m, oriented north–south, with six large perimeter stones visible and slight mounding. Date and purpose uncertain.

VS56 (NL646946) Boat-shaped stone setting, 9 × 3.1 m, oriented north north-east–south south-west, with 13 perimeter stones visible, including the prow stone. Date and purpose uncertain.

VS57 (NL648945) Low oval cairn, 2.4 × 1.3 m, not well-embedded and probably recent.

VS58 (NL648944) Arc of five stone blocks, a sixth to one side and a seventh in the centre. The centre block and two in the arc are set upright, while the remaining four blocks lie flat. The largest stones are 1.1 m and 1 m long, but the central stone is only 0.3 m high. The impression is of a modified and partly demolished stone ring, with a diam. c. 6 m and two stones removed from the south-east quadrant. The outlying stone, 0.75 m long, may have been removed from the south-west quadrant. Prehistoric stone ring?

VS59 (NL648943) Heavily ruined and embedded remains of oblong building, 6.5 × 4 m, walls 0.75 m wide, with a narrow door (0.75 m) in east-facing wall. Small blackhouse.

VS60 (NL647942) Two much-ruined and modified oblong stone buildings. A 8.7 × 5.1 m, entrance at north-east corner. B 5 × 4.4 m, entrance at south-east corner. House and byre?

VS61 (NL645942) Rough boulder-built rectangular stone structure, 6.8 × 4.7 m, with door in the south-east corner. Byre?

VS62 (NL643943) Stone setting outlining flat platform, 7.7 × 7 m. Possibly a building platform, but no trace of any stone building; more probably a garden plot.

VS63 (NL641940) A substantial earth/sand bank, running north–south across the saddle east of Ben Cuier. It was traced for about 550 m, its southern terminus at the point where it meets a rock formation. The southern section of the bank is 4–5 m wide and still stands 2 m high and runs for about 400 m. There is then a 15 m gap before another bank begins and swings slightly north-west to run for about 150 m downhill towards East Bay. This northern section of bank is quite different in character, being only some 1–1.5 m wide, steep-sided, and punctuated by occasional stone uprights. The bank has clearly been considerably weathered and naturally modified, particularly in its southern section, but its date is uncertain. Although it does not, apparently, reach either the north or south coast of southern Vatersay, it does appear to be a significant boundary between Eorisdale/Am Meall and the rest of the island to the west.

VS64 (NL641945) An impressive monolith, recumbent, 2.15 m long, 1.1 m wide at the base narrowing to 0.8 m below the rounded tip, and about 0.4 m deep in section. The stone lies 4 m east of the bank (VS63) and close by the point where the narrow northern section of bank picks up from the southern section. A connection between bank and stone cannot be demonstrated but not only is the juxtaposition suggestive, but the stone continues the alignment of the broad southern bank at the point where the narrow bank swings away north-westwards. Standing stone/boundary marker? of uncertain age.

VS65 (NL645946) A well-embedded circular stone structure, 2.5 m diam., on a small hillock. The walls are well-preserved, although there are traces of secondary modification. A shelter type C.

Zone M (Muldoanich)

M1 (NL687943) Turf and stone wall, about 40 m long, enclosing a small headland. Presumably a sheep pen.

M2 (NL687940) Thick-walled oblong building, 8.6 × 5.8 m, with door almost central in east wall, and a second door in north-west corner. Internal partition wall. Remains of three small thin-walled buildings, all around 3–4 m square, found close by, one in a stone-outlined enclosure to rear of main building. Blackhouse and outbuildings.

M3 (NL687938) A thick-walled structure, 7 × 4 m, with rounded north end and straight south end. A doorway 0.7 m wide is on the east side and gives into a small oblong room, 3 × 2 m, to the left, and a circular cell about 1.8 m diam. to the right. The wall of the cell is battered inwards and the cell may have had a corbelled roof. Too small to be a normal dwelling house, but too strongly and carefully built to be a casual shelter.

M4 (NL688936) A collapsed circular stone setting about 1.4 m diam. Shelter type A.

M5 (NL689940) A small cairn, 1.4 × 1.2 m, incorporating two large stones and many smaller, situated only 50 m from the highest point on the island.

M6 (NL689940) Much-destroyed and heavily embedded remains of a stone cairn about 2.8 m diam. as surviving. The modern trig. point is built on top of it. Possibly premodern.

M7 (NL689936) Collapsed and dispersed stone structure about 3.5 × 1.9 m. Shelter type C.

3. An Archaeological Survey on the Southern Outer Hebridean Islands of Sandray, Pabbay, Mingulay and Berneray

Patrick Foster and Roman Krivanek
with a contribution by Martin Kuna

Introduction

When Sheffield University first turned its attention to the archaeology of the Western Isles in 1988, the choice of which islands to work on was almost automatically decided by the local sea and air transport system operating between the mainland and the islands. At this time Vatersay had not been linked to Barra by the causeway, although a daily local ferry service put this island within the scope of the project. The archaeological investigation of the other, more remote, uninhabited islands to the south of Vatersay presented logistical problems that removed them from the general sphere of the University's work.

The archaeology of Barra proved to be wonderfully rich, containing many new and interesting aspects that would help rewrite the textbooks. However, the fact that the islands to the south of Barra were archaeologically almost virgin territory, combined with the tantalizing vision, seen daily as we worked on the site at Alt Chrisal, of their outlines stretching to the horizon proved a great and tempting attraction. The first excursions were taken aboard John Allen's motor launch on occasional weekend day trips, weather permitting, to the romantic island of Mingulay. Also, Callum Macneil with his fishing boat kindly provided the means to visit the island of Sandray. These initial all-too-brief glimpses showed that the archaeological potential of the southern islands was considerable and worthy of consideration.

Consequently a single day trip excursion to Sandray to conduct a survey was attempted in 1989. The survey team was landed by fishing boat that would return at the end of the day to collect the party. Immediately the weather became Hebridean, and, without shelter, all that could be done was just to wait miserably for the boat to return. This lesson proved that the only sensible method to undertake such a survey was to camp on the islands for an extended period of time, if only to cope with the vagaries of the weather.

In 1991, at the instigation of, and funded by, Historic Scotland, the University began a project to locate archaeological sites within a strip 50 m wide around the coastlines of as many of the islands as practical and to report on the current and any future possible threat to the sites by erosion. The sites found in the coastal erosion survey are marked with an asterisk in the catalogue below.

While the coastal erosion survey may be considered as a necessary initial step in the management of the island's threatened monuments, the limitation of the survey to erosion within 50 m of coastline may have been, in the light of experience, too limiting. For example, on Pabbay severe wind erosion has stripped much of the soil away down to bedrock well inland from the coast in the region of Allanish and An Cearcall, and on Mingulay many sites on the hill-tops, especially Carnan, are suffering greatly from a combination of wind erosion and peat deflation. In addition, probably the greatest threat to the archaeological monuments of the islands still remains that of burrowing rabbits, which inhabit a wide variety of sandy soil locations that are beyond the 50 m coastal strip. By taking the opportunity to attempt a comprehensive survey of all the monuments on each island, it is hoped that a better perception may be gained of the problems concerning both present and future threats.

In order to extend the survey to incorporate the uninhabited islands to the south of Vatersay, a set of logistical problems had to be overcome. The survey could not take place during the normal period of work in the islands unless a new project director came forward, since major excavations were in progress at Alt Chrisal and survey and excavations elsewhere occupied the remainder of the staff and students. By removing this survey project from the restriction of the university's fieldworking season it gained the advantage of greater flexibility so that work times, in consultation with Scottish Heritage, could be geared to periods that minimized the disturbance to the large bird colonies during the nesting seasons. This applied particularly to the islands of Mingulay and Berneray, since they have SSSI status.

Given the fact that the weather could severely curtail any fieldwork, time spent on an island would be at a premium. The time factor becomes even more acute when distance is added to the equation. To be economically viable, the survey team would have to spend an extended period encamped. The relatively high cost of island survey along with the tight time schedules, usually outside the normal times when the university is in the field, also negates the use of inexperienced randomly selected students who may or may not be capable of this type of field survey if not closely supervised.

Fortunately a set of circumstances evolved that solved many of these problems. In 1990, after a visit to Czechoslovakia, a fieldwork project between Sheffield University and the Institute in Prague had been organized, and this collaboration was expanded to allow Czech participation in the Hebrides SEARCH project. From 1992, starting with the survey of Berneray, the authors, occasionally assisted by members of the Department of Landscape Studies of the Institute of Archaeology in Prague (later expanded to include MA students from several Czech universities), agreed to undertake the archaeological exploration of the southern islands as a separate, but complementary project within the SEARCH project.

The survey has been supplemented by a number of excavations, some of which are reported below (Chapters 6 and 7), in order to provide a better understanding of the chronological range and function of the site types found in the survey and also to confirm site identification. Unfortunately, due to limited time and personnel numbers, this has been a limited exercise that has not addressed the problem satisfactorily and which, along with other archaeological considerations concerning the future of the uninhabited islands, should be included in any long-term planning.

Geology and Vegetation

The Hebridean island chain is basically formed from intensively metamorphosed Precambrian grey gneiss (Lewisian Gneiss) moulded by tectonic movements and subsequent episodes of erosion. Intrusive igneous activity in the Tertiary created a system of basaltic dykes through the country rock. The basalt, usually being more susceptible to erosion than the surrounding country rock, is being degraded and washed out of the dyke channels at the surface leaving sheer-sided defiles across the landscape. At the coastal margins dyke erosion is accelerated by the sea often faster than that of the stony postglacial clays that overlie the basalt, leaving a dangerously undercut deposit liable to collapse at any moment. These formations are often deeply incised into the coastline and can often provide sheltered landing places. In contrast the lines of rock faulting are often characterized by gullies and defiles of a more gentle profile. There are no formations of younger cover rocks, but glacially derived material was deposited over some areas, although the majority of this deposit was immediately subject to very active postglacial erosion, and the surviving residue can only

now be found in a variety of scattered locations. The effects of glacial scouring and polishing are readily apparent in the many exposed rock surfaces and play a major role in the appearance of the islands today.

Tectonic processes are responsible for much of the landscape modelling of the southern islands, but the level of their influence and intensity is different for each island. On Sandray the dyke systems and fault lines are generally orientated from north north-west to south south-east. Berneray and Mingulay share a number of dykes on a north to south alignment, but both islands have a small number of fault lines that are more randomly orientated. In comparison to the other islands Pabbay shows probably the most intensive and complicated system of fault lines that suggest a long unsettled geological history. The widest and deepest fault lines and dykes are orientated generally in west north-west–east south-east and north north-west to south south-east directions, but another set vary between east–west and north–south, a situation that has given Pabbay perhaps the most rugged landscape of all.

To soften the effects of these geologically remote events, the formation of sandy beaches have resulted in some aeolian dune formations and a tendency for wind-driven sand to plaster itself, quite thickly in places, over some of the hillsides. This has not only smoothed out the land surface profile, but enriched the generally acidic soils, encouraging a machair-type environment that greatly widens the plant diversity of the islands, while the deeper deposits of sand in the dune formations are dominated by marram grass.

In general the soils are characterized by very poor acid peaty podsols, gleys and heavily mineralized silty lithosols that support a range of moor and peat bog plant varieties. Although large areas of the landscape are of a boggy nature, there are no large floating bogs, but small localized ones can be found in some of the dyke bottoms. On the summits of the hills exposed areas of flat bedrock and hollows formed by peat deflation hold permanent ponds of rain water that support a micro environment with a limited range of fresh water plant varieties. In sheltered spots, prevalently on the more eastern aspects, small localized patches of scrub woodland survive, notably in the central glen on Pabbay and the northern glen of Alt á Mhuuilinn on Sandray.

The nature of the underlying geology controls the types of soil formation found on the islands and consequently the kind of vegetational cover that can be expected. This in turn plays a major part in determining the nature and extent of human settlement and land use that consequently has a great effect upon the type and distribution of the archaeological sites and monuments. This aspect will be addressed in volume 6 where field systems and agricultural regimes will also be discussed.

Methodology for the Southern Islands Survey

The generally rugged topography of the islands means that almost every square metre has to be visited. Many small shelters are tucked away in sheltered situations that may be hidden from all but the most intensive searcher. Even in areas of more level or gently sloped landscape, sites may be so well-embedded in rank vegetation or peat deposits as to be unobservable from a distance. As a positive counterbalance to such disadvantages, the islands are all relatively small, which allows a small number of experienced robust workers to undertake an intensive landscape survey and complete it within an acceptable time span. Fortunately each member involved in this survey was experienced in field survey methods and practice. This allowed the division of tasks to be maximized and the work was usually carried out on an individual basis. Roman Krivenek and John Pouncett usually undertook the time-consuming task of producing the measured drawings of selected monuments to enhance and supplement the general archive of field sketches.

The method of field survey was simply that each surveyor would set off from the camp site to their designated survey areas, surveying along a route that would change by a few metres each day, thereby eventually covering the whole island. Both the route and final survey area was often best covered by an irregular search pattern that matched the often rugged terrain. In such a landscape the traditional use of straight line transects and traverses, especially on some of the steep slopes encountered, is totally impractical.

Each monument was recorded with a measured field sketch on preprinted SEARCH project survey cards or in small notebooks as a minimum standard, along with a topographical description and a brief note outlining any outstanding features of construction, condition, local vegetation and location. The sites were fixed in the landscape by being immediately plotted on enlarged copies of 1:10,000 base maps on loan from the RCAHMS in Edinburgh. As many monuments as possible were recorded to scale as stone-by-stone measured drawings. Almost every site was photographed in at least one 35 mm format. Each site was given a unique site code consisting of two letters to identify the island, SY Sandray, PY Pabbay, MY Mingulay, BY Berneray (Barra Head), followed by an individual site number beginning from 1 (one) on each island.

Enclosure and field walls were also recorded and, although they are not as a rule listed in the general catalogue, they are illustrated on the island maps in the archive. In recording the enclosures and field walls no attempt has been made to use any peculiarities of constructional style or method as a basis for some chronological scheme. Although this form of analysis has been successful in other parts of the British highland zone, notably Derbyshire (Hodges 1991), experience has shown that this is not so easily mastered in the Hebridean context. Many of the Hebridean field walls travel for long distances, crossing over a variety of topographical and natural features. In such walls the manner of construction is often highly variable, reflecting the nature of the locality that is being traversed. If the area is wet grassland with little or no free surface stone, then the wall may be constructed entirely of turf that changes to a single stone monolithic wall and again into a wall of several stone courses as field stone building material becomes more readily available. Often stretches of convenient geological features, such as the sheer rocky sides of a dyke, are used as natural barriers linked by short stretches of walling. Such a variety of building styles within the length of a single wall line cannot be easily dated on visual constructional criteria alone.

The dating of monuments was generally not attempted unless there was some firm reason to believe that a date/period could be assigned. Note was taken of the topographical position, condition, orientation, if any, structural features and if significant, local vegetation.

During the survey, sites that were considered under threat for whatever reason were identified as being candidates for future excavation or refined recording. Sites were also identified where it was considered that excavation could provide an advance in knowledge concerning the date, function and form of the type. The maintained priority of this survey project was to produce a total archaeological landscape for each island and any excavations that supplemented and enhanced its results were a secondary consideration.

The survey undertaken here is as detailed and accurate as time and circumstances allow, but there is much still to be accomplished. On each island there are inevitably still some sites to be found that were missed and each monument ultimately deserves an accurate fully measured drawing.

The location of each monument, enclosure wall, stream and in some instances details of watershed, was ultimately marked on a set of ordnance survey maps provided by the RCAHMS and comprise a part of the archive, along with original field notebooks, drawings, photographs and other material, to be deposited with the Commission in Edinburgh. Although great care was taken to locate and fix each monument to its exact position on the ordnance survey map, a number of sites were difficult to place with absolute accuracy, often due either to the lack of local reference features or to the difficulty often encountered in relating topographical complexities between map and reality. Many monuments would benefit from being fixed in the landscape by satellite location methods (GPS).

Site Categorization

A problem continually encountered throughout the entire lifetime of the SEARCH project has been the difficulty in deciding the function, chronology and at times even the typology of the sites located in the various landscape survey programmes. During the early years of the project it had appeared all to easy to stride across the landscape identifying the monuments on a typological/functional basis and allotting them instant chronological labels. This early overconfidence was soon sensibly subdued in the light of experience gained mainly through the excavation of a variety of different sites. The excavations at Alt Chrisal (Foster 1995) showed that 'roundhouses' (T18 and T19), considered in the initial field survey to be Iron Age, were in fact datable to the Neolithic/Early Bronze Age. To compound the problem it was found that possible 'roundhouses' of a similar diameter found in the Borve valley appeared, on the basis of coarse handmade pottery found in them, to be mediaeval.

Excavation has also proved the fallibility of typological identification through visual surface examination. A presumed hut circle (B60) of 3 m diameter located in the Borve valley survey in 1988 was excavated in 1990 and shown to be D-shaped in plan once displaced stonework had been removed.

In general most misidentification results from two factors neither of which can be controlled. The first is the reuse of a site at a later period. Reuse of a site often entails the reorganization of much of the visible stonework, which then masks the nature of the original structure. The later structure then collapses, causing further masking. The potential wheelhouse (MY344) at Skipisdale, Mingulay, is an example of this. The identification of the original form was only possible after the clearance of some of the tumbled stonework originating from a large shelter constructed out of the upper stonework of the Iron Age structure.

Peat growth and rank vegetation may also mask the true nature of a site. Occasionally some resolution may be gained by probing for hidden stonework, but unless the monument is of some simple structural form this does not always produce an improvement.

Such problems have led to considerable discussion on how to present the survey results. Rather than allocate a misleading date or misinterpreted function it was decided to rely on a simple description based upon a limited range of site types and that any inferred comments should be restricted to subnotes on the survey cards. This may appear to be excessively cautious, but we believe that this will allow a clearer assessment of the sites unclouded by misguided preconceptions and interpretations.

The main site categories are as follows.

Blackhouses

From the 18th to the early/mid 19th century the blackhouse had an open fireplace, usually consisting of a pad of beach cobbles set into the floor. In terms of construction the superstructure of both the improved and unimproved blackhouses is the same, being of thick earth-filled, battered drystone walls, rectangular in plan with rounded corners and all roofed with turf or reed thatch and seaweed. The earlier blackhouse is likely to incorporate internal stalling for animals, a tradition that slowly declined towards the end of the 19th century. Traditionally, in the spring the byre end wall of the house would be dismantled and the manure removed, along with the soot-impregnated thatch of the blackhouse, and spread on the fields.

Improved blackhouses

Dating to the later part of the 19th century and built in the traditional manner, but with fireplaces and chimney stacks incorporated as an integral part of the end gable walls. Window places to hold framed glazing are now commonly inserted on either side of the entrance. The building material relies upon field stone and the robbed gleanings from other structures in the locality, but some quarried and dressed stonework may be used. Farm animals were now commonly kept in separate external byres, either built butted to one end of the house or at just a short distance to one side

Houses

modern houses constructed with local quarried stone set with mortar and roofed with slate or corrugated roofing sheets. Usually datable to the last decades of the 19th century. Rectangular in plan with thin walls and sharp angled corners formed by alternating quoin stones. This simple chronological sequence is naturally blurred considerably in reality since many of the earlier type of blackhouse were occupied, usually by a conservative older generation, as late as the early 20th century.

The structural definitions that are described below for roundhouses, wheelhouses and Atlantic roundhouses have been deliberately oversimplified to aid the categorization of sites and monuments often imperfectly seen in the field. A fuller discussion of the variability and distinguishing features of this type of monument is left to the chapters below concerning the detailed excavation of their kind.

Earth-houses

Only one monument that could be called an earthhouse has been located on the southern islands and that was identified only after excavation. This subterranean building (PY56) was found as a mass of stones, many slabs that measured over 1 m in length, apparently lying on the surface of the sand dunes of Pabbay. The area contains many other clusters of stone, which may be further examples of this type of monument (PY61 and 62, for example). Excavation revealed a well-preserved, drystone-built subterranean house whose floor level was at a depth of over a metre in places. No other comparable set of sites has been found on the other islands in the survey, but sites found on Fuday as part of the Barra survey may be similar (above p. 10).

Roundhouses

Circular constructions with walls of earth faced with stone or in some cases mainly just turf constructions with some stone revetting whose internal diameter exceeds two metres and with no internal divisions. This form of dwelling appears to be common for all the periods prior to the Norse occupation of the islands, although during the Iron Age this simple type is developed into distinctive forms of much greater size and elaboration. Few Iron Age examples have been proven for this simple form (but see p. 216) but the excavations at Alt Chrisal, Barra have revealed some examples (T18/19) to be Late Neolithic/Early Bronze Age in date. To eliminate confusion all roundhouses have been grouped into the pre-Iron Age period unless it can be proven that they are of another period.

Wheelhouses

An Iron Age development from the simple roundhouse distinguished notably by the construction of internal radial subdivisions. A detailed description of the constructional details may be gained from the excavation report on the wheelhouse T17 at Allt Chrisal (Chapter 4).

Atlantic roundhouses (duns and brochs)

A further Middle Iron Age elaboration on the roundhouse theme, but on a grand scale. Usually described as a defensive structure built as an expression of power and status. A broch is a tower-like construction of thick drystone galleried walls that contain a variety of cells, staircases and chambers. They are usually circular in plan, whereas duns are less regular in plan and do not generally contain such elaborate architectural features as the broch. However, there are many examples of hybrid structures linking the two types, the so-called galleried duns of Berneray and Sandray, for example, which give rise to much debate on the fine points of both similarities and differences of these building forms (Lethbridge 1952; Young 1961; MacKie 1965; Armit 1988a, 1990). Armit suggests a new classification of Atlantic roundhouse that incorporates all the architectural varieties

that may be encountered in these large monumental sites (Armit 1991, 1992) and it is this definition that will be followed here.

Forts/promontory enclosures

These are generally accepted as being Iron Age in date and to be of a defensive nature. Whether they were meant for permanent or semipermanent occupation or were just for use as an occasional refuge is rarely clear. They usually consist of a drystone wall enclosing some naturally strong position such as rocky hilltops or coastal promontories and are often devoid of related internal structures.

Shielings huts

These are dwellings that are more than just an overnight shelter and less than a permanently occupied house. They are only occupied seasonally and indicate the practice of transhumance, but they could also be for a variety of seasonal or occasional activities. They vary considerably in size, shape and complexity, but since they are occupied for many weeks they are usually constructed to encompass more than just a few square metres whatever their shape. Many are constructed with only a single room, but a subdivision or smaller attached annexe for storage is not uncommon. Their period of use is difficult to assess, and they represent a wide and varied date range that only terminates at some time in the twentieth century.

In terms of construction morphology and technique the dividing line between an individual shieling and a shelter may not exist. In this survey we have generally taken the position that a shelter is less complex and robust than a shieling, although a shieling may consist of a collection of basic shelters usually associated with other structures such as enclosures, stock pens, store rooms and other ancillary constructions.

Shelters

The shelter is one of the commonest monuments found throughout the islands and is primarily defined by the area of the internal floor space being more than one and less than four square metres. There are problems in distinguishing large shelters from shielings or small roundhouses. This is an important area of definition since it may also have chronological implications.

The separation of shelters from small cairn structures is just as problematic. Some shelters are no more than a few large stones pushed together covered with a piece of tarpaulin. A shelter intended for a limited period of time and hurriedly constructed could conceivably result in a small stone ring easily classed as a cairn in the survey. Conversely, a cairn could itself be converted into a small shelter becoming both types of monument at the same time. Most shelters, especially the smaller variety, do not appear to have regular entrances and their function as a personal over night or bad weather shelter is very much doubted. A more likely function for many of the shelters found is that of storage after the fashion of the St Kilda cleit (Harman 1997), but on a much smaller and less elaborate scale.

Peat dryers

This category of monument is rare on the southern islands except for Mingulay where it exists in great numbers and was in use in the early modern/modern period. In both structural architecture and function they have no relationship to the cleitean of St Kilda, although in ground plan alone their size and shape may be comparable (Harman 1997). Comparable monuments may be found in the Shetland islands of Foula (Baldwin 1996) and Out Skerries (Dey 1991) and on Faroe Isle (personal communication Noel Fojut).

The Mingulay examples appear in two variations of basic structural design. They are usually sited on slightly raised, dryer ground that may be prepared beforehand. The peat is then stacked and enclosed with a loose assemblage of stonework, sometimes in laid courses and sometimes as single upright stones leaning on to the sides of the stack. Judging by the amount of stone left at these sites, the actual 'walling' was not of great proportions. Presumably, some stone may have been laid on top of the stack. In this variation the stonework encompasses the stack completely. Overall dimensions vary from three to five or more metres long and a metre plus wide while shape varies from oval to subrectangular. The second variation is an open ended subrectangular shape with larger stones set as a 'facade' at the closed end and diminishing in size along the sides towards the open end. They are set longitudinally against a slight slope with the open end pointing up-slope. The interior usually appears as a low flat mound of peat soil that merges into the hillside at the open end. This variety is categorized as a peat dryer mainly due to its similarity of size, shape and location, and since no examples appear to have any significant structure that could suggest that they might be some form of burial chamber.

Cairns and mounds

A common and frequent monument on all of the islands surveyed that as a general body are placed in the pre-Iron Age period, apart from those early modern/modern examples, which are obviously stone clearance cairns within field systems, marker cairns and those erected by tourists. Several mounds of substantial size were found, but few of the cairns showed any distinction in size or structure, and none were as well-preserved and showed such architectural detail as the kerbed cairns on Fuday and Vatersay.

Chamber tombs

This monument type is characterized by the use of large monolithic slabs or boulders to form a burial chamber that is then covered by a mound of earth or stones. Without exception all of the monuments recorded in the survey have been degraded to a large extent and in many cases their identification without excavation must be far from certain.

Burial grounds

Each of the islands had a burial ground, and there was the historical suggestion that they were shared by associated chapels. However, apart from Mingulay, none was in evidence during the time of the survey, and the burial ground on Sandray had disappeared altogether, presumably under the shifting sand dunes. The burial grounds of Berneray, Pabbay and Mingulay were all mounded or incorporated mounds with a suggestion of stone cobble capping that may indicate an early Christian origin. Both Berneray and Pabbay have engraved stone cross grave markers in place, and in addition Pabbay has a Pictish symbol stone lying at the base of the cemetery mound. These burial grounds most likely cover a period of use spanning the early mediaeval to modern periods. On Berneray a small modern cemetery was made exclusively for the lighthouse keepers and their families, and on Mingulay a fine chapel house was built at the end of the 19th century.

Stone circles

There are several stone circles or rings, but, although this class of monument is allocated to the pre-Iron Age period, none of them are of such distinctive proportions that they could not be for some other purpose and belong in some other period.

Standing stones

The same comments as those made for stone circles apply exactly for standing stones.

The Landscape Periods

Lesser categories include a wide range of site types most of which are early modern/modern in date, such as roads, bridges, piers, winches, stone quarries, sheep dips, nausts, and so on. There are also a number of other, possibly prehistoric, sites that are not well-defined and are listed under miscellaneous. Cup marks are a common sight around the rocky coastlines, and since they are most likely to have been formed for grinding fish bait rather than as some prehistoric art form, they have not been included in the survey in detail.

Initially there had been some hope of reconstructing relatively accurate period landscapes on the basis of the survey results, but the difficulty in determining even the date, for the majority of the sites discovered, without the benefit of excavation, was rapidly acknowledged. Some elements can readily be seen to be of greater antiquity than others. On every island earlier field walls, for example, could be identified and separated from boundaries that were in more recent use, but categorically to determine their actual period of use is virtually impossible on the basis of visual examination alone. Great care must therefore be exercised in presenting any analysis of the survey results and in the reconstruction of the various landscapes represented by them. To be disabled completely by these restrictions would result in a very thin and uninformative report, and so, with not a little trepidation, an attempt will be made to suggest, for each island, a set of period landscapes.

Early modern and modern

This is taken as the 18th century to the present day. On Berneray there is an separate distinguishable landscape that concerns the Barra Head lighthouse. In this period can be found one of the most frequent of site types, the shelter, but unexpectedly no corn dryers were identified, although two mills were located.

Mediaeval and post-mediaeval

From the time of the Norse conversion to Christianity in the 10th/11th centuries AD to the late 17th century there are very few visible monuments, apart from the burial grounds, that can be attributed with certainty to any period within this time span. For almost a millennia there is a true archaeological dark age throughout the southern islands. Yet this covers probably the most important formative years of the islands between the 12th and 14th centuries, when they were part of the independent Kingdom of the Isles, a relic of which may be Kisimul Castle in Castlebay, Barra (McDonald 1997).

Early mediaeval or Norse

Viking raids began in the area at the later part of the 8th century, but actual settlement may not have occurred until much later, possibly in the middle of the 9th century with the conquest of the Hebrides by Ketil (Crawford 1987). Unfortunately, the Norse period is almost as blank as the later mediaeval periods except for a wealth of place names, some few finds of objects and possibly the enigmatic boat-shaped stone settings. All of the southern islands appear to contain a number of these monuments, and it is a general assumption that they belong to the Norse period. However, very few examples have been archaeologically tested, and those without helpful results. Recent excavations by Parker Pearson and Sharples on South Uist, though, suggest that Norse period settlements may be buried within the machair.

Iron Age

A period that encompasses a number of distinctive and easily recognizable monuments that include the Atlantic roundhouses (duns and brochs) and wheelhouses. There may be many smaller roundhouses that also belong in this period, but without excavation (such as that of SY14 on Sandray and MY348 on Mingulay, for example) or material ejected from rabbit burrows they must remain in the general prehistoric category. In this survey we have taken the Iron Age to include all of the Pictish period.

Pre-Iron Age

As in the Iron Age period the monuments in this period are usually degraded by stone robbing or erosion. Burial monuments are usually the most recognizable structures of this period, which covers both the Neolithic and the Bronze Age. Although there are no chamber tombs that can compare with the architectural grandeur or volume of stonework of Dun Bharpa on Barra, the southern islands do contain a number of monuments that may be the degraded remnants of chamber tombs of a lesser scale. There are also numerous cairns, some of which must certainly be funerary monuments. Excavations on Barra at Alt Chrisal (Foster 1995) clearly show that stone-built roundhouses may frequently be allocated to this date range. Therefore, in this survey all the well-embedded examples are grouped into this period. Here too are many of the miscellaneous sites from stone settings to standing stones and circles.

Mesolithic

The Mesolithic period does not make an appearance in the work of this survey due entirely to the total lack of evidence for its existence. The evidence for its impact on the landscape of the Western Isles has been deduced from the analysis of carbonized plant remains that indicate land clearance by fire in the late Mesolithic period (Edwards 1996). Mesolithic activities in the Inner Hebrides are well-documented (Mercer 1972; Wickham-Jones 1990, for example), but the raised beaches where these sites are often located do not form part of the Outer Hebridean landscape. While the west coast and inner islands were elevated, the western islands were depressed at the end of the last glaciation and low-lying coastal regions were flooded. In this way the Outer Hebrides, once a long single island with a backbone of volcanic mountains that stretched for over a hundred miles, became an island chain with its former low-lying coastal plains sunk beneath the waves. The Mesolithic population, from evidence found on the Inner Hebrides, appear to have spent a large part of their annual cycle exploiting the reserves of shell-fish, fish and birds found around the littoral zone. These areas are now up to three kilometres out to sea and therefore well out of reach for this survey.

Conclusion

Although the time taken to reach this point in the archaeological exploration and recording of the southern islands can be measured in years, the actual real time involved is measurable in weeks. Berneray received just over one week of survey time supplemented by a couple of day trip visits. Mingulay on the other hand received over a month of survey and excavation. Much has been achieved in this time, but the room for refinement, new discoveries and exploration is still considerable. This survey should only be

considered as representing the first few steps in a much longer journey.

Some Preliminary Results and Comments on the Digitization and Analysis of the Survey Data

Martin Kuna

Introduction

All sites were located on 1:10,000 Ordnance Survey maps on loan from the Royal Commission on

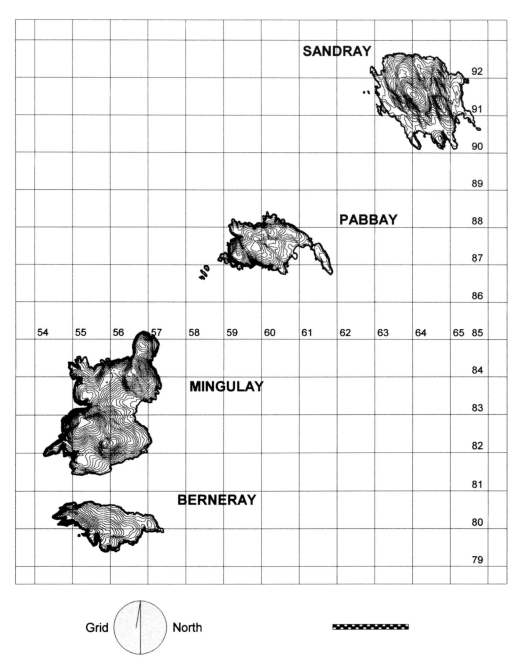

Figure 3.1 A relief map of the four southern islands with newly generated contours.

the Ancient and Historical Monuments of Scotland during work in the field. Their position was subsequently transformed into pairs of co-ordinates of the National Grid (NGR) and stored in computer files together with other information. The coordinates were read with an accuracy of 10 m—any attempt at greater accuracy would obviously be unsuccessful. The database of sites was transformed into digital maps using GIS software (Idrisi for Windows in this case).

To enhance computer visualization and analysis of site distribution, the relief of the islands was also transformed into a series of digital maps. Contour lines of the original maps were digitized and subsequently changed into digital elevation models (DEM) of the individual islands under study. Since the original contour lines are less suitable to be used as illustrations (for example, no lines are possible in the space between the top and bottoms of high cliffs because printed maps use other ways to display steep slopes) new vectors were generated to create a complete and continuous series of contour lines for the whole perimeter of the islands. The newly generated contour lines correspond to 10 m intervals of altitude and they are used in the following illustrations (Fig. 3.1). Considering the character of the maps, we must be aware of the fact that the original base maps, serving as the input information, are themselves quite generalized. For example, no dykes are displayed on the available maps, although we know from autopsy that dykes are important features in the real landscape, creating communication barriers and routes, points of shelter, controllers of hydrological patterns, etc. That is why digital landscapes in the present form should not be overestimated but used for appropriate analytical goals only.

Site frequencies

Table 3.1 shows the list of site types recognized during the survey and their frequencies on individual islands as well as in total. The sum of sites should be considered without the number of 'complexes' (type no. 31) since this category represents site clusters, the components of which were also listed in the database individually. The information on the frequency of individual type sites is illustrative, but should not be credited for any consideration in the problems encountered in defining site typology and classification. The same must be said about differences between individual islands falling mostly within the range of random variation. There must be some exceptions like 'mounds' (type no. 7) and 'peat dryers' (type no. 22) that appear almost exclusively on Mingulay, but not on other islands. This situation cannot be random, but has to be explained in environmental, historic or methodological terms.

Table 3.1 Site types and their frequencies on southern Outer Hebridean Islands.

Type	Berneray	Mingulay	Pabbay	Sandray	Total	Symbol
PREHISTORIC						
Roundhouse	3	1	0	4	*8*	small black square
Earthhouse	0	0	3	0	*3*	small black square
Platform	3	2	1	3	*9*	small grey square
Setting	1	2	7	3	*15*	small grey square
Cairn	10	81	56	45	*192*	small open circle
Chambered tomb	8	4	0	2	*14*	large black circle
Mound	0	31	0	0	*31*	small black circle
Standing stone	3	1	0	3	*7*	small open square
Stone circle	0	1	0	0	*1*	large open square
Atlantic roundhouse/Fort	2	1	1	1	*5*	large black square
Settlement	0	4	0	1	*5*	small black square
Total	*30*	*133*	*68*	*62*	*293*	
MEDIAEVAL AND MODERN						
Boat shaped stone setting	11	5	3	2	*21*	large open square
Burial ground	2	1	1	1	*5*	large black circle
Blackhouse	13	13	5	14	*45*	large black square
House	4	3	1	0	*8*	large grey square
Shelter	25	111	45	74	*255*	small open circle
Shieling	1	23	7	12	*43*	large open circle
Barn	8	3	5	1	*17*	small grey circle
Peat dryer	0	120	1	0	*121*	small black circle
Total	*64*	*279*	*68*	*104*	*515*	

Site distribution: some preliminary ideas (Table 3.1)

Prehistoric landscape

1. Domestic features (roundhouses, earth-houses, platforms and settings) seem to be located mainly with regard to easy access to the sea. Typically, prehistoric houses are located around open bays (all islands). In areas where the slope is most moderate the residential sites might appear even at greater distance from the shoreline (Mingulay Bay). This can be seen also in the histogram of altitudes (Fig. 3.2), showing a clear peak about 20 m, but gradually spreading as high as 140 m above sea level. There are several residential sites on Berneray appearing on the southern side of the island where the coast is higher, but even here the coast with the highest cliffs is avoided. We must be aware of the fact, however, that the set of known sites is very incomplete and many residential features may be buried below later occupation remains or destroyed if subsequent settlements were built in the same place. Strong spatial continuity is a striking aspect of most domestic sites on the islands. Of course, gradual building of higher living platforms and their occupation in many subsequent phases can be understood in both adaptive and social terms. From this point of view we could explain even the fact that one of the most attractive areas on the islands, the lower part of Mingulay Bay, seems to be rather empty on the map of the prehistoric occupation. It is highly probable that a large part of the expected mediaeval sites have also been either buried or destroyed here by early modern and later activities that naturally concentrate in this area.

2. Three types of sites may indicate funerary activities. Chambered tombs are most numerous on Berneray, with nine; a further three occur on Mingulay and two on Sandray. They mostly appear in the same area as domestic sites and a general correlation between these two types of sites may be predicted.

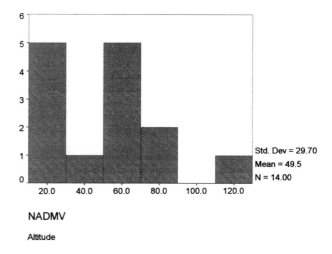

Figure 3.3 A histogram of the altitude of Megalithic tombs.

The same can be seen from Fig. 3.3, which shows similar altitudes for chamber tombs as for the domestic sites, with peaks at 20 m and 60 m above sea level. In contrast to this, mounds (typical only for Mingulay) and cairns (Fig. 3.4) are distributed more widely than domestic sites (Berneray?, Pabbay and Sandray), and on one island (Mingulay) they even display a complementary distribution. On Mingulay this is accentuated even more where the distribution of cairns shows a peak in altitudes above 100 m and the average altitude of cairns is 131 m This pattern, however, may again be partly caused by secondary factors, namely by the later recycling of stones from cairns in the settlement or field enclosure areas as building materials.

3. There are several marked clusters of mounds and cairns on Mingulay, prevailingly on the tops of the hills and close to sheer cliffs. It is tempting to think of these as prehistoric 'cemeteries' separated from residential areas. Without excavation, however, this suggestion cannot be clearly verified, mainly because

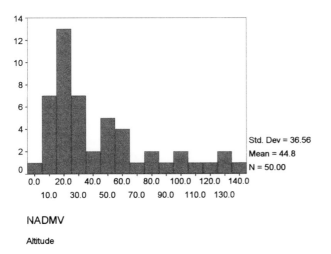

Figure 3.2 A histogram of the altitudes of 'prehistoric' sites.

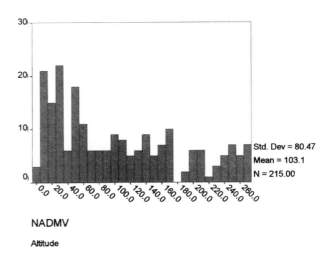

Figure 3.4 A histogram of the altitude of cairns and mounds.

both 'mounds' and 'cairns' are ambiguous site categories and the distribution of chambered tombs (which as a category are clearer) seems to be different. This is not surprising since they represent different funerary traditions (Bruck 1995), the chamber tombs being Neolithic and the cairns and mounds usually accepted as being Bronze Age in date.

4. There are seven sites described as 'stone circles'. Six of them, three on Berneray and three on Mingulay, are located along the southern coasts of the two islands and seem quite detached from the areas containing domestic sites. If stone circles are seen as ritual places this observation could make sense.

5. Standing stones seem to mark peninsulas (three times on Sandray and once on Berneray), but they may actually be marking the settlement bay areas that the peninsulas often enclose.

Iron Age landscape
There are few sites that can be specifically classified as Iron Age. The five known 'Atlantic roundhouses' and 'forts' are, however, very specific in their landscape setting. Sites of this type appear exclusively in dominant locations that were generally avoided or neglected in other periods. On Berneray there is one Atlantic roundhouse (BY17) and one Fort (BY16) close to the edges of cliffs on the western coast, fully exposed to the westerly gales. On Mingulay a Fort (MY376) occupies a large promontory on the west coast that is surrounded by the sea and high sheer cliffs. Pabbay has a single Atlantic roundhouse (PY10) built on a small low rocky peninsula on the north coast, while on Sandray there is one Atlantic roundhouse (SY70) perched on a high inland promontory, again exposed to the westerly gales. Locations of this sort can indicate that the Iron Age settlement pattern owes something to other factors than the purely practical. It seems that either strategic or symbolic reasons must have driven the construction of these sites in such locations. Other types of domestic sites belonging to the Iron Age are situated in less prominent places, often coinciding, as on Mingulay (MY384) and Sandray (SY14), with the main domestic settlement areas. Wheelhouses fall into this category, and, although their classification is more complex than generally thought (see Chapter 4), they can often be tentatively recognized in the field by their large diameter, circular stone ring-walls and the possibility of internal divisions, usually represented by a mass of displaced stonework within the ring-wall. On Sandray several of these structures (SY41 and 73) can be found in low-lying sheltered places close to fresh water, and they appear to mirror the generally dispersed modern settlement pattern. Mingulay is an exceptional island during the Iron Age period in that it has no apparent Atlantic roundhouse, Dun Mingulay being merely a wall across the neck of a promontory, but there are three possible wheelhouses (MY344, 345

and 346), all in close proximity to each other in the valley of Skipisdale. This site location is against the usual trend in that the wheelhouses are located in a valley without modern permanent settlement.

Norse and mediaeval landscape
Few sites belonging unambiguously to these periods were identified during the survey. It is an important fact that each of the islands had one (central) burial ground or cemetery in the modern era; the origins of these burial places in the early mediaeval period is probable, but difficult to prove directly in all cases. Unfortunately, the number of these monuments is relatively low, their date is mostly uncertain and even their landscape setting does not differ substantially from other types of monument. There is, however, a considerable body of evidence to show that many prehistoric sites were reused or continued to be used into the historic period, but this will be discussed more fully in SEARCH volume 6.

Early modern and modern
1. Domestic activities seem to follow the pattern set in prehistory of using the most suitable and preferred areas for occupation. There are settlement concentrations on the northern coastal lowlands of Berneray, in the broad eastern coastal valley of Mingulay Bay and in a similar, but smaller, eastern coastal valley on Pabbay. Only Sandray shows a slightly different pattern of scattered settlements around the island. The natural environment, in the form mainly of geologically controlled relief in relation to prevailing winds, plays the major role in determining this pattern of preferred settlement.

2. Around the residential clusters 'shelters' mostly appear in wide scatters without any clear preference in landscape setting. 'Shielings' as more elaborate shelters generally show a similar type of distribution, but in some cases it seems that these two types of sites may be spatially exclusive to some extent. On Mingulay, for example, shielings appear on the south-eastern slopes of the island, whereas shelters are spread predominantly on the hill-tops and in the northern part of the island. Shielings accompany residential activities more closely in this case, whereas the distribution of shelters is rather complementary to them. On Sandray we can see a similar type of distribution with shielings occurring in the vicinity of residential sites and shelters more widely scattered over the island. On Pabbay the situation may be different, but even here shelters seem to be, in contrast to shielings, more widely spread over the island and reach even higher locations. If shielings and shelters are the remains of a similar set of past activities, we would expect perhaps that the more elaborate sites, the shielings, would be predominantly situated at larger distances from residential sites if they were used as temporary dwellings within a transhumance type of

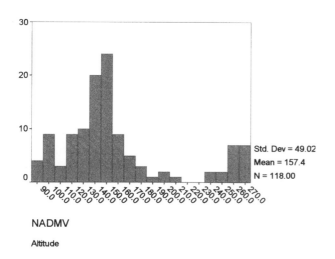

Figure 3.5 A histogram of the altitude of peat dryers.

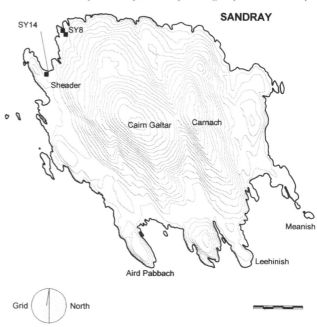

Figure 3.6 Sandray, showing topography, place-names, and excavation sites.

economy. The distribution shows, however, something different: some spatial correlation of the more elaborated structures with residential areas. This may perhaps be taken into account in any reconsideration of their original purpose.

3. Peat dryers are typical not only for their specific shape and construction, but also for a particular setting in the landscape. Their occurrence appears to be limited to the island of Mingulay, where they occupy the upper hill slopes and tops, and the high ridges between them (this clear preference is visible on Fig. 3.5). Their occurrence coincides with shelters, but is more or less exclusive with shielings. Considering their function a correlation of peat dryers with a particular type of environment is certain and is a subject that will be expanded upon in SEARCH volume 6.

Sandray Survey, 1990–1995

Introduction (Fig. 3.6)

Sandray is a rounded square shape (2.5 × 2.7 km) with many headlands jutting out to sea on the southern side. The island is greatly influenced by the underlying geology, which has been deformed by a period of tectonic activity creating a series of fault lines and intrusive dykes orientated in a north-east to south-east direction. This influence, especially on the east side, shaped the flattened sides of the island and its drawn-out peninsulas peculiar to that orientation. A projecting headland to the north-east creates a breakwater that has led to the formation of a long sandy beach down the flattened east coast from which subsequent dune formations have developed inland. Other small sandy beaches have formed in bays around the island's coastline, which has no dominant rocky cliffs that characterize many of the other islands. As a consequence Sandray is not noted for its bird colonies. The high ground is concentrated in the single great

207 m high hill of Cairn Galtar, which forms the central mass of the island. However, the faulting and intrusive dykes combined with uneven erosion has combined to divide off a part of Cairn Galtar to create a separate hill, Carnach, 180 m high, and thus one of the unusual features of Sandray, a rocky cliff facing inland.

The island is fortunate that other less dramatic and slower processes, resulting from glacial erosion, produced two large hollows scoured out of the surface during the last Ice Age. This gave Sandray the only fresh-water lochs in the southern islands, Loch na Cuilce, and a probable loch further to the east that became silted up from material washed down from the inland hill slopes. Today this is an extensive area of reed bed, which became an important source of thatching materials for both Sandray and the surrounding islands. On the east and west sides of the island, set back from the coastline, are the remnants of two long, glacially formed valleys, which are potentially the best agricultural lands on the island, but the east valley has become choked with wind-blown shell sand and dune formations.

These geological and natural processes have given Sandray a slight advantage in topographical variety and natural habitats over the other islands, but with around 80% of the island composed of rocky terraces and high plateaux and around 10% of sand and sand dunes the residue of decent agricultural land, even rough pasture of the higher ground, is limited. The coastline is less dramatic and easily approachable from many directions, being only 50% low rocky cliffs and more than 30% sloping rocky shelves. The coastal dykes give sheltered access, especially in the south, while the beaches with handy rocky stepped platforms at their sides give additional landing places to the north, east and south. There is even a cobbled storm beach on the west coast south of Sheader that can be used.

The bulk of the island is very rugged with many sheltered areas that have filled with bracken, heather and patches of scrub woodland. The spread of rank vegetation combined with the difficult uneven rocky terrain found in most of the rest of the island makes archaeological prospection very uncertain, and it is likely that a number of new sites could be discovered if further intensive research was undertaken in the future.

Human activity and habitation on Sandray is visibly shown by the 150 sites located in this survey. The chronological range of these sites is, as is normal for these islands, patchy, with most of the evidence leaning towards the early modern/modern and Iron Age periods. There is a disappointing lack of distinctly recognizable prehistoric burial monuments, which are the usual means by which Neolithic and Bronze Age occupation is safely identified in the islands. As described above access to the island is not difficult, but the natural environment and resources appear limited. While sustained, even continuous occupation is possible for all of the islands surveyed, the actual size of the population would be controlled by these limiting factor.

The potential for Sandray to support a relatively high population is revealed in the record of 40 individuals thought to be resident on the island in the year 1764 (Buxton 1995). A mediaeval population cannot be quantified on the data currently available, but it is recognized as existing in a similar fashion by the presence of a chapel, Cille Bhride, and associated cemetery, which is clearly marked as a circular enclosure on the OS map of 1880. In 1915 officers of the Royal Commission could not identify the chapel with confidence since it may have been incorporated into structures built in the area by shepherds, and of the graveyard nothing was found at all. The shifting sands appear to have obscured the site thoroughly since nothing has been seen of it during any of the many visits made during this current survey.

Finally, any account concerning Sandray cannot help containing a reference to the Vatersay Raiders, but the story of these modern local heroes is told in great detail in many other publications (Hunter 1995, for example). Suffice it to say that the Raiders reoccupied the deserted settlement at Sheader for a short time in 1908 during the final battle for land on Vatersay.

Royal Commission on the Ancient and Historical Monuments of Scotland National Monuments Record of Scotland

Sites entered in the National Monuments Record of Scotland that were known prior to this survey are:

1. NL69SE1 (NGR NL6511:9192). Chapel and burial ground of Cille Bhride (SY65). The RCAHMS report of 1915 states that only a corner of the lime-mortared stone foundations of the chapel can be seen. The site was noted as being largely occupied by a sheep dip tank. An OS visit (1965) found no trace of the site, but the sheep tank was still in place.
2. NL69SE2 (NGR NL6500:9200). Farm settlement. This site includes the remains of a house and two outbuildings plus enclosures. Extant from 0.3–1.0 m. Max. height.
3. NL69SW3 (NGR NL6375:9137). Dun (SY70). The RCAHMS (1928) locate the site on a high point of the south-west slope of Cairn Galtar. Wall galleries were visible in the southern half of oval? superstructure and there was an outer defence wall on the north side before entrance. OS visit (1965) adds an oval plan and dimensions, 16.0 m north–east by 12.0 m east–west. Outer northern defensive wall survives to six courses high at 1.7 m. The inside dun wall is visible to 0.5 m high with variable wall width averaging 4 m around circumference, and the outer wall is visible to 0.5 m high but covered in rubble.
4. NL69SW4 (NGR NL642:905). Buildings. Two cairns at NL64209059 and NL64309056 (SY43). OS 1-in. Map (1904), 2nd edition. Visit by OS (1965) found the two cairns located at the south-east end of the valley. Close to the shore at approximately 25 ft OD appear the remains of buildings. (A) A semicircle 8.5 m diam. wall of large stones standing to a maximum of 0.7 m high. The south side is eroded and no entrance was seen. (B) A complex of three irregular-shaped, c. 0.3 m high, drystone constructions. The north-west building has entrance to south and is encircled with 0.2 m high bank (?SY43). (C) Is a circular mound of earth and stones with an 8.0 m diam., standing 1.3 m high at NL6432 9055.
5. NL69SW7 (16) (NGR NL6312:9200). Buildings (SY13). Name Book (1878) Sheader 'a piece of ground formerly cultivated'. 1st edition 6-in. OS map (1880) shows two unroofed houses with an enclosure attached to a field wall. OS 1:10,000 map (1971) shows two unroofed houses, one with three compartments.

The 1990–1995 Survey

The convenience of Sandray to Barra inevitably led to the island being visited more often on a casual basis with day trips by student groups and project leaders beginning with a visit by the author aboard Callum MacNeil's fishing boat in 1990, and in 1991 the first abortive attempt was made to undertake a systematic survey sweep in one day by the author and Sarah Darnborough. That same year further day trips by various members of staff and students accumulated a number of sites and the net result was a semisystematic survey with additional unsystematically collected sightings of variable value. In 1995

Sandray was surveyed whilst excavations were conducted at Sheader SY13/14. Roman Krivanek conducted a week-long systematic survey of the island that not only assimilated and corrected all the earlier work but achieved a comprehensive photographic coverage.

Of the 144 sites found, 53 (37%) of them were within 50 m of the coastal or cliff edge. Because of the commitment to the excavations at Sheader not so many sites were drawn stone by stone to scale, but all were drawn with measured field sketches in notebooks. One notable exception was the stone-by-stone drawing of the standing buildings of the Sheader settlement by John Pouncett, which will be published in SEARCH volume 6.

Description and catalogue of sites and monuments
SY1 (NL6437:9233) Platform. *Location*: Upper valley slope. *Description*: Rectangular 13 × 10 m flat grassy platform butted against field wall. A few stones, up to 0.60 m in size, are set along the edges.
SY2* (NL6426:9246) Cairn. *Location*: Coastal bench. *Description*: Unstructured 2 m diam. Mound of earth and stones in the 0.40–0.90 m size range. *Note*: Not found in 1995 resurvey.
SY3 (NL6408:9245) Cairn. *Location*: Shelf on coastal slope. *Description*: Circular shape of 2 m diam. flattened mound with stones in the 0.40–0.80 m size range at the perimeter. *Note*: Eroding out on to bedrock, but some recolonization by heather.
SY4* (NL6352:9257) Shelter. *Location*: On flat coastal shelf above the foreshore. *Description*: Triangular-shaped setting with 1 m side lengths of flat laid stones up to 0.60 m long.
SY5 (NL6347:9245) Shelter. *Location*: Lower coastal slope. *Description*: Oval, 3 × 2.5 m, single cell with two large stones 0.90 × 0.60 m set on edge at north and south ends and other piled stones around perimeter in the 0.20–0.60 m size range. *Note*: Area under threat of erosion.
SY6* (NL6334:9246) Shelter. *Location*: Coastal valley floor. *Description* Circular 4 m diam. Low yet prominent mound surmounted by a single cell shelter built of several large stone slabs, up to 1 m in size, occasionally set on edge, at irregular intervals around the perimeter.
SY7 (NL6336:9238) Shelter. *Location*: Lower coastal slope. *Description*: Rounded square 2 × 2 m shape constructed of spaced stones up to 0.90 m in size.
SY8* (NL6326:9245) Complex of shelter and stone setting. *Location*: Coastal spur out to sea. *Description*: Oval shelter of piled stones with associated linear stone settings and a possible enclosure wall. *Note*: The possible enclosure wall on the west side of this complex has been undercut by wave action and is displaced on the foreshore bedrock. Further erosion of this site is to be expected. Minor excavation produced a small quantity of struck flints.

SY8a* (NL6326:9245) Shelter. *Location*: As above. *Description*: Oval single cell.
SY8b* (NL6326:9245) Stone settings. *Location*: As above. *Description*: Linear stone settings of unidentified function.
SY9* (NL6326:9239) Cairn. *Location*: Coastal shelf above foreshore. *Description*: Single circular cell 1 m diam. of stones up to 0.60 m in size. *Note*: 1995 survey showed fresh erosion of the site into the stream bed.
SY10* (NL6328:9234) Cairn. *Location*: Coastal bench. *Description*: Ovoid 1.2 m diam. Low mound that may have a set stone kerb and a large 1 m square slab could be a cap stone or fallen upright.
SY11* (NL6329:9232) Cairn. *Location*: Coastal bench on slightly elevated position 2 m from SY10. *Description*: Circular single cell, 2.5 m diam. with some stone set in a ring. *Note*: Could be a shelter.
SY12* (NL6322:9207) Standing stone. *Location*: Bottom of hill-slope to coast. *Description*: Standing stone 1 m high on the eastern side of the Sheader Bay settlement area.
SY13* (NL6312:9200) Settlement complex (Sheader). *Location*: On grassed-over shell sand dunes immediately above storm beach (Fig. 3.7). *Description*: Nucleated settlement of improved blackhouses of more than one phase, with associated barns and field enclosures. The 1908 settlement of the Vatersay Raiders at Sheader is composed of five improved blackhouses built in a row, but the fifth is stepped forward out of line to the north. Each has a fireplace and chimney built into the west wall and an entrance in the north wall. Several outbuildings and enclosures complete the settlement, however, there is more than a single phase of occupation and use represented here. Blackhouse (a) appears to overstep (c) and the possible outhouse or barn foundation wall (f) most likely belongs to an earlier 19th-century phase. An earlier set of blackhouses exist below the 1908 settlement that were built prior to abandonment in the clearance of 1835 and are depicted on the 1st edition OS map of 1880. An excavation of the floor area of house No. 4 (SY13A) of the 1908 settlement revealed a floor, fireplace and an earlier internal room division that indicate that at least some of the Raiders' houses may have been modifications of the earlier blackhouses. There is also the distinct possibility that some of the abandoned buildings were used and possibly modified by the shepherds in the post-clearance period. *Note*: Stone-by-stone survey of the settlement to be published in SEARCH volume 6.
SY13a* (NL6312:9200) Blackhouse. *Location*: As above. *Description*: Subrectangular, single room dry-stone structure, 9 × 5 m, rounded external corners, entrance to the north and fireplace/chimney in west wall. *Note*: Excavation revealed earlier house with open floor fireplace below present standing building (see excavation report in SEARCH volume 6).

Figure 3.7 A view of site SY13, the settlement mound at Sheader.

SY13b* (NL6312:9200) Blackhouse. *Location*: As above. *Description*: Subrectangular, 4.3 × 4 m, rounded external corners, entrance to the north and fireplace/chimney in west wall.

SY13c* (NL6312:9200) Blackhouse. *Location*: As above. *Description*: Subrectangular, 6 × 4 m, rounded external corners, entrance to north and fireplace/chimney in west wall. *Note*: This building appears to have been partly demolished for the construction of SY13A.

SY13d* (NL6312:9200) Blackhouse. *Location*: As above. *Description*: Subrectangular, 9.8 × 5 m, entrance to the north and fireplace/chimney in west wall.

SY13e* (NL6312:9200) Blackhouse. *Location*: As above. *Description*: Subrectangular, 7.2 × 4.4 m, entrance to north and fireplace/chimney in west wall.

SY13f* (NL6312:9200) Barn. *Location*: As above. *Description*: Rectangular, 6 × 4 m, wall foundation only with no visible entrance. *Note*: Could have several other functions, such as haystack stand etc.

SY13g* (NL6312:9200) Enclosure. *Location*: To the west of the settlement blackhouses except for SY13e that opens on to it. *Description*: Subrectangular, 17 × 14 m, low drystone wall with entrance to east into settlement enclosure SY13h.

SY13h* (NL6312:9200) Enclosure. *Location*: To north of the main blackhouse group. *Description*: Rectangular drystone walled enclosure, c. 29 × 14 m, with entrance to west into enclosure SY13g. Blackhouses a to d appear to open onto it, but all of its eastern and half of its northern extent is not visible. *Note*: Part of its northern line was revealed in the excavations (see above) as a revetted terrace wall.

SY14* (NL6312:9200) Settlement (Bronze Age to Iron Age, Sheader). *Location*: Stratigraphically below modern settlement SY13 on the Sheader shell-sand dunes. *Description*: Multiphase occupation deposits with several walls or partitions of single stone settings and post holes of more than one phase. Only the northern exposed edge of the mound was subjected to a limited tapestry excavation, and it is most likely that the structures become more substantial and more chronologically complex deeper inside the mound This assertion is reinforced by a C14 date taken from a limpet shell sample from a midden at the base of the site that gave a late Bronze Age date (see excavation report, Chapter 7). *Note*: Excavation report includes Iron Age pottery and faunal remains. Both SY13 and 14 are subject to severe storm erosion and large quantities of material is being washed out from the east side of the site mound. Structural damage is affecting buildings of all periods.

SY15* (NL6299:9210) Shelter. *Location*: On Sheader point peninsula. *Description*: Ovoid shape, 1.5 × 1 m, of spaced small stones in the 0.2–0.4 m size range. *Note*: May be a stone setting of unknown function rather than a shelter.

SY16* (NL6299:9205) Complex of cairn and chamber tomb. *Location*: On Sheader point peninsula. *Description*: Combination of a possible chamber tomb and later stone cairn (Fig. 3.8). *Note*: Erosion down to bedrock in places.

SY16a* (NL6299:9205) Cairn. *Location*: As above. *Description*: Circular 3 m diam. stone cairn mound at the south-eastern point of the chamber SY16b.

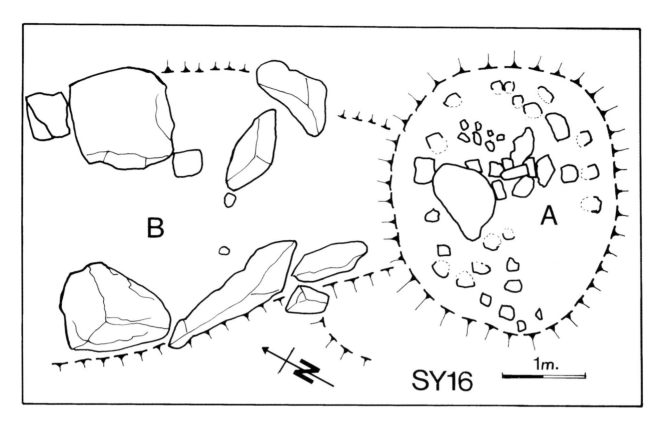

Figure 3.8 Site SY16, a stone cairn and possible burial chamber.

SY16b* (NL6299:9205) Chamber tomb. *Location*: As above. *Description*: Trapezoidal-shaped structure of large orthostats loosely forming a chamber of c. 4 × 2.5 m orientated north-west–south-east.

SY17* (NL6304:9195) Cairn. *Location*: Coastal peninsula. *Description*: Circular 1.2 m diam. Mound of piled stone, some up to 0.50 m in size. *Note*: Cairn is grassed over, but surrounded by denuded bedrock.

SY18* (NL6300:9203) Boat-shaped stone setting. *Location*: Coastal peninsula. *Description*: Pointed boat shape, 2.5 × 0.7 m, of single set stones in the 0.60 × 0.80 m size range sited on the Sheader headland, which is perhaps an expected location for a boat setting, but the form is less than perfect since pointed prow is missing. *Note*: Erosion to bedrock in places.

SY19* (NL6313:9184) Cairn. *Location*: Coastal edge of valley floor. *Description*: Circular 3 m diam. grassed-over piled stone (sizes up to 0.30m) mound. Sited near an enclosure wall. *Note*: Possibly a clearance cairn. 6 m from cairn SY20.

SY20* (NL6314:9183) Cairn. *Location*: Coastal edge of valley floor. *Description*: Circular 2 m diam. grassed-over piled stone (sizes up to 0.30m) mound. Sited near an enclosure wall. *Note*: Possibly a clearance cairn. 6 m from cairn SY19.

SY21 (NL6325:9180) Shieling complex (enclosure and shelters). *Location*: Valley floor. *Description*: Ovoid enclosure of single stone settings with three shelters or animal pens attached. This is typical of the type of site that we often classify as a shieling, but the structures are little more than shelters (B, C and D) with associated enclosures and pens formed of single stone settings (A). These are presumably stones put along the bottom of a wire fence to stop the livestock from pushing underneath the bottom wire.

SY21a (NL6325:9180) Enclosure. *Location*: As above. *Description*: Ovoid setting of single stones marking c. 10 m diam. Enclosure butted to rock face with entrance to south-east.

SY21b (NL6325:9180) Shelter. *Location*: As above. *Description*: 2 m square single cell shelter set inside, and incorporating part of, the enclosure wall. Entrance into the enclosure.

SY21c (NL6325:9180) Shelter. *Location*: As above. *Description*: Rectangular, 4 × 3 m, single cell shelter set externally to, but incorporating, the enclosure wall. Entrance into the enclosure.

SY21d (NL6325:9180) Shelter. *Location*: As above. *Description*: Rectangular, 1 × 0.60 m, single cell shelter at enclosure entrance. Form not clearly identifiable.

SY22 (NL6329:9181) Complex of roundhouse and shelter. *Location*: Bottom hill-slope to valley. *Description*: Circular mounded 5 m disc of displaced stone with shelter to one side (Fig. 3.9).

SY22a (NL6329:9181) Roundhouse. *Location*: As above. *Description*: Circular mounded disc of disarranged grassed over stonework, 5 m diam., designated as a roundhouse only on its merits as a large circular structure. Like many other monuments located close to or in areas of preferred settlement the possibility of

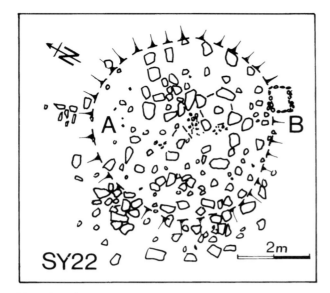

Figure 3.9 Site SY22, a collapsed stone roundhouse and later shelter.

stone robbing is very high and this site is situated to the east side at the northern end of the intensively used valley that runs south from the Sheader settlement. The disarranged state of SY22A, which masks its clear identification, is therefore no surprise.

SY22b (NL6329:9181) Shelter. *Location*: As above. *Description*: Square, 1 × 1 m, single cell shelter built on the south-east edge of the roundhouse wall circuit.

SY23 (NL6331:9178) Complex of enclosure and shelter. *Location*: Lower hill-slope to valley. *Description*: Oval enclosure and shelter or animal pen butted to rock crag face. *Note*: Slight platform.

SY23a (NL6331:9178) Enclosure. *Location*: As above. *Description*: Oval arc, 8 m radius, of spaced stones butted to rock crag face.

SY23b (NL6331:9178) Shelter. *Location*: As above within enclosure. *Description*: Insubstantial ovoid, single cell, 3 m diam., marked by a few stones around parameter and butted to rock crag face. *Note*: Alternative possibility is animal pen.

SY24 (NL6327:9142) Shelter. *Location*: Valley floor on slope of crag. Above wet area. *Description*: Circular single cell, 3 m diam., mounded with entrance to south-east. *Note*: Entrance well-defined by two stone slabs set on edge forming short passage. Could also be a chambered cairn.

SY25* (NL6314:9154) Cairn. *Location*: Coastal slope on cliffs. *Description*: Square single cell with 1 m sides formed of single 1 m long stone slabs set on edge. *Note*: This structure is set at the terminal end of a field boundary wall and may have been used as a marker for the wall during its construction.

SY26* (NL6317:9154) Cairn (clearance). *Location*: Lower coastal slope. *Description*: Circular, 2 m diam., grassed-over mound of stones standing 0.5 m high. *Note*: Within field system with lazy-beds.

SY27* (NL6318:9159) Cairn (clearance). *Location*: Lower coastal slope. *Description*: Circular, 2 m diam., grassed-over mound of stones. *Note*: Within field system with lazy-beds.

SY28* (NL6319:9155) Cairn (clearance). *Location*: Lower coastal slope. *Description*: Circular, 2 m diam., grassed-over mound of stones. *Note*: Within field system with lazy-beds.

SY29 (NL6327:9140) Complex of shelters. *Location*: Valley floor. *Description*: Three circular cojoining shelters covering an area 11 × 7 m. *Note*: Could be a shieling.

SY29a (NL6327:9140) Shelter. *Location*: As above. *Description*: Single cell oval, 4 × 3 m. *Note*: Stones of 0.6–0.9 m range.

SY29b (NL6327:9140) Shelter. *Location*: As above. *Description*: Single cell oval shape, 6 × 4 m. Stones of 0.6–1.2 m size range.

SY29c (NL6327:9140) Shelter. *Location*: As above. *Description*: Single cell ovoid, 3 m diam. Stones of 0.6–0.9 m size range.

SY30 (NL6330:9137) Cairn (clearance). *Location*: Valley floor. *Description*: Oval, 3.5 × 1 m, elongated stone mound (some scattered).

SY31 (NL6330:9143) Complex of three shelters. *Location*: Valley floor. *Description*: In an area of 6.5 × 4 m, three insubstantial shelters and a possible field wall in area of lazy-beds.

SY31a (NL6330:9143) Shelter. *Location*: As above. *Description*: Single oval cell, 2 m diam. with stones of 0.2–0.6 m size.

SY31b (NL6330:9143) Shelter. *Location*: As above. *Description*: Single subrectangular cell, 3 × 2 m with stones 0.2–0.6 m size.

SY31c (NL6330:9143) Shelter. *Location*: As above. *Description*: Single oval cell, 1 m diam. with stones of 0.2–0.6 m size.

SY32 (NL6334:9150) Complex of roundhouse and shieling. *Location*: Valley floor. *Description*: Circular thick wall of a roundhouse overlain by shieling hut and barn.

SY32a (NL6334:9150) Roundhouse. *Location*: As above. *Description*: Large single circular stone-faced wall, 10 m diam. and 1 m wide without visible internal divisions. Entrance to the east with northern arm of ring-wall turning and extending to the east. This site, like so many others, may require excavation to fully understand its structural history and function. The shieling could be many other things such as a byre or Sandray-style cleit, but its modern date is not in doubt. The roundhouse consists of a metre-wide double stone-faced wall and has no internal structures visible. There also appears to be a small annexe and a slightly narrower wall leading off from the entrance, features that are unusual for a roundhouse. The possibility that this structure is not a house but an enclosure associated with the shieling around which it is constructed cannot be ruled out.

SY32b (NL6334:9150) Shieling. *Location*: As above. *Description*: A substantially built single subrectangular house, 4.5 × 3 m, with stone-faced, 0.85 m thick walls and an entrance to the east. *Note:* Overlies the southern part of the roundhouse entrance.

SY32c (NL6334:9150) Store. *Location*: As above. *Description*: Mass of large rock slabs in formless setting on south side of shieling house. *Note*: Overlies possible annexe to roundhouse.

SY33* (NL6341:9105) Shelter. *Location*: Coastal shelf. *Description*: Single circular cell, 1.5 m diam., of piled stones up to 1 m in size. Entrance to north north-west.

SY34* (NL6356:9098) Shelter. *Location*: Coastal shelf. *Description*: Single circular, 3 m diam., cell of spaced stones of 0.3–0.6 m size.

SY35* (NL6403:9058) Blackhouse. *Location*: Coastal valley floor. *Description*: Unimproved blackhouse of subrectangular, 7 × 3.5 m, shape with very rounded external corners. Entrance to north and internal division built south from doorway. The back wall is a revetment against higher flat ground to the north. The single wall lines of vertically set stones suggests that the bulk of the superstructure was of turf, which would be unusual for a blackhouse of this time. As an alternative this building may be considered a shieling.

SY36* (NL6403:9041) Standing stone. *Location*: Cliff edge. *Description*: Set similar to SY12 but is smaller, being only 0.6 m above the ground surface. Similarly, it also commands a view of a bay area, being located on the cliff edge of the Aird Pabbach peninsula.

SY37 (NL6322:9148) Complex of cairn and platform *Location*: High knoll on valley floor. *Description*: Curved platform with cairn mound at eastern side.

SY37a (NL6322:9148) Cairn. *Location*. As above. *Description*: Circular 4 m diam. Mound of grassed over stones.

SY37b (NL6322:9148) Platform *Location*: As above. *Description*: Ovoid, 8 m diam., platform defined by stones set around leading edge.

SY38 (NL6404:9062) Complex of blackhouse and shelter. *Location*: Coastal valley floor. *Description*: Subrectangular unimproved blackhouse on platform with small later circular shelter to one side off the platform

SY38a (NL6404:9062) Blackhouse. *Location*: As above. *Description*: Very rounded subrectangular, 5 × 4 m, single cell unimproved blackhouse. No internal divisions or entrance visible. Walls stone-faced, earth-filled, 0.8 m wide, using stones up to 0.9 m in size. *Note*: Platform visible around northern edge with piles of stone against its lip.

SY38b (NL6404:9062) Shelter. *Location*: As above. *Description*: Circular, 2 m diam., single cell built five courses high. *Note*: Surviving height suggests very recent date.

SY39* (NL6405:9059) Shieling. *Location*: Coastal valley floor. *Description*: Oval, 12 × 8 m, single cell

of stones, 0.3–0.7 m size range, piled 0.5 m high in places. Entrance to the south.

SY40* (NL6407:9060) Shelter. *Location*: Coastal valley floor. *Description*: Single oval, 5 × 3 m, cell with stones in 0.2–0.9 m size range. Internal divisions suggested, but uncertain due to mass of collapsed and displaced stonework. *Note*: Possible shieling?

SY41 (NL6407:9066) Wheelhouse (Iron Age). *Location*: Coastal valley floor. *Description*: Circular, 9 m diam., with internal radial divisions set on large grassy platform Located close to a stream that originates in Loch na Culice, the site is within one of the early modern settlement areas and therefore liable to extensive stone robbing. *Note*: Iron Age pottery sherd found in rabbit burrow.

SY42* (NL6428:9057) Shieling complex. *Location*: Coastal above storm beach. *Description*: Subrectangular shieling shelter within complex of enclosure pens. Butted against rock crags. *Note*: Swept by storm waves.

SY42a* (NL6428:9057) Shieling. *Location*: As above. *Description*: Subrectangular, 3 × 2 m, single cell shieling hut of piled stones (or collapsed) with entrance to south.

SY42b* (NL6428:9057) Pen. *Location*: As above. *Description*: Oval, 7 × 4 m, animal enclosure pen.

SY43* (NL6429:9056) Shelter. *Location*: Coastal above storm beach. *Description*: Oval single cell, 7 m diam., much-disarranged walls standing to 1.75 m. *Note*: Collapsed roundhouse?

SY44* (NL6439:9053) Cairn. *Location*: Coastal rocky edge. *Description*: Circular, 1.5 m diam., damaged by burrowing.

SY45* (NL6478:9057) Complex of blackhouse and enclosure. *Location*: Edge of coastal dyke on Allt nam Brodach stream on blown sand soils covering old storm beach. *Description*: Isolated subrectangular blackhouse with enclosure.

SY45a* (NL6478:9057) Blackhouse. *Location*: As above. *Description*: Single cell square, 6 × 6 m, blackhouse with no entrance or internal divisions visible. *Note*: Shieling?

SY45b* (NL6478:9057) Enclosure. *Location*: As above. *Description*: Subrectangular, 20 × 10 m, enclosure to north of house.

SY46* (NL6498:9038) Shelter. *Location*: South slope to neck of Leehinish peninsula in area of exposed bedrock. *Description*: Insubstantial single cell ovoid, 3 × 2 m, of spaced stones some up to 0.7 m in size.

SY47* (NL6497:9036) Shelter. *Location*: Below SY46 on south slope to Leehinish peninsula. *Description*: Insubstantial square, 2 × 2 m, single cell shelter or natural feature.

SY48* (NL6508:9033) Shieling complex. *Location*: On cliff at east side of neck to Leehinish peninsula. *Description*: Unclear structures of possibly subcircular shape, very disarranged, set within enclosed area between denuded bedrock and stream *Note*: Site in state of erosion from stream. Exposed periglacial deposits 1.5 m deep reveal peat with much tree wood.

SY48a* (NL6508:9033) Shieling. *Location*: As above. *Description*: Oval, 5 m diam., of indistinct single cell marked by spaced stone settings.

SY48b* (NL6508:9033) Shieling. *Location*: As above. *Description*: Subcircular single cell, 3.3 m diam., of spaced stone settings.

SY48c* (NL6508:9033) Enclosure. *Location*: As above. *Description*: Curved wall of drystone enclosing an area, 15 × 10 m, bounded by a stream to the south enclosure and exposed bedrock top the north.

SY49 (NL6504:9052) Shelter. *Location*: Upper peninsula ridge. *Description*: Circular, 3 m diam., single cell of four spaced stone blocks 1 m in size. *Note*: Eroding out down to bedrock in south-east quadrant.

SY50* (NL6501:9051) Shelter. *Location*: On east coastal slope of Leehinish peninsula. *Description*: An unclear circular, 5 m diam. arrangement of large boulders that could be a cairn.

SY51* (NL6518:9083) Shelter. *Location*: On small coastal peninsula to south of Meanish beach on blown sand soil. *Description*: One side of an oval, 1.5 × 1 m, shelter? in area of lazy-beds. *Note*: Enclosure wall to north across peninsula.

SY52* (NL6543:9097) Cairn. *Location*: On neck of Meanish peninsula on blown sand soil. *Description*: Slightly mounded hollow oval, 1.7 × 0.5 m, setting of stones orientated north-east to south-west with a 'heel' stone at the south-west end and a curved 'bow' to the opposite north-east end.

SY53* (NL6540:9106) Cairn. *Location*: At the root of Meanish peninsula on blown sand soil. *Description*: Subrectangular flat setting of stones, 1.5 × 1 m, of stones.

SY54* (NL6499:9201) Complex of blackhouse and byre and two animal pens. *Location*: On sand dunes of Cille Bhride bay. *Description*: Complex covers an area of c. 20 × 10 m encompassing blackhouse, outbuildings and enclosures.

SY54a* (NL6499:9201) Blackhouse. *Location*: As above. *Description*: Unimproved rectangular, 10 × 5 m, single cell blackhouse with boulder wall foundations 1.2 m wide and entrance to the south-west. Some lengths of walling are not defined, especially the north-west corner. *Note*: Slightly defined enclosure walls connect to the north and east.

SY54b* (NL6499:9201) Barn. *Location*: As above. *Description*: Square, 4.2 × 4.1 m, single cell with internal stone square setting in north-east corner. *Note*: Possible kiln house?

SY54c* (NL6499:9201) Barn. *Location*: As above. *Description*: Subrectangular, 5 × 4 m, indistinct single cell wall foundation. *Note*: Possibly earlier version of SY54b.

SY54d* (NL6499:9201) Pen. *Location*: As above. *Description*: Rounded subrectangular enclosure, 7 × 5 m, marked with spaced stones that may have been put

down along the bottom of wire fencing to stop the stock from pushing underneath. *Note*: Further indistinct stone settings may indicate other enclosures.

SY55* (NL6484:9231) Shelter. *Location*: Low coastal cliff top. *Description*: Very indistinct rounded subrectangular or double rounded single cells, 10 × 5 m overall, marked by spaced and infrequent set stones and slightly raised platform.

SY56* (NL6478:9238) Shelter. *Location*: Low coastal cliff on peat soil. *Description*: Oval, 5.6 × 3.5 m, single cell slightly mounded. *Note*: At base of slope.

SY57* (NL6454:9245) Cairn. (clearance). *Location*: Low coastal plateau. *Description*: Semi-circular, 3 × 3 m, mounded earth and stone.

SY58* (NL6454:9248) Shieling complex. *Location*: Low coastal plateau with much denuded bedrock. Set close to stream. *Description*: Two indistinct rounded subrectangular huts. *Note*: Structure disarranged.

SY58a* (NL6454:9248) Shelter. *Location*: As above. *Description* Rounded subrectangular single cell, 7.6 × 4.8 m, not well defined. *Note*: Active erosion.

SY58b* (NL6454:9248) Shelter. *Location*: As above. *Description*: Subrectangular single cell, 1.8 × 0.8 m to the north-west of shelter (a).

SY59* (NL6448:9247) Shelter. *Location*: Low coastal plateau. *Description*: Subrectangular indistinct single cell, 2 × 1.5 m, on small mound. *Note*: Severe erosion, only north corner of wall well-defined.

SY60* (NL6449:9244) Shelter. *Location*: Low coastal plateau on grassy shelf. *Description*: A few spaced stones suggest an indistinct single cell, 2 × 1.5 m, oval structure. *Note*: Severe erosion.

SY61 (NL6450:9242) Shelter. *Location*: Low coastal plateau. *Description*: A disarranged collection of spaced stones suggest an oval structure, 3.5 × 3 m, but a few upright stones stand to 0.70 m. *Note*: Also possibly a cairn.

SY62 (NL6453:9236) Roundhouse. *Location*: Lower hill slope above coastal plateau. *Description*: Rounded shape with suggestion of internal structures, 5 × 4 m, slightly mounded. Described as a roundhouse on the same criteria as SY22A, which means that this 5 m diam. featureless mound of grassed stonework could also be a cairn, a designation that would suit its location on a natural platform on the northern coastal slope of Carnach. *Note*: Much internal collapse and no suggestion of internal radial divisions.

SY63* (NL6487:9215) Shelter. *Location*: Coastal shelf. *Description*: Rectangular single cell, 2.5 × 2 m, setting of single orthostats against crag bedrock. *Note*: Within enclosure.

SY64 (NL6515:9187) Complex of three shelters. *Location*: North-east coastal shell sand dunes. *Description*: Group of interconnected shelter constructions of various shapes defined by outlines of set stones occupying an area of 8 × 6 m. *Note* Threatened by erosion of sand soils.

SY64a (NL6515:9187) Shelter. *Location*: As above. *Description* Ovoid, 3 m diam., single cell opening into area (c).

SY64b (NL6515:9187) Shelter. *Location*: As above. *Description*: Subrectangular, 4 × 3 m, single cell with entrance to south.

SY64c (NL6515:9187) Shelter. *Location*: As above. *Description*: Not clearly defined except for single linear wall line north–south between (a) and (b) and a jumbled collection of stonework forming possible containment of an area c. 6 × 3 m.

SY65 (NL6512:9192) Burial ground (Cille Bhride). *Location*: North-east sand dunes. *Description*: Not located in survey. Whether the cemetery and chapel Cille Bhride was still in use in the early modern period could not be determined by the survey alone, but it is clearly marked as a circular enclosure with an internal building on the 1st edition 6-in. OS map of 1880—although it is also labelled as 'site of' chapel and 'disused' graveyard. These structures could not be found by the 1915 RCAHMS survey team (see above).

SY66 (NL6411:9231) Blackhouse. *Location*: Peat covered plateau shelf at edge of gully of Allt á Mhuilinn. *Description*: Subrectangular single cell, 4 × 3 m, unimproved blackhouse with stone-faced 0.9 m thick walls, corners rounded externally and opposing doorways east and west. *Note*: Possible platform. Erosion by weathering and rabbit burrowing.

SY67 (NL6414:9228) Cairn. *Location*: Peat-covered plateau shelf. *Description*: Mounded pile of stones 2 m diam. with sizes of 0.15–0.4 m. *Note*: Could be a clearance cairn.

SY68 (NL6418:9225) Complex of blackhouse and shelter. *Location*: Peat-covered plateau shelf overlooking gully of Allt á Mhuilinn. *Description*: Subrectangular, 5 × 2.5 m, unimproved blackhouse with later shelter built inside.

SY68a (NL6418:9225) Blackhouse. *Location*: As above. *Description*: The building is masked to some extent by displaced stone and has been subject to reuse as a shelter (B) that was built on top of one half of the partly deconstructed house. The underlying house appears to be a subrectangular single cell, approximately 5 × 2.5 m, unimproved blackhouse with thin walls c. 0.50 m thick and possibly opposing doorways north and south. Building blocks in 1.5–0.8 m range. These dimensions are more suitable for a shieling hut, but may be all that a single shepherd of the post-clearance phase would require.

SY68b (NL6418:9225) Shelter. *Location*: As above. *Description*: Mass of reused tumbled stone in squared construction, 1 × 1 m, forms single cell shelter inside eastern half of house.

SY69 (NL6365:9198) Shelter. *Location*: Mid hill-slope. *Description*: Oval, 3.5 × 3 m, with division into twin cells. Some walling standing to several courses, 0.50 m high. *Note*: Possibly built from material robbed from underlying reduced roundhouse.

SY70 (NL6376:9138) Atlantic roundhouse (galleried dun), Iron Age. *Location*: On prominent elevated spur formed by faulting along west flank of Cairn Galtar (Fig. 3.10). *Description*: A much-reduced unnamed galleried dun. Little can be added to the RCAHMS description (see above), apart from the locally told story that the walls were deliberately pushed down by a party of rabbit catchers to provide material for shelters at the base of the cliff. A shelter (SY130) does exist in the right place, but why rabbit catchers should be working and living at such an elevation is a mystery. *Note*: Many structural elements are still visible and worthy of an accurate building survey.

SY71 (NL6447:9110) Chamber tomb. *Location*: Inside dyke. *Description*: Subrectangular single cell, 3.5 × 2 m, of massive orthostats 0.7–1.7 m in size range standing up to 0.95 m high with what appears to be fallen lintel stones inside chamber. The rank fern and heather vegetation obscured more stonework than visible in the recorded field illustration. The site is located on a rock shelf of the lower slopes of Cairn Galtar overlooking the length of Gleann Mor glen to the south and south-east.

SY72 (NL6452:9121) Shieling complex. *Location*: Inside dyke formation of upper Gleann Mor, just above Allt nam Bodach stream. *Description*: Two subrectangular co-joining cells, 6 × 3 m, butted on north side of field wall across the dyke, from dyke east side to stream edge. *Note*: Against north wall of cell (b) is a mass of collapsed stonework that may prove to be another structure.

SY72a (NL6452:9121) Shelter. *Location*: As above. *Description*: Square single cell, 3 × 3 m, of stone and earth wall foundation with entrance to the east, butted to and using a field wall to the south.

SY72b (NL6452:9121) Shelter. *Location*: As above. *Description*: Square single cell, 3 × 3 m, built on to and cojoining the north wall of shelter (a). Built of earth and stone walls with entrance to the east. Piled stone mounded to the north may be another structure.

SY73 (NL6461:9109) Wheelhouse, Iron Age. *Location*: On the floor of upper Gleann Mor glen close to Allt nam Bodach stream. *Description*: The apparently oval shape of 9 × 7 m may be a distorted view due to collapsed and disarranged stonework. Some upright stonework defines part of walls and internal, possibly radial, divisions. The site is an eye catching mound of large disarranged stonework standing out against the surrounding dull vegetation as a bright green target caused by the rank fern growth that has invaded the structure, but has not been able to compete against the heather outside. The location of the site is deep within the glen of Gleann Mor and close to the stream Allt nam Bodach. *Note*: Needs some structural clarification by selective stone removal after accurate measured survey and then resurveying.

SY74 (NL6406:9110) Shelter. *Location*: South-west slopes of Cairn Galtar. *Description*: Circular single

Figure 3.10 Site SY70, the broch seen from the north-west.

cell, 2.5 m diam., of spaced stones with possible entrance to north-east. *Note*: Covered by heather.

SY75* (NL6309:9186) Shieling complex. *Location*: West coast of valley floor. *Description*: Rounded irregular subrectangular, building, 21 × 11 m, or cluster of cojoined cells that may be resolved into two main buildings set to one side of an oval enclosure.

SY75a* (NL6309:9186) Shieling. *Location*: As above. *Description*: Rounded externally, but more rectangular internally with a wall division forming two cells, overall dimensions 6 × 5 m, with possible doorway into building (b). *Note*: Slightly mounded and grassed over.

SY75b* (NL6309:9186) Shieling. *Location*: As above. *Description*: Rounded subrectangular building, 7 × 5 m, with three cells, one circular and two rectangular, that form either a separate shieling or an extension of building (a). *Note*: There is no apparent external doorway, but the internal connection between the two structures suggests that they form a single entity.

SY75c* (NL6309:9186) Enclosure. *Location*: As above. *Description*: Oval, 11 × 10 m, enclosure against south-east wall of building (b) formed by stone settings.

SY76 (NL6331:9208) Shelter. *Location*: Coastal hill-slope on shelf between dykes. *Description*: Oval single cell, 6 × 4 m, of spaced upright blocks, 0.5–1.5 m size range, standing up to 0.4 m high. *Note*: Erosion to bedrock in patches.

SY77 (NL6336:9219) Shelter. *Location*: Coastal hill-slope on small shelf. *Description*: Subrectangular single cell, 3 × 2.5 m, with stone and earth walls 0.6 m thick set against field wall. *Note*: No apparent entrance.

SY78 (NL6347:9225) Cairn. *Location*: Coastal hill-slope. *Description*: Oval single cell, 3.5 × 2.5 m, of spaced massive blocks up to 1 m in size. *Note*: Could be part of wall 10 at turning.

SY79 (NL6337:9225) Cairn. *Location*: Coastal hill-slope inside dyke. *Description*: Rectangular flat-topped mound, 4 × 3 m, of earth with some non-structural stones.

SY80* (NL6363:9257) Cairn. *Location*: Sloping coastal shelf, some erosion down to bedrock. *Description*: rectangular flat mound, 4 × 3 m, with some stones piled on top and to one side. *Note*: Covered by heather.

SY81 (NL6400:9238) Cairn. *Location*: Shelf sloping to dyke and stream of Allt á Mhuilinn. *Description*: Half-circle of spaced stones against natural boulders forming oval, 3 × 1.5 m, and platform. *Note*: Covered by heather.

SY82 (NL6412:9223) Cairn (mound) *Location*: Inside dyke mid-slope of Allt á Mhuilinn. *Description*: Circular, 7 m diam., grassed mound and a few random stones. *Note*: Covered by heather.

SY83 (NL6411:9226) Shieling. *Location*: Inside dyke mid-slope of Allt á Mhuilinn. *Description*: Rounded subrectangular single cell, 3 × 2.5 m, with earth and stone walls 0.6 m thick, entrance to south. *Note*: Covered by heather.

SY84 (NL6374:9228) Cairn. *Location*: Mid-slope shelf. *Description*: Oval single cell, 1.8 × 1.2 m, dry-stone walling displaced on west side on to denuded bedrock. *Note*: Severe erosion threat.

SY85 (NL6376:9224) Cairn. *Location*: Mid-slope shelf. *Description*: Circular, 2.5 m diam., mounded earth with some stones at edge, some displaced. *Note*: Threatened by wind erosion.

SY86 (NL6337:9190) Blackhouse. *Location*: Plateau on lower hill slope to Sheader. *Description*: Subrectangular single cell, 5 × 3.5 m, unimproved blackhouse, with 0.6 m thick walls that are externally rounded and built of banked earth and small stones, but internally they are stone-faced and sharply cornered. There are opposing entrances east and west. *Note*: Covered by heather.

SY87 (NL6346:9203) Shelter. *Location*: Plateau on lower hill slope. *Description*: Single cell formed by semicircular wall, 2 × 1.5 m, stone-faced internally and earth-banked externally, set against field wall with entrance to south.

SY88 (NL6344:9208) Complex of blackhouse and shelter. *Location*: Plateau on lower hill slope. *Description*: Subrectangular single cell unimproved blackhouse with shelter built later inside south-western corner.

SY88a (NL6344:9208) Blackhouse. *Location*: As above. *Description* Subrectangular single cell, 4.5 × 3 m, unimproved blackhouse with stone-faced walls of earth and stone 0.7 m thick. The structure appears to have been subject to some deconstruction and a small shelter (B) may have been built in one corner, but this has collapsed into an amorphous pile of stones. There may be opposing entrances, but only one is visible to the south, the other being covered with displaced rubble.

SY88b (NL6344:9208) Shelter. *Location*: As above. *Description*: Shapeless conglomeration of collapsed stonework, 1 × 1 m, may be shelter built inside south-west corner of blackhouse.

SY89 (NL6350:9206) Shieling. *Location*: Mid-slope inside dyke. *Description*: Building with two trapezoidal-shaped cells, 7 × 4 m, built against field wall and bedrock exposure. Entrance from the west with internal doorway leading into second room. Both cells measure 3.5 × 4 m and are constructed of drystone walling. *Note*: Masses of displaced collapsed stonework.

SY90 (NL6372:9212) Shelter. *Location*: Mid-slope plateau just inside northern head dyke. *Description*: Oval single cell, 3 × 2 m, with wall of single set stones, some on edge standing to 0.8 m in height, and earth packing. *Note*: Covered by heather.

SY91 (NL6370:9213) Complex of three shelters. *Location*: Same plateau as SY90. *Description*: Circular drystone walled shelter (b) enlarged by L-shaped drystone wall (a) extending from crag forming second shelter of similar internal area. A third circular shelter (c) with banked earthen walls is slightly apart to the west. All with entrances to the south. *Note*: wet hollow covered by heather.

SY91a (NL6370:9213) Shelter. *Location*: As above. *Description*: Subrectangular single cell, 3 × 2.5 m, built as additional annexe to shelter (b) by extending an L-shaped drystone wall out from the backing rocky crag against which they are built.

SY91b (NL6370:9213) Shelter. *Location*: As above. *Description*: Circular, 2.5 m diam., single drystone cell.

SY91c (NL6370:9213) Shelter. *Location*: As above. *Description*: Circular, 2.5 m diam., single cell of earthen walls.

SY92 (NL6367:9214) Shelter. *Location*: Mid-slope plateau. *Description*: Rectangular, 2.5 × 2.2 m, shape, inner space filled possibly with collapsed walling and earth.

SY93 (NL6375:9215) Shelter. *Location*: Mid-slope plateau. *Description*: Circular single cell, 1.8 m diam., composed of spaced stones. *Note*: Flat wet area.

SY94 (NL6377:9217) Shelter. *Location*: Mid-slope plateau. *Description*: Circular single cell, 2 m diam., ring wall foundation of small stones and earth. *Note*: Active erosion exposing bedrock.

SY95 (NL6411:9214) Shelter. *Location*: On side slope of Allt á Mhuilinn outside northern head dyke. *Description*: Superficially irregular single cell, 3 × 2.5 m, but distortion may be due to displacement and collapse. Constructed with large blocks, 0.5–1 m in size. *Note*: Could be an adapted chamber tomb.

SY97 (NL6413:9229) Complex of two shelters. *Location*: Lower-slope plateau overlooking dyke. *Description*: Two oval cojoined shelters using large stone blocks. *Note*: Stones 0.5–1 m range could be rebuild from earlier monument.

SY97a (NL6413:9229) Shelter. *Location*: As above. *Description*: Oval single cell, 4 × 3 m, built with large blocks 0.5–0.7 m.

SY97b (NL6413:9229) Shelter. *Location*: As above. *Description*: Oval single cell, 3.5 × 3 m, built of large blocks 0.5–1 m, possibly as an annex to (a), or the standing remains of an earlier structure.

SY99 (NL6451:9234) Cairn. *Location*: Lower coastal hill slope. *Description*: Rectangular, 3 × 2.5 m, stony platform. *Note*: Single visible upstanding stone 0.6 m high.

SY102 (NL6496:9150) Building. *Location*: Valley floor in eastern sand dunes. *Description*: Square, 4 × 4 m, building of drystone walling several courses high. Internal corner angles infilled with stone. The centre is paved by a circle, 1.5 m diam., of flat-laid stone slabs. An early modern date in the 18th century is assumed by the considerable amount of pottery and associated low denomination coinage of that period found in the area. *Note*: Area threatened by erosion and is littered with displaced stonework eroding out of the deflating dunes.

SY103 (NL6508:9155) Building. *Location*: Valley floor in eastern sand dunes. *Description*: Large oval building, 10 × 6 m, with thick banked earth walls around an internal narrow elongated oval slot. At one end this slot is marked by a bow of small stone. *Note*: Presumably of 18th-century date, possibly a kiln or dryer of some kind.

SY105* (NL6310:9185) Cairn. *Location*: Coastal valley floor. *Description*: Circular, 2.5 m diam., grassed mound with some embedded stones. *Note*: Severe damage by burrowing.

SY106 (NL6337:9164) Cairn. *Location*: Valley floor at bottom of hill slope. *Description*: Circular, 2 m diam., mound of stones embedded in earth standing 0.20 m high.

SY107 (NL6338:9159) Shelter. *Location*: Valley floor at bottom of hill slope. *Description*: Square, 3 × 3 m, single cell of set stones with entrance to south. *Note*: Covered by heather.

SY108* (NL6340:9107) Cairn. *Location*: Slope of rocky coastal knoll, Knock Noddimull. *Description*: Oval, 2 × 1.5 m, mound with surface stones scattered.

SY109 (NL6416:9090) Shelter. *Location*: Lower slope under rocky crags. *Description*: Circular drystone, 1.3 m diam., single cell built against field wall.

SY110 (NL6398:9074) Cairn (clearance). *Location*: Valley floor. *Description*: Circular, 1.8 m diam. Mound of stones. *Note*: Area of lazy-beds.

SY111 (NL6399:9073) Shelter. *Location*: Valley floor. *Description*: Circular single cell, 2 m diam., of drystone walling close to field wall. *Note*: Area of lazy-beds.

SY112 (NL6400:9074) Shelter. *Location*: Valley floor. *Description*: Square, 2 × 2 m, single cell with indistinct stony walls butted on to field wall. *Note*: Damage by burrowing.

SY113 (NL6399:9070) Platform. *Location*: Valley floor. *Description*: Subrectangular, 10 × 8 m, with piled stones at leading edge. *Note*: Erosion in places at edges.

SY114 (NL6335:9170) Shelter. *Location*: Base hill-slope to valley. *Description*: Sub-rectangular single cell, 2 × 1.2 m, internally obscured with collapsed stonework.

SY115 (NL6346:9157) Enclosure. *Location*: Lower hill-slope. *Description*: Semicircle, 8 × 5.5 m, of large stone blocks up to 1 m in size. *Note*: Could be reduced or overgrown roundhouse.

SY116 (NL6352:9138) Complex of two shelters. *Location*: Base of hill-slope to valley. *Description*: Rectangular drystone cojoined pair of shelters. Assess into cells uncertain. Stones in 0.4–1 m range, partly collapsed in places.

SY116a (NL6352:9138) Shelter. *Location*: As above. *Description*: Rounded subrectangular single cell, 2.5 × 2 m, with some upright set stones in wall.

SY116b (NL6352:9138) Shelter. *Location*: As above. *Description*: Square single cell, 3 × 3 m, drystone construction cojoined with shelter (a).

SY117 (NL6365:9121) Shelter. *Location*: Lower hill-slope on shelf. *Description*: Triangular stone setting, 3 × 2.5 m, and square platform 2 × 2 m. *Note*: Identification uncertain. Covered by heather.

SY118 (NL6405:9100) Shelter. *Location*: Mid-slope shelf. *Description*: Semicircular, 7 × 5 m, stone-faced wall over 1 m wide and built with massive blocks of up

to 1 m in size set butted against crag face. *Note*: Active wind erosion.

SY119 (NL6400:9099) Complex of two shelters. *Location*: Inside dyke lower hill-slope. *Description*: Double oval shelter on platform, (b) may be annexe to (a). Entrances not apparent. *Note*: Covered by heather.

SY119a (NL6400:9099) Shelter. *Location*: As above. *Description*: Oval single cell, 4 × 3 m, with 1 m thick walls using some stones set upright.

SY119b (NL6400:9099) Shelter. *Location*: As above. *Description*: Oval outward curved wall, 2 m, butted against wall of (a) forming annexe.

SY120 (NL6448:9107) Cairn. *Location*: Inside dyke. *Description*: Oval, 3 × 2.5 m, flattened grassy mound with stones set at western edge.

SY121 (NL6446:9184) Cairn. *Location* Shelf of hill-slope below Carnach cliff face. *Description*: Oval flattened grassy cairn mound, 4.5 × 3 m, with northern perimeter edged with set stone.

SY122 (NL6443:9162) Cairn. *Location* Inside dyke. *Description*: Circular, 1.2 m diam., of stone blocks. *Note*: Covered by heather.

SY123 (NL6448:9138) Shelter. *Location*: Inside dyke. *Description*: Oval single cell, 3.8 × 3 m, drystone construction of stones in range 0.2–0.5 m, standing several courses, 1.1 m, high, some fallen inside. Entrance to north. *Note*: Active erosion to bedrock. Possible shieling.

SY124 (NL6448:9140) Shelter. *Location*: Inside dyke. *Description*: Partly obscured square single cell, 2 × 2 m, earth and stone walls damaged by rock naturally falling into the dyke.

SY125 (NL6451:9125) Shelter. *Location*: Inside dyke. *Description*: Circular, 1.5 m diam., setting of stones on a slightly raised grassy platform.

SY126 (NL6426:9104) Shelter. *Location*: Mid hill-slope of Cairn Galtar. *Description*: Circular, 3 m diam., setting of stone, with a possible internal division, on a slightly raised platform. *Note*: Covered by heather.

SY127 (NL6338:9198) Cairn. *Location*: Inside dyke on lower hill-slope. *Description*: Circular, 1.2 m diam., stone setting, some upstanding 0.60 m high, on mound. *Note*: Covered by heather.

SY128 (NL6336:9203) Cairn. *Location*: Lower northern hill-slope. *Description*: Circular, 3.5 m, stone-edged mound surmounted by circle, 1.5 m diam., of stones, some standing 0.40 m high.

SY129 (NL6369:9156) Cairn. *Location*: Inside dyke mid hill-slope. *Description*: Circular, 1.2 m diam., ring of stones. *Note*: Covered by heather.

SY130 (NL6372:9137) Shelter. *Location*: Mid hill-slope shelf at base of cliff to galleried dun SY70. *Description*: Irregular-shaped single cell, 4 × 2.3 m, constructed from stone thrown down from the dun. *Note*: Presumably built by the rabbit catchers who destroyed much of the dun. Covered by heather.

SY131 (NL6375:9126) Shelter. *Location*: Lower hill-slope plateau. *Description*: Rounded subrectangular single cell, 3.5 × 3 m, earth and stone wall foundations with entrance to east. *Note*: Some erosion threat. Covered by heather. Possibly a roundhouse.

SY132 (NL6469:9047) Shieling complex. *Location*: Hill-slope coastal peninsula. *Description*: Interconnected multicellular building, 8 × 7 m, complex of four circular and rectangular rooms. *Note*: Much collapsed stonework. Similar in form to SY75.

SY132a (NL6469:9047) Shieling. *Location*: As above. *Description*: Rectangular single cell, 3.5 × 3 m, with south entrance and no direct access to the other rooms.

SY132b (NL6469:9047) Shieling. *Location*: As above. *Description*: Square single cell, 2 × 2 m, with party wall to (a), entrance through from (d), external exit to north, but there is no access to cell (c).

SY132c (NL6469:9047) Shieling. *Location*: As above. *Description*: Slightly oval single cell, 1.5 × 1.2 m, with entrance to north-east. Although it has a party wall with (b) there is no connection with the other cells.

SY132d (NL6469:9047) Shieling. *Location*: As above. *Description*: Circular single cell, 2 m diam., acts as ante chamber to cell (b). Entrance to south-east.

SY133 (NL6497:9043) Shelter. *Location*: Lleehinish peninsula. *Description*: Circular, 2 m diam., single cell of drystone walling, partly collapsed.

SY134* (NL6508:9090) Setting. *Location*: Bottom of hill-slope to southern beach and sand dunes. *Description*: Angular linear stone setting next to oval platform. *Note*: Turning of pathway from hillside.

SY135* (NL6550:9108) Standing stone. *Location*: East coast of Meanish peninsula. *Description*: Stone block 1.7 × 1.5 × 0.8 m in sandy soil. *Note*: Most likely a glacially derived boulder.

SY136* (NL6513:9204) Shieling complex. *Location*: Northern bay sand dunes. *Description*: Rectangular single cell drystone shelter with associated animal pen and enclosure. *Note*: Covered by blown sand.

SY136a* (NL6513:9204) Shelter. *Location*: As above. *Description*: Rectangular drystone single cell, 4.5 × 2 m, wall height 1.3 m, with entrance to north.

SY136b* (NL6513:9204) Pen. *Location*: As above. *Description*: Rectangular, 4 × 3 m, drystone wall aligned with south wall of shelter and once possibly butted to it.

SY136c* (NL6513:9204) Enclosure. *Location*: As above. *Description*: Rectangular stone setting, 10 × 3 m, set at right angles to the pen.

SY137 (NL6458:9157) Cairn. *Location*: Saddle north of Carnach hilltop. *Description*: Circular, 1.5 m diam., setting of spaced stones on slight mound. *Note*: Erosion down to bedrock locally.

SY138 (NL6409:9146) Cairn. *Location*: Plateau hilltop of Cairn Galtar. *Description*: Triangular pile of stones, 1.2 × 1.2 m, set as a pyramid 0.80 m high. *Note*: On denuded bedrock.

SY139 (NL6403:9155) Shelter. *Location*: Summit of Cairn Galtar. *Description*: Circular, 5 m diam., stone ring around trig. point on bedrock. *Note*: Severe erosion. Most likely modern.

SY140 (NL6402:9158) Cairn. *Location*: Summit of Cairn Galtar. *Description*: Circular, 1.4 m diam., pile of stones on bedrock. *Note*: Severe erosion, but covered by heather.

SY141 (NL6392:9155) Cairn. *Location*: Summit of Cairn Galtar. *Description*: Triangular, 1.2 m diam., pile of stones on bedrock. *Note*: modern.

SY142 (NL6348:9208) Cairn. *Location*: Lower hill-slope. *Description*: Circular, 1 m diam., group of stones on slight mound. *Note*: ?Early relict wall.

SY144 (NL6363:9196) Shelter. *Location*: Mid hill-slope. *Description*: Rectangular single cell, 3.5 × 2 m, of massive wall stones up to 1 m in size.

SY145 (NL6420:9175) Cairn. *Location*: Hill-slope shelf. *Description*: Circular, 1 m diam., stone ring on slight mound.

SY146 (NL6393:9165) Cairn. *Location*: Summit Cairn Galtar. *Description*: Triangular pile of stones, 1 m diam.

SY147 (NL6341:9154) Boat-shaped stone setting. *Location*: Base of hill-slope to valley. *Description*: Boat-shaped stone setting, 4 × 2.5 m, with blocks up to 0.6 m in size. *Note*: Covered by heather.

SY148 (NL6339:9143) Shelter. *Location*: Valley floor. *Description*: Rectangular single cell, 3 × 2.5 m.

SY149 (NL6320:9169) Complex of two shelters. *Location*: Valley floor. *Description*: Two circular cojoining shelters, 2.4 × 2 m. *Note*: Covered by heather.

SY149a (NL6320:9169) Shelter. *Location*: As above. *Description*: Circular, 1.8 m diam., single cell of spaced stone settings. *Note*: Covered by heather.

SY149b (NL6320:9169) Shelter. *Location*: As above. *Description*: Semicircle, 1 m diam., single cell annexe to (a). *Note*: Covered by heather.

SY150 (NL6324:9175) Roundhouse. *Location*: Valley floor. *Description*: Circular, 7 m diam., ring-wall of collapsed stonework on a mounded flat platform. To be confident that the identification of the structure described here is accurate much more work is required. The 7 m diam. allows for this to be identified as either an Iron Age or a pre-Iron Age building. The location of the site in the intensively used modern landscape of the valley south from the Sheader settlement means that it may have been subjected to intensive stone robbing.

Landscape period summaries

The early modern and modern landscape (Fig. 3.11)
The early modern settlement pattern is not focused on any one single township village like Mingulay and Pabbay or any wider, yet still concentrated, settlement area, such as that on Berneray. The pre-1835 settlement pattern is generally a dispersed one and

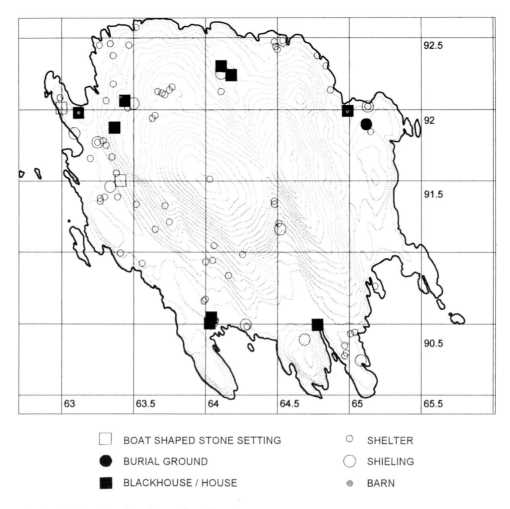

Figure 3.11 Sandray, showing the location of modern and mediaeval monuments.

traditionally it has been thought that there were three settlements on the island at, Sheader and Bagh Ban at the north-west and north-east corners respectively, and Bagh na Greot on the south coast (Buxton 1995), the main concentration being at Sheader. But the Bagh Ban area with its cemetery and chapel site could be expected to be the location of a further settlement concentration. However, there is only a single blackhouse there (SY54). This most likely belongs to the shepherds, although they may well have reoccupied an existing dwelling. There are four other single small blackhouses scattered along the northern part of the island, SY66, 68, 86 and 88. At Bagh an Greot there are two houses, SY35 and 38, from which at least one family emigrated to Nova Scotia, but strangely there is no settlement along the western side of the island between Sheader and Bagh an Greot, which contains some of the best agricultural land on the island, as the almost continuous lazy-beds and rig earthworks testify. There are plenty of adequate natural platforms attendant to this area that would provide decent house plots, and it is noticeable that the Iron Age dun

SY70 commands this region, but perhaps the westerly gales are a deterrent to all lesser forms of domestic habitation. The final blackhouse (SY45) of this dispersed settlement pattern is located at the sea end of the glen Gleann Mor where the small stream of Allt nam Bodach empties into a sea dyke.

The opposite coast to the east tells a very different story. Although it is an area of shifting dunes, occupation or some form of intense activity was taking place there at least during the 18th century. No houses are in evidence, but in areas where the dunes have deflated stone structures are appearing (SY103, for example) and at the northern end of the coastal strip considerable quantities of 18th-century ceramics, including handmade wares as well as porcelain, have been surface collected. Other finds from this area include domestic debris from metal fittings to oil lamps and low-denomination coins of the late 18th century.

The settlement pattern after the time of the clearance in 1835 became concentrated with the Vatersay Raiders occupying the Sheader settlement and, before them, the shepherds in the Bagh Ban area. Unlike the

Raiders the actual houses used by the shepherds are not so easy to identify. One of their houses must be SY54, but where the second house is located is not clear. Possibly the same drifting sands that covered the cemetery have hidden it or it may be located away from the bay area, for there are several small blackhouses along the north coast.

The commonest feature in the early modern/modern landscape is the shelter, which without confirmatory evidence must be allocated to this period on the grounds that most shelters are likely to be of a relatively recent date. There are also a number of buildings that are likely to be summer shielings that belong to this period, and some of the small blackhouses could in fact be more substantially constructed examples of this class of site.

The island is divided into large blocks of land by a system of long distance field walls in the same manner as Pabbay and Mingulay. The land division on Berneray is probably too unbalanced by the lighthouse landscape to be comparable. The better agricultural land on the west side, especially around Sheader, is divided and subdivided by a dense network of field walls comparable to the system around the bay village on Mingulay, which is contrary to Buxton's (1995) view that Sandray possesses few field walls. Roman Kravenik mapped most of the wall system in 1995.

Improved blackhouses. SY13A + B + C + D + E.

Unimproved blackhouses. SY13, 35, 38, 45, 54, 66, 68, 86, 88.

Shelters. SY4, 5 6, 7 8A, 15, 22B, 23B, 24, 29A + B + C, 31A + B + C, 33, 34, 38B, 40, 43, 46, 47, 49, 51, 55, 56, 59, 60, 61, 63, 64A + B + C, 68B, 69, 74, 76, 77, 87, 88B, 90, 91A + B + C, 92, 93, 94, 95, 97A + B, 107, 109, 111, 112, 114, 116A + B, 117, 118, 119A + B, 123, 124, 125, 126, 130, 131, 133, 136A, 139, 144, 148, 149A + B.
Sandray's total of 74 possible shelters (not including those thought to be part of shieling complexes) may be an indication that in more recent times its proximity to the inhabited islands of Barra and Vatersay may have encouraged more frequent visits by a variety of people, rabbit catchers, fishermen and shepherds, for example, who erected a variety of shelters for storage or personal shelter.

Shielings. SY21A + B + C + D, 32A + C, 39, 42A + B, 48A + B + C, 58A + B, 72A + B, 75A + B + C, 83, 89, 132A + B + C + D, 136A + B + C.

Miscellaneous sites and monuments. This group includes those isolated platforms and enclosures, all of which are at present impossible to date, along with some of the enigmatic structures that have appeared out of the deflating east coast dune system.

Platforms. SY1, 37B, 113.

Buildings. SY102, 103.

Burial ground and Cille Bhride chapel. SY65.

Mediaeval landscape (Fig. 3.11)
Presumably the cemetery and chapel Cille Bhride (SY65) was in use during this period and possibly, but less likely, also during the early mediaeval period. Probably one of the most obvious settlement sites for this period would have been that of the Sheader mound, SY13, but no recognizable features or ceramics were recovered from the excavations of SY14 or by surface collection.

Early mediaeval/Norse landscape (Fig. 3.11)
As usual little can be found of this landscape except two boat-shaped settings of stone that may be of the period, but neither are very convincing examples of the type.

Boat-shaped stone settings: SY18, 147.

The Iron Age landscape (Fig. 3.12)
Sandray, like both Berneray and Pabbay, has an Atlantic roundhouse dominating part of the landscape and there are also several sites in Gleann Mor that may be Iron Age wheelhouses. One Iron Age site (SY14) has been proven by excavation on the small sand dune system above the storm beach at Sheader. This site shows some affinity to a similarly situated site excavated on dunes in Mingulay Bay (MY384). Although it has not been possible to fully excavate either site they both appear to be constructed with insubstantial stone walling, most likely supporting or revetting turf constructions, of several superimposed phases. Sandray, like Mingulay, has enough landmass to provide a number of locations suitable for settlement sites and it is possible that during the later Iron Age the island was occupied to its maximum carrying capacity, giving home to a population that may have exceeded that of the known modern preclearance figure of 40 individuals.

Atlantic roundhouses. SY70. Sandray is unique in the southern islands in that its Atlantic roundhouse, a galleried dun, is not located in a coastal situation, but on a high crag cut out from the hill-slope of Cairn Galtar; it is still remote and aloof from any easy access. There can be little doubt that the decision to site the dun at such an inaccessible location had no other purpose than to deter and impress.

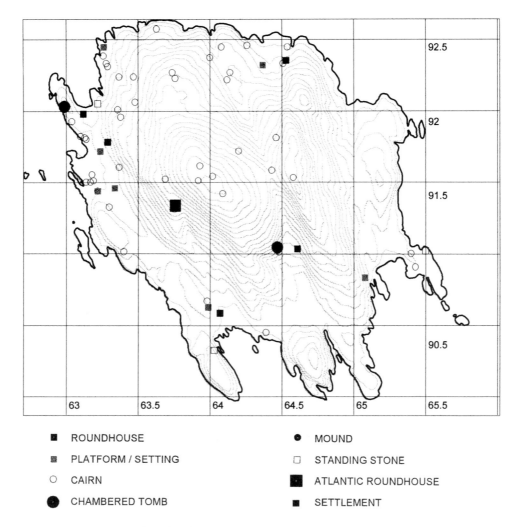

Figure **3.12** Sandray, showing the location of prehistoric monuments.

Wheelhouses. SY41, 73. The survey evidence for the identification of these two monuments is based upon a set of accumulative factors rather than any distinctly recognizable element. They appear circular and of a diameter that is within wheelhouse parameters. They are the focus of a considerable amount of stonework and display internal shapes that could be the distinctive radial compartments found in wheelhouses. Iron Age pottery has been collected from rabbit burrows at one of the sites.

Other settlement sites. SY14. The excavations carried out at the edge of the Sheader settlement mound revealed a series of relatively insubstantial Iron Age structural elements consisting of lines of one and two coarse stone walling with associated post holes. The restricted area excavated did not allow a sufficient area of the structures to be revealed for the purpose of definitive identification, however, from the evidence that was revealed it is clear that this site has much in common with the site excavated in the Mingulay dunes (MY384). Both sites may be representative of a

class of Iron Age domestic buildings, most likely of roundhouse form, built with low stone walls that most likely act as revetment or foundation to substantial turf-built walls.

The Pre-Iron Age landscape (Fig. 3.12)
Unfortunately Sandray has no pre-Iron Age sites that can be identified without qualification. The possible chambered tomb SY71 is a likely candidate, but this is only so on the grounds that very large stonework is evident rather than its actual recognizable morphological attributes.

Roundhouses. SY22A, 32A, 62, 150.

Megalithic/chamber tombs. SY16B, 71.

Standing stones. SY12, 36, 135.

Cairns. SY2, 3, 9, 10, 11, 16A, 17, 19, 20, 25, 26, 27, 28, 30, 37A, 44, 52, 53, 57, 67, 78, 79, 80, 81, 82, 84, 85,

99, 105, 106, 108, 110, 120, 121, 122, 127, 128, 129, 137, 138, 140, 141, 142, 145, 146.

Out of the total number of 45 cairns there are many that have dimensions in the region of 3 m, such as 16A, for example, but there are none that visibly display the architectural detail of the kerbed cairns of Fuday and Vatersay. A number are most likely field clearance cairns, such as SY19 and 20, which are located to one side of the good agricultural land to the south of the Sheader settlement. However, unlike Mingulay and Berneray, it is impossible on Sandray to separate out potential field cairns from cairns of other functions with certainty.

Conclusion

The lack of dramatic sea cliffs, a feature of all the other islands, probably gives the impression that Sandray is of less interest, especially when viewed from the sea. The long eastern beach is inviting but its bay is less formal and sheltering than those of Mingulay or Pabbay. Perhaps it is for these reasons that Sandray figures less as a port of call for tourist yachts. During our stay on the various islands, it was noticeable that Mingulay, Pabbay and even Berneray were continually visited by passing tourists and by those who took a day trip from Castlebay by motor launch, whereas Sandray appeared to be shunned by all except those who worked the sheep stock.

Yet neglected Sandray has a much more varied and interesting landscape, which, on more intimate knowledge gained by a long stay on the island, persuades me that Sandray is perhaps the most rewarding of all the islands.

When considering the future of archaeological research on the southern islands, Sandray must figure largely in any calculation. The lack of large nesting bird populations frees the island from any restrictions that could be encountered during the nesting seasons. The range of archaeological sites is comparable to the other islands and the sites at Sheader, which are continually threatened by coastal erosion, the seriously damaged galleried dun and the sites being revealed and damaged by the deflation and movement of the shell sand dunes on the east coast are all worthy of an intensive investigation. The presence of the loch and reed-bed area may be considered suitable for environmental research. Logistically, Sandray is very attractive, being close to Vatersay and Barra; the travelling distance is not only short from Castlebay, but sheltered for almost the entire journey. Personal experience has shown the island's rats to be clean, well-fed and friendly.

Pabbay Survey, 1992–1998

Introduction (Fig. 3.13)

A map of Pabbay shows an island shaped like a ragged rectangle that is around 3 km north–south and

1.7 km east–west, with the Rosinish headland jutting out to sea from one side, a cartographic clenched fist with an accusing finger pointing to the south-east. The Rosinish headland affords the only sheltered bay and beach at Bágh Bán even greater protection, ensuring its reputation as one of the better anchorages in the southern islands. The gentle glen that forms the backdrop valley to the bay and its beach is the natural location for any long-term settlement, as the clustered ruins of the 19th-century township indicate. In a north-westerly direction from the beach the wind has blown a mantle of shell sand over a wide area of the north-east corner of the island, which has developed into a lime-rich soil that encourages the growth of marram grass. The early 1880 OS map shows a wide swathe of apparently recently deposited or still mobile shell sand reaching from the beach to almost the furthest point on the north coast. Although material from the beach environs continues to be blown inland, almost all of the areas affected have long since stabilized and the area of exposed sand shown on the old map now corresponds to a landscape of the machair, with short, tightly knit grasses, mosses and other plants. This is a delightful area of the island much beloved by butterflies attracted to the abundant variety of wild flowering plants that grow there. Visually, the sharp division between the lime-rich shell sand soils and the rest of the island is a distinctive feature of the island, especially when seen on the approach into the bay from the sea.

The beach has provided enough shell sand for the formation of a large (up to 10% of the total land area) stabilized dune system inland from the foreshore. An 18th-century report on the islands (McKay 1980) describes Pabbay as being agriculturally spoilt because of the shell sand blowing over the settlement area and its surrounding arable fields. Whatever the configuration of the dune system, the environs of the bay, with its dry, grass-covered slopes to the north-east, provide a gentle landscape that is a natural focus for any settlement. With very few exceptions the rest

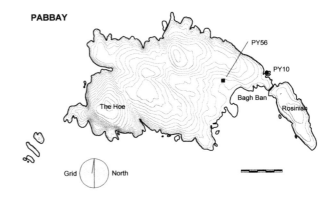

Figure 3.13 Pabbay, showing topography, place-names, and excavation sites.

of the island is an inhospitable combination of wet blanket peat and exposed wind-swept bedrock that accounts for around 80% of the land surface.

On Pabbay, like most of the other major islands, the basic bedrock of Lewisian gneiss is etched with a criss-crossed pattern of Palaeozoic basalt dykes, a rock more susceptible to erosion than the surrounding gneiss. This erosional differentiation results in one of the most distinctive features of the topography, the eroding basalt degrades and the dyke system is transformed into a series of straight, sheer-sided channels that also become an avenue for surface and bog water draining off the higher ground. A confluence of dykes at the heart of the island have produced one of Pabbay's notable landmarks, a small enclosed valley filled with wet peat soil, but sheltered enough to provide a suitable environment at one side for what can only be described as a small forest of scrub woodland. It is a dark place, silent and oppressive, out of the sun and away from the sounds of bird and seashore. Ben Buxton (1995) rightly describes it as 'a rather sinister place', and those who have lived on the island may also have felt the same for there are no indications of the valley being intensively used apart from occasional arable cultivation and the existence of a single small ring cairn of stones embedded in the soil (PY86).

A less 'sinister' place is an area of level grassy ground found to the south-west of the beach area. It is in a slight depression yet on higher ground than the settlement area in the bay and is consequently out of sight from there. As expected there appears to have been considerable activity here judging from the number of sites concentrated in the area. Most of the monuments, however, are not easily classified, being either just piles of stone or stone settings that have no apparent sense. In contrast the central area is occupied by a complex of enclosures with piled drystone walls standing up to 1.5 m high (PY53), and it is possibly the stone robbing to build these walls that may account for the muddled condition of the sites in the vicinity. These enclosures may be for a breed of small ponies reportedly allowed to graze on the island until sold as pit ponies. The area in general, although not convenient to the seashore, could be considered a preferred settlement area, but there is little structural evidence to indicate that anything other than agricultural activities took place here.

Another distinctive topographical feature of the island is the Rosinish headland extending south-east out to sea. The survey found it surprisingly little used in terms of monuments other than a few shelters, enclosures and the inevitable cairns. The headland is now a tidal island, but the 1880 OS map shows that it was originally connected to the main island via a natural arch, presumably an eroding dyke, which has since collapsed.

The general topography of the island is, apart from its rugged and in many areas barren nature, unremarkable. The highest point, The Hoe, stands at 171 m and the sea has yet to carve away its sides to produce the sort of spectacular cliffs that can be found on Berneray and Mingulay, although progress is being made in that direction with over 90% of the coastline being composed of rocky cliffs. There are some notable cliffs, especially around the north and the west coasts, but nothing to tempt the sea birds to colonize on a grand scale. One surprise held by the island, which can be approached on foot, but is better seen from the sea, is a great arch formed in the face of the northern cliffs by a massive rock fall that may be romantically described as a grand Romanesque blind arcade.

Royal Commission on the Ancient and Historical Monuments of Scotland National Sites and Monuments Record of Scotland

Only four monuments are listed in the National Monuments Record of Scotland archive. They are:

1. NL68NW1(NGR NL6128:8760). Dunan Ruadh (PY10). The remains of a broch or galleried dun. The RCAHMS (1928) reported that only a small portion of the south-western arc of the outer wall, incorporating a possible gallery, survived. The wall is 13 ft 6 in. wide and the mound of stone stands 7 ft high. The OS (1965) report adds that the wall is 4.6 m wide and they prefer the galleried dun classification.

2. NL68NW2 (NGR NL6072:8745). Cemetery, cross slabs, Pictish symbol stone, midden (PY55). J. Anderson (1897) describes the cemetery as a mound 10 ft high with a Pictish symbol stone lying on its flank, three incised cross slabs and reports that many human bones were found. He also describes a chapel measuring 31×14 ft built on the summit. A chapel is recorded on the island in 1549 by Munro, but Anderson's dimensions are impossible to fit on the point of this mound. This is illustrated by Wedderspoon's (1915) description estimating that there is space for only one grave at the summit. The OS (1965) visit resurrects the summit chapel with the description that all that remains of the chapel are some remnants of walling and scattered slabs on the slopes. The cross slabs are there but only two survive in place, the third is lying broken at the foot of the mound, and a shell midden was exposed in the lower east slope. From an illustration by Anderson, Mack (1997) classifies the symbol stone as a Pictish Class I stone with incised crescent and v-rod above a flower. A later cross is incised above.

3. NL68NW3 (NGR NL608:874). Middens, bones, bronze pin, pottery. Wedderspoon (1915) describes an area stretching east from the cemetery covered with numerous middens and hearths from which bones pottery and a bronze pin were recovered and sold at

Castlebay, Barra. The pin was dated as 7th century by Stevenson (1955).

4. NL68NW4 (NGR NL60:87). Worked flint. Flint flakes were found by A.A. Carmichael in 1872 among the fallen debris in what he thought of as an artificial recess within an immense natural cave. An accurate location for this cave cannot be gained from the description, the grid reference just locates the island as a whole. There are only two possible locations that could fit the description 'immense cave' known to the authors of the present survey. One is the great rock fall that resulted in the natural arch in the north coast cliff face. This is approachable on foot and there could have been some situation as described which has since been covered. The other is the natural dyke cave that existed across the neck of Rosinish headland at the time of Carmichael's visit. Nothing was found during the survey to add to the note of 1872.

The 1992–1998 survey

The survey of Pabbay began in 1992 and was continued by Roman Krivanek in 1995 and 1997. In 1998, while excavations of the broch PY10 were completed and the excavation of site PY56 was extended, the opportunity was taken to complete the photographic record of the island's sites. Some difficulty in pinning sites to their location points was experienced, especially in the desolate rocky landscape of the western side of the island, which accounts for the survey continuing over a three-yearly visiting period as sites were double-checked. The extra visits also provided the opportunity to draw more of the sites in detail to scale.

A total of 131 sites have been recorded of which 30 sites are within 50 m of the coastal edge. Only three sites (PY10, 54 and 55) have been previously reported in any detail (see RCAHMS above). Judging from the visual assessment given to each site during the survey, it would appear that almost all are of single-phase construction, although on excavation many may be found to have been reused or modified. Only two sites have been excavated on Pabbay, the Iron Age Atlantic roundhouse, Dunan Ruadh broch (PY10) and the late Bronze Age subterranean house (PY56).

Description and catalogue of the sites and monuments

PY1* (NL6161:8737) Cairn. *Location*: Coastal shelf on Rosinish peninsula. *Description*: Oval stone ring, 2.3 × 2 m, around 0.3 m high earthen mound. A larger circle of spaced stones, 4.6 × 5.6 m appears to have once been set around the perimeter of a much larger mound, but erosion has denuded much of the local area down to bedrock.

PY2 (NL6154:8732) Complex of shelters. *Location*: Shelf on Rosinish peninsula. *Description*: Two drystone shelters set side by side. Both shelters appear to

be constructed on top of, and possibly out of, some earlier structures that can now be seen only as shaped mounds partially obscured by the later buildings.

PY2a (NL6154:8732) Shelter. *Location*: As above. *Description*: Oval single cell, 3.5 × 2.5 m, with drystone walls slightly disarranged and no visible entrance.

PY2b (NL6154:8732) Shelter. *Location*: As above. *Description*: Circular single cell, 2.5 m diam., drystone walls and no visible entrance.

PY3 (NL6150:8730) Complex of shelters. *Location*: Backed on to a rocky crag face on a west-facing grassy plateau shelf of Rosinish peninsula. *Description*: Two square-shaped cojoined shelters, 6 × 3 m in total area. Their form is indistinct.

PY3a (NL6150:8730) Shelter. *Location*: As above. *Description*: Square, 3 × 3 m, single cell of spaced set stones.

PY3b (NL6150:8730) Shelter. *Location*: As above. *Description*: Rectangular, 3 × 2 m, single cell of larger stones in some disarray.

PY4 (NL6173:8697) Cairn. *Location*: On Rosinish peninsula exposed high point to west of cairns marked on the OS map. *Description*: Half-circle, 1 m diam., of stones and soil, probably the last remnants of a totally eroded cairn.

PY5* (NL6172:8691) Cairn. *Location*: On Rosinish peninsula. *Description*: Circular, 2 m diam., piles of stone standing 1.5 m high. *Note*: Marked on the OS map. Most likely modern.

PY6* (NL6173:8690) Cairn. As for PY5.

PY7* (NL6179:8706) Shieling. *Location*: Coastal cliff-top on Rosinish peninsula. *Description*: Subrectangular, 5 × 4 m, possibly internally subdivided, but collapsed stonework obscures definition. Built against and incorporating bedrock formations and against, but not including, a field wall through which an entrance has been opened into the shieling. Internal collapsed stonework may indicate subdivisions.

PY8* (NL6178:8710) Shelter. *Location*: Mid hill-slope shelf above coastal cliffs on Rosinish peninsula. *Description*: Subrectangular single cell, 3 × 2.5 m, with large blocks of stone up to 1.1 m in size, but tumbled stonework obscures true definition. *Note*: Could be a chamber tomb.

PY9 (NL6150:8735) Shelter. *Location*: Flat plateau ridge on Rosinish peninsula. *Description*: Only half-circle, 3 m diam., surviving of stone and earth walls of single cell set on slight mound. *Note*: Local erosion to bedrock.

PY10* (NL6128:8765) Atlantic roundhouse (broch Dùnan Ruadh). *Location*: On small north-east-facing coastal peninsula. *Description*: Excavated in 1996–97 (see Chapter 6). From the excavations came a range of Iron Age pottery fragments and considerable faunal remains and a 7th-century AD Pictish 'fist' pin from the upper deposits that indicates a long period of occupation from the Iron Age into the early mediaeval. When the excavation commenced only an arc of the main southern double outer ring-wall survived, with a small area of undisturbed internal occupational deposits protected within the arc. This is in contrast with the picture suggested by the 1st edition 6 in. OS map of 1880, which depicts a fully circular enclosure inside which a three-sided, subrectangular structure is situated with its open end to the east. No sign of this structure now exists or was evident at the time of excavation. The majority of the internal area as it would have been was bare unrelieved bedrock. A subrectangular shaped building is at odds with the known evidence for a circular broch structure, and consequently it is most likely to be a later construction of material stripped from the broch superstructure. The recovery of a 'fist' pin of Pictish date in a deposit of fish bones dumped over the broch main wall indicates a late occupation of the broch at a time when the superstructure was in a degraded state. Mediaeval pottery has also been recovered from the upper levels, and it is possible that the subrectangular building relates to this period. However, although some late occupation more than likely did occur on the remnants of the broch, it is even more likely that this particular illustrated structure is an early modern shelter or shieling that has been swept away by storms in the past hundred years.

Brochs and duns are not usually built in what may be considered preferred settlement locations and PY10 is no exception, being sited out on an exposed northern coastal promontory of the island. Whether this is the only occupation site for the whole of the island's population during the late Iron Age or whether there are other sites to be found buried in the dunes as on Mingulay (MY384), or under the peat, cannot yet be ascertained.

PY11 (NL6088:8778) Cairn. *Location*: Rocky hilltop above sand dunes. *Description*: Circular, 1.5 m diam., pile of stones. *Note*: Prominent exposed position and subject to active erosion.

PY12* (NL6033:8817) Cairn. *Location*: Coastal hill-slope shelf. *Description*: Disturbed pile of stones on 2 m diam. Mound.

PY13 (NL6025:8814) Cairn. *Location*: Mid hill-slope shelf. *Description*: Irregular circular, 2 m diam., collection of stone, some up to 1 m in size, that may be a disturbed cist cairn. *Note*: Local erosion to bedrock.

PY14* (NL6036:8824) Cairn. *Location*: Shelf on slope of northern coastal peninsula. *Description*: Circular disarranged stone ring, 1.7 m diam. *Note*: Embedded in soil, but local erosion to bedrock. Adjacent scattered natural stone.

PY15 (NL6036:8791) Cairn. *Location* Upper plateau at mouth of dyke. *Description*: Square, 2 × 1 m, slightly mounded platform area with set stones on leading edge.

PY16 (NL6031:8793) Complex of cairn and enclosure. *Location*: Upper hill-slope. *Description*: Possible circular cairn and oval enclosure wall.

PY16a (NL6031:8793) Cairn. *Location*: As above. *Description*: Circular, 1.5 m diam., indistinct eroded mound.

PY16b (NL6031:8793) Enclosure. *Location*: As above. *Description*: Oval, 6 × 4.5 m, of spaced stones forming possible enclosure.

PY17* (NL6018:8810) Shieling complex. *Location*: Lower coastal hill-slope shelf. *Description*: Group of shelters and cairns set within the perimeter of a subrectangular enclosure, 55 × 25 m, marked by piled, much-disarranged stone. All the components of the group are in a degraded state, with their structural stonework displaced and in places absent.

PY17a* (NL6018:8810) Shelter. *Location*: As above. *Description*: Circular stone ring, 5 m diam., greatly disturbed. May actually be a twin cell structure but stonework is indistinct.

PY17b* (NL6018:8810) Shelter. *Location*: As above. *Description*: Rectangular single cell, 8 × 5 m, with possible internal structures.

PY17c* (NL6018:8810) Cairn. (clearance) *Location*: As above. *Description*: 2 m diam. cluster of stones.

PY17d* (NL6018:8810) Cairn. (clearance) *Location*: As above. *Description*: Square pile of stones, 3 × 3 m.

PY17e* (NL6018:8810) Enclosure. *Location*: As above. *Description*: Indistinct subrectangular enclosure, c. 55 × 25 m, of piled and set stone with many gaps.

PY18* (NL5989:8797) Cairn. *Location*: Coastal hill-slope shelf. *Description*: Circular stone ring, 1.7 m diam., denuded cairn base. *Note*: Exposed place, eroded.

PY19* (NL5983:8791) Shieling. *Location*: Coastal shelf. *Description*: Subrectangular single cell, 4 × 2.7 m, built with substantial, well embedded, stone blocks in 0.5–0.6 m range. No entrance visible. *Note*: Severe active erosion has affected the structure on the north and east sides.

PY20* (NL5944:8800) Cairn. *Location*: Coastal shelf. *Description*: Oval mass of stone, 2.6 × 2.2 m, eroded to bedrock at edges. *Note*: Covered by heather.

PY21* (NL5941:8795) Shieling. *Location*: Valley floor. *Description*: Oval single cell, 5.5 × 4 m, of piled stone walls on dry platform. *Note*: Onset of erosion in patches to bedrock.

PY22* (NL5939:8806) Cairn. *Location*: Back of small rocky northern coastal peninsula. *Description*: Oval, 2.8 × 2.6 m, collection of stones on 0.60 m high mound. *Note*: Some displacement.

PY23* (NL5929:8806) Cairn. *Location*: Coastal bench. *Description*: Oval, 3.2 × 2.6.m, open ring of stones up to 0.6 m in size, on platform or mound 0.3 m high. *Note*: Some erosion.

PY24 (NL5932:8791) Shelter. *Location*: High plateau. *Description*: Oval, 3.5 × 2 m, of piled and set stone, 0.4–0.5 m size range, apparently without entrance, but with suggestion of central dividing wall.

PY25 (NL5947:8780) Shelter. *Location*: Shelf on upper hill-slope. *Description*: Circular single cell, 4 m diam., stone ring-wall difficult to determine structure due to coverage by rank heather.

PY26* (NL5949:8775) Shelter. *Location*: Coastal shelf overlooking exit gorge of western sea dyke Sloch Glansich. *Description*: Circular single cell, 2 m diam., stone ring of 0.2–0.6 m blocks with no visible entrance. *Note*: Covered by heather, but eroding out on west side.

PY27 (NL5961:8759) Peat dryer. *Location*: Mid hill-slope shelf. *Description*: Oval, 4.5 × 2.5 m, grassy flat-topped mound with widely spaced stone blocks of 0.5–1 m size range around perimeter. *Note*: An unexpected monument for Pabbay, but it is within the parameters of comparable peat dryers found on Mingulay.

PY28 (NL5956:8755) Shelter. *Location*: Hill-slope shelf. *Description*: Circular single cell, 2 m diam., stone ring-wall partly displaced. *Note*: Covered by heather.

PY29 (NL5954:8751) Shelter. *Location*: Shelf above dyke. *Description*: Half-circle, 5 m diam., of widely spaced set stones forming a single cell butted against crag face. *Note*: Possibly another indistinct circular feature close by.

PY30* (NL5934:8762) Boat-shaped stone setting. *Location*: Mid hill-slope bench of An Cearcall. *Description*: Boat shape, 5 × 2 m, outlined by large rock slabs along sides to unusually massed jumble of very large rock slabs at ?prow end. Just to the front of the southern pointed ?prow end is a massive slab that would serve well as a cap stone. *Note*: Could be a collapsed and disturbed chamber tomb.

PY31* (NL5933:8759) Cairn. *Location*: As PY30 above. *Description*: Small group placed stone, 0.5 m diam., on mound 0.5 m high. *Note*: Soil eroding from around stonework.

PY32 (NL5922:8733) Shelter. *Location*: Mid hill-slope shelf of The Hoe. *Description*. Subrectangular, 3 × 1.5 m, mass of collapsed stonework. *Note*: Could be a collapsed chamber tomb.

PY33 (NL5924:8731) Shelter. *Location*: Mid hill-slope between crags on The Hoe. *Description*: Circular, 5 m diam., single cell of drystone walling in a state of disarray.

PY34* (NL5913:8716) Shieling complex. *Location*: Coastal bench at base of hill-slope from The Hoe. *Description*: A mass of collapsed stonework, 11 × 7 m in area, but in which several shelter structures can be seen. *Note*: The site is difficult to approach and is in an exposed position liable to erosion.

PY34a* (NL5913:8716) Shelter. *Location*: As above. *Description*: Circular single cell, diam. 4 m, of large set slabs.

PY34b* (NL5913:8716) Shelter. *Location*: As above. *Description*: Oval single cell, 6 × 4 m, of large set slabs and piled stone, which may be more extensive, but

collapsed stonework obscures a large part of its possible floor area.

PY34c* (NL5913:8716) Shelter. *Location*: As above. *Description*: Possibly circular, diam. 3 m, single cell but largely collapsed.

PY35* (NL5923:8704) Shelter. *Location*: Coastal bench at base of The Hoe hill-slope. *Description*: Oval single cell, 3 × 2 m, of single stone foundation linking large natural rock fall boulders.

PY36* (NL5927:8699) Shelter. *Location*: Coastal bench at base of The Hoe hill-slope. *Description*: Circular single cell, diam. 2.2 m, using large 0.8–0.9 m, size blocks.

PY37 (NL5939:8720) Cairn. *Location*: The Hoe hill-top. *Description*: Circular, diam. 1 m, grassy mound with half circle of stones around western edge.

PY38 (NL6002:8709) Shelter. *Location*: Exposed hill-slope. *Description*: Circular, diam. 2 m, stone ring half-eroded away on to bedrock.

PY39 (NL6063:8724) Cairn. *Location*: Small hillock on edge of flat area. *Description*: Circular, diam. 1.5 m, low mound with some set stones on perimeter.

PY40 (NL6055:8716) Cairn. *Location*: Flat area on lower south-east slope to Bgh Bn. *Description*: Circular, diam. 1.2 m, low mound with some scattered stones.

PY41 (NL6055:8690) Cairn. *Location*: Exposed coastal shelf central Rubh' a' Charnain. *Description*: Oval, 2 × 1.9 m, open ring of large rocks in 0.7–0.8 m range.

PY42 (NL6055:8694) Shelter. *Location*: Self on slope south to Rubh' a' Charnain peninsula. *Description*: Square, 2 × 2 m, platform with stones set on two sides, south and west, with some collapsed jumble. *Note*: Between two streams. Erosion down to bedrock advancing.

PY43* (NL6052:8692) Shelter. *Location*: South facing coast bench on slope to Rubh' a' Charnain. *Description*: Oval, 3 × 2.3 m, partially collapsed circle of large stones up to 0.8 m in size. *Note*: Active erosion to bedrock in and around structure.

PY44* (NL6038:8685) Shelter. *Location*: Inside dyke on coast edge. *Description*: Oval, 2.7 × 2.5 m, single cell single set stone ring-wall with much other scattered stonework. *Note*: Covered by heather.

PY45* (NL6035:8697) Cairn. *Location*: Upper coastal shelf on south slope. *Description*: circular, diam. 3 m, mound with scattered stones. *Note*: Covered by heather.

PY46 (NL6038:8716) Well. *Location*: On slope inside wet dyke. *Description*: Rectangular single cell, 3.2 × 2.1 m, drystone box with three visible standing courses. This well or water catchment box is constructed on the lower slope of a dyke channel in a position where it can best accumulate the rain water run off from up-slope. The bottoms of these dyke channels always contain some running water even in summer, as they act as drains for the water-logged peat and blanket bog reservoirs that occupy the high ground of the island.

PY47 (NL6053:8720) Shelter. *Location*: Valley. *Description*: Subrectangular, 3.7 × 1.5 m, indistinct structure that appears to have one clear long and one short side of piled stonework with the suggestion of several inner divisions that could be no more than collapsed material. *Note*: Could be a peat dryer.

PY48 (NL6055:8720) Cairn. *Location*: On rocky knoll in valley. *Description*: Collection of assorted stones, 3.1 × 2.6 m, maximum size 1.15 m.

PY49 (NL6055:8722) Complex of shelter and platform. *Location*: Valley. *Description*: Circular mass of stonework, presumably mostly collapsed and disarranged, set on platform. Stone has most likely been robbed to construct the modern enclosures PY53 that are central to the valley.

PY49a (NL6055:8722) Shelter. *Location*: As above. *Description*: Circular, 4 m diam., mass of stonework suggesting a possible ring-wall with much disarranged material. *Note*: Could have been a roundhouse. Active erosion.

PY49b (NL6055:8722) Platform. *Location*: As above. *Description*: Possibly oval, 7.5 × 4 m, severely eroded.

PY50 (NL6058:8721) Complex of shelter and cairn. *Location*: Valley. *Description*: Circular single cell built next to an ?older mound of earth and stone.

PY50a (NL6058:8721) Shelter. *Location* As above. *Description*: Circular, diam. 1.5 m, single cell made with flat stones up 0.5 m in size.

PY50b (NL6058:8721) Cairn. *Location* As above. *Description*: Circular mound, 2 m diam., of stone and earth.

PY51 (NL6053:8726) Cairn. *Location*: Inside dyke. *Description*: Circular, diam. 1.2 m, low mound with half circle of set stones on perimeter to south. Interior hollow.

PY52* (NL5952:8704) Cairn. *Location*: Mid southeast hill-slope of The Hoe. On prominence. *Description*: Egg-shaped oval mound, 4.6 × 3 m, with stone ring 2.4 × 2 m at broad south end.

PY53 (NL6057:8723) Enclosures. *Location*: Valley floor. *Description*: Three irregular curvilinear cojoining enclosures, total area 30 × 35 m, with drystone walls standing 1.5 m high. *Note*: Reportedly built for breeding pit ponies. Enclosure (a) 25 × 15 m. Enclosure (b) 20 × 20 m. Enclosure (c) 25 × 20 m.

PY54 (NL6069:8748) Settlement complex. *Location*: Valley floor behind the beach to Bágh Bán bay on wind blown sand soils. *Description*: Township area, 80 × 70 m, includes blackhouses, outhouses, enclosures and burial ground. Identification of structures in the township core is complicated by post-abandonment modification and reuse, mainly for sheep control and dipping. The settlement and its area is worthy of a future detailed and accurate survey

Although the island became uninhabited in 1912 it was continuously used thereafter for sheep grazing and the settlement buildings with its enclosures became the natural centre at which to gather the flock together when necessary. Some of the house shells were subdivided or modified for various reasons connected with the flock and its handling. Additionally there are a number of wooden sheep pens erected to the south of the settlement. A full description of this settlement is to be published in SEARCH volume 6.

PY54a (NL6069:8748) Blackhouse. *Location*: As above. *Description*: Rectangular, 8 × 5 m, apparently unimproved blackhouse single cell with drystone walls 1.5 m wide and no visible fireplace or entrance. Orientated east to west. Unidentifiable internal structure at east end. East end appears to have been remodelled.

PY54b (NL6069:8748) Barn. *Location*: As above. *Description*: Square, 6 × 6 m, barn single cell with thick drystone walls and entrance to east. May originally have been a blackhouse slighted by later enclosure wall.

PY54c (NL6069:8748) Blackhouse. *Location*: As above. *Description*: Rectangular, 8 × 5 m, unimproved double cell blackhouse of drystone walls with internal division and thickening of inner southwest wall, which may be a later development.

PY54d (NL6069:8748) Blackhouse. *Location*: As above. *Description*: Rectangular, 13 × 6 m, single-cell unimproved blackhouse of drystone construction with entrance to south.

PY54e (NL6069:8748) Blackhouse. *Location*: As above. *Description*: Rectangular, 9 × 4.5 m, single-cell unimproved blackhouse of drystone construction, original south door blocked and new one opened in east end wall.

PY54f (NL6069:8748) Barn. *Location*: As above. *Description*: Rectangular, 4 × 3 m, two-cell barn of drystone construction with north entrance and narrow room partition wall foundation east–west.

PY54g (NL6069:8748) Barn. *Location*: As above. *Description*: Rounded square, 3 × 3 m, single-cell barn of drystone construction, entrance to the east. Appears to be an L-shaped addition butted on to surrounding walls.

PY54h (NL6069:8748) House, modern. *Location*: As above. *Description*: Rectangular, 12 × 5.5 m, single-cell modern house with thin sharp-cornered walls, entrance to east flanked by glazed windows, also a pair of glazed windows to the west, and with a fireplace and chimney built into each gable wall, north and south. Building stone is quarried, dressed and fixed with cement mortar. A concrete porch step to front entrance. The timber frame floor has long since rotted away, but the slots for roof joist timbers are still visible and the chimney pots are still in place. Buxton (1995) gives the name of the builder as Donald MacAulay of Castlebay, Barra, who constructed it, probably in the 1890s, for one of the Uist families that had replaced the old Pabbay population in the mid-19th century.

PY54i (NL6069:8748) Barn. *Location*: As above. *Description*: Square, 3 × 3 m, single-cell drystone built barn with entrance to north-east tacked on to the northern edge of the 'infield' enclosure system.

PY54j (NL6069:8748) Blackhouse. *Location*: As above. *Description*: Rectangular, 12 × 7 m, unimproved single-cell drystone blackhouse greatly modified in conjunction with the formation of the central enclosure PY54o.

PY54k (NL6069:8748) Sheep dip. *Location*: As above. *Description*: Square, 4 × 4 m, single-cell modern sheep-dip.

PY54l (NL6069:8748) Barn. *Location*: As above. *Description*: Rectangular, 6 × 4 m, single-cell drystone barn possibly a remnant of an original blackhouse.

PY54m (NL6069:8748) Sheep dip. *Location*: As above. *Description*: Rectangular, 13 × 6 m, single cell modern sheep dip.

PY54n (NL6069:8748) Sheep dip. *Location*: As above. *Description*: Rectangular, 8 × 4 m, modern single-cell sheep dip continuation of k.

PY54o (NL6069:8748) Enclosure. *Location*: As above. *Description*: Triangular, 20 × 17 m, modern late addition drystone enclosure appears to be connected with the sheep dips and building j.

PY54p (NL6069:8748) Enclosure. *Location*: As above. *Description*: Boot-shaped, 40 × 30 m, drystone-walled enclosure.

PY54q (NL6069:8748) Enclosure. *Location*: As above. *Description*: Area between settlement and rocky crags to west.

PY54r (NL6069:8748) Enclosure. *Location*: As above. *Description*: Not clearly defined as only a short length appears to survive, but an enclosure around the burial mound PY55 could be expected.

PY54s (NL6069:8748) Enclosure. *Location*: As above. *Description*: Indistinct, 30 × 20 m, walled enclosure.

PY54t (NL6069:8748) Enclosure. *Location*: As above. *Description*: Irregular-shaped, 40 × 25 m, drystone-walled enclosure between village and stream to south.

PY55 (NL6074:8750) Burial ground. *Location*: As above. *Description*: Oval shape, c. 15 m diam., artificially heightened natural sand to form a steep sided burial mound. Like the burial mound on Berneray it appears to be capped with beach cobbles and several stone grave markers are still in place, one with a cross pecked on one face. The well-known Pabbay symbol stone lies at the base of the mound where it was dropped after being removed from its position on the mound. No doubt it proved too heavy to completely carry away. The Pictish symbols pecked on to its surface have become weathered and are only visible with the best of oblique lighting. The inscription consists of a 'moon' crescent and V-rod over the so-called flower, all of which clearly places it as a Class I inscribed stone that could date from around the 7th century AD (Allen and Anderson 1993). The stone has either been reused as a later grave marker or converted in true Christian fashion by incising a cross above the Pictish symbols.

There is little evidence, in the form of grave furniture, for example, to be seen on the site of the cemetery (PY55) to indicate that the mound had been used for burial rites during the modern period. How frequently the priest from Barra visited the island is not clear, but there was some connection with Craigston church at least for a while in the early 19th century through Lachlan MacNeil of Pabbay, who paid an annual fee for retaining a seat there (Allen and Anderson 1993) and the well-used cemetery on Mingulay would also have been within easy reach from Pabbay.

PY56 (NL6076:8758) Earth-house. *Location*: In the sand dunes on north side of valley. *Description*: A trench was put across the site to find the contemporary land surface, which was expected to be at only a few centimetres under the turf, but after a day's excavation it was found at a depth of over 1 m (see excavation report below, p. 271). The site was subsequently opened further and excavations continued. The site is a multicellular house of interconnected circular and oval cells excavated into the sand dunes to a depth of over 1 m. A very few fragments of coarse, friable handmade late Bronze Age pottery and animal bone were recovered. The sunken levels of the building were back-filled with compacted sand to conserve the structure, but enough of the site was left visible and understandable in outline for anyone wishing to view the monument.

PY57 (NL6074:8757) Setting. *Location*: As above. *Description*: Scattered surface stones, diam. 3.5 m.

PY58 (NL6078:8757) Setting. *Location*: As above. *Description*: Surface stones, diam. 5 m, possibly part of sunken house.

PY59 (NL6078:8756) Cairn. *Location*: As above. *Description*: Circular pile of stones, diam. 1 m.

PY60 (NL6079:8755) Setting. *Location*: As above. *Description*: Surface stones, diam. 2.5 m, could be part of earth-house.

PY61 (NL6078:8756) Earth-house. *Location*: As above. *Description*: Arc of stones, diam. 4.5 m, may be cell of earth-house that includes 58, 59, 60 and 64.

PY62 (NL6079:8752) Earth-house. *Location*: As above. *Description*: An oval low mound with several arcs of stone that may represent the surface evidence of an earth-house.

PY63 (NL6078:8754) Cairn. *Location*: As above. *Description*: Pile of stones, 1.5 m diam., a little removed to the east from the 61 group.

PY64 (NL6077:8756) Mound. *Location*: As above. *Description*: Oval 9 × 2.5 m grassy mound.

PY65 (NL6074:8760) Setting. *Location*: As above. *Description*: Wide scatter, over 10 m area, of stones 0.2–0.7 m range. Possibly a further earth-house.

PY66 (NL6076:8759) Setting. *Location*: As above. *Description*: Thin scatter, 2.5 m in area, may belong to 61.

PY67 (NL6075:8751) Cairn. *Location*: As above. *Description*: Scatter of stones on small mound, 2 m diam., which may indicate a further earth-house, although it is located close to the burial mound and stream which also separates it from the other potential earth-house sites.

PY68 (NL6075:8753) Cairn. *Location*: As above. *Description*: Concentration of stones on mound, 3 m diam., on flat valley floor next to stream, but presumably on top of deep-dune sand deposit.

PY69 (NL6090:8773) Shelter. *Location*: Exposed rocky plateau to north of and above dunes. *Description*: Circular, diam. 1 m, single cell, but in state of collapse.

PY70 (NL6087:8771) Cairn. *Location*: Exposed rock plateau above dunes. *Description*: 1 m diam. Pile of a few stones.

PY71 (NL6034:8786) Enclosure. *Location*: Hill top plateau. *Description*: Broad arc of a few spaced stones, 8 × 4 m, butted to crag face form the suggestion of an enclosure.

PY72* (NL6032:8828) Shelter. *Location*: North-facing coastal shelf on mid hill-slope, bedrock. *Description*: Arc, diam. 1.5 m, of piled stones forming single cell against crag face.

PY73* (NL6015:8820) Cairn. *Location*: Northern lower hill-slope coastal bare shelf in prominent position. *Description*: Circular, diam. 1 m, small cairn of piled stone.

PY74 (NL6032:8787) Cairn. *Location*: Hill-top at end of dyke. *Description*: Surviving arc of stone ring, diam. 1 m, of small, 0.1–0.3 m range stones. *Note*: Area severely eroded down to bedrock.

PY75 (NL6031:8778) Cairn. *Location*: Hill-top wet hollow plateau. *Description*: Circular mound, diam. 4 m, of earth and stones 1 m high. *Note*: Erosion to bedrock on east side.

PY76 (NL6011:8796) Shelter. *Location*: North facing shelf mid hill-slope. *Description*: Oval, 5 × 2 m, single cell on platform but with only a few stone blocks in place. *Note*: Covered by heather.

PY77 (NL6017:8779) Shelter. *Location*: On shelf of west-facing slope into dyke. *Description*: Rectangular, 2.5 × 2 m, single-cell closely set stones on slight platform.

PY78 (NL6054:8757) Cairn. *Location*: High on slope inside dyke. *Description*: Circular, diam. 2 m, flat-topped mound with a few stones and some massive metre-sized blocks that may be natural fallen debris.

PY79 (NL6049:8761) Cairn. *Location*: High shelf on slope above dyke. *Description*: Oval, 3 × 2 m, stone ring on slight mound.

PY80 (NL6041:8758) Shieling complex. *Location*: Inside dyke. *Description*: Arc of drystone walling butted to rock face of dyke forms animal pen with a small rectangular single-cell shelter butted to dyke face and east wall of pen.

PY80a (NL6041:8758) Enclosure. *Location*: As above. *Description*: Arc, diam. 4 m, of drystone walling, several courses, 0.4–0.7 m, high, with an entrance to south is butted to the north dyke rock face.

PY80b (NL6041:8758) Shelter. *Location*: As above. *Description*: Rectangular, 3 × 1.5 m, rectangular drystone single cell standing several courses high up to 0.7 m and butted to the dyke rock face to the north and the enclosure wall to the west. *Note*: No entrance provided.

PY81 (NL6038:8759) Cairn. *Location*: High on slope inside dyke. *Description*: Subrectangular, 5 × 2 m, mounded platform with some scattered stone and further 1.5 m circular mound at leading edge.

PY82 (NL5983:6078) Cairn. *Location*: High exposed plateau. *Description*: Oval, diam. 2.2 m, ring of spaced stones around slight mound. *Note*: Whole area subject to erosion down to bedrock.

PY83 (NL5986:8783) Shelter. *Location*: High plateau shelf. *Description*: Oval, 3 × 2 m, single cell of piled stone walls much dispersed. Stones up to 0.70 m in size.

PY84 (NL5940:8787) Shelter. *Location*: Valley floor on bare rock shelf east of Allanish. *Description*: Oval, 5.5 × 3 m single-cell ring of loose stones with blocks up to 1 m in size. *Note*: Subject to erosion. Covered by heather.

PY85 (NL6022:8739) Cairn. *Location*: Prominent position on bare rock shelf above central valley to north. *Description*: Circular, diam. 1.2 m, mound with some stone partly eroded out. *Note*: Covered by heather.

PY86 (NL6014:8755) Cairn. *Location*: Side of central valley between converging dyke streams. *Description*: Circular, diam. 2 m, stone ring.

PY87 (NL5988:8749) Cairn. *Location*: Hill-top plateau. *Description*: Oval, 2 × 1.5 m, stone ring eroding on to bedrock.

PY88 (NL5957:8775) Complex of shelters and enclosure. *Location*: On stepped bench on slope down to valley at Allanish with dyke to Sloc Glansich steeply to the south. *Description*: Long thin oval enclosure marked by spaced set stones butted to rock crag face. Also butted to crag face are three single-cell shelters spaced apart within the enclosure. *Note*: Covered by heather.

PY88a (NL5957:8775) Shelter. *Location*: As above. *Description*: Subrectangular, 3 × 2 m, single cell of piled stones with entrance to north.

PY88b (NL5957:8775) Shelter. *Location*: As above. *Description*: Subrectangular, 3 × 2 m, single cell of piled stones using convenient fallen boulders in the construction.

PY88c (NL5957:8775) Shelter. *Location*: As above. *Description*: Subrectangular, 2.5 × 1.5 m, single cell of piled stone.

PY88d (NL5957:8775) Enclosure. *Location*: As above. *Description*: Elongated arc of set stones, 30 × 8 m, forms enclosure butted to crag rock face.

PY89 (NL5977:8749) Shieling. *Location*: High rocky shelf. *Description*: Oval, 6 × 5 m, single cell with earth and stone walls, but few stones are in place, most being scattered by erosion of the wall core. Entrance not visible. *Note*: Subject to erosion.

PY90 (NL5976:8746) Shieling. *Location*: High bench on slope. *Description*: Subrectangular, 5.5 × 4 m, single cell with substantial piled-stone walls, although erosion has displaced large parts. No entrance is visible.

PY91 (NL5976:8744) Shelter. *Location*: Prominent place on high bench of slope. *Description*: Oval, diam. 3.5 m, circle of large-spaced stone blocks some standing 0.8 m high.

PY92* (NL5941:8778) Cairn. *Location*: Side of valley floor above sea cliffs of Sloch Glansich inlet. *Description*: Ovoid, diam. 1.5 m, open stone ring against fallen rock.

PY93 (NL5959:8740) Boat-shaped stone setting. *Location*: Inside dyke at highest elevation. *Description*: Boat-shaped oval, 5 × 2 m, slight mound with some edging stones.

PY94 (NL5941:8716) Cairn. *Location*: Hill-top The Hoe on bedrock. *Description*: Circular mound, diam. 3 m, of earth and stone. *Note*: Covered by heather.

PY95 (NL5936:8728) Cairn. *Location*: Summit of The Hoe, 171 m, on bedrock. *Description*: Circular, diam. 0.8 m, stone pile.

PY96 (NL5984:8721) Shelter. *Location*: Mid hill-slope shelf plateau on bedrock. *Description*: Subrectangular, 2.5 × 2.5 m, single cell of piled stone walls, 0.4–0.70 m range, mostly collapsed.

PY97 (NL5983:8751) Shelter. *Location*: At head of dyke. *Description*: Possibly originally a square, 3 × 3 m, drystone single-cell structure, but is now in a state of collapse.

PY98 (NL6000:8743) Cairn. *Location*: East upper-slope denuded plateau. *Description*: Circular mound, diam. 1.2 m, edged with stone, many also scattered. *Note*: Covered by heather and subject to erosion.

PY99 (NL6004:8739) Cairn. *Location*: East upper-slope plateau. *Description*: Slight circular mound, diam. 1.5 m, with scattered stones.

PY100 (NL6040:8731) Shelter. *Location*: Inside dyke to central valley. *Description*: Probably a square, 1.5 × 1.5 m, single cell edged by stones, but the southern side has eroded out on to bedrock. *Note:* Covered with heather.

PY101 (NL6040:8734) Shelter. *Location*: Inside dyke to central valley. *Description*: Subrectangular, 2.5 × 2 m, single-cell possible shelter on platform against the dyke rock wall. Stones scattered. *Note*: Covered by heather.

PY102 (NL6038:8730) Shelter. *Location*: Inside dyke. *Description*: Circular, diam. 1.2 m, single cell with drystone walls standing 0.4 m high on mound. *Note*: Covered by heather.

PY103 (NL5999:8731) Cairn. *Location*: High plateau. *Description*: Rounded square, 2 × 2 m, mound with some edge stones in place, others scattered. *Note*: Subject to erosion.

PY104 (NL5983:8735) Cairn. *Location*: Denuded hill-top. *Description*: Circular, diam. 2 m, mound with scattered stones. *Note*: Subject to erosion.

PY105 (NL6012:8714) Shelter. *Location*: Rocky plateau slope. *Description*: Circular stone setting, diam. 3.5 m, utilizing natural boulders. *Note.* Covered by heather and subject to erosion.

PY106 (NL6047:8701) Boat-shaped stone setting. *Location*: Rocky plateau on lower slopes. *Description*: Pointed ovoid slightly mounded, 3.5 × 1.3 m, with edging stones. Mass of stone at prow-pointed end similar to PY30. *Note*: Subject to severe erosion that may have produced the apparent boat shape by the removal of material and resultant stone displacement.

PY107 (NL6053:8701) Cairn. *Location*: Rocky plateau. *Description*: Circular, diam. 2 m, pile of stone with oval platform at north end. *Note*: Subject to severe erosion.

PY108 (NL6052:8699) Shelter. *Location*: On south slope denuded shelf above dyke. *Description*: Circular, diam. 3 m, spaced stone ring eroding out on to bedrock. *Note*: Covered by heather.

PY109* (NL6057:8701) Shelter. *Location*: Inside dyke. *Description*: Arc of piled stones, 2 × 1.5 m, standing 0.80 m high forming single cell butted against rock face. *Note*: Inner platform grassed.

PY110 (NL6045:8726) Cairn. *Location*: Denuded plateau between dykes. *Description*: Circular, diam. 1.5 m, stone ring. *Note*: Covered by heather, but stone eroding out on to bedrock.

PY111 (NL6053:8725) Complex of shelters *Location*: Prominence at side of valley floor. *Description*: Two cojoining circular shelters of drystone walling. Some scattering.

PY111a (NL6053:8725) Shelter. *Location*: As above. *Description*: Circular, diam. 3 m, single-cell stone ring wall partly collapsed with no observable entrance.

PY111b (NL6053:8725) Shelter. *Location*: As above. *Description*: Oval, 4 × 3 m, single-cell drystone ring wall much collapsed.

PY112 (NL6062:8727) Cairn. *Location*: Plateau at side of valley floor. *Description*: Circular, diam. 1.8 m, open stone ring, 0.5–0.7 m size range, of closely set stone on slight mound.

PY113 (NL6060:8725) Cairn. (clearance) *Location*: Valley floor. *Description*: Circular pile of stone, diam. 1.5 m.

PY114 (NL6059:8724) Cairn. (clearance) *Location*: Valley floor. *Description*: Circular pile of stone, diam. 1.4 m.

PY115 (NL6059:8727) Shelter. *Location*: Valley floor. *Description*: Circular, diam. 2 m, spaced stone ring close to enclosure wall across valley.

PY116* (NL6164:8728) Cairn. *Location* Coastal shelf on Rosinish peninsula north-east facing. *Description* Circular, diam. 1.8 m, spaced stone ring.

PY117 (NL6020:8787) Cairn. *Location*: Denuded hill-top. *Description*: Circular, diam. 1 m, pile of stones.

PY118 (NL5987:8752) Cairn. *Location*: High plateau shelf. *Description*: Circular, diam. 0.9 m, pile of stones.

PY119 (NL6090:8772) Cairn. *Location*: Rocky shelf above dunes. *Description*: Circular, diam. 1 m, pile of stones.

PY120 (NL6095:8758) Stone setting. *Location*: High on side of valley in sand dunes. *Description*: Scattered stones, diam. 2 m area, which may indicate sunken feature.

PY121 (NL6118:8758) Well. *Location*: On high slope of wet peat bog at edge of rock exposure. *Description*: Known only from the 1st edition OS map, which indicates a well on the track leading to Dùnan Ruadh broch just before it reaches the final rise out of the bay. This site was not located in the survey.

PY122* (NL6081:8717) Fish-salting box. *Location*: Rocky foreshore. *Description*: Square concrete fish-salting box. *Note*: Natural landing place west of Sumula.

Landscape period summaries

The early modern and modern landscape (Fig. 3.14)
The benign landscape of the bay area unquestionably provides the best settlement habitat for the island's community at any period of its history. The early modern and modern settlement is in keeping with the limited size and topography of the island, being focused into a tiny village of tightly clustered build-ings (PY54). Apart from numerous shelters and a few enclosures of assumed recent date almost all of the post-mediaeval to modern structural elements in the landscape are concentrated in the bay area.

The settlement. PY54.

Shelters. PY2A + B, 3A + B, 8 9, 17A + B, 24, 25, 26, 28, 29, 32, 33, 35, 36, 38, 42, 43, 44, 47, 49A, 50A, 69, 72, 76, 77, 83, 84, 88A + B + C, 91, 96, 97, 100, 101, 102, 105, 108, 109, 111A + B, 115.
The 44 shelters recorded by the survey display a range of sizes, forms and possibly a variety of functions and ages are also represented. As with almost all of the sites surveyed, the shelters can be divided into various types.

Shielings. PY7, 19, 21, 34A + B + C, 80, 89, 90.

Peat dryers. PY27.

Wells. PY46, 121.

Salt box. PY122.

Enclosures and walled land divisions. PY17, 53, 54 O-T, 80, 71.
The Pabbay landscape, like most of the other main islands, is divided into blocks of land based on a system of long-distance field walls that commonly use

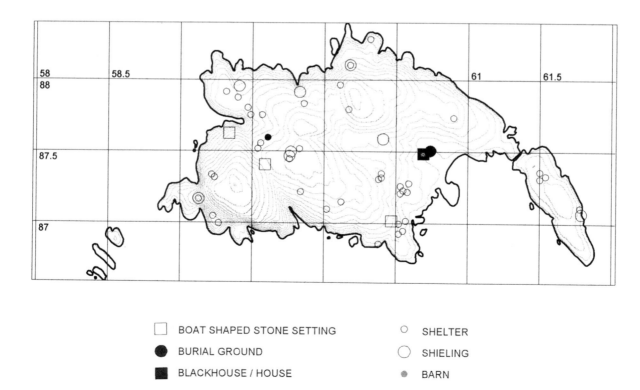

Figure 3.14 Pabbay, showing the location of modern and mediaeval monuments.

LEGEND:
- □ BOAT SHAPED STONE SETTING
- ● BURIAL GROUND
- ■ BLACKHOUSE / HOUSE
- ○ SHELTER
- ○ SHIELING
- • BARN

the natural dyke troughs that run in straight lines criss-crossing the island. Other smaller enclosures are created around the island using short stretches of wall between natural rock formations. Quite often they appear to make little functional sense. Some may be the remnants of old enclosures and this certainly may be true in the north-east area of the island, especially in the high dunes, where occasional fragments of field walls can be seen. Other enclosures are little more than small animal pens, that of PY80 and PY71, for example, but the enclosures of PY53 form a large complex of three cojoining, high drystone-walled pony corrals. Interconnected with the main settlement PY54 are a number of enclosure walls forming a small infield system. The cemetery mound PY55 is located to the north of a wall that could either be part of the settlement infield system, thus excluding it from the domestic area, or, less convincingly, it could be the surviving part of a cemetery enclosure that has collapsed into the stream around its north and eastern sides.

The mediaeval landscape (Fig. 3.14)
There are no sites that can be allocated to this landscape except possibly the cemetery-burial mound PY54, which, if the island was occupied, would have been in use. The funerary evidence in the form of burial rite and its expression in the form of inscribed grave markers suggest occupation since there are a number of simple cross-inscribed stones either in place on the cemetery mound or lying fallen around its sides. Although they cannot be securely dated to anything but the Christian period in general, it is likely that some of them may be as early as the mediaeval period. Of the supposed chapel at the summit of the mound there is no evidence.

The early mediaeval/Norse landscape (Fig. 3.14)
The recovery of a Pictish 'fist pin', dateable to around the 7th century AD, from the upper deposits of the broch Dùnan Ruadh (PY10) may be taken as evidence that the surviving broch structure, although much infilled with earlier deposits, was still used as a place of occupation. Another pin of similar date was found associated with midden material, pottery and bone apparently in an area to the east of the cemetery (see RCAHMS above), but this site has never been re-located.

There are three possible boat-shaped stone settings which, although they could represent Norse monuments and are listed as such, are not the most convincing examples of this class of monument.

Burial ground. PY55.

Boat-shaped stone settings. PY30, 93, 106.

The Iron Age landscape (Fig. 3.15)
The Iron Age landscape echoes that of the other periods, being focused upon a single monument of

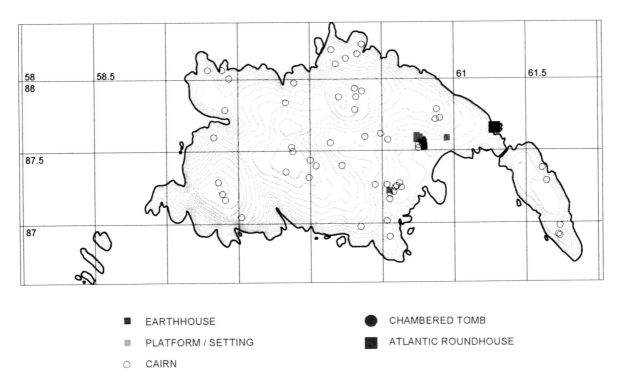

Figure 3.15 Pabbay, showing the location of prehistoric monuments.

91

great significance accompanied by a number of undated small sites. There is a high probability that some of the field walls may belong this far back in time, since in such a limited topography the division of land is also limited along almost predictable lines, and such land boundaries that do exist may have been simply used conveniently at all periods since their initial construction. How much the preferred settlement area was utilized at this time will not be clear until more of it can be excavated, but the excavation of PY56 in the dunes (see below) shows that much can be hidden from sight in the area.

Atlantic roundhouses. PY10 Broch Dùnan Ruadh (see excavation report, Chapter 6).

The Pre-Iron Age landscape (Fig. 3.15) settlement complex. PY56 to 68.

To the north of the cemetery mound and modern settlement a small stream runs down from the north of the island, first in a dyke formation at its upper reaches, then, as it begins to level out nearer the bottom of the valley, it cuts a deep channel into the shell sand of the dunes. On its northern side the land gently slopes upwards, but at the same time is modified by the bumps and ridges of the dune system. As part of that system, immediately across the stream from the cemetery is a long sand-covered ridge that provides some relatively level areas on which a number of sites, PY56–68, are located. Their general appearance is of vaguely structured stone settings and stone collections slightly embedded into the surface of the sand and partially obscured by marram grass. Initially it was thought that the ridge was of bedrock only thinly covered with sand and that the sites were therefore only moderately embedded, but the excavations at PY56 showed that in fact they are subterranean houses dug into the dunes at depths exceeding 1 m. Two further subterranean houses may be suggested at PY61 (of which PY59, 60 and 64 may be a part) and PY62 respectively. Other concentrated collections of disarranged stone have been noted at various locations in the dunes that cover the upper bowl of the valley.

These sites are very similar to sites EF located in sand dunes during a survey of the small island of Fuday (see p. 10).

Cairns unstructured. PY4, 5, 6, 11, 12, 13, 17C + D, 20, 22, 31, 40, 48, 50B, 59, 67, 68, 70, 73, 95, 113, 114, 117, 118, 119.

Cairns structured. PY1, 14, 15, 16, 18, 23, 37, 38, 39, 41, 45, 51, 52, 74, 75, 78, 79, 81, 82, 85, 86, 87, 92, 94, 98, 99, 103, 104, 107, 110, 112.

After shelters, cairns are the most frequent monument on the island and consequently, by sheer numbers alone, they are the monument most likely to be modified. Some of the cairns on Pabbay may be of very recent date, such as navigation markers erected by local fisherman to help steer clear of the inshore reefs. Field stone clearance is a common origin of cairns and Pabbay is said to have had ten acres of arable land under cultivation in 1891 (Buxton 1995), which would be the place to expect them. Areas of improved land clear of rough vegetation on the old OS map are located around the settlement, the dunes close to Dùnan Ruadh, the central 'dark' glen and the land around the corrals PY53 which should be the home of field stone clearance cairns, but apart from four examples in the area of PY53 there are none. Some cairns are on expected locations, such as headlands, hill-tops and prominent exposed coastal features, but the remainder are in diverse and often obscure places. Structured cairns can be described in general as being composed of a circular setting of stones or stone and earth enclosing an area of approximately 2 m². They often appear to be built on a small prepared mound or platform, although this could merely be the eroded out material from some superstructure since collapsed. Only one cairn, PY75, could be described as a significantly mounded earth and stone structure being an exceptional 4 m in diameter and standing a metre in height.

Conclusion

Pabbay rarely appears to have been populated by more than a few family groups at any one time and this appears to be reflected in the apparent lack of site diversity and even an absence of certain site classes that one would normally expect to find. Distinct roundhouse or hut circles are not in evidence and nor are chamber tombs. However, two sites, PY32 and 33, which have been described as shelters, could profit from a further detailed evaluation that may reveal them to be dismantled tombs. PY33 is without doubt a shelter, but there is a great deal of surplus disarranged stonework that might be the result of stone robbing for the shelter construction from some earlier, larger construction. In this respect Pabbay appears to be quite an archaeologically impoverished island when compared with even the smaller and topographically bland island of Berneray, where the ratio of archaeological sites to land area is much higher and the diversity greater. Without the Pictish symbol stone and the Iron Age broch Dùnan Ruadh the archaeological cupboard would appear bare indeed. The cover of shell sand over the settlement area and the late settlement itself are most likely obscuring a wealth of archaeological material of which the excavations at PY56 have only just allowed a small glimpse.

Mingulay Survey, 1991–1998

Introduction (Fig. 3.16)

Mingulay is a large, irregular, suboval-shaped island pinched in at the waist by the Bágh na h-Aoineig inlet on the west coast and the wide sandy beach of Mingulay Bay to the east, and with the 149 m high hill of Tom á Reithean extending out to the north. Its maximum dimensions are c. 3.8 km north to south by 3.1 km east to west. The island is dominated by a semicircle of massive hills, Hecla 219 m, Carnan 273 m, Tom á Mhaide 173 m and Macphee's Hill 224 m, that curve westwards around the bay area to form a wide sheltered amphitheatre-shaped valley. The combination of access to the sea via the bay; shelter by the hills from the westerly storms and a level area suitable for agricultural development in the broad glen make the bay area a natural preferred settlement location. The hill's tops may be mantled with thick wet peat formations, but they also provide extensive relatively even slopes that are generally well drained. Two other coastal valleys exist, Skipisdale to the south and another facing Bay Sletta to the east. Neither benefit from sandy beaches at the sea's edge, although Skipisdale does have possible cobble-floored landing places in eroded dyke formation inlets. The overall topographical configuration provides considerable areas of rough grazing pasture and valuable workable peat deposits that account for over 40% of the total Mingulay land surface, while only 30% of the island area is taken up by very rocky terraces and dykes. More than 70% of the coastline is of high

inaccessible rocky cliffs, but the remainder is of low sloping shelves, beaches and dyke inlets that afford good access. Only around 5% of the ground coverage is occupied by shell sand dunes, of which about half are relatively stable, encouraging a marram grass environment. However, the influence of the sand dunes is much more widespread, mainly due to wind-blown sands that have enriched large areas of the valley and the hillsides, especially the southern lower slopes of Macphee's Hill and the north-western slopes of the valley bowl. Rabbits have taken advantage of these sandy soils to make burrows and investigations of their outcast spoil has produced quantities of presumably early modern handmade pottery fragments that indicate not the presence of archaeological sites, but the practice of manuring and cultivating these self-improved lands. These figures and attributes suggest that of all the southern islands Mingulay is the most conducive to permanent or long-term settlement. The earliest documentary proof of this is a short description of Mingulay, made in the 16th century, as being two miles long, inhabited and well-manured, good for fishing and corn (Monro 1994).

Settlement is eminently apparent in Mingulay Bay by the presence of a large haphazardly clustered collection of ruined blackhouses, a burial ground and further ruined buildings in the vicinity that include several more blackhouses, a modern school, a mill and a modern priest's house/chapel. Any earlier occupation in such an intensively used area is either masked or destroyed, but there can be little doubt that if the island was occupied at any time this would always have been the naturally preferred location. To some extent this assumption is already proven with finds of possible Bronze Age flintwork from the area of the dunes and a perforated mace from deep deposits in the valley, the excavation of a minor Iron Age site, also in the dunes, and possible early mediaeval objects from the burial ground. However, although earlier settlement may always have been represented in the Mingulay Bay valley there are other dispersed upstanding settlement buildings in the valley of Skipisdale of obvious importance that may date from the Iron Age, if not earlier. There is also a small nucleated settlement composed of small houses on the low coastal slopes of Hecla that may be of Mediaeval date.

Successful settlement depends on many factors that interrelate with the basic elements of people and animals—the land, sea and, climatically, the sky. An informative exercise is to draw a flow chart showing the pattern of this relationship with commodities, produce, production, etc. Such a flow chart has been produced for the island of St Kilda (Harman 1997: Fig. 7) 40 miles to the west and Mingulay's similarity to that island (it was once called 'the nearer St Kilda' [Jolly 1883]) negates the need to reproduce another version here for it serves both islands well.

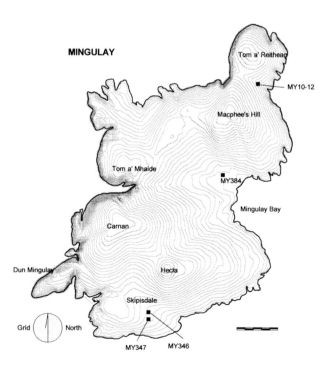

Figure 3.16 Mingulay, showing topography, place-names and excavation sites.

One of the resources shared by the two islands are the large sea bird colonies that inhabit the magnificent cliffs and smaller associated islands and stacks. Mingulay's west coast cliffs, especially those shared by Carnan and Ton Mhaide, are comparable to and quite as breathtaking as those of Oiseval and the Mullach's on St Kilda, even if they are on a grander scale. Bird catching on the cliffs of St Kilda is well-documented as early as Martin Martin's tour in the 17th century. Mingulay does not benefit from such detailed documentary evidence compared to St Kilda, but it is recorded that they owed a barrel of manx shearwaters as rental (Serjeantson 1998)—simple proof that they also gathered the avian harvest.

The St Kilda-type cleitean is not to be found on any of the islands in the survey. There are shelters all around the landscapes and there are barns near or next to the blackhouses of the settlement, but nothing that competes with the architectural sophistication found on St Kilda. Both Muir (1885) and Harvie-Browne and Buckley (1888) describe the Mingulay blackhouses as primitive and poor and perhaps this is reflected in their other buildings too.

Once the inhabitants had left the island Mingulay began to take on the mantle of a romantic and mysterious place in true Gaelic tradition, culminating in the composition of the songs 'Mingulay Boat Song' and 'Song to the Isle of Mingulay'. Also, the fact that the descendants of Mingulay still live, holding their heritage and ancestral home dear, keep its memory alive. Today Mingulay is the most visited of the uninhabited islands, with regular day trips by motor launch from Castlebay, and there are groups, both official and unofficial, who stay for longer lengths of time. Such attention brings with it the hazard of deterioration through use, a subject raised by Ben Buxton (1995) at the end of his book.

Royal Commission on the Ancient and Historical Monuments of Scotland National Sites and Monuments Record of Scotland

1. NL58SE1 (NGR NL566:827). Crois an t-Suidheachain. Site of cross (MY76). Described in the RCAHMS 1928 survey report as three stone structures or settings where open-air mass was said to be held. A central rectangular structure, c. 3×2.5 m internally is flanked by a similar, but slightly smaller structure, c. 2×1.2 m, to the north. A large slab of stone c. 1.2 m long, set on edge, divides the internal space of this structure giving one compartment (the west) the appearance of a short cist. On the other flank, angled to the south-east, is a suboval setting c. 1.20 m across with a large block of stone $0.55 \times 0.45 \times 0.55$ m. All other stones barely appear above the ground. (See RCAHMS field notebook of 1915 for field sketch of the site.) In addition T. Muir (1885) records a circle of stones surrounding three cells and a central heap. This situation is recorded on the 1st edition 6 in. OS map of 1880, although four structures are depicted set in a circle within the enclosure. No trace of this site was found during the 1965 OS visit.

2. NL58SE2 (NGR NL5649:8328). St Columba's chapel and village burial ground (MY88). No such chapel was known by the inhabitants at the time of Muir's visit in 1885 and the graveyard was in a ruinous state. A visit by the OS in 1965 reported the burial ground as a sandy knoll enclosed by a low wall of boulders within which a few modern headstones and crosses stood, the whole being obscured by drifting sand. However, a second visit by the OS in 1973 reported: '[W]hat appears to be the remains of the chapel are visible on the summit of the knoll. It consists of the west end of a rectangular building 3 m long and up to three courses high. Further details are obscured by drifting sand.' Historic Scotland's scheduling document of 1997 states: 'At the heart of Mingulay village is an oval burial enclosure around a low mound. This is the site of St Columba's chapel. This is certainly of pre-Reformation date, but has no secure early history and shows just a few protruding coursed stones to hint at the presence of a small rectangular foundation.' Marked on the 1st edition 1880 6-in. OS map as 'site of St Columba's chapel'.

3. NL58SE5 (NGR NL5648:8328). Midden. Wedderspoon (1915) found a denuded shell midden on a bare ridge at the north end of a bay on the east side of Mingulay. It adjoins the hillock on which stands the burial ground. Apart from shells, the midden contained hammer-stones split by fire, bones and teeth. The OS visit of 1965 apparently managed to find the midden site on the north-west side of the burial ground, but only a few shells were visible. Two 'basin-stones' from the midden were found in the chapel enclosure and measured c. $0.7 \times 0.5 \times 0.2$ m with a large groove or hollow in the centre. This type of grinding stone or saddle quern has been used continually in the islands since Neolithic times and some examples have been found during this survey of the southern islands in or at some of the early modern houses, BY57 and MY83, for example. It therefore cannot be used to date the midden. The site was not located in the current survey, although scatters of shell were noted in many areas around the village, but the stones were found close to the modern priest's house/chapel (MY87). The author removed them to a position close to the northern enclosure wall for safety.

4. NL58SE6. (NGR NL5653:8330). Iron Age pottery (MY384). Iron Age pottery sherds were found by Mrs V. Pritchard in 1959 and donated to the National Museum of Antiquities (HR 1212–1214). The site could not be found in 1965 by the OS, but in 1971 up to 200 sherds were found during a survey of the island, but no evidence of settlement (information from Mr Phillips, Engineering Faculty, UCL). The OS also visited the site in 1971. This survey in fact included an

unpublished small excavation of the site mound that is referred to in the excavation report below.

5. NL58SE7 (NGR NL5641:8341). Modern priest's house and chapel (MY87). The building is situated on higher ground above the village and to the north-west of the burial enclosure. Wedderspoon described it in 1912 as being erected a few years ago on the site of an older building, of which nothing remained but a shapeless heap of stones. When digging the foundations, a small stone bowl was found, and is at present in the chapel. Several boulders were also found with cavities hollowed out of the flat upper surface. These are preserved in the chapel enclosure. The OS in 1965 found the chapel ruinous and disused with no trace of earlier buildings and the stone bowl was not evident.

6. NL58SE8 (NGR NL5649:8327). Coins and pins. Several ancient coins and bronze pins were found some years ago in the graveyard by the midden (NL58SE5) and were disposed of in Castlebay, reports Wedderspoon (1915).

7. NL58SE9 (NGR [A] NL5654:8342). Enclosures (hut circles). Situated in an area of blown sand and rock outcrops are the remains of two enclosures. The first consists of a circle of vertical slabs about 4 m in diameter with two orthostats in the south-west quadrant, presumably representing an entrance. 2 m to the south, the tops of about six slabs protrude from the sand, forming a semicircle with similar dimensions to its partner. The Iron Age midden (MY384) is about 10 m to the north-west (NGR [B] NL5659:8335). Situated in an area of rock outcrop with erratics are two enclosures. The first consists of a levelled area enclosed by upright slabs utilizing erratic blocks, giving a diameter of c. 4 m. A slight revetment is visible on the downhill side. 5 m to the south-west is a similar enclosure, not so well defined and measuring c. 3.8 m in diameter. Reported by the OS in 1973.

8. NL58SE10 (NGR NL5598:8329). Enclosure (MY75A + B). Situated on gently sloping pasture land are the remains of an oval enclosure measuring internally 5.5 m north–south by 4 m within a wall of large vertical slabs. The enclosure has been levelled into the hillside and revetted front and back. A small recent sheep pen (shelter) has been constructed in the interior. Although the enclosure lies close to several shielings (NL58SE26) its construction is possibly indicative of a prehistoric house site. Reported by the OS in 1973.

9. NL58SE11 (NGR NL5651:8213). Shieling hut (MY194). Situated on gently sloping ground are the remains of a small rectangular bothy or shieling overlying a revetted oval platform measuring 10.5 m northeast–south-west by 7.5 m. About 15 m to the south is a similar turf-covered platform with no overlying structure. While the bothy is clearly a secondary structure, it is possible that the two platforms are the sites of houses. Reported by the OS in 1973. See excavation report in SEARCH volume 6.

10. NL58SE12 (NGR NL565:834). Iron Age pottery and a flint scraper. On the north side of Mingulay Bay, centred about 15 m above sea level, a very large spread of shells and bone, containing sherds of typical Hebridean Iron Age pottery. Donated to Glasgow Museum by J. Davies. See also the report in *Discovery and Excavation, Scotland*, 1973, 28–29.

11. NL58SE13 (NGR NL5650:8342). Cist (possible) (MY389). A possible cist is situated c. 15 m south-west of the smaller cairn (NL58SE17). The structure measures c. 1.5 m east–west by 1 m. Its north side is composed of a vertical slab 1 m long, while the south side has two slabs, one up to 0.7 m high; the east end is a transverse slab, and the west end is formed by smaller stones. Alternatively the structure could be part of the wall of a recent building (Buxton 1981).

12. NL58SE14 (NGR NL5668:8312). Noosts (MY32). Three seaward-facing structures, probably boat noosts, c. 5 m above HWM with an expanse of smooth gently sloping rock to seaward. The noosts are composed of upright slabs up to 0.7 m high (Buxton 1981).

13. NL58SE15 (NGR NL5620:8334). Axe-hammer. A fragment of perforated cobble, tentatively identified as an axe-hammer, was found in 1975 250 m south south-west of the modern chapel (MY87) in a soil test pit at a depth of 0.6 m (Buxton 1981).

14. NL58SE16. (NGR centred NL565:832). Township with field system. There is a long passage describing the village and its environs from the Historic Scotland scheduling document of 1997 that repeats much of the information concerning the chapels, burial ground and cross. Buxton's 1981 dissertation investigates the village in great detail, mapping and numbering all the houses. To summarize the village particulars entered in the record: the village comprises about 30 buildings plus a priest's house/chapel and schoolhouse. The east side of the village is becoming inundated with sand dunes. A new schoolhouse and several further houses are built near to the well made track that leads to the landing place at Aneir. The village has developed organically and there is considerable evidence for earlier occupation in the area. The village was finally abandoned in 1912.

15. NL58SE17 (NGR NL5652:8343). Cairns. 8 m west of the Iron Age site (MY384) are two small cairns, the larger c. 3.5 m across, horse-shoe shaped in plan and 0.6 m high. The other lies 4 m to the south-west and is c. 2.5 m across. Both cairns appear to be stratigraphically earlier than the midden. In the east edge of the larger a rim of Iron Age type pottery was found in 1971 (Buxton 1981).

16. NL58SE20 (NGR NL5565:8382). Enclosure. Oval enclosure, 3.3 × 2 m, defined by vertical slabs. Not a peat cleit. OS visit of 1973. (In an area of many peat dryers or cleits.)

17. NL58SE21 (NGR NL5680:8223). Structure (MY35). A group of about eight rectangular, oval

and circular 'cells', adjoined by walling, the whole laid out in a half-circle. OS visit of 1973.

18. NL58SE22 (NGR NL5560:8204) (MY344); (NGR NL5554:8187) (MY345); (NGR NL5563: 8170) (MY346). Structures. Three groups of up to 12 oval and circular 'cells'. Each group adjoined by walling, passages, with several constructional phases. Much ruined, no corbelling visible. OS visit of 1973. Three unroofed structures are depicted on the 1st edition 6-in. OS map of 1880, but they are not shown on the current 1989 1:10,000 OS map (RCAHMS 1997). (These three separate rectangular structures are located in the area of MY345, which is a large, generally circular complex unit. At the time of mapping in 1880 it is possible that the three buildings represent a small settlement that was being occupied at that time as tradition suggests or that they are early modern shielings built on and around the earlier settlement structure of MY345.)

19. NL58SE23 (NGR NL5575:8165). Enclosures (MY42 structure). Rectangular platform of massive construction, 2.4×3.4 m (NGR NL5563:8163) (MY347). Rectangular enclosure of massive construction about 2.1×3 m enclosed by several vertical orthostats, small extension to west. OS visit of 1973.

20. NL58SE24. (NGR NL560:825). Shieling huts (MY111). Remains of a trapezoidal shieling and three suboval shielings with side chambers. OS visit of 1973.

21. NL58SE25 (NGR NL55:83). Cleits (For example, MY273). Along the ridge between Tom á Mhaide and Macphee's Hill and usually situated in exposed positions on rock outcrops, are about 25 peat cleits in varying stages of disintegration. Where best-preserved they basically consist of a low rectangular platform of stone, revetted by vertical slabs, measuring overall about 5×2 m. Other platforms are now reduced to elongated turf-covered mounds, or subrectangular settings of vertical slabs. The cliets occur in peat-cutting areas throughout the remainder of the island (e.g. NGRs NL556:827; NL565:839). OS visit of 1973.

22. NL58SE26. (NGR NL557:832). Shieling huts; cleit (MY65 Peat dryer, possibly MY66, 68 and 67 shelters). Remains of three oval shielings and a peat cleit. OS visit of 1973.

23. NL58SW1 (NGR NL5477:8230). Fort, Dun Mingulay (MY376), promontory fort. It is defended by a stone wall built across the end of the peninsula facing the approaching ridge. The wall has for the most part disappeared, but in one place shows an outer face of drystone building standing some 0.9 m in height (RCAHMS 1928). The OS survey of 1965 adds: '... is defended by high sheer cliffs on three sides and a grass-covered dry-stone wall c. 1.6 m thick. The outer face of the wall is visible along the whole of its length to a maximum height of 1.6 m, but only a vague trace of the inner wall face remains. The entrance, about 1 m wide, appears to be at the south end of the

wall. A grass covered earthen bank, 4.5 m wide and 0.8 m high extends 20 m in a NW direction from the inner face of the wall at a point midway between the North and South ends, but this appears to be a secondary feature.' A further OS visit in 1973 records internal features: '[O]n the south slopes of Dun Mingulay are several unclassifiable structures (MY372-5 Shelters). The best preserved is an oval cell measuring internally 3×2.2 m within three courses of corbelled walling. Other structures include a 3-sided structure about 1.5 m square and two wall-courses high; also the remains of another oval cell and several amorphous piles of stone. These structures are all situated in exposed positions and cannot be related to each other or the dun.'

The 1991–1998 survey

On a brief visit in 1991 the village and surrounding area of Mingulay Bay was the initial basis for what became an extended series of long-stay systematic field surveys during the years to 1998. Apart from Patrick Foster and John Pouncett the survey teams were composed entirely of senior members of the Department of Landscape Studies of the Institute of Archaeology in Prague, except for the final year when MA students from Charles University, Prague, prepared measured drawings of the major monuments in Skipisdale and the village MY35. The survey work was enhanced by a limited number of small excavations during 1996 and 1998. The teams are extremely grateful to John Allen for getting them on and off the island and to the Sheep Stock Company for allowing us the use of the schoolhouse.

Mingulay is the largest island of the southern group and its multiple hills are of massive proportions, which, if flattened out, would form a considerable area of landscape. There are around 400 sites on the island, some scattered, some densely grouped. Approximately 10% of the sites are within 50 m of the cliff or coastal edge.

Although we have taken great pains to be accurate, it is recognized that in some areas away from the modern field systems site location is difficult. Roman Krivanek has checked the whole survey on the ground against the map plots. Even the sites that crowd the plateau ridge that forms the back of Mingulay Bay valley, with its many angular and stepped rocky formations, have been difficult to plot. Often trying to find a previously plotted site has proved to be a problem, incurring many frustrating hours of quartering the landscape. Mingulay is the one island in this survey that would benefit most from a resurvey using GPS.

Description and catalogue of the sites and monuments

MY1 (NL5685:8357) Standing stone. *Location*: Shelf on hill-slope. *Description*: Sited on the south flank of

Macphee's Hill at the north end of Mingulay Bay, close to the possible chamber tomb MY2 and several artificially constructed platforms of unknown date and function (MY3 and 4). This is the only standing stone of note on the island that has clearly been erected and is not the result of natural processes. The dimensions of the stone as seen above ground level, 0.8 m high by 0.6 × 0.18 m in section, are substantial, but not comparable to the massive standing stones found on Barra at Brevig and Borve. The presence of other large randomly scattered stone blocks close by casts some doubt on MY1 functioning as a free-standing monolith and not part of a robbed chamber tomb similar to MY2 just a few metres to the east.

MY2 (NL5688:8357) Chamber tomb. *Location*: Level bench on slope close to standing stone MY1. *Description*: Circular, diam. 1.7 m, hollow mound with large boulders, largest being 1 × 0.90 × 0.15 m. *Note*: Could be natural since there is no chamber or other architectural aspect that can substantiate its inclusion in this class of site other than the massive size of the blocks of stone that are lying here, which suggest that some significant monument might have been dismantled.

MY3 (NL5686:8359) Platform. *Location*: Bench on slope. *Description*: Square, 11 × 11 m, grassy platform levelled up from hillside. Leading edge revetted with stones. 0.3–1 m in size, especially on the west side. *Note*: May be associated with the ?road MY4, which this platform butts up to.

MY4 (NL5691:8358) Platform. *Location*: Bench on slope. *Description*: Grassy platform 30 m long and 3 m wide, banked up along the southern edge and at each terminal end set into the base of a natural rise in the hillside. There is no formal stone revetting, but a single set stone alignment runs from the top of the platform leading edge, down its banked slope and along the base of the bank out beyond the east end of the platform. MY4 initially appeared to be a road construction leading east around the girth of Macphee's Hill for ponies bringing in peat cuttings, but on closer examination it was clear that there was no extension of it in any direction and the ends appeared closed as a step down. Perhaps disuse and erosion have masked what may have once appeared as a clear route, partly artificial in construction and partly just an unmodified route across the landscape. There is some similarity to the road MY86, used for bringing peat from the area to the north of Macphee's Hill around the west side and up on to the ridge between Tom á Mhaide and Macphee's Hill. Although there is a scatter of various monuments around the east side of Macphee's Hill, peat cutting appears to be much less of an activity than around the other sides of the valley as the distribution of peat dryers indicates. *Note*: If this monument is part of a road track around the side of the hill it is inexplicable that it should have distinct banked ends.

MY5 (NL5709:8357) Shieling. *Location*: Edge of plateau bench on hillside. *Description*: Rectangular, 7.5 × 4.8 m, earth and stone walls internally stone-faced. Consists of small living room with fireplace built into the west wall and a bench seat along the side of the dividing compartment wall. An entrance through this wall leads to an external entrance in the north wall. The eastern end of the building is divided up with cross walls of single stones set on edge making three small stalls for sheep. *Note*: Fully excavated. Report in SEARCH volume 6. A fragmented iron spade, possibly for digging peat, was found in the excavations.

MY6* (NL5715:8371) Shieling complex. *Location*: Plateau bench on hillside. *Description*: Oval single cell with wind shield and store annexe. *Note*: Damaged from extensive rabbit burrowing. Excavation with a trench across the southern part of the structure did not produce any material finds except some rusted fragments of what may have been a bucket. Report in SEARCH volume 6.

MY6a* (NL5715:8371) Shelter. *Location*: As above. *Description*: Oval, 3.5 × 3 m, single cell of placed stone with entrance to west opening into area protected from the wind by an extension (c) westward of the southern ring-wall. To the east a curved wall extending east from the southern ring-wall forms a single-cell open-ended (north) annexe (b) of similar proportions and construction to the main shelter.

MY7 (NL5710:8372) Shieling. *Location*: Plateau bench on hillside. *Description*: Oval, 12 × 7 m, double cell with walls of earth and stone, some of which may represent internal wall facing stone. *Note*: Some burrowing.

MY8* (NL5731:8375) Enclosure. *Location*: Grassy shelf on stepped coastal cliff. *Description*: Long curved wall, 6 × 3 m, butted against rock face.

MY9* (NL5720:8406) Cairn. *Location*: Grassy shelf on stepped coastal cliff. *Description*: Circular, 3 m diam., mound of earth with few stones. *Note*: Inside area of naturally slumped peat soil. Could be natural.

MY10 (NL5694:8446) Cairn. *Location*: Inside dyke. *Description*: Oval, 3 × 2 m, flat-topped mound with ring of stone around upper perimeter. *Note*: Excavated site, see Chapter 7, p. 307. Covered by heather.

MY11 (NL5696:8447) Cairn. *Location*: Inside dyke. *Description*: Circular, 2 m diam., piled ring and mound of stones eroding onto exposed bedrock. Surviving upright stones set inside ring of flat-laid stones may be remnant of small cell, but most of the stonework is displaced. *Note*: Active erosion. Excavated, see Chapter 7, p. 307.

MY12 (NL5693:8448) Cairn. *Location*: Inside dyke. *Description*: Oval, 1.7 × 1 m, stone ring with slight internal mound. *Note*: Active erosion. Excavated, see Chapter 7, p. 307.

MY13 (NL5699:8421) Peat dryer. *Location*: Shelf on stepped coastal slope. *Description*: Subrectangular,

4.5 × 3 m, small platform edged with stones. *Note*: Covered by heather.

MY14 (NL5707:8414) Complex of cairn and mound. *Location*: Shelf on stepped coastal hillside. *Description*: An earthen mound, slightly hollowed, with a few stones around the summit, appears to have a small ring of stones set on the east side. *Note*: The shelf is grassy, but bedrock is being exposed.

MY14a (NL5707:8414) Cairn. *Location*: As above. *Description*: Circular partly surviving stone ring, diam. 1 m, on flattened side of mound.

MY14b (NL5707:8414) Mound. *Location*: As above. *Description*: Circular mound, diam. 3 m, of grassed-over earth with some scattered stone around the flattened, slightly hollowed summit.

MY15 (NL5657:8357) Shelter. *Location*: Against dyke rock face. *Description*: Rectangular, 2 × 1.3 m, single cell of piled stone walling set against the rock face of a dyke below rock overhang.

MY16 (NL5698:8370) (Fig. 3.17) Cairn. *Location*: Inside dyke. *Description*: Circular, diam. 2 m, pile of small stones with a suggestion of set kerb stones. Hollowed and many stones displaced. *Note*: May have been reused as a shelter.

MY17* (NL5717:8409) Cairn. *Location*: Shelf on stepped coastal hillside. *Description*: Oval, 3 × 2 m, mound with scattered stone.

MY18 (NL5699:8421) Cairn. *Location*: Shelf on stepped coastal slope. *Description*: Subrectangular, 3 × 2 m, single cell slightly mounded with walls, stones up to 0.8 m in size. *Note*: Could be a shelter.

MY19 (NL5694:8426) Cairn. *Location*: Stepped coastal slope. *Description*: Circular, diam. 1.8 m, slight mound with a few spaced large upright stones around perimeter.

MY20 (NL5697:8431) Cairn. *Location*: Stepped coastal slope. *Description*: Circular, diam. 1.5 m, pile of stone.

MY21 (NL5692:8436) Cairn. *Location*: Stepped coastal slope. *Description*: Circular, diam. 1.5 m, ring of stones at one end of a larger oval mound.

MY22 (NL5686:8436) Cairn. *Location*: Stepped coastal slope. *Description*: Subrectangular, 4 × 2 m, mound with a few side stones.

MY23* (NL5710:8456) Cairn. *Location*: Stepped coastal slope. *Description*: Oval, 5 × 3 m, possibly single cell with some set upright stones and much more collapsed material.

MY24* (NL5720:8474) Enclosure. *Location*: Stepped coastal slope. *Description*: Oval, 6 × 4 m, enclosure of single large set stone butted against crag rock face.

MY25* (NL5666:8478) Shelter. *Location*: Stepped coastal slope. *Description*: Subrectangular, 3.5 × 2 m, single cell of earth and stone walls, but stonework is very scattered.

MY26* (NL5665:8474) Shelter. *Location*: Cliff edge. *Description*: Circular, diam. 2 m, single cell, open-sided to east with some set upright stones. *Note*: Active erosion.

MY27 (NL5672:8470) Peat dryer. *Location*: Lower coastal slope. *Description*: Rectangular, 1.8 × 1.4 m, single cell orientated east–west. Central flat mound with a stone facade at west sea-facing end. *Note*: South side destroyed by large collapsed burrow.

MY28 (NL5677:8468) Shelter. *Location*: Lower slope. *Description*: Subrectangular, 2.5 × 1.6 m, single cell with stonework severely eroded on the east side. *Note*: Could be a peat dryer. Covered in heather.

MY29 (NL5676:8464) Peat dryer. *Location*: Lower slope. *Description*: Rectangular, 5 × 2 m, single cell with low mound in centre edged with spaced stones to a substantial facade at the west end where large flat slabs, originally set on edge, have fallen. The east end blends into the hillside.

MY30 (NL5678:8466) Cairn. *Location*: Lower slope. *Description*: Circular, diam. 1.2 m, mound, edged on western side with set upright stones as partial ring wall.

MY31 (NL5681:8465) Peat dryer. *Location*: Lower slope. *Description*: Rectangular, 5 × 2 m, single cell orientated west–east with low flat mound edged with stones. West end facade mostly eroded on to bedrock. East end blends into hillside. *Note*: Active and severe erosion under way.

MY32* (NL5667:8311) Noost. *Location*: Low cliff edge grassy bench. *Description*: Boat-shaped open-ended (to the sea) subrectangular spaced stone settings used to lash down upturned boats when out of service.

MY33 (NL5692:8252) Cairn. *Location*: Coastal plain. *Description*: Circular, diam. 1.5 m, slightly mounded with some stones in half-circle ring-wall.

MY34* (NL5700:8239) Shelter. *Location*: Coastal plain. *Description*: Oval, 2 × 1.8 m, single cell with

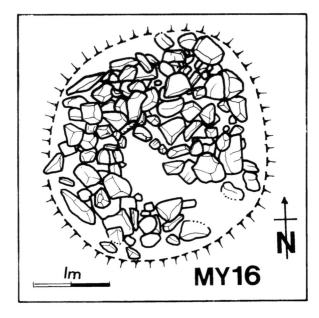

Figure 3.17 Site MY16.

ring-wall of piled and occasionally set upright stones. *Note*: Covered by heather.

MY35 (NL5680:8223) Shieling complex. *Location*: Coastal plain. *Description*: A complex of small dwellings and associated barns and clearance cairns in an area 44 × 30 m. The complex as a whole appears to be built on a prepared platform. The dating of this monument is problematical, two small sondage trenches opened in the hope of finding datable material did recover Iron Age pottery sherds, but they appear to predate the standing buildings and appear to belong to some earlier settlement. The supposed dwellings are not true blackhouses. Judging from a small excavation across one of the larger buildings they are small, generally square internally, consisting of a small single cell with a seating bench around the internal walls. The walls are generally stone-faced with small stones. On the present evidence the hoped-for mediaeval or earlier dating of this monument, apart from whatever is lying below the present buildings, cannot be sustained, and the most likely function for this group of dwellings is that of regular seasonal use as a shieling complex. Further use in modern times is most likely and some of the buildings may have been modified and other shelters constructed. Excavation report will be in SEARCH volume 6.

MY35a (NL5680:8223) Shieling. *Location*: As above. *Description*: Subrectangular, 6 × 5 m, single cell. Entrance to the north.

MY35b (NL5680:8223) Barn. *Location*: As above. *Description*: Oval, 4 × 3 m, single cell. Store for (a).

MY35c (NL5680:8223) Enclosure. *Location*: As above. *Description*: Oval, 12 × 10 m, enclosure formed by closing off what may have originally been an opening for livestock giving access between the upper and lower fields. *Note*: Most likely a later addition.

MY35d (NL5680:8223) Shieling. *Location*: As above. *Description*: Subrectangular, 6.5 × 4.5 m, single cell with entrance to the west that appears to be in a different constructional style to the other buildings, and it also appears to be superimposed over other features. Consequently, it may therefore be a later addition to the complex.

MY35e (NL5680:8223) Barn. *Location*: As above. *Description*: Oval, 7 × 4 m, single-cell ?store for (d). Could be shieling.

MY35f (NL5680:8223) Cairn. (clearance) *Location*: As above. *Description*: Circular pile of stones, 2 m diam.

MY35g (NL5680:8223) Shelter. *Location*: As above. *Description*: Oval, 4 × 3 m, possible collapsed shelter built with a stone setting of three large monoliths to the east.

MY35h (NL5680:8223) Shieling. *Location*: As above. *Description*: Subrectangular, 6 × 5 m, single cell. Entrance to the north.

MY35i (NL5680:8223) Barn. *Location*: As above. *Description*: Subrectangular, 4 × 3 m, barn to ?(h).

MY35j (NL5680:8223) Shieling. *Location*: As above. *Description*: Subrectangular, 5 × 3.5 m. Entrance open end to west.

MY35k (NL5680:8223) Shieling. *Location*: As above. *Description*: Subrectangular, 6 × 5 m, entrance to north-east. *Note*: Possibly a later rebuild.

MY35l (NL5680:8223) Shieling. *Location*: As above. *Description*: Subrectangular, 7 × 6 m, single cell. Entrance to north.

MY35m (NL5680:8223) Shieling. *Location*: As above. *Description*: Subrectangular, 7.5 × 5.5 m, single cell later rebuilt and divided into two cell structure?

MY35n (NL5680:8223) Barn. *Location*: As above. *Description*: Square, 3 × 3 m, single-cell barn for (m).

MY35o (NL5680:8223) Shieling. *Location*: As above. *Description*: Subrectangular, 5 × 3.5 m, double cell. Entrance obscure.

MY35p (NL5680:8223) Barn. *Location*: As above. *Description*: Subrectangular, 3 × 2 m, entrance to north. Barn to ?(q).

MY35q (NL5680:8223) Shieling. *Location*: As above. *Description*: Subrectangular, 5 × 4.7 m, single cell built over change in underlying ground surface. Entrance to ?east.

MY35r (NL5680:8223) Shieling. *Location*: As above. *Description*: Square, 4 × 4 m, single cell. Entrance obscure.

MY35s (NL5680:8223) Barn. *Location*: As above. *Description*: Oval, 5 × 4 m, or collapsed shelter?

MY36 (NL5678:8214) Shelter. *Location*: Bottom of slope to coastal plain. *Description*: Oval, 3.6 × 1.5 m, single cell with field wall crossing south end. Spaced orthostats of large size, some standing to 1 m in height. This could be the surviving larger stones of a chamber tomb robbed of all other material for the field wall.

MY37 (NL5656:8199) Shieling complex. *Location*: Bottom slope to coastal plain. *Description*: Oval single-cell shelter (a) with single-stone thick walls standing up to five courses high. Entrance is to the east. A small storehouse is attached at the back. Set on a platform (c) with attached walls extending from the east and west to form an enclosure (b) of the buildings and partially the platform. Curved stone settings around the outer southern edge appear to have no functional relationship and may be part of an earlier underlying monument. There is almost 2 m of mounded elevation, which also suggests a hidden site below.

MY38 (NL5634:8195) Shelter. *Location*: Lower hillslope. *Description*: Possible circular, 3.5 m diam., shelter of a few piled stones (a) overlying subrectangular mound with scattered stones (b) that makes little structural sense. This may be a reused site that the cover of heather does little to clarify.

MY39 (NL5622:8192) Shelter. *Location*: Lower hillslope. *Description*: Circular, 1 m diam., single cell of single stone thickness, five drystone courses high butted to field wall.

MY40 (NL5604:8184) Shieling. *Location*: Lower hill-slope. *Description*: Subrectangular, 3 × 2.5 m, single cell with earthen wall containing little stone. Well defined, but gaps confuse entrance location, however, it is most likely on the eastern side. Set into the hillside and with a revetted platform to the south.

MY41 (NL5600:8176) Shelter. *Location*: Lower hill-slope. *Description*: Circular, diam. 1.5 m, single cell of drystone ring-wall standing four courses high. Built against field wall.

MY42 (NL5576:8166) Setting. *Location*: Valley floor. *Description*: Rectangular, 2.5 × 2.1 m, setting of large slabs that may represent the robbed-out remains of a monument of considerable size.

MY43 (NL5563:8154) Shelter. *Location*: Shelving coastal slope. *Description*: Circular, diam. 2 m, single cell with arc of set stone ring-wall around southern edge. *Note*: Active severe erosion to bedrock.

MY44* (NL5547:8152) Shelter. *Location*: Shelf on stepped coastal slope. *Description*: Rectangular, 2.1 × 1.5 m, single cell of spaced set stones against field wall at its terminal.

MY45 (NL5534:8152) Shelter. *Location*: Shelf on stepped coastal slope. *Description*: Subrectangular, 1.5 × 1 m, single cell of placed stones butted to large naturally placed boulder. A half-oval enclosure 8 × 4 m curves out from either side of the shelter to the edge of a steep slope that may be a deliberate cutting into the hill-slope, forming a level platform within the enclosure.

MY46* (NL5530:8147) Shelter. *Location*: Shelf on stepped coastal slope. *Description*: Ill-defined oval, 2 × 1.5 m, single cell of widely spaced embedded stones occupying half the area of an oval platform, 4 × 2 m, marked by spaced small stones around the perimeter.

MY47 (NL5527:8147) Shelter. *Location*: Shelving cliff slope. *Description*: Oval, 2.3 × 1 m, single cell with stone ring-wall built against enclosure wall that connects it to MY48.

MY48 (NL5525:8148) Shelter. *Location*: Shelving cliff slope. *Description*: Oval, 3.5 × 1.5 m, single cell built against enclosure wall. Stonework collapsed.

MY49* (NL5519:8145) (Fig. 3.18) Stone circle. *Location*: Flat shelf above cliff. *Description*: MY49 can be found on a flat, grass-covered and very gently sloping area that leads down to the denuded rock that exists in an irregular strip just above the foreshore along the extreme southern coastline of the island. This circle, of not very large stones set in a 7 m diam. ring, looks out to Berneray and the nearer islands of Geirum Mor and Beag to the south, a situation not dissimilar to the stone circle at the north end of Barra at Scurrival, which looks to South Uist. A smaller circle of c.1 m diameter is set against the southern inner edge of the main ring, and opposite the only upstanding stone, 0.4 m high, in the circle at the north point.

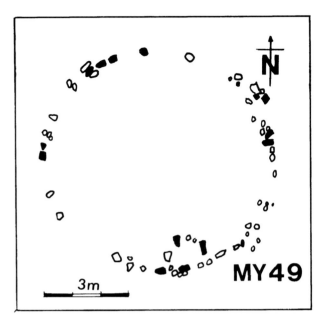

Figure 3.18 Site MY49.

MY50* (NL5514:8146) Cairn. *Location*: Shelf above cliff. *Description*: Oval, 3 × 2 m, pile of stones. *Note*: Erosion to bedrock.

MY51 (NL5677:8456) Shelter. *Location*: Inside dyke. *Description*: Circular, diam. 2 m, single cell mounded with a few spaced stones at the edge. A tail of mounded soil extends to the north with scattered stones. Could be natural.

MY52 (NL5683:8459) Shelter. *Location*: Inside dyke. *Description*: Circular, diam. 2 m, half-circle of upright stones with circle completed by slight bank.

MY53 (NL5696:8351) Cairn. *Location*: Bench on slope. *Description*: Circular, diam. 1.5 m, single cell of large stones placed in ring, but some are displaced.

MY54 (NL5696:8353) Shelter. *Location*: Bench on slope. *Description*: Square, 1.5 × 1.5 m, single cell of a few stones set on edge around a slightly banked wall of earth. Entrance possibly from southern corner.

MY55 (NL5566:8418) Cairn. *Location*: Coastal valley floor. *Description*: Circular, diam. 2 m, mound with a half-circle of kerbstone in place.

MY56* (NL5518:8444) Shelter. *Location*: Promontory cliff. *Description*: Subrectangular, 6 × 3 m, single cell of large blocks of stone denuded of soil. *Note*: Active erosion threat.

MY57* (NL5517:8448) Shelter. *Location*: Promontory cliff. *Description*: Circular ring of rocks, 2.5 m diam., lying on exposed bedrock. Other scattered stones all around. *Note*: Severe active erosion.

MY58* (NL5501:8408) Peat dryer. *Location*: Cliff plateau. *Description*: Subrectangular, 5 × 2 m, single cell with slight mound edged by stones rises to facade while opposite open end merges with the hill-slope.

MY59 (NL5505:8407) Peat dryer. *Location*: Cliff plateau. *Description*: Subrectangular, 5 × 2 m, single cell, slight mound edged with stones except at open end where the mound merges with the hill-slope.

MY60 (NL5503:8410) Peat dryer. *Location*: Cliff plateau. *Description*: Subrectangular, 5 × 2 m, single cell with slight mound edged with stones, but front end has been eroded away. At the rear open end the mound merges into the hill-slope.

MY61 (NL5506:8410) (Fig. 3.27) Peat dryer. *Location*: Cliff plateau. *Description*: Subrectangular, 5 × 2 m, single cell with facade at one end, opposite open end where the slight mound merges into the hill-slope. The mound is hollowed in the centre.

MY62 (NL5520:8371) Peat dryer. *Location*: Mid slope shelf. *Description* Subrectangular, 6 × 2 m, single cell has facade front to north-east, edged by stones along sides and the slight mound merges with the hill-slope at the rear open end.

MY63 (NL5517:8367) Setting. *Location*: Mid-slope shelf. *Description*: A cross-shaped setting, 4 × 3.5 m, of large stones. *Note*: Surrounded by active peat erosion.

MY64 (NL5519:8361) Shelter. *Location*: Mid-slope shelf in prominent position. *Description*: May originally have been circular, but much stonework displaced to give oval, 4.8 × 3.8 m. Constructed of large blocks and thin slabs, many of which are set on edge around the outer ring. The centre is mounded, possibly from fallen material. Possible entrance to north. *Note*: Rabbit burrowing and wind erosion active. Could be a disassembled peat dryer.

MY65 (NL5575:8321) (Fig. 3.27) Peat dryer. *Location*: Mid slope shelf to valley. *Description*: Sub-rectangular, 5 × 2 m, mounded single cell. Many edging stones in place, but some on the eastern side are scattered.

MY66 (NL5573:8321) Shelter. *Location*: Mid-slope shelf to valley. *Description*: Irregular circle, 1.5 m diam., single cell built against large boulder and field wall.

MY67 (NL5579:8318) Shelter. *Location*: Mid-slope shelf to valley. *Description*: Oval, 3 × 2 m, single cell of large stones, some set upright with no entrance.

MY68 (NL5582:8315) Shelter. *Location*: Mid-slope shelf to valley. *Description*: Circular, diam. 3 m, single cell of spaced-stone ring open to west.

MY69 (NL5575:8319) Shelter. *Location*: Mid-slope to valley. *Description*: Rectangular, 1 × 0.8 m, single cell of drystone walling several courses high, much tumbled. Butted to field wall and without entrance.

MY70 (NL5578:8330) Shelter. *Location*: Mid-slope to valley. *Description*: Circular, diam. 2 m, single cell of tumbled drystone walling.

MY71 (NL5583:8329) Shieling. *Location*: Mid-slope shelf of valley on slight rise. *Description*: Square, 3 × 3 m, with 1 m thick walls rounded at the corners. No entrance visible and outlines generally indistinct except for the east wall, which stands three courses high at 0.50 m.

MY72 (NL5664:8198) Cairn. *Location*: Low on coastal bench. *Description*: Circular, diam. 1 m,

mound of earth and stone.

MY73 (NL5619:8196) Shieling complex. *Location* Lower mid hill-slope. *Description*: Oval enclosure platformed into hillside with leading edge stone revetted. An entrance on to the platform is from the west next to three small shelters.

MY73a (NL5619:8196) Shelter. *Location*: As above. *Description*: Circular, diam. 1 m, single cell, very indistinct.

MY73b (NL5619:8196) Shelter. *Location* As above. *Description*: Oval, 3 × 2.5 m, single cell with ragged ring-wall on a slight earthen bank.

MY73c (NL5619:8196) Shelter. *Location*: As above. *Description*: Oval, 3 × 2 m, single cell of earth and stone ring-wall butted against hillside slope bedrock.

MY73d (NL5619:8196) Enclosure. *Location*: As above. *Description*: Oval, 12 × 7 m, enclosure with entrance to west platformed into hillside with stone revetting along leading edge.

MY74* (NL5589:8153) Cairn. *Location*: Cliff edge of valley floor. *Description*: Irregular ovoid, 1.5 m diam., mound with scattered stones.

MY75 (NL5598:8329) (Fig. 3.19) Complex of kerbed cairn and shelter. *Location*: Bottom of slope to valley. *Description*: Circular kerbed cairn with later square shelter built just off-centre inside the cairn ring.

MY75a (NL5598:8329) Kerbed cairn. *Location*: As above. *Description*: Circular, diam. 5 m, slight mound with a kerb of stones set upright around the perimeter. Single cell with some scattered stones inside and a later shelter.

MY75b (NL5598:8329) Shelter. *Location*: As above. *Description*: Square, 2 × 2 m, single cell of piled and set stones. Built slightly to the west of centre inside the cairn kerb ring.

MY76* (NL5664:8276) Place of cross (Crois an t-Suidheachain). *Location*: Cliff edge of coastal bench. *Description*: Noted from OS map. Now only a 4 × 4 m platform with a few embedded formless stones in evidence. See RCAHMS above.

MY76(2) Chamber tomb. Shown on the 1st edition 6 in. OS map of 1880 as four small subrectangular structures standing in a circle on a stone-edged platform where, in early modern times, open-air mass was conducted (presumably before the chapel house was constructed). The 1915 RCAHMS field notes and description of this site suggest that one of the structures could once have been a cist, judging by the small chamber formed by massive stone slabs set on edge. The location at this southern point of Mingulay Bay opposite that of sites MY2 and MY1 on the northern side is typical of the territorial marking around a settlement area that is not uncommon in the Neolithic and is similar to such arrangements in the Borve Valley on Barra.

MY77* (NL5661:8289) Cairn. (clearance) *Location*: Cliff edge of coastal bench. *Description*: Circular, diam. 3 m, grassed-over mound of piled stone. *Note*:

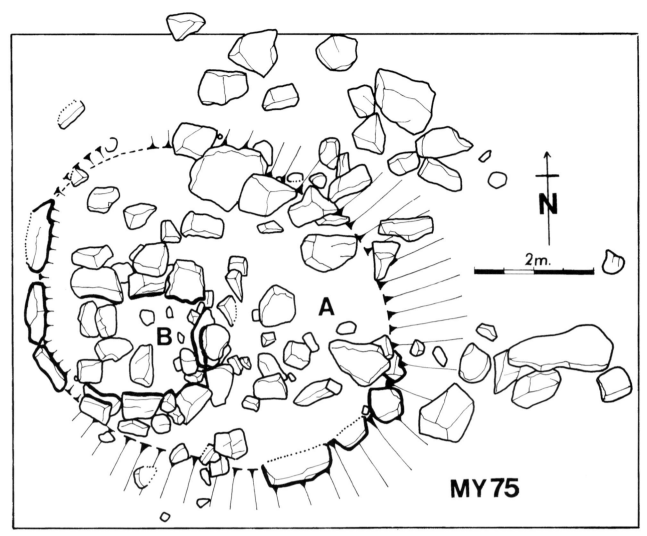

Figure 3.19 Site MY75.

Rabbit burrows and sheep treading have exposed interior.

MY78 (NL5654:8286) School classroom and house (modern). *Location*: Cliff edge of coastal bench. *Description*: A new school classroom was built in 1881 to the south of the village, at the side of the road leading to the landing place at Aneir. The building is a large single classroom built of quarried dressed stone with a large window in the south gable wall. The east wall incorporates a fireplace with chimney stack and gives space for the entrance and windows facing the sea. The roof was of stone slate from the mainland, but it now stands a roofless shell. This building replaced the old school for boys and girls, which can still be found as a wall foundation and enclosure at the north edge of the village close to the Iron Age site MY384. Three years later in 1884 a two-storey schoolhouse wing was added facing south and butted to the west wall of the school classroom. This gave a more than modest accommodation for Mr Finlayson, the schoolteacher (Buxton 1995). To this complex was added an enclosure of square plan and a set of outside toilets, unique in the southern islands!

Today the schoolhouse is kept roofed and locked and is used by the members of the Sheep Stock Company for accommodation and storage. The enclosure has been adapted, with pens and dip for working the sheep with the outside toilets turned into separate kennels for the sheepdogs (they tend to argue when housed together).

MY79 (NL5651:8294) House (modern). *Location*: Cliff edge bench. *Description*: MY79 is a modern house two storeys high built with stone gable ends of quarried stone fixed with mortar that incorporate a fireplace and chimney stack. In contrast the other walls were constructed of only corrugated iron sheets fixed on a timber framework. This style of the late 19th century is found elsewhere in the islands. This, Mingulay's sole example, however, does not stand, and lies as two great fallen reminders of the power that can be unleashed by the Hebridean wind, a storm of 1989 in fact (Buxton 1995).

MY80 (NL5654:8300) Blackhouse. *Location*: Coastal bench. *Description*: This is John Sinclair's house (Buxton 1995), an improved rectangular drystone-built blackhouse (a), 13 × 6 m, with integral fireplaces and chimney stacks built into each gable end east and west and a small subrectangular barn (b), 4.5 × 3.5 m, butted to the east gable wall. Oddly the fireplace backs are not uniform in shape being square-backed in the west wall and semicircular in the east. Another subrectangular barn (c), 5.9 × 4.5 m, with east-facing doorway, is located 5 m further to the east. The house is located south from the village by the side of the road after it has passed over the ridge that forms the southern edge to Mingulay Bay and dropped down again on the approach to the schoolhouse. It is therefore out of sight from the village area and its front door and windows face towards the school 100 m to the south. A photograph of 1905, in the possession of the Barra Historical Society, shows the windows glazed and the roof thatched, but the side barn appears to be in a dilapidated condition. Buxton (1995) suggests that Sinclair built his house in 1868 when he moved from Berneray, since it does not appear on a map of 1861–63. In his construction he managed to procure several blocks of quarried and dressed stone and his walls appear thinner, with sharp angled corners in keeping with more modern fashion. Both barns have blocks of quarry-drilled stone in their fabric. A subrectangular, 25 × 13 m, enclosure (d) to the north is butted to the house walls.

MY81 (NL5605:8336) Barn. *Location*: Bottom of slope to valley floor. *Description*: Subrectangular, 2 × 1.5 m, single-cell barn with greatly reduced earth and stone walls.

MY82 (NL5627:8308) Shelter. *Location*: Valley floor. *Description*: Square, 2.5 × 2.5 m, single-cell platform with a few stones at the edge located inside the village infield system.

MY83 (NL5644:8279) Blackhouse. *Location*: Lower coastal bench. *Description*: An improved single-cell rectangular blackhouse, 12.5 × 6.75 m, situated to the west of the school facing south and out of sight of the village. Square-backed fireplaces are built into each gable wall, both positioned slightly to the south of centre, and there are south-facing windows on each side of the door set in a front wall that may have been rebuilt entirely in a more modern style. A large saddle quern was found amongst collapsed stonework from the north wall and placed on display just to the east of the doorway. The inside of the house has been recently modified by the construction of a drystone, L-shaped wall (C), most likely a sheep pen. To the west of the blackhouse is what appears to be an older subrectangular construction (B), 9 × 5.5 m, with a door to the south and a small window to the north, but no visible fireplaces. It is built at an angle to the blackhouse, but by distorting its shape manages to place the entire length of its eastern wall against the west wall of the blackhouse. Both buildings occupy a platform cut into the bank of a stream that flows west to east at their rear.

MY84 (NL5642:8332) Blackhouse. *Location*: Valley floor, village environs. *Description*: One of the many improved blackhouses to be found in the main village group, but it is outstanding in that it has some dressed and quarried stone, some with quarry drill holes visible.

MY85* (NL5514:8446) Cairn. *Location*: On promontory cliff edge. *Description*: Circular, 1.5 m diam., pile of stones standing 1 m high, most likely a modern navigation marker.

MY86 (NL5660:8448) Road. *Location*: Cliff-top to valley floor to ridge-top. *Description*: MY86 has a well-defined and constructed road bed, with revetting against the hillside, which runs from the north of Macphee's Hill at the cliff edge of Creag Dhearg, maintaining the same contour line and appearing to aim directly at the metre-high tumuli mound of MY277 on the skyline of the ridge between Tom á Mhaide and Macphee's Hill. Only at the cliff edge and out on to the valley mountainside at Macphee's Hill is the road artificially constructed. The rest of its route appears to be an unmodified path that loses itself among the peat dryers on the ridge around the tumuli. Presumably, from that point the ponies were guided down the slope to the village by whatever route was easiest. The peat carried along this route would have been cut in the area of a saddle and geological dyke between Macphee's Hill and Tom á Reithean where a number of peat dryers are also located.

MY87 (NL5641:8343) Priest's house and chapel (modern). *Location*: Valley floor. *Description*: Built in 1898 in the solid modern Hebridean fashion of the late 19th and early 20th centuries, with mortared quarried stone masonry cavity walls rising to two storeys, knitted at the corners with large quoin stones. The ground floor comprises the living quarters for visiting priests, while the upper storey, reached by an external staircase on the north gable end, is a long open room that served as the chapel. The front prospect, which faces Mingulay Bay to the east, has three dormer windows to light the chapel, the central dormer gable being adorned with a small stone cross finial. The roof is covered with stone slate most likely brought from the quarries near Oban on the mainland. The building is set within its own drystone-walled square enclosure. This description is how the site appeared when I first observed it in 1991, but sadly this picture is not true today. Bought privately in 1975, renovation and repair of the house began, but the project was not successful. The house was locked and abandoned, and began to once again deteriorate. The final years of the house were captured on film in a sad sequence that ends in total, irreparable collapse and destruction. Our first sighting in 1991 showed a hole in the rear west roofing slate. Regular storms succeeded in steadily enlarging this wound. In 1993 a ferocious storm removed many roof slates, some of which were found 300 m away. It was clear that a process of major structural damage was under way. The wind appeared to have shifted the roof tie-beam frame forwards, pushing the front facade of the house outwards in a bulge. The pressure on this bulging wall began to show at the edges, with vertical cracks that ran from top to bottom next to the quoin stones. Over the years this crack became more pronounced and even the quoin stones themselves began to shift.

In 1994 the extent of the damage was assessed. The hole in the roof was considerably larger and the upper front southern quoin stones had fractured. Masonry was also falling from the front dormer window surrounds. Internally the front wall outer skin had moved forward by half a metre, while the inner skin had been held back by the upper floor joists, but these had now been pulled out of their sockets and the inner wall skin was moving outwards. In 1996 many of the upper quoins had fallen out completely and in a storm in 1997 the front elevation and the entire roof collapsed. Our last visit in 1998 still found the back wall, the gable ends with chimney stacks and most of its inner timber framing and the upper chapel floor still standing, but now open to the weather.

MY88 (NL5652:8331) Burial ground and chapel. *Location*: Valley floor, village environs. *Description*: The burial ground was used into modern times, as the recent concrete grave stones indicate, and the last burial there in 1910 of Anna Ruairidh Dhomhnaill, the midwife of Mingulay who had moved to Sandray, is well-documented (Buxton 1995). The burial ground is accepted as the site of a mediaeval chapel dedicated to St Columba, but this was no longer visible except possibly for a few coursed stones that may have been one of the walls. The morphology of the burial ground is similar to other early examples in the islands, with a mounded interior surrounded by a drystone wall.

MY89 (NL5698:8226) Cairn. (clearance) *Location*: Coastal bench. *Description*: Circular, diam. 2 m, pile of stone within field system associated with MY35.

MY90 (NL5561:8310) Peat dryer. *Location*: Shelf at mid hill-slope. *Description*: Oval, 4.6 × 2 m, low flat mound with many stones set on edge around the sides and as a possible facade at the eastern end.

MY91* (NL5547:8317) Peat dryer. *Location*: Cliff-top shelf. *Description*: Oval, 2.3 × 1.9 m, remnant of a very badly eroded monument that is presumed to be a peat dryer. One side is still in position with a line of stones set on edge, but most of the rest are displaced out on to denuded bedrock. *Note*: Severe active erosion.

MY92 (NL5544:8308) (Fig. 3.27) Peat dryer. *Location*: Cliff-top shelf. *Description*: Rectangular, 4 × 1.8 m, low flat mound edged on three sides with set stones many of which are still in a vertical position. At the open end to the west the mound merges into the hillside.

MY93 (NL5534:8305) Cairn. *Location*: Shelf on cliff-top. *Description*: Circular, diam. 2 m, possibly kerbed, grassed mound.

MY94 (NL5534:8364) Peat dryer. *Location*: Upper hill-slope. *Description*: Oval, 4.5 × 2.5 m, low flat mound with a few stones that may have been set around the edges, but most are scattered at random over the mound area.

MY95 (NL5541:8361) Peat dryer. *Location*: Upper hill-slope shelf. *Description*: Rectangular, 4.5 × 2.5 m, scattered arrangement of stones set on an oval low flat mound.

MY96 (NL5544:8362) Peat dryer. *Location*: Upper hill-slope. *Description*: Rectangular, 4.7 × 3.5 m, single cell based on a platform bounded by stone on three sides in a disarranged state. The open southern end of the mound merges into the hillside. *Note*: Scattered stones.

MY97 (NL5522:8347) Boat-shaped stone setting. *Location*: Upper hill-slope shelf. *Description*: Boat-shaped, 7 × 3.5 m, single cell, upright stones standing 0.4 m high at the eastern corner. Orientated east–west.

MY98 (NL5539:8345) (Fig. 3.27) Peat dryer. *Location*: Ridge plateau. *Description*: Oval, 4.5 × 3 m, low flattened mound edged with stone and emphasized substantially at the western end facade.

MY99 (NL5541:8348) Shelter. *Location*: Ridge plateau. *Description*: Oval, 4 × 3 m, single cell of small scattered surface stones. *Note*: Could be dispersed cairn.

MY100 (NL5541:8349) (Fig. 3.27) Peat dryer. *Location*: Plateau. *Description*: Oval, 5 × 2.1 m, low flat mound edged with piled stone.

MY101* (NL5536:8344) Peat dryer. *Location*: Ridge plateau. *Description*: Subrectangular, 7 × 4.5 m, very low flat mound with a few upright stones still in place, but mostly displaced and thinly scattered along the sides.

MY102 (NL5534:8350) Peat dryer. *Location*: Ridge plateau. *Description*: Subrectangular, 5 × 1.9 m, low flat mound with some side stones in place but others collapsed inwards. *Note*: Covered by heather.

MY103 (NL5527:8348) Cairn. *Location*: On slope. *Description*: Oval, 1.7 × 1.6 m, collection of a few stones on a small square platform.

MY104 (NL5632:8284) (Fig. 3.20) Cairn. *Location*: Lower back slope of coastal valley. *Description*: Circular, 1.5 m diam., collection of stones with a slight ring bank of earth in which a massive upright 1.2 m long and 0.70 m high is set on the northern edge.

MY105 (NL5611:8269) Shieling complex. *Location*: Lower valley hill-slope. *Description*: Oval shape, internal divisions, 7.5 × 5.5 m ellipse with circle inside.

MY105a (NL5611:8269) Shieling. *Location*: On slope. *Description*: Oval, 7.5 × 5.5 m, single-cell ellipsoid of a banked earthen wall foundation with a few stones embedded.

MY105b (NL5611:8269) Shelter. *Location*: On slope. *Description*: Circular, diam. 1.5 m. A mass of stonework piled within and on the oval bank. A particular mass of stones forms a wall across the inside of the oval while the rest are disarranged all around the eastern end.

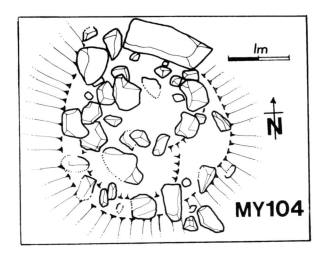

Figure 3.20 Site MY104.

MY106 (NL5607:8271) Shieling. *Location*: Lower valley hill-slope. *Description*: Subrectangular, 6 × 3 m, double cell composed of a square room 3 × 3 m of banked earthen wall foundation edged in places with set stones. Butted to this on the eastern side is a second subrectangular room 3 × 2 m. There is no apparent entrance and some of the stonework is displaced. *Note*: Covered by heather.

MY107 (NL5607:8275) Shieling. *Location*: Lower valley hill-slope. *Description*: Oval, 8 × 5 m, double cell very similar to MY106 except that the individual rooms are circular. The main room is 3 m diam. with 1 m thick earthen walls edged in places with stonework. An entrance may exist to the north. The second room of 2 m diam. is cojoined on the south-western side. No entrance is visible to this room. *Note*: Covered by heather.

MY108 (NL5613:8253) Peat dryer. *Location*: Mid hill-slope. *Description*: Subrectangular, 6 × 2.7 m, very low mound with stones set along the sides and a substantial stone-built facade at the east end. The west end is open and the mound merges into the hillside.

MY109 (NL5610:8254) Shieling complex. *Location*: Mid hill-slope. *Description*: Complex covers an area of approximately 14 × 7 m composed of a main oval hut 109d and a set of smaller huts or storerooms whose walls all cojoin at the rear of the main building. A small shelter appears to have been constructed at a later date inside the small hut 109b.

MY109a (NL5610:8254) Shieling. *Location*: As above. *Description*: Oval, 3.5 × 3 m, single cell of earthen and stone wall foundations internally faced with stone, but showing no apparent entrance.

MY109b (NL5610:8254) Shieling. *Location*: As above. *Description*: Subrectangular, 4 × 3 m, single cell of earthen and stone walls faced with stone and with no apparent entrance.

MY109c (NL5610:8254) Shieling. *Location*: As above. *Description*: Oval, 3 × 2 m, single cell of earthen walls, stone-faced internally and with no apparent entrance.

Cojoined to the rear, eastern, wall of the main building.

MY109d (NL5610:8254) Shieling. *Location*: As above. *Description*: Oval, 4 × 3.5 m, single cell with earthen walls, partly stone-faced inside, with a south entrance.

MY109e (NL5610:8254) Shelter. *Location*: As above. *Description*: Circular, 1.5 m diam., single-cell shelter built at a later date inside 109b.

MY109f (NL5610:8254) Setting. *Location*: As above. *Description*: Oval, 4 × 2.5 m, group of stones that may be a robbed-out building or a construction of a less substantial structure than the others in the complex.

MY110 (NL5607:8256) Shieling. *Location*: Mid hill-slope. *Description*: Oval, 7.5 × 3.7 m, single cell with the north part surrounded by an earthen bank while the rest of the area appears to be filled with displaced stonework. Dimensions and shape suggest the possibility that this could be a peat dryer.

MY111 (NL5602:8257) Shieling. *Location*: Mid hill-slope. *Description*: Oval, 6 × 5 m, double cell of stone-lined earthen wall foundations and with an entrance facing north. A smaller ?annexe or storeroom opens from the eastern side of the main room.

MY112 (NL5589:8261) Shieling. *Location*: Mid hill-slope. *Description*: Oval, 6.5 × 4.6 m, single cell formed with earth and stone walls, stone-lined internally and with an entrance to the west.

MY113 (NL5586:8258) Shelter. *Location*: Mid hill-slope. *Description*: Oval, 6 × 5.8 m, platform into hillside with single-cell shelter of set stones around leading edge.

MY114 (NL5616:8237) Cairn. *Location*: Mid hill-slope. *Description*: Oval, 4 × 1.9 m, mound of earth and stones. *Note*: Partly covered by heather, but the west side has eroded and the stonework is exposed.

MY115 (NL5617:8226) Peat dryer. *Location*: Upper hill-slope plateau. *Description*: Rectangular, 3 × 1.5 m, low flat platform with masses of piled stone around the south-western end and along the sides leaving the north-eastern end open. Much of the stonework has tumbled inwards. *Note*: Severe and active erosion has reduced the peat soil to bedrock all around the western sides spilling out the stonework from its original position along the edges.

MY116 (NL5610:8229) Peat dryer. *Location*: Upper hill-slope plateau. *Description*: Oval, 6.5 × 4 m, low mound with a mass of displaced stones around the edges, and with a few still in fixed upright positions. A possible facade is at the northern end.

MY117 (NL5585:8227) Cairn. *Location*: Hecla hill-top. *Description*: Oval, 5.5 × 3 m, low mound with a few stones around the edges. *Note*: Could be a peat dryer.

MY118 (NL5586:8229) Shelter. *Location*: Hecla hill-top. *Description*: Oval, 4 × 3.5 m, very slight mound with a few scattered stones. *Note*: Active erosion of the southern half. Could be a cairn.

MY119 (NL5577:8238) Shieling. *Location*: Hecla–Carnan hill saddle. *Description*: Oval, 8 × 6 m, double cell similar to MY106/7. The metre-thick earthen wall foundations are edged in places by large slabs set upright. There is no apparent entrance. The overall oval shape is modified by being pointed at one end and rounded at the other. A cross-wall divides the building into two rooms.

MY120* (NL5481:8211) Peat dryer. *Location*: Cliff-top. *Description*: Oval, 5 × 4 m, collection of stones some of which are set upright. Could be a peat dryer.

MY121* (NL5481:8199) Shelter. *Location*: Cliff-top. *Description*: Rectangular, dimensions unknown, several stones appear to be purposely set. *Note*: Could be natural.

MY122 (NL5518:8199) Shelter. *Location*: Cliff edge. *Description*: Circular, 4 m diam., of flat-laid stones that could be a degraded shelter or hut circle.

MY123* (NL5504:8167) Cairn. *Location*: Coastal shelf. *Description*: Circular, 2.7 m diam., earthen mound with a few stones.

MY124* (NL5512:8160) Setting. *Location*: Cliff-top. *Description*: Setting of stones that may be a natural formation. No dimensions.

MY125 (NL5605:8279) Setting. *Location*: Lower valley hill-slope. *Description*: An area, 10 × 8 m, of stonework some set in a curved line, but generally not making any overall structural sense. *Note*: Severely eroded.

MY126 (NL5604:8281) Peat dryer. *Location*: Lower valley hill-slope. *Description*: Oval, 8 × 4.5 m, low mound with stones set around the front eastern end as a facade. From the facade a few stones are set along each side. The western end is open and the mound merges into the hillside.

MY127 (NL5571:8274) Cairn. *Location*: Upper hill-slope. *Description*: Oval, 6.2 × 5.5 m, mound with some scattered stone and one large stone in an off-centre position. It may originally have been circular, but it has spread out of shape.

MY128 (NL5633:8218) Enclosure. *Location*: Mid hill-slope. *Description*: Oval, 19 × 12 m, arc of closely placed stones butted in at the ends to natural rock formations.

MY129 (NL5626:8219) Shelter. *Location*: Mid hill-slope bench. *Description*: Square, 4 × 4 m, open-sided single cell of large stones, height 0.6 to 0.9 m, set upright around the south end of an oblong mound.

MY130 (NL5631:8286) Shelter. *Location*: Shelf on lower valley hill-slope. *Description*: Subrectangular, 6 × 4 m, single cell of stone-faced earthen wall foundations set against a field wall of single-stone thickness. There is no apparent entrance.

MY131 (NL5624:8290) Shelter. *Location*: Shelf on lower valley hill-slope. *Description*: Square, 2.5 × 2.5 m, single cell of earthen walls lined with stones set on edge, but many have become displaced. *Note*: The

displaced stonework may be a rebuild into a much less robust shelter occupying only a part of the area.

MY132 (NL5631:8332) Mill. *Location*: Valley floor. *Description*: The Mingulay mill was built to the west of the village by John MacKinnon around 1890 on a stream fed by a number of channels draining the field system in the valley bottom. Constructed with a vertical wheel to drive the shaft on which the millstones were mounted, it closely resembles the mill on Berneray, which MacKinnon not only may have copied but may also have used parts stripped from since it went out of use at this time (Buxton 1995). Although some of the walls are over a metre thick, the construction is surprisingly flimsy in comparison to the usual solid walled Hebridean buildings, and just during the few years of the survey it has been possible to observe considerable deterioration in the superstructure. The mill is square in plan, 3.9 × 3.7 m, with the wheel housing built a further 1.3 m out over the stream to the south. On the northern side may have been a lean-to shelter either for working or for storage while working. The internal dimensions of the milling room that housed the millstones are 2m × 1.2 m. These millstones can at present be found half-way to the beach. They were no doubt to be taken aboard one of the many vessels that call in unannounced, but, they being large and heavy, it would appear that the attempt to relieve the island of its portable, saleable objects was abandoned. Ideally, their return to the mill site to be permanently fixed there would be desirable.

MY133 (NL5619:8331) Shelter. *Location*: Valley floor. *Description*: Circular, 2 m diam., single cell against a field wall. *Note*: Within the field system.

MY134 (NL5644:8377) Cairn. *Location*: Shelf on upper hill-slope. *Description*: Circular, 2 m diam., very slight mound with stonework around most of the edge. *Note*: Active erosion is threatening the western side.

MY135 (NL5645:8379) Shelter. *Location*: Shelf on upper hill-slope. *Description*: Half-circle, 2 m diam., arc of stonework mostly set on edge, like the front facade of a peat dryer, forming a single cell with an open end to the north. Set on a platform angled into the hill-slope.

MY136 (NL5645:8382) Shelter. *Location*: Shelf on upper hill-slope. *Description*: Circular, 2 m diam., single cell of stacked stone walling open to the south-east.

MY137 (NL5647:8384) Cairn. *Location*: Shelf on upper hill-slope. *Description*: Oval, 3.5 × 3 m, mound with a few stones at the edges, but not forming a full circle.

MY138 (NL5644:8384) Peat dryer. *Location*: Shelf on upper hill-slope. *Description*: Oval, 4 × 2.5 m, low flat grassy mound with a few scattered stones.

MY139 (NL5648:8387) Complex of shelters. *Location*: Shelf on upper hill-slope. *Description*: Oval platform, 3 × 2 m, occupied by two circular shelters.

MY139a (NL5648:8387) Shelter. *Location*: As above. *Description*: Circular, 2 m diam., single cell, half-circle of piled stone with an open side to the east.

MY139b (NL5648:8387) Shelter. *Location*: As above. *Description*: Circular, 1 m diam., single cell, half-circle of spaced stones with an open side to the east.

MY140 (NL5646:8386) Shelter. *Location*: Shelf on upper hill-slope. *Description*: Circular, 2.5 m diam., single cell composed of a few stones set on a platform, but the eroded disorganized state of the monument could allow it to be other things, such as a degraded peat dryer, for example.

MY141 (NL5652:8385) Shelter. *Location*: Shelf on upper hill-slope. *Description*: Rectangular, 2.1 × 1.9 m, single cell of internally stone-faced earthen wall foundations mounded at the southern end and open at the northern. At the northern end the mound merges into the hillside. This could be the facaded front of a degraded peat dryer.

MY142 (NL5655:8385) Shelter. *Location*: Shelf on upper hill-slope. *Description*: Oval, 2.7 × 2 m, half-circle of stones set upright, forming the southern side of a small single cell shelter.

MY143 (NL5649:8390) Shelter. *Location*: Shelf on upper hill-slope. *Description*: Subrectangular, 3.5 × 2.5 m, single cell of collapsed stonework, especially on the southern side, set on a platform. Could be a cairn.

MY144 (NL5650:8393) (Fig. 3.21) Cairn. *Location*: Upper hill-slope. *Description*: Oval, 4.1 × 3.9 m, flat-topped mound with stones set intermittently around the edges. *Note*: Possibly a kerbed cairn. Severely eroded and damaged by rabbit burrowing.

MY145 (NL5661:8378) Shelter. *Location*: Shelf on upper hill-slope. *Description*: Subrectangular, 3.9 ×

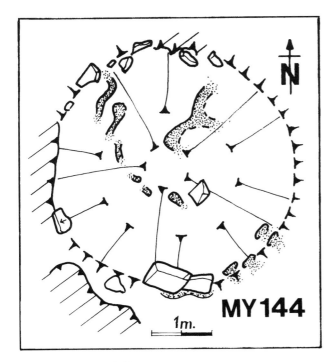

Figure 3.21 Site MY144.

2.2 m, single cell of collapsed stonework. Although some are still set upright in place, the rest are scattered.

MY146 (NL5659:8385) Shelter. *Location*: On slight prominence on upper hill-slope. *Description*: Subrectangular, 2.5 × 2.3 m, single cell with stonework on three sides intact, but open to the north.

MY147 (NL5655:8389) Peat dryer. *Location*: Inside dyke on upper hill-slope. *Description*: Oval, 4 × 2 m, low flat mound with a piled stone facade at the south-eastern end. At the open north-west end the mound merges with the hill-slope.

MY148 (NL5642:8392) Shelter. *Location*: Shelf on upper hill-slope. *Description*: Subrectangular, 4.5 × 3.5 m, single cell on platform, sloped to the bedrock. There is only stonework surviving at the leading edge. *Note*: Could be a peat dryer. Partly eroded.

MY149 (NL5645:8404) Cairn. *Location*: Upper hill-slope shelf in dyke. *Description*: Oval, 3.7 × 2.5 m, earthen mound with a few stones at the edges. *Note*: Half of the mound on the west side is eroded away.

MY150 (NL5643:8400) Peat dryer. *Location*: Shelf on upper hill-slope. *Description*: Oval, 5.6 × 2 m, low flat mound with a set stone facade that has partly collapsed down the slope at the south-western end. Few other stones are to be seen. *Note*: Wind erosion is attacking the western edge.

MY151 (NL5648:8399) (Fig. 3.27) Peat dryer. *Location*: Upper hill-slope shelf. *Description*: Oval 5 × 2 m mound standing a metre high with a facade of stones set on edge. Very little stonework is to be seen in the rest of the monument. *Note*: Considerable rabbit burrowing throughout and wind erosion.

MY152 (NL5660:8426) Shelter. *Location*: Upper hill-top shelf. *Description*: Oval, 4 × 2 m, single cell, upright stone 0.7 m high.

MY153 (NL5663:8420) Shelter. *Location*: Upper hill-top shelf. *Description*: Oval, 4 × 3.5 m, single cell of a few stones set in earthen bank ring-wall. Stonework on north side, but south-west side has suffered from erosion.

MY154 (NL5680:8389) Shelter. *Location*: Mid hill-slope shelf above dyke. *Description*: Oval, 2.2 × 1.2 m, low flat mound with some single stones set in line along the top edge, especially the southern side, forming a possible single cell. *Note*: Covered by heather.

MY155 (NL5690:8394) Peat dryer. *Location*: Shelf on steep mid hill-slope. *Description*: Subrectangular, 4.6 × 2.7 m, mound that has mostly eroded away, but the southern facade of stones set on edge is prominent. *Note*: Active and severe erosion.

MY156 (NL5690:8387) Shelter. *Location*: Mid hill-slope. *Description*: Subrectangular, 3.5 × 3 m, low mounded platform with large slabs placed around one end and the sides, forming an open-ended single cell.

MY157 (NL5656:8407) Peat dryer. *Location*: Upper hill-top shelf. *Description*: Rectangular, 4.2 × 2.5 m,

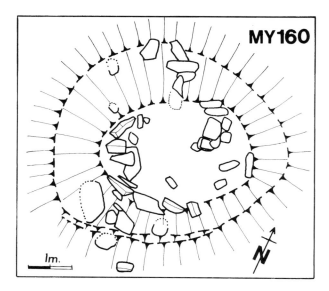

Figure 3.22 Site MY160.

low flat mound edged with stone, some set on edge with a few others scattered out of place. At the southern end the structure is under the shelter of a large fallen boulder.

MY158 (NL5653:8404) Mound. *Location*: Upper hilltop valley. *Description*: Oval, 3.3 × 2.3 m, grassy mound with a few stones.

MY159 (NL5654:8416) Mound. *Location*: Upper hilltop shelf. *Description*: Oval, 4 × 3 m, grassy mound with a few stones.

MY160 (NL5652:8412) (Fig. 3.22) Kerbed cairn. *Location*: Upper hill-top shelf. *Description*: Oval egg-shaped mound 5.5 m across at its widest point, with some stonework set on the perimeter and some in displaced secondary positions.

MY161 (NL5603:8300) Peat dryer. *Location*: Slight prominence on a shelf of the lower valley hill-slope. *Description*: Oval, 3 × 2 m, low mound edged with large stones. The north-west edge may once have been open-ended. Many stones have been displaced. *Note*: Subject to erosion.

MY162 (NL5597:8300) Boat-shaped stone setting. *Location*: Lower valley hill-slope. *Description*: Boat-shaped, 4.2 × 2 m, low mound orientated east–west, with the pointed end to the east. Several large stone blocks are placed around the upper edge.

MY163* (NL5539:8343) Complex of shelters. *Location*: Ridge plateau. *Description*: Two square cojoined shelters with placed stone, single-thickness, single-course, walling.

MY163a* (NL5539:8343) Shelter. *Location*: As above. *Description*: Square, 1.5 × 1.5 m, single cell.

MY163b* (NL5539:8343) Shelter. *Location*: As above. *Description*: Rectangular, 2.1 × 1.5 m, single cell with opening to the west.

MY164 (NL5541:8351) Cairn. *Location*: Ridge plateau in dyke. *Description*: Circular 5 m diam. slight mound with a few stones at the edge. *Note*: Could be natural.

MY165 (NL5544:8354) Peat dryer. *Location*: Ridge plateau. *Description*: Subrectangular, 7 × 2.4 m, low flat mound with some small scattered stones around the sides. Eroded down to bedrock at sides.

MY166 (NL5545:8351) Mound. *Location*: Ridge plateau. *Description*: Oval, 2.8 × 1.5 m, grassy mound with several stones around the edge. *Note*: Active erosion threatens from the west where denuded bedrock can be seen.

MY167 (NL5537:8356) Peat dryer. *Location*: Ridge plateau. *Description*: Oval, 7 × 2.5 m, low flat mound with a linear scatter of stones along the western side and a group of scattered stones on the eastern side. A single large block of stone at the northern end may be the remnant of a facade.

MY168 (NL5538:8354) Shelter. *Location*: Ridge plateau. *Description*: Circular, 1.5 m diam., very slight mound with several stones set in a circle around the edge forming a possible single cell.

MY169 (NL5533:8355) Peat dryer. *Location*: Ridge plateau. *Description*: Oval, 6 × 2 m, flat-topped mound with a pointed facade of set stone slabs at the north-eastern end. The opposite end is open and the mound merges into the hillside through the gap.

MY170 (NL5556:8346) Peat dryer. *Location*: Ridge plateau. *Description*: Subrectangular, 4 × 1.5 m, low flat mound with stones placed around the south side to a rounded facade of stonework at the east end. The other side and end have few stones in place.

MY171 (NL5555:8351) (Fig. 3.23) Cairn. *Location*: Ridge plateau. *Description*: Oval, 1.5 × 1 m, pile of stones, some few scattered out on to exposed bedrock. *Note*: Threatened by erosion.

MY172 (NL5551:8348) Peat dryer. *Location*: Ridge plateau. *Description*: Oval, 4.5 × 2.3 m, low mound with stones along the south side and the eastern end, which may form a facade. *Note*: Active erosion to bedrock from south.

MY173 (NL5548:8343) Cairn. *Location*: Ridge plateau. *Description*: Oval, 1.8 × 1.5 m, low mound with stones up to 0.3 m in size set around the edges. Could be a shelter.

MY174 (NL5535:8353) Shelter. *Location*: Ridge plateau. *Description*: Oval, 1.6 × 1 m, single cell formed with a ring of stones set in the shelter of a large boulder. *Note*: Active wind erosion.

MY175 (NL5531:8350) Peat dryer. *Location*: Ridge plateau. *Description*: Oval, 3.5 × 2 m, low flat mound with an arc of stones forming a slightly disarranged facade at the southern end. There is very little other stonework. The northern end merges into the hill-slope.

MY176 (NL5533:8360) Peat dryer. *Location*: Edge of ridge plateau. *Description*: Subrectangular, 6 × 3 m, low flat mound edged with stones, some set upright and standing to 0.3 m.

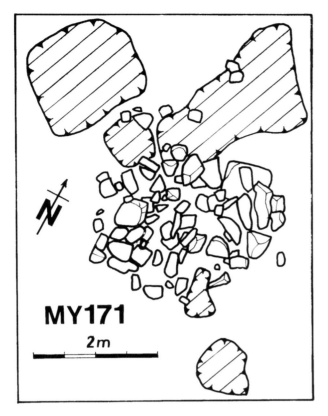

Figure 3.23 Site MY171.

MY177 (NL5530:8358) Cairn. *Location*: Edge of ridge plateau. *Description*: Circular, 1.7 m diam., slightly mounded with stones around the edges. *Note*: Wind erosion damage from the north.

MY178 (NL5527:8354) Peat dryer. *Location*: Edge of hill-top plateau. *Description*: Subrectangular, 4.5 × 3 m, low flat mound with large blocks of stone along the sides, but apparently open at the ends.

MY179 (NL5531:8363) Cairn. *Location*: Upper hill-slope. *Description*: Oval, 2.9 × 2.4 m, low mound of earth with intermittently set stones around the edges.

MY180 (NL5530:8367) Shelter. *Location*: Upper hill-slope. *Description*: Circular, 2 m diam., single cell formed with piled stones, but many have fallen down slope.

MY181 (NL5526:8351) Shelter. *Location*: Ridge plateau. *Description*: Circular, 4 m diam., very flat mound with a ragged circle of stones forming a single cell with a possible entrance to the north-east. The stone walling appears collapsed and scattered outwards.

MY182 (NL5529:8351) Shelter. *Location*: Ridge plateau. *Description*: Sub-rectangular, 5 × 3 m, platform with an ill-defined circle of spaced and scattered stones on top.

MY183 (NL5535:8348) Shelter. *Location*: Ridge plateau. *Description*: Circular, 1.2 m diam., single cell formed with a few placed stones. *Note*: Subject to active erosion with bedrock being exposed.

MY184 (NL5534:8347) Cairn. *Location*: Ridge plateau. *Description*: Oval, 2 × 1.5 m, grassy mound. *Note*: scattered stones.

MY185 (NL5536:8346) Cairn. *Location*: Ridge plateau. *Description*: Circular, diam. 1.5 m, slight grassy mound with several large blocks set around the edge.

MY186 (NL5618:8370) Cairn. *Location*: Mid-valley hill-slope. *Description*: Oval, 2.5 × 1.5 m, low mound with several large blocks placed around the edges.

MY187 (NL5629:8371) Shieling. *Location*: Mid-valley hill-slope. *Description*: Square, 4 × 4 m, single cell of stones. There is considerable displaced and scattered stonework.

MY188 (NL5626:8389) Shelter. *Location*: Upper-valley hill-slope. *Description*: Oval, 2.5 × 2.5 m, single cell with a possible entrance to the north-east set on a small mound.

MY189 (NL5569:8338) Shelter. *Location*: Hill-slope to valley. *Description*: Subrectangular, 8 × 4 m, double cell butted against face of dyke rock wall and also using an enclosure wall that crosses the dyke. Both the enclosure wall and the shelter walls are constructed of piled stones, many of which have fallen and are locally scattered.

MY190 (NL5644:8255) Shelter. *Location*: Lower hill-slope shelf. *Description*: Circular, 2.6 m diam., single cell stone ring, but many of the stones appear disarranged. *Note*: Covered by heather.

MY191 (NL5648:8227) Shieling complex. *Location*: Bottom of mid-slope on sloping bench. *Description*: Rectangular platform and enclosure attached to the inside of the island head dyke wall. A shelter on the platform is butted to the head dyke.

MY191a (NL5648:8227) Enclosure and platform *Location*: As above. *Description*: Rectangular, 10.5 × 5.6 m, enclosure on grassy platform.

MY191b (NL5648:8227) Shelter. *Location*: As above. *Description*: Rectangular, 2 × 1.5 m, single-cell stone shelter inside the enclosure and butted against head dyke wall with entrance into the enclosure to the west.

MY192 (NL5653:8223) Cairn. *Location*: Lower hill-slope bench. *Description*: Oval, 2.5 × 3 m, mound with a few stones set and scattered. On a slight platform

MY193 (NL5655:8221) Cairn. *Location*: Lower hill-slope bench. *Description*: Circular, 2 m diam., grassy earthen mound with a few scattered stones both on and off the mound.

MY194 (NL5651:8213) Complex of roundhouse and shieling *Location*: Lower hill-slope. *Description*: Rectangular shieling with stone-faced, earth-filled walls, standing many courses high. The building stands on a circular mound, 10 m diam., with a small circular stone setting on its northern side. *Note*: Excavated: site report in volume 6 forthcoming.

MY194a (NL5651:8213) Roundhouse. *Location*: As above. *Description*: Circular, 10 m diam., revetted mound, but excavation has shown that the mound is formed by an internal stone-faced wall of which the revetting of the mound is the outer face. Not enough of the structure was revealed to determine its true form and function. A later shieling hut was constructed on the upper levels.

MY194b (NL5651:8213) Shieling. *Location*: As above. *Description*: A substantially built rectilinear, 4 × 3 m, single cell with upstanding stone-faced walls filled with earth. A doorway faces the sea to the south-east, but was partly filled, as was the interior, with fallen stone and earth. The work as a whole was set on a stone-revetted mound of an earlier construction. On the northern side is a small circular setting of stone and downslope is a further stone-revetted mound on a platform, but without any crowning structure. The southern half of the building was excavated and found to contain, under the fallen infill of stone and earth, a thick laminated deposit representing a long sequence of peat fires. The back wall of an earlier building was revealed, the fire deposits rested immediately upon it flowing down into the hollow of the interior. For some reason the walls of the lower building had not been utilized as a foundation and the later shieling hut had been constructed partly in and partly over the earlier walls. The interior of the earlier building had obviously been visible as a hollow and this had been used to give shelter inside for the occupants and their fireplace. Dating evidence for the upper building rests on a sherd of 19th-century china. The earlier deposits and structures were not disturbed.

MY195 (NL5673:8244) Shieling complex. *Location*: Lower hill-slope bench. *Description*: Oval enclosure on a levelled slope with shieling hut inside.

MY195a (NL5673:8244) Enclosure. *Location*: As above. *Description*: Oval, 23 × 10 m, enclosure with a small subenclosure at the south-west side that has one definite shelter in the southern corner and another possible shelter at the opposite end.

MY195b (NL5673:8244) Shieling. *Location*: As above. *Description*: Subrectangular, 5 × 4 m, single cell hut inside the enclosure.

MY196 (NL5660:8227) Peat dryer. *Location*: Lower hill-slope bench. *Description*: Subrectangular, 6.7 × 3 m, low flat mound with a few stones around the sides and a fallen facade of stones at the northern end. *Note*: Covered with heather.

MY197 (NL5664:8226) Peat dryer. *Location*: Lower hill-slope slope bench. *Description*: Oval, 3 × 1.4 m, low, slightly concave centred mound, with a stone facade of stones set on edge at the east end. Set side stones get more widely spaced as they approach the open west end.

MY198 (NL5652:8210) Mound. *Location*: Lower hill-slope bench. *Description*: Oval, 8.8 × 7 m, low grass-covered mound with the south side faced by stone blocks.

MY199 (NL5658:8212) Shelter. *Location*: Lower hill-slope bench. *Description*: Oval, 2.1 × 1.9 m, single cell

horseshoe-shaped, low earth and stone wall foundation set on platform cut into hillside.

MY200 (NL5637:8210) Peat dryer. *Location*: Steep mid hill-slope. *Description*: Oval, 5.5 × 3.8 m, low mound with large stone blocks and slabs in size range 0.7–1 m set at the edges. *Note*: Covered by heather.

MY201 (NL5626:8207) Shelter. *Location*: Mid hill-slope. *Description*: Oval, 4.5 × 3 m, very slight mound with a ring of stones around the edge forming a single cell. *Note*: Covered by heather.

MY202 (NL5529:8280) (Fig. 3.24) Cairn. *Location*: Carnan hill summit, 273 m. *Description*: Oval, 5.5 × 4.5 m, double circle of set ring stones forming solid flat cairn around the modern trig. point 273 OD. There are other scattered stones. Although there may be some modern displacement and probably additional material recently collected here around the survey point, there is a high probability that the core of an ancient cairn was used for the emplacement of the marker.

MY203 (NL5531:8276) Peat dryer. *Location*: Carnan hill-top plateau. *Description* Oval, 10 × 5 m, low flat mound with displaced stonework at the southern end. There is little other stonework along the sides and the opposite end appears to merge into the hill-slope. *Note*: On an eroded platform

MY204 (NL5533:8278) Peat dryer. *Location*: Carnan hill-top plateau. *Description*: Subrectangular, 4 × 2 m, low flat grassy mound with several stones set around the edges.

MY205 (NL5528:8276) Peat dryer. *Location*: Carnan hill-top plateau. *Description*: Rectangular, but greatly disfigured by erosion, 5.6 × 2 m remnant of a mound with one surviving stone-lined edge on the western side. *Note*: Severe active erosion has destroyed much of this monument.

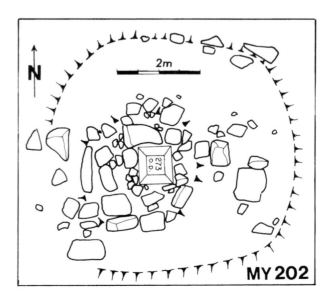

Figure 3.24 Site MY202.

MY206 (NL5527:8275) Peat dryer. *Location*: Carnan hill-top plateau. *Description*: Oval, 4.4 × 4.3 m, low-flat topped mound with a few stone slabs set around the perimeter. *Note*: Active erosion is degrading the site from several directions revealing bedrock.

MY207 (NL5521:8276) Cairn. *Location*: Carnan hill-top plateau. *Description*: Oval, 4 × 3.2 m, mound of earth with depressed centre. There are a few visible stones.

MY208 (NL5524:8271) Peat dryer. *Location*: Carnan hill-top plateau. *Description*: Oval, 6 × 4 m, low flat mound with some scattered displaced stonework. The northern end merges with the hillside. The 4 m width includes material spreading off the mound.

MY209 (NL5521:8272) Mound. *Location*: Carnan hill-top plateau. *Description*: Circular, 2 m diam., earthen mound with a slight hollowing of the top. Apart from two stones at the southern edge it is stone-free. *Note*: Some wind erosion is evident.

MY210 (NL5523:8281) Peat dryer. *Location*: Edge of hill-top plateau. *Description*: Subrectangular, 5.5 × 2.6 m, low mound with a few stones placed around the perimeter. *Note*: Active peat deflation on western edge of mound.

MY211 (NL5525:8283) Peat dryer. *Location*: Edge of hill-top plateau. *Description*: Oval, 4.5 × 3.2 m, low mound with a few displaced stone blocks scattered around. *Note*: Severe active erosion deflating the mound.

MY212 (NL5529:8288) Cairn. *Location*: Shelf on the edge of hill-top plateau. *Description*: Oval, 5.5 × 5 m, grassy bank of earth with scattered stone on a platform. *Note*: Could be a degraded peat dryer.

MY213 (NL5523:8284) Peat dryer. *Location*: Edge of hill-top plateau. *Description*: Possible shapeless, 4 × 2 m, remnant of low peat mound now almost totally eroded away leaving some displaced stone.

MY214 (NL5527:8284) Peat dryer. *Location*: Edge of hill-top plateau. *Description*: Probably a rectangular, 4.5 × 4.3 m, mound with a single cell of stone around the edges. Now severely deflated and partly dissolved into pools of standing water. What may have been the original stone facade at the southern end is still intact.

MY215 (NL5534:8288) Cairn. *Location*: Edge of hill-top plateau. *Description*: Oval, 4.4 × 4.2 m, mound severely eroded revealing its internal stonework and displacing it. *Note*: Active erosion threat.

MY216 (NL5528:8282) Cairn. *Location*: Hill-top plateau. *Description*: Oval, 3.7 × 3.1 m, small mound with some stones around the perimeter.

MY217 (NL5546:8280) (Fig. 3.25) Peat dryer. *Location*: Hill-top plateau. *Description*: Possibly an oval or subrectangular, 7.5 × 5.5 m, peat mound with a mass of displaced stonework. Some stonework may still be in place as the perimeter retaining wall but perhaps as much as a third of the mound has dissolved into a large pool of standing acidic water. *Note*: Severe active deflation in progress.

MY218 (NL5543:8274) Peat dryer. *Location*: Hill-top slope. *Description*: Oval, 5 × 3.5 m, low mound with a few spaced stones around the perimeter. The northern end merges into the hillside.

MY219 (NL5546:8274) Peat dryer. *Location*: Hill-top slope. *Description*: Oval, 7.5 × 3.8 m, low mound with a few stones around the perimeter.

Figure 3.25 Site MY217.

MY220 (NL5544:8272) Mound. *Location*: Hill-top slope. *Description*: Oval, 2.5 × 1.8 m, grassy mound with a few stones at the southern end.

MY221 (NL5542:8269) Mound. *Location*: Hill-top slope. *Description*: Oval, 3 × 2 m, grassy mound with a few stones at the southern end.

MY222 (NL5547:8275) Peat dryer. *Location*: Hill-top slope. *Description*: Oval, 4 × 2.5 m, low flat mound with a few large stone slabs, in the 0.5–0.8 m size range, lying in displaced positions.

MY223 (NL5555:8273) Cairn. *Location*: Hill-top slope. *Description*: Oval, 3 × 1.5 m, flat mound with a mass of displaced stone blocks at the southern edge of what may have been a facade. The northern end merges into the hill-slope. This monument has many of the characteristics of a peat dryer.

MY224 (NL5560:8274) Peat dryer. *Location*: Upper hill-slope. *Description*: Subrectangular, 4.8 × 3.3 m, low flat mound with stone slabs set around the edges. *Note*: Active erosion degrading the southern edge of the mound.

MY225 (NL5560:8279) (Figs 3.26, 3.27) Peat dryer. *Location*: Upper hill-slope. *Description*: Subrectangular, 5.5 × 2.5 m, low mound with stones set on edge along the northern side. The southern side stonework is mostly displaced and tumbled inwards. A facade at the eastern end is built up with four to five courses of flat stones.

MY226 (NL5556:8282) (Fig. 3.27) Peat dryer. *Location*: Upper hill-slope. *Description*: Rectangular, 5 × 3 m, setting of stone with many still in upright positions around the sides. The southern side appears in a state of collapse. The structure is set on an oval mound.

MY227 (NL5550:8284) Shelter. *Location*: Upper hill-slope. *Description*: Circular, 2.6 m diam., single-cell ring of set stones.

MY228 (NL5551:8287) Shelter. *Location*: Upper slope bench. *Description*: Oval, 4.4 × 3.3 m, single-cell stone ring around flat mound top.

MY229 (NL5555:8288) Shelter. *Location*: Upper hill-slope. *Description*: Rectangular, 3.5 × 3.4 m, single cell of stones set around edges. Erosion has caused the displacement of stonework making any identification of a possible entrance difficult. *Note*: Active erosion.

MY230 (NL5558:8289) Cairn. *Location*: Upper hill-slope shelf. *Description*: Oval, 4.5 × 3.3 m, flat mound of earth with the remains of a stone ring built around the upper edge. *Note*: Some active erosion.

MY231 (NL5564:8289) Shelter. *Location*: Upper hill plateau. *Description*: Square, 3 × 3 m, single cell of small placed stones, but erosion has displaced most of the alignments and the site is almost leached down to the bedrock.

MY232 (NL5546:8285) Mound. *Location*: Edge of hill-top plateau. *Description*: Oval, 5.6 × 4 m, hollow-topped grassy mound with a few visible embedded stones around the upper edge.

MY233 (NL5542:8283) Mound. *Location*: Hill-top plateau. *Description*: Oval, 3.5 × 2.5 m, grassy mound with a few stones visible at the north-eastern edge.

MY234 (NL5538:8283) Mound. *Location*: Hill-top plateau. *Description*: Oval, 5 × 4.5 m, grassy mound of peat soil. *Note*: Active erosion beginning to deflate northern edge of mound.

MY235 (NL5539:8285) Cairn. *Location*: Edge of hill-top plateau. *Description*: Circular, 1.5 m diam., collection of piled stone.

Figure 3.26 Site MY225.

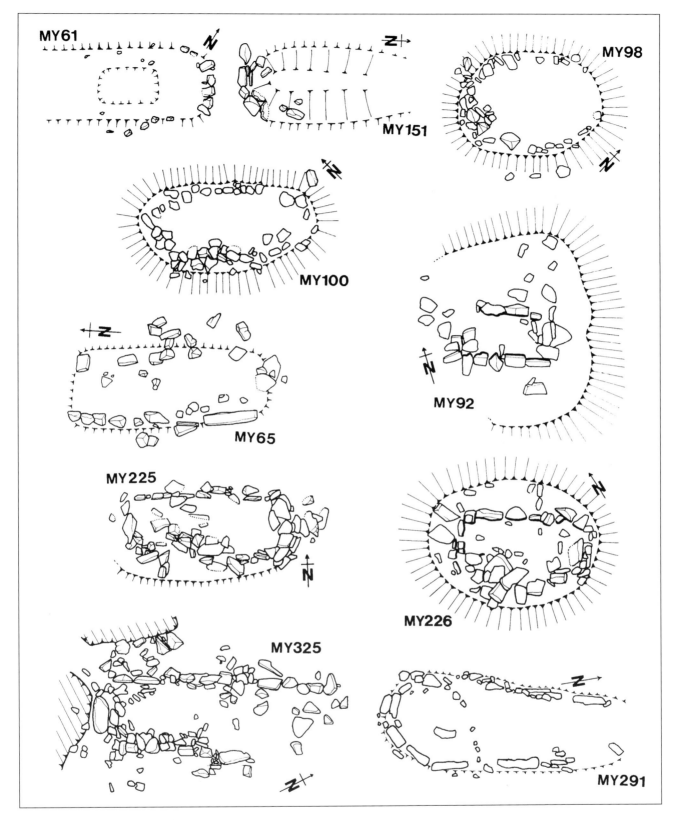

Figure 3.27 A selection of peat dryers.

MY236 (NL5526:8293) Peat dryer. *Location*: Upper hill-slope. *Description*: Oval, 5 × 4 m, low flat-topped mound with a U-shaped stone setting around the eastern end forming a facade.

MY237 (NL5529:8296) Mound. *Location*: Upper hill-slope. *Description*: Oval, 3 × 2 m, grassy stone-free mound.

MY238 (NL5524:8296) Mound. *Location*: Upper

hill-slope. *Description*: Circular, 2.5 m diam., grassy stone-free mound.

MY239 (NL5530:8301) Mound. *Location*: Shelving upper coastal hill-slope. *Description*: Circular, 2.5 m diam., grassy stone-free mound.

MY240 (NL5535:8302) Mound. *Location*: Shelving upper coastal hill-slope. *Description*: Circular, 2.5 m diam., grassy stone-free mound.

MY241* (NL5530:8310) Mound. *Location*: Cliff edge. *Description*: Circular, 2.5 m diam., grassy stone-free mound.

MY242* (NL5531:8307) Cairn. *Location*: Cliff edge. *Description*: Circular, 2.5 m diam., grassy mound with a few stones set on a platform.

MY243* (NL5525:8306) Mound. *Location*: Cliff edge. *Description*: Circular, 2.5 m diam., grassy stone-free mound.

MY244* (NL5522:8304) Mound. *Location*: Cliff edge. *Description*: Circular, 3 m diam., grassy stone-free mound.

MY245* (NL5520:8320) Mound. *Location*: Shelving coastal upper hill-slope. *Description*: Circular, 2 m diam., grassy stone-free mound.

MY246 (NL5522:8300) Mound. *Location*: Shelving upper coastal hill-slope. *Description*: Circular, 2.5 m diam., grassy stone-free mound.

MY247 (NL5521:8298) Mound. *Location*: Upper hill-slope. *Description*: Circular, 2.5 m diam., grassy stone-free mound.

MY248 (NL5519:8295) Mound. *Location*: Upper hill-slope. *Description*: Circular 2.5 m diam. grassy stone-free mound.

MY249 (NL5525:8300) Mound. *Location*: Upper hill-slope to cliff edge. *Description:* Circular, 2.5 m diam., grassy stone-free mound.

MY250 (NL5684:8475) Peat dryer. *Location*: Hill-top. *Description*: Oval, 3.7 × 1.7 m, slight flat mound with a mass of stonework at the southern end forming a facade and as a thinner stone line along the sides. The northern end is open and the mound blends into the hillside. *Note*: Active erosion has stripped the peat soil at the southern end in front of the facade.

MY251 (NL5671:8475) Shelter. *Location*: Shelf on mid hill-slope. *Description*: Oval, 2.8 × 2.6 m, single-cell ring of stones on a mound. *Note*: Badly eroded at the south-western edge. Could be a cairn.

MY252 (NL5674:8472) Peat dryer. *Location*: Upper hill-slope. *Description*: Subrectangular, 2.8 × 2.3 m, low flat mound with a massive stone slab, a metre long, set on edge as a facade at one end. There are a few side stones, but they have mostly fallen away. *Note*: Severe damage from rabbit burrowing and wind erosion.

MY253 (NL5684:8467) Shelter. *Location*: Upper hill-slope. *Description*: Oval, 3.3 × 3 m, single cell formed with large stone blocks. *Note*: Could be natural.

MY254 (NL5563:8349) Cairn. *Location*: Ridge plateau. *Description*: Oval, 3.6 × 2 m, low grassy mound with remnant of stone ring around upper edge. Other stones are scattered.

MY255 (NL5564:8351) Cairn. *Location*: Ridge plateau. *Description*: Circular, 2.5. diam., low grassy mound with a scatter of stones around the edges.

MY256 (NL5564:8353) Peat dryer. *Location*: Ridge plateau. *Description*: Oval, 6 × 4.5 m, low flat mound with a U-shaped stone setting around the eastern end forming a facade. There are a few other scattered stones down the length of the mound.

MY257 (NL5562:8355) Complex of shelters. *Location*: Ridge plateau in small dyke. *Description*: Two oval single-cell shelters of half-circle piled stones.

MY257a (NL5562:8355) Shelter. *Location*: As above. *Description*: Oval, 3.5 × 2.5 m, single cell with a half-circle of piled stone walling, open to the east and set on a slight flat mound.

MY257b (NL5562:8355) Shelter. *Location*: As above. *Description*: Oval, 2 × 1.5 m, single cell with a half-circle of piled-stone walling, open to the east and set on a small flat mound.

MY258 (NL5566:8356) Peat dryer. *Location*: Ridge plateau. *Description*: Subrectangular, 3.3 × 2.1 m, low mound with considerable stonework along the western side and southern end. Much more stonework is displaced and fallen down-slope.

MY259 (NL5567:8351) Cairn. *Location*: Ridge plateau. *Description*: Oval, 1.2 × 1 m, grassy mound with substantial piled stone ring around upper edge. Some stone displaced down mound sides.

MY260 (NL5566:8349) Peat dryer. *Location*: Ridge plateau. *Description*: Subrectangular, 6.5 × 3.7 m, low flat mound with a mass of piled stones around the sides and the southern end. The northern end is open and the mound merges into the hillside.

MY261 (NL5567:8345) Peat dryer. *Location*: Edge of upper ridge plateau. *Description*: Oval, 5 × 2.3 m, grassy mound with a ring of placed retaining stone slabs, many still upright, around the upper edge.

MY262 (NL5572:8351) Peat dryer. *Location*: Edge of ridge plateau. *Description*: A very rounded subrectangular, 4.5 × 3 m, low flat mound with a group of slightly displaced stones at the eastern end which probably once formed a facade. Some of these blocks are in the 0.3–0.6 m size range.

MY263 (NL5576:8354) Peat dryer. *Location*: Edge of ridge plateau. *Description*: Subrectangular, 5 × 2.5 m, low flat mound with a few scattered stones on top and to one side, but the east end has a facade of large set stones while the opposite end is open. The mound merges into the hillside through this gap.

MY264 (NL5572:8362) Peat dryer. *Location*: Ridge plateau. *Description*: Oval, 7.5 × 4.1 m, low flat mound with stone placed around the edges.

MY265 (NL5570:8365) Peat dryer. *Location*: Ridge plateau. *Description*: Subrectangular, 5 × 1.9 m, mound surmounted by a substantial retaining ring of piled stone much collapsed, but some still set upright. Many large slabs in 0.9–1 m range.

MY266 (NL5583:8366) Peat dryer. *Location*: Ridge plateau. *Description*: Oval, 6 × 1.8 m, low flat mound with stones set along the sides to a pointed end. *Note*: Could be a boat-shaped stone setting.

MY267 (NL5554:8362) Peat dryer. *Location*: Ridge plateau. *Description*: Subrectangular, 4.5 × 1.5 m, low flat mound with a mass of piled stone at the northern as a facade. The southern end is open and the mound merges into the hillside through this gap in the stonework.

MY268 (NL5572:8370) Peat dryer. *Location*: Ridge plateau. *Description*: Subrectangular, 6 × 1.5 m, low flat mound with displaced large stones around the edges of the mound. A facade of set stones is in place at the north-west end. The main structure is on a platform 6.8 × 3 m that may be natural or a product of the dryer degrading and spreading.

MY269 (NL5577:8372) Peat dryer. *Location*: Upper hill-slope. *Description*: Subrectangular, 4 × 1.6 m, structure that is most likely to be a peat dryer, but the stonework is disorganized and erosion has severely affected the site.

MY270 (NL5565:8381) Shelter. *Location*: Shelf on edge of ridge plateau. *Description*: Oval, 2 × 1.5 m, single cell of stones placed in an oval shape on an oval mound, with an entrance probably from east side.

MY271 (NL5570:8376) Peat dryer. *Location*: Ridge plateau. *Description*: Subrectangular, 4 × 1.9 m, very low flat mound on a small grassy platform A few stones are in place along the southern side of the mound, but the rest is degrading and spreading to the north where a few scattered stones mark the original side of the mound. *Note*: Active erosion is removing the peat soil from the eastern edge.

MY272 (NL5569:8373) Peat dryer. *Location*: Ridge plateau. *Description*: Subrectangular almost oval, 3.5 × 2.5 m, flat-topped mound with dispersed stones around the outer edge and with several displaced off the mound altogether.

MY273 (NL5584:8374) Peat dryer. *Location*: Upper ridge plateau. *Description*: Rectangular, 4.5 × 2.6 m, very slight mound edged in places with placed stones. Front south edge may have been originally have had a stone facade, but active erosion has dissolved much of the peat soil along this edge displacing stones. The opposite end has no retaining stones and merges into the hillside.

MY274 (NL5626:8417) Peat dryer. *Location*: Shelf on upper hill-slope. *Description*: Oval, 70 × 3.5 m, mound with several spaced stones around the northern end and partly along the sides from there.

MY275 (NL5625:8419) Peat dryer. *Location*: Shelf on upper hill-slope. *Description*: Oval, 5.6 × 2.8 m, mound with a stone surround and piled at the northern end as a facade.

MY276 (NL5619:8417) Mound. *Location*: Shelf on upper hill-slope. *Description*: Oval, 7 × 3.5 m, grassy mound with a few stones in evidence. *Note*: Could be natural.

MY277 (NL5620:8411) Mound. *Location*: Ridge plateau. *Description*: Oval, 6.4 × 4.8 m, 1 m high mound of earth and stones, some scattered. *Note*: Some active erosion.

MY278 (NL5620:8414) Peat dryer. *Location*: Ridge plateau. *Description*: Oval, 4.6 × 3.5 m, very slightly mounded with several spaced stones around the edges. *Note*: May be natural.

MY279 (NL5621:8415) Peat dryer. *Location*: Ridge plateau. *Description*: Oval, 4.5 × 3.5 m, mound with several spaced stones around the edges. *Note*: Being subjected to active erosion on the western side.

MY280 (NL5619:8416) Peat dryer. *Location*: Ridge plateau. *Description*: Subrectangular, 5 × 2.5 m, scatter of stones in a vague semblance of form. There is no mound and the area is severely eroded down to bedrock, but a large stone slab set on edge in a position where the facade may have been expected lends some weight to its identification as a site.

MY281 (NL5617:8417) Peat dryer. *Location*: Ridge plateau. *Description*: Oval, 4.5 × 2.6 m, mound, 0.7 m high with a stone facade around the northern high end. At the southern end the mound merges into the hillside.

MY282 (NL5612:8416) Peat dryer. *Location*: Ridge plateau. *Description*: Oval, 4.6 × 2.1 m, low flat mound with many set vertical stones.

MY283 (NL5607:8418) Peat dryer. *Location*: Shelf on upper hill-slope. *Description*: Subrectangular, 4.3 × 3 m, low flat mound with several stones set around the edges.

MY284 (NL5604:8420) Peat dryer. *Location*: Shelf on upper hill-slope. *Description*: Oval, 4.2 × 2.8 m, flat-topped mound with several stones set around the edge. *Note*: Active erosion.

MY285 (NL5616:8410) Peat dryer. *Location*: Ridge plateau in dyke. *Description*: Oval, 5.2 × 3.5 m, eroded and misshapen low flat mound with a dense scatter of stones along the eastern side. There are some stones around the north end and west side. *Note*: Active and severe erosion down to bedrock, especially to the south.

MY286 (NL5615:8409) Cairn. *Location*: Ridge plateau in dyke. *Description*: Oval, 1.8 × 0.9 m, single course stone setting forming a single cell with a possible entrance to the south.

MY287 (NL5612:8408) Setting. *Location*: Ridge plateau in dyke. *Description*: Setting of stones covering an area of 2.2 × 2 m. *Note*: Could be natural.

MY288 (NL5614:8407) Peat dryer. *Location*: Ridge plateau in dyke. *Description*: Oval, 3.2 × 3 m, low flat mound with spaced stones around the perimeter, especially numerous along the western side.

MY289 (NL5624:8410) Peat dryer. *Location*: Ridge plateau. *Description*: Subrectangular, 7.4 × 3 m, low flat mound with a scatter of stones along the sides and a set stone facade at the northern end. The southern end appears to have originally been open, although the stone scatter makes this unclear.

MY290 (NL5626:8410) Peat dryer. *Location*: Ridge plateau. *Description*: Subrectangular, 4.5 × 2.5 m, slight mound with rounded ends and a few spaced stones set at one end that may serve as a facade.

MY291 (NL5624:8407) (Fig. 3.27) Peat dryer. *Location*: Ridge plateau. *Description*: A low long flat-topped subrectangular mound, 5.5 × 1.9 m, with a rounded southern facade, fronted end and well-defined sides edged with many upright stones. The northern end is open and here the mound merges into the hillside.

MY292 (NL5624:8403) Peat dryer. *Location*: Ridge plateau. *Description*: Oval, 3 × 2 m, low flat mound that merges into the hillside to the south. A stone facade at the north end is formed by a disarranged and tumbled collection of stones.

MY293 (NL5622:8401) Boat-shaped stone setting. *Location*: Ridge plateau. *Description*: Oval, 2.6 × 1.5 m, with a pointed end to the north north-east, set on a low natural prominence. Stones are set or placed all around the perimeter, but there is no mound inside. *Note*: There is damage from rabbit burrowing. This could also be a shelter or peat dryer.

MY294 (NL5622:8399) Boat-shaped stone setting. *Location*: on slope. *Description*: Oval, 3.4 × 2.5 m, single-cell, upright stones in front. *Note*: Boat shape but could be peat dryer.

MY295 (NL5620:8496) Shelter. *Location*: Ridge plateau. *Description*: Oval, 2 × 1.8 m, mound with a single-cell stone ring around the upper edge. There is no entrance.

MY296 (NL5599:8420) Peat dryer. *Location*: Shelf on upper hill-slope. *Description*: Oval, 4 × 2.8 m, low flat mound with most of the revetting stonework eroded out on to denuded bedrock. *Note*: Severe active erosion, especially along the western flank.

MY297 (NL5621:8411) Peat dryer. *Location*: Ridge plateau. *Description*: Oval, 4 × 2.7 m, low mound with a mass of stonework piled at the north-west end, which may be the remnants of a collapsed facade. *Note*: Active erosion and rabbit damage.

MY298 (NL5613:8401) Shelter. *Location*: At edge of dyke on plateau. *Description*: Semicircle, 3 × 2.7 m, of set stones open to the east where presumably the sides have fallen into the dyke.

MY299 (NL5604:8402) Shelter. *Location*: At edge of dyke on plateau. *Description*: Oval, 3.5 × 3 m, single-cell ring of stones on slight mound. *Note*: Covered by heather.

MY300 (NL5624:8418) Shelter. *Location*: Shelf on upper hill-slope. *Description*: Circular, 1.8 m diam., slight flat mound with a half-circle of stones set around the northern edge. The southern half has been eroded down to bedrock.

MY301 (NL5612:8405) Shelter. *Location*: Ridge plateau in dyke. *Description*: Circular, 1.8 m diam., very low flat mound with a few spaced stones around the edge forming a single cell. *Note*: Active erosion on the western side.

MY302 (NL5609:8399) Cairn. *Location*: Ridge plateau in dyke. *Description*: Circular, 4.2 m diam., earthen mound with a scatter of stones on the surface.

MY303 (NL5609:8395) Peat dryer. *Location*: Upper hill-slope. *Description*: Oval, 7 × 5 m, slight flat mound with large blocks, up to 1 m in size, around the northern end as a facade. A few further stones are set along the sides. *Note*: Active erosion has destroyed the peat soil at the south-eastern corner down to bedrock.

MY304 (NL5584:8381) Peat dryer. *Location*: Upper ridge plateau. *Description*: Subrectangular, 5 × 3 m, low mound with a considerable amount of piled retaining stonework especially along the west side and around the north end in what may be classed as a facade.

MY305 (NL5589:8375) Shelter. *Location*: Ridge plateau. *Description*: Circular, 2.5 m diam., single cell with walls of piled and set stone with many blocks around the 0.5 m size. No entrance is visible.

MY306 (NL5589:8389) Peat dryer. *Location*: Ridge plateau. *Description*: Rectangular, 4.1 × 2.2 m, setting of placed stones, still in their original last use positions, with a few scattered outside. Both sides and end walls have a stone edge.

MY307 (NL5583:8385) Shelter. *Location*: Upper ridge plateau. *Description*: Oval, 4 × 3 m, earthen-walled single cell with half-circle of stones piled and set around the north-western side.

MY308 (NL5576:8384) Cairn. *Location*: Shelf slope of upper ridge. *Description*: Oval, 3.7 × 2.5 m, slight mound with a mass of stone that makes little structural sense. Although superficially cairn-like it is just as likely that the stonework forms the retaining walls of a peat dryer.

MY309 (NL5592:8374) Peat dryer. *Location*: Ridge plateau. *Description*: Subrectangular, 4.6 × 3.5 m, area marked by a line of stones still in position along the south-western side even though this whole area is subject to active erosion that has left the stonework on bare bedrock. The southern end is built up to form a facade while the rest of the perimeter is marked by scattered and displaced stonework.

MY310 (NL5590:8380) Shelter. *Location*: Ridge plateau. *Description*: Oval, 3 × 2 m, single cell formed by a ring of stones with no entrance.

MY311 (NL5593:8377) Peat dryer. *Location*: Edge of upper ridge plateau. *Description*: Subrectangular, 5 × 2 m, low flat mound of peat earth bounded by large stone slabs, 0.9–1 m in size, some still in place set on edge, but mostly fallen. *Note*: Some active peat erosion.

MY312 (NL5593:8370) Shelter. *Location*: Shelf on upper slope. *Description*: Oval, 6 × 3.5 m, ill-defined single-cell ring of earth and stone. *Note*: Under active erosion threat.

MY313 (NL5592:8382) Shelter. *Location*: Ridge plateau. *Description*: Circular single-cell shelter of piled stonework that appears to have been constructed out of another structure, possibly a peat dryer, of subrectangular shape, 4.6 × 3.5 m, but only a possible built up facade is all that remains to identify it.

MY314 (NL5588:8385) Peat dryer. *Location*: Ridge plateau. *Description*: Subrectangular, 4.4 × 1.9 m, low flat mound with a stone revetment around both sides and a facade of upright set slabs standing to a metre in height at the south-west end. The southern end is open. *Note*: A large area of erosion down to bedrock is advancing at the south-western edge. Rabbit burrows infest the mound.

MY315 (NL5595:8386) Peat dryer. *Location*: Ridge plateau in dyke. *Description*: Oval, 5.8 × 4.2 m, flat mound with collapsed stone facade at the southern end. The sides stones are scattered and displaced. *Note*: Many burrows are dug into the mound.

MY316 (NL5598:8380) Shelter. *Location*: Ridge plateau. *Description*: Oval, 2 × 1.8 m, single cell formed by a circle of set or placed stones with a possible entrance to the south-east.

MY317 (NL5594:8389) Boat-shaped stone setting. *Location*: Ridge plateau. *Description*: Boat shape, 2 × 1.2 m, single cell with a pointed end to the south edged with stone blocks as a facade. No further blocks outline the rear or side. Could be a peat dryer.

MY318 (NL5589:8389) Peat dryer. *Location*: Ridge plateau. *Description*: Oval, 3 × 1.8 m, low flat mound with a facade of a single embedded stone set on edge. Side stones are few and spaced out. *Note*: Active and severe erosion down to bedrock along the western flank.

MY319 (NL5587:8392) Peat dryer. *Location*: Upper-ridge plateau. *Description*: Subrectangular with rounded ends, 4.5 × 2 m, with many retaining upright stones still in place along the sides. The north-west end is built up to a facade while at the opposite end little stonework is evident.

MY320 (NL5583:8392) Shelter. *Location*: Upper-ridge plateau. *Description*: Oval, 3.5 × 2.8 m, mound with a half-circle stone ring around one side and a flat bank tailing out from the unenclosed side. The stone ring, with some stones set on edge, may in fact be the facade to a much-reduced peat dryer, the bank being the main body.

MY321 (NL5585:8395) Shelter. *Location*: Ridge plateau. *Description*: Oval, 4 × 3.5 m, platform cut into the hill-slope on which a low mound edged with a ring of stone is sited. There is no entrance. *Note*: There is extensive burrowing damage.

MY322 (NL5597:8396) Peat dryer. *Location*: Ridge plateau. *Description*: Rectangular, 4.5 × 2.5 m, low mound graded into the hillside to the south-east.

A stone facade to the north-west is much disarranged and there are a few stones set along the western side.

MY323 (NL5592:8392) Shelter. *Location*: Ridge plateau. *Description*: Circular, 1.3 m diam., slightly mounded with a scatter of stones around the upper edge forming a single cell. Could be a cairn.

MY324 (NL5590:8401) Peat dryer. *Location*: Ridge plateau. *Description*: Oval, 6 × 2.5 m, low mound with some stone along the western side and also to a lesser extent along the eastern. The front facade at the northwest end has fallen and the area is degraded down to bedrock.

MY325 (NL5597:8396) (Fig. 3.27) Peat dryer. *Location*: Ridge plateau. *Description*: Rectangular, 6.5 × 2.2 m, long structure with stone sides of set and piled rock. A southern facade is composed mainly of single large blocks. The northern end is open and here there are some scattered displaced stones in and around the structure. *Note*: Internally badly damaged by burrowing.

MY326 (NL5607:8393) Peat dryer. *Location*: Edge of upper ridge plateau. *Description*: Oval, 5.3 × 2.5 m, low flat mound of peat earth with a scatter of disarranged stonework on the top and sides. *Note*: Active erosion threat.

MY327 (NL5605:8387) Peat dryer. *Location*: Ridge plateau. *Description*: Oval, 3.5 × 1.2 m, boat-shaped setting of stones without a mound. The stonework to the rear, rounded, south-western end is scattered, while the front pointed end sides are edged with stone. *Note*: Covered by heather.

MY328 (NL5603:8406) Mound. *Location*: Ridge plateau in dyke. *Description*: Circular, 2 m diam., grassy stone-free mound. *Note*: Could be natural.

MY329 (NL5612:8393) Cairn. *Location*: Upper hill-slope. *Description* Oval, 4.2 × 2.9 m, mounded jumble of stone. The dimensions indicate that this could be a disarranged peat dryer.

MY330 (NL5610:8393) Shelter. *Location*: Upper hill-slope. *Description* Oval, 1.9 × 1.2 m, slightly mounded with a few spaced stones at the edges. Set against a large naturally placed boulder.

MY331 (NL5612:8386) Peat dryer. *Location*: Upper hill-slope. *Description*: Oval, 9 × 4.5 m, low mound with spaced stones around the edges and a few scattered inside. *Note*: Active erosion has reduced the south and west sides in places to bare bedrock.

MY332 (NL5610:8384) Shelter. *Location*: Upper hill-slope. *Description*: 3.4 × 2 m single cell suggested by a scatter of stones on a low mound. *Note*: Denuded bedrock intrudes. Could be natural deposit.

MY333 (NL5600:8384) Shelter. *Location*: Edge of upper ridge plateau. *Description*: Square, 2 × 2 m, single cell could originally have been any shape since almost all of the stonework is displaced. *Note*: Active and severe erosion threat.

MY334 (NL5607:8390) Shelter. *Location*: Upper hill-slope. *Description*: Oval, 3 × 2.8 m, single cell formed by spaced placed stones. *Note*: Damage from burrowing and erosion to bedrock.

MY335 (NL5600:8375) Peat dryer. *Location*: Upper slope at edge of ridge plateau. *Description*: Oval, 5.5 × 3.5 m, low flat mound with a spaced stones placed around the upper edge and with many others scattered on and off the mound. *Note*: Covered by heather.

MY336 (NL5596:8364) Peat dryer. *Location*: Shelf at edge of ridge plateau. *Description*: Oval, 4 × 2.8 m, low flat mound with spaced stones set around the upper edge and a few fallen to the side. *Note*: Covered by heather.

MY337 (NL5590:8363) Peat dryer. *Location*: Shelf on upper hill-slope. *Description*: Oval, 3.7 × 1.9 m, low flat mound with stones at the sides and southern, rather pointed, end. The northern end is open.

MY338 (NL5551:8221) Peat dryer. *Location*: Lower-valley hill-slope. *Description*: Oval, 7.7 × 5 m, setting of large blocks without an internal mound. Some of the stonework is displaced.

MY339 (NL5550:8227) Shelter. *Location*: Lower valley hill-slope. *Description*: Rectangular, 7 × 4.5 m, single cell of large stones, some piled and some set on edge with an opening in the wall up slope to the north, set on a platform into the hillside. *Note*: Possibly constructed from the stonework of an earlier monument.

MY340 (NL5545:8227) Complex of two shelters and a pen. *Location*: Lower-valley hill-slope. *Description*: Oval area, 8 × 7.5 m, with two shelters and a scatter of stones that may represent former animal pens.

MY340a (NL5545:8227) Shelter. *Location*: As above. *Description*: Subrectangular, 1.8 × 1.7 m, single cell of a few set, spaced stones.

MY340b (NL5545:8227) Shelter. *Location*: As above. *Description*: Subrectangular, 1.7 × 1.5 m, single cell formed by a few set, spaced stones.

MY340c (NL5545:8227) Pen. *Location*: As above. *Description*: Oval, 6 × 3.5 m, indistinct enclosure composed of scattered stones.

MY341 (NL5532:8210) Peat dryer. *Location*: Lower-valley hill-slope. *Description*: Oval, 7 × 5 m, low flat mound with a ring of stones, many on edge, set around the perimeter.

MY342 (NL5545:8209) Complex of two shelters. *Location*: Lower-valley hill-slope. *Description*: Two shelters set on a revetted platform of an earlier site.

MY342a (NL5545:8209) Shelter. *Location*: As above. *Description*: Circular, 2 m diam., single cell of piled stones widely open to the south-west. This could be a wind-break.

MY342b (NL5545:8209) Shelter. *Location*: As above. *Description*: Circular, 2 m diam., single cell formed by a wall of double stone thickness with a south entrance.

MY343 (NL5552:8218) Shelter. *Location*: Lower-valley hill-slope. *Description*: Rectangular, 2.5 × 2.1 m, single cell formed by a number of set stones. Degraded on the north side.

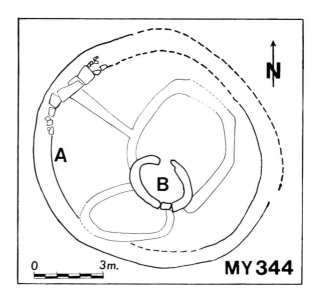

Figure 3.28 Site MY344.

MY344 (NL5560:8204) (Fig. 3.28) Complex of wheelhouse and shelter. *Location*: Lower hill-slope of valley. *Description*: Circular, mostly collapsed and displaced stonework except for small area that shows lower curved walling of large stone blocks. A modern shelter is constructed on top of the earlier site and uses stone taken from it.

MY344a (NL5560:8204) (Fig. 3.29) Wheelhouse. *Location*: As above. *Description* Circular, 12 m diam., located to one side at the back of Skipisdale valley, aloof from the other major sites on the valley floor. It is a very visible site being surrounded by bright green vegetation that targets a considerable mass of displaced stonework. A modern shelter (b) has been erected in the centre of the mass. Around the shelter the general impression is of total chaos with displaced stonework at all angles. However, at ground level a number of large blocks of stone can be seen forming the edge of a large disc-shaped structure. No internal features can be recognized, but the structure is most likely a wheelhouse.

MY344b (NL5560:8204) Shelter. *Location*: As above. *Description*: Oval, 2.5 × 2 m, single cell with drystone walls of several courses, 1.5 m high, built in the 1920s (Buxton 1995).

MY345 (NL5555:8187) (Fig. 3.30) Settlement complex. *Location*: Valley floor. *Description*: A fragment of Iron Age pottery was found ejected from a rabbit burrow in the slope down to the stream that runs east–west immediately to the south of the site. The site, however, is a complex of more than one phase and almost certainly more than one period. The various buildings are contained in an area of c. 30 × 40 m. The earliest visible structure appears to be a large circular stone foundation approximately 12 m in diameter situated at the west end of the site, and it is from the vicinity of this building that the pottery sherd was

Figure 3.29 Site MY344.

recovered. The ring-wall is c. 1 m thick and appears to be of single thickness, which suggests that if it is Iron Age in date, it is either a wheelhouse or a roundhouse. No internal wall divisions were evident, but general structural collapse and stone robbing may account for that. Over and around the ring-wall are a number of later, smaller buildings of all shapes and sizes that continue in an interconnected line to the east for

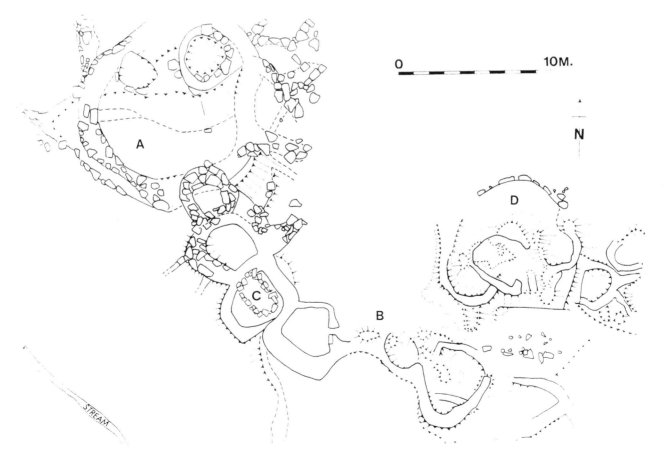

Figure 3.30 Site MY345.

c. 20 m where the building line turns, after a small gap, to continue for a further 20 m to the north. Some of the structures are most likely the shelters that could form a shieling complex of the early modern/modern period and it is also quite likely that Pictish-period occupation may have continued on the site, expanding out from the ring-wall building. Continuous settlement in a valley like Skipisdale is always a possibility and this site is the most likely location for it, but in such a complex of continually reused buildings and building materials it cannot be determined by survey alone.

MY346 (NL5564:8171) Settlement complex. *Location*: Valley floor. *Description*: Located lower down the valley on the west bank of the stream MY346 presents much the same site profile as MY345. There is a large circular building at the western edge of the complex with later structures overlying it and spreading to the east. A small excavation trench was opened alongside inside the east wall of the ring-wall (see above). This showed the main wall to be constructed of massive stone blocks, some of which weigh in excess of 1 ton, forming a single-face internal revetment to a 1 m wide turf, earth and stone wall. An unstructured hearth was found against the inner wall face at a high level in peat soil that most likely relates to a recent use of the site as a shieling or shelter. A rough stone floor was encountered and excavation ceased at this point since there was no intention to remove undisturbed archaeological features or significant deposits at this stage. The expected dating evidence did not appear and the peat soil infill down to the floor level was burrowed by rabbits to such an extent that it is arguable whether any material remained in these levels that was not disturbed. Presumably the floor encountered represents the last permanent occupation of the building before the accumulation of peat soil and fallen stonework infilled much of the interior. Overlying the ring-wall and these upper deposits is a 'D'-shaped early modern/modern shelter standing several drystone courses high. This was used to contain the spoil from the excavation that was left open so that informative details of the ring-wall elevation could be seen (Fig. 7.17).

MY347 (NL5564:8164) Chamber tomb. *Location*: Elevated plateau of valley floor. *Description*: Rectangular, 4.9 × 2.3 m, of two possible cells formed with massive vertically placed stone. Structurally it appears to have been robbed less severely than usual and a number of the large orthostats are still in their original position. A limited half-section was excavated (see excavations, p. 309) that revealed a burnt soil surface at what may have been the original ground surface— this was left intact. Burnt soils are a common feature of such monuments, but burnt soils from hearths and perhaps heather clearance have been found under less significant monuments (Branigan 1995a: 161).

MY348 (NL5551:8181) Shelter. *Location*: Valley floor. *Description*: Rectangular, 5 × 3.6 m, drystone single cell standing many courses high to 0.8 m with an entrance to the east. Butted against infield enclosure wall that appears to be associated with the settlement site MY345.

MY349 (NL5573:8190) Cairn. *Location*: Lower-valley hill-slope. *Description*: Circular, 8 m diam., grassed mound, 1.5 m high. *Note*: Possibly a kerbed cairn. Some active erosion caused by animal scraping and deflation of the central mound area.

MY350 (NL5575:8189) Shieling. *Location*: Lower-valley hill-slope. *Description*: Rectangular, 5 × 2 m, single cell of metre-thick earthen wall foundations faced internally with stone. Entrance is to the east on to a platform

MY351 (NL5646:8231) Peat dryer. *Location*: Shoulder of hill. *Description*: Oval, 4 × 2 m, half-circle of a few stones around the edge of a low mound. *Note*: In field system covered by heather.

MY352 (NL5636:8237) Mound. *Location*: Shoulder of hill. *Description*: Oval, 4 × 2.5 m, low flat-topped mound with a scatter of stones, some set around the edge. *Note*: Covered by heather.

MY353 (NL5642:8245) Shelter. *Location*: Shoulder of hill. *Description*: Oval, 3 × 2.2 m, single cell of spaced embedded stones in a ring around the edge of a slight flat-topped mound. *Note*: In field system covered by heather.

MY354 (NL5691:8376) Shieling. *Location*: Mid hill-slope. *Description*: A possibly subrectangular, 4 × 2 m, single cell of collapsing stone walling that makes definition difficult. Possibly part of the same building is a larger, oval, single-cell stone setting of just a few spaced stones and slabs, some quite large. All are sites on a platform. They could also represent a shelter built over an earlier, much larger, site.

MY355 (NL5689:8379) Complex of pen and shelter. *Location*: Mid hill-slope in dyke. *Description*: Half-circle enclosure pen set against the dyke rock wall with a shelter set to one side.

MY355a (NL5689:8379) Pen. *Location*: As above. *Description*: Circular, 6 m diam., half-circle wall of spaced stones set on a platform and butted to the dyke wall.

MY355b (NL5689:8379) Shelter. *Location*: As above. *Description*: Possible circular, 1.3 m diam., single cell, but mostly it appears to be a mass of tumbled rock. Set at the eastern end of the enclosure.

MY356 (NL5642:8273) Complex of barn and pen. *Location*: Lower-valley hill-slope. *Description*: Subrectangular, 10 × 5 m, single-cell barn and pen.

MY356a (NL5642:8273) Barn. *Location*: As above. *Description*: Square, 5 × 5 m, single cell with rounded external corners and entrance to the east.

MY356b (NL5642:8273) Pen. *Location*: As above. *Description*: Subrectangular, 4 × 3 m, pen of single spaced monoliths.

MY357 (NL5641:8271) Barn. *Location*: Lower valley hill-slope. *Description*: Subrectangular, 6 × 5 m, single cell with north entrance against wall.

MY358 (NL5523:8275) Mound. *Location*: Hill-top plateau. *Description*: Oval, 5.5 × 3 m, grassy mound with several stones at the edge.

MY359 (NL5526:8274) Cairn. *Location*: Hill-top plateau. *Description*: Oval, 8 × 6 m, earthen mound with the centre hollowed.

MY360 (NL5524:8273) Mound. *Location*: Hill-top plateau. *Description*: Oval, 6 × 5 m, grassy mound. *Note*: Damaged by peat digging and subject to active wind erosion.

MY361 (NL5518:8256) Peat dryer. *Location*: Upper hill-slope edge of hill-top plateau. *Description*: Sub-rectangular, 10 × 4 m, low flat mound with a few retaining stones at the sides.

MY362 (NL5515:8245) Cairn. *Location*: Shelf on upper hill-slope. *Description* Circular, 1.6 m diam., very slight mound with a few stones. *Note*: Probably natural.

MY363 (NL5564:8178) Shieling. *Location*: Valley floor. *Description*: Oval single cell, approximately 4.5 × 4 m, marked by stone revetting and edge stones that are in position, but much of the monument is a mass of collapsed stone. Set against a field wall.

MY364 (NL5533:8167) Peat dryer. *Location*: Shelf on slope of low coastal plateau. *Description*: Oval, 5.5 × 2.8 m, low flat mound with piled stone retaining walls around the western side.

MY365 (NL5533:8163) Cairn. *Location*: Shelf on slope of low coastal plateau. *Description*: Oval, 3 × 2.3 m, piled stones very badly eroded with many large stones falling away out on to denuded bedrock.

MY366 (NL5531:8185) Shelter. *Location*: Low plateau. *Description*: Subrectangular, 3.7 × 1.5 m, slight mound with spaced stones set around the edges except for the north end that is open. This shelter is built off centre on top of a circular, 6 m diam., flat platform mound with a few stones set at the eastern edge. It is most likely that this platform is an earlier site.

MY367 (NL5531:8189) Shelter. *Location*: Low plateau. *Description*: Oval, dimensions unknown, mound with stone half-circle.

MY368 (NL5707:8395) Mound. *Location*: Shelf on mid hill-slope. *Description*: Triangular, 2 m sided, flat-topped pile of grassed-over stones.

MY369 (NL5704:8402) Peat dryer. *Location*: Shelf on mid hill-slope. *Description*: Oval, 5 × 2 m, low flat mound with dispersed stone retaining walls around some parts of the mound edge. The eastern end has a facade of vertically set stones.

MY370 (NL5674:8465) Shelter. *Location*: In dyke. *Description*: Subcircular, 2.6 × 1.9 m, single cell of spaced stone blocks. *Note*: Covered by heather.

MY371 (NL5646:8418) Shelter. *Location*: Shelf on upper hill-slope. *Description*: Square, 1.5 × 1.5 m, low flat mound with stones set around the edge forming a single cell with no entrance.

MY372* (NL5449:8213) Cairn. *Location*: Coastal shelf. *Description*: Oval, 1.4 × 1 m, probably modern piled stone.

MY373* (NL5457:8206) Shelter. *Location*: Coastal shelf. *Description*: Oval, 3.4 × 3.3 m, single cell of stone ring-wall, two courses high of large 1 m sized blocks. Entrance to the east.

MY374* (NL5453:8207) Shelter. *Location*: Coastal shelf. *Description*: Oval, 3.5 × 3 m, single cell formed by large 1 m sized blocks of stone set upright on a natural platform

MY375* (NL5462:8208) Stone circle. *Location*: Coastal slope of Dun Mingulay. *Description*: Oval, 4 × 3 m, of large 1 m sized blocks set in a circle. Although large in size it is also possible that this is a shelter.

MY376* (NL5478:8231) Fort. Dun Mingulay (?Iron Age). *Location*: Coastal promontory. *Description*: Dun Mingulay is a so-called defended promontory fort consisting of a wall across the narrow neck of the promontory. No contemporary structures were found inside the defended area (see RCAHMS above for full details).

MY377 (NL5620:8287) Shelter. *Location*: Shelf on lower-valley hill-slope. *Description*: Rounded subrectangular, 3.5 × 3 m, single cell, with no apparent entrance, butted against a field wall. *Note*: Part of infield system.

MY378* (NL5523:8306) Peat dryer. *Location*: Cliff edge. *Description*: Rectangular, 7 × 5 m, low flat mound with retaining stones placed on edge along the sides at the eastern end. The western end is open and the mound merges with the hillside through this gap. Some stones have become displaced.

MY379* (NL5526:8300) Mound. *Location*: Shelf on upper coastal hill-slope. *Description*: Oval, 5 × 3 m, mound of grassed-over stones.

MY380* (NL5522:8308) Cairn. *Location*: Cliff edge. *Description*: Circular, 5 m diam., grassed earthen mound.

MY381 (NL5533:8409) Shelter. *Location*: Valley floor. *Description*: Square, 2.5 × 2.5 m, low mound with some stones around the edges and a further disorganized mass inside. Could be a cairn rearranged into a shelter.

MY382 (NL5625:8400) Peat dryer. *Location*: Upper ridge plateau. *Description*: Subrectangular, 3 × 1.5 m, low flat mound with only three stones as a facade at the south end. *Note*: Active erosion threat to the east side.

MY383 (NL5600:8304) Setting. *Location*: Shelf on slope. *Description*: 3 × 2 m. A few, apparently set, stones on platform.

MY384 (NL5655:8342) Roundhouse (Iron Age). *Location*: Coastal valley floor, sand dunes. *Description*: Initially this site appeared as a midden deposit eroding out of a mound in the area of dune deflation to the west of the dunes system at the north end of Mingulay Bay. Iron Age pottery fragments, animal bone, shell, fire-fractured stones and charcoal have been reported and recovered from this site over a period of many years and some small trenches were excavated in 1971. The continual erosion of this site encouraged the team, in consultation with Historic Scotland and Scottish Nature, to conduct a limited excavation across the eroding face of the mound (see further, Chapter 7). A sequence of stratified deposits and drystone structures were found superimposed one on top of the other, which, apart from possible modern structures and deposits at the top, are wholly Iron Age in date. The structures and deposits rest upon the surface of a shell sand dune that itself is scarred by the marks of cross-ploughing. Since only the face of the mound was excavated, it was not possible to determine exactly the nature of the buildings represented, but the walling was all of single stone width even though some of them were constructed with massive orthostats (wall 4). The most likely form is that of a roundhouse constructed of stone revetted turf walls.

MY385 (NL5651:8308) Village road. *Location*: Valley floor to lower coastal bench. *Description*: The village road begins on the west side of the township and wends its way up out of the valley of the bay, past the schoolroom and house (MY78), past the site of Crois an t-Suidheachain (MY76) and on to the landing place and crane emplacement at Aneir. For much of its route the road bed is metalled, sometimes paved with large stone slabs and edged with stone blocks. Two well built drystone bridges span small streams, one almost at its end in the village and one just to the south of the school. The bridge at the village end is in a dangerous state with some of the main spanning stones fallen into the stream and should be considered worth repairing before its original form becomes lost in its eventual and inevitable total collapse.

MY386* (NL5667:8278) Well. *Location*: Cliff edge lower coastal bench. *Description*: The well at the Aneir landing place was located on the rocky face at the edge of the road to the crane site and is a bowl-shaped hollow pecked out of the bedrock.

MY387* (NL5679:8272) Crane emplacement. *Location*: Cliff side. *Description*: A concrete base, 3×3 m square, and fittings for a crane are still visible at the landing place at Aneir that is marked on the 1st edition of the OS 6-in. Map. Apparently it was hardly used, to the extent that an iron ladder provided for it was never fitted in place and still lies rusting where it was left at the roadside.

MY388 (NL5651:8298) Blackhouse. *Location*: Lower coastal bench. *Description*: MY388 is opposite John Sinclair's house (MY80) on the road from the village to the landing place at Aneir. The close proximity, albeit on opposite sides of the road, of the two properties makes it difficult to determine whether this is a separate small blackhouse or a drying kiln house belonging to Sinclair. The building is a double cell,

9.5×5.5 m, subrectangular traditional construction with no apparent window openings and a single entrance to the north. Internally there is a dividing wall making two rooms and in the west room a round-backed fireplace is built into the gable wall.

MY389 (NL5652:8337) Chamber tomb. *Location*: Valley floor. *Description*: Possible rectangular chamber, 3.5×1.7 m, has one 2 m long side stone, which appears to be in its original place, set on edge. There may be several other large stones still in place, but most of the other stonework looks displaced. Being so close to the village, it is almost against the north wall of the old schoolhouse enclosure, it will have suffered from much interference and stone robbing and in this respect it is surprising that it has survived at all.

MY390 (NL5651:8344) Complex of cairns. *Location*: Valley floor. *Description*: Two small cairns on slope of gully at the sand dune margin.

MY390a (NL5651:8344) Cairn. *Location*: As above. *Description*: Circular, 1 m diam., grassed pile of stones.

MY390b (NL5651:8344) Cairn. *Location*: As above. *Description*: Circular, 1 m diam., grassed pile of stones.

MY391* (NL5688:8342) Bridge. *Location*: Cliff edge. *Description*: Dimensions unknown, stone bridge over sea gully on north side of bay. On unmarked route to landing place.

Landscape period summaries

The modern and early modern landscape (Fig. 3.31)
The early modern and modern history of Mingulay is thoroughly documented by Ben Buxton (1981, 1995), essential reading for anyone interested in the Western Isles. His detailed coverage of this period renders any attempt to discuss it further at any length unnecessary. Equally with so much attention already concentrated on the village area it was considered a duplication of effort to include it in the Sheffield survey. Dr Mary Harman, SNH area officer for Uist and Barra, drew a measured plan of the burial ground enclosure, and to duplicate her excellent work was also considered unnecessary.

The Township. Situated on the western fringe of the dune system that rises steeply from the beach of Mingulay Bay. The houses and enclosures that form the village complex appear to be partly built on solid rock and partly on old shell sand beach or dune accumulation. Many of the houses are slowly being filled and covered by shell sands, but in places small active streams are deeply cutting through the sand becoming a danger to any wall foundations in their vicinity. The beds of these streams provide a rich source for objects washed out from different levels of the substratum underlying the buildings of the present village. A collection of handmade early modern pottery fragments has been accumulated and will be reported on in SEARCH volume 6.

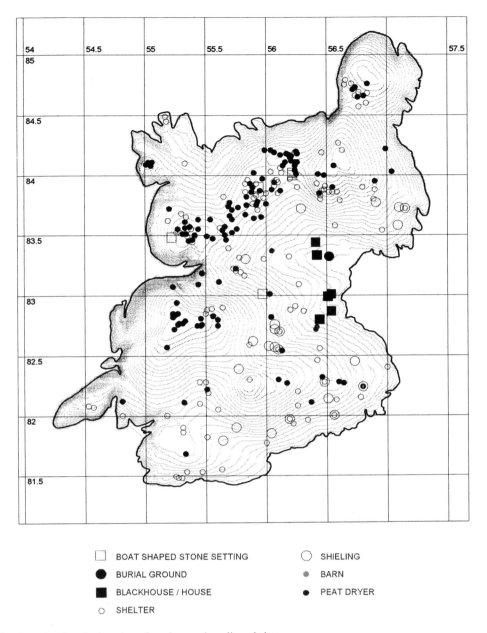

BOAT SHAPED STONE SETTING   SHIELING

BURIAL GROUND   BARN

BLACKHOUSE / HOUSE   PEAT DRYER

SHELTER

Figure 3.31 Mingulay, showing the location of modern and mediaeval sites.

The houses are all drystone constructions built with field stone, but some larger slab-like blocks are most likely derived from prehistoric monuments that must have undoubtedly existed in this preferred settlement area.

There is some indication of light stone quarrying around the edge of the valley, but this is impossible to date, however, several of the drystone-built houses display stone blocks dressed and with quarry drill holes, MY84, for example. There are several modern houses built in the closing years of occupation that are distinguished as being constructed in two storeys, with high thin cemented walls and higher gable ends to take either corrugated iron or stone slate-covered roofs. These houses are all built outside the village area and include the priests chapel house MY87 and the later schoolhouse and room MY78. Several blackhouses, MY 80 and MY83 for example, are located away from the village area.

The priest's chapel house. MY87.

Blackhouses. MY80, 83, 84, 388.

Barns. MY81, 356, 357.
Buildings that are here called barns are recognized as being small square or rectangular buildings, without fireplaces that are built in a similar manner to the blackhouse and whose walls are expected to be standing many courses high. Their function may be that of

storage or byre and they will be in the settlement area and its immediate field system. There are several barn-like structures within the township, which, as part of the village, have not been included.

Shielings. MY5, 6, 7, 35, 37, 38, 40, 42, 71, 73, 105, 106, 107, ?109, 110, 111, 112, 119, 187, 191, 194, 195, 350, 354, 363.

Only a few of the monuments that have been called shielings show the more substantial construction and clustered groupings that can be found on the mainland, such as at Coire Bhorradail, North Argyll, where an exceptional group of over 50 structures are gathered. On small islands one cannot expect great clusters, although MY35 might be such a complex. Three sites, MY5, MY6 and MY194, have been subject to excavation in order to clarify their date and function and will be fully reported in SEARCH volume 6. These three examples of possible shielings show the wide variety of structures that can be expected of this slightly ambiguous category of site as found in the southern islands.

Shelters. MY15, 25, 26, 28, 34, 36, 39, 41, 43, 44, 45, 46, 47, 48, 51, 52, 54, 56, 57, 64, 66, 67, 68, 69, 70, 75B, 82, 99, 105, 113, 118, 121, 122, 129, 130, 131, 133, 135, 136, 139A + B, 140, 141, 142, 143, 145, 146, 148, 152, 153, 154, 156, 163A + B, 168, 174, 180, 181, 182, 183, 188, 189, 190, 199, 201, 227, 228, 229, 231, 251, 253, 257A + B, 270, 295, 298, 299, 300, 301, 305, 307, 310, 312, 313, 316, 320, 321, 323, 330, 332, 333, 334, 339, 340A + B, 342A + B, 343, 344, 348, 353, 355, 366, 367, 370, 371, 373, 374, 377, 381.

110 shelters may appear to be an overly massive number even for such a large island, but when one considers that there are 1,100 cleitean on St Kilda with more on the surrounding smaller islands (Harman 1997), then perhaps such a figure does not appear so amazing. The real stumbling block in placing these numerous small monuments into their active role in the living landscape is our general ignorance of the actual function or functions of any one of them. In a rapid survey like this one it is rarely possible to expend a great deal of time at each location when larger, more complex, therefore probably more important, monuments demand attention. Judging from the number located in each of the peat-drying areas many appear to be shelters erected for intermittent but regular use, especially in uncertain weather while working the peat beds. Others may be mistaken identifications and be cairns of one form or another and vice versa. However, if one accepts the need for cold- or at least well-aired storage in the manner of a cleit then many of them could be intended for this use. Storage facilities in and around the village are solid walled barns built for warmth and shelter which are most likely byres for cattle and ponies, there are no, even primitive, cleitean forms that allow the free

circulation of air for cold storage. It is known that sea birds were collected on a much less intensive scale than on St Kilda and storage in small shelters may have been all that was required.

Peat dryers. MY13, 27, 29, 31, 58, 59, 60, 61, 62, 65, 90, 91, 92, 94, 95, 96, 98, 100, 101, 102, 108, 115, 116, 120, 126, 138, 147, 150, 151, 155, 157, 161, 165, 167, 169, 170, 172, 175, 176, 178, 196, 197, 200, 203, 204, 205, 206, 208, 210, 211, 213, 214, 217, 218, 219, 222, 224, 225, 226, 236, 250, 252, 256, 258, 260, 261, 262, 263, 264, 265, 266, 267, 268, 269, 271, 272, 273, 274, 275, 278, 279, 280, 281, 282, 283, 284, 285, 288, 289, 290, 291, 292, 296, 297, 303, 304, 306, 309, 311, 314, 315, 318, 319, 322, 324, 325, 326, 327, 331, 335, 336, 337, 338, 341, 351, 361, 364, 369, 378, 382.

The control of fire is necessary for many basic needs such as cooking, warmth, industrial and craft work, light and much more. The home fire also has significant importance within the family group, which may be expressed in the seating arrangements around the hearth and the fact that the domestic fire was always kept alight. The central fire in the Iron Age wheelhouse T17 at Alt Chrisal (see below) is over half a metre of laminated peat ash, indicating that this tradition may have a long history. There may be very practical reasons for this practice since it cannot always have been easy to light a fire in such a damp environment without modern matches or lighters. In an environment like that found in the Outer Hebrides fire may be considered one of the requirements for survival, therefore the fuel necessary to maintain it assumes a similar importance.

The fact that areas of woodland were once a common feature of the islands in the past can be seen by the physical presence of submerged woodland at the edge of Borve Headland, Barra. Such woodland certainly may have existed on the southern islands in the improving postglacial epoch, although this may be less certain in the case of Berneray. However, areas of the sheltered environment necessary for the generation and continued survival of such woodland are limited on these smaller islands, and with the impact of human activity and settlement in the Neolithic, if not before (Edwards 1990), local supplies would soon have been exhausted. However, analysis of the archaeobotanical samples recovered from the Neolithic site at Alt Chrisal indicate that a wide variety of tree species were growing locally during at least part of that period (Boardman 1995). Not only would the limited supply of timber be needed for fires, but also for building and other activities. The formation of peat and its use as a fuel may therefore be considered an important factor in the survival of island communities throughout the ages until the use of alternative fuels became feasible in recent times.

Mingulay with its rich deposits of peat became a source of supply for the less-endowed islands of

Pabbay and especially Berneray, which has virtually no peat beds. Evidence for working the peat is extant and takes the form of extensive areas of reduced landscape where peat has been extracted, a road MY86 constructed to aid the ponies in carrying creels full of peat down to the village and a peat-drying structure sometimes referred to as a cleit. The Mingulay peat dryer (cleit), however, bears no resemblance to those sophisticated buildings constructed on St Kilda and commonly recognized as the ideal cleitean.

The Mingulay peat dryers are very simple structures, and unlike the St Kilda cleitean that were used as a multipurpose store, are used simply to stop the drying peat from blowing away. However, a group of boat-shaped and U-shaped stone settings on St Kilda that were considered to be Bronze Age burials on the basis of a C14 date of 1833 BC are quite likely to be peat dryers by their close similarity to those on Mingulay, which would support Harman's contention that the date could derive from relict peat debris within the structure (Harman 1997: 60).

Almost always they are sited on a natural prominence or constructed platform that would put the base of the peat stack above the general ground level to keep the base of the stack dry. Such a prominence could and most likely does include earlier monuments rearranged to form a suitable base. This would be in keeping with the St Kilda examples that have recently been excavated revealing earlier cairns underlying them (Harman 1997).

The Mingulay peat dryers have a wide range of ground plans, sizes and building methods (Fig. 3.27). Some are apparently constructed with a minimum of materials and effort while others show that time, effort and not a little skill have been put to use. Mingulay appears to be the only island in the survey that has this type of monument in significant numbers (there are 120). Therefore, a boat-shaped stone setting on Berneray, for example, is not confused as a peat dryer, but on Mingulay such an oval-shaped monument does not automatically fall into a separate boat category. This makes all of the boat-shaped monuments on Mingulay suspect, and, although they have been allotted a separate categorization and put into the Norse period, it is likely that many of them, if not all, are in fact peat dryers. MY97, for example, shares the same topographical environment and location with the peat dryers on Tom á Mhaide and morphologically appears to fall between either category.

Peat dryers appear to be quite specific in their site location, which raises doubts on the identification of any that have been found outside their perceived distribution range. MY364, for example, is an isolated individual on the plateau to the west of Skipisdale and its oval, almost boat, shape adds further possible doubt to its present identification. They are sited in the peat-cutting areas and in that respect they indicate the regions of the island where the peat formation was

worth extracting. There are a scattered few on the more plateau-inclined east slope of Hecla, a denser pattern on the flattened summit of Carnan, while the flattened summit of Tom á Mhaide, with an extension along the plateau ridge top towards Macphee's Hill, shows the greatest and densest concentration of all. There are a few scattered around Macphee's Hill and there are two small groups of four, one on the west side of the saddle between Maphee's Hill and Tom á Reithean and the other on the cliff-top plateau to the north of Sloc Chiasigeo inlet on the north-west coastline. These locations are all at generally high elevations on relatively flat, badly drained plateau-like areas that, not surprisingly, always appear wet whatever the weather. Steep hill-slopes, which are generally self draining with only localized boggy spots, are devoid of peat dryers, as are the valley bottoms of Mingulay Bay and Skipisdale.

Mills. MY132.

Roads. MY86, 385.

Wells. MY386.
The well label is misleading since the prevalent solid igneous geology is not easily penetrated without modern drilling equipment, consequently most wells on the islands in reality concern water catchment. Considering the high annual rainfall in the islands this seems a sensible and practical approach. The many streams that exist also provide adequate water as long as any dead sheep are removed regularly.

Noosts. MY32.
Noosts are open ended boat shaped stone settings built just above the tidal high water mark with their open end facing the sea on the point of the southern arm of Mingulay Bay. They were used to secure small boats when they needed to be out of the sea for long periods, in winter for example. Noosts are a common feature in the Northern Isles where their Norse originating name is also commonly used, but this does not mean that they automatically date from that period. The Mingulay examples were in use in the early modern/modern period (Buxton 1995). Buxton made a plan of the visible stones for his dissertation of 1981 which we were able to improve with just a few more hidden stones found by probing. There is also a substantial revetment wall of vertically set stone slabs along the front edge of the grassy bench on which the Noosts are built which may be related to them.

Crane/derrick. MY387.

The mediaeval landscape (Fig. 3.31)
Early references to a chapel of St Columba sited in the enclosed burial ground of the township would indicate that it is most likely that a settlement of

some form existed in the area during the mediaeval period, although no recognizable mediaeval pottery has yet been recovered from the village area. The survey did not locate any immediately recognizable mediaeval house structures in the rest of the island's landscape.

Burial ground and chapel. MY88.

The Norse/early mediaeval landscape (Fig. 3.31)

Boat-shaped stone settings. MY97, 162, 293, 294, 317. Although these stone settings are boat-shaped, it is almost certain that they are all peat dryers. Their locations are all in the areas where the peat dryers are thickest on the ground.

Burial ground and ? chapel. MY88.
The earliest monument of the period in the region is the Pictish symbol stone on Pabbay, which is dated to the 7th century, but the Christian cross carved at the top is a later addition. The monastery on Iona was flourishing in the 6th century and St Columba was active there at this time, but there is no record of him ever visiting the isles so any dedications to him are most likely to be mediaeval in date. However, several bronze pins that may have been late Pictish were found in the area of the burial ground (RCAHMS above), but on the present evidence no date can be put on the acceptance of Christianity and the commencement of Christian burial rituals in the southern islands.

The Iron Age landscape (Fig. 3.32)
One of the surprises of Mingulay's settlement pattern concerns the absence of a major Iron Age Atlantic roundhouse in the island. Even the much smaller island of Berneray displays what once must have been a galleried dun or broch of monumental proportions dominating the western approaches as does the modern lighthouse today. There is almost certainly a wheelhouse (MY344) in Skipisdale and it is quite likely that the two substantial circular structures of MY345 and MY346 are also wheelhouses, but none of these three sites has the dominance of a broch. They are much less demanding and more settled in their domestic agricultural surroundings. True there is Dun Mingulay, which, although large and certainly dramatic in its setting, is largely a natural product of the geology. There are no magnificent structures to dominate, quite the contrary, the interior is untouched except for a few modern shelters. All that it can claim is the remnants of an enclosure wall across the narrow neck of its approach. The dun is in fact a promontory fort that may have served as a defensible refuge. Mingulay, although the largest island and generally the one best suited for settlement, is unique among the southern islands in that during the Iron Age it possesses no settlement of higher status than a

wheelhouse. Did Mingulay come under the lordship of Berneray centred on the significant and symbolic galleried dun there? If so then it might explain the substantial wheelhouse and other buildings in Skipisdale, opposite and within easy distance of Berneray, in contrast to the meagre structural occupation evidence from Mingulay Bay, the natural preferred settlement area.

Settlements. MY35, 345, 346, 384 (RCAHMS NL58SE6 [4]).
MY345 and 346 appear to be contemporary settlements of the Iron Age, possibly wheelhouses that have been occupied and expanded at later periods of time. They are located on either side of the main valley stream that flows down Skipisdale glen to the sea in a south-easterly direction. Both sites are located within a curvilinear enclosure system that occupies the central area of the valley floor and with which they are almost certainly contemporary at some period. The possible shieling complex MY35 has produced Iron Age pottery sherds from excavations into the premodern levels that indicate an early presence of some kind. The excavations on the midden mound MY384 have revealed a sequence of structures and deposits containing considerable Iron Age pottery, and, although the true structural form of the monument is still not known, it is thought most likely to be a sequence of Iron Age roundhouses.

Wheelhouses. MY344.

Forts: Dun Mingulay. MY376 (RCAHMS NL58SW1 [23]).

The Pre-Iron Age landscape (Fig. 3.32)
Possible chamber tombs, burial cairns and mounds, along with a small collection of flintwork, indicates a pre-Iron Age presence on the island, but no certain examples of domestic sites have been located during the survey.

Roundhouses. MY194.
MY194 is a circular structure partly obscured by later buildings that cannot be accurately planned or identified as a roundhouse, consequently its categorization is arbitrary to a large extent.

Chamber tombs. MY2, 76, 347, 389.
There are no megalithic burial monuments on the island that are completely architecturally convincing, but perhaps the greater concentration of population on this island led to a more intensive use of the available stone resources that inevitably led to most of the early monuments being dismantled over the ages.

Cairns. MY9, 10, 11, 12, 14, 16, 17, 18, 19, 20, 21, 22, 23, 30, 33, 50, 53, 55, 72, 74, 77, 85, 89, 93, 103, 104.

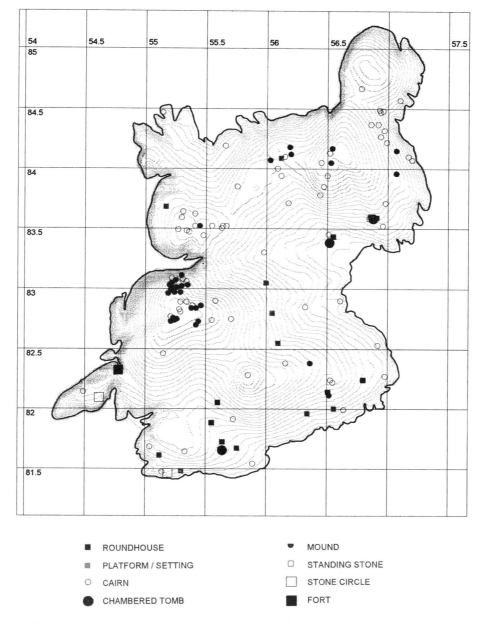

■	ROUNDHOUSE		▼	MOUND
■	PLATFORM / SETTING		□	STANDING STONE
○	CAIRN		□	STONE CIRCLE
●	CHAMBERED TOMB		■	FORT

Figure 3.32 Mingulay, showing the location of prehistoric sites.

114. 117, 123, 127, 134, 137, 144, 149, ?164, 171, 173, 177, 179, 184, 185, 186, 192, 193, 202, 207, 212, 215, 216, 223, 230, 235, 242, 254, 255, 259, 286, 302, 308, 329, 349, 359, 362, 365, 372.

As with all of the islands Mingulay has a wealth of cairn-like structures, some of which may be collapsed shelters. Some will be the result of field stone clearance and some may just be stone accumulation stores for future building work. A few will possibly be of ritual significance and be for burial or disposal of the dead.

Kerbed cairns. MY75A, 160.

At least two monuments may be kerbed cairns, but there may be many more, especially in areas where

they may have been reused in the construction of peat dryers.

Mounds. MY158, 159, 166, 198, 209, 220, 221, 232, 233, 234, 237, 238, 239, 240, 241, 243, 244, 245, 246, 247, 248, 249, 276, 277, 328, 352, 358, 360, 368, 379, 380.

Most, if not almost all, of these monuments may be cairns that have become overgrown with vegetation or are natural postglacial formations. Of all the possible exceptions to this observation MY277 is outstanding, being a mound of earth and stone standing over a metre high. This tumuli stands on the ridge, at the north end, between Tom á Mhaide and Macphee's Hill. It is not visible from Mingulay Bay, but if observed from the opposite side of the ridge it is a prominent feature of the skyline.

Standing stones. MY1.

Stone circles. MY49.

Platforms. MY3.
Artificially created platforms are not uncommon in the hilly landscape of the islands and even on level ground they may still be found as method of raising a structure or building above often wet, boggy ground. Such platforms are generally included in the description of the monument that they underpin, however, a small number of platforms do not appear to have any related buildings and it may be that they were the foundation for some temporary accommodation, such as the fishermen's shacks that were common in the late 19th century around Vatersay Bay.

Miscellaneous undated structures

Numbered enclosures. MY8, 24, 128.
Enclosures and field walls were all mapped when and where possible and form a separate section within the survey along with geological, hydrological and botanical observations.

Stone settings. MY63, 124, 125, 287, 375, 383.
Stone settings, that is, groups of stones that have perhaps been deliberately arranged but which do not make any recognizable form. The reason for their lack of shape is most likely because they have either been deliberately disarranged or subjected to stone robbing.

Conclusion
Mingulay has a wealth of archaeological sites, over 400 of them, and, although the majority may be considered repetitions on the same theme and, therefore of less interest, as a collection they achieve an importance beyond the individual. The peat dryers as a group, for example, illustrate a significant occupation that must have played an important part in the lives of the inhabitants. The numerous cairns and shelters likewise have their part to play in the social and economic history of the island. Apart from these examples, there are a large number of sites that are individually important and have the potential to provide new and revealing information. The apparent absence of a major Iron Age building in the form of a broch or dun, for example, which may have an importance in its own right, cannot detract from the potential of the Iron Age sites that are known to exist. Already excavations at the apparently minor site at MY384 have provided much new information relating to the period and a careful investigation of the sites in Skipisdale may provide answers to many questions that relate to more than just the Iron Age period. Somewhere, either under the peat or under the deposits and features of a later site, there must be the evidence for occupation during the pre-Iron Age periods. The mediaeval and Norse periods are just as enigmatic and sites of these periods must certainly exist hidden somewhere.

Berneray or Barra Head Survey, 1992

Introduction (Fig. 3.33)

Of the formerly inhabited islands included in the survey Berneray is the smallest, being only 3 km long from east to west and 1.3 km wide from north to south and is also the southern most island of the Outer Hebridean chain. This gives it the dubious honour of being the remotest island in the group and one that could be considered the least suitable for permanent settlement.

Normally the first view of the island is from the north as one travels down the island chain from Barra. The initial impression is its sriking greenness, for the northern aspect is tipped at such a steep angle that most of the island's grassy interior is in plain view. The second impression may be that the island is not conducive to permanent settlement with such a limited area available for agricultural use, although over 60% of the available land surface is grassy, the rest being rocky terraces. The coastal topography of the island, over 70% high rocky cliffs and only 20% low shelving rock, does little to encourage settlement, offering few sheltered areas and no bays or beaches, even along the north coastline, which shelves relatively gently to the sea in comparison to the spectacular high sheer cliffs that face the sea to the south and west. The axis of this elongated oval island is east–west, leaving most of the land surface open to the westerly gales that regularly sweep in from the Atlantic.

Stories about the ferocious weather on Berneray are numerous and often concern the lighthouse perched 178 m high on the lofty cliffs of the Stron an Duin promontory at the western end of the island. For example, Miss Isabella Bird visited the island in 1863

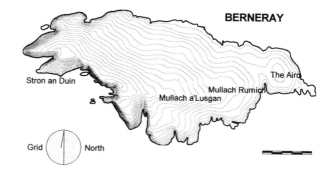

Figure 3.33 Berneray, showing topography and place-names.

and tells of the times, often counted in weeks, when the lighthouse families cannot 'stir outside the lighthouse walls, without the risk of being blown over the cliff—the fate of a former light-keeper' and the times when the lighthouse enclosure, which is over 600 ft (190 m) above sea level must be drained because it 'is so full of water from drifting surf that they open the scuppers to let it out' (Bird 1866). Robert Stevenson, the designer of the lighthouse, reported an occasion when a horse and cart of the hauliers that was bringing supplies up to the construction site was blown over and 'both shafts were broken and the body of the cart blown into the air' (quoted in Buxton 1995).

This daunting description does not paint a completely true picture and there is much to soften the apparent disadvantages. The wide range of monument types found during the archaeological survey suggest that the island was permanently occupied for long periods of time. However, only when the island's past is investigated in much greater depth, and it is probable that only an extensive programme of archaeological excavation is able to produce the required data, can questions concerning population figures, periods of settlement or types of social structure be addressed. To some extent the carrying capacity of the island may be judged from our knowledge of the resident population in recent times. Census figures available for 1841 show that the island maintained 6 inhabited houses occupied by a total of 30 individuals, not counting the lighthouse keepers and their dependants. These figures vary only slightly during the nineteenth century, rising in 1881 to 10 inhabited houses with a population of 57 individuals. In 1911 the census shows only the 3 lighthouse families occupying the island.

Whether these figures may be used as a genuine basis for calculating earlier populations is difficult to determine, but the limited land area available for agricultural use may indicate that the island could rarely support more whatever the social structuring. Although the agricultural potential of the island is comparatively low, a variety of root and tuber vegetables, oats and barley were grown in the last century. The lazy-beds that were required to bulk up the thin soils for growing these crops can still be seen, usually around the homesteads, since the rest of the land was used for grazing. Sheep, goats, ponies and cattle were noted by Bird in the description of her visit in 1863 aboard HMS *Shamrock* (Bird 1866), but it is most likely that she mistook the ponies used to haul supplies up to the lighthouse as part of the normal native stockholding.

However, the sea in the vicinity of Berneray was noted for its rich stocks of white fish and was consequently used as a base by fishermen from neighbouring islands. In the late 19th century as many as 20 fishermen were in temporary occupation and can be added to the population figures (Buxton 1995).

William Chambers, a commissioner for the Northern Lights and joint editor of *Chambers' Information for the People* encyclopaedia, describing his tour of inspection to the lighthouse in 1866, goes so far as to describe the area as being 'not a half or one tenth part fished' with ling and cod 'jostling each other in their anxiety to be caught and eaten' (Chambers 1866). Offshore fishing could be and was supplemented by line fishing from the shore, as numerous cup marks hollowed into the rocks and used for grinding fish bait indicate.

Possibly surpassed only by those of Mingulay and St Kilda, the monumental, 190 m high sea cliffs to the south and west of the island, which can appear so daunting and inhospitable, provide an equally rich resource in the form of sea birds and their eggs. The bird population includes many different species, but puffins, guillemots, razorbills, fulmars and kittewakes are the commonest birds caught. This important source of protein, available in apparently inexhaustible quantities, was exploited by the islanders, who also managed an additional small economic benefit from the sale of feathers for bedding (Bird 1866).

The lack of beaches is in no way a deterrent to settlement on the island or a significant barrier that prevents the movement from sea to land and back. In fact it is far easier to step ashore from a boat hooked on to the rock shelves of the north coastline than to attempt a landing on any beach unless it is from a modern flat-bottomed inflatable dinghy. The gentle rocky slopes of that shoreline provide many places where a boat may easily be hauled up out of the sea and securely lashed down.

Probably it is the island's remoteness that renders permanent settlement a precarious option today. The journey from Castlebay on Barra can take many hours even by motor launch. To the fishermen of the 19th and earlier centuries the same journey would have been considered a major undertaking and yet such a distance appears to have been acceptable.

Berneray, unlike most of the other inhabited and formerly inhabited islands, has no significant peat deposits. This is due almost entirely to the overall steep angle imposed upon most of its land surfaces, which allows much of the rainwater rapidly to drain off. Whether there was ever any tree growth on the island is doubtful considering its generally exposed nature. Even if woodland had existed the island is so small in area that it would have been quickly exhausted by the first few generations of settlers. Since until modern times peat was the only fuel available in quantity, it has therefore always been an essential requirement for successful settlement in the islands and the lack of it may be considered a considerable impoverishment. In 1866 it was reported that peat had to be brought over from Mingulay and that the people of Berneray were thought poorer in comparison to those of the other islands because they lacked their own deposits (Buxton 1995). It is possible that a similar solution to this problem was undertaken from a very early period, possibly in the Neolithic, since the need for fuel is a universal constant in the development and survival of any community.

Royal Commission on the Ancient and Historical Monuments of Scotland National Sites and Monuments Record of Scotland

The 13 sites known prior to this survey are recorded in the National Monuments Record of Scotland. They are:

1. NL58SE3 (NGR NL5674:8029). Chapel and burial ground (BY55). T.S. Muir (1885) noted no objects of antiquity. No dedication in Name Book 1878. The RCAHMS visit (1928) found no trace of the chapel and the OS visit (1965) found no certain trace of the chapel or burial ground.
2. NL58SE4. Standing stone 7 ft high and an altar to St Christopher. M. Martin c. 1695. Not found during the OS visit (1965).
3. NL58SE18 (NGR NL5647:8039). Hand crane.
4. NL58SE19 (NGR NL5520:8010). Burial ground (BY19). The OS (1965) record a 19th-century cemetery for lighthouse personnel.
5. NL58SE27 (NGR NL564:803). Stone circle (Osborn's Well). No further information, but mentioned by Thom (Thom 1967).
6. NL58SE28 (NGR NL5647:8040). Concrete Pier (BY85). No further information.
7. NL58SE29 (NGR NL567:803). Cup-marks. One on stone slab, two on wall to north of chapel NL58SE3 (BY55). OS (1965).
8. NL58SE30 (NGR NL55:80). Horizontal water mill (BY90). No further information.
9. NL58SE42/2 (NGR NL563:802). The Aird. Township, mill, chapel (BY53, 54, 57 etc.). Eleven roofed buildings including mill, three unroofed, several enclosures and head dyke. OS 6-in. Map (1880). One roofed, eight unroofed, enclosures. OS 1:10,000 map (1989).
10. NL58SW3 (NGR NL5485:8057). Dun Briste (BY16). OS 6-in. Map 1880. RCAHMS visit (1928). Promontory fort. Wall across 75 ft long by 5/10 ft wide. Two rows stone slabs on edge. No entrance. Within enclosure, against wall several hut circles up to 12 ft diam. OS (1965). Surveyed at 1/10 (560). As above, but four shelters, not hut circles.
11. NL58SW4 (NGR NL5485:8023). Dun (Stron an Duin, lighthouse promontory) (BY17). The main wall of the dun, across the promontory, is described by Miss Bird in 1863 (1866) as being about 30 ft high and this is after being reduced by the lighthouse builders. Thomas (1890) describes the same wall 25 years later as being 95 ft long, 15 ft wide and 13 ft high with the remains of two galleries visible south of the entrance. A plan by Anderson (1893) shows the south end complete. Visited by RCAHMS in 1915, found the height

to be only 9 ft. Described as a Galleried Dun (Feachem 1963). Visit by OS (1965) nothing further added.
12. NL58SW5 (NGR NL549:802). Cairn or dolmen noted by Muir (1885) down-slope below the lighthouse. Visit by OS (1965), not found.
13. NL58SW7. Lighthouse (BY18). Built by Robert Stevenson. Operational 1833. Bibliography: Munro 1979; Allardyce and Hood 1986.

The 1992 survey

Berneray was chosen as the first of the southern islands to be surveyed because its small land area appeared to be of manageable proportions suitable for testing our survey methods and gaining valuable experience in living and working on these remote islands for weeks at a time. This pilot survey was undertaken in 1992 solely by the authors and was planned to last for just over one week. At this stage investigative archaeological excavations were not considered appropriate.

For survey purposes the island could be divided into convenient parcels of land defined by either topographical features or manmade boundary walls. The west end of the island is neatly divided off from the rest of the island by the high straight enclosure wall that defines the lighthouse land holding. At the east end of the island a block of land, the Aird, which runs out to the sea at Nisam Point, is also divided from the rest of the island by an enclosure wall or head dyke that is the eastern end of the infield enclosure system belonging to the main area of early modern settlement. This enclosure land stretches along, and occupies, most of the lower slope along the northern coastline. A large block of land is enclosed from the head dyke and occupies the south-east corner of the island. The bulk of the remaining central portion of the island is not enclosed, but it can be easily divided into three blocks separated into southern, central and northern areas by the tarmac road leading to the lighthouse and the crest of the ridge Mullach á Lusgan. Each surveyor took one of these blocks of land each day and simply traversed backwards and forwards across it until satisfied that the area had been examined and recorded in as detailed a manner as possible in the time available.

The relatively smooth surface of the island enabled the ground to be speedily covered and made the monuments comparatively easy to spot; however the identification of many early monuments was hindered by later stone robbing. Stone robbing, always a factor in such a survey, is perhaps elevated in the scale of importance on Berneray. Although Berneray is composed of solid igneous rock there are few exposures where it can be won with ease. The nature of the rock, its hardness, and, where accessible along the north shore, its smoothness, allow for little ease of extraction to those without the tools or technology. Loose rock or field stone, the usual source for nonquarried building material, is available in only limited dispersed quantities around the island since the soil cover appears quite stable. There are no great erosion points where the underlying postglacial debris is exposed apart from a thin strip around the edge of the coastline and in the out-wash from the edge of decaying dykes and there are no mountainous formations producing scree deposits. Therefore building stone may always have been a relatively scarce commodity and until the lighthouse quarry was in operation it is most likely that most of the stone for building was acquired by robbing it from the obsolete structures of past generations.

A total of 89 sites were located during the survey of which the majority are previously unknown, a not unexpected situation since this was the first systematic survey of the island's archaeological monuments. Previous reports of the island, especially those of the 19th century or earlier, were usually made after only a short visit and perhaps the remoteness and smallness of the island gave the impression that little would be found here. During later visits by the Ordnance Survey and the Royal Commission most of the short time ashore necessarily involved checking the earlier reports. Out of the total sites recorded 26 (29.2%) were within the 50 m coastal strip.

No archaeological excavation was undertaken on this island although an opportunity was taken to clear some of the rank nettles and iris tubers from the cemetery mound (BY55). This action was of great benefit for it not only gave an insight into the nature and construction of the mound, but it also revealed a number of interesting stone markers. Argument

against archaeological excavation on the basis that these islands are protected by SSSI status and too remote to be threatened by anything other than natural processes can be countered by the example of the 19th-century mill seriously damaged by recent drainage work to the side of the road leading to the lighthouse.

Site description and catalogue
BY1* (NL5642:8035) Roundhouse. *Location*: Bottom of coastal hill-slope. *Description*: BY1 is located in the northern settlement area close to the foreshore. The overall diameter is 4.7 m with 1 m thick walls of stone and earth surviving to a height of 0.3 m. The entrance is, as tradition and the prevailing winds dictate, to the east.
BY2* (NL5625:8054) (Fig. 3.34) Chamber tomb. *Location*: Rocky prominence at bottom of coastal hill-slope. *Description*: BY2 is built low down on the north coast, just 5 m above the foreshore, to the west of the settlement area. The structure is composed of two massive stone slabs, one 1.4 m long and 1 m high and the other 1.7 m long and 0.8 m high, placed parallel to each other on a low mound with their axis east–west. There is some smaller stone between them partially blocking the east end and also around them, and a large irregular-shaped flat slab, 1 × 1.4 m, lying to one side to the north, which could either be another side stone or a cap stone. From the east the site is prominent against the low skyline. Other stones on the approaches from the east and more so from the west suggest some remnant of a 'processional way' originally leading to the monument, but this is not certain. *Note*: Damaged by burrowing and sheep scraping.

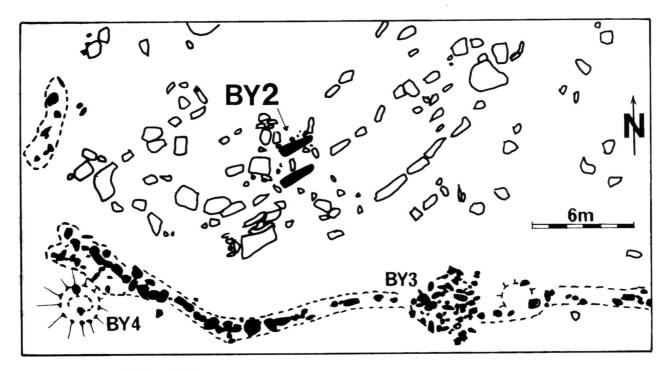

Figure 3.34 Sites BY2, BY3, and BY4.

BY3* (NL5624:8053) (Fig. 3.34) Shelter. *Location*: Bottom of coastal hill-slope. *Description*: Circular, diam. 3.8 m, single cell with 1.4 m thick stone faced earthen walls standing 0.5–0.75 m high. Entrance to south-west. *Note*: Enclosure wall butts to rear wall.

BY4* (NL5623:8054) Shelter. *Location*: Bottom of coastal slope. *Description*: Circular, diam. 4 m, single cell with 1.5 m thick spread earthen walls standing 0.2 m high. No apparent entrance.

BY5* (NL5619:8052) Cairn. (clearance) *Location*: Bottom of coastal hill-slope. *Description*: Circular, diam. 1.5 m, pile of stones inside field system with lazy-beds. Some outer ring stones set upright.

BY6* (NL5610:8057) Enclosure. *Location*: Bottom of coastal hill-slope. *Description*: Oval, 11 × 8 m, dry-stone walled enclosure standing 1 m high without entrance. Much tumbled material.

BY7 (NL5591:8048) Boat-shaped stone setting. *Location*: Above scarp line of lower hill-slope. *Description*: boat shape, 4 × 1.7 m, prow pointed to north to sea. Stones set along sides, some loose and tumbled, and as a division across the centre.

BY8* (NL5587:8057) Enclosure. *Location*: Bottom of coastal hill-slope. *Description*: Subrectangular, 29 × 35 m, enclosure marked by stone linear settings and revetted edges. Some internal divisions.

BY9* (NL5586:8057) Cairn (clearance). *Location*: Bottom coastal hill-slope. *Description*: Pile of stones, diam. 2 m, on mound, many large, up to 1.6 m in size set upright. *Note*: Within BY8.

BY10 (NL5583:8053) Setting. *Location*: Lower coastal hill-slope. *Description*: Oval, 4 × 2 m, structure very much overgrown. The structure is indistinct, but it is definitely not rectangular as depicted on the OS map.

BY11 (NL5579:8047) Shelter. *Location*: Lower coastal hill-slope. *Description*: Sub-rectangular, 1.4 × 1.1 m, single cell of drystone walling standing to seven courses high with entrance to east. *Note*: Set against enclosure wall.

BY12 (NL5578:8050) Shelter. *Location*: Lower coastal hill-slope. *Description*: Rectangular, 4 × 2.2 m, shelter divided by a cross-wall into two cells set end on against enclosure wall. The 2 m square cell nearest the enclosure wall has a raised floor of stone that may be to provide a dry bench bed. The entrance cell is marked by set stones only.

BY13* (NL5576:8055) Shelter. *Location*: Bottom of coastal hill-slope. *Description*: Circular, diam. 2.2 m, single-cell stone ring-wall with entrance to the east. *Note*: Set against enclosure wall.

BY14 (NL5541:8055) Shelter. *Location*: Lower coastal hill-slope. *Description*: Circular, diam. 3.4 m, single-cell stone ring-wall and a possible entrance to the east. Single block lying flat inside is 1.4 m.

BY15 (NL5524:8049) Cairn (clearance). *Location*: Lower coastal hill-slope. *Description*: Pile of stones, diam. 2 m, on line of enclosure wall.

BY16* (NL5485:8057) Fort Dun Briste (Iron Age). *Location*: Cliff-top promontory. *Description*: BY16 is labelled on the 1880 6 in. OS maps as Dun Briste and on the 1989 1:10,000 map as Dun Bristle. The monument consists of a stone wall built across the neck of a small promontory. The wall is approximately 23 m long, constructed as a double row of stone slabs set upright, some measuring 0.9 m long by 1.5 m high. At the southern end the two wall lines are spaced 3.3 m apart and at the northern end 1.6 m apart, the space between shows some evidence of being filled

Figure 3.35 Site BY17, the Barra Head lighthouse and the Iron Age dun wall in the foreground.

with small stones and presumably earth, but the earth has all been washed out and few of the stones are left. There is no apparent entrance and the interior is devoid of any associated structures; although four small shelters are built against the inside of the wall they are almost certainly of early modern date.

BY17* (NL5485:8023) (Figs 3.35, 3.36). Atlantic roundhouse (Iron Age galleried dun). *Location*: Cliff-top promontory. *Description*: A galleried promontory dun showing evidence of having once been a massively built structure worthy of the title stronghold. The original form and size of the superstructure now appears to be lost, but it once may have occupied all of the promontory Stron an Duin to the west of the present position of the lighthouse (Fig. 3.35). There is every reason to suspect that when the lighthouse, its ancillary buildings, enclosure walls and pavements were being constructed, not only was the interior of the dun used as a stone quarry, with stone blasted out of the bedrock, but that most of the dun superstructure, including all its interior structural stone fittings, were robbed out for the same purpose. Drill holes still survive on blocks of granite in the quarry area and nothing of the dun survives, apart from a section of its eastern wall. The survival of the east wall is not hard to understand considering the exceptionally high winds encountered up on this cliff-top. As Miss Bird (1866) recounts, the top of the wall was lowered to allow better vision, but the builders of the lighthouse were not so stupid as to totally remove an excellent windbreak that had already proved its ability to withstand the Hebridean weather for over a thousand years.

The presence of a gallery, still visible today and proof of architectural complexity, on the inside of the surviving portion of the east wall, plus the sheer massiveness of the masonry stone from which it is constructed, suggest that at least that part of the wall circuit did once reach a considerable height. Perhaps Miss Bird's apparent estimate of 30 ft at its highest point is not so incredible.

The surviving east wall does not terminate when it reaches the sheer cliffs of the south side of the promontory, but for a short distance curves round and follows the line of the cliff edge. This continuation is of much lighter construction and may not have served as a continuation of the gallery. However, it does indicate that the wall circuit may originally have been complete. The size of the blocks of masonry used to construct the visible remains of the east wall are truly massive (Fig. 3.36), some measured at 2 × 1.35 m in size and fitted together in a skilful interlocking manner, the whole given a slight batter. The walling of the northern portion of this wall, including the present doorway, is of different later construction and was almost certainly built up at the termination of serious quarrying in the interior. The logic behind this assertion lies in the fact that it would not have been possible to work the quarry, removing large quantities of material, without demolishing a working way through the dun walls. This would have been rebuilt afterwards to maintain the windbreak afforded by the walling as a whole. The change in building technique in this part of the wall is clear and it is possible to distinguish reused lintel stones from the internal gallery inserted into the new work as long stabilizing stones. The size, style and butt joint of

Figure 3.36 Site BY17, a detail of the massive masonry of the dun.

the doorway prove it to be alien to the dun, as is the walling around the north side.

Inside the dun some of the gallery lintel stones were still visible, but not the inner ring-wall. How much undisturbed deposit remains is not possible to estimate, but if the gallery was open or revealed, as it must have been during the lighthouse building, then it was certainly investigated if only for curiosity. Regardless of that probability some carefully targeted excavations could still reveal important information as to surviving deposits, structural details and hopefully some dating material. Important noninvasive work could be undertaken by accurately planning the remains and drawing stone by stone elevations to scale.

The relationship between the two duns is difficult to illustrate; although they share similar locations, their forms are sufficiently different to eliminate any suggestion that their functions have a common denominator other than defensive potential. BY17 was most certainly residential and was most likely occupied over a long period of time, while BY16 is only a single monolithic wall enclosing the internal area of a promontory with no apparent internal structures to suggest long-term occupation. That they are contemporary is probable and at present, with so little information available, the most acceptable answer is that the two are part of the same social organization and that one is for human habitation and one is for the safe keeping of livestock—house and byre on a grand scale.

There are no visible field walls directly associated with either of the duns and the lack of any trace of field walling in the vast bulk of the island, west, south and central, would suggest that this part of the island was always open land until the lighthouse enclosures were imposed upon it. Because of the tight schedule less time was taken with the monuments that had already received some attention and the dun was given only a cursory inspection. A short visit, however, was long enough to gain some useful impressions and indications of where further work would be of value.
BY18* (NL5490:8025) (Fig. 3.35) Lighthouse (modern). *Location*: Cliff-top. *Description*: Circular lighthouse tower within a rectangular enclosure complex with ancillary buildings. The lighthouse was designed by Robert Stevenson (1772–1850) and built in 1830–33.
BY19* (NL5520:8009) Burial ground (modern). *Location*: Cliff-top. *Description*: Circular, diam. 10 m, 19th-century cemetery consisting of a high circular wall of quarried and dressed stone mortared with cement. Located on the south cliff edge within the outer light-house field enclosure. Entrance is via a small wooden gate (now almost rotted away) on the eastern side. Inside several memorial wall plaques in poor condition have fallen from the walls. *Note*: Constructed specifically for the Protestant lighthouse keepers and their dependants.

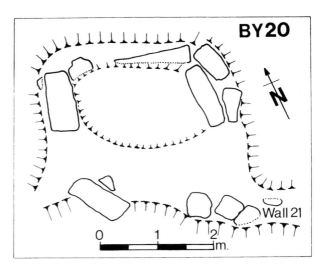

Figure 3.37 Site BY20.

BY20 (NL5633:8014) (Fig. 3.37) Chamber tomb. *Location*: Mid northern hill-slope on prominent knoll out from prominent break in the hill-slope. *Description*: BY20 is located inside the settlement area high on its southern edge. The tomb appears to have been used as a point of reference when the head dyke (wall BY21) was first laid out, as it incorporates the south side of the monument in its course from east to west. The actual junction is not clear and requires careful excavation to truly determine the sequence of events. From the settlement area lower down to the north the monument stands prominent on the skyline even though most of its stonework appears to have been robbed away, possibly in the construction of wall BY21. One large upright remains on the eastern side, but most of the rest are well-embedded stones of some lower part of the structure. Subrectangular, 3 × 1.5 m, embedded side stones and single orthostats only survive stone robbing.
BY21 (NL5613:7968) Enclosure. *Location*: On south-east slope. *Description*: Rectangular, 110 × 50 m, of piled stone walls with internal sub-divisions.
BY22 (NL5591:7980) Complex of shelter and enclosure. *Location*: Bottom of southern slope of Mulliach á Lusgan. *Description*: Oval enclosure with shelter centrally placed.
BY22a (NL5591:7980) Shelter. *Location*: As above. *Description*: Oval mound, 4 × 3 m, with oval single cell, 3.3 × 2.3 m, ring of stones, in size range 0.5–1.2 m, set vertically.
BY22b (NL5591:7980) Enclosure. *Location*: As above. *Description*: Subrectangular, 65 × 24 m, enclosure walled with stones up to 1.9 m in size set on edge.
BY23 (NL5591:7977) Complex of mound and shelters. *Location*: Slope of southern plateau. *Description*: Oval mound with rounded shelter with further rectilinear shelter adjacent.
BY23a (NL5591:7977) Shelter. *Location*: As above. *Description*: Circular, diam. 1.5 m, group of stones set

in semblance of round shelter, but with disarranged stonework, is built on the north-west flank of a 2.5 m diam. Mound.

BY23b (NL5591:7977) Shelter. *Location*: As above. *Description*: L-shaped stone setting built west from the mound, 3 × 1.75 m, which could form a shelter or may be part of a larger building that includes (a).

BY24 (NL5579:7982) Shelter. *Location*: Base of south slope from Muliach á Lusgan. *Description*: Single-stone subrectangular, 5 × 3 m, construction with stones less than 1.4 m in size, almost hidden in the grass. It is located on a platform in a flat area on a bench of the upper crags on the south side of Mullach á Lusgan.

BY25* (NL5577:7980) Chamber tomb. *Location*: On plateau slope south of Muliach á Lusgan. *Description*: Several upright stones set on low oval mound suggest a possible original chamber of 2.5 × 2 m. A single large slab of 1.25 m length appears out of place, diagonally situated pointing into the centre of the chamber.

BY26* (NL5591:7942) Shelter. *Location*: Cliff-top. *Description*: Rectangular, 2 × 1.5 m, single cell of coursed drystone walling using a large 1.5 m sized boulder for one side. No entrance.

BY27* (NL5583:7943) Shelter. *Location*: Cliff-top. *Description*: Oval, 3 × 2 m, single cell of stones, some upright, butted to large round boulder. Possible entrance to south.

BY28* (NL5598:7957) Boat-shaped stone setting. *Location*: South cliff-top. *Description*: A low oval mound, 5.25 × 4.25 m, is surmounted by a stone setting of spaced blocks some of which appear displaced. They form no clear structure, but do suggest the elongated cell, 4 × 2.5 m, of a possible boat-shaped setting. However, this identification is very tentative.

BY29 (NL5605:7960) Shelter. *Location*: On east slope from high plateau. *Description*: Oval shape, 2 × 1.5 m, single cell of a few small blocks forming a broken ring-wall foundation.

BY30 (NL5587:7958) Cairn. *Location*: High plateau. *Description*: Circular, 2 m diam., mound of grassed-over stone.

BY31 (NL5585:7970) Boat-shaped stone setting. *Location*: On plateau. *Description*: A low oval mound, 5 × 3 m, with several irregularly spaced stone blocks around the high perimeter that suggest a boat shape, but overgrown and indistinct.

BY32* (NL5601:7959) Shelter. *Location*: On plateau slope. *Description*: Oval, 4 × 3.1 m, single cell of widely spaced stones.

BY33 (NL5618:7958) Roundhouse. *Location*: Slope to south cliff. *Description*: Half-circle, 4 m diam., single cell of set stones, many upright. Ring-wall is only a single stone thickness, less substantial than should be expected for a roundhouse. This site therefore could be no more than a shelter.

BY34 (NL5616:7969) Shelter. *Location*: On slope to south cliff from plateau. *Description*: Circular, 2.7 m diam., single cell with walls of piled and set stones, some large, in the 0.65–1.5 m size range. *Note*: Within enclosure BY21.

BY35* (NL5639:7966) Shelter. *Location*: South cliff-top. *Description*: Rectangular, 2.6 × 2 m, single cell of large stones, some on edge, 0.6–1 m size range.

BY36* (NL5661:7969) Shelter. *Location*: On slope to south cliff edge. *Description*: Subrectangular, 2 × 1.7 m, single cell with wall of coursed and set stones. Wall thickness in some places several stones wide. *Note*: Set against field wall.

BY37 (NL5662:7972) Boat-shaped stone setting. *Location*: On slope to south cliff edge. *Description*: Stones set in a possible boat shape on a slight mound, other stones scattered, single cell, 4.5 × 2.5 m. *Note*: Stone robbing is likely.

BY38* (NL5664:7966) Boat-shaped stone setting. *Location*: Natural prominence on slope to south cliff. *Description*: Oval, 10 × 5 m, single cell of stones spaced in outline, well-embedded into slight mound. *Note*: A field wall down to the cliff edge uses one side of the boat setting in its alignment. Stone for the wall has most likely been robbed from the monument.

BY39 (NL5665:7976) (Fig. 3.38) Cairn. *Location*: On slope to south cliff edge. *Description*: Circular, 2.5 m diam., stone ring with many stones set upright on slight mound.

BY40 (NL5665:7979) Cairn. *Location*: Plateau. *Description*: Pile of stones with no clear structure or form, could be tumble from adjacent field wall.

BY41 (NL5661:7981) Enclosure. *Location*: Plateau. *Description*: Large semicircle of spaced stones butted to side of a broad earthen ramp.

BY42 (NL5656:7981) Oval setting. *Location*: Plateau. *Description*: Oval shape, 5 × 3 m, of embedded stones. Totally obscured by heather.

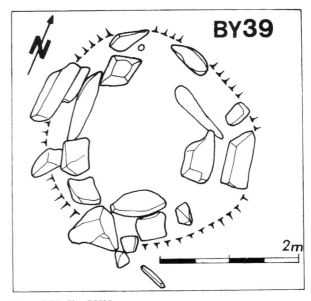

Figure 3.38 Site BY39.

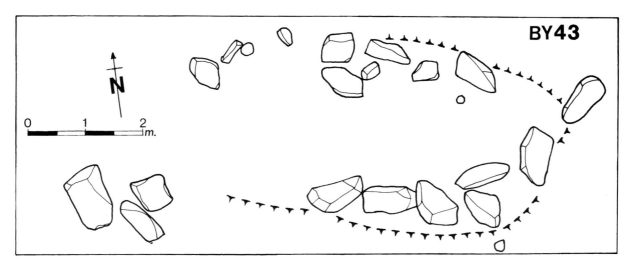

Figure 3.39 Site BY43.

BY43 (NL5654:7982) (Fig. 3.39) Boat-shaped stone setting. *Location*: Flat area on slope. *Description*: Oval, 7 × 4 m, single cell of large blocks set along sides in a possible boat shape, also some stones scattered. *Note*: Similar to BY38, both similar to some of the Mingulay peat dryers.

BY44 (NL5651:7982) Shieling complex. *Location*: Platform against hill-slope. *Description*: Rectangular shieling house, 1.4 × 3.1 m, single cell with 0.7 m thick stone-faced walls and entrance to the east. Set on a 10 m diam. arc of a slightly mounded platform set against the hill-slope. A south entrance in the platform is approached by a ramp.

BY45 (NL5651:7989) (Fig. 3.40) Boat-shaped stone setting. *Location*: Plateau. *Description*: A narrow pointed boat shape, 9 × 3 m. Only one side is well-defined with set stones. The other side appears to be displaced and slightly scattered.

BY46 (NL5651:7986) Shelter. *Location*: Plateau slope. *Description*: Circular, 2.3 m diam., single cell with several large slabs of 0.65 m size set on edge. Smaller stones are set around raised flat internal platform. *Note*: Could be a reduced cairn.

BY47* (NL5682:7993) Shelter. *Location*: On slope to cliff edge. *Description*: Rectangular, 2.2 × 1.1 m, single cell with single-stone thick walls butted to field wall—entrance to south-west.

BY48 (NL5711:8011) Boat-shaped stone setting. *Location*: Plateau on the Aird peninsula. *Description*: Oval setting, 5 × 2 m, of stones, some scattered, makes possible boat shape.

BY49 (NL5713:8008) Boat-shaped stone setting. *Location*: Plateau on the Aird peninsula. *Description*: Several stones set in a curved line, 4.5 m long, with several others making a pointed prow shape.

BY50 (NL5703:8013) Complex of cairn and standing stones. *Location*: Hill-top point of the Aird. *Description*: Piled stone cairn on the point of the hill with two possible standing stones close by. A curved line of set stones is to the south.

BY50a (NL5703:8013) Cairn. *Location*: Point of hilltop, the Aird peninsula. *Description*: Piled stones, diam. 3 m, degraded and possibly modern.

BY50b (NL5703:8013) Standing stone. *Location*: The Aird peninsula hill-top. *Description*: Small standing stone.

Figure 3.40 Site BY45.

BY50c (NL5703:8013) Standing stone. *Location*: The Aird peninsula hill-top. *Description:* Small standing stone.

BY51 (NL5710:8020) Shelter. *Location*: North slope the Aird plateau. *Description*: Circular stone setting, diam. 1.5 m, forming single cell butted to a few stones set along the curving edge of a natural depression of the peat on the hill-slope. *Note*: A further possible shelter 6 m to the north-west.

BY52 (NL5680:8013) Cairn. *Location*: Bottom of hill-slope. *Description*: Circular, diam. 5 m, of earth and stone. *Note:* Within the settlement area field system so could be a clearance cairn.

BY53* (NL5688:8026) Complex of houses and platform *Location*: Bottom coastal plain. *Description*: Two rectangular improved blackhouses built at right-angles to each other forming an L shape that retains a raised and revetted platform. Modified after abandonment to provide a modern set of stock pens with concrete sheep dip.

BY53a* (NL5688:8026) Blackhouse. *Location*: As above. *Description*: Rectangular single cell with 1.5 m thick drystone walls, a curved back fireplace in the south end wall and a blocked entrance to the west. Assuming that the doorway is approximately in the middle of the wall then the length of the building is around 10 m and its internal width is 3.1 m. A gated doorway has been cut through the east wall giving access to the enclosure (d). A further door has been cut through the wall in the position where the north end fireplace would have been giving access into the pen (c).

BY53b* (NL5688:8026) Blackhouse. *Location*: As above. *Description*: The largest of the two houses, a rectangular, 14.4 × 7.2 m, single cell with 1.5 m thick drystone walls, a square-backed fireplace in the east end wall and an entrance to the north. Assuming that the end west wall is original, then an entrance has been cut through it, where the fireplace could have been, to give access to the pen (c). A further opening has been cut to the north of the east fireplace and a sheep dip chute inserted that gives passage to a dip tank just inside the house. *Note*: There is no direct access to the platform enclosure to the south between the houses.

BY53c* (NL5688:8026) Pen. *Location*: As above. *Description*: Rectangular single cell of drystone, 1.5 m thick walls, with internal dimensions of 5.3 × 3.8 m built in the angle of the two blackhouses using the west wall of house (b), but possibly reconstructing the north end of house (a) to allow for more internal space. A gated doorway to the north and one to the west give access to the open field system. Doorway to the south into house (a) and east into house (b) complete the sheep control system. The animals can be driven through the dip in house (b) and on into the pen and so on to house (b) with an exit to the raised platform enclosure or they can be cut out into temporary fenced pens at the north doorway of house (b) and the north or west exits from the pen.

BY53d* (NL5688:8026) Platform. *Location*: As above. Description: Rectangular, 15.5 × 6.5 m, raised platform built inside the angle of the two blackhouses providing an enclosure with access from house (a) only. The leading edges are revetted with piled stone to the south and set upright stones to the east. Presumably the enclosure was completed with temporary wire fencing.

BY54 (NL5681:8026) Cairn. (clearance) *Location*: Coastal plain. *Description*: Piled stones, diam. 2 m, within settlement field system

BY55* (NL5675:8031) Burial ground complex of blackhouses, enclosure, platform and mound. *Location*: Coastal plain. *Description*: Subcircular drystone walled enclosure (40 × 25m). Within the enclosure the ground is generally raised up to the height of the outer wall-top. Located in a central position within the eastern half is an unenclosed burial mound capped with cobbles and with several grave markers visible, but it is now largely covered by rank iris and nettle overgrowth. Judging by the grave markers and other scattered stones, the area of burial appears to have spread off the mound from the north and out into the enclosure. The cemetery is later reorganized with the introduction of a drystone wall that bisects the enclosure north–south. Along its course, and incorporated in it, are two square earth and stone single-cell buildings (i and h). One (i), in a central position, also appears to be dug into the burial mound, while the other (h) is to the south close to the enclosure wall where a small additional length of walling forms a small square single cell ?barn (c) between the wall and building (h). Building (h) is cut by a subrectangular building of blackhouse proportions (d) that stands inside the cemetery enclosure while also incorporating that wall as its south-east elevation. There is an entrance north-west into the burial ground, but whether an entrance through the south-east wall to the outside was in use at the same time is at present not known. A second smaller square building sits squarely on top of (d) using this second entrance. The two blackhouses (a) and (b) appear normal dwellings, but any of the other buildings could serve as a chapel.

BY55a* (NL5675:8031) Blackhouse. *Location*: As above. *Description*: Subrectangular, 7 × 4.5 m, single-cell drystone improved blackhouse with an entrance to the west. The walls are approximately 1 m thick and there is a fireplace built into the north end wall. The building is on the outer side of the cemetery enclosure wall, but incorporates it as its eastern rear wall.

BY55b* (NL5675:8031) Blackhouse. *Location*: As above. *Description*: Subrectangular, 7.5 × 4.5 m, single-cell improved blackhouse almost identical to (a), but with the fireplace built into the south end wall. *Note*: A grinding saddle quern stone was found in the collapsed stonework by the fireplace.

BY55c* (NL5675:8031) Barn. *Location*: As above. *Description*: Square, 4 × 4 m, single cell inserted between the cemetery enclosure wall and building (h). The small length of walling put across the gap seems to be a later addition.

BY55d* (NL5675:8031) Blackhouse. *Location*: As above. *Description*: Subrectangular, 9 × 5 m, single cell with earth and stone wall 0.8–0.90 m thick. There is a definite doorway into the cemetery to the north-east and it is possible that the doorway through the enclosure wall to the south-east used by building (e) may also be used by (d). It is impossible to determine whether this building is a blackhouse dwelling or of some other function, such as a chapel, but its location inside the enclosure suggests that it may be a religious building.

BY55e* (NL5675:8031) Barn. *Location*: As above. *Description*: Square, 4 × 4 m, single-cell barn-sized building with walls of earth and stone constructed on top of and inside (d). The only doorway is to the outside through the enclosure wall to the south-east.

BY55f* (NL5675:8031) Building. *Location*: As above. *Description*: The true form of this structure is unclear from the surface evidence. It appears to be about 6 m across and to consist of a raised platform of earth and stone that most likely represents a buried walled structure.

BY55g* (NL5675:8031) Burial mound. *Location*: As above. *Description*: Circular, diam. 10 m, flat mound capped with stone cobbles. Building (i) appears to be dug deeply into the western side, which, if true, may suggest that the importance of the mound had been diluted when this took place. Grave markers and other scattered stones to the north of the mound suggest that the burial area had spread off the mound in that direction, which would support the possibility that the mound itself was no longer of prime importance. Two small areas were cleared of undergrowth, which revealed the cobble surface and two grave markers, one with a simple pecked cross and the other with a cup mark.

BY55h* (NL5675:8031) Building. *Location*: As above. *Description*: Square, 8 × 8 m, single cell apparently without any formal entrance, appearing as a grassy mound with internal shaped hollow. The earth and stone walls stand 1 m high and are over 2 m wide in places. The south-east corner is cut by building (d). The burial ground north–south dividing wall appears to be connected to the north-west corner, continuing to the enclosure wall from the south-east corner. In the space to the south is building (c).

BY55i* (NL5675:8031) Building. *Location*: As above. *Description*: Subrectangular, 5.5 × 5 m, single-cell building with walls of earth and stone up to 2 m thick, standing 1 m high and without any apparent entrance. This mound-like building is built from the east side of the north–south dividing wall and cuts into the west side of the burial mound.

BY56* (NL5655:8036) Garage. *Location*: Bottom slope to coast edge. *Description*: A storehouse was built a few metres along the tarmac road from the shore, which has since become the garage for the tractor and trailer that now transports supplies up to the lighthouse on those occasions when the maintenance engineers are in residence. *Note*: Not fully recorded.

BY57 (NL5655:8032) Blackhouse (a) with barn (b). *Location*: Low on slope to coast edge. *Description*: Rectangular, 10.3 × 6.1 m, possibly double-cell, improved blackhouse (a) with 1 m thick round-cornered walls, entrance to the north, 3.2 m from the west end corner, and a collapsed fireplace set in the east end wall. A single stone internal division, just west of the entrance, is set north–south making a slight revetment to a raised platform in the west end. A single-cell drystone barn, 4 × 3.3 m square, also with an entrance to the north, is butted to the west external wall of the blackhouse. The complex is built on a platform into the hillside. *Note*: A hollow saddle quern is placed in front of the north blackhouse wall.

BY58 (NL5653:8030) modern house (a) (the 'Giant's House') with barn (b). *Location*: Low on slope to coast edge. *Description*: Rectangular, 12 × 6.2 m, with 0.8 m thick walls, possibly originally a single cell using quarried, dressed, and in the east fireplace machine-cut, stone pointed with cement. The building has been extensively modified, possibly in parts rebuilt and was last used as a sheep dip and stock yard. The eastern half of the house appears to have been rebuilt into a lean-to type of temporary accommodation for visiting shepherds. The east end gable wall was raised square with additional sloping raised sides on top of the north and south wall. A sloping corrugated tin roof may have been fixed. The fireplace at this end may already have been rebuilt since in its construction is some quarried and machine-cut stonework. A doorway to the south appears to have been blocked and a window to the north reduced. From the probable position of the original front north door (there are two threshold paving stone slabs in the floor at this point) the wall was opened both front and rear and wooden gates inserted to fill the gap. To make an enclosed room in the lean-to half of the building a cross wall with north doorway was built and the whole of the interior rendered with mortar. The west wall, with what appears to be an original fireplace, remains intact with two wall stubs of the north and south walls forming an enclosure before the lean to. In the south end of this enclosure is a sheep dip leading to an external concrete apron and a stock yard that runs the outside length of the house. 1.5 m from the west wall of the house is a square barn (b), 6.2 × 6 m, single cell with an entrance to the north. The house was called the 'giant's house' because it was reputedly the home of 'Big Peter' or the 'Barra Giant' (Pádraig Mor) (personal communication, John Allen) who stood 2.06 m (Buxton 1995).

BY59 (NL5650:8023) Well. *Location*: Lower slope to coast. *Description*: Square enclosure, dimensions not recorded, around a disused well head and pump housing. *Note*: Built for lighthouse use.

BY60 (NL5575:8014) Well. *Location*: Midslope. *Description*: Disused pump-house and well. Not surveyed.

BY61 (NL5644:8019) modern house. *Location*: Lower slope to coast. *Description*: Rectangular single-storey modern house of several rooms built for the lighthouse hauliers. Roof now in state of collapse. Interesting graffiti. Not surveyed.

BY62 (NL5658:8014) (Fig. 3.41) Chamber tomb. *Location*: Midslope on low lateral ridge. *Description*: Circular setting of stones, set upright or on edge, around the perimeter of a 3 m diam. turf mound. The largest slab is 1.4 m long. Located on a slight ridge running across the hillside it is seen against the skyline from the lower settlement area.

BY63 (NL5656:8011) Platform *Location*: Midslope. *Description*: Possible platform but only one short line of revetting stone visible. Very indistinct. Not surveyed or photographed.

BY64 (NL5654:8015) Shelter. *Location*: Mid-slope. *Description* Circular, diam. 3 m, single cell of small stones, up to 0.6 m in size, mostly scattered, but with possible entrance to east.

BY65 (NL5682:8013) Shelter. *Location*: Small hillock on saddle valley floor. *Description*: Square, 2 × 2 m, single cell of set upright stones .

BY66 (NL5663:8021) Complex of roundhouse, blackhouses, barn and enclosure. *Location*: Lower slope to coastal bench. *Description*: BY66 is of indubitable antiquity since it is overlain by a later building, but the actual date of its construction is as usual not determinable. Unfortunately circumstances did not allow sufficient time for a creditable survey. The structure is

a substantial circular wall of earth and stones approximately 5 m diam. and 1 m thick with just one side of an east-facing entrance visible. The other side of the entrance is obscured by the later square-shaped early modern buildings. This whole group of buildings is set within an enclosure that itself may be of some early date. The later rectangular buildings appear to be the outbuildings of the early modern homestead BY67. The complex deserves a detailed measured survey and some selective excavations to elucidate the phasing sequence, to date that sequence and to determine the possible functional purposes of the various elements.

BY66a (NL5663:8021) Roundhouse. *Location*: As above. *Description*: Not clearly seen, but possibly a 5 m diam. roundhouse mounded and with a wide mound slope radiating from the core area.

BY66b (NL5663:8021) Blackhouse. *Location*: As above. *Description*: Possible blackhouse or earlier subrectangular house, 8 × 5 m, most likely single cell with 0.8 m thick walls of earth and stone with an entrance to the east.

BY66c (NL5663:8021) Enclosure. *Location*: As above. *Description*: Irregular curvilinear enclosure, 24 m across at its widest, of earth and stone walls.

BY66d (NL5663:8021) Barn. *Location*: As above. *Description*: A square, 4 × 4.5 m, single cell with earth and stone walls siting squarely over part of house (b) using the same entrance out on to the enclosure.

BY66e (NL5663:8022) Blackhouse or earlier. *Location*: As above. *Description*: Subrectangular, almost oval, 8 × 5 m, building of earth and stone walls, a single cell without any entrance apparent. This building overlies the possible mounded roundhouse, but appears to predate all the other structures.

BY66f (NL5663:8022) Barn. *Location*: As above. *Description*: An L-shaped wall built off the north wall of building (b) may be a single-cell barn of approximately 5 × 4 m square. The wide open side faces west, away from the enclosure. A slight suggestion of a wall at the opposite end of building (b) could be a further barn.

BY67 (NL5661:8022) Blackhouse. *Location*: bottom of slope to coastal bench. *Description*: Subrectangular, 10 × 6 m, single cell with doorway facing to the north. Two staggered platforms, situated in front and to the south of the house, are picked out as revetted stone arcs. *Note*: This house is only 7 m to the west of the complex BY66 and may be associated with it.

BY68* (NL5661:8031) (Fig. 3.42) Chamber tomb. *Location*: Bottom of coastal slope. *Description*: BY68 is located much lower down the slope than some of the others, well into the settlement area at around the 20 m contour, but it is prominently displayed upon a possibly natural circular mound, 6.5 m diam., of post-glacial solifluction deposit of mixed soil and stone. Two slabs over 1 m in length are set on edge forming a single straight line, presumable one side of a robbed-out rectangular chamber. In the central area on the

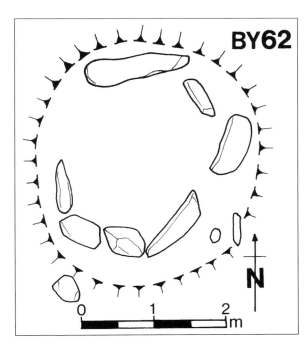

Figure 3.41 Site BY62.

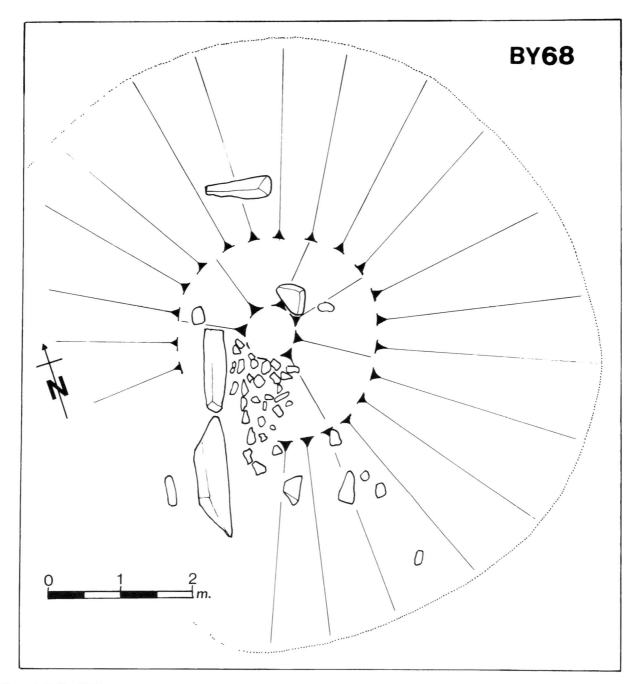

Figure 3.42 Site BY68.

mound summit is a mass of small stones. Other stones of varying sizes are scantily scattered locally. *Note*: Notable damage from burrowing.

BY69 (NL5676:8025) (Fig. 3.43) Chamber tomb. *Location*: On natural hillock on coastal plain. *Description*: BY69 is located to the east of BY68 at a similar elevation and on a similar presumably periglacial oval mound, 7.5 × 4.5 m, of earth and rubble. The mound is surmounted by the possible remnants of a once rectangular chamber of orthostats. Now only four survive spaced almost equally around the mound summit in an oval configuration, 1.25 × 2.25 m. The shape is also rectangular at about 2 m to each side with one northern slab still set on edge.

BY70 (NL5628:8017) Complex of house and barn on platform. *Location*: Lower midslope. *Description*: Subrectangular blackhouse with internal compartments and a later dividing wall. A detached subrectangular barn stands to the east and a metalled haystack stand is sited to the north. All stand on a large stone front-revetted platform. The house is approached from the north by a track via a ramp up on to the platform.

BY70a (NL5628:8017) Blackhouse. *Location*: As above. *Description*: Sub-rectangular, 10 × 6 m, improved blackhouse; drystone shell of 1 m thick walls, rounded at the corners and with an entrance to the north. A fireplace is built into each gable end.

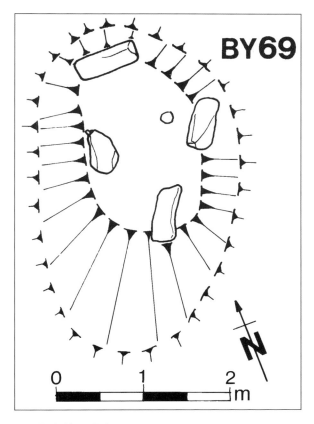

Figure 3.43 Site BY69.

Internally the floor space is divided into a number of platform room bases against the south wall that are edged with stones and separated with walkways at the normal ground level. This form of internal arrangement has not been noted in the survey before, although a similar example was seen on a visit to the island of Kerrera in the Inner Hebrides. At some later date the internal area was divided by a cross wall butted to the south wall making a separate room to the east of the front entrance.

BY70b (NL5628:8017) Barn. *Location*: As above. *Description*: Subrectangular, 7.3 × 5.5 m, drystone single cell with 1.1 m thick walls and an entrance to the south. The barn is 1.8 m to the east of the blackhouse.

BY70c (NL5628:8017) Platform *Location*: As above. *Description*: Irregular area that fronts the farmstead to the road. The leading edge is a series of staggered revetted steps forming a wavy frontage. At a later date the area has been subdivided by rectangular walled enclosures that formalize the local farmyard landscape.

BY71 (NL5648:8025) Cairn. *Location*: Lower coastal hill-slope. *Description*: An unstructured mound of earth and stone approximately 1.5 m diam. sited on a large natural boulder. Could be natural .

BY72 (NL5643:8023) Shelter. *Location*: Lower coastal hill-slope. *Description*: Oval, 4 × 3.5 m, disarranged single cell, but still with some embedded ring-wall stones.

BY73 (NL5626:8022) Standing stone. *Location*: Lower midslope. *Description*: Single standing stone, 1.2 m high with a section of 0.47 × 0.26 m. Stands by roadside like a gatepost, but there is no local recollection of such a gate existing.

BY74 (NL5626:8023) Haystack stand. *Location*: Lower midslope. *Description*: Circular, diam. 11 m, haystack stand of embedded grassed-over stones.

BY75 (NL5623:8025) Enclosure. *Location*: Lower midslope. *Description*: Irregular (zig-zags in places) to rectangular enclosure using some large single orthostats 1.1–1.9 m in size taken from chamber tomb BY76. The enclosure uses the dismantled tomb as a turning corner point. *Note*: Cut by lighthouse road.

BY76 (NL5625:8026) (Fig. 3.44) Chamber tomb. *Location*: Lower midslope. *Description*: BY76 is a classic example of a megalithic chamber tomb used first as a reference point and then as a stone source in the construction of a later enclosure wall. The tomb is set on a mound of soil and rubble, possibly periglacial in nature, with two slabs of stone set on edge and parallel with each other. The largest is 1.5 m long and the overall size of the existing remnant chamber may have been a 2 × 2 m square, but the original chamber could have been more rectangular. The line of the field wall from the monument is south by south-west, pivoting at the tomb to head north. The field wall on its southern line directly from the tomb is constructed using massive slabs of over 1 m in length set on edge that have obviously been dragged off the tomb. The rest of the enclosure wall is constructed of markedly smaller stones.

BY77 (NL5627:8022) Blackhouse. *Location*: Lower midslope. *Description*: Subrectangular, 7.4 × 5.2 m, single cell of drystone walling with an entrance to the north. The walls vary in thickness from 1 m to 1.5 m.

BY78 (NL5615:8032) Stone setting. *Location*: Lower midslope. *Description*: An area of the hillside covered with a confused scatter of stone with no apparent structural integrity. Could be natural uncleared landscape or the remnants of some robbed-out structure.

BY79 (NL5626:8023) Blackhouse. *Location*: Midslope. *Description*: Subrectangular, 5 × 4 m, single-cell barn with walls 1.2 m thick and an entrance to the east is the result of extensive remodelling of a blackhouse originally 8.5 × 5 m with an entrance to the north. The platform of the dismantled half of the blackhouse extends east from the present barn structure. There is much displaced stonework locally.

BY80 (NL5627:8022) Mound. *Location*: Lower midslope. *Description*: Shapeless mound of earth and stone that could be boat-shaped but is most likely natural.

BY81 (NL5633:8030) Boat-shaped mound. *Location*: Lower hill-slope to coast. *Description*: Boat-shaped mound of earth and stone, 4.5 m long and 2.5 m wide, with a pointed end to south-west up-slope away from the sea. At the opposite end a stone slab makes a flat

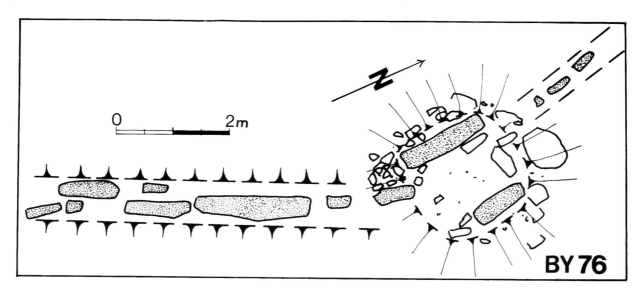

Figure 3.44 Site BY76.

end. The stonework is not structured. *Note*: Most likely a natural colluvial deposit.

BY82 (NL5634:8006) Shelter. *Location*: Midslope plateau, on side of mound for possible chamber tomb BY84. *Description*: Square, 2 × 2 m, single-cell stone setting with possible entrance to the north-east. *Note*: Stone probably taken from the possible chamber tomb.

BY83 (NL5635:8004) Shelter. *Location*: Midslope plateau on side of mound for possible chamber tomb BY84. *Description*: Rectangular, 2.5 × 2 m, single cell of set stone with open side to south. *Note*: Stone probably taken from the possible chamber tomb.

BY84 (NL5635:8005) Chamber tomb. *Location*: Mid-slope plateau. *Description*: A 7 m diam. circular mound surmounted by two large stone slabs set on edge parallel to each other. No other stonework appeared to exist in the rank overgrown grass that covered the area, but two early modern shelters (BY82/BY83) built on the edges of the mound most likely were constructed from material taken from the tomb. Unfortunately, the weather virtually closed down work within minutes of arrival on the location. *Note*: The area off the mound is generally stone-free and very boggy.

BY85* (NL5648:8040) Pier. *Location*: Coast edge on foreshore bedrock. *Description*: modern concrete platform and ramp down below high water mark. Although a tarmac-surfaced road was immediately built linking the landing place and the site of the lighthouse, no provision was made for the easy handling of materials on to the island, which indicates the ease with which it was possible to disembark and transfer materials on the rock shelves of the north shore. A derrick was installed later to help with some of the more awkward and heavy items needed for the lighthouse, but the construction of the pier did not take place until around 1870.

BY86 (NL5710:8019) Shelter. *Location*: Hill-slope. *Description* Circular, diam. 1.5 m, small single cell butted against the wall.

BY87 (NL5498:8032) Building (modern). *Location*: Hill-top slope. *Description:* Rectangular double-cell structure in corner of upper lighthouse enclosure. *Note*: From OS map only, not surveyed.

BY88 (NL5494:8030) Building (modern). *Location*: Hill-top. *Description*: Square single-cell structure within centre of lighthouse upper enclosure. *Note*: From OS map only, not surveyed.

BY89 (NL5671:8023) Enclosures. *Location*: Bottom of hill slope to coastal plain. *Description*: Two small cojoining enclosures within the settlement area. (a) Oval approximately 20 m diam. (b) Subrectangular 30 × 15 m. They appear to overlie a field boundary wall of the larger field system of the settlement area.

BY90 (NL5643:8019) Mill. *Location*: Lower slope to coast. *Description*: Not visible as a building, only some coursed drystone walling in the side of the road drainage trench. Some of its stonework has been laid as a base for the drainage trench, including a shattered millstone. *Note*: Severely damaged by cutting of drain by lighthouse authority.

BY91 (NL5648:8040) Road. *Location*: On hill-slope between lighthouse and pier. *Description*: modern single track road with tarmac surface. *Note*: Coordinates of pier.

Landscape period summaries

The early modern and modern landscape (Fig. 3.45)
Much of the modern landscape, that is, those features belonging to the 19th and 20th centuries, can be taken directly from the Ordnance Survey map. The modern landscape may be further divided between those features belonging to the lighthouse and those belonging to the indigenous population. The lighthouse

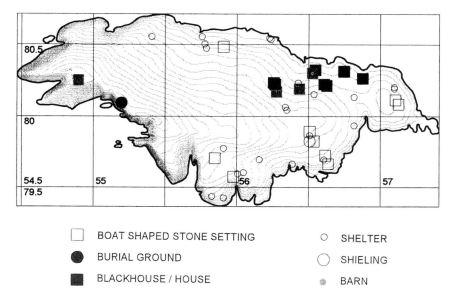

BOAT SHAPED STONE SETTING   ○ SHELTER

● BURIAL GROUND   ◯ SHIELING

■ BLACKHOUSE / HOUSE   ◉ BARN

Figure 3.45 Berneray, showing the location of modern and mediaeval monuments.

landscape has been imposed upon the topography of the island with no regard to the previous established order of an evolved landscape. The early modern landscape, unlike that of the lighthouse, has its origins so well embedded in the past that there can be difficulty in dividing some of its elements into the conventional periods of history and prehistory. The areas of preferred settlement and intensive land use are almost inevitably determined by the topography of the island, and in the case of Berneray its influence on access to fresh water, the sea and shelter from the prevailing wind is very strong.

The more easterly portion of the northern coastal area is the only area where these factors can be linked. Almost all of the fresh-water streams run to the north coast; the shelving coast along this area is virtually the only stretch where landings from the sea are practical. Of shelter there is barely any, but the curve of coast and hillside give this area a little more than much of the rest of the island. The only other area that affords some degree of shelter, and is therefore to be considered, is the land to the south and east of Mullach á Lusgan and to the south of Mullach Rumich. Little fresh running water is to be found here, but, being sheltered, relatively level and reasonably well drained, the agricultural possibilities are obvious. The complex of enclosures indicate that this agricultural potential was exploited, but that the other disadvantages of the area discouraged permanent settlement in the early modern period and most likely to every other period as well.

Permanent settlement on the island therefore naturally focuses on the north coast lowland, especially towards its eastern extent. It is here that all the early modern houses are to be found located within the borders of the head dyke. The area itself is a complex of field walls, some defining enclosures, others just short lengths that make no immediate sense within the overall pattern. The western stretch of the northern lowland, to a much lesser degree, has a few field walls that extend the areas of enclosure.

The pattern shows that some of the field walls, especially those that are intermittent or obviously only remnants, whatever their location, are survivals of earlier enclosures abandoned whenever the system was modified. However, because of the natural focus of the settlement to one preferred area, even the current enclosure walls, including the head dyke, may in reality belong to settlement periods of much greater antiquity. There is no reason why some of the field walls in this landscape should not be belong to the first period of settlement on the island. Unless robbed away or covered by blanket peat a wall will remain a visible part of the landscape and can remain in use throughout time if it is conveniently situated. No attempt will therefore be made to fit the field walls into any of the recognized periods, but this should not detract from their value for they are worthy of much more research.

Besides the field walls the early modern landscape contains several other clearly defined features:

Improved blackhouses with chimneys. BY53 (at least two houses set at right angles to each other with sheep dip and pens), BY55A and B (part of the cemetery complex, two separate houses set into the cemetery perimeter wall), BY58 ('Giant's' house with sheep dip and pens), BY70A.

Houses of rectangular shape, usually using mortar to fix the stonework and to give both internal and

143

external surfaces to the walls. In some cases the stone employed displays quarry drill holes. There are usually, but not always—note 55A and B—two fireplaces, one at each gable end, which are built as an integral part of the wall with chimney shafts leading to chimney stacks. These houses are all still standing to some degree, often to roof height, but in nearly every case, except for the haulier's house (BY61), the roofs have rotted completely away. These buildings can all be dated at least to the late 19th century. Many of them are still used as sheep pens and have been modified with sheep dips etc. by the grazing committee that still keep several hundred sheep on the island.

Unimproved blackhouses without chimneys. BY55D (part of cemetery complex, set into cemetery perimeter wall), BY57, 66, 67, 77, 79, possibly 44.

These houses are usually of subrectangular shape with rounded corners, and with no evidence for integral built-in fireplaces. Walls are earth-filled and rarely standing above a single course, but often of similar dimensions of ground plan to later houses. Some, however, appear as quite small, more square in ground plan, and may actually be barns rather than houses, BY44 and 79, for example. These houses are impossible to date without excavation. Their manner of construction has changed little since possibly even the later mediaeval period. The house excavated at Alt Chrisal on Barra (Foster 1995), which was inhabited in the late 18th to early 19th century, is a large example of this type of dwelling. Some examples are known to have been occupied very late in the 19th century, especially by the older generation, who did not incline to living in the more modern houses then becoming standard. That some of these houses could be much earlier cannot be ruled out.

Shieling. BY44.
BY44 is the only possible shieling on the island. Located appropriately on the grassy plateau slopes close to the enclosures of the high southern grazing land below the backbone ridge of Mullach á Lusgan.

Shelters: Round. BY3, 4, 11, 13, 14, 22A, 27, 29, 32, 34, 36, 46, 51A + B, 64, 72, 82A.

Shelters: Square. BY12, 23, 35, 47, 65, 82B.
Most Berneray shelters conform to Branigan's type A (Branigan 1995), having walls of single-stone thickness whether one or more courses high. Exceptions to this are shelters BY3 and 4, which are built like tiny hut circles. They are circular single-cell structures with internal areas of 1 m diam enclosed by double stone-faced walls, 1.5 m thick, packed with soil. There are no multicellular examples.

Burial Ground. BY55.

Stone clearance cairns. BY5, 9, 15, 52, 54, 71.
All of these small stone cairns are located within the northern coastal lowland enclosures and are therefore assumed to be associated with the clearance and cultivation within them during the early modern period.

Haystack stands. BY70, 74.

The modern landscape of the Commissioners of Northern Lights
The lighthouse. BY18.

Cemetery. BY19.

Garage. BY56.

Well and water pump. BY59.

House. BY61.

Concrete landing pier. BY85.

Enclosures. To complete the lighthouse landscape an ambitious programme of wall building resulted in the enclosure of the entire western end of the island, approximately 25% of the land area.

mediaeval and Post-mediaeval landscapes
(Fig. 3.45)
The only monument that may belong to this period is the burial ground BY55.

The Early mediaeval/Norse period (Fig. 3.45)
The Early mediaeval period is almost as blank as that of the rest of the mediaeval and Post-mediaeval except for a number of boat-shaped stone settings.

Boat-shaped stone settings. BY7, 28, 31, 37, 38, 39, 43, 45, 48, 49, 80, 81.
Three of these monument types are to be found in the settlement enclosures of the northern coastal strip, which is not their usually expected type of location. In this light the doubts expressed about BY80 and 81 concerning their structure and form at the time of their recording becomes significant, that is, that they could most likely to prove to be natural geomorphological shapes formed at the end of the ice age and would benefit from excavation to prove their status. In contrast BY7 has an acceptable shape, but there are quantities of displaced fallen stone at its edges that suggest some form of upstanding structure, a condition at odds with other examples of this monument type.

All of the other boat shapes are on the high ground, away from the settlement area, overlooking the sea to the south or in a similar situation on the Aird headland, exactly the sort of location that one would expect of them Of this group the least positive is BY49 on the Aird headland, which is composed of only a single curved setting of stones.

The Iron Age Landscape (Fig. 3.46)
Of the Iron Age landscape only the Atlantic round-house (galleried dun) BY17, perched high on the tip of Stron an Duin promontory and immediately to the west of the lighthouse can be positively allocated to this period. Dun Briste, situated on a promontory to the north and at a lower elevation from BY17, is generally assumed to be a type of promontory fort and is included in this survey as such.

Atlantic roundhouses. BY17.

Forts. BY16.

The Pre-Iron Age landscape (Fig. 3.46)
The commonest sites found in this landscape are its burial monuments, cairns and megalithic chamber tombs and in this respect Berneray is rather unusual in the apparently high number of possible chamber tombs when compared with the other islands, and again in contrast with the scarcity of possible prehistoric cairns. The possible chamber tombs are all located within the northern settlement enclosure complex, usually in a position of prominence. Their proximity to the settlement area makes them convenient either as sources of building stone or for use in some other form Consequently they are robbed of stone or

modified in some way and can rarely be identified with total confidence.

Megalithic tomb. BY2, 20, 25, 62, 68, 69, 76, 84.

Cairns. BY30, 39.
These two cairns are located on the southern side of the island on the far side of Mullach Lusgan, away and out of sight from the settlement area.

Roundhouses. BY1, 33, 66.
There are surprisingly few roundhouses or hut circles represented in the survey, although considering the focus of settlement in such a restricted area, and the propensity for site reuse, it is quite likely that many more roundhouses do exist but are obscured by later sites. BY66, for example, is such a site that has not been completely hidden by later reuse.

Miscellaneous structures

Oval/subrectangular structures. BY10, 24, 42.

Standing Stones. BY50b, 50c, 73.

Platform. BY63.

Setting. BY78.

Conclusion
Berneray may well have always sheltered some small community ever since the Neolithic, but without archaeological excavation it will be difficult to prove such a possibility. In all probability such a small island

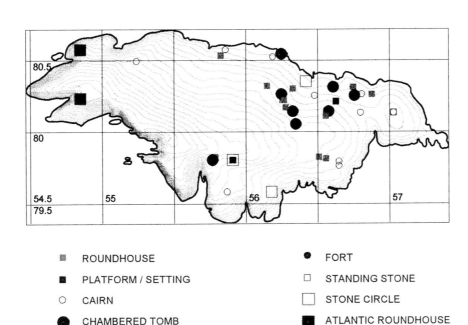

Figure 3.46 Berneray, showing the location of prehistoric monuments.

■	ROUNDHOUSE	●	FORT
■	PLATFORM / SETTING	□	STANDING STONE
○	CAIRN	▭	STONE CIRCLE
●	CHAMBERED TOMB	■	ATLANTIC ROUNDHOUSE

is most likely to have been unoccupied for long periods of time throughout the past few millennia, but the survey has shown that there is a range of premodern sites that, if investigated, could give a high information return for a small archaeological investment. The fact that the island has a limited land surface area yet is capable of sustaining a small resident population, as proven by the survival of such a community in modern times, could make research into the dynamics of such an environment very desirable.

4. The Excavation of Iron Age and Later Structures at Alt Chrisal T17, Barra, 1996–1999

Patrick Foster and John Pouncett

Introduction

Excavations at Alt Chrisal T17 were directed by Patrick Foster with the assistance of John Pouncett. The report presented below was written and compiled by John Pouncett. Post-excavation analysis was undertaken with the assistance of a number of individuals, in particular Emma Gowans, Joanna Paxton, Rachel Bannon and Carolyn Elford. Illustrations were produced by John Pouncett, with the exception of Figures 4.29–4.37 (inclusive), which were drawn by Emma Gowans.

Alt Chrisal T17 (National Grid Reference NL642978) is located on the lower slopes of the Tangaval massif (Fig. 4.1). The Tangaval massif is a horst block of Lewisian Gneiss aligned from northeast to southwest (Gilbertson and Grattan 1995). It is criss-crossed by a network of Palaeozoic faults and Tertiary dykes, which divide the massif into a series of discrete 'parcels' of land. The wider impact of these features upon the topography of the Western Isles and their implications for the inhabited landscape are discussed elsewhere (Kuna, p. 61). The Lewisian Gneiss is locally overlain by glacial and periglacial deposits (Hall 1996). These deposits have been subject to intensive erosion and weathering. The surface of the underlying bedrock has been smoothed by the action of the Pleistocene ice sheet, rendering the overlying deposits susceptible to mass movement (Gilbertson, Grattan and Pyatt 1996). Thin acid soils derived from the reworked till cover much of the Tangaval massif. Accumulations of soil only survive where they are retained by natural hollows or manmade structures.

The site lies on the southern coast of the Tangaval peninsula, close to the eastern margin of a 'parcel' of land defined by the streams of Alt Ghortein and Alt Chrisal. It is situated towards the rear of a natural terrace overlooking the Sound of Vatersay, at a height of approximately 30 m OD. To the south-west, the site of Dun Caolis is clearly visible across the water. A series of stone built structures have been constructed upon the level surface of this terrace (Fig. 4.2), the most prominent of which are the Ben Tangaval roundhouse, the adjoining rectangular building and the adjacent enclosure. The Ben Tangaval roundhouse was initially identified as an Atlantic roundhouse (Armit 1992: 163), but was subsequently reinterpreted as an aisled roundhouse or wheelhouse (Branigan and Foster 1995: 35). During the course of the SEARCH survey of the Tangaval massif, a series of structural elements were identified within the roundhouse. These structural elements were interpreted as radial piers: the distinctive spoke-like features from which the term 'wheelhouse' is derived.

There is a long tradition of research into the stone-built roundhouses of the Scottish Iron Age (see Armit 1992; Parker Pearson and Sharples 1999). Structural typologies have been drawn up on the basis of the presence or absence of architectural features. These typologies have become increasingly blurred: the majority of stone-built roundhouses are in an advanced state of collapse; and many of the excavated sites show distinct similarities in both spatial organization and monumental architecture. An amended system of classification has recently been proposed, recognizing the distinct architectural traditions of Atlantic Scotland (Armit 1990b, 1991). This system differentiates between 'simple' Atlantic roundhouses (c. 800–400 BC) with substantial, undifferentiated wall circuits, and 'complex' Atlantic roundhouses (4th century BC onwards) with elaborated or galleried walls. The 'complex' roundhouses, including both brochs and duns, show increased evidence for internal subdivision. They are broadly contemporary with the highly formalized architectural tradition of the aisled roundhouse or wheelhouse.

Relatively little is known about the later prehistory of Barra, few Iron Age sites have been excavated on the island. The most recent excavations are those of the 'complex' Atlantic Roundhouse at Dun Cuier and the aisled roundhouse at Allasdale (Young 1955, 1952 respectively). Recent excavations on South Uist, employing such techniques as magnetic susceptibility and phosphate analysis, have shown the potential for shedding new light on the Hebridean Iron Age (Parker Pearson and Sharples 1999). A complementary programme of fieldwork was planned for Alt Chrisal T17, however, extensive environmental sampling was abandoned due to widespread rabbit disturbance. The surface of the site had been badly disturbed by rabbit activity, accordingly an assessment of the impact of rabbit infestation on the structures and associated deposits was integrated into the

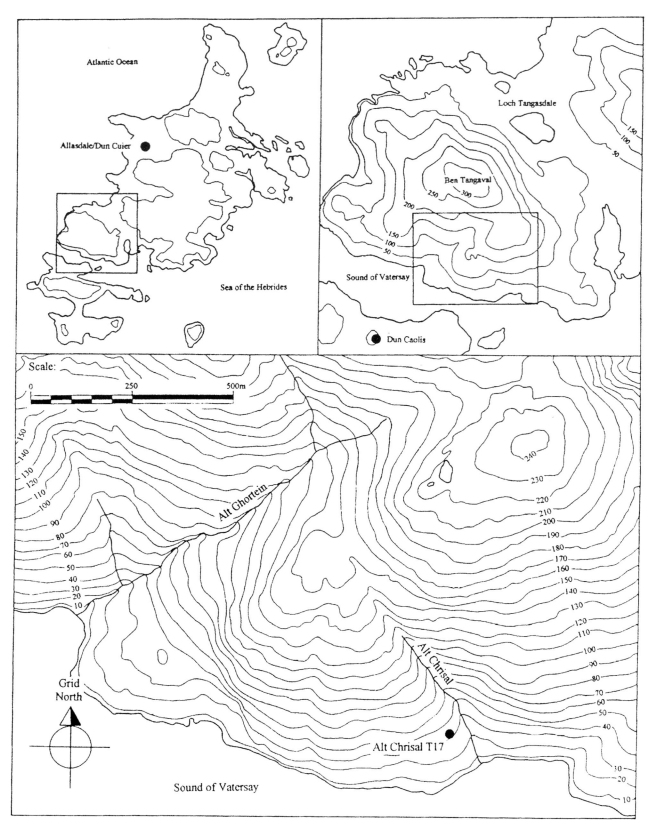

Figure 4.1 Location map showing relationship to other excavated sites.

initial project design. The impact of bioturbation upon archaeological sites has been emphasized by the recent publication of a Technical Advice Note on *Burrowing Animals and Archaeology* (Historic Scotland 1999).

The Ben Tangaval roundhouse is one of a series of Iron Age structures built along the southern coastline of the Tangaval Peninsula (Branigan 1995b: 201–204, Fig. 7.2). Three other wheelhouses were identified during the course of field survey, however, these have

Figure 4.2 The aisled roundhouse during the course of excavation, facing south.

subsequently been reinterpreted as roundhouses (see p. 336). Alt Chrisal has provided a focus for settlement from the Neolithic onwards (Branigan 1995b). Between 1989 and 1994, a number of sites were excavated in the vicinity of the stream (Foster 1995). These structures were associated with a series of 'dwellings' or 'farmsteads' dating from the Neolithic to the early twentieth century. Although no later prehistoric component was identified within the excavated landscape, T17 was noted as the probable locus of Iron Age activity in the Alt Chrisal region. The structures identified at the site were thought to be broadly contemporary: the rectangular building being comparable with the Kiln House at Allasdale.

During the course of research, the framework within which the site was to be interpreted shifted dramatically. First, excavation revealed a series of structures dating from the Early Iron Age to the 18th or 19th century. The structural sequence was much more complex than first thought, with the super-imposition of one structure upon another and the persistent reuse and modification of existing structures. Secondly, preliminary analysis of the assemblages of pottery and worked stone has shown that there is a significant quantity of residual and intrusive material throughout the depositional sequence. The degree to which human activity has dictated the deposition of material culture, and the extent to which rabbit burrowing has caused the migration of artifacts, was greatly underestimated.

A preliminary account of the excavations at Alt Chrisal T17, between 1996 and 1999, is presented below. In light of the above observations, discussion has been kept to a minimum: further interpretation would be meaningless without an understanding of the impact of human agency and rabbit infestation on site formation processes. All finds from the site were recorded three-dimensionally, the coordinate data being integrated with the catalogue of finds. Spatial analysis of this data set will allow assessment of the impact of burrowing on artifact distributions. Once the nature and extent of disturbance is understood, consideration of the discard patterns inherent within the distribution of artifact should enable discussion of the use of space within and around the Ben Tangaval roundhouse (cf. Last 1998; Neustupný 1998). The results of this analysis will be published at a later date.

The Excavations, 1996–1999

Alt Chrisal T17 was excavated over four seasons between June 1996 and July 1999. Once the extant structures had been planned, the site was stripped of vegetation and the stonework derived from recent collapse was removed. The site was divided into quadrants by perpendicular baulks, establishing two sections through the depositional sequence. Excavation in 1996 focused on the rectangular structure at the northern extent of the site, and the upper levels of the enclosure to the east of the roundhouse. The lower levels of the enclosure were excavated during the following season. During 1997, the emphasis of work shifted to the reduction of the deposits within the interior of the roundhouse. Once the wall circuit had been fully defined, the baulks were removed to allow correlation of deposits across the site. A series of structures were identified within the upper levels of the site. These were dismantled once they had been planned and recorded. Reduction of the interior of the site continued in 1998. Towards the end of the 1998 season, the vestiges of an earlier structure were identified beneath the Ben Tangaval roundhouse. A small team of excavators returned to the site in 1999 to define the full extent of this structure.

The Structural and Stratigraphic Sequences

The Atlantic roundhouse

The Lewisian Gneiss is locally overlain by postglacial colluvium. Widespread iron panning has prevented the percolation of ground water into the subsoil, resulting in the intensive mineralization of overlying deposits. The base of the depositional sequence is characterized by a compact gritty deposit (context 184), tentatively interpreted as a mineralised soil. This deposit has been subject to extensive weathering and has been worked out across much of the site. It only survives where retained by later structures, that is, beneath the wall circuit of the Ben Tangaval roundhouse. A stone structure, possibly an Atlantic roundhouse, is built

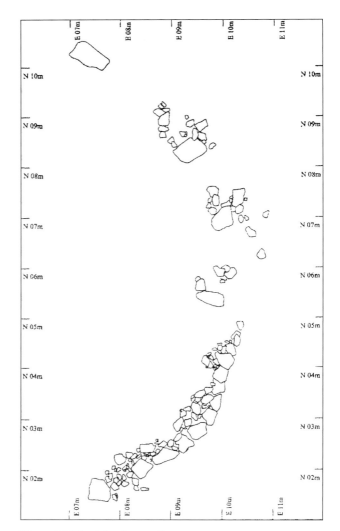

Figure 4.3 The Atlantic roundhouse.

Figure 4.4 The early Iron Age structure incorporated into the wall circuit of the Ben Tangaval roundhouse, facing north.

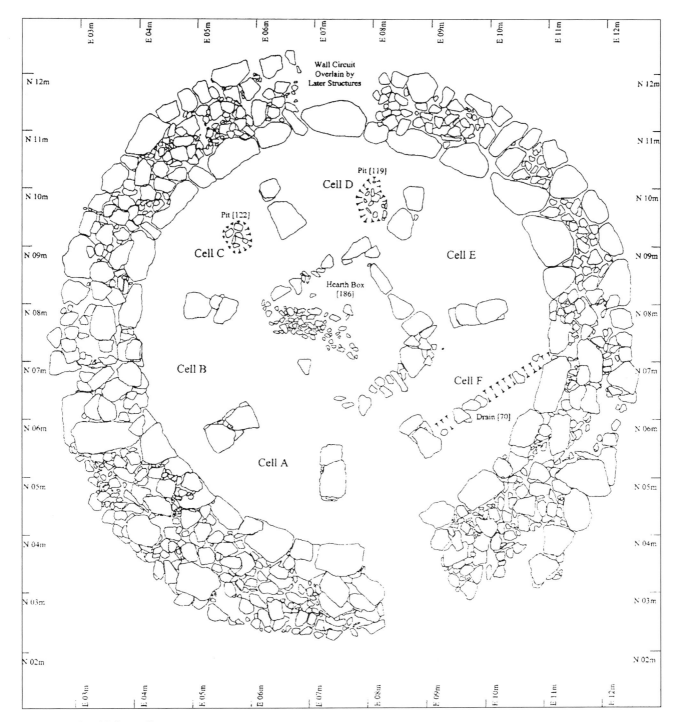

Figure 4.5 The aisled roundhouse.

upon the truncated surface of the mineralized soil (Fig. 4.3). The centre point of this structure is situated approximately 2.2 m to the west of that of the later roundhouse. It is constructed from a double thickness wall, approximately 1.6 m wide, comprising a rubble core faced with two 'skins' of drystone walling. This method of construction is employed within many of the structures identified at Alt Chrisal T17. At the northern extent of the site, the arc of walling is bonded into the subsoil. Whilst the base of the wall would have been subject to intensive iron panning, it is possible that the lower courses of stonework lay within a shallow foundation trench. The arc of walling is best preserved where it is incorporated into the wall circuit of the Ben Tangaval roundhouse (Fig. 4.4). Only an arc of walling approximately 12.5 m in length survives, the remainder of the structure has been destroyed. The paucity of displaced stonework associated with the arc of walling would suggest that the masonry was dismantled and used in the construction of the later structure; the wall, in effect, being used as a stone quarry. On the basis of the surviving arc of walling, the external diameter of this structure would have been approximately 10.9 m in diameter (internal ø c. 7.7m). The estimated size of this structure is comparable to other Atlantic roundhouses identified on Barra and North Uist, falling within the lower end of the range for such structures (Armit 1992: 102–103, Ill. 11.1). Thirty stone-built roundhouses, with diameters in the range of between 8 m and 12 m, were identified during archaeological survey on Barra and Vatersay (see p. 334).

Following the construction of the Atlantic roundhouse, a homogenous, organic silt (context 114) was deposited across the site. There is no marked differentiation between the material deposited on either side of the arc of walling. However, throughout the depositional sequence it is difficult to identify discrete deposits or layers. The boundaries between contexts are often diffuse, and one context may only be differentiated from the next by a subtle variation in colour or composition.

The aisled roundhouse

An aisled roundhouse, the structure referred to as the Ben Tangaval roundhouse, was subsequently built upon the site of the Atlantic roundhouse (Fig. 4.5). The aisled roundhouse has an internal diameter of approximately 6.3 m. It is smaller than many of the excavated sites in the Western Isles. Structural analysis has shown that free-standing structures, such as that at Alt Chrisal, tend to be smaller than the revetted structures found with the machair (Armit 1992: 107).

The wall circuit of the aisled roundhouse is formed by a substantial double-thickness wall approximately 1.4 m wide, constructed from unhewn blocks of Lewisian gneiss. A single course of stonework rests upon a 'raft' of flat stones laid down to mark out the ground plan of the building prior to construction. Towards the southern extent of the site, the outer edge of the wall circuit has collapsed where burrowing has undermined the wall core. The wall circuit stands to a height of 1.1 m. Allowing for the pitch of the roof, this would have provided ample clearance within the interior of the roundhouse. Consideration of the methods of construction employed by the roundhouse builders (below) would suggest that the wall stood no higher. A series of smaller, upright stones have been incorporated into the inner face of the wall circuit at regular intervals (Fig. 4.6). Recent excavations at Cnip, on Lewis, have shown that a series of votive deposits were placed behind the wall of wheelhouse 2 (Armit 1996: 156). The upright stones within the wall circuit of the Ben Tangaval roundhouse may have sealed similar deposits. Three of the putative 'plugs' were removed, and in each instance the exposed fabric of the wall had been heavily disturbed by burrowing, rendering any interpretation meaningless.

Seven radial piers (piers 1–7) were identified within the interior of the aisled roundhouse. The piers survive to a height of up to four courses, approximately 0.7 m. However, at the northern extent of the site, piers 3 and 5 have been reduced to a single course: structural collapse echoing the truncation of deposits. The piers, each two stones deep, were built using a technique similar to the wall circuit. In each instance, the stone blocks forming the inner face of the pier

Figure 4.6 An upright stone inserted into the wall of the aisled roundhouse within cell E, facing north-east.

were carefully selected to present the veneer of a dressed surface (Fig. 4.7). A similar phenomenon was observed at Kilpheder, where the inner faces of the piers were pecked smooth by stone pebble mauls (Lethbridge 1952). The inner face of pier 4 was formed by a single block of Lewisian Gneiss, re-erected during the course of excavation (Fig. 4.8). Each of the piers is offset from the wall circuit by a distance of between 0.47 m and 0.83 m, defining a narrow passage or aisle around the circumference of the interior: hence the term aisled roundhouse.

At Kilpheder the piers were connected to the wall circuit by stone lintels, set at a height of approximately 1.2 m (Lethbridge 1952). A corbelled roof sprang from the stone lintels, rising to an estimated height of approximately 3.35 m within the interior of the roundhouse. Whilst the Ben Tangaval roundhouse is smaller than that at Kilpheder, the constructional techniques and structural proportions of Hebridean aisled roundhouses are highly standardized (Armit 1992). Although no lintels were found *in situ* at Alt Chrisal, it is likely that the piers were connected to the inner face of the wall circuit. Possible lintels stones were found within the rubble fill of the site (Fig. 4.9). Furthermore, the nature of the displaced stonework within the upper levels of the roundhouse is consistent with material derived from the collapse of a corbelled structure. This structure would have supported a thatch roof, the apex of which would have been approximately 4 m above the ground surface.

Figure 4.7 The 'dressed' inner face of pier 2, facing west.

Figure 4.8 Pier 4, facing north-east.

153

Figure 4.9 Displaced stonework in the vicinity of cell F, facing east.

Primary occupation

The radial piers impose a distinct spatial order on the use of space within the aisled roundhouse (Giles and Parker Pearson, in press). Access to the interior of the roundhouse was gained through a narrow passageway between piers 1 and 7 (Fig. 4.10). This passage opened on to a central area, approximately 3.7 m in diameter, bordered by six dial cells (cells A to F). While each of these cells would have had a corbelled roof, it is likely that the passageway leading to the southern entrance remained uncovered. It has been suggested that the dial cells were entered from the aisle rather than from the interior: the axis of movement reinforcing the importance of the central living area (Lethbridge 1952). However, at many sites the aisle would have been too low and narrow to allow easy passage around the circumference of the roundhouse (Reid 1989). The logistics of movement dictate that the dial cells were entered from the interior of the roundhouse. Each of the radial cells was excavated separately and a section was established through the interior of the roundhouse (Fig. 4.11).

The southern entrance

An apron of mixed ash and organic silt, context 109, was identified in the vicinity of the southern entrance. This spread represents an accumulation of midden material derived from the sweeping out of the interior of the roundhouse. Analysis of the midden deposits at Dun Vulan, South Uist, has shown that the interior of

Figure 4.10 The south-facing entrance to the aisled roundhouse, facing north.

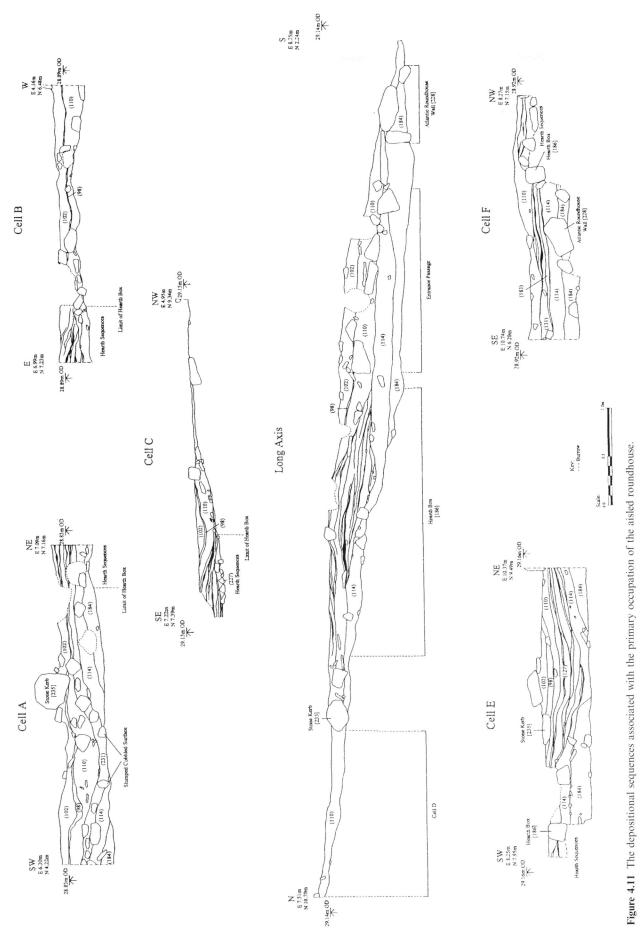

Figure 4.11 The depositional sequences associated with the primary occupation of the aisled roundhouse.

the site was swept out at regular intervals (Parker Pearson, Giles and Sharples 1999a). The pottery and animal bone derived from these deposits was more fragmented than that recovered from the rest of the site. While little pottery was recovered from the midden deposits at T17, only sherds above 5 mm in diameter were retained during the course of excavation. At some point during the lifetime of the aisled roundhouse, the practice of sweeping out the interior of the building was abandoned. The interior of the roundhouse is filled with a series of deposits derived from the continuous build-up of occupational debris. Although discrete deposits were identified within each of the radial compartments, the deposits within the passageway between piers 1 and 7 were indistinguishable from the primary depositional sequence, context 110. The only deposit associated with the primary occupation of the aisled roundhouse was a discrete lens of ash, context 209, adjacent to pier 1.

The central area

A rectilinear stone setting (approximately 2.2 m by 2.3 m) dominates the interior of the roundhouse, occupying nearly half of the available floor space. This stone setting, or hearth box, is offset from the internal face of each of the piers by a distance of between 0.28 m and 0.42 m. While it would have restricted movement around the interior of the building, access to the radial cells could still be gained from the central area. The stone setting, constructed from a series of irregular stone blocks laid end to end, retained ash deposits associated with three distinct hearth sequences (Fig. 4.12). Although the western edge of the hearth box had been destroyed, the limit of the stone setting could be reconstructed from the maximum extent of these ash deposits. A section was excavated through the hearth box and associated deposits (Fig. 4.13). The hearth sequences had been disturbed by rabbit activity; the loose, dark fill of the rabbit burrows contrasting sharply with the brightly coloured ash.

The base of the hearth was constructed from a pad of irregular stones bedded within a compact gritty deposit, context 227. This fire-damaged surface had been heavily disturbed and largely worked out. Remnants of this surface were only recorded within the north-western corner of the hearth box. It is uncertain whether the base of the hearth box perhaps represents the continuation of the cobbled floor discussed below. The earliest hearth sequence associated with the rectilinear stone setting, contexts 170–80, is broadly contemporary with the discrete deposits identified within each of the radial compartments. However, the later hearth sequences, contexts 148–69, and contexts 135–47, postdate these deposits. They are overlain and sealed by context 110 and thus seem to have accumulated during the primary depositional sequence.

Following the abandonment of the practice of sweeping the floor of the roundhouse, ash from the central hearth was spread throughout the interior of the building. The deposits within each of the radial cells are comprised of layers of organic silt interspersed with ash. These deposits are best preserved in cells E and F where numerous discrete layers of

Figure 4.12 The ash deposits associated with the hearth box, facing north.

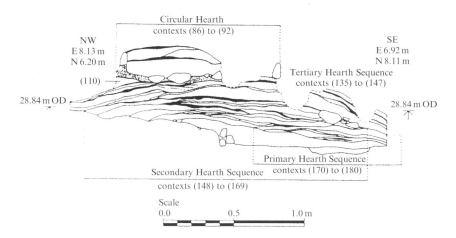

Figure 4.13 Section through the hearth sequences associated with the central hearth.

ash were recorded. At Dùnan Ruadh, Pabbay, thin layers of shell sand were spread within the interior of the roundhouse to create a 'clean' floor surface (see p. 235). It is possible that the ash from the central hearth of the Ben Tangaval roundhouse was strewn across the floor for a similar purpose. The only distinct floor surface identified at Alt Chrisal T17, that associated with the secondary occupation of the aisled roundhouse, was comprised of a compact layer of ash approximately 5 cm thick.

Cell A

The floor of the aisled roundhouse was covered by a continuous cobbled surface constructed from irregular blocks of Lewisian Gneiss. This surface is best-preserved in cell A (Fig. 4.14) where the cobbled floor extends up to the edge of the hearth box and behind piers 1 and 2. Cobbled or flagged floors are found within a number of Hebridean roundhouses, for example, that at Clettraval, North Uist (Scott 1948). It is likely that the midden deposit extending out of the southern entrance was derived from the sweeping of the cobbled floor. Sweeping was possibly abandoned once material had become embedded in the surface and the cobbles had been partly obscured. The cobbled floor is overlain by an accumulation of organic silt and ash, context 231: occupational material accumulating over a prolonged period of time. This deposit becomes more compacted towards the edge of the hearth box, where it was presumably subject to heavily trampling. Cell A has been undermined by an extensive network of rabbit burrows, context 125. The cobbled surface and overlying deposits have slumped into the void created by these burrows.

Cell B

Further traces of the cobbled floor were found within cell B against the edge of the hearth box, and the southern elevation of pier 3. No discrete deposits were identified within cell B. As with the earlier Iron Age

structure, the deposits at the north-western extent of the site, that is, those within cells B C, and D are heavily truncated and have been largely worked out.

Cell C

A subcircular pit was cut into the subsoil within cell C (Fig. 4.15). The pit, surviving to a depth of 0.08 m, was approximately 0.42 m in diameter. Prior to the

Figure 4.14 The cobbled surface, context 129, within cell A, facing south-west.

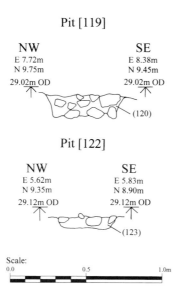

Pit [119]

NW — E 7.72m N 9.75m 29.02m OD

SE — E 8.38m N 9.45m 29.02m OD

(120)

Pit [122]

NW — E 5.62m N 9.35m 29.12m OD

SE — E 5.83m N 8.90m 29.12m OD

(123)

Scale: 0.0   0.5   1.0m

Figure 4.15 The subcircular pit, context 122, within cell C and the subcircular pit, context 119, within cell D.

creation of the cobbled floor within the interior of the roundhouse, a number of pits were excavated towards the rear of the site. These pits, filled with rubble derived from the collapse of the cobbled surface, are sealed by the primary depositional sequence. They are associated with the primary occupation of the aisled roundhouse. Similar pits have been identified at other comparable sites in the Western Isles, where circumstances have permitted the excavation of the lower levels of the site (Armit 1996). Large numbers of pits were identified at Kilpheder (Lethbridge 1952) and Sollas, North Uist (Campbell 1991). In both instances, the pits appear to postdate the construction of the roundhouse, no pits being found beneath the radial piers. They perhaps represent votive or ritual deposits associated with the 'investiture' or primary occupation of the building. The spatial distribution of these pits is restricted; the majority of the pits at both Sollas and Kilpheder are located towards the rear of the roundhouse (Armit 1996). Furthermore, the nature of the objects buried within the pits is indicative of structured deposition, over one-third of the pits at Sollas contained overtly 'ritual' deposits (Campbell and Finlay 1991). The majority of the 'ritual' deposits at Sollas were comprised of complete or partially dismembered animal skeletons. Animal bone does not survive within the acid soils at Alt Chrisal. Only a single sherd of pottery was recovered from the fill of the pit, context 123, within cell C.

Cell D

A second pit was cut into the subsoil within cell D (Fig. 4.15). This subcircular pit, approximately 0.52 m in diameter and surviving to a depth of up to 15 cm, was slightly larger than that in cell C. The rubble fill of the pit, context 120, was sterile.

Cell E

The cobbled floor discussed above has been heavily disturbed within cell E. Surviving only as a discontinuous layer of stonework, it is overlain by a series of occupational deposits grouped together as context 127. These deposits, and the underlying cobbled surface, have slumped into the middle of the cell, dipping towards a marked unconformity in the upper surface of context 114 (Fig. 4.1). This unconformity, with moderate to steep sloping sides, may represent the cut of a third pit. Unfortunately, due to the intensive mineralisation of the lower levels of the site, the cut of this putative pit was not identified during the course of excavation.

Cell F

A stone-lined drain was inserted into the upper surface of context 114 within cell F. This drain, constructed from two, closely spaced, parallel rows of stone blocks, lay at a tangent to the wall circuit. It ran from the deepest part of the site, close to the northernmost point of pier 7 towards the roundhouse wall. The stone-lined drain is less substantial than the capped drain within the aisled roundhouse at Allasdale (Young 1952). It is perhaps comparable to the drainage channels identified at Dùnan Ruadh (see pp. 237–8). The drain is sealed by a series of occupational deposits, context 131 and context 183. It is uncertain as to whether the drain remained open, or whether it was covered. The cobbled floor surface within cell F heavily disturbed by rabbit burrowing, has largely been destroyed.

The primary depositional sequence

The discrete deposits identified within each of the radial cells are sealed by an accumulation of organic silt, the primary depositional sequence (context 110). While it appears to be homogenous, this deposit represents the continuous build up of occupational debris over a prolonged period of time. Where ash is not present it is difficult to define discrete layers within the peat. Subtle changes in the colour or composition of the soil are difficult to detect. The primary depositional sequence is thus likely to represent a series of occupational deposits, and can, in effect, be treated as a continuously shifting floor surface. This pattern of deposition persisted during the secondary occupation of the aisled roundhouse and after the abandonment of the site. Following the deposition of context 110, the aisle between the radial piers and the wall circuit was blocked up. The deposits beneath the rubble blocking were assigned separate context numbers to allow rapid identification of the materials deposited behind each pier. In each instance, the underlying deposits had been heavily disturbed by rabbit activity, the stonework blocking the aisle providing a focus for burrowing. Bulk samples were taken from

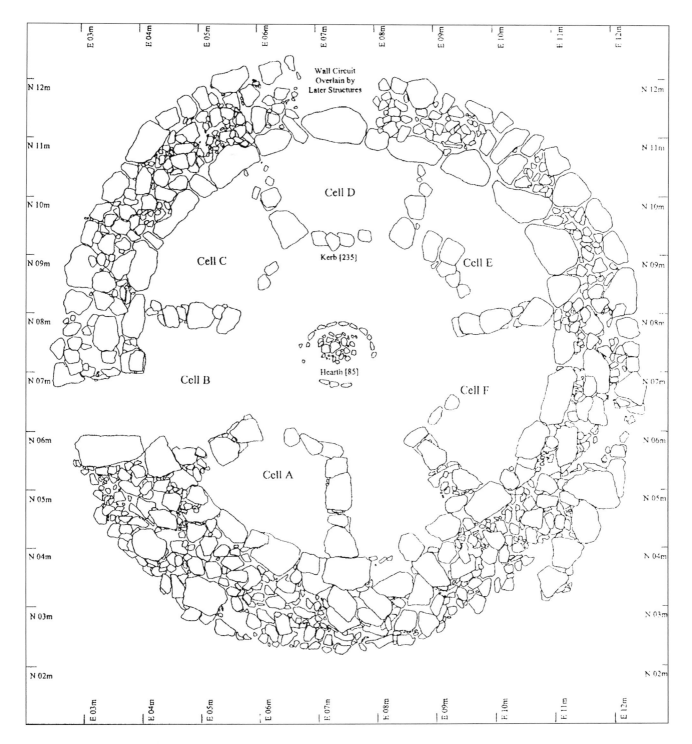

Figure 4.16 The modified aisled roundhouse.

the midpoint of each of the radial cells to test for the presence of carbonized plant remains and to assess whether the species present within each cell would reflect fundamental differences in the use of space within the roundhouse. Whilst it would have been desirable to have a comparable set of samples from the modified roundhouse, that is, from the secondary depositional sequence (context 102) the deposits associated with the later use of the structure were too heavily disturbed to allow bulk sampling.

Secondary occupation

Shortly after the primary occupation of the structure, the aisled roundhouse underwent a series of structural modifications (Fig. 4.16):

1. The south facing entrance was blocked and a new doorway created to the west. The original entrance was blocked by a series of flat stone slabs, stacked one on top of the other.
2. The aisle around the periphery of the interior was closed. The space between each of the radial piers and the inner face of the wall circuit was blocked with drystone walling (Fig. 4.18).

Figure 4.17 The section excavated through the depositional sequence within cell E, facing north.

Figure 4.18 The rubble wall blocking the space between pier 6 and the wall circuit, facing south.

Figure 4.19 The circular hearth associated with the secondary occupation of the aisled roundhouse, facing east.

3. A low stone kerb, one course high, was constructed linking the inner faces of each of the piers. This kerb formalized the boundary between the central area and the radial cells.
4. A circular hearth, approximately 0.8 m in diameter, was built within the central area (Fig. 4.19). This new, smaller hearth dramatically increased the available floor space.

The changes in the internal architecture of the Ben Tangaval roundhouse perhaps represent a transformation of the way in which space was used within the interior of the building.

The central hearth

The central hearth associated with the secondary occupation of the aisled roundhouse is defined by a circular stone setting. This stone setting is constructed from a series of rounded beach pebbles, some of which have been removed and may have been reused as cobble tools. The base of the hearth is lined with a layer of postglacial clay, context 134. This compact clay surface is overlain by a series of ash deposits, contexts 86, 87, 88, 91 and 92. Ash from the central hearth was spread throughout the interior of the building to create a compact floor surface, context 98. While this layer of ash represented the only distinct floor surface within the interior of the aisled roundhouse, extensive rabbit disturbance prevented systematic sampling for magnetic susceptibility and phosphate analysis.

The secondary depositional sequence

The ash floor is sealed by the secondary depositional sequence, context 102. As with the primary deposi-

tional sequence, this deposit represents the continuous build-up of occupational debris over a prolonged period of time.

After abandonment

Following the abandonment of the aisled roundhouse, a number of stone built structures were subsequently built at Alt Chrisal T17 (Fig. 4.20). Displaced stonework, contexts 54 and 68, derived from the collapse of the roundhouse was used in the construction of these later structures. The site was also reused intermittently by those tending animals or seeking shelter from the elements. Discrete ash lenses, derived from *in situ* burning, were found throughout the upper levels of the site. These ash deposits represent temporary hearths lit within the confines of the abandoned wall circuit. They are often sealed beneath a stone slab or a pile of smaller stones, presumably placed over the hearth to extinguish the flames. Three temporary hearths, contexts 60, 94 and 96, were associated with the initial abandonment of the aisled roundhouse. Once the corbelled roof of the roundhouse had collapsed, the surface of the site was subject to intensive weathering. A formal hearth was constructed upon the weathered surface of the secondary depositional sequence, context 74. This hearth was defined by a rectilinear stone setting, 1.04 m × 1.30 m (Fig. 4.21). It was constructed from three stone slabs set in an upright position. The stone setting retained an accumulation of ash, context 78, interspersed with lenses of charcoal. It was associated with a series of dumps of ash and pottery, contexts 63, 69 and 79.

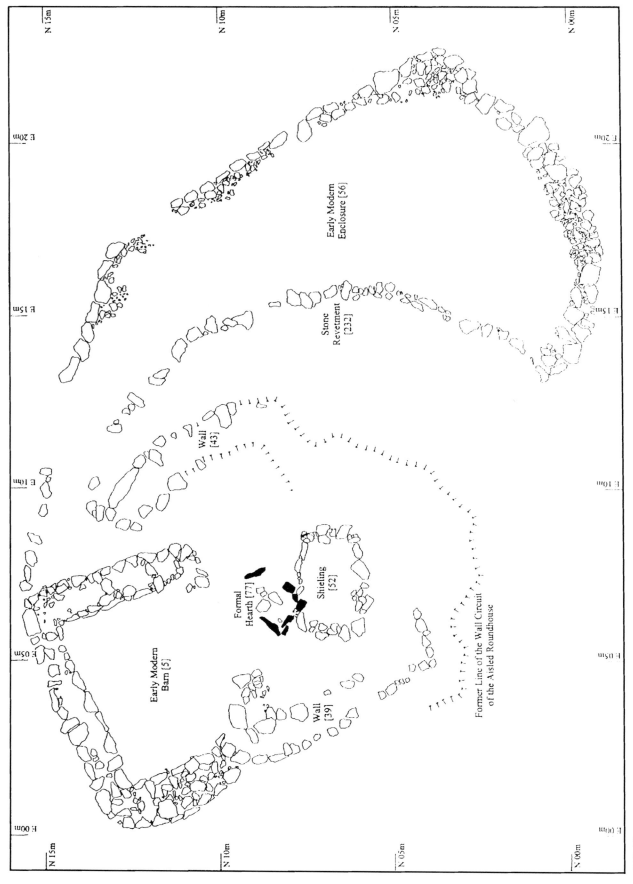

Figure 4.20 The stone structures postdating the abandonment of the Ben Tangaval roundhouse.

Early Modern Enclosure [56]

Stone Revetment [232]

Wall [43]

Early Modern Barn [5]

Formal Hearth [77]

Shieling [52]

Wall [39]

Former Line of the Wall Circuit of the Aisled Roundhouse

Figure 4.21 The formal hearth constructed upon the weathered surface of the secondary depositional sequence, facing north-east.

The tertiary depositional sequence

The weathered surface of the site is sealed by the tertiary depositional sequence, context 66. This deposit represents the build up of material over a long period of time, during which the site continued to be used episodically. A series of discrete ash lenses (contexts 20, 22, 24, 34, 72 and 84) associated with temporary hearths were identified close to the inner face of the abandoned wall circuit. The tertiary depositional sequence is also associated with two stone-built struc-

tures. Access to these structures was gained via a gentle slope created by the collapse of the stone slabs blocking the southern entrance to the aisled roundhouse. The displaced stone slabs are associated with a loose unconsolidated deposit, context 121.

The shieling. During the accumulation of the tertiary depositional sequence, a shieling was inserted into the interior of the abandoned roundhouse (Fig. 4.22). This small shelter, approximately 3.8 m by 2.3 m,

Figure 4.22 The shieling inserted into the tertiary depositional sequence, facing east.

appears to have been sunk into the contemporary ground surface. It is constructed from a series of irregular stone blocks; a number of which have been stood upright. A small hearth, context 28, was identified within the interior of the shieling. While no formal stone setting was detected, this hearth was associated with an accumulation of ash 20 cm thick. The northern wall of the shieling appears to have been built on top of an accumulation of iron rich silt, context 126. A similar deposit, context 99, was banked up against the external face of this wall. The origin and interpretation of these deposits are uncertain. Following the abandonment of the shieling, a discrete layer of rubble (context 80) derived from the collapse of the structure formed within the tertiary depositional sequence.

The subrectangular building. A large sub rectangular building, measuring 9.9 m by at least 6.7 m, was built towards the rear of the site. This structure, overlying the wall circuit of the aisled roundhouse, has largely been destroyed. The northern wall of the sub rectangular building was demolished prior to the construction of an early modern barn (see below). Only two short sections of walling survive (Figs. 4.23, 4.24).

Figure 4.24 The east wall of the subrectangular building, facing south-east.

The building is constructed from a double thickness wall, approximately 1.2 m wide, with an earthen core. To the west, the return of the outer skin of the wall can be traced by a line of smaller stones possibly laid down to mark out the plan of the building prior to construction. To the east, while the stonework has mostly collapsed, the return of the wall can be traced by a slight break in slope where surface deposits have slumped into rabbit burrows following the line of the structure. No discrete deposits associated with this building were identified during the course of excavation. The displaced stonework, context 61, derived from the collapse of the subrectangular building was clearly differentiated from that associated with the earlier structures.

The stone revetment

A stone revetment was built to the east of the aisled roundhouse (Figs. 4.25, 4.26). This curvilinear wall, offset by a distance of approximately 2 m, runs parallel to the wall circuit of the aisled roundhouse. It is built upon the upper surface of an accumulation of organic loam, context 81. This deposit, sealing the midden in the vicinity of the southern entrance of the aisled roundhouse, is broadly contemporary with the secondary depositional sequence. It is associated with two

Figure 4.23 The west wall of the subrectangular building, facing north.

Figure 4.25 The revetted enclosure, facing north.

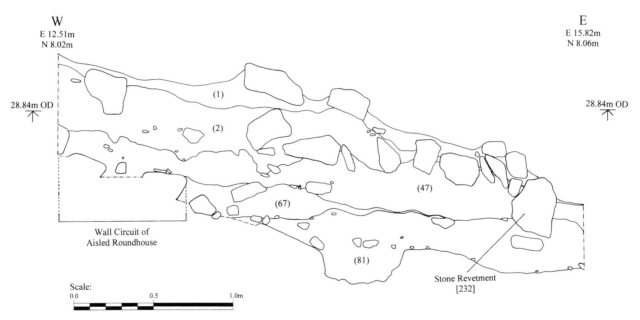

Figure 4.26 Section through the deposits associated with the stone revetment.

dumps of ash, contexts 106 and 107. The upper surface of this deposit has been subject to intensive weathering and is sealed by a coarse gritty deposit, context 67. This heavily mineralized deposit is equivalent to the iron-rich silt sealing the wall circuit of the aisled roundhouse. It is comparable to the weathered surface, context 74, identified within the interior of the site. Two discrete ash lenses (contexts 30 and 65), associated with temporary hearths, were identified within the area enclosed by the stone revetment. The weathered surfaces of the wall circuit and the revetted enclosure are sealed by an accumulation of organic

silt, context 47. This deposit is equivalent to the tertiary depositional sequence. The subrectangular building described above is built upon the upper surface of this deposit.

The exterior of the aisled roundhouse

The deposits identified within the revetted enclosure can be correlated with those to the south and the west of the aisled roundhouse (Fig.4.27). While the depositional sequence associated with the stone revetment could be traced along the southern face of the wall circuit, the deposits at the western extent of the site

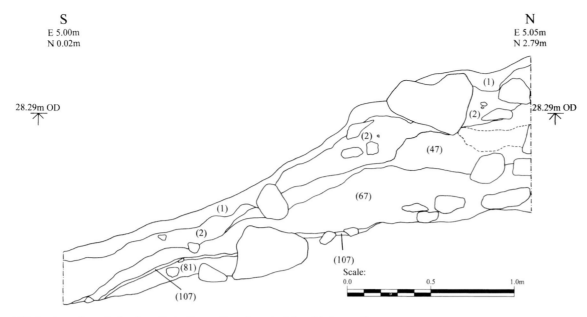

Figure 4.27 Sections through the deposits to the south and west of the aisled roundhouse.

had been heavily truncated. A series of temporary hearths (contexts 31, 36 and 38) were identified upon the weathered surface of the subsoil, context 26, to the west of the aisled roundhouse. The ash deposits associated with these hearths are sealed by an accumulation of organic silt, context 17, equivalent to the tertiary depositional sequence.

The early modern structures

Most recently, a series of early modern structures were built in the vicinity of the site (Fig. 4.28). These structures are possibly associated with the blackhouse excavated at Alt Chrisal T26 (Foster 1995). A rectangular building, approximately 7.7 m × 5.5 m, was built towards the northern extent of the site. This building, incorporating part of the subrectangular building described above, was constructed from a substantial double-thickness wall roughly 1.3 m wide. It was constructed upon the upper surface of context 13, an accumulation of organic silt that can be correlated with the tertiary depositional sequence. Although no formal hearth was identified within the rectangular

Figure 4.28 The Early Modern barn and enclosure, facing south.

building, a discrete ash lens (context 12), associated with a temporary hearth, was identified at the interface with this deposit. Two distinct layers were identified with the interior of the building (contexts 10 and 11), however, the absence of any internal features would suggest that the structure was used for storage rather than for occupation or stalling animals. In the absence of a formal hearth or stone-lined drain the rectangular building has been interpreted as a barn, as opposed to a blackhouse or byre. An elongated enclosure, defined by an orthostat wall, was constructed towards the eastern extent of the site. This enclosure, abutting the external face of the early modern barn, incorporates part of the stone revetment to the east of the aisled roundhouse. An agglomeration of stones, context 58, towards the south-east extent of the enclosure is probably derived from the 'improvement' of the enclosed land. The enclosure retains an accumulation of organic silt, context 4 that has been disturbed by recent cultivation.

Unstratified and intrusive deposits

The upper levels of the site have been heavily disturbed by rabbit burrowing and have largely been reworked. An accumulation of loose organic silt (context 2), the spoil ejected from rabbit burrows, covers much of the site. Active rabbit burrows were found and recorded within all levels of the site. Many of the burrows followed the line of the stonework associated with the manmade structures. Pottery and other artifacts were recovered from rabbit burrows intruding into cell A (context 125), the hearth box (contexts 133 and 182), the primary depositional sequence (contexts 113 and 188), the central hearth (context 90) and the secondary depositional sequence (contexts 101 and 116). The deposits associated with the stone-built structures at Alt Chrisal T17 had also been disturbed by rats. Two rat nests (contexts 62 and 111), containing an abundance of pottery and limpet shells, were found with the materials deposited against the wall circuit of the aisled roundhouse. Finds were also recovered from the deposits used to backfill the site in 1998 (contexts 235, 236, 239, 240, 243 and 245). These deposits were removed during the course of later excavations, and materials from the backfill of each of the radial cells were recorded separately.

Coarseware

Jane Timby, with Emma Gowans and John Pouncett

Introduction

A total of 5,600 sherds of pottery, weighing 33.257 kg were recovered during excavations at Alt Chrisal T17. This assemblage represents a minimum of 81 vessels. The sherds have been badly fragmented and many

severely worn or abraded. However, conjoining sherds were noted both within and between contexts. Preliminary examination of the pottery would suggest that the assemblage contains a significant proportion of intrusive and residual material. Further detailed analysis of the pottery will be undertaken at a later date, as part of the assessment of the impact of rabbit infestation upon the site.

Fabric types

Twelve broad fabric types were identified during macroscopic examination of the pottery assemblage. These fabric types are differentiated largely on the basis of the range of inclusions. The majority of the pottery would have been fired either in a bonfire or a clamp kiln. Variations in the colour and hardness of the pottery can largely be attributed to the method of firing.

B1: A moderately hard, sandy textured brown ware distinguished by the presence of occasional very coarse, angular, igneous inclusions (<5 mm) alongside finer fragments.

B2: A slightly finer version of B1 occurring in various shades of grey, black and brown. General fabric type characterized by poorly sorted, sparse to moderate inclusions including occasional fragments of quartzite ≤5 mm.

B3: A finer version of B2 with better-sorted inclusions, usually ≤1 mm general fabric type.

B4: A B2/B3 variant with an even, blackened (burnished?) external surface.

B5: A hard, compact dark grey ware with pale brown surfaces. Organic or sand-tempered ware with sparse fine inclusions.

B6: A fine, slightly porous dark brown ware with occasional sand inclusions (visible at ×20 magnification).

B7: A hard, compact dark grey ware with brown surfaces, similar to B5. Contains a scatter of fine mica inclusions and occasional larger fragments of gneiss but no organic matter.

B8: A B2 variant with a high density of well-sorted inclusions, generally ≤3 mm.

B9: An orange brown or pale orange ware with darker core. Characterized by frequent biotite mica inclusions.

B10: A distinctive fine, red ware with sparse, fine mica and quartz inclusions.

B11: A rare orange ware with a grey core. Thick, poorly wedged fabric with sparse igneous intrusions ≤5 mm.

B12: A hard, coarse red brown ware with a high density of igneous inclusions ≤1 mm.

There would appear to be little differentiation between the fabric types found within and between contexts. While fabrics B6, B11 and B12 appear to have a restricted distribution, the low frequency of these fabric types renders any interpretation meaningless. The raw materials, derived from the reworked glacial till, appear to have remained constant throughout the history of the site.

Vessel Forms

Only one complete vessel profile was identified within the assemblage of pottery (Fig. 4.36.1, page 177). This vessel, a shallow bowl with moderate to steep sides and a simple undifferentiated rim, was found within

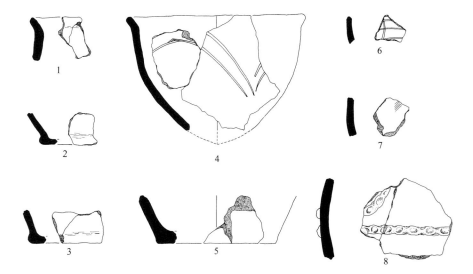

Figure 4.29 Coarseware: pottery from the Atlantic roundhouse.

the early modern enclosure. Near-complete profiles were also recovered from the deposits associated with the Atlantic roundhouse and the stone revetment. These vessel forms included a deep bowl with a slightly everted rim and rounded base (Fig. 4.29.4), and a round bodied vessel with a concave neck (Fig. 4.35.9, page 176). In the absence of further profiles, consideration of vessel form must rely upon the classification and interpretation of rims and bases.

Rim types
103 rim sherds, representing six distinct rim types, were recovered during the course of excavation.

Type 1:   Simple undifferentiated rounded rims. Includes jars and shallow bowls, ranging from 64 mm to 368 mm in diameter.
Type 2:   Slightly everted rims. Includes bowls, ranging from 147mm to 159mm in diameter.
Type 3:   Everted rims. Includes flared jars and globular vessels, ranging from 118 mm to 229 m in diameter.
Type 4:   Rounded out-turned rims. Includes globular vessels, ranging from 159 mm to 221 mm in diameter.
Type 5:   Expanded squared rims. Includes wide diameter bowls, up to 410 mm in diameter.
Type 6:   Simple undifferentiated squared rims. Includes wide diameter bowls, up to 351 mm in diameter.

Types 1 and 2 are ubiquitous and are found throughout the depositional sequence. The remainder of the rim types would appear to be slightly later in date. Types 3, 4 and 5 are first found within the deposits associated with the primary occupation of the aisled roundhouse, whilst type 6 emerges during the primary depositional sequence.

Base types
106 base sherds, representing five distinct base types, were recovered from Alt Chrisal T17.

Type I: Flat bases with moderate to steeply sloping sides, ranging from 104 mm to 133 m in diameter.

Type II: Footed bases with moderate to steeply sloping sides, ranging from 98 mm to 295 mm in diameter.
Type III: Flared bases with moderate sloping sides, ranging from 114 mm to 267 mm in diameter.
Type IV: Slightly flared bases with moderate to steeply sloping sides, ranging from 107 mm to 192 mm in diameter.
Type V: Undifferentiated bases with slightly sloping sides (bowls?), up to 128 mm in diameter.

Although types I and IV are found throughout the depositional sequence, the base types would appear to have a more restricted distribution than the rim types. Types II and III are only found within the lower levels of the site, that is, within the deposits associated with the aisled roundhouse and the underlying structure. In contrast, type V is only found within the upper levels of the site and would thus appear to be much later in date.

Surface treatment

The coarseware is handmade using a variety of techniques including 'tongue and groove' (Figs. 4.31.3; 4.36.1, page 177). In a number of instances, the surface of the vessel had been smoothed or wiped, or a coarse slip had been applied to the external surface of the vessel. Similar surface finishes have been noted at Allasdale (Young 1952) and Sollas (Campbell 1991). Analysis of the pottery from Dùnan Ruadh has suggested that wiping or smoothing is confined to the central zone of the vessel and that the coarse slip is only applied to the lower zones.

Use wear

Approximately 42% of the sherds show evidence for blackening or sooting on the external and or internal surface of the vessel. Soot or carbonized residues are usually confined to the lower portion of the vessel. A number of sherds also show evidence for the repair of broken vessels. Perforated or 'drilled' sherds were recovered from the deposits associated with the primary occupation of the aisled roundhouse (Figs. 4.30.5, 4.31.11). Similar sherds were noted within the pottery assemblage from the other excavated sites at Alt Chrisal, where it was suggested that leather thongs were threaded through the holes to bind a broken vessel together (Gibson 1995).

Impressed wares

The most common impressed wares are those decorated with finger or fingernail impressions. This form

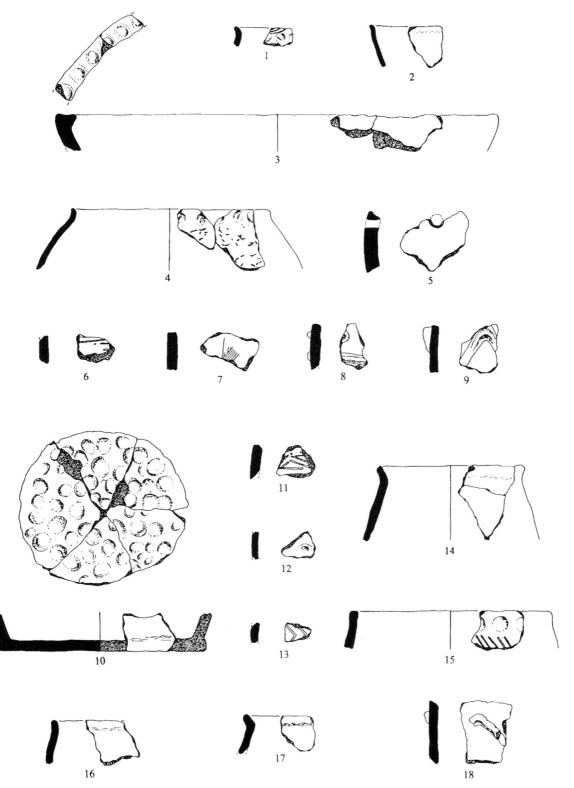

Figure 4.30 Coarseware: pottery from the aisled roundhouse.

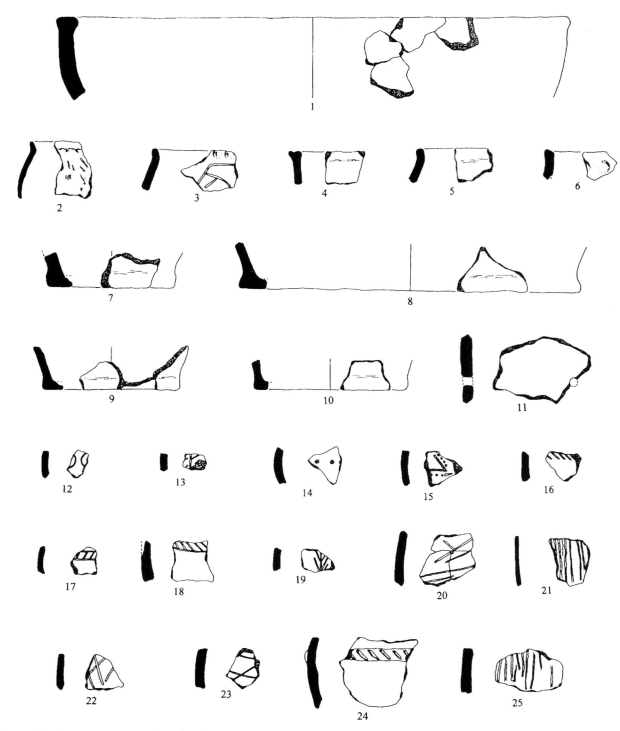

Figure 4.31 Coarseware: pottery from the primary depositional sequence.

of decoration may be confined to the upper surface of the rim (Fig. 4.30.3), but is more often than not found within the zone beneath the rim (Fig. 4.30.4) or around the edge of the base (Fig. 4.32.6). Finger-pressed rims and bases are largely confined to the lower levels of the site. While they may be indicative of the techniques of manufacture, it is thought that the regularly spaced finger impressions represent an early form of decoration (Mike Parker Pearson, personal communication). A single sherd from the primary

depositional sequence was decorated with impressed circles (Fig. 4.31.12). Similar sherds were recovered from the aisled roundhouse at Allasdale, where it was suggested that the impressions were created by a circular-headed pin (Young 1952: 92). These 'pin stamped' sherds are characteristic of the Hebridean Iron Age (Young 1966: 48). A number of sherds from the primary and tertiary depositional sequences were decorated with impressed dots (Fig. 4.31.14). These dots, created by a round or slightly squared pointed

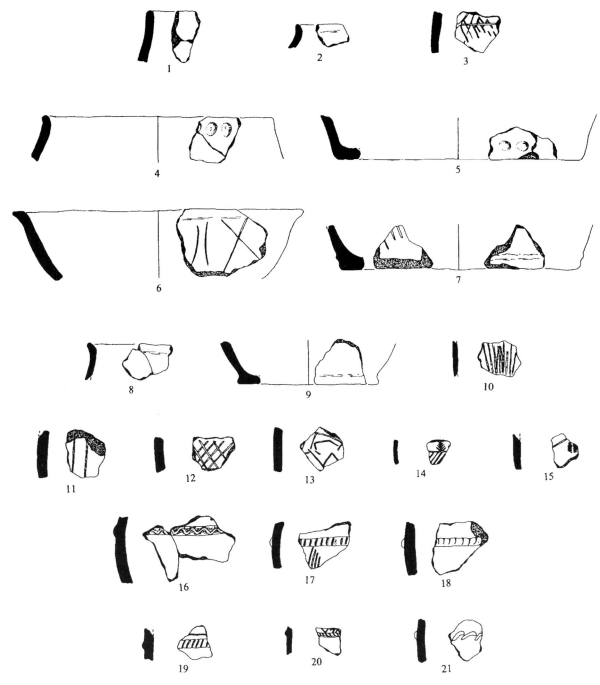

Figure 4.32 Coarseware: pottery from the secondary depositional sequence.

object, were sometimes associated with incised lines (Fig. 4.31.15). Similarly, a handful of sherds were decorated with irregular impressions created by pushing an object, possibly a small bone, into the surface of the vessel and then twisting it in a circular motion. In one instance, the resulting impression strongly resembled an eye (Fig. 4.30.12).

Incised wares

A wide range of incised wares, decorated with linear and curvilinear designs, was observed within the pottery assemblage. However, as a result of the fragmentary nature of the pottery, it is often difficult to differentiate distinct motifs. The description and interpretation of the incised decoration is dependent on the preservation of sherds. In many instances only a small, undiagnostic proportion of a design is visible. The earliest forms of incised decoration, coincidentally those found throughout the depositional sequence, include parallel diagonal lines (Figs. 4.29.8, 4.31.16) and chevrons (Fig. 4.30.13). Initially the zones of decoration appear to be unbounded, however, later forms were defined by single or multiple incisions

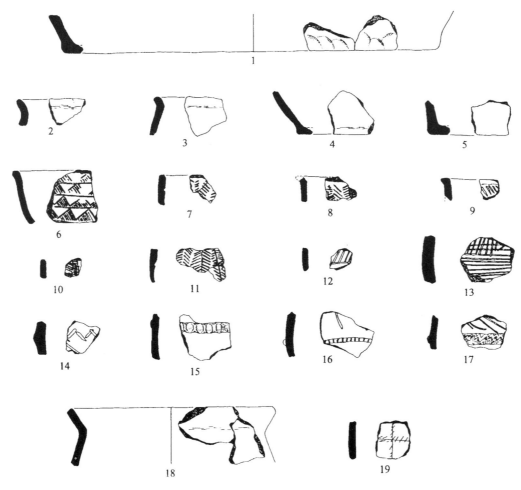

Figure 4.33 Coarseware: pottery from after abandonment.

(Figs. 4.31.18, 4.34.10). A distinct variant of this form (Fig. 4.31.17), the ladder design, was found within the primary and tertiary depositional sequences. Additional forms of incised decoration, including lattice (Fig. 4.32.12), feather (Fig. 4.32.14) and multiple herringbone designs (Fig. 4.33.11), are found within the deposits associated with the occupation and reuse of the aisled roundhouse. A number of less frequent incised motifs were identified within the pottery assemblage. These include sherds decorated with freestyle or geometric designs (Figs. 4.31.2 and 20) and infilled triangles (Fig. 4.33.6). Finally, the surface of a number of vessels is decorated with deep 'vertical' scored lines, possibly created by a comb (Fig. 4.32.10). Similar sherds were recovered during excavations at Dun Vulan (LaTrobe-Bateman 1999: 70).

Cordoned wares

Vessels decorated with both applied and pinched cordons were recovered from Alt Chrisal T17. In both instances the cordon runs around the body of the vessel, and later forms, where the cordon is positioned at the neck of the vessel, are absent. Vessels decorated with applied cordons appear to be slightly earlier in date than those with pinched cordons (Young 1966).

The earliest cordoned wares, those associated with the primary occupation of the aisled roundhouse and the underlying structure, are decorated with an applied freestyle cordon (Figs. 4.29.8, 4.30.8). An additional fillet of clay is applied to the body of the vessel above the cordon. It is perhaps comparable to the exaggerated applied wavy line cordons (Fig. 4.30.9) found within the deposits associated with the primary occupation of the aisled roundhouse. Other applied decorative styles include wavy line cordons with impressed or incised vertical lines (Figs. 4.32.17–18), finger-pressed cordons (Fig. 4.33.15) and tooled cordons where the fillet is shaped into shallow ripples (Fig. 4.32.21). Two main variants of pinched cordon were identified. Simple undecorated forms were differentiated from those ornamented with incised decoration (Figs 4.33.14 and 17). In a number of instances, the zone above the cordon is decorated with incised lines (Fig. 4.33.17).

The Atlantic roundhouse

A small assemblage of pottery was recovered from the deposits associated with the structure beneath the aisled roundhouse (Fig. 4.29). The assemblage consisted of 97 sherds (total mass 973 g) with an average mass of 10.03 g per sherd. Forty-four sherds were recovered from the mineralized soil (context 184) upon which the earlier Iron Age structure was built. These included 2 rim sherds (type 1) and 4 base sherds (types I, II and III). Only one base sherd (type I) was recovered from which the diameter of the vessel could be estimated (Fig. 4.29.5). While the majority of the pottery from context 184 was undecorated, 3 decorated sherds representing a range of decorative styles were identified. These sherds were decorated with incised perpendicular lines (Fig. 4.29.6), a vertical band of fine diagonal incisions (Fig. 4.29.7), and an applied freestyle cordon (Fig. 4.29.8). A further 53 sherds were recovered from the deposit associated with the arc of walling (context 114). These included 2 conjoining sherds from a bowl (158 mm in diameter and approximately 114 mm deep) with a slightly everted rim and rounded base (Fig. 4.29.4). The bowl is decorated with curvilinear incisions that formed pointed arches around the body of the vessel. It is comparable with the incised bowls recovered from Neolithic and Bronze contexts at Alt Chrisal T26 (Gibson 1995; Fig. 4.32.68) and is thus thought to be residual.

The aisled roundhouse

A total of 197 sherds (weighing 1,946 g), with an average sherd mass of 9.88g, were recovered from the deposits associated with the primary occupation of the aisled roundhouse (Fig. 4.30). The vast majority of this pottery was derived from cell F, and only 11 sherds were recovered from the other radial cells. It has been suggested that the concentration of artifacts within Iron Age roundhouses is greatest within the area to the right of the entrance (Giles and Parker Pearson, in press). Whilst the concentration of pottery within Cell F would appear to support this assertion, the disparity between the radial cells can largely be attributed to the truncation of the deposits towards the north-western extent of the site.

Over 170 sherds were recovered from the occupational deposits within cell F (contexts 131 and 183), including 11 rim sherds (Types 1–5) and 7 base sherds (types I–IV). Sherds from the type 2 rim were also found within the primary depositional sequence (context 110). Approximately 14% of the sherds associated with the primary occupation of the aisled roundhouse were decorated, representing a range of decorative styles. These included sherds decorated with irregular impressed designs (Fig. 4.30.12), incised chevrons (Figs. 4.30.11 and 13), closely spaced fine diagonal incisions (Fig. 4.30.7), an applied freestyle cordon (Fig. 4.30.8) and an applied wavy line cordon (Fig. 4.30.9). A rim sherd decorated with both finger impressions and a band of incised diagonal lines was found within context 131. Partial profiles were recovered from a number of vessels. Four sherds from a

large bowl, approximately 348mm in diameter, were found within the accumulation of ash (context 183) at the base of the radial cell (Fig. 4.30.3). This bowl had an expanded squared rim, the upper surface of which had been decorated with regularly spaced finger impressions. Two conjoining sherds, forming part of a globular vessel at least 156 mm in diameter, were recovered from the same context (Fig. 4.30.4). This vessel, constructed from a hard, organically tempered fabric, had a rounded out turned rim (type 4) decorated with finger impressions. A complete flared base (type III) was also found within context 183 (Fig. 4.30.10). The internal surface of the base was covered by shallow finger impressions. Similar 'finger-pressed bases' were recovered from Dun Vulan (LaTrobe-Bateman 1999: 216) and Sollas (Campbell 1991; microfiche 2 D3). Finally, a single sherd from an undecorated jar approximately 118 mm in diameter, with an everted rim (type 3) was found within the organic loam (context 131) sealing the accumulation of ash.

Seven sherds of pottery were recovered from Cell E. These included 2 rim sherds (types 2 and 3) and a body sherd decorated with an exaggerated applied wavy line cordon (Fig. 4.30.18). The remainder of the pottery associated with the primary occupation of the aisled roundhouse was undifferentiated. Three body sherds were recovered from the accumulation of organic silt and ash (context 231) in cell A while a single sherd of pottery was derived from the fill (context 123) of the shallow pit cut into the subsoil within cell C. A further 14 sherds were recovered from the midden deposits (context 109) in the vicinity of the southern entrance.

The primary depositional sequence

A moderate assemblage of pottery was recovered from the primary depositional sequence (Fig. 4.31). This assemblage contained 494 sherds (total mass 4,472 g) with an average mass of 9.05 g per sherd. The vast majority of this assemblage was derived from context 110 or from the deposits behind the radial piers. However, 13 sherds were recovered from the hearth sequences associated with the rectilinear stone setting, including a rim sherd (type 4) from context 148 (Fig. 4.31.5) and a base sherd (type I) from context 135. Whilst only a handful of sherds were found behind piers 4, 5 and 7 (contexts 242, 248 and 251 respectively), a small group of 19 sherds was found behind pier 6 (context 238). A further 458 sherds were recovered from the interior of the aisled roundhouse, and these included 9 rim sherds (types 2–6) and 18 base sherds (types I–IV). One of the type 5 rim sherds formed part of a vessel also found within the secondary depositional sequence (context 102). Approximately 6% of the sherds from the primary depositional sequence were decorated.

A wide range of decorative styles were identified, including sherds decorated with: finger impressions (Fig. 4.31.6); impressed circles (Fig. 4.31.12) or dots (Figs 4.31.13–4.31.15); bands of incised diagonal lines (Figs. 4.31.16–18), incised feather motifs (Fig. 4.31.19), freestyle linear designs (Figs. 4.31.3 and 20) or lattices (Figs. 4.31.22–23); and applied cordons (Fig. 4.31.24). In addition, a number of sherds decorated with scored vertical lines were found within contexts 110, 160 and 238. These sherds were derived from a minimum of two vessels; sherds from these vessels were also found within the compact ash floor (context 98) sealing context 110 and the secondary depositional sequence (context 102).

The secondary depositional sequence

A total of 951 sherds (weighing 6,567 g) with an average sherd mass of 6.91 g were found within the secondary depositional sequence (Fig. 4.32). Nine sherds, including 2 rim sherds (type 1), were recovered from the deposits associated with the central hearth. A further 326 sherds were associated with the compact ash floor (context 98). The remainder of the pottery associated with the secondary occupation of the aisled roundhouse was derived from the accumulation of organic silt (context 102). The assemblage of pottery from the secondary depositional sequence contained 18 rim sherds (types 1–6 inclusive) and 18 base sherds (types I–IV). Sherds from one of the type 4 rims belonged to a vessel also found within the tertiary depositional sequence (context 66). Approximately 4% of the assemblage was decorated, with cordoned wares becoming more frequent. Sherds were decorated with finger impressions (Figs. 4.32.4 and 5); scored vertical lines (Fig. 4.32.10); incised chevrons (Fig. 4.32.3), parallel lines (Fig. 4.32.11), lattices (Fig. 4.32.12), geometric designs (Fig. 4.32.13) or feather motifs (Figs. 4.32.14 and 15); applied wavy line (Fig. 4.32.16), impressed (Fig. 4.32.17), incised (Fig. 4.32.18) or tooled cordons (Fig. 4.32.21); and pinched cordons (Figs. 4.32.1 and 20). A number of sherds exhibited scratch marks created by rabbits (Figs. 4.32.7 and 17). Only 2 sherds were recovered from the secondary depositional sequence from which partial profiles could be reconstructed. A single sherd, decorated with fine linear and curvilinear incisions, belonged to a shallow bowl with an everted rim (Fig. 4.32.5). This vessel, approximately 230 mm in diameter, was constructed from a hard fabric that had been fired at a high temperature. Another sherd formed part of a bowl or globular vessel, at least 114 mm in diameter, with a footed base (Fig. 4.32.9).

After abandonment

Over 900 sherds of pottery (weighing 3,008 g) with an average sherd mass of 3.29 g were recovered from the deposits associated with the abandonment of the aisled roundhouse (Fig. 4.33). Sherds from the weathered surface of the secondary depositional sequence had been heavily trampled, hence the lower average mass. The majority of the pottery was derived from context 74, however, 66 sherds were recovered from the ash deposits (contexts 63, 69, 78 and 94) associated with the formal hearth built within the abandoned wall circuit. A further 21 sherds were found within one of the discrete ash lenses (context 94) derived from *in situ* burning. The pottery associated with the abandonment of the aisled roundhouse included 13 rim sherds (types 1–6 inclusive) and 15 base sherds (types I–IV). Only one partial profile was reconstructed. Two conjoining sherds from the ash deposit within the formal hearth, formed part of the rim of a flared jar at least 172 mm in diameter (Fig. 4.33.18). Approximately 4% of the pottery was decorated, the assemblage being predominated by complex linear designs and cordoned wares. A wide range of decorative styles was identified, including sherds decorated with finger impressions (Fig. 4.33.1); incised infilled triangles (Fig. 4.33.6); multiple herringbone designs (Figs. 4.33.7–11) or horizontal and diagonal lines (Figs. 4.33.12 and 13); applied finger-pressed (Fig. 4.33.15) or incised cordons (Fig. 4.33.16); and pinched cordons with incised ornamentation (Figs. 4.33.14 and 17). Furthermore, one of the sherds derived from the ash deposits associated with the formal hearth (context 94) was decorated by an incised cross with hatched limbs.

The tertiary depositional sequence

The largest assemblage of pottery was associated with the tertiary depositional sequence (Fig. 4.34). This assemblage contained 1,290 sherds (total mass 6,347 g) with an average mass of 4.92 g per sherd. The majority of these sherds were derived from the accumulation of organic silt (contexts 66 and 121) and the discrete ash lenses associated with temporary hearths. While the majority of these ash deposits contained only a handful of pottery, a group of 99 sherds, including 2 rim sherds (type 1), was found within one of the temporary hearths (context 84). Small groups of pottery were also associated with the shieling inserted into the interior of the site (contexts 53, 80, 99 and 126), and the sub rectangular building overlying the abandoned wall circuit (contexts 45 and 61).

Over 1,000 sherds were recovered from the accumulation of organic silt, context 66. A further 16 sherds were found within the loose deposit (context 122) associated with the collapse of the stone slabs blocking the southern entrance to the aisled roundhouse. The pottery from contexts 66 and 121 included 13 rim sherds (types 1, 3, 5 and 6) and 13 base sherds (types I, IV and V). Only one partial profile was identified; namely, a wide bowl, approximately

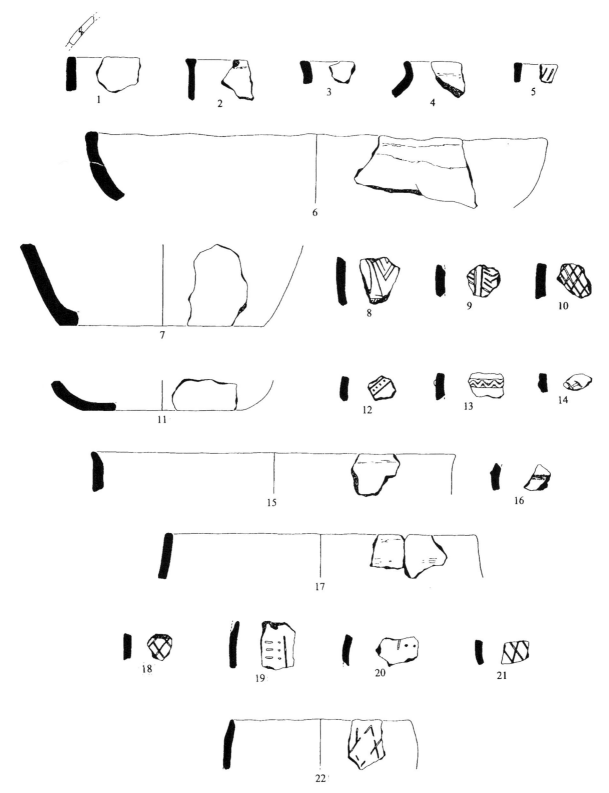

Figure 4.34 Coarseware: pottery from the tertiary depositional sequence.

364 mm in diameter, with a simple undifferentiated rounded rim (Fig. 4.34.1). Only 2% of the sherds from these deposits were decorated. Fewer decorative styles were represented. Decorated sherds include those with impressed dots and incised lines (Fig. 4.34.12) incised chevrons (Fig. 4.34.9), herringbone designs (Fig. 4.34.10) or lattices (Fig. 4.34.11); applied wavy line cordons (Fig. 4.34.13); and pinched cordons (Figs. 4.34.14 and 16).

A total of 96 sherds were found within the deposits associated with the shieling built within the abandoned wall circuit. The majority of these sherds were found within the iron-rich silts deposited in the vicinity of the northern wall of the shieling (contexts 99 and 126). However, a number of sherds were found within the fabric of the wall and the displaced stonework associated with the collapse of the structure. The group of pottery associated with the shieling contained 4 rim sherds (types 2, 5 and 6) and 3 base sherds (types I and IV). Approximately 7% of the sherds were decorated. A limited repertoire of decorative styles was represented, sherds being decorated with either impressed dots and incised lines (Figs. 4.34.19 and 20) or incised lattices (Figs. 4.34.18 and 21).

Only 13 sherds were recovered from the deposits associated with the subrectangular building built towards the northern extent of the site. A single undecorated body sherd was found within the displaced stonework derived from the collapse of this building. The remainder of the pottery was derived from the earthen core (context 45) of the substantial double-thickness wall. A rim sherd (type 1) decorated with an incised lattice was found within the wall core (Fig. 4.34.22). This rim was derived from a vessel, possibly a jar or bowl, approximately 154 mm in diameter.

The stone revetment

A total of 416 sherds (weighing 3,216 g) with an average sherd mass of 7.73 g were found within the deposits associated with the stone revetment (Fig. 4.35). Only 41 sherds were recovered from the accumulation of organic loam upon which the stone revetment was built (context 81). These included 3 rim sherds (type 4) and 1 base sherd (type V). In contrast, 152 sherds were recovered from the weathered surface of this deposit (context 67). A further 87 sherds, including 7 base sherds (types I and IV), were recovered from one of the piles of ash, context 106, dumped upon the weathered land surface. Only a single body sherd was recovered from the second ash dump, context 107. The remainder of the pottery from the revetted enclosure was derived from the accumulation of organic silt (context 47) sealing context 67 and the weathered surface of the abandoned wall circuit. Very few decorated sherds were recovered from the

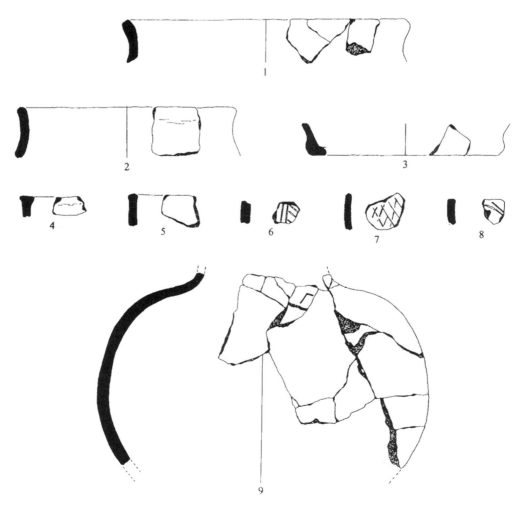

Figure 4.35 Coarseware: pottery from the stone revetment.

176

deposits associated with the stone revetment. The range of decorative styles was very restricted and is confined to incised linear designs (Figs. 4.35.3–8). One near-complete vessel profile was recovered from the upper levels of the revetted enclosure. A group of conjoining sherds forming part of a round-bodied vessel, approximately 262 mm in diameter, with a concave neck were found within context 47. This undecorated vessel is similar to a vessel associated with the abandonment of the stone-built roundhouse at Dun Vulan (Parker Pearson and Sharples 1999: 199).

The exterior of the roundhouse

Few sherds of pottery were found outside the roundhouse. Only 32 sherds (weighing 165 g), with an average sherd mass of 5.16 g, were found within the deposits at the western extent of the site. No rim sherds, base sherds or decorated sherds were recovered from these deposits.

The early modern structures

A moderate assemblage of pottery was recovered from the deposits associated with the early modern structures (Fig. 4.36). This assemblage contained 557 sherds (total mass 2,970 g) with an average mass of 5.33 g per sherd. The vast majority of these sherds were derived from the deposits associated within the enclosure to the east of the aisled roundhouse (contexts 4 and 58). These deposits have been heavily disturbed by recent cultivation, and the fragmentary nature of the assemblage reflects this fact. Few rim sherds, base sherds or decorated sherds were recovered from the deposits associated with the early modern structures. However, a number of sherds are worthy of note. These include the complete profile of a

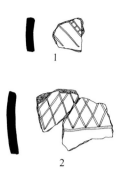

Figure 4.37 Coarseware: pottery from the unstratified or intrusive deposits.

small shallow bowl, approximately 146 mm in diameter and 45 mm deep, with a simple undifferentiated rim (Fig. 4.36.1), and the partial profile of a narrow jar or globular vessel, at least 70 mm in diameter, with a simple upright rounded rim (Fig. 4.36.2). A small, rectangular handle or foot (Fig. 4.36.3) was also found within the deposits associated with the early modern enclosure. This 'handle' was constructed from a hard fabric, fired at a very high temperature.

Unstratified and intrusive deposits

The remainder of the pottery assemblage from Alt Chrisal T17 was derived from unstratified or intrusive deposits (Fig. 4.37). Over 500 sherds of pottery were recovered from the spoil ejected from rabbit burrows (context 2), whilst only 64 sherds were associated with active burrows (contexts 101, 113, 188 and 125). Thirty sherds were found within the rat nests (contexts 62 and 111) close to the wall circuit of the aisled roundhouse. A further 10 sherds of pottery were recovered from the deposits used to backfill the site in 1998 (contexts 235, 236, 239, 240, 243 and 245). Only two sherds are illustrated from unstratified or intrusive deposits: a particularly fine example of an incised ladder design (Fig. 4.37.1), and a decorated sherd where the zone above the pinched cordon is decorated with an incised lattice (Fig. 4.37.2).

Discussion

Until recently, few stratified assemblages of pottery have been recovered from Iron Age sites in the Outer Hebrides. Existing chronologies have been challenged (Topping 1987; Lane 1990). The ceramic phases identified by Scott (1948) and Young (1966) have been refined (e.g. Campbell 1991). Furthermore, recent programmes of radiocarbon dating have improved the resolution of existing chronologies (Parker Pearson and Sharples 1999: 210–211). A series of distinct ceramic phases were identified with the pottery assemblage from Alt Chrisal, T17. These phases, primarily based on stratigraphic relationships, can be correlated with those from other Hebridean sites.

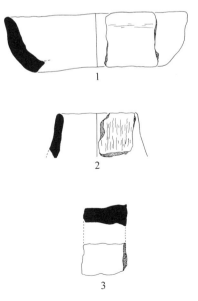

Figure 4.36 Coarseware: pottery from the early modern structures.

0. Deep bowls with slightly everted rims and rounded bases. Decorated with incised curvilinear designs. Neolithic?
1. Plain, undecorated vessels with undifferentiated rounded (recurved?) rims. Possibly equivalent to Dun Vulan Phase 1a dated to the 1st centuries BC/AD.
2a. Globular vessels with rounded out turned rims and footed or finger-pressed bases. Decorated with finger impressions beneath rim, impressed dots and incised linear designs, chevrons or lattices. Equivalent to Dun Vulan Phase 2 and Sollas Phase A1 dated to the 1st/3rd centuries AD.
2b. Globular vessels with everted rims. Decorated with incised feather motifs, ladder designs and lattices. Applied cordoned wares are also represented. Equivalent to Clettraval phase 1a, Dun Vulan Phase 3 and Sollas Phase A2 dated to the 1st/3rd centuries AD.
3. Bowls with slightly everted or simple undifferentiated squared rims. Decorated with incised multiple feather motifs, herringbone designs and infilled triangles. This phase also appears to be associated with the transition between applied and pinched cordons. Equivalent to Dun Vulan Phase 4 and Sollas B1 dated to the 2nd/4th centuries AD.
4. Plain, undecorated jars or globular vessels with flared rims (exaggerated everted forms). Equivalent to Dun Vulan Phase 6 dated to the 6th/9th centuries AD.
5. Vessels with simple, upright undifferentiated rims. Decorated with impressed dots and/or incised linear designs. Norse?
6. Undecorated, round-bodied vessels with slightly concave necks. Mediaeval—comparable to Dun Vulan Phase 7 dated to the 14th/16th centuries AD.

These ceramic phases provide a chronological framework within which the development of the site can be interpreted. However, any interpretation must be tempered with an understanding of the residual and intrusive materials found throughout the depositional sequence. Whilst a significant number of sherds from the same vessels were found within different parts of the stratigraphic sequence, the nature and extent of this problem is not yet understood. More detailed analysis, including refitting and spatial analysis of sherd distributions, is required to resolve these issues.

Plant Remains

Helen Smith

Introduction

Bulk soil samples were taken from seven contexts on the site for the retrieval of plant remains and other environmental material. One sample was taken from a mineralized deposit (context 114) associated with the early Iron Age 'simple' Atlantic roundhouse (phase 1). Samples were also taken from the aisled roundhouse (phase 2) and from an accumulation of occupation material (context 110) that was deposited across the interior of the roundhouse. The interior of the structure was subdivided, by radial piers, into a series of compartments. The samples were taken from the centre of six of the compartments, labelled A–F in a clockwise direction, starting with the compartment immediately to the west of the south-facing entrance.

The central area of the structure contained a hearth box, but there were no samples available from this feature. Questions of interest related to possible differences between the plant remains from the phase 1 and phase 2 deposits, and the possibility of internal differences, in the radial arrangement of the aisled roundhouse, being reflected in the plant remains collected from the individual compartments.

Methods

The samples varied in size, ranging from 18 to 26 litres. Samples were processed on site using a water separation/flotation tank (Kenward, Hall and Jones 1980) where light material was collected as coarse and fine flots (1 mm and 300 micron mesh sieves) and heavy material as residue (1 mm mesh). The samples were examined using a low-powered binocular microscope at ×15–×80 magnification. Fine flots were scanned for their contents and heavy residues were sorted. Identifications were made using a modern seed collection in the University of Bournemouth and the Institute of Archaeology, University College of London, and with reference to illustrations and descriptions in Godwin (1975). Identifications were often limited to genus or family owing to the poor preservation of much of the material. Details of modern habitats were obtained from Stace (1997); Pankhurst and Mullin (1991); Clapham, Tutin and Moore (1989) and Rose (1981). The nomenclature is according to Stace (1997).

Results

Charred and uncharred plant remains were recovered from the coarse flots of the bulk samples (no remains were recovered from the fine flots or the heavy residues). In all cases the number and range of items recovered from the samples was extremely limited and the preservation of the plant remains was poor. The assemblage included cereal grains and the seeds of wild species plus the charred remains of animal dung. The contents of individual samples are listed in Table 4.1. The densities of plant remains were recorded per sample, thus enabling comparison between different contexts and samples. Both the number of cereal grains per litre and the number of items per litre (excluding nonquantifiable fragments of grain, modern seed and dung) have been calculated.

Resolution of the data

In all samples there was a limited quantity and range of plant remains and the state of preservation of the material recovered was poor. Some of the cereals have a vesicular outer surface, which could indicate extremely hot temperatures during the carbonization of the material. In such circumstances, some taxa may have been lost due to preservational biases, which might account in part for the limited range and

The Excavation of Iron Age and Later Structures at Alt Chrisal T17, Barra, 1996–1999

Table 4.1 Alt Chrisal: identified plant remains by context.

Hordeum vulgare							
grains (hulled)	6	3	2		5	5	2
indet (frags)	7					12	1
Chenopdium sp.					1*		
Polygonum sp.			1			3	
Polygonum sp. (small)						3	
Apiaceae							
cf. *Conium maculatum*		1					
Plantago sp.						1	
Galium sp.						1	
Asteraceae							
2 species represented			2				
Carex sp. (biconvex)			1			2	
Carex sp. (trigonous)		1				1	
Poaceae							
several species represented						2	1
Indeterminate	2	6	4	2	5		
Stalk	1						1
Bud	1						
Dung fragments		10					
Cereal grains per l. deposit	0.27	0.12	0.11	0	0.23	0.2	0.10
No items per l. deposit	0.45	0.42	0.56	0.08	0.45	0.72	0.19

S.A.R. = Simple Atlantic Roundhouse
*possibly modern seed

quantity of material in the assemblage. Postdepositional factors resulting in preservational biases might also account for the limited quantity and range of material, such as the mechanism and speed of incorporation of the material into the deposits (trampling and maintenance activities associated with an occupation surface), and any postburial disturbances (rabbit burrowing).

Most of the seeds of wild taxa have only been identified to generic level, due to the poor preservation of the plant material. When identifications are limited to the generic level, the information relating to the ecological requirements of the plants is limited to only the most general descriptions of the habitats. This is the case with the plant remains recovered from the Alt Chrisal samples.

Crop plants
Barley (*Hordeum* sp.) is the most frequently represented cereal in the samples, from both phase 1 (the early Iron Age, 'simple' Atlantic roundhouse) and phase 2 (the aisled roundhouse). Where identification of the grain was possible, barley was of the hulled variety. No rachis internodes were recovered, which may have indicated whether the two-row species (*Hordeum distchon*) or the six-row species (*Hordeum vulgare*) were present. Twisted (lateral) grains were identified, however, which indicates the presence of six-row barley, but there were insufficient grains to determine the actual ratio of asymmetrical to symmetrical grains and hence whether only six-row barley or both six-row and two-row barley were present (based

on the 2:1 ratio of twisted and straight grains in six-row barley). No other cereals were recovered from the samples from Alt Chrisal.

Wild species
The number and range of seeds representing wild taxa is limited. The wild taxa include plants that are common on arable land, disturbed and waste ground, and/or grassland and heath. Taxa identified as knotweeds (*Polygonum* spp.) bedstraw (*Galium* sp.), plantain (*Plantago* sp.), the daisy family (Asteraceae) and Apiaceae (cf. Hemlock (*Conium maculatum*) could represent vegetation from arable fields and/or disturbed and trampled places.

Seeds of taxa associated with grassland and heathland include sedges (*Carex* spp.) and the grasses (Poaceae). Plantain (*Plantago* sp.) possibly grew in grassland.

Materials collected for fuel
Many of the samples contained charcoal, some of which represents fragments of small diameter round wood. The wood of heather and other heathland shrubs was traditionally used as fuel, although these shrubs grow in areas where peat and turf are cut for fuel, and so may have become charred incidentally during peat burning. Other materials may have been used as fuel, such as dung. In one sample, from compartment A fragments of dung were recovered that were charred and appeared to represent dung of sheep/goat. These may have been accidentally or deliberately imported.

Distribution of the plant remains

Phase 1: Early Iron Age, 'simple' Atlantic roundhouse

Only one sample was taken from the phase 1 deposits, a mineralized deposit (context 114) associated with the early Iron Age, 'simple' Atlantic roundhouse. This was located near to the southern side of the roundhouse (in the vicinity of 'compartment A', in the overlying structure). Very few carbonized plant remains were recovered from the phase 1 sample. These include six barley grains, a stalk and bud and two indeterminate seeds (Table 4.1).

Phase 2: Aisled roundhouse

Very few items were recovered from the samples taken from the compartments inside the aisled roundhouse from the occupation layer, context 110. Barley is present in all of the samples, together with a small number and range of weed seeds (Table 4.1).

Overall, in the phase 2 deposits (context 110), there is very little difference in the material recovered from the six different compartments sampled (A–F). The highest density of items occurs in the sample from compartment E (0.72/litre), compared to 0.08–0.56/litre for the other samples. The density of cereal grains in all samples is low (ranging from 0 to 0.23/litre) and the range and number of seeds of wild taxa is greatest in sample E although the total number is still quite low.

Conclusion

In general, very few plant remains were recovered from the phase 1 or phase 2 samples and these provide little evidence of activities related to the use of either structure. Similarly, on the basis of the plant remains recovered, it is not possible to suggest any significant difference between the phase 1 and phase 2 deposits.

The paucity and poor preservation of the plant remains recovered from the samples creates a number of other problems relating to the interpretation of the assemblage. Such problems hinder an understanding of the modes of arrival of the botanical material on the site, and limit the interpretations relating to the utilization of plant resources, the location of arable land, crop husbandry practices and crop processing activities that might otherwise be gleaned from the plant remains.

Hulled barley (*Hordeum* sp.), including six-row barley (*H. vulgare*), is the only cereal crop represented at Alt Chrisal. The grain is in association with a small number and range of weed seeds and charcoal fragments. The type and proportions of chaff and weed seeds incorporated with cereal grain might reveal something about the stages of crop processing represented and as such might provide information about the agricultural techniques employed (Hillman 1981). However, the small numbers of cereal grains and weed seeds, and the absence of cereal chaff within the samples recovered from the site, limit any interpretations related to the use and consumption of plant resources.

Archaeologically, charred grains accompanied by few weed seeds might have resulted from accidents during crop processing, such as the parching of grain prior to threshing and winnowing, or in cooking. The weeds might represent waste from cleaning operations or contaminants remaining with the crop. The few occurrences of contaminants may also reflect differential destruction and/or the poor preservation of the material, as a result of the conditions of charring (Boardman and Jones 1990; Wilson 1984). Most of the plant material is exploded and has a vesicular outer surface that would suggest poor preservation of the less robust species and components during charring.

The predominant habitats indicated by the weed seeds are damp and disturbed ground and cultivated fields: the grasses (Poaceae), sedges (*Carex* spp.), plantain (*Plantago* sp.), goosefoots (*Chenopodium* sp.), knotweeds (*Polygonum* spp.), bedstraws (*Galium* sp.), carrot family (Apiaceae) and daisy family (Asteraceae). These might indicate cultivation on wetter land typical of the blackland or peatland, where the site is situated, or the low-lying areas of machair that are prone to flooding in the winter and spring months and/or the importation of materials from the heathland.

It is possible that the weed seeds recovered from the occupational deposits do not represent contaminants of the cereal crop. These seeds may represent the deliberate collection of materials for other purposes (such as roofing materials or flooring) or they may have arrived at the site incidentally, on feet, clothes or animals or incorporated within the deliberately collected materials (such as turf or peat collected as fuel). Distinguishing between these different categories and potential routes is problematic without more detailed habitat information. Plant material might also have been removed at a number of different stages in the crop processing sequence, which would in turn be difficult to identify without larger numbers of remains of both cultivated and wild plants. Furthermore, the overlap that is possible between these different activities (i.e. the burning of crop-processing waste and/or the accidental or deliberate burning of building materials and rubbish in fires which might be built of peat or turf) means that interpretation of the data is limited.

Discussion

At other Iron Age sites on the southern Outer Hebrides, where plant remains have been collected, the material is very similar to that recovered at Alt Chrisal. At Dun Vulan, South Uist (Smith 1999), Kildonan, South Uist (Valamoti 1989), Hornish Point,

South Uist and Baleshare, North Uist (Jones, in press) hulled six-row barley is the dominant cereal species represented, with oats, rye and wheat present in very low numbers. In the samples from Alt Chrisal it is possible that the low number of items accounts for the difference in cereal types present.

Historically, 'black oat', 'small oat' or 'bristle oat' (*Avena strig.osa*) was a traditional crop of the Hebrides, along with Common oat (*A. sativa*) and rye (*Secale cereale*). Wheat was not considered to be suited to cultivation on the Outer Hebrides, although there were attempts to reintroduce it in historical times. Traditionally the barley has been grown on blackland, peatland and machair, although the blackland is generally better suited to productive barley cultivation than the machair, despite a recent emphasis on the machair as good agricultural land (Grant 1979). Unlike the machair, which is easily exhausted and prone to destabilization without periods of fallow, blackland can tolerate continual cropping (Smith 1994)

Ethnographic studies (Smith 1994) and historical data indicate that the cultivation potential and husbandry requirements of each land type are quite specific. Blackland, which is more loamy in character, is least prone to exhaustion if fertilized sufficiently using dung (or seaweed, if dung is in short supply), and can tolerate almost constant cropping. The blackland can, however, be patchy, shallow and/or wet. Historically, such characteristics precluded the use of a plough (and/or social factors denied access), which determined/dictated the need to work the ground through the labour intensive methods of hand cultivation (Smith 1994). Traditionally, the grain crop, barley, was preferably grown on the good areas of blackland in the first year of a rotation and received all of the available phosphate-rich dung. Oats were grown in the succeeding one or two years, without additional manure.

In contrast, the machair is easier to work with a plough, owing to the open expanses that it generally forms. The calcareous sandy ground is, however, easily exhausted after the first year of cultivation and periods of fallow and fertilization are necessary to produce a decent crop and avoid destabilization of the ground. Other problems related to the cultivation of machair include low levels of organic matter, a deficiency of nitrogen, phosphorus, copper and manganese and alkalinity above the optimum for most crops (Grant 1979). Although the water content of the machair can be low in dry periods, some areas are prone to waterlogging or flooding when rainfall is high and can become inaccessible as a result (Grant 1979; Boyd 1979, 1990). The use of fertilizer can provide essential organic matter and supplement the deficient elements. Seaweed was used preferentially, and, if available, dung was also used (Smith 1994). The machair was more usually treated as an outfield,

with two or three years of cultivation followed by a period of fallow, the length of which depended on land capability and availability. Oat crops were most commonly associated with the machair, although barley and rye were sometimes grown, with barley always planted in the first year of the rotation.

In recent times, an emphasis has been placed on the machair as the best arable land. This is, however, more a reflection of a change of emphasis in the nature of farming, that is, the cultivation of barley as a grain crop on the blackland has been abandoned in favour of the cultivation of fodder crops (mixed barley, oats and rye) on the more vulnerable but easily worked machair (Smith 1994). This practice has been facilitated by the decreased demand for fertilizer on the blackland and by the fact that fodder crops require less fertilizer than the grain crop (Smith 1994). From an archaeological perspective, it would be interesting to find evidence relating to the nature of the arable land used for cereal cultivation, as this would throw light on the farming strategies adopted, the emphasis of animal versus arable husbandry and in turn might elucidate more complex issues relating to the location of settlements within the landscapes. Unfortunately the assemblage from Alt Chrisal is too small to address such questions. The environmental evidence recovered from contemporary sites, in combination with more botanical evidence in general, is likely to provide a better understanding of the use of the highly varied landscape in the Outer Hebrides.

Flaked Stone

Caroline Wickham-Jones and John Pouncett

Introduction

A total of 172 pieces of flaked stone were recovered from the excavations at Alt Chrisal. Only 12 pieces of flaked stone were recovered from the deposits associated with the aisled roundhouse and the underlying structure. In contrast, 125 pieces of flaked stone were recovered from the deposits associated with the abandonment and reuse of the site. The remainder of the assemblage was derived from the spoil ejected from rabbit burrows.

Raw materials
During the course of excavation, 166 pieces of worked flint were recovered. Where pieces retained cortex, the rounded and abraded nature of the cortex suggests that the raw material might have been derived from beach pebbles. Indeed, three flint pebbles were recovered from Alt Chrisal T17. While these would have afforded little in the way of workable flint, they do indicate the nature of the raw materials used. Although flint does not outcrop locally, flint nodules are found

as glacial erratics within the local boulder clay (Peacock 1991). Flint nodules may be found as beach pebbles where the sea has scoured out deposits of boulder clay. A number of sources of beach flint have been identified on the island of Barra (Dickens n.d.).

Although the majority of the assemblage is comprised of worked flint, a single piece of worked coarse stone and five pieces of worked mudstone were recovered from the site. Whilst the derivation of the coarse stone is uncertain, sources of mudstone have been identified close to the Mesolithic and Neolithic site of An Corran at Staffin Bay on the Isle of Skye (Saville and Miket 1994). These raw materials may be indicative of contact with the Inner Hebrides. However, the presence of glacial erratics derived from the marine troughs flanking the Outer Hebridean archipelago and the Inner Hebrides is well documented within the Western Isles (Peacock 1991). It is likely that these pieces of flaked stone, as with the worked flint, were produced from raw materials derived from glacial erratics.

Condition

The majority of the assemblage of flaked stone was unabraded. Only 14 pieces showed signs of abrasion that could not be attributed to use wear. Approximately one-third of the assemblage of flaked stone was patinated. The conditions leading to the development of a patina are complex and varied. One factor, however, is exposure to light. Accordingly, the pieces of patinated stone may have been exposed on the ground surface for a prolonged period of time. The low frequency of abraded pieces would suggest that any exposed material remained relatively undisturbed prior to burial. One of the pieces of flaked stone shows evidence of two separate episodes of working. Additional flakes had been removed from the flake-scarred, patinated surface of the piece of flint. Similar pieces of reworked stone have been identified within the lithic assemblage derived from earlier excavations at Alt Chrisal T17 (Wickham-Jones 1995). Twenty pieces of burnt flint were recovered during the course of excavation. The presence of burnt material is unsurprising considering the large number of temporary hearths within the upper levels of the wheelhouse.

Core working

Four cores were identified within the lithic assemblage. These included two bipolar cores (e.g. Fig. 4.38.6) and two prepared platform cores (e.g. Fig. 4.38.10). One of the prepared platform cores shows evidence for microlithic retouch or use wear along the edge of one of the 'striking platforms'. This core may have been reused as a scraper or as a strike-a-light. Approximately 30% of the flakes recovered from the site have been struck from bipolar cores. This technique of core working would have been ideally suited to a lithic industry based upon the production of stone tools

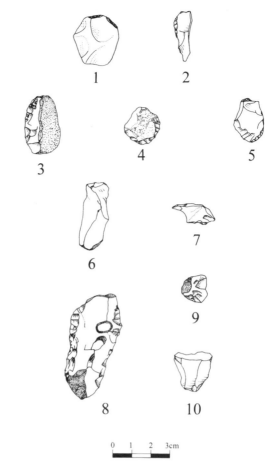

Figure 4.38 Flaked stone.

from beach pebbles. The flint pebbles recovered during the course of excavation would have yielded little in the way of workable flint. However, the character and composition of the lithic assemblage would appear to suggest that these pebbles are typical of the raw materials used at Alt Chrisal T17. The majority of the flint flakes recovered from the site are associated with the removal of cortex, rather than the trimming of stone tools. Only a handful of flakes exceeded 30 mm in length or width. The majority of flakes were short and squat; very few blade-like flakes were recovered from the site. This is unsurprising given the nature of the raw materials upon which the local lithic industry was based. In addition to the flint flakes, 47 pieces of miscellaneous debitage were recovered from the site. This material was probably derived from the reduction of flint cores or the testing of flint nodules.

Lithic traditions

Two distinct stone-working traditions can be identified within the assemblage. First, that based upon the production of retouched pieces. Seven scrapers were identified within the assemblage of worked stone, including two end scrapers (e.g. Fig. 4.38.5), two side scrapers (e.g. Fig. 4.38.3) and a fine thumbnail scraper (Fig. 4.38.4). One of the scrapers was manufactured from a fine-grained mudstone; coarse flakes had been removed from the dorsal surface of the piece of stone to create a crude scraper (Fig. 4.38.1). Other retouched pieces included three retouched flakes (e.g. Figs. 4.38.2 and 7), the broken base of a small bifacial leaf point (Fig. 4.38.9) and a plano-convex knife (Fig. 4.38.8). These pieces of worked stone, characteristic of the Neolithic or Bronze Age, were mostly derived from deposits associated with the reuse of the site after abandonment. Only one piece of retouched worked stone, the crude mudstone scraper, was found within 'prehistoric' contexts. Secondly, that based upon the production of strike-a-lights. Ten pieces of flaked stone show use wear, along one or more edges, characteristic of use as a strike-a-light. The majority of the strike-a-lights were recovered from the early modern enclosure or from the spoil ejected from rabbit burrows.

Discussion

The assemblage of flaked stone recovered from Alt Chrisal T17 is relatively small, however, it is much larger than those recovered from other comparable sites in the Outer Hebrides. Only a single piece of struck flint was recovered from the excavations at Dun Vulan (Parker Pearson *et al.* 1999b: 230–32). Similarly, only four pieces of flaked stone were recovered from the aisled roundhouse at Allasdale (Young 1952). The small size of the lithic assemblages from such sites no doubt reflects the fact that flint was no longer a particularly important resource. The vast majority of the pieces of flaked stone were derived from the deposits associated with the later occupation of the site. While the use of stone implements would have continued into the Iron Age and beyond, the majority of the assemblage appears to predate the stone-built structures at the site. Just under half of the assemblage was derived from the revetted enclosure and early modern enclosure adjacent to the Iron Age roundhouse. The abundance of worked stone within these deposits may be indicative of the use of the enclosures for the purpose of cultivation. Many of the retouched pieces are intrusive and appear to be broadly contemporary with the 'Neolithic' bowl recovered from the deposits associated with the Atlantic roundhouse. It is likely that this material represents an earlier phase of activity at the site, an episode not represented in the stratigraphic sequence. Any speculation about the nature of earlier 'prehistoric' activity of the site should be tempered with an awareness of the extensive evidence for Neolithic and Bronze settlement elsewhere in the locality (Foster 1995).

Coarse Stone

John Pouncett

Twenty-nine pieces of coarse stone were recovered from Alt Chrisal T17. The size of this assemblage is broadly comparable to that from Dun Vulan (Parker Pearson *et al.* 1999b: 230–32), but is considerably smaller than that from A' Cheardach Mhor (Young and Richardson 1959: 150, 156). Stone tools were manufactured from a variety of raw materials. Over half of the assemblage was manufactured from Moinian psammite or Torridonian sandstone. While neither rock outcrops locally, both may be found as glacial erratics. Sedimentary and metasedimentary rocks derived from the Scottish mainland have been identified in abundance on the Pleistocene beaches of the Outer Hebrides (Peacock 1984). The raw materials used at Alt Chrisal were perhaps derived from the relict beach at Cliad, to the north of the Tangaval Peninsula. Two of the pieces of coarse stone are burnt on one surface, suggesting localized contact with heat. These may have been removed from the ring of stones defining the circular hearth associated with the secondary occupation of the aisled roundhouse.

A range of tools was identified on the basis of morphology and use wear characteristics:

1. Hammer stones: larger cobble tools with coarse abrasion to one or more edges.
2. Pounders: cobble tools with minor abrasion at one or both ends of the long axis of the pebble.
3. Rubbers: cobble tools with one or more worn surfaces or facets.
4. Miscellaneous: including loom weights, manuports, split pebbles, stone discs and whetstones.

While the majority of the pieces of coarse stone are unremarkable, a number are particularly worthy of note. First, a 'square' stone rubber with four bevelled and carefully maintained working surfaces was found within the deposits associated with the structure beneath the aisled roundhouse. Secondly, one of the cobble tools from the tertiary depositional sequence had been reused as a sharpening stone. Thirdly, a loom weight manufactured from a piece of granite was found within the spoil ejected from rabbit burrows. Fourthly, one of the stone rubbers found within the deposits associated with the stone revetment had been used in a manner that created a ridge around the circumference of the pebble. Finally, two conjoining pieces of a split pebble were found within the primary depositional sequence behind pier 2 and within cell E. There is little differentiation in the distribution of coarse stone objects or raw materials throughout the depositional sequence, suggesting continuity in both the patterns of procurement and usage.

Atlantic roundhouse

3617 context 114. A mudstone rubber measuring 61 × 58 mm with a thickness of 29 mm. Square, highly polished pebble with four bevelled, heavily abraded edges.

3618 context 184. A granite rubber measuring 154 × 87 mm with a thickness of 31 mm. Broken fragment of a rounded beach pebble with a prominent flattened surface.

Aisled roundhouse

1987 context 109. A sandstone rubber measuring 64 × 41 mm with a thickness of 25 mm. Rounded beach pebble with a well defined flattened surface. The edges of the pebble are rounded through use.

2150 context 183. A piece of burnt sandstone measuring 85 × 67 mm with a thickness of 38 mm. Rounded beach pebble with burnt edges and traces of soot or an organic residue on the upper surface. The lower surface of the pebble appears to be slightly flattened.

Primary depositional sequence
3575 context 110. A sandstone rubber measuring 86 × 71 mm with a thickness of 63 mm. Rounded beach pebble with one flattened end.

3596 context 237. A gneiss hammer stone measuring 156 × 99 mm with a thickness of 72 mm. Rounded beach pebble with coarse abrasion at one end.

3604 context 110. A split sandstone pebble measuring 59 × 42 mm with a thickness of 15 mm. Broken fragment of a rounded beach pebble that conjoins with 3606.

3606 context 247. A split sandstone pebble measuring 95 × 80 mm with a thickness of 46 mm. Broken fragment of a rounded beach pebble, with minor abrasion at one end, that conjoins with 3604.

3610 context 110. A sandstone rubber measuring 99 × 70 mm with a thickness of 37 mm. Rounded beach pebble with abrasion at both ends of the long axis.

Secondary depositional sequence
2381 context 102. A quartzite pounder measuring 105 × 67 mm with a thickness of 45 mm. Rounded beach pebble with marked abrasion at one end and slight (natural?) abrasion at the other.

2911 context 102. A gneiss pounder measuring 82 × 48 mm with a thickness of 28 mm. Rounded beach pebble with slight abrasion at one end.

2932 context 102. A quartzite pounder measuring 53 × 44 mm with a thickness of 30 mm. Rounded beach pebble with slight abrasion at both ends of the long axis.

2945 context 102. A quartzite manuport measuring 59 × 51 mm with a thickness of 27 mm. Rounded beach pebble with no obvious signs of abrasion or wear.

3193 context 102. A quartzite pounder measuring 91 × 74 mm with a thickness of 44 mm. Rounded beach pebble with abrasion at both ends, resulting in the formation of two distinct worn surfaces. At one end the ridge between the two surfaces runs parallel to the circumference of the pebble; at the other it runs at a slight tangent.

3400 context 102. A quartzite pounder measuring 73 × 64 mm with a thickness of 36 mm. Rounded beach pebble with minor abrasion on all edges. The upper surface and the edges of the pebble have been slightly burnt.

Tertiary depositional sequence
1074 context 66. A quartzite pounder measuring 106 × 76 mm with a thickness of 46 mm. Rounded beach pebble with minor abrasion at both ends of the long axis. A partially flattened surface has formed at one end of the pebble.

1183 context 66. A granite disc measuring 63 × 55 mm with a thickness of 14 mm. Flat irregular piece of granite with a highly polished surface formed by a series of fine, concentric striations.

1556 context 66. A quartzite rubber measuring 106 × 75 mm with a thickness of 52 mm. Rounded beach pebble with one flattened surface and minor abrasion to both ends. Fine striations run parallel to the long axis of the worn surface of the pebble.

1690 context 66. A micaceous psammite rubber measuring 82 × 57 mm with a thickness of 33 mm. Rounded beach pebble with a well defined flattened surface.

2089 context 66. A granite hammer stone measuring 168 × 101 mm with a thickness of 76 mm. Large tapering beach pebble with coarse abrasion at the narrow end.

2226 context 66. A quartzite sharpening stone measuring 95 × 83 mm with a thickness of 48 mm. Rounded beach pebble with minor abrasion to all edges. A shallow groove has been cut or worn into the polished upper surface of the pebble.

Stone revetment
1864 context 65. A granite rubber measuring 101 × 93 mm with a thickness of 48 mm. Rounded beach pebble with two working surfaces. The edges of both surfaces have been heavily abraded, creating a ridge around the circumference of the pebble.

2094 context 47. A quartzite rubber measuring 76 × 56 mm with a thickness of 29 mm. Rounded beach pebble with a slightly flattened surface and one burnt edge.

Early modern structures
96 context 10. A perforated whetstone measuring 29 × 27 mm with a thickness of 12 mm. Broken fragment of a micaceous psammite whetstone with convex surfaces, the profile of the lower surface being more pronounced. The internal edge of the whetstone appears to have been cut by a circular countersunk hole.

536 context 4. A quartzite pounder measuring 103 × 62 mm with a thickness of 43 mm. Rounded beach pebble with marked abrasion at one end and minor abrasion at the other. The upper surface of the pebble has been slightly polished suggesting reuse as a sharpening stone.

Unstratified and intrusive
758 context 2. A granite loom weight measuring 99 × 91 mm with a thickness of 54 mm. Irregular wedge-shaped loom weight with a bulbous butt defined by a pecked and worn groove.

3507 context 241. A granite hammer stone measuring 134 × 115 mm with a thickness of 71 mm. Large rounded beach pebble with coarse abrasion at one end.

3567 context 243. A gneiss hammer stone measuring 157 × 112 mm with a thickness of 71 mm. Large rounded beach pebble with coarse abrasion to one end.

3585 context 254. A granite pounder measuring 104 × 49 mm with a thickness of 35 mm. Elongated rounded beach pebble with one partially flattened surface and minor abrasions at both ends of the long axis.

Metalwork

Emma Gowans

A total of 113 metal objects were recovered from the site at Alt Chrisal T17. These included 109 iron objects, a copper alloy brooch, a copper alloy buckle, a brass shotgun cartridge and a piece of folded lead. The vast majority of the metalwork was derived from the deposits associated with the abandonment and reuse of the site. Very few metal objects were found within the deposits associated with the aisled roundhouse or the underlying structure. Approximately 75% of the pieces of metalwork are fragments of iron nails. The remainder of the metal objects are catalogued below with the exception of one piece of iron that disintegrated before recording took place. A number of the pieces of metalwork are worthy of special note. For instance, a gin trap and a metal rod, used to set traps, were found within the deposits associated with the secondary occupation of the aisled roundhouse and the abandonment of the site respectively, indicating rabbit disturbance at a considerable depth within the interior of the site. Furthermore, part of the body of an 18th or 19th-century cauldron was also found within the deposits associated with the abandonment of the aisled roundhouse. A number of other iron plates and fittings thought to be part of this cauldron were recovered from the upper levels of the site or from the spoil ejected from rabbit burrows. The widespread distribution of these objects is a further illustration of the extent to which rabbits have disturbed the site.

Aisled roundhouse

Secondary depositional sequence
1714 context 102. A gin trap measuring 300 × 132 mm, with extensive corrosion to the trig.ger plate and the jaws. The trap is constructed from a series of separate components connected to a base plate: the trigger plate is mounted on a single rivet; the spring is secured in place by a square-headed bolt; and the jaws, each mounted separately, are attached by two split pins.

2877 context 98. A fragment of a copper alloy brooch measuring 29 × 11 mm with a plate thickness of 1.5 mm. The brooch is comprised of an elongated plate with rounded corners that is upturned at either end. One of the upturned ends survives intact and is slightly thicker than the plate, measuring 3 mm. Unfortunately, the brooch is too corroded and fragmentary to allow further discussion.

After abandonment. 1215 context 74. An iron stud with a rectangular head measuring 19 × 16 mm. The shaft of the stud, 17 mm in length, is bent flat against the rectangular head.

1262 context 74. A concave sheet of iron, possibly part of the body of an iron cauldron, measuring 138 × 120 mm with a thickness of 4 mm.

2474 context 74. An iron rod, 298 mm long and 5.3 mm in diameter, probably used to push gin traps down rabbit burrows.

2489 context 74. An iron bolt, 87 mm long and 8 mm in diameter, with a rectangular head measuring 28 × 23 mm.

Tertiary depositional sequence
465 context 66. Four corroded pieces of iron that possibly form part of the iron cauldron. First, a broken piece of a flat rectangular plate, possibly a cauldron fitting, measuring 128 × 43 mm with a thickness of 4 mm. Secondly, a broken fragment of a perforated concave/convex plate measuring 94 × 36 mm with a thickness of 4 mm. A small hole, 7 mm in diameter, has been drilled through one end of this rectangular plate. Finally, two amorphous lumps of corroded iron measuring 47 × 33 mm and 59 × 50 mm respectively.

809 context 66. A fragment of an iron knife blade, close to the join between the blade and the tang, measuring 14 × 14 mm with a thickness of 2 mm.

1114 context 66. An angular fitting or bracket made from a single sheet of iron measuring 68 × 35 mm, with a trapezoidal cross section tapering from 7–5.5 mm in thickness.

1458 context 97. A perforated iron plate measuring 166 × 35 mm with a thickness of 4 mm. Distorted, elongated iron plate with rounded ends. Although extensively corroded, a small circular hole, 6 mm in diameter, can be identified at one end of the plate.

1700 context 66. A fragment of an irregular iron plate measuring 54 × 46 mm with a thickness of 4 mm The slight concave/convex curve of the plate suggests that it might be part of the body of the iron cauldron.

Stone revetment. 1300 context 47. An iron bolt, measuring 51 × 14.3 mm, with a hexagonal head 16 mm across. A fragment of a square nut, 33 × 33 mm, is corroded onto the shaft of the bolt.

1614 context 67. A fragment of a sub rectangular iron plate, measuring 58 × 23 mm with a thickness of 2.8 mm. Two ridges run along the middle of the plate, parallel to its long axis. This plate is possibly one of the fittings for the iron cauldron.

Early modern structures. 15 context 12. An elongated D-shaped copper alloy buckle measuring 31 × 22 mm with a thickness of 2 mm. Whilst the pin is missing from the buckle, the cross bar remains intact.

136 context 4. A fragment of an iron knife blade measuring 23 × 9 mm with a thickness of 4 mm.

146 context 4. A fragment of the rim of the iron cauldron constructed from a sheet of iron measuring 36 × 36 mm with a thickness of 6.5 mm.

Unstratified or intrusive. 697 context 2. A piece of folded lead measuring 22.5 × 11.6 mm with a thickness of 5 mm.

707 context 2. A fragment of an iron knife blade, with the tip and tang missing, measuring 18 × 15 mm with a thickness of 3 mm.

712 context 2. A fragment of an irregular iron plate measuring 95 × 62 mm. The plate is constructed from a single sheet of iron, 2 mm in thickness, folded double and hammered flat.

750 context 2. Three fragments of an iron plate (38 × 28 mm, 41 × 29 mm and 120 × 47 mm) constructed from a sheet 1.3 mm thick folded double.

800 context 2. Two irregular fragments of a convex iron plate, possibly one of the fittings for the iron cauldron. The fragments, measuring 43 × 40 mm and 45 × 30 mm, both have a sheet thickness of 4 mm.

821 context 2. A fragment of an iron 'hook', measuring 23 × 16 mm with a rectangular cross section approximately 10 × 11 mm, probably the link securing the handle to the main body of the iron cauldron.

827 context 2. An amorphous piece of iron measuring 38 × 19 mm with a thickness of 9 mm.

886 context 2. A fragment of an iron plate measuring 34 × 26 mm with a thickness of 5 mm.

1213 context 2. A fragment of an iron knife blade, with the tip and tang missing, measuring 43 × 17 mm with a thickness of 4.3 mm (tapering to 3.2 mm).

1283 context 2. A fragment of a perforated iron plate, measuring 30 × 26 mm, constructed from a single sheet of iron, 2.8 mm thick, folded double. A hole, 16 mm in diameter, has been drilled through the midpoint of the plate.

1769 context 2. A brass 12 bore shotgun cartridge, 22 mm in diameter, made by Eley of London and bearing the trademark EBL. Although the sleeve is largely missing, part of the brass sleeve is preserved between the shell casing and the cork wadding at the base of the cartridge.

Early Modern Pottery

Patrick Foster

A small assemblage of early modern pottery was recovered during the course of excavation at Alt Chrisal T17. The assemblage was comprised of 55 sherds (total mass 855 g), with an average sherd mass of 15.5 g, representing a minimum of 14 vessels. Ceramic wares, including salt-glazed white, stone or earthenwares, tin glazed white-ware and lead glazed reduced-ware, were differentiated on the basis of fabric type and surface treatment. A number of decorated sherds were also identified, including those decorated with underglaze transfers and hand-painted designs. Whilst similarities were noted with the assemblage of early modern pottery from the excavation of the blackhouse at Alt Chrisal (Foster 1995: 117–18), direct comparison of the assemblages was not attempted. More detailed analysis will be undertaken at a later date as part of a reinterpretation of Post Medieval settlement in the locality. Sherds derived from the same vessels, including conjoining sherds, were found both within and between contexts. For instance, two conjoining sherds from the neck of a stoneware water bottle were found within the tertiary depositional sequence. Similarly, sherds from a large earthenware bowl were found within the tertiary depositional sequence, the revetted enclosure and the spoil ejected from rabbit burrows. While the majority of the early modern pottery was found within deposits associated with the abandonment and reuse of the site, a single piece of salt-glazed earthenware was found within the primary depositional sequence behind pier 2. The deposits beneath the rubble blocking of the aisle, between the wall circuit and each of the radial piers, have been heavily disturbed by rabbit activity. As such, the presence of early modern pottery within the lower, 'prehistoric', levels of the site is unsurprising.

Glass

Emma Gowans and John Pouncett

Bottle glass

Twenty-one pieces of bottle glass with a total mass of 146 g were recovered during the course of excavation. The bottle glass represents a minimum of two vessels, which may be distinguished on the basis of colour. While three broad groups of glass thickness (1.5–2 mm, 2 mm and 2–3 mm) can be identified, further differentiation is impossible due to the degree of variation in glass thickness exhibited by a single bottle. The assemblage of bottle glass included fragments of a broad-shouldered bottle with an upright neck, possibly a sherry or port bottle. A twist stressed within the neck of the bottle would suggest that this vessel was blown and not moulded. The outer surface of each of the pieces of bottle glass is abraded or scratched. Only a handful of pieces show signs of wear on the inner face. It can be suggested that the pieces of bottle glass with internal wear are those that have been subject to disturbance and movement after breakage or deposition. The vast majority of the bottle glass is derived from the deposits associated with the reuse of the site after abandonment or the spoil ejected from rabbit burrows, however two pieces were found within the lower levels of the site. A piece of pale blue glass was recovered from the deposits associated with the structure beneath the aisled roundhouse, and a piece of pale green glass was found within the primary depositional sequence behind pier 6. Both pieces are further indication of the depth to which rabbits have disturbed the site, and the extent to which burrowing has resulted in the migration of artifact.

Window glass

Eleven pieces of window glass, weighing a total of 21 g, were recovered from the site at Alt Chrisal. The assemblage of window glass represents a minimum of two panes of glass, 1.75 mm and 2.25 mm in thickness. Whilst a single piece of a third possible pane of glass was identified, its thickness is greater than that of normal window glass. This small splinter of glass may in fact be a piece of bottle glass. The vast majority of the window glass was derived from the tertiary depositional sequence or from the spoil ejected from rabbit burrows, however, a single piece of window glass was recovered from the uppermost deposit (context 10) within the early modern barn.

Calcined Bone

Eleven pieces of calcined bone, weighing a total of 21 g, were recovered during the course of excavation. None of the fragments of burnt bone were large enough, or sufficiently well-preserved, to allow identi-fication or speciation. Two of the pieces were highly fragmented. Five pieces of calcined bone were derived from the circular hearth associated with the secondary occupation of the aisled roundhouse. Similarly, a single fragment of burnt bone was found within one of the hearth sequences associated with the primary occupation of the aisled roundhouse. The remainder of the calcined bone was derived from the primary and tertiary depositional sequences.

Small Finds

Emma Gowans

Spearhead

A corroded but well-preserved iron spearhead, measuring a total length of approximately 116 mm, was recovered from a dump of ash associated with the formal hearth built upon the weathered surface of the secondary depositional sequence (Fig. 4.39). This spearhead has a leaf-shaped blade, measuring 74 × 27 mm with a thickness of approximately 3 mm, and a contiguous clefted socket, 42 mm in length and 17 × 15 mm in cross-section. As there are so few spearheads found in Iron Age contexts in Scotland comparison is difficult, however, the spearhead is comparable

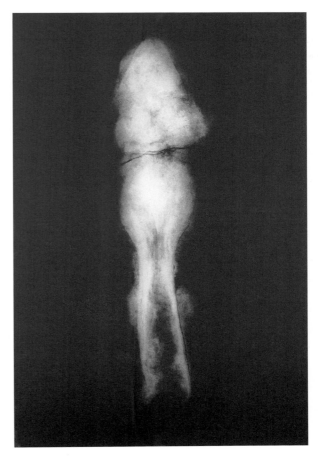

Figure 4.39 The leaf shaped spearhead.

to Swanton group C1 (Swanton 1973). Group C1 is described as a small leaf-shaped blade of the simplest kind that measures between 100 and 200 mm long. There are a variety of profiles within the group, but the majority have relatively stout blades that curve firmly and regularly from the broad socket junction to the tip. The broadest part of the blade is either just below or at the middle of the blade. The socket is usually half the length of the entire spearhead, with the cleft stretching right up to the blade junction. Group C1 spearheads are found in large numbers throughout Anglo-Saxon England, for instance, at Fairford in Gloucestershire and Chesseldown on the Isle of White, and can be dated to between the mid 5th and late 6th century AD. This date correlates with the pottery (Ceramic Phase 4) recovered from the deposits associated with the abandonment of the aisled roundhouse. Whilst the presence of a type of spearhead found in Anglo Saxon England is surprising, it is not unprecedented. A Swanton Group D2 spearhead was found during the course of excavation at Scalloway, Shetland (Campbell 1998a: 159).

Shale bangle

A fragment of a substantial shale bangle, with an external diameter of approximately 110 mm (internal ø 78 mm), was recovered from the deposits within cell F (Fig. 4.40). Just over one quarter of the bangle has survived in tact. It has a semicircular cross section, between 12 mm and 16 mm in thickness, with a slightly convex inner face. Scott (1948) notes the presence of bone or lignite armlets at Iron Age sites on South and North Uist. However, while fragments of a less

substantial shale bracelet were recovered from Cladh Hallan on South Uist (Mike Parker Pearson, personal communication), there is little or no published information about shale bangles from excavated sites in the Outer Hebrides. Parallels are therefore drawn with those few shale and serpentine artifacts recovered from sites in Shetland. A fragment of a serpentine armlet or bangle was recovered from an Iron Age hut circle at Underhoull (Tommy Watts, personal communication). Similarly, a fragment of an unfinished bangle (internal ø 75–80 mm) manufactured from canneloid shale was found during the excavation of a Norse site at Unst (Steffan Stummann, personal communication). The Alt Chrisal bangle was found within the primary depositional sequence. Pottery from this deposit (Ceramic Phase 1) suggests a 1st–3rd-century AD date for the bangle, that is, Mid to Late Iron Age. Whilst the bangle is probably 'native', shale bracelets are also common in Roman Britain. The presence of Roman material within the stone-built roundhouses in the Outer Hebrides has been used as one of the criteria for establishing a chronology for the Scottish Atlantic Iron Age (Armit 1991).

Spindle whorls

Three spindle whorls were recovered from the site at Allt Chrisal T17 (Fig. 4.41). A broken fragment of a spindle whorl, measuring 32 × 16 mm with a thickness of 13 mm, was recovered from the spoil ejected from rabbit burrows. This spindle whorl, manufactured from a piece of metamorphosed sandstone, has convex surfaces the lower of which appears to be slightly polished through wear. Similarly, a blank spindle whorl or gaming piece, measuring 40 × 33 mm with a thickness of 15 mm, was found within the tertiary depositional sequence. The lower surface of this subcircular metamorphosed sandstone object is slightly polished through use. A third spindle whorl, measuring 28 mm in diameter with a thickness of 12 mm, was recovered from the tertiary depositional sequence. Both surfaces of this spindle whorl are polished with use. This spindle whorl, manufactured from a piece of steatite, can be dated to the Norse period and is thought to be associated with the shieling inserted into the interior of the abandoned wall circuit. Spindle whorls, made from a variety of materials, have been

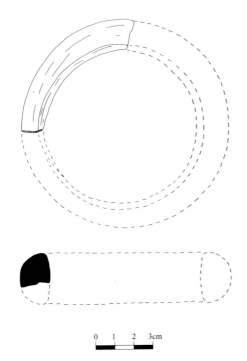

Figure 4.40 The shale bangle.

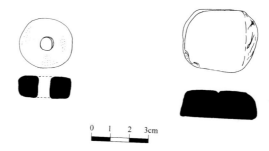

Figure 4.41 The spindle whorls.

found at many comparable sites in the Western Isles. A bone spindle whorl, decorated with concentric circles and parallel lines, was found during the course of excavation at A' Cheardach Mhor (Young and Richardson 1959: 168). Similarly, a spindle whorl, made from a sherd of pottery with incised decoration, was recovered from the wheelhouse at Kilpheder (Lethbridge 1952: 185). Stone spindle whorls comparable to those found at Alt Chrisal T17 were found during the course of excavations at Sollas (Campbell 1991: 163–64).

Pumice

An irregular piece of pumice, measuring 67.8 × 61.6 mm with a thickness of 31.7 mm, was found within the tertiary depositional sequence. The piece of pumice has shaped facets, and some of the edges are smoothed through use. Worked pumice has been found at a number of comparable sites in the Outer Hebrides. Thirteen pieces of worked pumice, those with one or more flat surfaces, were found during the course of the earlier excavations at Alt Chrisal (Branigan and Foster 1995: 144–48). The majority of these pieces of pumice were recovered from the Neolithic deposits beneath the early modern blackhouse T26, or from the deposits associated with the prehistoric platform T26A. Ten pieces of worked pumice were recovered from the midden deposits and the adjacent broch revetment wall at Dun Vulan (Parker Pearson and Sharples 1999: 32).

Crucible

A small fragment of a crucible base, measuring 27 × 20 mm with a wall thickness of 3–4 mm, was found in the spoil ejected from rabbit burrows. This slightly vitrified crucible, albeit unstratified, is the only evidence for metal working at the site. Evidence for metalworking has been found at other Hebridean Iron Age sites. A broken crucible, 6 lb of slag and a fragment of an open mould were recovered during the course of excavations at Dun Cuier (Young 1952: 299). Similarly, a broken crucible, with the residue of bronze working remaining on the lip, was found at A' Cheardach Mhor (Young and Richardson 1959: 157). Further evidence for metalworking at Iron Age sites has been recovered from Dùnan Ruadh, Pabbay (p. 270).

Clay pipes

Three fragments of clay pipe were recovered from the site at Alt Chrisal T17. First, a broken clay pipe stem, measuring 34 mm in length with a diameter of 7 mm, was found in the spoil ejected from rabbit burrows. Secondly, a fragment of a clay pipe stem, measuring 43 mm in length with a diameter of 8 mm, was derived from the tertiary depositional sequence. Thirdly, a

piece of clay pipe stem, measuring 27 mm in length with a diameter of 7 mm, was recovered from the deposit associated with the early modern enclosure.

Coins

Only two coins were recovered during the course of excavations, the first a Scottish penny (date 1793?), the second a badly worn halfpenny. Both coins were recovered from the spoil ejected from rabbit burrows.

Discussion

Preliminary analysis of the artifact assemblages recovered during the course of excavations has provided a chronological framework within which the site can be interpreted. A series of distinct phases of activity were identified at Alt Chrisal T17, described below.

Phase 0: residual material (Neolithic?)

Earlier prehistoric ceramics and worked flint were dispersed throughout the depositional sequence at Alt Chrisal T17. These artifact were not associated with any structural elements, however, the lower levels of the site have been heavily truncated. While the stone tools and pottery may be residual material associated with the nearby Neolithic stone working platform, it is possible that they represent an earlier phase of activity at the site. Consideration of the spatial distribution of these objects may confirm the presence or indicate the locus of any earlier prehistoric activity.

Phase 1: the Atlantic roundhouse (1st centuries BC/AD)

The earliest stone structure identified during the course of excavation was a short arc of walling, approximately 12.5 m in length. This substantial double-thickness wall is best-preserved where it is incorporated into the wall circuit of the later aisled roundhouse. It is thought to represent part of the wall circuit of an Atlantic roundhouse, with an external diameter of approximately 10.9 m The deposits associated with this structure were heavily truncated and there was little or no differentiation between the deposits either side of the stone wall. Further interpretation of this structure is purely conjectural.

Phase 2: the aisled roundhouse (1st/3rd centuries AD)

The Ben Tangaval roundhouse, a free-standing aisled roundhouse approximately 9.1 m in diameter, was subsequently constructed on the site of the Atlantic roundhouse. This substantial stone-built roundhouse was identified during the course of field survey and provided the initial impetus for excavation at the site. Seven free-standing radial piers were identified within the interior of the roundhouse. The piers, supporting the roof of the structure, impose a distinct order on the use of space within the interior of the building. They define a central area bordered by a series of radial cells, each of which would have had a corbelled roof. A narrow passage or aisle runs around the periphery of the interior. The interior of the round-house was entered through a doorway to the south. It is dominated by a rectangular stone setting retaining the ash deposits associated with the central hearth. The interior of the roundhouse was initially covered by a cobbled surface and was swept out at regular intervals. Midden material derived from floor sweepings was identified in the vicinity of the southern entrance. The practice of sweeping out the interior was abandoned early on, and the site was subsequently witness to the continuous build up of occupational debris.

Phase 3: secondary occupation of the aisled roundhouse (2nd/4th centuries AD)

After an initial period of occupation, the Ben Tangaval roundhouse underwent a series of structural modifications: the southern doorway was blocked and a new entrance was created to the west; the aisle around the periphery of the interior was blocked; a low stone kerb was constructed linking the inner faces of each of the radial piers; and a new, circular hearth was built at the centre of the roundhouse. These modifications represent a transformation in the internal architecture of the roundhouse that is perhaps associated with the restructuring of the way in which space is used within the building. A compact layer of ash is spread throughout the interior of the roundhouse. This layer of ash, containing an abundance of pottery, represents a discrete floor surface. It is sealed by an accumulation of silt loam comparable to the build up of occupational debris associated with the primary occupation of the aisled roundhouse.

Phase 4: abandonment and intermittent reuse of the site (6th/9th centuries AD)

Structural collapse followed the abandonment of the aisled roundhouse. The surface of the site was exposed to the elements and surface deposits were reworked to form a compact mineralized deposit. After abandonment the site continued to be used on a regular basis. First, the abandoned wall circuit was used intermittently by those seeking shelter from the elements. Discrete ash lenses associated with small fires or temporary hearths were found throughout the upper levels of the site. Secondly, the site was temporarily reoccupied on a number of occasions. A series of stone structures built from displaced stonework derived from the collapse of the aisled roundhouse were iden-

tified at the site (see below). The deposits associated with these structures are largely homogenous and it is difficult to identify discrete deposits associated with the individual structural elements. As such, phasing of the later periods of occupation at the site is less secure. A formal hearth, constructed from upright stone slabs, was built within the interior of the ruined roundhouse. This hearth does not appear to be associated with any other structural elements, and thus perhaps represents a continuation of the tradition of intermittent reuse suggested by the temporary hearths.

Phase 5: the shieling (Norse?)

Subsequently a small shieling was inserted into the interior of the site. The extant structure of the formal hearth (Phase 4) was incorporated into the fabric of the shieling. This shieling again suggests intermittent reuse of the site by those seeking shelter, perhaps whilst tending animals. It has been tentatively dated to the Norse period through its association with a steatite loom weight.

Phase 6: the mediaeval building (14th/16th centuries AD)

After further collapse of the superstructure of the aisled roundhouse, a subrectangular building was built towards the rear of the site. Traces of this structure only survive where the extant structure of the Iron Age wall circuit provided a stable foundation. The remainder of the building has collapsed where burrowing has undermined the stonework. However, it should be noted that the former extent of the structure could still be traced where slumping had occurred along the line of the rabbit burrows that had contributed to its collapse.

Phase 7: the early modern barn and enclosure (18th/19th centuries AD)

Finally, a small barn was built towards the north-west corner of the site. This rectangular structure incorporated stonework from the northern wall of the mediaeval building (Phase 5). A large enclosure, defined by an orthostat wall, was built against the barn, towards the eastern extent of the site. This enclosure appears to have been used for the purposes of cultivation. The deposits within the enclosure are poorly sorted, containing ceramics and other artifact associated with all periods of activity at the site. Within recent years the upper levels of the site have been heavily disturbed by rabbit burrowing and have largely been reworked. The site is sealed by an accumulation of loose silt—the spoil ejected from rabbit burrows.

5. Excavations on Barra and Vatersay

Keith Branigan and Colin Merrony

Excavation of B55

Colin Merrony

B55 is an unusual stone enclosure lying at about 80 m OD high up in the Borve Valley and commanding excellent views down the valley and westwards out to the sea beyond. The monument consists of an irregular stone circuit with a low mound in the centre. The stones stand between 0.25 and 0.60 m high. The central mound stands up to 0.2 m above the surrounding ground level. A survey of the visible structure was completed in 1992. This was followed up in 1995 when an area of 10 × 7 m was excavated. This area covered the south-east quadrant of the site from the central mound out to approximately 1 m beyond the enclosing line of stones.

Removal of the turf revealed a dark, sandy silt, highly organic topsoil across the entire excavated area. Within this there were some darker, black organic-rich lenses. A similar dark deposit made up the central mound. Removal of the topsoil revealed soft brown subsoil into which the stones of the monument had been set. The stones appeared to have a small amount of packing of smaller stones at their base. Within the line of stones running through the excavated area there were two areas of small stones that had no larger stones set into them This suggests that there may have been at least two more large stones, now missing, in the line of stones (Fig. 5.1).

While the excavation revealed the possible location of two more stones, the form of the monument suggests that it may have been extensively altered and that many other stones may also no longer be in their original position. The area upon which this enclosure stands is a roughly oval platform about 18 m east–west and 12 m north–south. The ground then slopes away on all but the east side. The most substantial slope is down to the west and north-west, down the Borve Valley. There are enough upright stones to suggest the main area of this oval platform may have once been enclosed by a ring of about 12 stones.

Today the stones form a line running east–west (of closely spaced stones) which then turns and runs southwards, with less closely spaced stones, for approximately 10 m. There is the suggestion of a curving line running westwards from near the end of this line round to a U-shaped feature or 'cove' that lies at the western end of the platform This arrangement of stones is about 3.5 m long and 2 m wide with its 'open' end to the south–east. From here there are occasional stones near the edge of the platform running back towards the beginning of the north–south line (see Fig. 5.1). It is easy to imagine that the U-shaped feature, the east–west line of stones and perhaps the stone at the southern end of the north–south line could be later alterations of the monument and have been constructed using stones taken from the original ring or oval.

The evidence from the excavation, which suggests the possible definition of two locations where upright stones may have stood, supports this idea. Unfortunately the upright stones investigated in the excavated area are not set into substantial sockets dug into the subsoil. This probably means that, even if considerable further excavation is conducted on the platform, it may prove impossible to conclusively demonstrate the presence, or otherwise, of previous positions for stones along the line of the imagined ring or oval.

The central mound is made up of a soft, black, silty-clay, organic-rich deposit. This deposit was featureless and relatively stone-free and produced no artifact material. There is no positive evidence from the excavated deposits to clarify what the central mound may have been, or may have been for.

Overall within the excavated area the deposits are generally less than 0.4 m deep overlying the natural gritty subsoil. In most places the deposits are much less than this in depth. Even in the central mound the maximum depth of deposits is only just over 0.4 m. No artifactual material was recovered during the excavation. Apart from the possible position of one more stone there were no cuts or features defined in the excavation.

The deposits revealed in the excavation follow a simple sequence, and it has been demonstrated that the large stones are only shallowly set into the ground, perhaps with a limited amount of packing of small stones. It is possible that the position of one or more (now missing) stones has been defined. Other than that no additional information was revealed that could help with an interpretation of this enigmatic site.

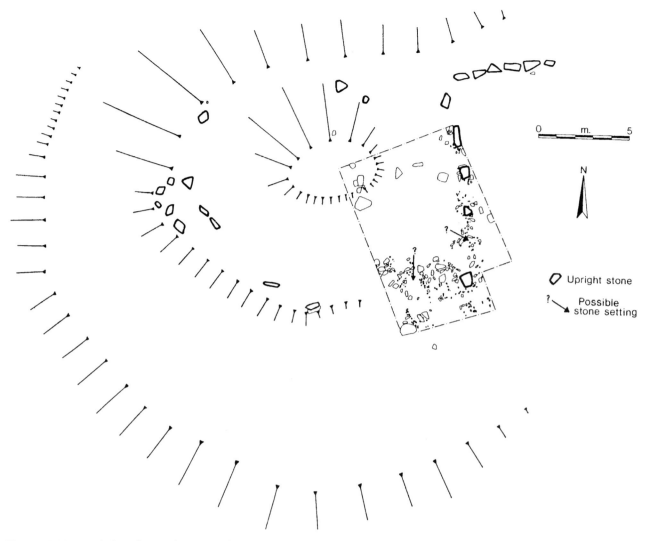

Figure 5.1 Measured plan of stone ring B55 and sampling excavation.

The Excavation of Kerbed Cairn VS7, South Vatersay

Colin Merrony

The kerbed cairn of VS7 lies on a ridge to the west of Dun Vatersay. This cairn is adjacent to the steep rocky drop down to a small inlet of the sea to the south. Immediately north and west of the cairn the ground slopes gently down and the faint lines of lazy-bed cultivation are visible. To the north of the culti-vated ground is a small steep sided valley. A second kerbed cairn, VS6, also lies on this ridge 30 m north-west of VS7. VS7 is overlooked by Dun Vatersay and by a ridge of hills to the south but has views of Bagh Siar to the north.

VS7 is circular with a diameter of 8.3 m and a maximum height of 0.8 m. There is a small kink in the alignment of the kerb on the south side at the position where an arc of stones runs southwards from the cairn and curves round to the east. A 1 m gap in the kerb

was visible on the west side of the cairn as well as a 0.5 m gap on the north-west side. The kerb was fairly visible prior to excavation. Inside the kerb the cairn was overgrown with short grass. There was a clear hollow visible in the top of the mound. This hollow was approximately circular with a diameter of 1.2 m and a maximum depth of 0.2 m.

Excavation

The excavation was conducted by laying out four quadrants across the mound. A 0.5 m baulk was left between each quadrant that resulted in sections running north-west to south-east and north-east to south-west across the mound. The area of excavation was extended beyond the area of the cairn by forming each quadrant into a rectangle rather than following the edge of the kerb. The turf was removed from the entire excavated area. The east and west quadrants were fully excavated (down to the buried ground

VS7

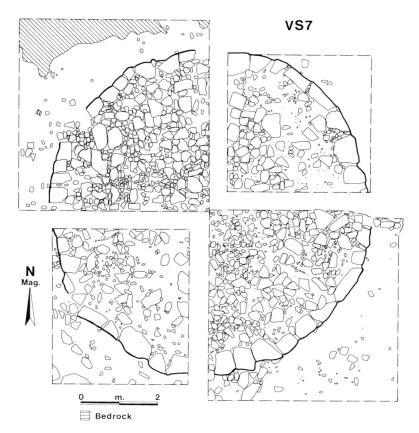

N
Mag.

0   m.   2

☰ Bedrock

Figure 5.2 Plan of cairn VS7 after removal of turf and topsoil.

surface under the cairn), while the north and south quadrants were only deturfed and the top layer of stone removed (Fig. 5.2).

After the removal of the turf the underlying soil was carefully removed by hand to reveal the stone cairn. This upper layer of the cairn (context numbers 002/104/202/302) was made up of a dark-grey, sandy, organic-rich deposit that contained approximately 40% stones. These stones were primarily small, up to 0.1 m but with some larger stones, up to 0.25 m (Fig. 5.3). This upper deposit covering the entire mound was clearly a mixture of stone and soil laid down together, and is not the result of stone being placed over the mound and then soil gradually filtering down in between the stone as a turf layer formed above. A small amount of artifactual material (pottery and flint) was recovered from this deposit.

Once the surface of this upper deposit of the cairn had been planned this deposit was removed in the east and west quadrants. The upper deposit lay within the line of the kerb (003/105/203/303), which was made of large stones (up to 1 m in length and 0.5 m thickness) laid flat on the buried ground surface (006/109/204/407) that underlay the cairn (Fig. 5.4). The upper deposit of the cairn had not tumbled over the kerb, but appears to have been carefully placed within the kerb and with a sloping upper surface sufficiently shallow to ensure that stones did not subsequently spill over the kerb. Clearly therefore the kerb must have

been in place before the upper deposit of stone and soil was deposited. The upper deposit of the cairn also lay directly on the buried ground surface in the outer part of the cairn. Removal of the upper deposit also revealed a central structure to the mound made up of very large stones around a central area of medium-sized stones.

Removal of the upper deposit revealed that the hollow in the centre of the top of the cairn was sitting above a part of the upper deposit that was relatively stone-free. There was no evidence of collapse underneath the upper deposit in the centre of the cairn. Consequently, either the cairn was constructed with the hollow in the top (and with relatively little stone in the upper deposit underneath it) or, perhaps more plausibly, the hollow represents an attempt at some point in the past to dig into the top of the mound. However, it was not possible on the excavated evidence to establish with any certainty which of these alternatives produced the hollow in the top of the mound.

Within the east quadrant a small area of harder brown sandy-silt (110) was defined within the upper deposit (104). Area 110 was an irregular shape of approximately 0.3 m diameter, but with poorly defined edges. Excavation revealed that it was about 0.18 m thick and tapering at its base. It was suspected that this deposit was formed by burning and represented the hearth of a small fire used during construction

Figure 5.3 The south-west quadrant of cairn VS7 after removal of turf and topsoil, showing bedrock in foreground, missing kerbstone, small stones of cairn, and inner ring of large stones.

of the cairn. Analysis of the magnetic susceptibility of samples taken from this deposit strongly supports the hypothesis that this is a hearth.

Within the southern quadrant removal of part of the upper deposit (202) around the junction between the outlying arc of stone (207) and the kerb (203) revealed an irregular oval-shaped area of light brown sandy-silt (209) underlying 202 but overlying the buried ground surface (204). While this deposit was

not as hard or as thick (it was only about 0.05 m thick) as 110, it was suspected that this may also be an area of burning. Time did not permit this area to be fully excavated, but magnetic susceptibility samples were taken. The results from the analysis of these samples did not support the idea that this deposit had been subject to any burning. While we may be able to say that this feature was not a hearth, no positive interpretation can be offered.

Figure 5.4 The NE quadrant of cairn VS7 after removal of turf, showing the large kerbstones in this quadrant.

The excavation adjacent to the junction of the outlying arc of stones (207) and the cairn did not reveal any clear relationship between the two features. It seems likely that the two features were deliberately associated, however, it was not possible to define if the two features were contemporary, or if 207 is later than the cairn, or if part of 207 was destroyed and then the cairn built over the site of it.

After removal of the upper deposit it was possible to collect samples for pollen analysis from the eastern quadrant. A series of samples were collected from across the buried ground surface (109) and also from underneath the kerb (105). The sample from underneath the kerb was taken as a small monolith given a complete profile through 109. The other samples were spot samples collected from a cleaned surface of 109. Details of the results of the pollen analysis are given below. Cleaning of the buried ground surface produced a small amount of artifactual material.

After removal of the upper deposit in the east and west quadrants it was clear that the cairn contained a substantial central structure. Initially it appeared that the central structure comprised a central area of medium-sized stones, up to 0.3 m, forming an approximately circular feature 2.8 m in diameter, which was surrounded by a double row of large stones, up to 0.8 m in length, 0.6 m wide and 0.5 m thick (Fig. 5.5). These large stones (004/108/205) were standing almost upright but leaning slightly in towards the centre as if they had been placed into position upright and then eased over so they leant against the central structure, at an angle of up to approximately 20° from the vertical. While this initial impression was broadly correct, the central structure eventually proved to be more complex in its construction.

The large stones were removed in the east and west quadrants. They stood directly on the buried ground surface (006/109) and were leaning up against a central structure that must have been constructed before the large stones were placed in their current position. The central structure comprised a number of components. The medium-sized stones visible within the double row of larger stones proved to be a mound of stones placed over a carefully built central cairn of medium- to large-sized stones (0.3–0.5 m diam.). The boundary between the mound of stones (005/107) and the built central cairn (401) was quite clear as 401 was carefully constructed to produce an even facing. On the outside 401 appeared to look like a small corbelled construction, however upon excavation it proved to be a solid cairn built over and around a central deposit.

Both the double row of large stones (004/108) and the inner mound of stones (005/107) were removed with the baulks still in place. The sections were then drawn, as it was clear that to successfully dismantle the central structure the central 2 m of the baulks would have to be removed to create an adequate working space. The central structure (401) was a roughly circular, carefully built, solid cairn approximately 1.5 m in diameter. This was built above a circular platform of flat stones (406) approximately 1 m in diameter (Fig. 5.6), which was standing directly on the buried ground surface (407). Sitting on 406 and within 401 was a cremation deposit. This deposit consisted of an upper deposit of many small rounded

Figure 5.5 The central structure of cairn VS7, and in the foreground the large stones of the inner ring.

Figure 5.6 The central platform of cairn VS7.

pebbles (beach pebbles) within a soft, dark-brown sandy matrix (402). Some of the pebbles were fractured as if damaged by heating. Underneath this was a black silty clay with occasional sandy lenses within it (403/404/405). This deposit, which was over 0.2 m thick, contained cremated bone and occasional fractured beach pebbles (Fig. 5.7). The frequency of pebbles increased towards the base of this deposit. The entire cremation deposit was collected so that the fragments of bone could be recovered for analysis in the laboratory. Details of this analysis are given below.

There were no clear signs of burning around the cremation deposit. However, in order to investigate the extent of burning, samples for magnetic susceptibility analysis were taken from the cremation deposit and from the buried ground surface (407) immediately below the stone platform (406). These samples were taken from less than 0.2 m apart and, given the high temperatures required in order to cremate a body, it is inconceivable that the sample from the buried ground surface would not have been affected by the burning had the cremation taken place in the position of the cairn. In order to further investigate the extent of any burning and to provide a background level to compare with the magnetic susceptibility levels of the central area, samples were collected from the buried ground surface (006) on a regular grid across the western quadrant out as far the kerb. Details of the magnetic susceptibility analyses are given below. However, in summary, while the cremation deposit had clearly been subject to high temperatures, none of the samples from the buried ground surface (including

the sample from 407) showed any sign of having been heated. It seems certain that the cremation represented by the deposit in the centre of VS7 took place away from the site of the cairn. The presence of beach pebbles within the deposit perhaps suggests that the cremation may have taken place on or near a pebble-rich surface, such as a beach. However, the same result would be achieved by the deliberate addition of beach pebbles to the pyre prior to or during cremation. The resulting deposit must have then been collected up and brought to this site and placed on the stone platform (406).

The excavation recovered 18 sherds of prehistoric pottery and 9 pieces of flint. All of this material came from the upper deposit within the cairn or from cleaning the surface of the buried ground surface beneath the cairn. The central cremation deposit contained no surviving grave goods.

A magnetometer survey was conducted over an area extending for 20 m immediately around the cairn using a Geoscan FM18 Flux-gate Gradiometer. This produced no significant magnetic anomalies that could have been associated either with the site of the cremation pyre or with further deposits of cremated bone. These findings are consistent with the excavation of the area immediately outside the kerb, which revealed no associated structural remains or deposits of any kind. While this does not prove that the cremation did not take place within this area, as the deposits may not have survived, it does add weight to the suggestion that the cremation took place some distance away, perhaps nearer the shoreline.

Figure 5.7 Soil mixed with cremated bone fragments and pebbles on the central platform of cairn VS7.

The cremation deposit

Elizabeth Rega, Duncan Robertson and Andrew Chamberlain

The skeletal material recovered from the excavation of VS7 in 1995 on Barra consisted of 24 fragments of heavily calcined bone, imbedded in an organic-rich matrix. Because of their fragmentary and extremely friable condition, the bone fragments were brushed clean when necessary for identification, but subjected to no further cleaning.

The skeletal material consists of small (4 cm) fragments, the majority of which appear to be derived from the cortical bone found in the limb bones. Although specific identification to bone element is not possible for the majority of cases, the bone is clearly mammalian in origin and the texture is consistent with the assessment of human. There are no fragments that are clearly faunal in origin. The identifiable fragments, which include a splinter from the ilium and a section of an ulnar midshaft substantiate an assignment of human. The fragment of ulna is characteristically triangular in cross-section—given its size and robustness, in spite of shrinkage, it is likely that the remains represent minimally one individual, an adult older then sixteen. This individual was muscular and robust, and therefore probably, but not definitely, male. The figure of one individual is a minimum and the presence of two or more individuals cannot be excluded.

The bone material is heavily calcined, white and chalky in appearance. Several fragments display a decided bluish cast to the bone. No fragments display any reduction or signs of incomplete burning. Every fragment manifests multiple parallel cracks indicative of warping, cracking and shrinkage under high cremation heat. It is important to note that these are not cut marks indicative of defleshing. It is unlikely that the bone contains sufficient organic content to permit direct radiocarbon dating.

Table 5.1 Bone fragments from the cremation deposit in cairn VS7.

Find no.	Description
SVX1-13	Long bone
SVX1-21	? Metatarsal or metacarpal
SVX1-22	Indeterminate
SVX1-23	Indeterminate
SVX1-24	Indeterminate
SVX1-25	Cortical bone
SVX1-26	Femur shaft
SVX1-27	Cranial vault and long bones
SVX1-28	? Long bone epiphysis
SVX1-29	Indeterminate postcranial bone
SVX1-30	Cortical bone
SVX1-31	Tibia
SVX1-32	? Radius
SVX1-33	Cranial vault and long bones
SVX1-34	Postcranial
SVX1-35	Ulna (?left side)
SVX1-36	Long bone
SVX1-37	? Humerus
SVX1-38	? Rib
SVX1-39	Indeterminate
SVX1-40	Long bone
SVX1-41	Indeterminate
SVX1-42	? Ulna
SVX1-43	Long bone, ? femur shaft

The high heat of cremation in this case, which probably but not certainly attained at least 600 degrees centigrade, may have been produced by several factors, including a well-fuelled and well-constructed fire and constant oxygen supply, perhaps by high winds or human production of air circulation. However, a very important factor is also the fat content of the dead body or bodies themselves. An obese individual will combust hotter and will cremate more quickly than a very thin one, due to the oxidation of the lipids, which themselves burn very hot.

Magnetic susceptibility analysis

Colin Merrony and Derilyn Frusher

Magnetic susceptibility is a measure of the susceptibility of a material to becoming magnetized when placed within a magnetic field and is dependent on the crystal structure of the iron oxide compounds present within the sample. Variations in the magnetic susceptibility of soils can provide valuable information about the presence of areas of archaeological activity on a site, as the structure of the iron oxide particles (and consequently the level of magnetic susceptibility) may be altered by such factors as burning of material or by the breakdown of organic matter deposited in antiquity.

In this analysis samples were collected in the field and brought back to the laboratory. The samples were dried overnight in an oven at below 100°C. Large particles were removed from the samples and then each sample was weighed and its magnetic susceptibility was measured using a Bartington MS2b Susceptibility Bridge connected to an MS2 meter. The results were normalized to give a value per 100 g. Thirty-four samples were analysed and the results are given in the table below, and shown graphically in Figure 5.8.

The results from the analysis of samples taken from the buried ground surface (006/109) proved to have consistently low results, with all returning values

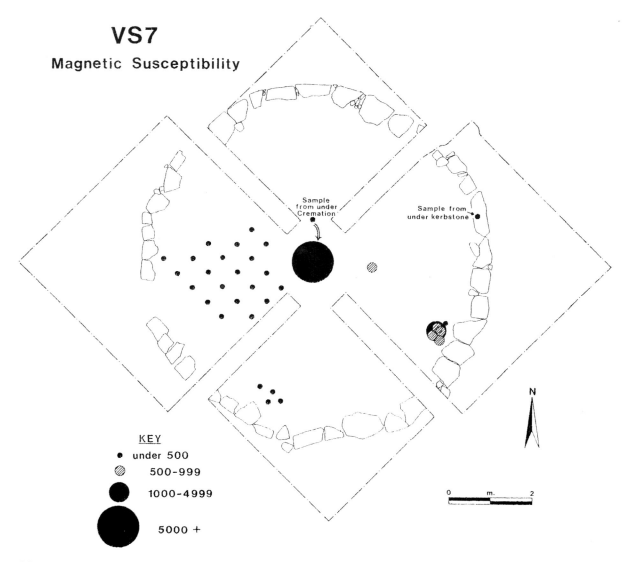

Figure 5.8 The magnetic susceptibility plots at cairn VS7.

below 500 (except for sample 5B, which was taken because it looked like a small patch of burning and so is not representative of the general background value of the buried ground surface—it may well represent a small area of burning from some time prior to the cairn's construction).

The area of suggested burning in the east quadrant (110) produced values between 570 and 1190, therefore supporting the hypothesis that this is an area that has been subject to limited heating, perhaps as a result of a small hearth. This deposit is within the structure of the mound and so represents a period of small-scale heating during the process of constructing the mound (note this is, however, after the construction of the central structure within the mound, and is during the period of the deposition of the upper deposit of the mound). The other suggested substantial area of burning (209), which was in the southern quadrant, produced a value of 390. When this is compared to the samples from the buried ground surface around this feature (204), which produced values from between 130 and 360, and to the general variability of the background values, this value cannot be taken to con-

clusively demonstrate that 209 is a burned deposit. However, the value is high enough to allow the possibility that this deposit has been subject to low-temperature heating.

The sample from the cremation deposit produced a value of 21,860; this is nearly 20 times the next highest value and is more than 100 times the value of the sample taken from immediately underneath the stone platform (which produced a value of 141). This strongly supports the hypothesis that the deposit within the central structure of the cairn has been subject to very high temperature burning. It also supports the interpretation that this burning must have taken place away from the site of the cairn, otherwise the samples from the buried ground surface would have had much higher values.

Soil pollen analyses

Kevin Edwards and Robert Craigie

Abstract

During the excavation of kerbed cairn VS7, soil samples for pollen analysis were taken in an attempt

Table 5.2 Magnetic susceptibility results from cairn VS7.

Sample Number	Quadrant	Context Number	Result (SI Units/100 g)
1	W	006	114.56
2A	W	006	162.75
2B	E	109 (under kerb)	128.41
3	W	006	99.55
4A	S	204	361.65
4B	W	006	167.48
5A	W	006	150.61
5B	E	109 (under 107)	799.12
6	W	006	167.57
7A	W	006	252.80
7B	E	110	579.06
8A	W	006	151.55
8B	E	110	1188.02
9	E	104	365.38
10A	W	006	6.36
10B	E	110	667.82
11A	W	006	340.54
11B	E	110	713.34
12A	W	006	263.43
12B	E	110	574.32
13	W	006	263.73
14	W	006	134.52
15	W	006	141.09
16A	W	006	484.08
16B	S	209	390.42
17A	W	006	369.53
17B	S	204	299.50
18A	W	006	305.90
18B	S	204	130.30
19	W	006	126.88
20	W	006	7.13
21A	W	006	385.89
22	CENTRAL	405	21860.14
23	CENTRAL	407	141.71

to determine local land use or more general environmental conditions at the time of construction of the cairn. The data indicate that the cairn was built upon a vegetational cover dominated by a heath-grassland mosaic, which may have developed from more extensive heathland under the influence of grazing. There is also the possibility that hazel was being conserved as part of a coppice system.

Introduction

During the excavation of kerbed cairn VS7, soil samples were taken from beneath the structure and submitted for pollen analysis. The intention was to ascertain whether palynological data would reveal evidence for local land use or more general environmental conditions during or immediately prior to the construction of the cairn. The data yielded interpretable evidence and form the basis of the following account. These and those from the companion cairn VS4B (below) are the first pollen analyses from the island of Vatersay.

Samples, laboratory methods and data presentation

The soil samples derive from two types of contexts. Four spot samples (S6–9) came from 0.5 cm thick slices of material spaced at different points immediately beneath basal cairn boulders within the eastern quadrant. Three samples (M1, 5, and 9) were extracted from a small monolith tin that contained a soil column from immediately beneath a kerbstone in the eastern quadrant 4 m from the cairn centre. Sample locations are indicated in Figure 5.9.

Samples were subjected to standard KOH, HCl, HF and acetolysis pretreatments and suspension, unstained, in silicone oil of 12,500 cSt viscosity (Faegri and Iversen 1989). Pollen counts of 300 identifiable terrestrial pollen were made in addition to aquatic and cryptogam taxa and to pollen and spores deemed indeterminable (unidentifiable due to breakage, crum-

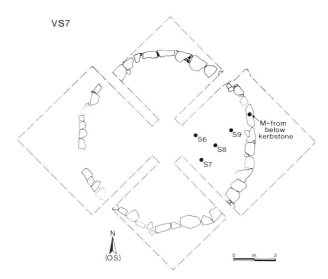

Figure 5.9 The locations from which pollen samples were recovered under cairn VS7.

pling or corrosion; crumpling was the major problem). Palynomorph identification was to the lowest taxonomic level. The computation and construction of pollen diagrams (Figs. 5.10–5.12) were achieved with the computer programs TILIA and TILIA(GRAPH) (Grimm 1991). Pollen and spore taxa are expressed as percentages of total land pollen (TLP) and palynomorph and plant nomenclature follows Bennett (1984) and Stace (1997) respectively. The English common names of taxa are indicated in the diagrams alongside their Latin botanical names.

Discussion

It is well known that the pollen and spore content of soils is subject to various processes (e.g. differential palynomorph survival and movement within profiles) that reduces sample integrity when compared to data derived from peat or lake sediments (Dimbleby 1985). The low counts for resistant spores (e.g. Pteropsida)

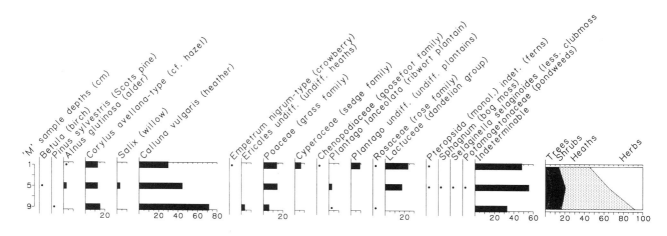

Figure 5.10 Percentage pollen and spore diagram for the monolith from beneath the kerbstone in cairn VS7. ● Indicates less than 2% TLP.

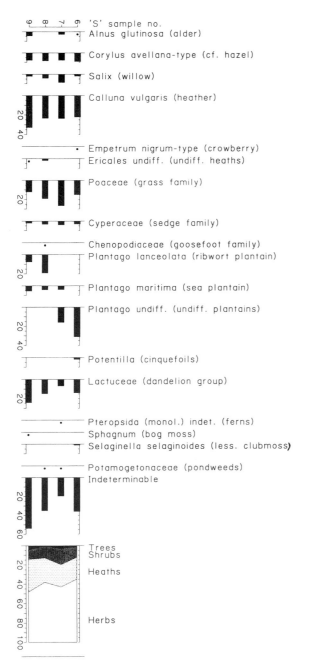

Figure 5.11 Percentage pollen and spore diagram for the spot samples from beneath the cairn boulders in VS7. • Indicates less than 2% TLP.

ceae and Lactuceae. If the top sample from the monolith is penecontemporaneous with the spot samples (assuming the latter to be approximately contemporaneous), then they would be expected to show a similarity in pattern. This may be borne out by the results of a detrended correspondence analysis (DECORANA, Hill 1979) based on those taxa, represented in both series and which exceed 5% TLP in at least either the monolith or the spot series (*Corylus*, *Salix*, *Calluna*, Poaceae, Cyperaceae, *Plantago lanceolata*, *Plantago* undiff., Lactuceae). The analysis places samples M1 and M5 close to spot samples S9 and S6 in a graph plot of sample scores (Fig. 5.12).

The monolith series (Fig. 5.10) would appear to show a sequence that represents changing vegetation, even if the chronology is unknown. Essentially, the basal pollen spectrum is dominated by heather, which is reduced up-profile in favour of grasses and pollen of dandelion-type. The local vegetation is interpreted as a heath-dominated flora that gave way to grassland habitats, possibly culminating in a heath-grassland mosaic. The extension of grassland may have been a product of grazing, whereby natural manuring increased the nutrient content of heathland soils. It is quite possible that wind-blown additions of calcareous sand from the adjacent machair assisted in this process. Apart from *Plantago lanceolata* (the *Plantago* undiff. category could also be derived from crumpled ribwort plantain grains) and Lactuceae (cf. *Leontodon* and *Taraxacum* spp.), the grassland may have contained poorer elements, including sedges (Pankhurst 1991). All of these types may also have been constituents in the machair, which may have contributed some, but not the majority, of the pollen. *Corylus avellana*-type is a constant representative and probably reflects hazel growing nearby (the pollen type includes hazel and bog myrtle, and, although both are found in the southern Outer Hebrides today, hazel is thought the more likely).

The diagram of spot samples must be read as a penecontemporaneous series, and not as a depth profile, hence the orientation of Figure 5.11. As in the surface spectrum of the monolith, the assemblages are dominated by grass-heathland in which plantain and Lactuceae are especially prominent, but in which sea plantain and cinquefoils (cf. *Potentilla erecta* [tormentil], and *P. anserina* [silverweed]) would also thrive. Once again, the good representation for *Corylus* suggests the growth of hazel shrubland in the pollen catchment area.

Conclusion
The pollen data indicate that the site upon which Vatersay cairn VS7 was later to be built had a vegetational cover dominated by heather. It is likely that grazing over this surface encouraged the extension of grassland and that the area became characterized by a heath-grassland mosaic that formed the local

and the fact that, although high, the indeterminable taxa counts are dominated by crumpled pollen grains, suggests that palynomorph survival has not been a problem in the Vatersay samples. Movement of pollen and spores would probably only apply to the monolith samples, and even there, assuming that the soil matrix formed *in situ* and is not a mixed body (palynomorph concentrations decrease with depth, as would be anticipated), the changes in microfossil spectra with depth are capable of interpretation.

The spectra from both spot and monolith samples series have a number of abundant taxa in common, namely *Corylus avellana*-type, *Calluna vulgaris*, Poa-

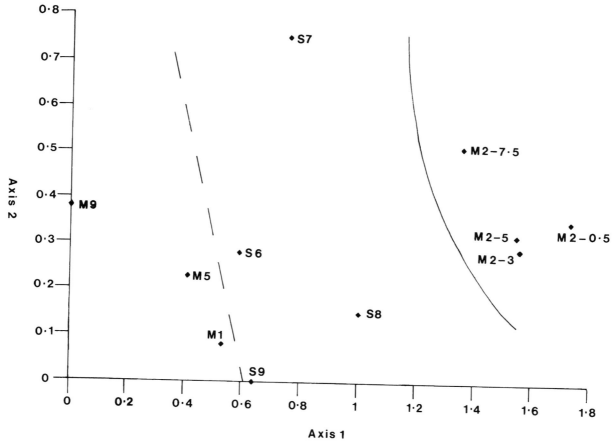

Figure 5.12 Graph plot of sample scores on the first two DECORANA axes for the soil pollen samples from cairns VS7 and VS4B.

vegetation when the cairn was built. Off-site floristic elements from the nearby machair and especially from hazel shrubs contributed to the pollen rain at all times during the period of microfossil deposition.

The taxa revealed in the Vatersay samples are all to be found in other published peat and lake sediment profiles from the southern Outer Isles (e.g. Bennett *et al.* 1990; Brayshay and Edwards 1996; Whittington and Edwards 1997; Brayshay *et al.* this volume). In comparison with sequences of Bronze Age date from Barra, the Vatersay cairn samples differ most markedly in containing virtually no *Betula*. Given the expected ubiquity of birch, this probably indicates the local nature of the pollen spectra from Vatersay, or the fact that any birch had been overexploited by this time. This makes the level of *Corylus* representation all the more interesting, and raises the possibility that hazel was being conserved as part of a coppice system.

The finds

Pottery

Keith Branigan

Eighteen sherds (total weight 110 g) were recovered, mostly from the upper-cairn material. The pottery can be divided into two quite distinct fabric groups.

Fabric 1 (15 sherds) is a gritty fabric with many small (1 mm) gneiss inclusions, and a few larger angular inclusions up to 7–8 mm, fired medium-hard to a purplish-brown colour. The surface is smoothed and speckled with mica. Most sherds were around 10 mm thick. Fabric 2 (3 sherds) is a fine, dense material with smaller gneiss inclusions than fabric 1 a slightly sandy surface texture, and fired soft-medium to a dark grey-black. Sherds are 7–8 mm thick. The entire assemblage could represent the remains of just two vessels, one of each fabric, although we cannot confirm this.

There were no decorated sherds, no rims, bases or carinations. There is thus no direct evidence for their date. Fabric 1 is very similar to that used for some of the larger jars from the Neolithic activity platform at Alt Chrisal (Gibson 1995), and the only sherd to be found in the precairn soil was a sherd of this fabric, but the similarity may well reflect the limited clay sources available to local potters. A sample sherd of fabric 1 was submitted to I. Bailiff and S. Barnett at the University of Durham and an OSL (Optically Stimulated Luminescence) determination was produced (for brief details of the procedure, see p. 206). The estimation of age for the sherd from VS7 was as follows:

Ref.	Age (years)	Random error (years)	Overall error (years)
DurOSL-234-2q1	4000	±380	±500

This very broad bracket suggests a date within the later Neolithic or earlier Bronze Age. It also suggests that VS7 is considerably earlier than VS4B, a second excavated cairn 200 m to the north from which a sherd was also dated by OSL (see p. 207). In this respect, it may be significant that the fabrics of the 18 sherds from VS7 were quite different to those of the 15 sherds from VS4B.

Flint artifacts

Caroline Wickham-Jones

There were nine flaked flint artifacts from the cairn VS7.

All of the pieces are made of pebble flint. There is one core, a bipolar core made on a small pebble. It does not appear to have had many flakes removed, no doubt because of its small size. There are three other flakes with evidence of bipolar knapping, but there is some evidence that platform reduction was also used.

The flakes are not generally in as good condition, or as regular, as those from the cairn VS4B, but there are also two retouched pieces from this site. No. 3 is a small blunt awl, recovered from the turf layer, and no. 9 is a broken flake that has some retouch, though it is not possible to classify it closely.

The assemblage is very small and all but two artifacts have come from the east quadrant: no. 3 came from the west and no. 20 from the north. The material is divided more or less evenly between that which came from the turf and topsoil (five pieces) and that from the cairn material (four pieces). There is no clear patterning in the spatial distribution, but this would not be expected given the small size of the assemblage. It would therefore seem that the flints were associated with the building and the use of the cairn, though they do not add much to the interpretation, or dating of the site. None of the artifacts offers any close chronological parallels, though the awl is of a type that occurs in the later Neolithic and Bronze Age.

Discussion

VS7 has clearly been constructed to contain the remains of a single cremation, probably of a single

Table 5.3 Flint artifacts from cairn VS7.

Type	Turf and Topsoil	Cairn Material
Core	1	
Debitage Flakes		1
Regular Flakes	3	2
Retouched Flakes	1—awl	1—miscellaneous
Total	5	4

adult, perhaps a male. The cairn is constructed directly on the existing ground surface in an area that was probably pasture. The underlying soil is thin and it would seem necessary that most, perhaps all, the stone (and soil) required for its construction was brought from some distance away.

The cairn has been constructed by laying out a circular kerb and building a central structure. Whether these were done at the same time or one before the other cannot be determined. All that can be said is that both were in place before the covering of stone and soil that forms the upper layer of the cairn was deposited. The central construction consists of an almost circular stone surface made up of thin stone flags laid directly on the old ground surface. Upon this was placed the cremation deposit. It is not possible to define where the cremation took place; however, it clearly did not take place on the site of the cairn. The cremation deposit included a substantial number of beach pebbles many of which were fractured perhaps as a result of heating, possibly during the cremation itself. It is possible that these pebbles became incorporated into the cremation deposit as a result of the cremation taking place on the beach, with the pebbles getting scraped up with the rest of the deposit prior to its transportation up to the site of the cairn construction. It may be, however, that the pebbles have been deliberately added to the pyre material at some point, perhaps to make a reference to the shore or perhaps as a reference to cooking as they are identical to stones that would have been used as 'pot boilers'. The deliberate inclusion of these stones may represent some aspect of the identity of the interred individual, although the reference remains unclear given the limited evidence from the excavated remains. Whatever the reason, the pebbles became incorporated in the cremation deposit. They, along with the remains of the pyre, were placed on the stone platform and then a carefully constructed drystone cairn was built over it. This cairn was well faced to produce a coherent structure in itself. This could well have stood on its own for some time, although it is not possible to determine whether this was the case or whether the rest of the cairn was built over this central structure immediately.

The rest of the cairn was constructed by piling medium-sized stones over the central structure and then placing large stones upright adjacent to this and leaning them inwards so they were pressing inwards against the central structure with an angle of 10–20° from the vertical. This whole construction was then covered with a layer of stone and soil to produce a mound within the boundary of the kerb.

The kerb itself is not continuous; it has two gaps, on the west and north-west. The evidence from the excavation did not demonstrate that stones had ever been in these positions. It is possible that stones had been removed to create these breaks in the perimeter, however, there was no direct evidence for this. In addition to the two gaps in the kerb, on the south side there is a 'misalignment' or kink in the kerb. It did not appear from the excavated evidence that this was the result of later disturbance. It may be that this change in alignment is due to the proximity of the arc of stones that runs south and east from this point. Time constraints did not permit the further investigation of this arc of stones.

It may be that some disturbance of the cairn has occurred in the past resulting in the hollow in the top of the cairn. However, if this is late disturbance then it is very minor and did not result in damage to the central structure. It is possible, however, that this hollow is part of the original construction of the cairn, although this would be a unique feature among the cairns so far identified on Vatersay.

The date of 4,000 years BP ±500 places this perhaps as much as a millennium earlier than the site of VS4B described below. While these dates are consistent with monuments of this form they demonstrate that kerbed cairns had a long currency as funerary structures. If the total of 30 kerbed cairns known from Vatersay represents anything like the real number of cairns constructed then these monument are representing the burial of only a tiny proportion of the human population of the island.

The Excavation of Kerbed Cairn VS4B, South Vatersay

Keith Branigan

The kerbed cairn at VS4B was the largest of four such cairns discovered, in a close-set row oriented north-west, east south-east–west north-west, during field survey in 1992. Further kerbed cairns were found on south Vatersay during the same survey, and a larger number were found on north Vatersay during surveys conducted in 1990–92. Altogether, at least 30 kerbed cairns are now known on Vatersay (out of a total of 222 sites and monuments) while there are only 6 possible examples from Barra (out of 960 sites and monuments). The kerbed cairns clearly form an important component of the archaeological record on Vatersay and excavation of two examples was therefore undertaken in the hope of establishing their date, their purpose, and their structural history.

Cairn VS4B sits on top of the ridge than runs from Dun Vatersay down to the end of Traigh Siar at Sloc Mhartuin; today the ridge is used for cattle pasture and there is no trace of lazy bedding or other recent cultivation. The kerbed cairn group here is at 35 m OD, overlooking Bagh Siar but in turn itself overlooked by Dun Vatersay. To the north, across the other side of Baigh Siar, the small valley with a complex of at least 19 further kerbed cairns is clearly

visible, while to the south the cairns at VS6 and VS7 can be seen. Prior to excavation a careful study was made of the cemetery area designated VS4 and a fourth, much destroyed, cairn was confirmed immediately north-west of cairn C making a row of four cairns in line. To the west of cairns A and B a fifth possible cairn was located, marked by a slight mounding and a few possible kerbstones. On balance it was decided that this feature was more probably debris disturbed and removed from the adjacent cairns than a cairn itself.

Excavation

Excavation of cairn B was undertaken by laying out four quadrants for excavation with two 30 cm baulks at right-angles to each other, preserved across the entire diameter of the cairn. The contexts in each quadrant were separately numbered and recorded, those in the south-east quadrant were numbered from 001, those in the south-west from 101, in the north-west from 201 and in the north-east from 301. When the small inner cairn was reached, contexts were numbered only in the sequence beginning 001 (Figs. 5.13, 5.14).

Once the turf was removed the topsoil (002, 102, 202, 302) was carefully cleared from over the underlying stone cairn. The kerb proved to enclose a circular area 7.7 m in diameter. At an early stage of this operation it became clear that, within the kerb of large stone blocks, the bulk of the uppermost stone cairn material (003, 103, 203, 303) was comprised of small stones of 10–20 cm in size, many of which were well weathered. Some much larger blocks of stone were also visible, and there was a suggestion of an inner ring of large blocks, and also a central capping of larger stones (Fig. 5.15).

On a kerbstone just west of south, an apparently deliberately shaped piece of gneiss was lying. It was regularly shaped, 21.5 cm long and 7.5 cm wide, and it is tentatively identified as an ard tip rough-out. Just to the east of the north–south section, but higher up the cairn, a second piece of shaped gneiss was noted during cleaning. This was smaller, and wedge-shaped, measuring 11 × 4.8 cm, tapering to an edge at the broad end. It looks like a stone axe but the material of course is unsuitable for such a tool, and if it was intended to represent an axe then it must have done so in a purely symbolic manner.

Once the cairn had been planned stone by stone, the cairn material began to be removed. Beneath the covering of small, mostly weathered stones, larger blocks of stone were exposed (004, 104, 204, 304) and a clear inner ring of large stones, diameter around 4.5 m, could be seen (Fig. 5.16). Stone blocks between the outer kerb and the inner ring were then removed to show that the latter was an inward-leaning rough revetment constructed around a inner cairn (005, 105,

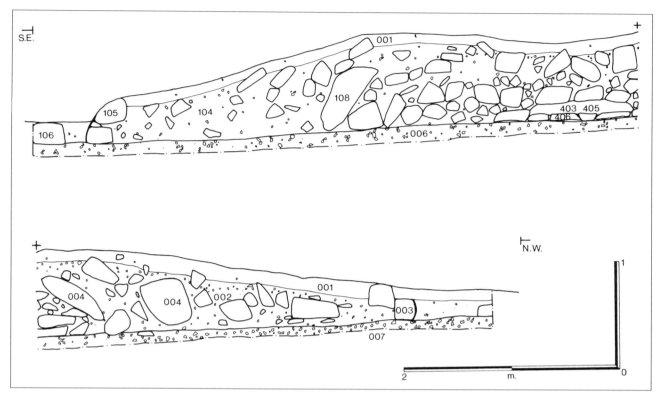

Figure 5.13 A section through cairn VS7.

205, 305) covered with more medium to small stones. In the north-west quadrant these stones were found to partly cover a long regularly shaped stone 103 × 30 × 20 cm that lay at an angle of about 35°, partly covered by the stones of the revetment and partly resting on the inner cairn (Fig. 5.17). When the small stones and revetment were removed over the whole area, the inner cairn proved to be covered with a 5–10 cm thick deposit of fine black slightly sandy soil (006) itself revetted with a single ring of largish stone blocks. Beneath the black soil was a thin (7–8 cm) burnt spread of small angular stones mixed with a few white beach pebbles (007), forming a low oval mound 2.5 × 1.5 m resting on a rough kerb of medium-sized gneiss blocks (Fig. 5.18).

This spread in turn overlay a 2–4 cm thick deposit of brown soil and unburnt field stones (008), partly resting on four flat slabs of stone. These slabs proved to sit immediately over an orangey-brown rather clayey hump of material with areas of red and brown burnt material, flecks of charcoal and small decayed fragments of bone (009). This deposit, apparently pyre material, was about 12 cm deep at its centre and ringed by an oval of small stone blocks (011), measuring 2 × 1.5 m (Fig. 5.19).

A few of these blocks showed signs of discolouration from heat on their inside faces, but none showed such traces on their exterior sides. The removal of the pyre material revealed a small heap of weathered cobbles (010) discoloured by heat at the centre of the

area (Fig. 5.20). The cobbles rested on a few thin slabs of stone which in turn rested on a thin deposit of fine, dark brown, slightly sandy soil with few stones (012) which overlay bedrock and was also found beneath the stone blocks that outlined the pyre area. Immediately north-west of the oval pyre area six stone blocks (013) were set flat into the dark-brown gritty basal soil (306), forming a neat arc outside the line of the oval pyre deposit.

The fine, dark-brown, slightly sandy soil (012) found beneath the central pyre area was found spread across the whole of the cairn area (and was designated 014, 106, 206, 306), overlain in most areas directly by the lowest stones of the cairn material itself. It varied in depth from 2 to 6 cm. It was almost stone-free, but contained 4 pieces of flint and 15 sherds of pottery, the latter all found close together in a shallow depression just above bedrock. A slightly paler brown soil, with a gritty texture (015, 107, 207, 307) was thinly spread across the site, beneath 014 and immediately over bedrock.

The finds

There were no grave goods or funerary offerings of any kind in or around the pyre and the inner cairn. Finds came from the cleared ground surface beneath the cairn, from the fine black soil overlying the pyre debris, from the body of the cairn and from the surface of the cairn.

205

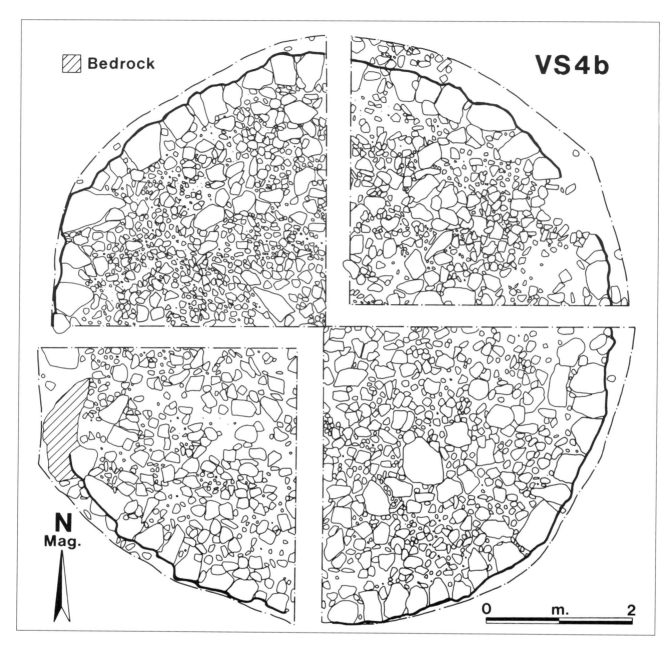

Figure 5.14 Plan of cairn VS4B after removal of turf and topsoil.

Metal
Three joining fragments of a bronze ring found in the cairn material (003). The ring was penannular, the circular-section bar flaring into a simple trumpet terminal. Diam. approx. 5 × 4.5 cm. It appears to be a simple version of a 'cloak fastener' of the type found in LBA assemblages (Fig. 5.22).

Pottery (C. Cumberpatch and K. Branigan)
Fifteen sherds (total weight 95 g) in a single fabric, possibly from the same vessel, were recovered from a small area in context 014. The fabric is coarsely tempered and contains abundant angular quartz and other gneiss-derived grains, and occasional large rock fragments (up to 8mm). The sherds come from at least

one thick-walled vessel up to 20 mm thick. In the absence of any decorated or rim sherds it is difficult to place this material chronologically, but it bears a resemblance to M/LBA thick-walled material from South Uist.

An OSL date was obtained for one of the sherds by I. Bailiff and S. Barnett of the University of Durham, who report:

We tested the thermoluminescence response of the quartz inclusions but found that their characteristics were not suitable for dose evaluation. We then turned to OSL. Since the very small quantities of quartz extracted from the ceramic body limited the range of tests that it was possible to make we turned to samples of quartz extracted from Iron Age pottery. We settled on a procedure and were able to arrive at an evaluation

206

Figure 5.15 The south-west quadrant of cairn VS4B.

of the palaeodose for both samples. Because of the limited number of tests we have some reservations but think the outcome should be good enough for period placement.

The result of this procedure was an estimation of age as follows:

Ref.	*Age* (years)	*Random error* (years)	*Overall error* (years)
DurOSL-234-1qi	3050	±290	±400

This is obviously a very broad bracket, but it suggests that the sherd is probably pre-Iron Age and either Middle or Late Bronze Age.

Heavy stone artifacts
Three stone artifacts were recovered during the excavation, none of which could be identified as specific tools with certainty, but all of which were found in

Figure 5.16 The inner revetment in the NE quadrant of VS4B.

Figure 5.17 The 'standing stone' sealed beneath the inner revetment stones and over the inner cairn in the north-west quadrant of VS4B.

Figure 5.18 The oval central mound covering the pyre material, VS4B.

significant positions, which persuades us that they were indeed deliberately made and deposited artifacts.

1. A stone ard tip made of local gneiss (Fig. 5.23.1). Length 24.5 cm, width at tip 5.0 cm. Apart from being quite different to any other of the stones and small boulders incorporated in

the cairn, this item was found under the turf and topsoil, lying immediately on a kerbstone in the south-west quadrant. It was probably never used, nor meant to be used; we believe it was an imitation or symbolic tool like number 2 below. Stone ard tips are not well known from the Western Isles, but are well documented in the Northern Isles from the 3rd to the 1st millennia BC (Rees 1979: 6–40).

Figure 5.19 The pyre material in cairn VS4B.

Figure 5.20 Cobbles sealed beneath the pyre material of VS4B.

2. A stone axe rough-out of local gneiss (Fig. 5.23.2). Length 11.5 cm, width at tip 5.0 cm. This item was found amongst the top stones of the cairn (003) almost at the centre of the monument, and stood out amongst the rounded and irregular stones around it. With its bevelled profile and straight sides it looks like an imitation of a metal axe rather than a stone one, which would befit the Bronze Age date of the cairn.

3. An oval 'rubber' of Torrodonian sandstone (Fig. 5.23.3) partly stained by burning, and with clear wear marks on its flattened side. Length 14.2 cm, max. width 6.5 cm. The rubber was found on the thin slabs overlain by the fire-marked cobbles (010) beneath the pyre material.

Flaked lithic material (C. R. Wickham-Jones)
A total of twenty-one pieces of worked stone were recovered from the excavation of the cairn at SV4B. With the exception of one flake of quartzite all of these were of flint.

Flint. The flint assemblage is unusual in that it comprises generally good-quality unbroken pieces and there is very little debitage (Table 5.4). There are two cores, both of which are bipolar, and one chunk, but half of the assemblage is made up of regular flakes, and there are, in addition two blades and three retouched pieces: two end scrapers and a notched piece.

The surviving cortex indicates that the assemblage is made on pebble flint, as is common throughout the Western Isles. The cores indicate that bipolar knapping was common, but there are also some pieces with platform remnants, indicating that platform reduction was also used, and again this is a common feature of many local assemblages. Many of the regular flakes

are large (Fig. 5.24), and though they are mostly corticated, there is very little edge damage on them and there are surprisingly few broken pieces.

The retouched pieces comprise two end scrapers and a notched piece. The end scrapers (nos. 1 and 6) are both made on regular flakes, and one (no. 1) is unusual because the retouch has cut through corticated flint and so seems to have been done at some time after the piece was originally knapped. They are of similar sizes and both have retouch on the distal end with narrower butt ends. The notched piece (no. 5), is made on a blade, and the retouch is very small and shallow to form a slight notch that could, in fact, be simply a result of accidental damage.

Quartzite. The quartzite flake is a large (40 × 29 × 12 mm) piece that appears to have been struck from a cobble tool, such as a hammerstone. It may well have been the result of accidental damage.

Discussion. Not surprisingly in such a small assemblage there are no pieces that are chronologically or culturally significant, and there is limited technological information to be gleaned. Nevertheless, there are certain points of interest. The low debitage content of the assemblage suggests that it has derived from the use, or specific deposition, of stone tools rather than their manufacture. Most of the pieces are corticated, but they are generally in good condition. There are few broken pieces and there is little visible edge damage. None of the pieces is obviously burnt.

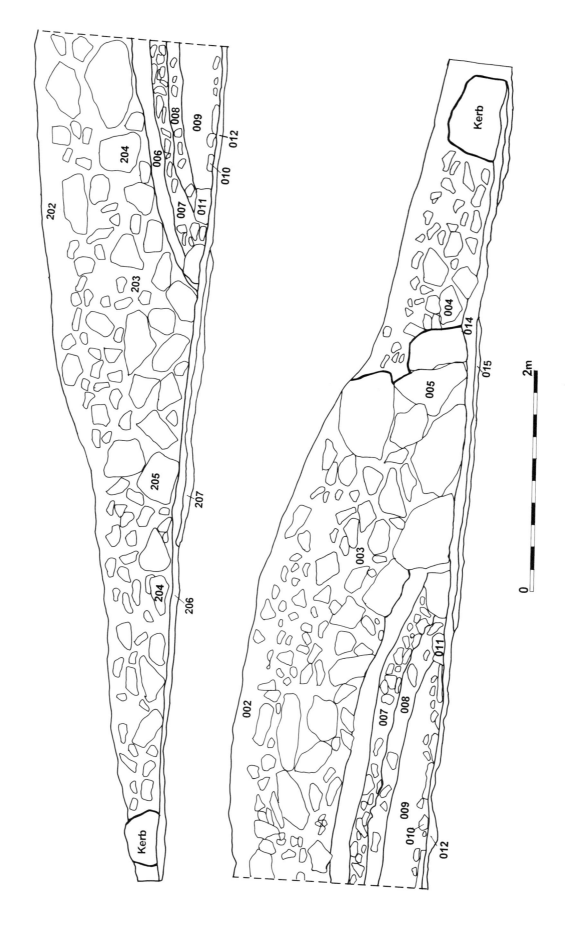

Figure 5.21 A section from west (left) to east (right) across cairn VS4B.

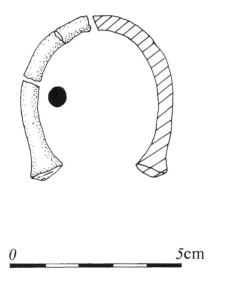

0 _____ 5cm

Figure 5.22 A bronze cloak fastener found in the cairn material of VS4B.

Nearly half of the pieces come from the main cairn material (Table 5.4). With regard to location, almost all of the pieces were located within the southern half of the site (Table 5.5). Two-dimensional coordinates were recorded for most of the artifacts, but there is no patterning visible when these are plotted out. The flints seem to have been generally scattered throughout the cairn material, but this lack of patterning is hardly surprising given the small size of the assemblage.

Conclusions. The nature of the site would suggest that this is not a common domestic assemblage and this is supported by the lithic material itself. There is very little waste or knapping debris and the pieces are generally in a good condition. There are not many formally retouched tools, but this is a small assemblage and it does contain an unusually high proportion of regular unbroken flakes. The material was

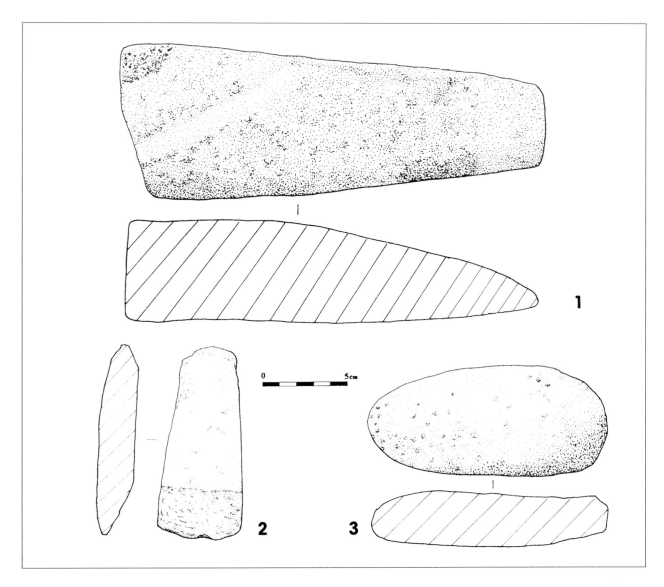

Figure 5.23 Three heavy stone artifacts from cairn VS4B. 1. An ard tip rough-out. 2. an axe rough-out. 3. Sandstone rubber.

211

Table 5.4 Breakdown of the flint assemblage from cairn VS4B by type and context.

Type	Topsoil	Main Cairn	Inner Cairn	Construction	Pre-Cairn
Cores		1			1
Chunks		1			
Blades		2			
Debitage			1		1
Flakes					
Regular Flakes	2	2	1	3	2
Retouched Pieces	1	2			
Total	3	8	2	3	4

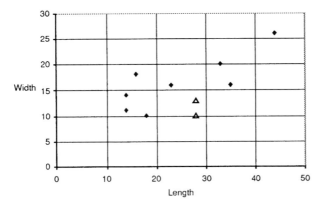

Figure 5.24 Size of regular blades and flakes from VS4B (in mm).

apparently generally scattered across the site and is clearly closely associated with the cairn. Only four pieces were found in the precairn surface and most of the assemblage comes from the construction and main and inner cairn levels. Unless the precairn surface was thoroughly cleared before construction this would seem to suggest that the lithics became incorporated into the site during the building, use and alteration of, the cairn. Interestingly, none of the lithics were burnt. Though there was evidence for cremation this seems to have taken place elsewhere, and this may well be supported by the unburnt nature of the lithics.

Soil pollen analyses

Kevin J. Edwards and Robert Craigie

Abstract
During the excavation of kerbed cairn VS4B, soil samples for pollen analysis were taken in an attempt to determine local land use or more general environmental conditions at the time of construction of the cairn. The data indicate that the cairn was built upon a vegetational cover dominated by grassland, richer than that at VS7, and it may have developed from a heath-grassland mosaic. This, and the virtual absence of hazel pollen, suggests that cairn VS4B postdates nearby kerbed cairn VS7.

Introduction
During the excavation of kerbed cairn VS4B, soil samples were taken from beneath the kerb and submitted for pollen analysis. The hope was not only to produce evidence for local land use and environment during or immediately prior to the construction of the cairn, but also to obtain comparative data to set beside those obtained from cairn VS7 (above).

Samples, laboratory methods and data presentation
Four soil samples (M2–0.5, M2–3.0, M2–5.0, M2–7.5) were extracted from a small monolith tin that contained a soil column from immediately beneath a kerbstone (context 014) in the south-eastern quadrant 3.7 m from the cairn centre (Fig. 5.14). Laboratory methods, palynomorph identification, and diagram construction were as detailed above (p. 200). It was possible, however, to achieve counts of 300–500 identifiable terrestrial pollen, which is likely, at least in part, to explain the greater representation of taxa in Figure 5.25.

Discussion
As was also the case for the cairn VS7 samples, the low counts for resistant spores and the fact that,

Table 5.5 The location of the flint assemblage in cairn VS4B.

Type	SE Quadrant	SW Quadrant	NW Quadrant	NE Quadrant
Cores	1	1		
Chunks	1			
Debitage Flakes	2			
Blades	1	1		
Regular Flakes	3	5		2
Retouched Pieces	2		1	

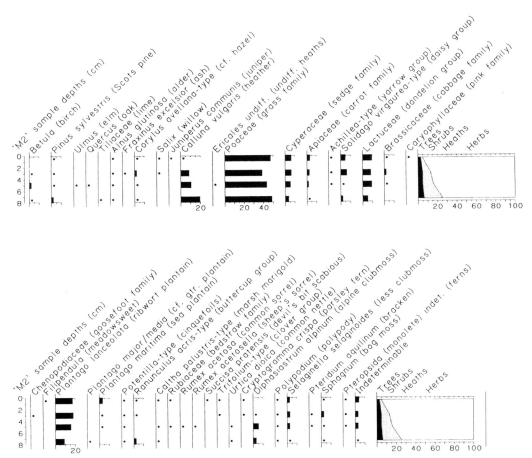

Figure 5.25 Percentage pollen and spore diagram for the monolith from beneath the kerbstone of VS4B. (● Indicates less than 2% TLP).

although high, the indeterminable taxa counts are low, suggests that differential palynomorph survival has not been a major problem in the cairn VS4B samples. There is, however, a marked decrease in palynomorph concentrations with depth (not displayed diagrammatically), implying possible degradation if the palynomorphs are long-lived, but an interpretable pattern in the spectra seems evident.

Essentially, the samples are dominated by undifferentiated Poaceae (grass family) pollen throughout and with other indicators of grassland (e.g. *Plantago lanceolata* and Lactuceae) and heathland (e.g. *Calluna vulgaris* and Cyperaceae), and mosses that may be found in both habitats (e.g. *Diphasiastrum alpinum* and *Selaginella selaginoides*). It is notable that the *Calluna* values decrease up-profile, while *Plantago lanceolata* representation rises. The impression is one of a mixed heath-grassland giving way to a dominant and possibly quite rich grassland. The grass and ribwort plantain pollen percentages are greater than those found beneath the stones of cairn VS7 and heather pollen values are lower. Tall-herb and other taxa are well represented in the herbaceous assemblages, with Apiaceae, *Achillea*-type, *Solidago virgaurea*-type (cf. *Bellis* [daisy]), Lactuceae (cf. *Leontodon* and *Taraxacum* spp.), Brassicaceae, *Potentilla*-type, *Ranunculus acris*-type and *Rumex spp.* The apparent richness of the

assemblages, when compared to those of VS7, may not only indicate the benefits accruing from wind-blown additions of calcareous sand and/or pollen from the adjacent machair, but could indicate the intentional improvement of soils around cairn VS4B by manuring or even the construction of plaggen-like soils from additions of sand, seaweed, or other organic refuse (Whittington and Edwards 1993; Davidson and Simpson 1994). The fossil flora includes elements that, although present naturally, are also typically anthropochorous, including Apiaceae, *Solidago virgaurea*-type, Lactuceae, Caryophyllaceae, Chenopodiaceae, Brassicaceae, *Plantago lanceolata*, *P. Major/me diam.*, *Ranunculus acris*-type, *Rumex acetosa*, *R. acetosella*, *Trifolium*-type, *Urtica dioica* and *Pteridium aquilinum*; cereal-type pollen is absent.

There is a marked dearth of tree and shrub pollen, which suggests that there were no local arboreal pollen producers to compare with the inferred hazel sources close to cairn VS7. Given the proximity of the cairns and the prolonged period over which *Corylus* persisted in the pollen rain of the Outer Hebrides (Brayshay and Edwards 1996; Brayshay *et al.* this volume) this would suggest that the pollen spectra beneath cairn VS4B postdate those of VS7. Less certainly, this may be reinforced by the strong grassland indications following upon a heath-grassland assemblage at VS4B—the most recent spectra at VS7 having been developing towards a heath-grassland. The differentiation of assemblages in the DEC-ORANA plot (Fig. 5.12), with the deeper VS7 monolith samples clustering towards the left of the diagram, the samples from immediately beneath the cairn boulders in the centre, and finally the mono-lith samples from cairn VS4B towards the right, would appear to represent a biostatistical depiction of this patterning.

Interpretation

The events leading to the construction of the cairn and the construction sequence itself appear to be much more complex than the apparently simple nature of the monument might lead one to expect. The monument is certainly a funerary structure, and the construction of the cairn to cover pyre debris including human bone suggests that the monument falls within the tradition of such funerary monuments in British prehistory.

The pollen analyses suggest that the cairn was erected in a landscape of mature grassland. It should be noted that on this exposed west-facing ridge, where powerful westerlies prevail, the pollen count will be dominated by pollen transported from the headland of Huilish Mhor to the west. Our impression at the time of excavation was that the monument was constructed on land that had been under cultivation at some time prior to the building of the cairn. The basal soil (014/106, 206, 306) was fine, rather sandy, mostly stone-free and had the appearance of being a tilled soil. This identification is strengthened by the evidence of small field stones (008) used as one of the deposits to cover the pyre, and of the much larger quantity of field stones used to cover the cairn after its completion (003). The relationship between cultivated land that may have been a small plot rather than a field system and funerary monument is perhaps reflected by the ard tip rough-out found on the kerb of the cairn.

Before the cairn was built, however, the area on which is was to be constructed appears to have been cleared almost down to bedrock—the surviving depth of soil below the cairn and the pyre would have been totally insufficient for crop production. Equally there was no trace of a buried land surface under the cairn; that is, deposits 014, 106, 206, 306 appear to be the truncated remains of the former topsoil.

The next step in the creation of the monument is uncertain. The oval of stone blocks to delineate the pyre area was certainly laid on to the clean, cleared surface, but whether it was preceded or succeeded by the laying of the arc of six stones to the north-west of the pyre area is uncertain. The arc of stones appears to follow the line of the oval pyre area and one is tempted to conclude that the arc is secondary to the pyre area therefore, but this is not conclusive. The

significance of this arc of six stones is not at all clear, but they were certainly deliberately and carefully positioned to form a neat alignment.

A few slabs of stone were laid on the soil within the outlined oval area together with a stone rubber, and a group of cobbles were laid on the slabs. It was on these cobbles that the pyre material itself was placed. We do not believe, however, that the pyre was built and lit here, nor do we believe, therefore, that the body of the deceased was cremated at this spot. Our reasons for this view are as follows. It is clear that the pyre debris was never a very large feature at all. The area covered by the pyre debris was only about 1 m in diameter, and the deposit at its deepest was only 10 cm thick. The pyre material appeared to consist almost entirely of burnt peat material and very small fragments of bone. That is, apart from a small flecks of charcoal, there were no substantial remains of the fuel used on the pyre. Yet the absence of any cremated bone apart from very small fragments suggests that the corpse had been completely consumed by the fire. Equally, the only signs of exposure to heat on both the cobbles under the pyre debris and the stone blocks encircling the pyre were very limited in both intensity and extent. The blocks, for example, only showed traces of heat only on a few inside faces. Taken together, the evidence strongly suggests that the pyre material was brought here from elsewhere. The evidence for some charring of the underlying material suggests either that the pyre material was brought here fresh and still hot from the cremation itself or that a symbolic small-scale recreation of the pyre material took place at the time the burial was made and the cairn erected. Evidence recovered in the excavation of cairn VS7 170 m to the south of VS.4B strongly supports this conclusion (see above).

After the deposition of the pyre material, four flat slabs were laid over the pyre and covered by a thin layer of the cultivated soil (008). This layer was too thin ever to have been intended as a major part of the covering cairn and its deposition must have been in some way symbolic, and presumably linked to the use of cultivated land for the siting of the monument and to the deposition of the ard rough-out on the kerb after the cairn was completed.

This deposit was in turn covered by a spread of burnt stone cobbles and beach pebbles (007). We suggest that the burnt cobbles most probably came from the site of the primary cremation. The alternative, that they were originally part of the deposit of cobbles on which the pyre material was placed when the monument was begun, is untenable. They are larger than the burnt cobbles beneath the pyre material and cannot in any case have been taken from there without removing the pyre material, which was of course found *in situ*. Whether the beach pebbles indicate that the primary pyre was on or close to the beach is unclear, and on the limited quantity of pebbles from VS4B (about a dozen) we would not press this argument. The evidence from VS7, however, certainly suggests that beach pebbles were deliberately collected and selected for use in the covering of the pyre material in that cairn.

The low oval cairn formed by these deposits was now covered with a thick layer of pure fine blackish soil with very few stones (006), which may have come from a midden or occupation deposit but was clearly well sorted before deposition, since it contained only two flint flakes. The enlarged cairn or mound was now encased in stone, with medium-sized stones (005, 105, 205, 305) covering the 'dome' and larger blocks forming a very rough basal ring to hold up the smaller stones.

It was at this point that the tall regularly shaped stone slab was placed at an angle of about 45° over the stones in the north-west quadrant, before the main inner revetment of large stone blocks was put in place. These blocks were placed over the base of the big stone slab, so that the point in the sequence at which the slab was inserted into the cairn can be pinpointed exactly. What cannot be so accurately fixed, however, is the point at which the stone slab was brought to the site. A key question arises—was the stone slab already on the site before the funerary monument began to be erected, or was it brought here from elsewhere to be incorporated into the monument? If the stone slab was already here, probably upright as a 1 m high standing stone, then we have the intrig.uing situation where a funerary cairn is built to incorporate an existing monument.

Unfortunately we have no clear evidence as to whether the stone was already *in situ* or was brought here specifically to be built into the cairn. It is true that we found no 'stone hole' at the base of the stone or anywhere near it, but we have to remember that the soil had apparently been removed almost down to bedrock before the funerary monument began to be built. The stone could have stood in a hole 15–20 cm deep, and no trace of such a hole would remain. On the other hand, if the stone was here before the cairn was begun, then it stood in the middle or on the edge of what we believe was a cultivated area. In any event, the incorporation of the stone into the cairn must be regarded as a significant event. It is so clearly quite different to all the other smaller, irregular blocks and boulders used in the cairn that it must have been deliberately incorporated. Whether its incorporation was intended simply to lay claim to the prestige and symbolism that went with the standing stone, or whether it was more directly linked to the deceased who was commemorated by the cairn, must remain unknown. It is worth noting, however, that a standing stone was set into the kerb of the cairn EF2 on Fuday, and fallen monoliths were recorded at the paved cairn of T214 and the apparently similar cairn of G35. That is, we have at least four Bronze Age cairns with associated standing stones, sufficient to suggest that standing stones may have had a significant role in the funerary practices and beliefs of the Bronze Age populations of these islands.

After the stone had been laid across the inner cairn, a revetment of large stone blocks was built around the circumference and the inner cairn completed with a capping of medium to large blocks (004). The outer kerb was either laid out now or at some earlier point in the sequence. There is no direct evidence for the place of the outer kerb in the construction sequence, except that it was laid directly on the cleared subsoil just above bedrock and that it was in place before the outer ring of cairn material was put there. The only obvious difference in the size of the kerbstones around the circumference was that the smallest stones were concentrated in the southern arc, but it is not clear whether this was either deliberate or significant.

The space between the kerb and the inner cairn revetment was filled with a spread of medium to large stone (004) blocks to form a low platform around the central, inner cairn. Finally, small field stones (003) were deposited over the entire cairn, which on completion had a profile like an upturned soup bowl. The final covering of predominantly small field stones may have been no more than an energy-saving device for the builders, given that we believe the monument was built on cultivated land. On the other hand, it may have held a deeper significance for those involved in the funerary rites and/or the wider community. The choice of arable land on which to build the cairn is somewhat surprising—the surrender of a valuable resource that would have taken considerable effort to clear and cultivate. We have already noted the stone rubber (for use with a saddle quern?) deposited at the centre of the mound and the base of the inner cairn, and the apparently symbolic layer of cultivated soil spread over the pyre material within the inner cairn. The final acts of agricultural symbolism may have been the deposition of an imitation axe on the cairn and an ard tip rough-out on the kerb. In this context the covering of the cairn with field stones may have been not only a symbolic act but also one in which every member of the local community could be involved. It may have been part of a recurrent arable theme running through the construction of the monument and the rites that accompanied it.

The material culture that appears to have been deliberately incorporated into the cairn is impoverished—a rubber, an imitation axe, an ard rough-out and possibly a small quantity of chipped stone—and even the quantity of bone from the original cremation is very limited. But to set against this appearance of material impoverishment is the remarkably complex sequence of construction and the apparently rich symbolism of the process. We identify no less than 16 phases in the construction of this apparently simple monument. While some of these phases were undoubtedly very closely connected in time, they each seem to have been an important part of a highly structured process. Furthermore that process seems to have been designed to incorporate a variety of different symbols. We have stressed the arable symbolism, which seems to be a recurrent theme, but we should also note the incorporation of the stone monolith, the inclusion of beach pebbles in the stones that cover the pyre material and the deposit of occupation or midden soil that was brought to cover the inner cairn. Even the limited quantity of lithic material was concentrated in the southern half of the cairn, and according to Wickham Jones (above) 'is not a common domestic assemblage'. It is not easy to envisage how the lithics were accidentally incorporated into a cairn comprised almost entirely of field stones and larger blocks.

The distribution of the lithics and the contexts in which they were found are suggestive of deliberate deposition. There seem to be symbolic statements here that concern other arenas of life in the islands—the sea, the home, and perhaps the ancestral tradition.

The chronological position of this monument is not as well fixed as one might wish, but the OSL date of 3050 BP with an error of ±400 years suggests a Middle/Late Bronze Age date, not inconsistent with the fragment of a cloak-fastener from the body of the cairn material, nor contradicted by the pottery found beneath the cairn. The nearby site of VS7, however, produced a considerably earlier date, and it is interesting that the pollen evidence from the two cairns supports an earlier date for VS7 (p. 213).

A LBA/EIA Occupation Site in the Borve Valley: B54

Keith Branigan

Site B54 was discovered in 1988, the first year of the project, and aroused great interest at the time. It is situated at about 70 m OD on a flat, rather boggy shelf of land that looks straight down the valley to Borve

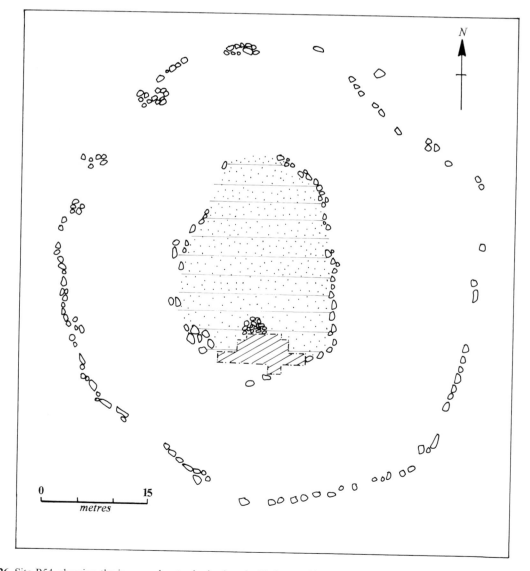

Figure 5.26 Site B54, showing the inner and outer kerbs, lazy-bedded grass hillock, and location of excavation trench.

headland. Immediately behind, the hillside rises to a plateau at about 100 m OD on which there are scattered shieling sites, while immediately north-east of site B54 a small knoll overlooking the site has the remains of what appears to be a robbed and modified stone ring (site B55, p. 191). To the north, the great chambered cairn of Dun Bharpa is clearly visible on the skyline.

B54 itself comprises three main elements on the surface (Fig. 5.26). At the centre of the area is a low grassy mound with traces of lazy bedding very clearly visible. Since it drains well into the boggy ground on all sides, this natural hillock has obviously attracted both sheep and possibly cattle in the past, and their manuring has helped to enrich the soil. An episode of relatively recent cultivation is therefore not unexpected. The hillock is oval and at its south end there are stray blocks of stone embedded in the cultivation area, a heap of stones or boulders, and a second smaller heap at the south-west corner.

Around the perimeter of the hillock, where the green manured grass meets the bog vegetation, there is an incomplete but apparently once-continuous stone kerb. This is comprised of stone blocks, mainly about 30–50 cm long, laid end-to-end to enclose an oval or slightly egg-shaped area about 35 m × 20 m. The third element to the site is an outer kerb of similar type but employing somewhat larger stones and measuring about 70 m × 57 m. This outer kerb fringes the damper ground around the west and east sides but has to cross it at the northern and southern ends.

The site is quite spectacular if approached from the east, the outer kerb being clearly visible, with the bright green mound at its centre, as one comes over the edge from the upper plateau. The proximity of the stone ring at B55, the clear view to (and from) Dun Bharpa on the northern skyline and the curious morphology of site B54 itself inevitably raise the possibility that this is some form of ritual monument of Neolithic or Bronze Age date.

Closer examination of the two kerbs, however, at once raises the probability that they are relatively recent constructions. They appear to be single stones of modest size, not resting on any underlying structure but rather on, or just in, the vegetated surface. They are not, for the most part, well-embedded and this suggests they have not been in their present position for many centuries, let alone millennia. Since the crofters of Borve and Craigston have no oral tradition which explains why and when these two oval stone rings were constructed we believe they most probably belong to the earlier modern period. It seems likely that the inner kerb at least was broadly contemporary with the lazy-bedding on the central mound and may have represented stones removed in cultivation and placed along the edge of the hillock, possibly to support wooden fence posts around it. The purpose of the outer kerb is unclear.

Excavation

Excavations were undertaken at the southern end of the central mound or hillock to confirm that the mound was essentially a natural feature rather than manmade, and to investigate the possibility that the blocks of stone heaped at this end may have come from a structure that preceded and was disturbed by, the lazy-bed cultivation. Initially a trench 12.5 × 1.5 m was laid across the southern end of the mound on its short east–west axis (Fig. 5.26). Below the turf in a fine medium-brown stone-free tilled soil (context 2) we soon encountered small sherds of handmade pottery and pieces of flint. In the centre of the trench, midway across the mound, we encountered more of this material as well as stone blocks and traces of a deeper deposit of dark-brown soil flecked with charcoal and burnt stone. At this point we therefore opened a 5 × 3.5 m extension in the central area. Three further small extensions were added to this area as excavations progressed in order to answer specific questions. The total area excavated in trench 1 eventually amounted to 40 m².

These excavations confirmed that that mound was a natural hillock with bedrock overlain by an orangey-yellow clay (context 20) that contained small chips of stone and had a gritty texture. This undisturbed natural was found immediately below the lowest disturbed and manmade deposits. At the west end of the area these deposits were the base of the tilled soil (context 4), but in the central and eastern areas of trench 1 more complex deposits were found that we could divide into four phases.

Phase 1 (Fig. 5.27)

Over much of the central area, natural was overlain by a charcoal-rich sticky black soil (context 15) containing a few broken sherds of pottery. This deposit ran up to a line of well-worn stone slabs set to form an alignment that could be traced for ten slabs (2.35 m) north–south before it appeared to meet the remains of a similar alignment running roughly east–west. Owing to the cutting of the furrow at this point, only two slabs could be traced to the west and one to the east. The degree of wear on these slabs was such that they must have been exposed and in use for a considerable time, and they must have been continually walked on (Fig. 5.28). We therefore interpret them as the remains of a path rather than any sort of structural foundation. Immediately east of the path there was no trace of the sticky black soil but instead a deposit of well-embedded stone cobbles (context 18) into which was set a line of four slabs, beyond which further cobbles were found extending down to the eastern limit of the trench. Where cobbles were missing a darkish-brown stony soil was found (context 14), again containing small quantities of pottery. The only other features that were related to context 15 and therefore fall in

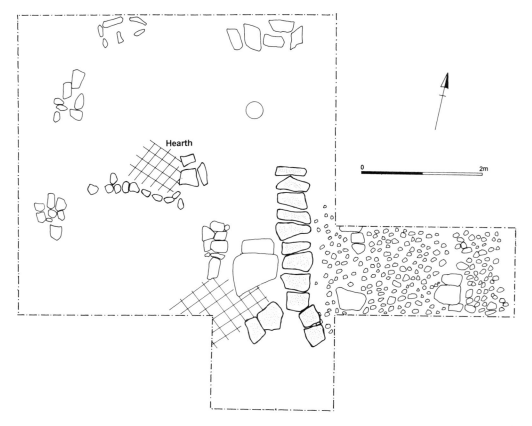

Figure 5.27 Phase 1 and 2 features at site B54.

phase 1 were a large block of stone 0.75×0.6 m and 0.45 m tall, set immediately next to the path, and a small cist-like structure up against the western baulk and somewhat isolated from the path and cobbles. This measured 0.5×0.27 m and was outlined by seven

small stone slabs set on edge (two were badly decayed). The feature was only about 6 cm deep and filled with a dark-brown sticky soil (context 17) from which came three sherds and a small whetstone. There was no trace of burning and it is unlikely to have been a small hearth setting. Equally the shallow depth suggests it can scarcely have acted as a storage bin. Its function is therefore uncertain; perhaps it was a standing for some moveable object or furnishing. Contexts 14, 15 and 17 yielded a total of only 21 sherds and a small sandstone whetstone.

Phase 2 (Fig. 5.27)

Over most of the central area of excavation context 15 was overlain by an orange-brown sandier soil flecked with charcoal (context 8). This also ran up to and overlay the flagstones of the phase 1 path, and spread over the first 50 cm of cobbling to the east of the flagstones. Set in this soil in the central area were five spaced clusters of small stone slabs and blocks. There is nothing in either their size or disposition to suggest they were the remains of a substantial stone foundation, but equally, they do not appear to have been purely random dumps of stone in this deposit. A cluster of three slabs near the centre of the area was associated with a thin area of burnt soil and charcoal and a linear arrangement of small stones suggestive of a short-lived hearth area. To the north-east of this feature was a single post hole, 25 cm across narrowing

Figure 5.28 The well-worn paving slabs of phase 1 at B54.

Figure 5.29 The damaged stone-lined drain of phase 2 overlying the phase 1 slabs, B54.

to 10 cm at its base, and 20 cm deep with traces of the burnt stump of the post.

Cutting across the south end of the phase 1 path was a damaged stone drain comprised of small blocks and slabs set upright in two parallel lines, with four covering slabs still in position and two more slipped into the gully (Fig. 5.29). The drain could be traced for 2.5 m before it gave out at the north-east end, and had been clearly destroyed by a furrow of the lazy bedding at the south-west. A metre west of the drain,

up against the south baulk of the excavation, a bright orange and red area of clayey soil with traces of charred fibrous material (context 19) 1.25 × 0.5 m appeared to be the remains of a fire, possibly of a peat or turf stack. To the east of the drain, the phase 1 cobbles were mostly covered with a dark silty soil (context 10), among which there were patches of secondary cobbling. The impression was of an area in which mud or silt accumulated and into which cobbles were occasionally dumped to firm it up. From contexts 10, 8 and 6 (a lens of very dark-brown soil with much charcoal and burnt stone flecks, overlying context 8 on the west of the central area) came a total of 248 sherds of pottery, three pieces of pumice and a single flint flake.

Phase 3 (Fig. 5.30)
In the central area contexts 6 and 8 were overlain by a dark-brown slightly sandy soil with many red and black flecks (context 5). This relatively thin deposit (2–5 cm thick), was very similar to context 6 and may have been essentially the higher level of the same deposit, but it differed from context 6 in one important stratigraphic respect. Context 5 ran up to a curving line of stone blocks found in the west–north-west part of the central area, and also ran up to a similar but shorter arc of blocks in the north-east quarter; context 6 in contrast, ran beneath the stones in the west–north-west arc.

The stone blocks were clearly the remains of a stone-founded circular structure that had been largely destroyed by the furrows of the lazy-bedding and was preserved only beneath the extra depth of soil on one of the ridges. The two heaps of stone at this end of the

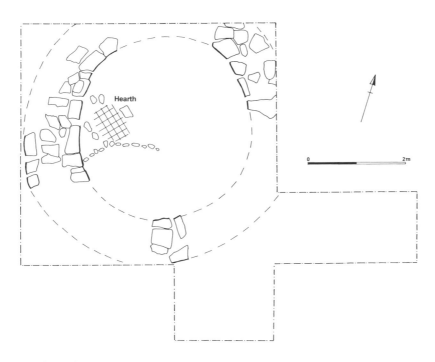

Figure 5.30 Phase 3 features at site B54.

hillock almost certainly represent the destroyed remains of walling dug out of the furrows by the lazy-bed cultivators. Four sizeable blocks of stone almost certainly from the wall were found in the base of the southernmost furrow, just outside the line of the wall. A further five blocks on the south side, again in the very base of the furrow, appeared to be *in situ*.

Enough of the foundations survived (Fig. 5.31) to show that the stones were laid to form a foundation about 1.2 m wide. The two surviving arcs of foundation suggest a structure that was slightly oval, 6.5 × 5.75 m overall enclosing a floor area of about 15 m². The facing stones in the foundation level were mostly set on their long axis, and at one point three courses survived, so that the stone foundations certainly rose well above floor level. On the other hand the quantity of stone in the two surface heaps was certainly insufficient to raise the circuit wall more than three or four courses high, and even if the stones of the inner kerb originally came from this circular foundation it would have been no more than five or six courses (perhaps 0.6–0.7 m) high. We therefore believe it unlikely that the structure was built entirely of stone. Its superstructure was probably of turf, although the nature of the roof is uncertain. There was no evidence at all for any ring of posts to support the roof, such as has been found in roundhouses with stone foundations like those at Cul a'Bhaile on Jura (Stevenson 1984).

Context 5 with its many charcoal and burnt stone flecks was found within the stone wall foundation and clearly represents an occupation deposit. Against the western arc of walling an area of black soil with many small pieces of charcoal and lumps of burnt stone

(context 9) formed a roughly circular area about 0.75 m across, around which five slabs of stone were scattered. This appears to be the remains of a hearth. Immediately south of it an alignment of small stones ran from the wall inwards towards the centre of the house for 1.5 m. The stones themselves are far too small to have been part of a structural element but their alignment was absolutely clear and plainly artificial. We believe they must mark the line of an internal partition of some sort, most probably of light wickerwork. This would have had the effect of shutting off the hearth area from the south-west quadrant of the building.

There were no other recognisable features inside the structure and it was impossible to identify where the original entrance lay. From the occupation deposit (contexts 5 and 9) 87 sherds of pottery, two flint blades and two flakes, a quartz flake and a stone rubber were recovered.

Phase 4

Contexts 5 and 9 were sealed over much of the centre of the area by a hard deposit of iron-pan (context 11), which was overlain by a silty greyish-brown soil (context 7) sitting in the roughly circular depression formed by the iron-pan. This in turn was overlain by an orange-brown worked soil (context 4), quite compacted, that appeared to be the base of a cultivated soil above (contexts 2 and 3) and extended over the whole of the cultivated area. The fine medium-brown cultivated soil (context 2) was almost stone-free, and at the east end of the area became finer and almost silty (context 3) as it followed the dip of the

Figure 5.31 The inner face of the stone-founded roundhouse of phase 3, B54.

natural mound and ran down to meet the boggy land that surrounds it.

This phase is essentially the early modern cultivation episode that was responsible for the destruction and removal of the remains of the stone-founded building and the disturbance of its occupation deposit. The material from this was scattered through contexts 2 and 3 and included 166 sherds of handmade pottery, 15 pieces of flint and 2 of quartz, 2 pieces of pumice, a stone rubber and a fragment of a whetstone. The pottery was notably broken into small pieces and heavily weathered; over 70% of the sherds were smaller than 2 cm square.

The finds

Pottery (C. Cumberpatch and K. Branigan)

A total of 522 sherds, all handmade, were recovered from site B54, with a combined weight of 4,415 grams. Of these 166 (32%) came from the uppermost contexts associated with early modern cultivation and these were notably weathered, abraded and small.

As usual the range of fabrics was limited and fabric types are identified mainly on the basis of variations in the quantity and size of the inclusions. Five fabrics were identified:

1. Fabric A is a coarse, very variable fabric with abundant quartz grains, rock fragments and mica. There are variations in texture within this fabric group, and it includes both thin- and thick-walled vessels.
2. Fabric F is a soft, dense slightly soapy fabric containing sparse fine inclusions of quartz and biotite in a dark-grey matrix.
3. Fabric H is a sandy fabric containing sparse fine inclusions (including quartz and biotite) in a dark-grey matrix, and it has a distinctive laminated fracture.
4. Fabric J is a hard, uneven, rather muddy fabric containing large, soft, angular rock fragments, quartz and mica.
5. Fabric K is a soft light-brown muddy fabric containing fine quartz, mica and occasional rock fragments, and may be a variant of fabric J.

The breakdown of the assemblage by context and phase is given in Table 5.6

The assemblage as a whole is dominated by the ubiquitous fabric A which makes up 93% of the total. It will be seen that the only fabric found in phase 1 is fabric A but in a group of only 21 sherds the absence of other fabrics may not be significant. In phase 2 fabric H is a minor component (5%) of the assem-

blage, and fabrics J and K appear to replace it as minor constituents (9% and 5%) in phase 3. Fabric F only appears in the cultivated soils of phase 4 and although this may be fortuitous, the two rims in this fabric (pots 15 and 16) may both be of Roman-Iron Age date, later than the material in phases 1–3.

In assessing the chronology of this assemblage we are much indebted to Mike Parker Pearson for allowing us to see material from his excavations at Cladh Hallan on South Uist and for providing us with information about the stratified sequence and C14 dating there.

Phase 2 pottery (Fig. 5.32). While the small group from phase 1 included no rims, bases or decorated sherds, the larger group from phase 2 contexts yielded 8 rims, 2 bases and one complete profile.

Pots 1–5 are all straight or slightly incurved bucket-like vessels with flat or only slightly curved plain rims. All these vessels are made in fabric A. The slightly bulbous rim of pot 1 is found in the lowest, LBA, levels at Cladh Hallan C14 dated to c. 1150–900 BC. Rims 2–5 are paralleled in the Cladh Hallan levels C14 dated to 700–400 BC.

Pots 6 and 7 from phase 2 deposits are very similar rims in the same fabric, from more bowl-like forms. The rim forms belong in the same group as no. 5.

Pot 8 with finger impressions around the inside of the rim is unusual and has no parallels at Cladh Hallan.

Pots 9 and 10 are two flat bases. The former, in fabric A may come from a bucket-shaped vessel, but the latter, in fabric K may come from a bowl with inturned rim. It may in fact be the base that goes with the rim of pot 11, from a phase 3 deposit.

Phase 3 pottery (Fig. 5.32). Only three rims were found in phase 3 contexts.

Pot 11 in fabric K is the upper part of a rather shallow bowl with inturned rim, and three rather uneven incised lines around its shoulder. It may well be from the same vessel as the base, pot 10, in which case it is residual from phase 2. Similar forms are found at Dun Vulan in the construction material of the broch (LaTrobe-Bateman 1999: 214, type 8).

Pot 12 is also probably residual. Made in fabric A it is another example of the straight-sided jar with a slightly rounded rim.

Table 5.6 The pottery assemblage by fabric and context at site B54.

Fabrics	A	F	H	J	K
Context 2/3/4/7	157	4	2	—	3
Context 5/9	75	—	1	7	4
Context 6/8/10	234	—	12	1	1
Context 17/15/14	21	—	—	—	—
Total	487	4	15	8	8

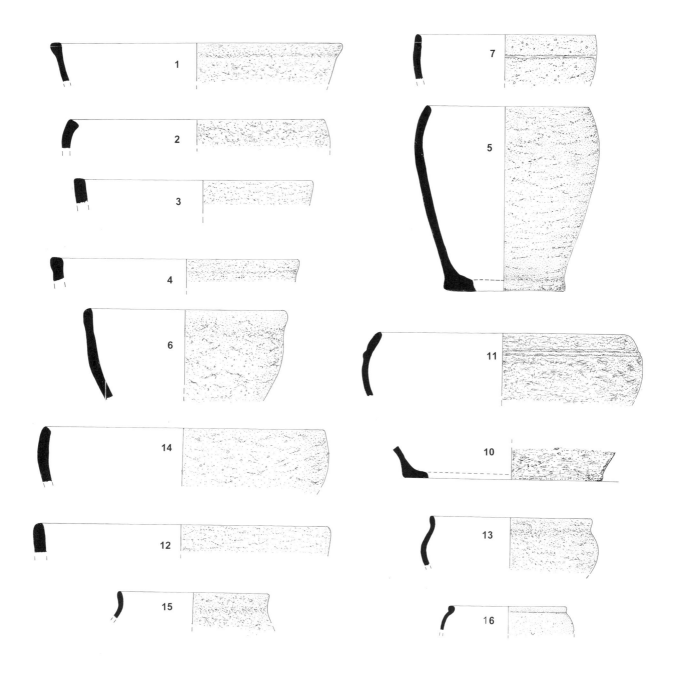

Figure 5.32 Pottery from site B54.

Pot 13, in fabric J is a rather fine small bowl with a marked waist and an upright rim. At Dun Vulan this is form 11, found in all phases (LaTrobe-Bateman 1999:214, type 11).

Pottery from disturbed contexts (Fig.5.32). Three rims were found in disturbed levels.

Pot 14, in fabric A is almost certainly residual—another example of the slightly inturned bucket rim of LBA/EIA type.

Pot 15, in fabric F is a slightly everted jar or bowl rim, of Dun Vulan type 11.

Pot 16, also in fabric F is a small bead-rimmed jar of a type likely to belong in the early centuries AD.

Comments. The rim forms suggest a date for phases 1 and 2 in the LBA/EIA transition, but it should be noted that fabrics A H and J found in phase 1 and 2 deposits are all much harder and finer than the Cladh Hallan fabric in which similar forms were made and used there. The fabrics are much closer to those in use at Dun Vulan in the MIA. This is obviously problematic in arriving at a probable date for our small assemblage. On balance we feel that forms have to be given precedence over fabrics. Fabrics, in a society where pottery production was highly localized, could well vary considerably from one island to another, although any significant differences attributed to an improved technology would have to be given due weight. The forms from phase 2 in particular seem to form a coherent group with LBA/EIA parallels at Cladh Hallan, and we believe this is their likely date range. Pots 11 and 13 from the phase 3 roundhouse might argue for a significantly later date for that structure but the Dun Vulan evidence is simply that both types were in use when the broch was being built. How much before that the forms may have come into use is unclear at present. Nevertheless we recognize there is still something of a problem in the dating of the three phases of occupation, since we believe that phase 3 followed on quickly and directly from phase 2 and was itself relatively short-lived. A date range of 5th–3rd centuries BC for all three phases might just about encompass all the strands of evidence.

Flaked stone and pumice (C.R. Wickham-Jones)

The assemblage comprises 32 pieces, including 22 flint artifacts, 6 pieces of pumice, 3 of quartz, and 1 coarse stone tool.

Flint. The breakdown of the flint assemblage is set out in Table 5.7.

Where cortex survives it is abraded and indicates that a pebble source of flint was used. Indeed, there is one flint pebble in the assemblage, though it is very small and therefore unlikely to have served as a potential core. Because of the small size of the assemblage there is little technical detail to be obtained, though it may be noted that there is evidence for the use of both bipolar and platform knapping. This is not unexpected where pebble nodules were worked.

Table 5.7 Breakdown of the flint assemblage by type at site B54.

Type	Quantity
Pebble	1
Chunks	6
Blades	2
Regular Flakes	11
Scrapers	2

The assemblage comprises primarily regular flakes, with two blades and two scrapers, though there is also some debitage. This general nature suggests that it has derived from the use of tools rather than their manufacture. Indeed, the debitage pieces may well have been used alongside the more formal tools. Traces of damage from use are impossible to detect in analysis such as this without microscopic work. The scrapers, however, are both undercut on the edge, which may be a sign of use, and one (no. 29) appears to have been resharpened. They are both circular thumbnail scrapers, and this is a fairly common type throughout prehistory.

Quartz. Three pieces of quartz were recovered from the excavation and these include two regular flakes. The evidence is slight, but it is clear that quartz was used to supplement the flint when necessary. This is not surprising as quartz is relatively easy to come by and was certainly worked on many sites in the Hebrides.

Pumice. There are six pieces of pumice all of which are very rounded. They must have been brought on to the site from a nearby beach, presumably for use.

Pumice lumps with signs of wear are fairly common on archaeological sites throughout the Hebrides, though none of the pieces from Borve Valley has very clear indications of use. Beach pumice tends to be naturally rounded, though pumice is also friable and therefore easily worn down if it is used for smoothing or rubbing skins or other materials. Two pieces, however, do have fine grooves that may have come from working points, such as bone or antler needles. These grooves are much less pronounced than on other pumice tools, however (Wickham-Jones 1990: 130, Ill. 88) and they could have been formed naturally.

Coarse stone. There is one coarse stone tool, no. 18, a small whetstone on an elongated soft sandstone cobble. It is 67 mm long and has naturally squared-off sides with longitudinal striations. The two ends are also very rounded, possibly from use as a rubbing tool, but this may also be natural and due to the soft nature of the stone.

Context. With regard to the context of the material the evidence is rather disappointing. Most of the pieces come from the topsoil. Four of the flint artifacts come from an occupation soil recorded as early Iron Age and these include the two blades as well as two regular flakes. The quartz flake was also recovered from this phase, but there was no pumice. The two pieces of pumice with fine grooving do, however, come from a context that has been identified as late Bronze Age or early Iron Age and this also contained a regular flint flake and the flint pebble.

223

Culture and chronology. Culturally the assemblage is also disappointing because there is nothing that has any clear parallels or indications as to date. The whetstone is obviously a tool that by context must date to later prehistory but it is not of a type that was specific to any period. The lithics are all of types that were quite common throughout prehistory, and pumice has also been recovered from sites of all periods.

Conclusions. The assemblage is a small one that clearly reflects some use of local flint and quartz, together with some pumice. It does not provide any clues as to when this might have taken place, but associated artifacts indicate that it was in later prehistory and this could be supported by the presence of a small whetstone in the topsoil, though this could also have come from much more recent times. It may also be noted that the use of stone tools, while still a factor of later prehistoric sites, had reduced considerably in importance in later prehistory, and this would be quite in line with the sort of assemblage considered here.

Interpretation

A low natural hillock, about 35×25 m, was occupied at the LBA/EIA transition. The excavation has revealed the remains of a cobbled yard area flanked by a well-worn paved path, but the domestic focus of occupation presumably lay nearby since there was a low density of occupation material in the excavated area. The degree of wear on the paving stones suggests that this first phase of occupation lasted years rather than months (Fig. 5.28). In time silty deposits accumulated on the yard surface, which was patchily resurfaced and a drain built across the line of the paved path. West of the drain and former path, occupation became more intensive, with a hearth or fireplace, perhaps a windbreak and other minor structural features.

This phase may have been short-lived, because an oval stone-founded house was constructed over these features, and the location of its hearth and internal partition closely mirrored that of the fireplace and windbreak of the phase 2 occupation (Fig. 5.30). Furthermore the phase 3 occupation deposit accumulated directly on that of phase 2. This house, with an internal area of about $15 m^2$, was probably built four or five courses high in stone, and the superstructure completed in turf. The pottery from its occupation includes bucket-shaped storage vessels of LBA/EIA type. The handful of pebble-flint tools include two blades and two thumbnail scrapers, which, together with pieces of pumice, were probably used for cleaning animal skins. No faunal or plant material was found so that there is no direct evidence for the economy that supported this occupation. The limited quantity of artifact material, the relatively shallow occupation deposit and the apparently simple internal structural features all suggest that occupation of this house was short-lived. Whether or not there was more activity, and more prolonged activity, elsewhere on the hillock is not known, and could only be demonstrated by further excavation.

Subsequently the hillock was apparently abandoned for use of any kind until the early modern period when it was lazy-bedded and brought into cultivation.

Excavations outside Scurrival Cave (E16), Eoligarry

Keith Branigan

Evidence for the Mesolithic exploitation of the Outer Hebrides remains elusive. To test the hypothesis that Mesolithic peoples exploiting the coastal fringe now submerged off the west coast of Barra would have made use of the small cave below Dun Scurrival, which overlooks this submerged area, a trench $5 m \times 1 m$ was excavated at one side of the platform outside the cave in June 1998.

The cave itself (Fig. 5.33) is really no more than a rock shelter, a narrow triangular gap between two massive blocks of rock. At its broadest, by the entrance, it is only 2 m across and this narrows gradually over a distance of 16 m to a point where no further penetration is possible. Facing south-west, the cave and the platform immediately outside it provide a good observation point over Traigh Eias and, when the western seaboard of Barra was further west, a low-lying coastal zone perhaps up to a mile wide. In good weather, the cave and platform would make a good base from which to exploit the resources of both Traigh Mhor cockle beach and the marine resources off the west coast. A small headland immediately west of the cave also shelters it from the worst of the westerlies. However, even in June it was found that the platform could be exposed to bad weather from the south/south-west, and that rain could penetrate up to 3 m inside the cave entrance.

Visits to the cave in 1988 and 1991 had revealed no clear evidence of any human use of the cave, and the only identifiable fragments found among half a dozen bones collected from the cave floor were of sheep. However, in 1989 we were shown a human skull by an islander who told us that he had personally seen this skull recovered from the cave. We believe this skull still to be on the island. It is of course undated, and it may be relatively recent—perhaps from a body interred here after being washed up on the beach below. Ships have certainly been wrecked on Greian headland to the south and the wreckage thrown up on to the beach at Traigh Eias (Gilbertson *et al.* 1996: 83–84).

In seeking to sample the site we were anxious to disturb as little of any potential deposits as possible. We therefore excluded any excavations inside the

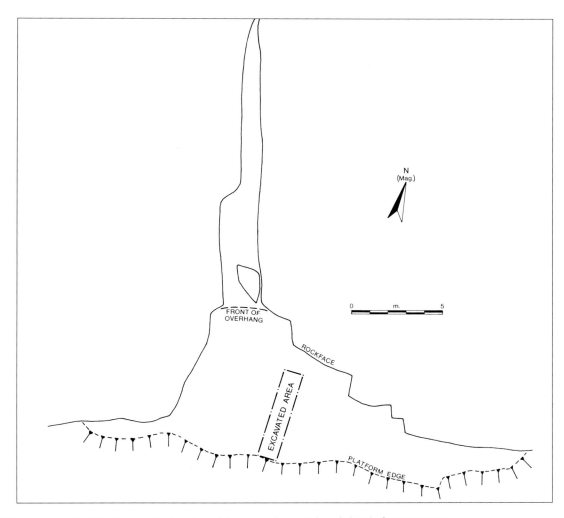

Figure 5.33 A plan of site E16, showing the location of the excavation trench and the platform revetment.

cave, where the available area is so small that any excavation would inevitably involve a significant proportion of the total cave area. We therefore turned our attention to the platform outside the cave. The platform that fronts the cave measures 8 m from front to back and 13 m across and is surrounded by large stone blocks that form a reasonably regular revetment and create the impression of an artificially created platform. At the back of the platform, close to the rock face in which the cave is situated, there are suggestions of a raised area, possibly with a revetment of small stones blocks.

The excavation

We laid out our trench so as to leave this raised area untouched. The trench ran from the southern edge of this raised area to the inner face of one of the large blocks that form the platform revetment, and was 5 × 1 m in size.

Below topsoil a deposit of silty black hill-wash (context 2) contained a small mixed assemblage of mediaeval and earlier pottery, flint pebbles and quartz chunks. The top of a saucer quern showed in this

deposit, but was found to be embedded in the top 10 cm of the underlying deposit (context 3). Context 3 was a dark rather sandy soil with small lumps of gneiss, up to 20 cm thick, in which both handmade pottery and flint and quartz flakes were found. This in turn overlay a soft sandy-brown soil with very few stones, which varied slightly in colour and texture at various points in the trench (contexts 4 and 6). Within this deposit, at the top (cave) end of the trench, there was rough stone paving forming a platform in which was set a small hearth area 25 × 20 cm (context 11). Rabbit activity had partly disturbed this feature. Further sherds, animal bones and lithic material were found in this deposit (6), though none was directly associated with the hearth and platform. Towards the bottom end of the trench a lighter-coloured yellowy-brown lens of soil about 0.5 m in diameter within context 6 appeared to be of no significance, but it may have been a small pit since it contained three pieces of pumice, the only context (8) in which pumice was found in the excavation. Cut into context 6 but overlain by context 3 was a shallow 60 cm wide band of sandy-brown soil mixed with many small lumps of stone, which ran across the top end of the trench.

Within this material (context 5) were two flint blades and two flakes.

Context 6 was found to lie against one of the large blocks forming the revetment of the platform and accumulated after the block came to rest in that position. However, the block sat on the top of the immediately underlying deposit (context 10), suggesting that it may have been moved into place during the early occupation of the site. It is possible therefore that the revetment is a manmade feature.

At the top end of the trench, context 6 overlay a slightly clayey yellow-brown soil with small angular stones and flecks of charcoal (context 7). This material formed a low bank across the north-east corner of the trench, anchored as it entered each side if the trench by a block of stone. It appears that context 7 represents the edge of the low roughly revetted platform that was noted in the survey of the area in front of the cave.

Context 10, a soft sandy loam mottled light reddish and dark brown, and containing many small fragments of weathered rock was 30–45 cm deep. It appeared to be a natural deposit but it yielded 27 sherds, animal bones and odd flecks of charcoal. It may represent a deposit of material washed downslope from the platform area (context 7) above. Beneath context 10, a similar soft sandy loam of lighter colour and with more angular fragments of stone (context 12) was probably the weathered surface material of the basal deposit—a greyish-yellow fine soil mixed with many large and angular lumps of stone (context 13), which the angle of deposition suggests had fallen from above. Bedrock was reached at a depth of 1.68 m (Fig. 5.34).

The finds

Pottery (C. Cumberpatch and K. Branigan)
The excavations produced an assemblage of 139 sherds weighing a total of 1,552 grams. The range of fabrics was limited and such distinctions as were made were on the basis of the quantity of large (2 mm+) rock fragments and varying proportions of the finer grade angular quartz and other gneiss-derived inclusions:

(a) Fabric A is a coarse, very variable fabric with abundant quartz grains, rock fragments and mica. There are variations in texture within this fabric group, and it includes both thin- and thick-walled vessels. The latter include the clearest examples of slab construction. This is the dominant fabric from this site.

(b) Fabric C is a coarsely tempered fabric containing abundant angular quartz and gneiss-derived grains, and occasional large rock fragments (up to 8 mm).

(c) Fabric E is a finely textured, relatively dense fabric with angular quartz grains up to 1.5 mm, but mostly 0.8–1 mm.

(d) Fabric F is a soft, dense rather soapy fabric containing sparse fine inclusions of quartz and biotite in a dark-grey matrix.

(e) Fabric G is very distinctive, lacking dense medium gritty inclusions typical of other fabrics. It contains sparse, large (to 5 mm) rock fragments. The sherds have very uneven, hand-modelled surfaces, apparently smoothed when the vessel was in the process of drying.

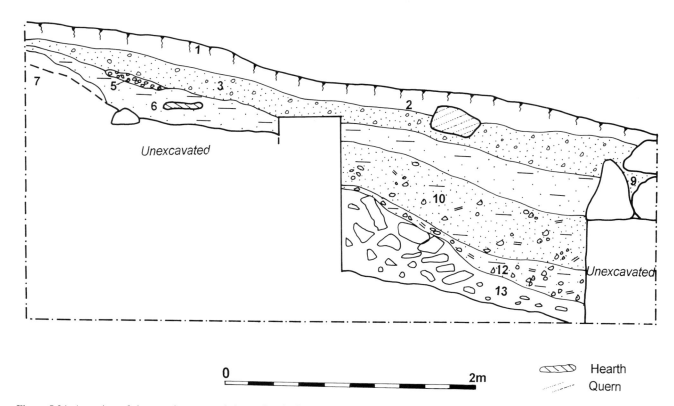

0 ———————————— 2m

◁▭▷ Hearth
·‒‒·‒ Quern

Figure 5.34 A section of the trench excavated down the platform at E16.

Table 5.8 The pottery assemblage by fabric and context at site E16.

	Fabric A	Fabric C	Fabric E	Fabric F	Fabric G
Unstratified	2	—	—	—	—
Context 3	19	2	3	2	—
Context 4/6	76	—	—	—	2
Context 7	6	—	—	—	—
Context 10	24	—	—	—	3
Total	127	2	3	2	5

There were two very simple rounded rims, and no bases or decorated sherds, so that chronological definition is difficult. Comparison with material from SEARCH excavations on South Uist suggest it is probably of MIA date. The two rims may have come from a straight-sided bucket form like Dun Vulan type 1 and a hole-mouthed jar like Dun Vulan type 8 (LaTrobe-Bateman 1999: 213) and several thick-walled body sherds of slab construction are similar to some material from the earlier levels at Dun Vulan (LaTrobe-Bateman 1999: 214). Fabrics C and E we believe to be late mediaeval or early modern.

The distribution of sherds through the deposits is as shown in Table 5.8.

Heavy stone artifacts (Keith Branigan)
Context 4/6 produced 17 heat-fractured large pebbles (upwards of 10 cm diam.) that we believe were used as pot-boilers. Three further examples were found in context 10. In context 4/6 there were also three rounded pebbles of 10–15 cm diam. that showed signs of pounding or hammering on one, usually rather flattened, side. The same deposit also yielded two elongated oval pebbles 11 and 14 cm long, each with signs of wear and smoothing on one side; these appear to have been used as polishers or possibly quern rubbers.

A large saucer quern was found well-embedded in the top of context 6 and was presumably in use at the time when the upper part of this deposit was accumulating. Made of a gneiss block about 60 × 50 cm, it had a well-worn circular depression about 35 cm diameter and 3.5 cm deep on one face.

Flaked lithic material (C.R. Wickham-Jones)
A total of 66 pieces of stone were recovered from the 1998 excavations at Dun Scurrival. Most of these were worked and they included 23 pieces of flint, 41 pieces of quartz (of which 30 may be natural, but at least 11 are artifactual), 1 piece of quartzite and 1 piece of coarse stone (Table 5.9).

The Flint. The flint is based on abraded pebble nodules that are most likely to be of local beach origin. It includes three pebbles, all of which have had at least one flake removed, and which probably represent the type of raw material available to the knappers. It is likely that the removal of flakes from these pebbles was a result of the testing of the material for further working, one piece at least (no. 33) is of such poor quality that it would be likely to have been discarded after this process. The other two pieces may have been set aside for future work that never took place.

The flint includes 14 regular flakes, but very little debitage. There is one bipolar core and one debitage flake, as well as three chunks. Bipolar knapping would be a good option for the working of pebble nodules, such as those here, and its use is confirmed by the regular flakes, of which 6 are bipolar while only 2 have platforms and 6 are indeterminate. Similarly, the size of the regular flakes accords well with the size of the bipolar core. More detailed technological information is unavailable due to the small size of the assemblage.

There is one retouched flake amongst the assemblage: a strange double-notched piece (no. 15). This is made on a segment of a large flake that has been

Table 5.9 Breakdown of the lithic assemblage by type and material at site E16.

	Flint	Quartz	Quartzite	Coarse Stone
Pebble	3			
Chunk*	3	30		
Bipolar core	1	1		
Debitage flake	1	1		
Regular flake	14	9		
Retouched flake	1			
Polished flake				1
Skaill knife			1	
Total	23	41	1	1

* Many of the quartz chunks may be natural.

retouched with irregular flaking on the two steep sides of the break. The retouch has formed a marked concavity on each edge to give a waisted appearance to the tool. No direct parallels to this piece are known to the author.

The Quartz. On first sight quartz would appear to be of more importance in the assemblage than flint, but this is a misleading impression due to the collection of quartz chunks. Quartz was certainly used to supplement the flint artifacts and there is one quartz core, so it is likely that some of these chunks do result from the working of quartz, but many are likely to be natural. Flint does seem to have been the preferred raw material for the knappers.

Among the quartz chunks are two very large pieces that may well represent the sort of raw material which was collected for working. Interestingly one (no. 21), appears to be of vein quartz, while the other (no. 29) has an abraded cortex and seems to be from a pebble nodule. The quartz core is a bipolar core. The use of bipolar knapping is often associated with quartz working so it is not surprising to find it here and indeed all nine of the regular quartz flakes show signs of bipolar knapping. There is only one debitage flake of quartz, and no pieces with secondary working.

Other stones. One flake of a coarser stone (no. 5) was recovered from the excavations, and this is a very interesting piece because it appears to be polished on one surface. The polishing is slightly unusual in that there are no marked striations of the sort usually visible on, say, polished axes, but the surface of the flake has a gloss that does not appear natural. It would seem to have come from the polishing of a naturally smoothed surface. Frustratingly, this is clearly a flake from a larger tool, the nature of which is no longer apparent.

The assemblage also includes a flake of quartzite (no. 28), and this, too, is interesting because it is in the form of a skaill knife. Skaill knives comprise flakes removed from rounded cobbles and their function is uncertain, though a possible use in butchery as flensing knives has been researched (Clarke 1989). In reality, it is likely that they served many different purposes.

Assemblage context. The context of the assemblage is shown in Table 5.10. The material is spread fairly consistently throughout the excavated contexts, with more material in context 6, which also provided the main evidence for human activity. Much of the quartz, including especially the chunks, was recovered from context 2 below the turf, and this probably represents the background level of broken quartz lumps in the area. Most of the obviously worked quartz was recovered from lower contexts, and this would seem to support the argument that many of the upper quartz chunks are natural.

Table 5.10 The lithic assemblage by context and raw material at site E16.

Context	Flint	Quartz	Quartzite	Coarse Stone
2	2	26		
3	5	9		
4	1	1		
6	9	4	1	1
7	1			
9	1			
10	3	1		
12	1			

Discussion. The assemblage is a small one in which quartz has been used to supplement flint. The raw materials are all local and the knappers seem to have preferred the bipolar technique, which would, indeed, be particularly suited to the knapping of this sort of raw material.

Though the assemblage is not large it is comprised primarily of regular flakes and there is little debitage. This suggests that it derives mainly from the use, rather than the manufacture, of stone tools. Tools may well have been made elsewhere, away from the area investigated, but the small size of the assemblage would also suggest that stone tools were not that important. This might be supported by the likely cultural affinities of the site. The rest of the artifactual material suggests a date in later prehistory or the mediaeval period, and the flaked stone artifacts would not disagree with this. Skaill knives are common in the Neolithic and early Bronze Age, but they do occur on other sites and none of the other pieces has any clear chronological or cultural parallels. As a rather gross rule, later sites have fewer stone tools, and this would be quite in accordance with Dun Scurrival, though the stone tool assemblage from any site must also depend on other factors, such as the type of activity undertaken.

Animal bone

Judith Cartledge

The excavation of a sampling trench down the platform outside the cave produced 54 fragments of animal bone, of which 37 came from context 6 and the remainder from context 10. The identifications are given below in Table 5.11.

The species identified were sheep/goat, cattle, pig and rabbit. In addition a single sample submitted to A. Jones proved to be a basioccipital from a large gadoid fish, probably a hake. The bones show some signs of erosion. Most of the bones were fragments and the number of loose teeth indicates high fragmentation. The bone in best condition was a complete rabbit tibia, which is presumably intrusive (for rabbit disturbance see the description of the excavation

Table 5.11 The faunal sample from site E16.

Layer	Quantity	Animal	Bone	L/R	Proximal Fusion	Distal Fusion	Gnawing	Fresh Break	Burnt	Age Estimate	Max. Length (mm)	Mandible D4
6	1	Cattle	Metapodial fragment					0	Black	Adult		
6	3	Cattle	Tooth					0				
6	1	Pig	Phalange 1 complete		PF	DF		0		Adult		
6	1	Rabbit	Mandible fragment	Left				0				
6	1	Sheep/Goat	Mandible fragment	Right				0				12
6	1	Sheep/Goat	Metacarpal barrel					0				
6	1	Sheep/Goat	Metacarpal distal			DF		0		Adult		
6	1	Sheep/Goat	Tibia barrel	Right				1				
6	1	Sheep/Goat	Tibia barrel					0		Adult		
6	1	Sheep/Goat	Tibia distal	Left		DNF		0	Black	Sub adult		
6	10	Sheep/Goat	Tooth					0				
6	1	Sheep/Goat	Ulna fragment					0				
6	13	Unidentified	Unidentified					0				
6	1	Unidentified	Vertebra					0				
10	1	Cattle	Femur proximal					0	Black	Adult		
10	2	Cattle	Tooth					0				
10	1	Rabbit	Humerus proximal	Left	PNF			0		Sub adult		
10	1	Rabbit	Tibia complete	Right				0		Adult	87.8	
10	1	Sheep/Goat	Astragalus complete	Left				0		Adult		
10	1	Sheep/Goat	Phalange 1 fragment				Rodent	0		Adult		
10	1	Sheep/Goat	Tibia barrel	Left				1		Adult		
10	1	Sheep/Goat	Tibia distal	Right		DF		1		Adult		
10	1	Sheep/Goat	Femur distal	Left		DNF		0		Juvenile		
10	1	Sheep/Goat	Ulna fragment	Left				0		Juvenile		
10	1	Unidentified	Rib					0				
10	4	Unidentified	Unidentified					0				
10	1	Unidentified	Vertebra					0				

above). Context 6 was associated with a hearth (context 11) and some of the bone from both contexts shows signs of burning. A bone from context 10 had been gnawed by rodents. Evidence of butchery could not be detected but this could be due to the small size of the sample.

It is not possible to interpret ratios since such a small fragmented sample is likely to favour more robust bone, that is, bones from adult animals and larger species. However, most of the identified bone came from sheep/goat, some of which was very immature, a pattern that is not dissimilar to the evidence at Dun Vulan.

Interpretation

Our interpretation of this stratigraphy and material is that there were three successive periods of usage of the platform outside the Scurrival cave, represented by context 3 by contexts 4, 6 and 8 and the platform and hearth (context 11), and by context 10.

The first occupation of the area represented in the excavated trench is marked by context 10. There is no suggestion that this is itself an occupation deposit, but the soil apparently accumulated while the area up-slope from the trench was occupied, possibly marked by the low revetted platform just in front of the cave. The large blocks of stone that make up the lower revetment rested on the top of this deposit and must therefore have arrived there after the cave and/or the area immediately outside it were occupied. Although it is possible that the blocks represent a natural rock fall, the fact that they form a revetment for an extended platform area, that in places they stand two blocks high and that their arrival in position was preceded and followed by human occupation all strongly suggest that the blocks were deliberately placed here by the people who were utilizing the cave.

Utilization of the enlarged platform was apparently never very intensive and may well have been nothing more than seasonal or occasional usage. At some point after the use of the platform began, a small hearth was constructed surrounded by an area of rough stone paving. Most of the pot-boilers, and all the hammer stones and polishers/rubbers were found in deposits broadly contemporary with the hearth. Together with the evidence of sherds with fire marks and soot accretions, and the limited quantity of animal bone recovered, food preparation seems to be the principal activity attested. The limited lithic material would fit into this scenario, although the three pieces of pumice from context 8 may have been used for cleaning skins.

The platform seems to have been used sporadically in the late mediaeval and/or early modern period, and the saucer quern would still have been on the surface at this time, if it was not actually brought here then. On present evidence, however, the principal period of use was the MIA. Although a single example of a quartzite skaill knife might hint at some earlier use of the site, there was no evidence for Mesolithic occupation of the platform

Cleaning of a Midden Section at Borve Broch (B5)

Keith Branigan

Immediately to the north of the broch at site B5, a midden can be seen eroding out of the steep bank about the sea dyke that flanks the broch to the east.

It appears to run without a break for a distance of at least 20 m northwards and may well spread further but the erosion scar ceases at this point. We have made annual visits to the site over the last five years to check material eroding from the midden. In 1999 a slump had revealed a section of the midden at its northern end and the opportunity was taken to clean this section back 10 cm along a 1 m length. In view of the opportunistic circumstances and the small amount of material excavated (approx. 0.15 m³) sieving procedures were not undertaken.

The midden deposit at this point is just 15 cm thick, composed of dirty, dark-grey sand and containing shells, bone and pottery. The midden sits on a deposit of clean sand, and is overlain by further wind-blown deposits that are in turn sealed by the thin topsoil and turf of the machair.

Pottery

Only six small sherds were collected in 1999, four of the 'Iron Age fabric' found at other broch sites and in middens at Eoligarry (see p. 334) and two of a coarser, dark-brown fabric. No rims or bases were present, but one fragment had a twisted clay cordon. A larger sherd with a similar cordon was recovered from the eroding face two years previously. Cordons of this type are common in the MIA but certainly continue in use into the LIA.

Animal bone

Judith Cartledge

Borve broch produced 44 fragments of animal bone, in addition to the fish bones reported on below. These

Table 5.12 The faunal assemblage recovered from the midden at site B5.

Quantity	Animal	Bone	L/R	Proximal Fusion	Distal Fusion	Gnawing	Fresh Break	Age Estimate
1	Cattle	Metacarpal proximal	Left	PF		Carnivore	2	Adult
1	Cattle	Metatarsal fragment					1	Juvenile
1	Cattle	Metatarsal fragment					1	Juvenile
1	Cattle	Metatarsal fragment					1	Juvenile
1	Cattle	Skull fragment					0	
1	Sheep/Goat	Calcaneum fragment	Right	PNF		Carnivore	0	Sub adult
1	Sheep/Goat	Humerus proximal	Left	PNF			0	Sub adult
1	Sheep/Goat	Metacarpal fragment					0	Adult
1	Sheep/Goat	Metacarpal fragment					0	Adult
1	Sheep/Goat	Metatarsal barrel	Right				0	Adult
1	Sheep/Goat	Pelvis acetabulum and pubis	Right				0	Adult
1	Sheep/Goat	Pelvis acetabulum, ischium, ilium	Left				2	Sub adult
1	Sheep/Goat	Phalange 2		PF	DF		0	Adult
1	Sheep/Goat	Skull fragment					0	
1	Sheep/Goat	Tooth					2	
3	Unidentified	Rib					0	
21	Unidentified	Unidentified					0	
5	Unidentified	Vertebra					0	

came from a midden context associated with a small quantity of MIA pottery. The small amount of bone was in good condition with little sign of erosion. Two of the bones had been heavily gnawed by a carnivore, perhaps a dog. No butchery marks were identified. Identifications are as shown in Table 5.12.

Fifteen of the fragments were identified to species as sheep/goat and cattle. With such a tiny sample it is not possible to make any interpretation of ratios. However, most of the bone came from sheep/goat and this bone came from both young and adult animals. Three of the four cattle fragments were from very young animal/animals.

Fish bone

Andrew Jones

Forty fish bones were recovered from the midden material. All of these were large gadoid fishes in the region of 100–130 cm total length. Bones of hake, *Merluccius merluccius*, were the most common and comprised eight precaudal vertebrae, one caudal vertebra, two quadrates, two maxillae, two dentaries (in four fragments) and one vomer (broken into two fragments). The presence of similar-sized bones from the left and right hand side of the fish suggests they all came from the same individual.

Cod, *Gadus morhua*, was represented by six precaudal vertebrae, three caudal vertebrae, two quadrates (one left, one right) and fragments of a single articular. As with the hake remains, all these bones may have been originally from the same animal.

The only other bone to be identified was a single quadrate of a large ling, *Molva cf. Molva*. In addition there were approximately ten unidentifiable fragments, all of which were probably from large gadoid fishes.

In brief, the collection consists of the selected remains of three kinds of large gadoid fish—hake, cod, and ling. All parts of the skeleton, head, trunk and vertebrae were represented for hake and cod and it is possible that the assemblage is derived from only three individuals. This would not be at variance with the very limited area from which the remains were recovered.

Comments

The eroding midden at this site has been kept under a watching brief in case it yielded significant artifact material which might help to fix its chronology. It appears to be probably of MIA-LIA date, although only small amounts of pottery have been recovered and of this only two sherds point to this date range. However, since at least at the northern end where it is eroding most actively, the midden is only 15 cms deep and is overlain by no further midden strata, it is likely to have been in use for a relatively short period. There

is no reason to doubt that it is contemporary with IA occupation of the broch, and although we cannot be sure it seems likely that the midden began immediately outside the broch wall.

It therefore provides a parallel case to the midden found and partly excavated outside the broch at Dun Vulan on South Uist (Parker Pearson and Sharples 1999, 97–130). Parker Pearson and Sharples (1999, 348) argue that the very existence of a substantial midden outside the broch might be seen as a symbolic statement of the control over fertility of the soil on the machair. The Borve headland broch certainly stood on the edge of a substantial area of machair, on which incidentally, there are traces of a rectilinear field system of unknown date.

The animal and fish bones recovered from the section cleaning were felt worthy of analysis, despite the very small sample, because so few sites on Barra have yielded any faunal material at all. There is nothing in the mammal bones which needs comment, and with probably only three individuals represented in the fish bones comment here must obviously be limited too. The absence of any saithe, abundant at Dun Vulan, is probably attributable to the fact that the bones from Borve were recovered without sieving. On the other hand the appearance of Hake, albeit the one individual, adds another to the short list of sites in the island chain where it is attested (Ceron-Carrasco and Parker Pearson 1999, 282). All three species identified at Borve can be caught in shallow water off-shore.

Excavation of an Oval Enclosure, E11, on the North Coast of Barra

Keith Branigan

This site was discovered during coastal erosion survey in 1993 and was partly excavated in 1994. The site is located in a slight hollow some 40–50 m from the sea. Between the enclosure and the sea is bare, eroded rock and the erosion presently reaches to within 1 m of the enclosure.

The enclosure consists of a continuous ring of stone blocks and boulders set edge to edge to form an oval 15 × 13 m (Fig. 5.35). The stones are very well embedded, especially on the south side where soil has slipped or washed downslope into the hollow. It is thus impossible to be certain of the exact number, but there are at least fifty stones in the circuit and probably more. The stones vary between 0.3 and 1 m in length, and are mostly 0.3–0.5 m tall. On the west side however two stones each about 0.7 m high are stood upright with a gap about 0.5 m wide between them, apparently marking an entrance.

It was decided to excavate a quadrant of this monument since it is under imminent threat from wave

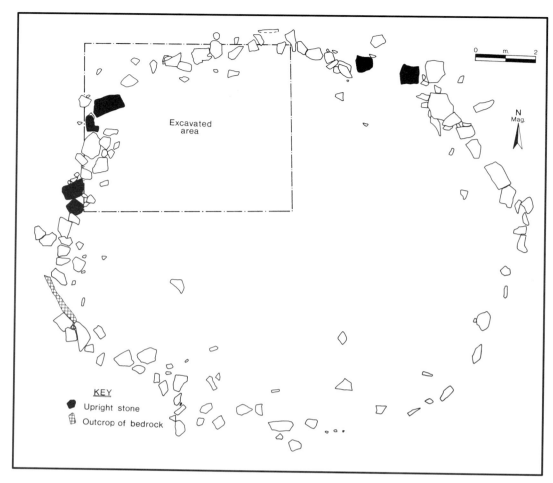

KEY

⬣ Upright stone

▦ Outcrop of bedrock

Figure 5.35 A plan of stone ring E11, showing the location of the excavated quadrant.

erosion and it presented some similarities to site T169 (Branigan 1995, 170–76) which proved to be a LBA activity site with a considerable quantity of lithic material.

The excavation

The north-west quadrant was stripped of its turf to reveal a root-filled sticky dark-brown peaty soil (context 2) that had accumulated as a result of wash and creep on this lowest side of the enclosure. Beneath this a gritty greyish-brown loam about 15 cm deep (context 3) overlay a paler grey soil of similar texture (context 4) that sat on the bedrock. There was no trace of any occupation deposit although the base of the enclosure stones and other structural features all rested on the pale grey soil, which appeared to represent the pre-enclosure level.

The enclosure itself proved slightly more elaborate than it appeared on the surface. Inside the stone ring, a band of smaller stone blocks about 0.6 m wide was found along the entire length of the excavated quadrant (Fig. 5.36). Although we considered the possibility that they were collapsed stones from the enclosure ring itself, we quickly disposed of this explanation. The stones were mostly much smaller than the stones

forming the ring and the ring stones themselves were too narrow ever to have been the foundation for any sort of superstructure. Furthermore the band of smaller stones inside the ring was too regular in width and too well 'packed' to have been the result of a process of collapse. We believe this inner band, or 'bench' as we labelled it (context 5), was a deliberate structure. Since it was only one stone high and had an uneven surface, we do not suggest that it was a 'bench' in the normal sense. A careful surface inspection of the circumference revealed traces of this bench around the entire circuit. Its purpose is obviously unclear, but we believe it is best explained as the base on which a turf superstructure or wall was built, the ring of enclosure stones acting as basal revetments on the outside of such a wall.

About 2.5 m left of the entrance the bench was interrupted for a distance of about 1 m, the only stone in this area (context 6) being a single water-rounded oblong block set against the edge of the bench. The feature gave the impression of a 'noost', perhaps with a pillow stone, but that may be too fanciful. Inside the enclosure and bench only two other features were noted. More or less on the centre-line of the enclosure, a tightly packed cluster of water-worn stones (context 7) formed a small stone plinth or base

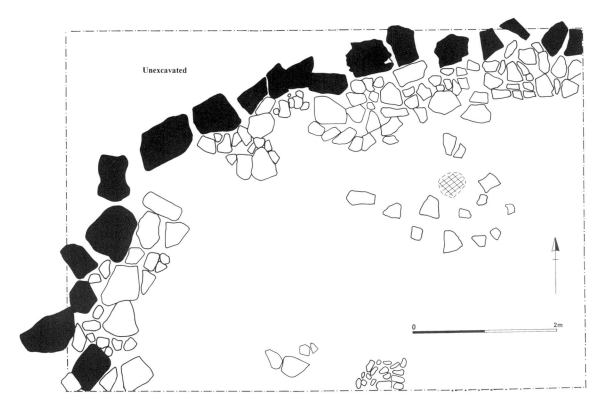

Figure 5.36 A plan of features in the excavated area of E11 (cross-hatching indicates an area of burning; kerb stones shaded black).

about 0.5 m square (Fig. 5.37). Between this base and the 'bench' there was a scatter of smallish stone slabs including an arc of about a dozen stones that looped around a small area of compacted burnt soil with small pieces of charcoal. Whether the stones marked the line of some temporary windbreak to protect the small fire is uncertain, but there was no visible trace of a superstructure of any kind.

Figure 5.37 The stone 'Plinth' near the centre of stone ring E11.

The finds

The only artifactual material recovered were eight pieces of quartz from context 3 which is contemporary with the construction of the enclosure. These were examined by C.R. Wickham-Jones. There were two chunks and six flakes. Of the flakes, one was primary, one secondary and four were inner. They suggest a prehistoric use of this enclosure but cannot be dated any more closely.

Interpretation

The enclosure has points of similarity and difference to T169 for which a calibrated C14 date of 793–522 BC was obtained (Branigan 1995: 174). That structure was a smaller oval, 7.5 × 6 m, in which the stones did not form a continuous circuit but were spaced out. It provided no evidence for a 'bench', and although, like E11, it yielded no pottery it produced 363 pieces of flint, 2 hammer stones and 1 piece of quartz. It was, however, in a sheltered spot just above the sea and turf was used to build a windbreak inside it.

It is tempting to think that both were 'activity sites' perhaps associated with exploitation of marine resources, although the marked difference in the use of lithics suggests that the activities were not the same. But E11 was probably not as well placed as T169 for exploiting marine food sources and it remains possible that E11 was a sheep pen, albeit a rather elaborately constructed one.

6. Excavations on Pabbay, 1996–1998: Dùnan Ruadh (PY10) and the Bàgh Bàn Earth-House (PY56)

Patrick Foster and John Pouncett

Dùnan Ruadh (PY10)

Excavations at Pabbay PY10 were directed by Patrick Foster with the assistance of John Pouncett. This report was written and compiled by John Pouncett. Illustrations were produced by Patrick Foster with the exception of Figures 6.19–6.21, which were drawn by Jane Timby.

Dùnan Ruadh (National Grid Reference NL 61288765) is located on the northern coastline of Pabbay, overlooking the Sound of Pabbay (Fig. 6.1). It is built upon a small rocky peninsula close to the narrow isthmus between Rosinish and the remainder of the island. The site of the galleried dun of Cairn Galtar on the island of Sandray is visible across the water to the north-east. While the lower slopes of the rocky peninsula are washed by the sea, the spur affords a natural plateau upon which a stone-built roundhouse was constructed. This structure, a 'complex' Atlantic roundhouse, described variously as a broch (RCAHMS 1928) or a promontory dun

(RCAHMS National Monuments Record of Scotland, 1965, No. 21383) is in an advanced state of decay. Storm seas have accelerated the natural collapse of the structure and only a short arc of walling survives towards the southern extent of the peninsula where it is protected from the action of the waves. Excavations at Dùnan Ruadh were initiated in response to the continued destruction of the site, witnessed during the course of archaeological survey.

The site is shown on the first edition 6 in. Ordnance Survey map (1880) where it is depicted as a circular structure. Although the representation of Dùnan Ruadh as a circular structure could be attributed to the use of cartographic symbols, a subrectangular building is shown within the wall circuit—additional detail that cannot be explained in terms of iconography. No trace of this second structure was found within the interior of the site, however, deposits associated with the reuse of the site after the abandonment and partial collapse of the wall circuit were identified during the course of excavation. The site was excavated over two seasons, during June 1996

Figure 6.1 PY10: Dùnan Ruadh, facing north-east.

234

Figure 6.2 PY10: the internal elevation of the wall circuit at the full extent of excavation, facing south-west.

and July 1997. Prior to commencement it was assumed that the wall survived to a height of two or three courses. At the full extent of excavation, however, the wall stood to a height of up to seven courses (Fig. 6.2). An accumulation of occupational deposits in excess of 1 m was banked up against the inner face of the wall, dispelling the anathema that the site was little more than a promontory enclosure once and for all.

The structural and stratigraphic sequences

An arc of walling approximately 15.8 m long and 3.3 m wide was uncovered during the course of excavation (Fig. 6.3). The remainder of the super-structure of the stone-built roundhouse had been destroyed by the action of the sea. On the basis of the surviving arc of walling, the external diameter of the roundhouse would have been approximately 19 m (internal ø 12.4 m). The wall circuit was constructed from two substantial double-thickness walls, cross-braced at regular intervals. In each instance, the internal and external faces of the wall were constructed from unhewn blocks of Lewisian Gneiss. The blocks of stone were smaller and more versatile than those used in the construction of the Ben Tangaval round-house; the local Lewisian basement fracturing to create regular pieces of stone well-suited to use in dry-stone walling. A series of features, a narrow passage-way (the Gallery) and two corbelled cells (chambers A and B), were incorporated into the wall circuit—architectural elaboration that would have been impos-sible at Alt Chrisal. The external skin of the wall circuit appears to have been rebuilt at some point.

Two possibilities arise, either the wall circuit was rebuilt and strengthened after an episode of collapse, or the roundhouse was built upon the site of an earlier building, the extant structure of which was incorpo-rated into the fabric of the wall circuit. While the former explanation is most plausible, the later is not unprecedented. Two apertures, each opening into one of the corbelled cells, were built within the internal face of the wall circuit (Fig. 6.4). A small, perforated plug made from a sheep long bone, the purpose of which is uncertain, was also incorporated into the inner face of this wall (Fig. 6.5).

The interior

The wall circuit is built directly upon the uneven surface of the rocky plateau. An accumulation of occupational material is preserved against the inner face of the substantial wall, trapped within a pro-nounced hollow within the bedrock. A section was excavated through the depositional sequence within the interior of the site (Fig. 6.6). Whilst only a small proportion of the interior of the site was preserved *in situ*, a series of excavated features and structural elements were identified during the course of excava-tion (Fig. 6.7). The accumulation of occupational material was comprised of a series of sandy loam deposits interspersed with layers of shell sand. These layers of sand, spread to create a clean living surface and tentatively interpreted as floor levels, provide a basis for phasing the interior of the site and the associated features.

Phase 1a. The base of the depositional sequence is characterized by an organic silt deposit (context 36).

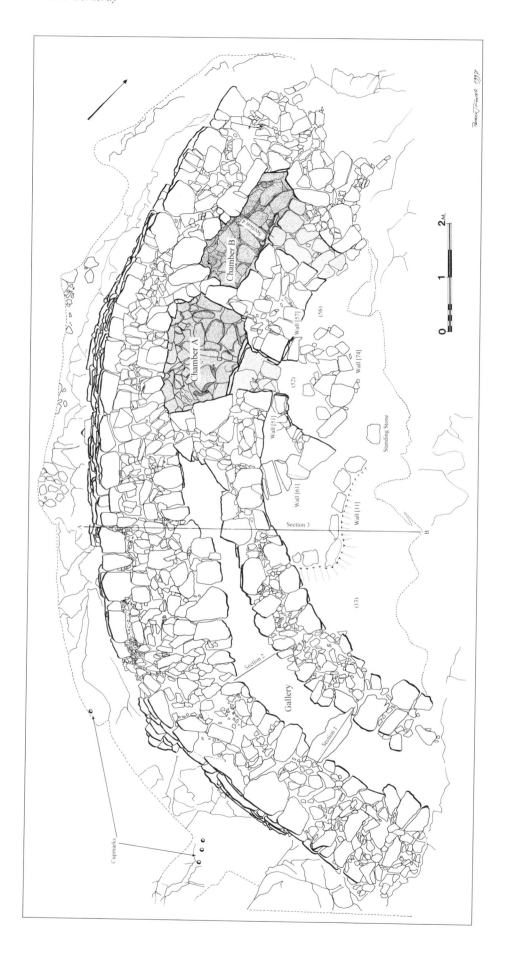

Figure 6.3 PY10: the extant arc of the wall circuit.

Figure 6.4 PY10: the apertures within the inner face of the wall circuit, facing south-east.

Figure 6.5 PY10: the perforated plug incorporated into the fabric of the wall circuit.

This intermittent layer of silt at the interface with the bedrock is comparable to the thin acid soils that mantle the exposed surface of the rocky peninsula nowadays. It is sealed by an accumulation of sandy loam (contexts 35 and 33). A small rectangular pit, measuring 0.65×0.42 m with a depth of 0.12 m, has been cut into the upper surface of this deposit. This pit, filled with a greyish-brown sandy loam (context 32), contained the articulated remains of an adult sheep. Whilst burials of articulated bone are common within Hebridean wheelhouses (Armit 1996), such deposits are rarely found within Atlantic roundhouses. Nevertheless similar burials were found elsewhere at Dùnan Ruadh. The pit is sealed by an accumulation of iron-rich sandy loam (context 31), the upper surface of which has been heavily disturbed, resulting in the formation of a greenish-brown clay loam (context 25). This reworked deposit contains an abundance of ash and is perhaps associated with the construction or initial occupation of the site.

Phase 1b. A layer of clean shell sand (context 30) has been spread across the surface of context 25. Prior to the creation of this shell sand floor, a stone lined drain was sunk into the interior of the site (Fig. 6.8). A narrow slot, lined with upright slabs of Lewisian Gneiss, ran diagonally from the deepest point of the interior towards the inner face of the wall circuit. This drain, filled with a loose sandy-silt deposit (context 29), contained a small assemblage of articulated animal bone. The shell sand floor and stone-lined drain

PY 10   Section A-B

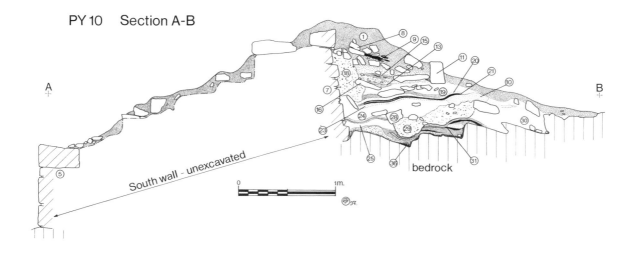

Figure 6.6 PY10: section excavated through the depositional sequence within the interior of the site.

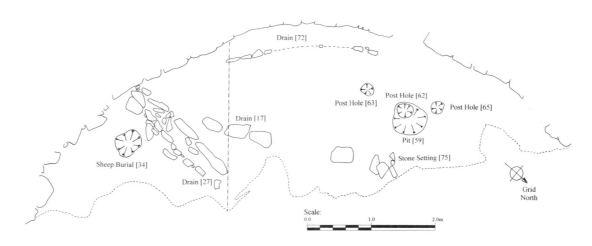

Figure 6.7 PY10: excavated features and structural elements identified within the interior of the site.

are sealed by an accumulation of sandy loam (contexts 24, 26 and 70). A small stone setting, approximately 0.44 m × 0.38 m, was inserted into the upper surface of this deposit. This rectilinear setting appears to have been a socket for a displaced stone upright found nearby. The upright may have once formed part of an internal partition. Evidence for internal subdivision has been found at many comparable sites, for example, at Bu on Orkney (Hedges 1987).

Phase 1c. Prior to the collapse of the stone upright, a second layer of clean shell sand (context 23) was spread throughout the interior of the site. The second shell sand floor is sealed by a continuous layer of ash (context 21). This compact ash deposit can be likened to the floor surface associated with the secondary occupation of the aisled roundhouse at Alt Chrisal T17 (above p. 157). A discrete lens of burnt material (context 22) was found within a shallow hollow within the upper surface of the layer ash. This lens, containing articulated animal bone, is possibly the vestige of a

second, truncated, pit. At some point during the history of the site, the deposits associated with phase 1 were subject to localized disturbance resulting in the formation of a mixed deposit (context 48). This reworked material, close to the edge of the site, may be the product of recent erosion or burrowing.

Phase 2. A third layer of clean shell sand (context 20) seals the compact layer of ash described above. The creation of shell sand floor appears to correspond to the abandonment of the system of internal subdivision established by the stone setting and associated upright. Two new stone-lined drains were sunk into the contemporary ground surface, the first draining the periphery of the wall circuit, the second servicing the interior of the site. The later drain appears to have replaced the stone-lined drain found within the lower levels of the site (phase 1b). Unlike the earlier drain, it appears to have been capped by a series of flat stone slabs. Both drains were filled with loose sandy silt (contexts 18 and 71 respectively). Two

238

Figure 6.8 PY10: the stone-lined drain associated with phase 1b.

discrete lenses of ash (context 67) and burnt shell (context 68) were deposited against the inner face of the wall circuit close to the aperture leading to chamber A. The stone-lined drains were sealed by an accumulation of brown sandy loam (context 19). Two subcircular post-holes, each approximately 0.2 m in diameter with a depth of 0.05 m, were inserted into the upper surface of this deposit (Fig. 6.9). The post-holes, offset from the wall circuit by a distance of approximately 1 m, appear to form part of a screen or partition in front of the opening to chamber A. Although a third post-hole was identified in the vicinity of the aperture, it is impossible to tell whether it is associated with this alignment. The third post-hole, also approximately 0.2 m in diameter, was truncated by a pit inserted into the upper levels of the site.

Phase 3. Following the deposition of a fourth and final layer of clean shell sand (context 58), sealing the

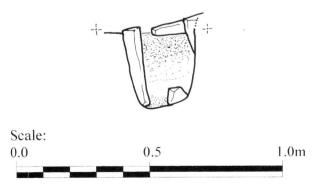

Scale:

Figure 6.9 PY10: the post hole associated with phase 2.

post-holes associated with phase 2 a series of stone structures were constructed within the upper levels of the site. The earliest of these structures were two short lengths of 'walling', the first (context 11) running at a tangent to the wall circuit towards the eastern extent of the site, the second (context 61) running perpendicular to the wall circuit close to the aperture leading to chamber A. Both were constructed from a single course of blocks of stone-laid end to end, inviting a comparison with the stone-lined drain associated with the primary occupation of the Ben Tangaval round-house (above p. 158). However, the interpretation of these features, neither surviving in its entirety, must remain open to question. The two walls are abutted and overlain by an accumulation of mixed sandy loam (contexts 10 and 10w). This deposit appears to be associated with the abandonment of the site. Overlying deposits contain an abundance of displaced stone-work derived from the collapse of the wall circuit.

Two arcs of drystone walling (contexts 51 and 57) were subsequently constructed within the interior of the abandoned wall circuit, either side of the aperture leading to chamber A. These walls appear to form part of a cellular building, the remainder of which has since been destroyed. The relationship between this structure and that shown on the first-edition OS map is not known. A circular pit, approximately 0.45 m in diameter, was inserted into the space defined by the two arcs of walling (Fig. 6.10). This pit, filled with a dark-brown sandy loam (context 60), appears to be broadly contemporary with a sheep burial found against the southern face of wall 11. The articulated remains of an adult sheep were buried within a

Scale:
0.0   0.5   1.0m

Figure 6.10 PY10: section excavated across the circular pit associated with phase 3.

shallow pit, 0.12 m deep, backfilled with loose sandy silt (context 48) and covered by a flat stone slab. Both features are sealed by an accumulation of mixed sandy loam (contexts 12, 13, 15 and 55). The cellular structure was subsequently modified to create a temporary shelter with the construction of a short, curvilinear rubble wall (context 74). The longevity of this shelter is uncertain, however a discrete dump of midden material (context 52) was deposited within the interior of the structure.

The upper levels of the site have been disturbed by structural collapse and have been reworked to form a loose sandy loam (context 8). Two discrete ash lenses (contexts 9 and 49) were identified within this reworked deposit, suggesting intermittent reuse of the abandoned site.

The gallery

A narrow passageway or gallery was constructed within the wall circuit of the stone-built roundhouse (Fig. 6.11). Towards the eastern extent of the site, the gallery is blocked by a stone lintel set approximately 0.4 m above the bedrock (Fig. 6.12). This lintel, linking the two faces of the wall circuit, no doubt served to provide structural stability. Two sections were excavated through the depositional sequence within the gallery (Fig. 6.13). The gallery itself is filled by an accumulation of dark-brown sandy loam (context 41) sealed by displaced stonework derived from the collapse of the abandoned wall circuit (contexts 6 and 43). A discontinuous layer of coarse sand (context 53) was identified at the interface with the bedrock, suggesting that the floor of the gallery was exposed prior to the accumulation of these deposits. While the fill of the gallery is largely homogenous, the deposits beneath the stone lintel appear to

Figure 6.11 PY10: the western extent of the gallery, facing west.

Figure 6.12 PY10: the stone lintel at the eastern extent of the gallery, facing west.

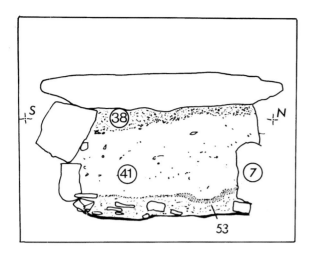

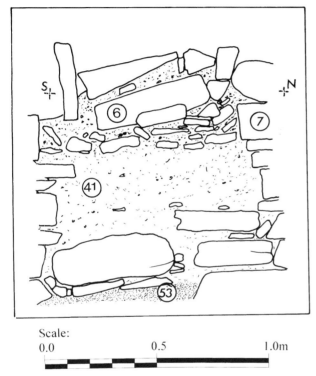

Scale:

0.0   0.5   1.0m

Figure 6.13 PY10: sections excavated through the depositional sequence within the gallery.

have been reworked by the action of ground water, resulting in the formation of a localised deposit of black organic silt (context 38). Following the abandonment and collapse of the wall circuit, a series of dumps of midden material were deposited on top of the wall circuit. This material (contexts 37 and 42) appears to be associated with the cellular building within the interior of the site.

The wall chambers
Two corbelled cells, chamber A (Fig. 6.14), and chamber B (Fig. 6.15), were also built within the wall circuit of the Atlantic roundhouse. A section was excavated through the depositional sequence within

each of the wall chambers (Fig. 6.16). In contrast to the gallery, the two corbelled cells had carefully constructed stone flag floors. Both were filled with an accumulation of dark-brown sandy loam (contexts 54 and 44 respectively) that predates the abandonment of the roundhouse. The depositional sequence within chamber A was sealed by displaced stonework (context 45) derived from the collapse of the corbelled roof of the cell (Fig. 6.17). Structural collapse was followed by intermittent reuse of the site, with midden material being dumped upon the abandoned wall circuit (Fig. 6.18). Discrete deposits of this material were identified within the vicinity of each of the corbelled cells (contexts 39 and 40 respectively).

The exterior
An accumulation of dark-brown sandy loam (context 3) was deposited against the exterior of the stone-built roundhouse. This deposit had been heavily truncated, surviving only where it was protected by the displaced stonework (context 2) associated with the collapse of the wall circuit. Four shallow hollows, less than 0.1 m in diameter, had been worn into the surface of the bedrock towards the eastern extent of the site. These hollows were probably associated with the preparation of bait—the cup-shaped indentations being formed by the action of grinding. A small fire had also been lit on the surface of the bedrock, resulting in the formation of a discrete layer of compact ash (context 4).

The pottery

Jane Timby

Excavations at Pabbay yielded a moderately large assemblage of some 3,697 sherds weighing 33.9 kg. The sherds were of mixed condition with many very fragmented pieces due to the friable nature of the material. No complete profiles were recovered, and although several joins were noted within and occasionally across contexts the latter was not extensively pursued. The assemblage was sorted macroscopically into broad fabric groups based on the density and size of inclusions, following the guidelines recommended by the prehistoric Ceramics Research Group (PCRG 1997). Details of surface finish and decoration were noted where present along with any evidence of use.

Fabric types
In contrast to some of the other island assemblages (e.g. Sandray, Barra), the Pabbay assemblage showed few distinctive traits in terms of fabric composition. Most of the sherds are variations of the coarse local fabric, the mineral components deriving from the local Lewisian gneiss. A broad distinction was made between coarsewares (P1), and finer wares (P2), where the inclusions were noticeable sparser and finer. Six

Figure 6.14 PY10: chamber A, facing north.

other fabrics were recorded but these generally formed very small groups.

P1: A handmade, sandy-textured ware with variable amounts of crushed igneous rock temper, larger fragments up to 7–8 mm. Surface colour varies from orange to orange-brown, brown, grey or black. Sherds can be quite friable.

P2: A much finer ware. Fine rock inclusions are still visible but the larger fragments are 1 mm or less in size. Sherds are generally carefully smoothed or wiped and frequently decorated. Many have a pale orange-brown or pale grey coloration.

P3: A brown-orange fabric with a black inner core. The paste contains fine biotite mica and very fine inclusions (less than 0.25 mm) and has a finely porous texture. Uneven exterior surface.

P4: A compact hardware with a noticeably higher density of ill-sorted crystalline rock fragments in the paste.

Figure 6.15 PY10: chamber B, facing east.

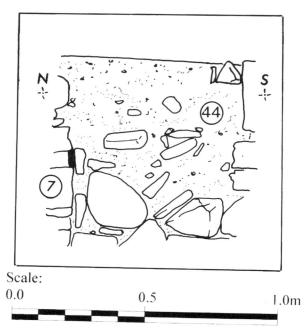

Scale:

Figure 6.16 PY10: Sections excavated through the depositional sequences within chambers A and B.

Figure 6.17 PY10: the displaced stonework derived from the collapse of the corbelled roof of chamber A, facing north-east.

Figure 6.18 PY10: the midden material sealing the depositional sequence within chamber B, facing east.

Inclusions reach up to 5 mm. Generally grey-brown or black in colour with thinner-walled vessels (5–6 mm).

P5: A moderately fineware with fairly hard, compact walls distinguished by a high frequency of biotite mica. The mica flecks are mostly fine with some examples up to 1 mm across.

P6: A fairly fine ware, generally orange-brown with a dark-grey inner core. The paste contains a sparse but ill-sorted density of igneous rock inclusions, coarser fragments up to 6 mm. The ware is distinguished by the presence of very fine, sparse organic impressions on the surfaces and in the core of the fabric. The finely comminuted material is probably dung.

P7: A black ware containing a sparse scatter of fine white inclusions (up to 1 mm), probably crushed shell. The paste is very finely micaceous but no other coarse components are visible.

P8: A single oxidized orange sherd with a coarse rock-temper similar to P1. The sherd is distinguished by having a sparse scatter of voids with white reaction rings (approximately 1 mm diameter), perhaps from salts or calcareous inclusions? These are particularly noticeable on the interior surface and in the core of the fabric.

P00: Very small thumbnail-sized sherds and crumbs were not sorted but grouped together as code P00.

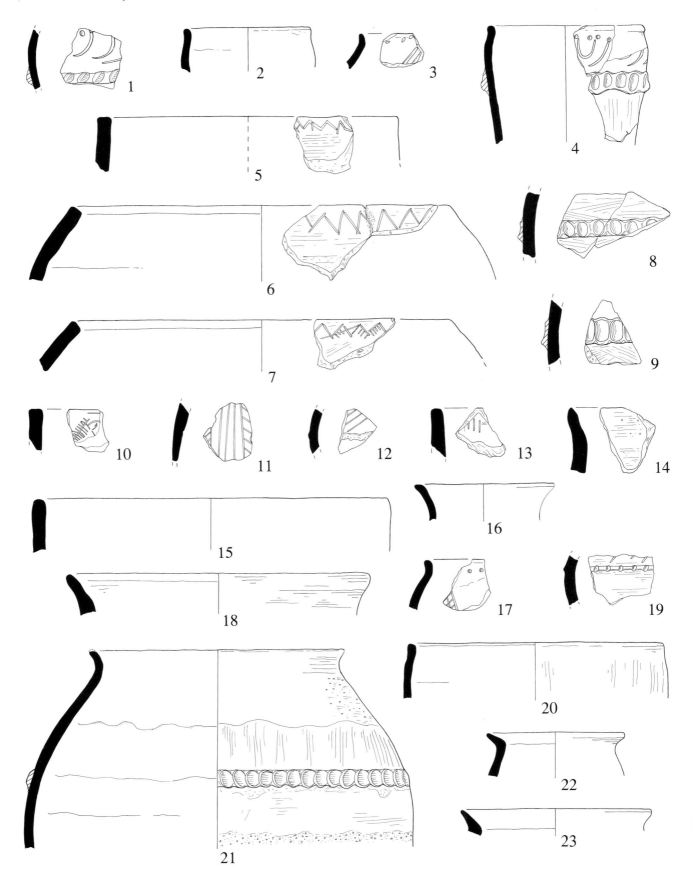

Figure 6.19 PY10: the pottery.

244

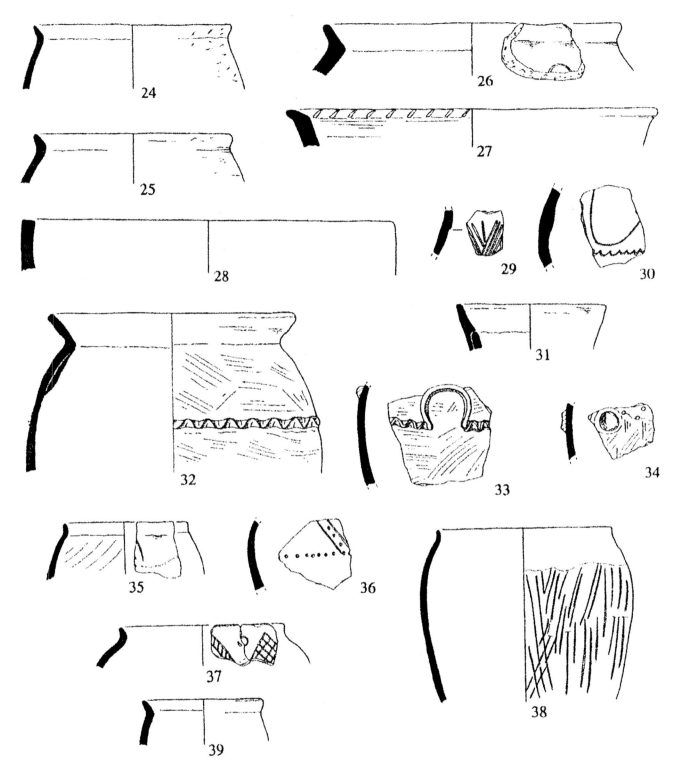

Figure 6.20 PY10: the pottery.

Vessel forms

All the vessels were hand-built including the use of the 'tongue-and-groove' technique (e.g. Fig. 6.20.31) characteristic of the Hebrides. As there were no complete vessels and many of the rim sherds were very fragmentary, the rims were coded according to shape. Seven main types were distinguished:

A: expanded either internally or externally or both (e.g. Fig. 6.20.27).

B: sharply everted with a flat internal face (e.g. Figs. 6.19.22–23, 6.20.24–26, 32 and 39).

C: simple undifferentiated vertical rim with a squared (C1), (Fig. 6.19.5, 10 and 13), or rounded top (C2) (Figs. 6.19.20, 6.20.31), or very short vertical rim (C3) (Fig. 6.20.35 and 38).

245

D: curved wall, undifferentiated rim (Fig. 6.21.43).

E: flaring everted simple rim (Fig. 6.19.16 and 21).

F: rounded out-turned rim on a globular bodied vessel, either slightly beaded (F1) or simple unthickened (F2) (Figs. 6.19.3–4, 17, 6.20.37, 6.21.42).

G: plain inturned, slightly squared rim (Figs. 6.19.6–7, 6.21.49).

A variety of vessel forms were clearly present including large bucket-shaped, thick-walled types with upright (C) or slightly incurving (G) rims (e.g. Figs. 6.19.6–7, 6.20.28); slack-sided jars with simple rims (Fig. 6.19.4) and more globular-bodied forms with slightly everted rims (e.g. Fig. 6.20.24–25 and 32). One particularly unusual carinated sherd with a burnished surface from context 6 could possibly be an import (M. Parker-Pearson, personal communication). The base sherds were simple unelaborated flat forms. None of the bases showed any decoration or evidence of thumb impressions on the basal pad as noted in other assemblages such as Alt Chrisal, Barra (p. 169) and Sollas, North Uist (Campbell 1991).

Surface treatment

A wide variety of surface finishes were identified. Sherds were classified according to whether the exterior of the sherds were oxidised (orange, orange-brown) or reduced (grey, grey-brown, black), and according to surface finish where discernible. Surface finishes included smoothing, burnishing, fine wiping, coarser brushwood wiping (leaving pronounced striations) and the application of a coarse slip. Burnishing does not appear to have been commonly used and only five sherds have been recorded that show a well-burnished surface finish. Several sherds, possibly from nearer the base of vessels, had a roughened slipped surface. This surface frequently splits away from the body of the vessel. A similar phenomenon has been noted on sherds from Sollas (Campbell 1991: 150) where haematite was added to the slip and from Tigh Talamhanta, Isle of Barra (Young 1952). The various surface treatments identified above may prove fairly meaningless, as it is clear that some vessels (e.g. Fig. 6.19.21) show several or all of these traits in different zones on the same pot. Wiping is often confined to the central zone and the use of slip to the lower zones. The sherd size is too small to assess whether such patterning is consistent across the vessel range. Some surfaces may also be the result of use or postdepositional changes. A high proportion of the sherds was also heavily sooted, thus effectively masking any surface finish.

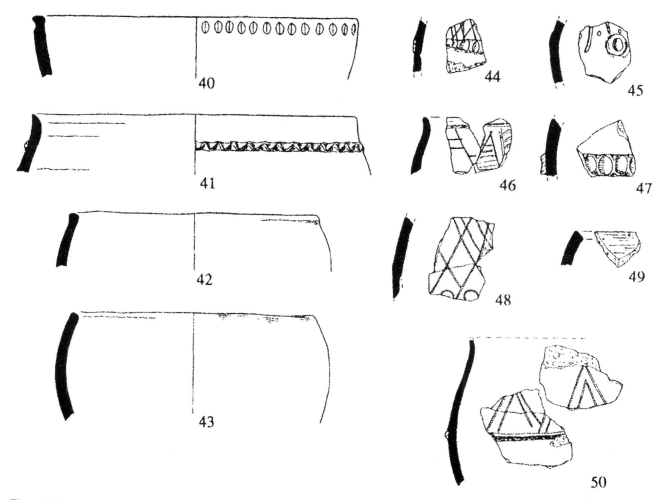

Figure 6.21 PY10: the pottery.

Decoration

Approximately 8.4% of the sherds by count showed some form of decoration. A wide repertoire of styles and motifs are represented with examples of most of the range illustrated. Following the system developed by Topping (1987) the decoration is divided into incised, applied and impressed wares. As observed elsewhere, the decoration on the pottery at Dun Ruadh can be found in three zones: around the rim (e.g. Fig. 6.21.40–41), as a cordon around the body of the vessel (e.g. Figs. 6.19.21, 6.20.32–33) and as an incised design or other ornament in the zone between these (Figs. 6.20.26 and 30, 6.21.50).

Linear incised decoration is one of the commonest styles present and is a characteristic feature of wheelhouse pottery. While the majority of the examples in this category have been executed using a fairly sharp tool producing a sharp fine line, there are a few examples with a more grooved incision or lightly tooled pattern. The designs are particularly diverse including single and multiline or nested chevrons, parallel diagonal or vertical lines, tramlines, lattice, infilled chevrons and fir-trees. Classification to a certain extent is reliant on the area of design available. The majority of the designs use straight lines, the use of curvilinear schemes, arcs or circles being much rarer. A single fragmentary example of a finger-grooved curvilinear pattern is present in the assemblage from the interior.

Applied decoration is mainly restricted to various forms of cordon. The three basic types are a fine fillet of clay applied to the vessel and pushed into a wavy line using a blunt tool or finger; a wider thumb-pressed cordon; and a thin plain horizontal cordon. All three types may be further embellished with incised slashes or impressions, in one case possibly using a small bird bone. The wavy-line type is the most common accounting for 67.5% of the cordoned sherds. Many cordoned vessels have other forms of decoration above the cordon, usually incised designs. Other forms of applied decoration include applied indented oval bosses and a single example of an inverted 'horseshoe'. There are no examples of the type of freestyle applied decoration seen on the sherds from Alt Chrisal, Barra (p. 172). Impressed decoration is less common and is restricted to impressed dots or stab marks, finger depressions and ring-stamps, mainly in association with other decorative techniques. One sherd has a cordon that appears to have been impressed with the end of a small bone.

Use wear

A high proportion of the sherds shows blackening or heavy sooting on both the internal and external surfaces. In many cases the heaviest sooting was confined to the central zone of a vessel, coinciding with the cordon. This cordon was presumably positioned just above the fire in the smokiest zone to facilitate handling out of the heat. Both decorated and plain vessels, coarse and finewares showed evidence of such use. No limescale residues were identified on the sherds examined.

The interior

The section into the interior deposits yielded the largest of the five excavated assemblages, some 2,391 sherds (24,811 g) with an average sherd size of 10.4 g. Pottery was recovered from some 32 individual contexts distributed throughout the depositional sequence. Perhaps not surprisingly, this is the most diverse of all the groups of pottery. It is also the only group with a relatively stratified sequence.

Phase 1a. The first ceramic material, a single oxidized coarseware (fabric P1) decorated with incised lines, came from the black organic silt (context 36) immediately above the natural. Twenty further coarseware sherds came from context 35 above; one of which also had incised linear decoration. Finishes are mainly plain with a single coarse slipped sherd. The sheep burial inserted into the upper surface of this deposit contained a small assemblage of 51 sherds (355 g). This material was not particularly well preserved despite coming from a pit context, with an average sherd size of just 7 g, possibly reflecting abandonment or sweepings. Three rim sherds (forms C3, E and F) were present (Fig. 6.19.2–3) and 4 decorated pieces. One sherd had an applied wavy-line cordon, 1 an applied thumbed cordon combined with curved incised lines and stabbed dots (Fig. 6.19.1), 1 rim sherd a combination of diagonal lines and stabs (Fig. 6.19.3) and 1 sherd an incised groove. The accumulation of orange-brown loam (context 31) immediately above this feature yielded just 6 sherds including a vessel with a thumbed cordon and curved-line decoration (Fig. 6.19.4) similar to one of the sherds from the pit fill. The succeeding brown clay loam (context 25) was particularly prolific producing 649 sherds (6,420 g). Several fineware sherds (4% by count) appear for the first time and 74 sherds (11.4%) have some form of decoration. Twenty-two rims, predominantly types B and C from a minimum of 11 vessels are present. The decoration includes applied cordons, both thumb-pressed types and wavy-line types and incised decoration, in seven cases in combination with the cordons. The only example of a fir-tree design came from this group (Fig. 6.19.10). Other designs include lattice, chevrons, infilled chevrons, diagonal and vertical lines. There is quite a marked similarity between this assemblage and that from context 44 in chamber B perhaps suggesting some contemporaneity.

Phase 1b. The shell sand floor (context 30) and associated drain above context 25 proved to be aceramic and thus presumably represent a period of disuse. An accumulation of grey sandy loam above this (contexts 24, 26 and 70) produced 206 sherds (3,552 g) with a higher than average sherd size of 17 g. The group mainly comprises coarsewares with a single fineware. Two new fabric types appear (namely P4 and P5). Eleven rim forms are present, B C1, C2, C2/ E, E and G. Eleven sherds (5%) show some form of decoration: 7 with applied cordons (both thumbed and wavy-line), some with additional incisions or notching; 2 with incised decoration; and 1 with a combination of incised tramline and dots and one with finger depressions. There are no very obvious differences between this group and the material below, although the sample of featured sherds is perhaps statistically too small to analyse. The introduction of the new fabrics and a greater range of rim forms may prove to have some chronological meaning.

Phase 1c. Small groups of pottery were associated with the shell sand floor (context 23) and the continuous layer of ash (context 21) associated with phase 1c. Fabrics P1, P4 and P6 were present but no finewares. In all cases the rim types present were restricted to form B. Where these deposits had been reworked, context 48 yielded a new fabric type, P7.

Phase 2. A small assemblage of pottery was recovered from the shell sand floor (context 20) sealing context 21, and further groups of pottery were associated with contexts 16, 18, 19, 71, 67 and 66. Vessel forms include everted jars (rim type B), along with rim types C1 and C2. Shell sand floor context 58 produced a single sherd of coarseware.

Phase 3. The accumulation of sandy loam (contexts 10 and 10w) sealing the stone walls associated with the cellular building built within the upper levels of the site produced a moderately large assemblage of some 551 sherds (4,800 g). Apart from a general absence of finewares there is little to distinguish this material from earlier groups. Vessel forms include rim types B C1 and C2, with the addition examples of rim types A and D. One vessel from context 10, with unusual slash decoration on the rim (Fig. 6.20.27), joins a sherd in context 55 above. Other decoration includes applied wavy-line cordons and incised chevrons, curvilinear designs and lattices. One sherd has a shallow groove across it rather than a sharp incised line. Apart from context 55, which produced some 59 sherds, most of the deposits within the upper levels of the site produced few sherds.

The gallery
The gallery produced around 273 sherds (2,496 g) with an average sherd size of 9 g. This material was more fragmented than that from the interior. The assemblage differs slightly in some respects from those derived from chambers A and B lacking the finer

element and the emphasis on decoration so dominant in the wall chambers. Vessel forms are mainly plain C1 or C2 types, with single examples of rim types E and G. Only 6% of the sherds from the gallery were decorated. Applied, incised and impressed forms of decoration were all present.

Chamber A
Chamber A produced a total 227 sherds (2,278 g) with an average sherd size of 10 g. Overall, the group is dominated by fabric type P1, with finer fabric, P2, accounting for 16% of the sherd count. Two sherds of fabric P3 were also present. Only 14 rim sherds were recorded, 10 examples of rim type B, 2 of C2 and 2 C3. Twelve decorated sherds were noted, 8 with applied cordons, 1 with incised decoration, two with cordons and incised decoration and 1 with a combination of incised and impressed decoration (Fig. 6.20.37). The lowest excavated surface, context 73, produced 15 undifferentiated coarseware sherds. Above this, context 54 produced 61 plain coarseware sherds, including two rims (rim types C2 and C3). The largest group from chamber A came from the collapsed wall, some 142 sherds (1,338 g). Two examples of jars with everted rims (form B) were present. All the decorated sherds from the chamber A assemblage came from this group. The uppermost horizon, context 39, had just 9 sherds, including another everted rim.

Chamber B
B produced a larger assemblage than A some 530 sherds (6,417 g) with an average sherd size of 12 g. The entire assemblage came from the accumulation of brown sandy loam, context 44. The group contained a relatively high proportion of fineware sherds accounting for 8% (by count), although many may derive from a single vessel. Most of the finewares were decorated with intersecting diagonal lines, applied cordons combined with incised chevrons, diagonal lines or lattices. Decorated sherds include those ornamented with finger impressions beneath the rim, thumb-pressed cordons and ring-stamping. Overall the decorated sherds account for 12% of the group. The vessel forms show a slightly different emphasis to chamber A for example, there is only one everted rim jar (rim type B). Other rim types present include types C2, D, F and G.

The exterior
The assemblage from the exterior comprises just 48 sherds (total mass 461 g) with an average sherd size (10 g) comparable to the assemblages from the interior of the site. This assemblage is dominated by fabric type P1, however, fabric types P4 and P6 are also present. Featured sherds are scarce and include examples of rim types B and D and two sherds with applied cordons.

Discussion

The ceramic assemblage from Pabbay, the first to be recorded from the island, shares many traits with middle Iron Age assemblages from elsewhere in the Hebrides in terms of fabric, form and decorative technique. Particularly close parallels can be made with the assemblages recently reanalysed from the 1957 excavations at Sollas, North Uist (Campbell 1991), and from older published material from A'Cheardach Mhor, South Uist (Young and Richardson 1959) and Tigh Talamhanta, Barra (Young 1952).

The pottery recovered from Dùnan Ruadh, Pabbay, appears fairly consistent both horizontally across the different zones and vertically through the depositional sequence. Although minor variations are observable between the different site subdivisions, the sample is unbalanced by the pronounced variation in quantity across the site and the generally low incidence of featured sherds. There is a suggestion of slightly better-quality material, in terms of the relative proportion of finewares and decorated wares, in chamber B compared with the other areas. A consideration of the incidence of the different surface finishes across the site showed no discernible differences other than perhaps a higher incidence of slipped sherds in the interior. The recurrence of traits throughout the sequence perhaps hints at a moderately short period of occupation.

Sollas perhaps provides one of the most useful published comparanda of material as the assemblage is of comparable size, has been studied in depth and has the added benefit of independent dating (Campbell 1991). As at Pabbay the fabrics encountered are very homogeneous, the only significant variant being the addition of organic temper. This ware appears to be specifically linked with the earlier levels of the site, predating the construction of the wheelhouse. A potentially similar fabric at Dùnan Ruadh, fabric P6, occurs in insufficient quantities to detect patterning but as such may represent the end of a tradition.

Most of the incised designs found on the Pabbay, pottery can be paralleled with examples in the Sollas, assemblage, which appears to contain almost the entire known repertoire of styles and motifs in the Hebrides. The presence of burnished sherds at Pabbay however, is not paralleled at Sollas and these could perhaps either be seen as imports or the development of a local style. The phasing at Sollas allows certain patterns to be detected. For example, the earlier phase (phase A) is characterized by vessels with incised decoration generally without cordons, which show a marked increase in the later phase (phase B2). Stamped decoration is also generally restricted to the earlier phase. The building of the wheelhouse at Sollas (phase B1) coincides with both the highest incidence of incised decoration and with the greatest variety of designs (Campbell 1991: 154). The use of channelled decoration at Sollas is generally found in period B2. Grooved sherds are notably scarce at Pabbay as are the wide finger-channelled sherds present in small quantities at Sollas and well represented at Clettraval, North Uist (Scott 1948: Pl. VIII).

The construction of the wheelhouse at Sollas also coincides with the introduction of everted rim pottery. Everted rim pottery features in many wheelhouse assemblages, particularly from the earlier levels, for example: A'Cheardach Mhor (Young and Richardson 1959); A'Cheardach Bheag, South Uist (Fairhurst 1971); Clettraval (Scott 1948); Tigh Talamhanta (Young 1952); and Dun Cul Bhuirg, Iona (Topping 1985). Radiocarbon dating at Sollas has suggested a date of construction for the wheelhouse in the late 1st or early 2nd century AD, thus confirming the traditional view that places decorated Iron Age pottery in the last few centuries BC and the early first century AD (Campbell 1991).

Recent reviews of Hebridean pottery have challenged the traditional sequences, largely established through work by Young (1966), and have identified various problems of dating (e.g. Topping 1987; Lane 1990). It has been emphasized that the pottery of the Western Isles does not appear to conform to a straightforward evolutionary sequence, and few of the observable decorative and other traits can be regarded as chronologically sensitive (Ibid.). It is clear from such assessments that it may be dangerous to extrapolate dates from other sites on the basis of the pottery sequence alone.

While it would thus perhaps be inappropriate at this stage to try and tie down the Pabbay assemblage too tightly chronologically, certain key features can be highlighted. The assemblage at Pabbay is a clear indication of middle Iron Age occupation on this island. The assemblage has many traits in common with other wheelhouse assemblages across the Hebrides, notably Barra, South and North Uist, Tiree and Iona. Recent work at Sollas, in particular, has identified a number of trends that can be mirrored, to a certain extent, in the assemblage at Pabbay. First, the presence of organic-tempered ware, which, if not a local phenomenon, appears to be an earlier feature at Sollas, along with stamped sherds and infrequent cordons. Secondly, the low incidence of organic sherds and stamped sherds at Pabbay and the appearance of cordoned wares throughout the sequence might suggest a later phase of occupation. Unfortunately there are no radiocarbon dates associated with Sollas phase A (prewheelhouse) to tie down this part of the sequence. It is also not entirely certain that there is complete continuity between phase A and the construction of the wheelhouse.

Conversely, the low numbers of groove- or channel-decorated sherds at Pabbay, and the absence of any double-cordoned vessels more typically associated with the later phase at Sollas, could suggest that

Pabbay was abandoned at a slightly earlier date. Alternatively, in view of its more isolated position the Pabbay potters may be more conservative, perpetuating traditional styles. The appearance of everted rim pottery relatively low in the interior sequence at Pabbay might suggest that the dun, like Sollas, dates from around the 1st or 2nd centuries AD. However, certain elements within the pottery might be earlier (M. Parker Pearson, personal communication). Although the sample of material below context 25 is small, the absence of everted rim forms and the occurrence of a decorative style (Fig. 6.19.1–4) not found later in the sequence might hint at a period of occupation predating the introduction of everted rim pottery.

Comparison of the Pabbay assemblage with those from other recently excavated sites in the Outer Hebrides, namely Mingulay, Sandray and Barra, indicates a few similarities and differences. There is, for example, less variety in terms of paste in the Pabbay assemblage compared to the groups from the other islands, possibly a reflection of a single limited period of occupation. The other groups are more chronologically diverse. Although all the assemblages appear to have a middle Iron Age component, both Sandray and Mingulay show only a small proportion of decorated wares. The greatest similarity is between Barra and Pabbay, where there is considerable overlap in the use of incised and applied decoration. The range of decoration at Barra, however, is more diverse showing a number of different asymmetrical elements, which might hint at a different chronological or functional emphasis or the development of a more idiosyncratic style.

Faunal remains (excluding birds)

Jacqui Mulville (mammals) and C. Ingrem (fish)

Introduction

There is abundant evidence for Iron Age activity on the islands but little exists in terms of faunal reports (Finlay 1984). There have been a number of wheelhouse excavations that have produced bone; at the Udal (Finlay 1984), Sollas (Finlay 1991), Northton (Finlay 1984), Baleshare (Halstead, in press), Hornish Point (Halstead, in press), Cill Donnain (Kildonan; ul Haq 1989), Cnip (unpublished; see Armit 1996: 148–50), A'Cheardach Mhor (Young and Richardson 1960) and A'Cheardach Bheag (Fairhurst 1971). Of all these only the first seven have produced assemblages of any size. There were no assemblages retained from the aisled roundhouse of Tigh Talamhanta (Young 1952) and Clettraval (Scott 1948).

Very few duns or brochs in the Outer Hebrides have been excavated and of these only Dun Vulan has detailed faunal evidence. Dun Cuier (Young 1955) is only recorded as a species list; there is no detailed record of the bones recovered from Dun Thomaidh

(Beveridge and Callander 1931) and the small excavation of Dun Carloway on Lewis produced no bone (Tabraham 1977). The Iron Age excavations at Pabbay, Mingulay and Sandray offer an opportunity to explore the use of animals on small island sites and to compare and contrast this with other Iron Age assemblages from the Western, Northern and Inner Isles.

Method

Species identification. The mammal bone was identified using the reference collection at the Faunal Remains Unit, University of Southampton. Wherever possible, sheep and goat were distinguished (Boessneck 1969), but where diagnostic features were absent due to fragmentation or poor preservation, they were classified under a single heading. Fragments that could not be identified to species level were classified as 'cattle-size' or 'sheep-size'. Fragments were recorded using a zoning method following Serjeantson (1991), zones being recorded when over 50% present. Ribs were recorded when the head was present and vertebrae (except axis and atlas) when over 50% of the centrum was present.

The fish remains were also identified at the Faunal Remains Unit, University of Southampton, with the aid of the comparative collection. Where possible fragments were identified and recorded to species and element, although in some cases it was only possible to assign fragments to family. In particular, the difficulties of distinguishing between members of the cod family meant that often elements could only be assigned to the family Gadidae. Vertebrae were recorded as either precaudal (anterior abdominal) or caudal (abdominal and caudal).

Quantification. The total number of fragments (NISP) was calculated for all species, while the minimum number of elements (MNE) and the minimum number of individuals (MNI) were calculated for the most common taxa. As the recording method indicates the zones present on each bone, the minimum number of each element present (MNE) could be calculated. From this it was possible to estimate the minimum number of individuals (MNI) that must have been present on site to form the bone assemblage recovered. NISP counts tend to be biased towards the larger species as larger bones suffer greater fragmentation and produce higher counts. MNI counts were calculated to reduce this bias. The percentage survival of each element was also calculated following Brain (1981), where the number of each element present is expressed as a percentage of the most frequently occurring element (i.e. the number expected if all the skeleton was present).

Ageing and sexing. Wear stages were recorded for dp4s, P4s and permanent molars of the domestic species using Grant (1982) and grouped into age stages following the methods of Halstead (1985), Payne (1973) and O'Connor (1988). The fusion stage of postcranial bones was recorded and related age ranges taken from Getty (1975). Loose epiphyses were recorded but excluded from analysis of the fusion information because to the possibility of counting a single bone twice by recording as unfused both the shaft and the epiphyses. Neonates were identified from their size, texture and state of fusion. These bones are very small and porous and no postnatal fusion has occurred. The percentage of neonates was calculated as the proportion of all long-bone shafts with recorded fusion information described as neonatal.

It was only possible to separate the sexes using morphological characteristics of pig canines. Although it is possible to detect the sexual composition of a population through metrical analysis, the number of measurements produced for individual bones and species was small and precluded any conclusions.

Measurements. Measurements taken on cattle, sheep/ goat, pig and horse bones, following von den Driesch (1976), Davis (1992) and Payne (1969) are contained within the site archive. Fish measurements were taken according to Morales and Rosenlund (1979), where this was not possible, size relative to the comparative specimens was noted. Measurements were compared with those listed in publications of other contemporary sites.

Gnawing, butchery and burning. For all identified bones gnawing and butchery marks were recorded. Butchery marks were described as 'chop' or 'cut' marks. Their position was recorded if considered particularly meaningful, but was not used for quantitative purposes. Gnawing marks made by carnivores and rodents were noted. Burning on bones was recorded as either present or absent.

Recovery. Bone was recovered by troweling and hand-picking.

Results
A total of 3,781 mammal and fish bones were recorded. For analysis this material was divided into the three ceramic phases. The majority of the mammal bone fragments derive from the contexts dating to the 1st–3rd century AD (Table 6.1). About half as much bone was recovered from the 6th–9th century AD, with the 2nd–4th century AD producing only a small number of recorded specimens (NISP). For fish the largest amount of material came from the latest phase, less than half this amount was recovered from the earliest phase with a small quantity recovered from the 2nd–4th centuries.

The condition of the mammal bone was excellent, with little erosion noted. Less than 1% of bone was

Table 6.1 Site PY10: mammals: number of identified specimens.

	1st–3rd	2nd–4th	6th–9th	Total	%
Sheep	1211	36	653	1900	79
Cattle	191	31	120	342	14
Pig	20	1	8	29	1
Red deer	1	1	5	7	<1
Otter	0	32	41	73	3
Common Seal	22	0	14	36	1
Atlantic Seal	16	0	5	21	0
Total	1461	101	846	2408	
Seal	6	0	3	9	
Whale	1	1	7	9	
Cattle size	25	1	10	36	
Sheep size	111	6	80	197	
Total	1604	109	946	2659	

gnawed or burnt, suggesting the excellent preservation of surface information and neonatal bone. Little of the bone was butchered, 8–14% . Fish bone showed only three records of charring, no butchery and no gnawing.

Species present
The number of fragments of mammal bone identified to species was 2,408, with a further 251 identified to broader size or family groups (Table 6.1). Domestic farm animals dominated. Sheep comprised the majority of identified bone with smaller amounts of cattle and pig present. Wild species included red deer, Atlantic seal, common seal, otter and a range of cetacea.

Considering the site as a whole, sheep accounted for nearly 80% of numbers of identified specimens. Cattle made up only 14%, with other species present at only 1–3%. The relative abundance using the minimum number of individuals (MNI) calculation shows a similar pattern (Table 6.2). There is slight increase in the proportion of the population that other species make up with a corresponding decrease in sheep. For wild species only a single individual per phase was identified.

The number of fish bones identified to species or species group was 1,122 (Table 6.3). Nineteen species

Table 6.2 Site PY10: mammals: minimum number of individuals.

	1st–3rd	2nd–4th	6th–9th	Total	%
Sheep	26	3	12	41	60
Cattle	5	3	4	12	18
Pig	2	1	2	5	7
Red deer	1	1	1	3	4
Otter	0	1	2	3	4
Atlantic Seal	1	0	1	2	3
Common Seal	1	0	1	2	3
				68	

Table 6.3 Site PY10: fish: number of identified species.

	1st–3rd	2nd–4th	6th–9th	Total	%
Tope	1			1	<1
Herring		5		5	<1
Common Eel	1	4	2	7	0
Conger Eel	19		13	32	3
Pollack	18		32	50	4
Saithe	44	14	153	211	19
Cod	5		19	24	2
Haddock	1			1	<1
Ling	9		16	25	2
Large Gadid	34	5	79	118	11
Small Gadid	15	3	10	28	2
John Dory		1		1	<1
Scad	5		4	9	0
Red Sea Bream	84	34	212	330	29
Black Sea Bream			1	1	<1
Sea Bream	40	20	52	112	10
Balan Wrasse	82	5	50	137	12
Wrasse	6	1	2	9	0
Lesser Weaver		1		1	<1
Mullet?			2	2	<1
Gurnard		4		4	<1
Sea Scorpion		1	2	3	<1
Flatfish	6	4	1	11	0
Total	370	102	650	1122	

were represented: tope (*Galeorhinus galeus*), herring (*Clupea harengus*), common eel (*Anguilla anguilla*), conger eel (*Conger conger*), pollack (*Pollachius pollachius*), saithe (*Pollachius virens*), cod (*Gadus morhua*), haddock (*Melanogrammus aeglefinus*), ling (*Molva molva*), John Dory (*Zeus faber*), scad (*Trachurus trachurus*), red sea bream (*pagellus bogaraveo*), black sea bream (*Spondyliosoma canbtharus*), ballan wrasse (*Labrus bergylta*), lesser weaver (*Trachinus vipera*), mullet (*Mugilidae*), gurnard (*Triglidae*), sea scorpion (*Taurulus bubalis*) and flatfish.

Cod family fish (Gadidae) and sea bream are the dominant families, comprising 41% and 39% respectively of the identifiable assemblage (Table 6.3). The most abundant species was red sea bream and saithe was the most numerous of the gadids. Ballan wrasse are also well represented. There are 32 fragments of conger eel and few fragments of other species recorded.

The domestic food animals
As noted above, sheep predominate in the Pabbay assemblage. They dominate the 1st–3rd and the 6th–9th centuries by a large degree using both the NISP and MNI calculation (Tables 6.1, 6.2). For the intervening period cattle and sheep show a more even distribution, however, the sample size for this phase is small and the results should be treated with caution. There is a change over time, with sheep becoming less dominant with a corresponding increase in the numbers of cattle.

Sheep
A consideration of the parts of the sheep skeleton present can indicate how these animals were utilized (Tables 6.4–6.6). Figure 6.22 uses the minimum number of elements (MNE) to demonstrate the relative abundance of sheep elements (after Brain 1981). Although shown for all three phases, the small number of bones in the second phase (36 fragments) precludes any detailed analysis of this distribution. For the earliest and latest assemblages a range of elements are present in similarly high percentages. The only elements that are underrepresented are the small phalanxes. There is a slight difference between the two phases in that the later phase has a higher relative abundance of most elements and a slight shift in emphasis toward the major meat-bearing long bones; the scapula, humerus, pelvis and femur. This pattern suggests that during both phases whole animals were bought to site with a possible importation of prime meat parts in the later phase. The generally higher relative abundance in the later phase indicates more identifiable fragments recovered. This may reflect less fragmentation of the bone; a possible result of a reduced emphasis on marrow extraction, or a change in disposal patterns.

Age. The timing of death of sheep can be examined through the fusion data from the long bones (Table 6.7). In all phases a quarter to a half of the earliest fusing bones remained unfused indicating an early death for many sheep. After the first year the proportion of unfused bone steadily increases, with less than a quarter of the latest fusing bones have fused. Sheep are dying young, many during their first year with few surviving to adulthood. The proportion of neonatal bone remained constant at between 4 and 7% for all three phases, suggesting little difference in the mortality rates for newborn lambs. Fusion information suggests that many animals are surviving birth but being slaughtered before their first year. The earliest phase has the highest percentage of unfused bone in the first year.

Dental eruption and wear is a further source of ageing evidence (Table 6.8; Fig. 6.23). As only three jaws were recovered in the 2nd–4th century there is no detailed discussion of that phase. The cumulative mortality indicates that a third of the jaws came from animals dying before they were six months old and half of all sheep were dead by the end of their first year. Only in the earliest phase was there evidence of any animals over three years old, the oldest aged mandible came from an individual of only 4–6 years. Overall there is a peak in the age of death at age stages B (2–6 months) and E (2–3 years). This indicates both the early slaughter of lambs, before the first winter, and later slaughter of young adults.

The size of the sheep assemblage and the presence of neonates suggest a breeding population. Many sheep

Table 6.4 Site PY10: abundance of elements: 1st–3rd century.

	Sheep	Cattle	Pig	Red deer	Common Seal	Atlantic Seal	Seal	Whale	Cattle Size	Sheep Size
Horncore	19	2								
dP4	3	2								
LM3	4	1								
Occ. Condyle	19	2								
Premaxilla	6	1				2				
Mandible	51	11	1			1				
Lower Canine			1							
Hyoid	3	1							1	
Scapula	44	9	2			1				
Humerus	48	11	2		1					
Radius	43	10	1	1	1					
Ulna	47	6								
Magnum	14	3								
Metacarpal	43	3	1							
Pelvis	48	9	2		1					2
Femur	63	9			2					
Patella	11		1							
Tibia	69	7	1		1					
Astragulus	20	7			1					
Calcaneum	24	11				1				
Nav. Cuboid	13	4								
Metatarsal	44	5								
Metapodial	24	10			8	2				
1st Phalanx	101	15	2		5	4				
2nd Phalanx	47	13	2		1	2				
3rd Phalanx	48	8	1			1			1	
Rib	78	9					5		3	63
Tooth										
VC01	13	4				1				
VC02	13	1			1					1
VC	32	8	3							13
VT	118								10	12
VL	47									
Sacrum	8									2
V. Caud.	7	8							3	3
Vert. Frag.	39	1					1		7	15
Unid								1		
Total	1211	191	20	1	22	15	6	1	25	111

survive the first few months only to die later in the autumn of their first year. A few animals are kept until sexually maturity to breed but even these are slaughtered after only a couple of seasons. As sheep reach sexual maturity early the high rate of slaughter could have been sustained. This method of sheep rearing does not focus on secondary products, indeed the lambs were quickly slaughtered for meat, although wool may have been gathered off the retained breeding population. Such a high rate of early slaughter indicates that overwintering sheep was not undertaken for most of the flock. Sheep lose condition over the winter and an early slaughter of lambs would be efficient if fodder was in short supply. Such a pattern of death also suggests that sheep manure was not important as a fertilizer, this could suggest extensive agriculture or the use of other material, such as seaweed, to improve the soil.

Articulated bone groups. During the recording of the site a number of articulated bone groups were noted.

The majority were composed of neonatal animals. In the earliest phase, two contexts in the gallery contained paired elements. Context 6 revealed pairs of horncores, humeri, radii, femora and tibiae, whilst context 41 contained a pair of radii and metatarsi. These elements were all from immature individuals. They may represent the partial burial of two individuals.

The interior revealed partial skeletons in three contexts 24, 32 and 35. Context 24 contained an individual represented by most of its skeleton; the head, spine, limbs, toes and tail were present. Fusion suggests an individual of five months (distal humerus and proximal radius fused, pelvis unfused and scapula fusing) whilst the dentition suggests around six months (first molar coming into wear in the right jaw but not yet in wear in the left). Butchery revealed evidence of head removal with knife cuts across the occipital condyles and the first cervical vertebra. Further butchery indicated the carcass had been split at the pelvis, with cuts at the distal humerus,

Table 6.5 Site PY10: abundance of elements: 2nd–4th century.

	Sheep	Cattle	Pig	Red deer	Otter	Whale	Cattle Size	Sheep Size
Occ. Condyle	1							
Premaxilla					2			
Mandible	6	3			1			
Scapula					1			
Humerus		1			2			
Radius	4	2			1			
Ulna	2	1			1			
Metacarpal		2						
Pelvis	3	1			1			
Femur	4			1				
Patella		1						
Tibia	1		1					
Astragulus		2			1			
Calcaneum	5				1			
Nav. Cuboid	1	3						
Metatarsal		1						
Metapodial	2				3			
1st Phalanx	3	8						
2nd Phalanx	1	3						
3rd Phalanx		1						
Rib					9		1	6
VC02		1			1			
VC	1				6			
VT	1				1			
VL	1							
V. Caud.					1			
Vert. Frag.		1				1		
Unid								
Total	36	31	1	1	32	1	1	6

proximal radius and ulna suggesting disarticulation at the elbow joint. This points to the animal being consumed and subsequently discarded complete.

Context 32 contained a second older individual. The dental wear patterns gave an age of two to three years, while the fusion suggested an animal between three and three and a half (proximal femur fused, distal femur and distal radius fusing, other late-fusing bones unfused). Again, the majority of the skeleton was present. This animal also showed butchery associated with disarticulation; cut marks were present around the humerus-radius joint. Knife cuts on the proximal metapodials are likely to be associated with skinning.

A pair of articulated front legs were recovered from context 35, consisting of scapula, humorous, radius and ulna. The bones in this part skeleton were unfused indicating a young animal of less than 3–4 months old.

Context 44 in chamber B contained a pair of unfused radii, one pair of metatarsi and a complete pelvis. These were all from immature or neonatal animals.

In the second phase context 16 had a pair of radii and ulna and calcaneum from immature animals. Context 45 contained a pair of metacarpi, pelves and femora; all except the pelves were unfused.

The prevalence of these articulated bone groups is perplexing. In other parts of Britain, the placing of such bone groups in pits has been interpreted as having a 'ritual' significance (Hill 1995), while at the site of Hornish Point there was a pit containing a human skeleton with other ritually deposited remains of animals (Barber *et al.* 1989). At Pabbay, however, the articulated bone was not recovered from cut features. Some of the 'burials' suggest feasting; events where single animals were slaughtered, consumed and quickly disposed of before bones became dispersed. The small size of these young animals may result in their total consumption at one sitting, with the resulting debris immediately cleared. However, while one of these animals is very young and small the other is a mature animal and would have provided a reasonable quantity of meat. If such a method of consumption and clearing often occurred why are articulated bone groups so rare in animal bone assemblages? The placement of the two most complete 'burials' within the interior suggest a deliberate placement of these animals as foundation or sealing deposits.

The many pairs of bones scattered through the contexts are more difficult to explain. It is clear that the animals had pairs of bones disposed of together rather than dispersed. These elements probably

Table 6.6 Site PY10: abundance of elements: 6th–9th century.

	Sheep	Cattle	Pig	Red deer	Otter	Common Seal	Atlantic Seal	Seal	Whale	Cattle Size	Sheep Size
Antler				4							
Horncore	5										
dP4	1	3									
Occ. Condyle	9	1	1								
Premaxilla	6										
Mandible	20	10	1								
Hyoid	2										
Scapula	26	8									
Humerus	30	4	1		1						
Radius	40	10			1		1				1
Ulna	12	1	1								
Magnum	3	2									
Metacarpal	23	4									
Pelvis	29	4	1								1
Femur	38	6			2	1					
Patella	4	2									
Tibia	35	6									
Astragulus	7	6									
Calcaneum	19	1									
Nav. cuboid	5	1									
Metatarsal	16	2	1	1							
Metapodial	11	5			7	5	2				
Os penis											
1st Phalanx	66	13			4	4	1				2
2nd Phalanx	37	8	1		4						
3rd Phalanx	12	6									
Rib	65	6			12		1			2	30
Tooth											
VC01	8	1								1	2
VC02	2	2									6
VC	18	1									16
VT	42	3			2					1	
VL	39				4						
Sacrum	2	1			2	2					1
V. Caud.	3					2				1	1
Vert. frag.	17	3			2				3	5	20
Maxilla	1		1								
Unid									11		
Total	653	120	8	5	41	14	5	3	11	10	80

belong to partial burials that were not fully recovered or identified.

Butchery. Sheep butchery is shown in Table 6.9. A range of elements have evidence of cut and chop marks, with the former more common. Between 8 and 20% of bones were butchered, the highest level being found in the small 2nd–4th century sample.

Three horncores show signs of removal by chopping and three skulls were split open, presumably to extract the brain. Cut marks on mandibles are likely to be associated with removal of the tongue and cheek meat. In many cases vertebra had been split, indicating butchery of the carcass by suspending and halving, however, such division was not universal. In one of the 'burials' the pelvis also shows signs of carcass division. The ribs had cut marks associated with removal of meat. Long bones bore evidence of skinning on the metapodials, dismembering at the joints, particularly at the humerus-radius joint, and on the astragalus.

Cattle

An examination of the relative abundance of elements (Tables 6.4–6.6; Fig. 6.24) reveals the parts of the cattle skeleton that are found on site. The small assemblage of cattle bone makes interpreting these results difficult, and for 3rd–6th century impossible.

The range of bones present indicate that all parts of the skeleton were present, which suggests the local slaughter of at least some animals. Few, if any, of the skull bones were recorded, although the presence of cattle mandibles suggests that at least part of the head was present. In the earliest phase bones of the upper

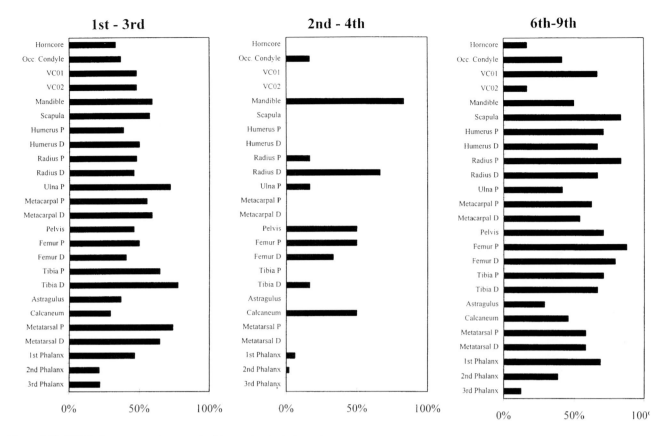

Figure 6.22 PY10: sheep: percentage survival by anatomical element.

Table 6.7 Site PY10: sheep: fusion data.

	1st–3rd				2nd–4th				6th–9th			
	Unfused	Neonate	Fused	% Unfused	Unfused	Neonate	Fused	% Unfused	Unfused	Neonate	Fused	% Unfused
Humerus D.	7	2	13						2		8	
Radius P.	10		15				1		3		19	
Scapula	7	3	16						4		12	
Pelvis	15	2	10		1		1		6	1	8	
<1 year	39	5	54	45	1	0	2	33	15	1	47	25
Tibia D.	20	6	14						6		5	
Metacarpal D.	16	2	16						8		4	
Metatarsal D.	21		10						4	1	5	
<2 years	57	8	40	62	0	0	0	0	18	1	14	58
Calcaneum	15		8		3		1		12	2	1	
Femur P.	22	1	11				1		17	2	3	
Humerus P.	7	1	5						9	1	1	
Radius D.	19		7		3				9		2	
Ulna P.	17	1	7						7		1	
Femur D.	14	1	2				1		11	2	2	
Tibia P.	18	8	8						5		4	
<3.5 years	112	10	48	72	6	1	2	78	70	7	14	85

	Neonates	Total	% Neonates		Neonates	Total	% Neonates		Neonates	Total	% Neonates
	23	311	7		1	11	9		9	165	5

Table 6.8 Site PY10: sheep: mandibular wear stage.

Stage	Age	1st–3rd	2nd–4th	6th–9th	Total	Cumulative Mortality
A	0–2 months	5		1	6	15%
B	2–6 months	6	1	2	9	38%
C	6–12 months	4		1	5	51%
D	1–2 years	2	2	1	5	64%
E	2–3 years	5	1	3	9	87%
F	3–4 years	4			4	97%
G	4–6 years	1			1	100%
		27	4	8	39	

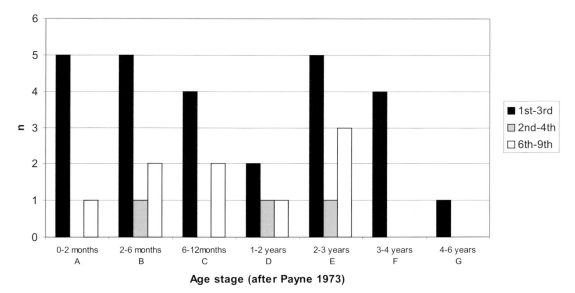

Figure 6.23 PY10: sheep: mandibular wear stages.

forelimb, the pelvis and the lower hindlimb are common, whilst metapodials and toes are relatively rare. In the latest phase, scapula and radius predominate in the forelimb and astragalas in the hind with bones of the lower limbs scarce. The small quantity of lower limb bones, metapodials and toes compared to the prime meat upper limb bones suggests the importation of some meat on the bone. In addition, the general underrepresentation of all elements suggests that at least some bone was neither recovered nor identified. This may be a product of fragmentation of the bone during marrow extraction.

Age. The small number of cattle bones present on the site means that only a cautious interpretation of fusion evidence can be made (Table 6.10). The data suggest that for all phases cattle died very young. Only in the latest phase is there evidence of animals greater than three years old. The proportion of neonatal bone reflects this ranging from 20 to 50%.

The evidence from tooth eruption and wear is also sparse but indicates mostly very young animals (Table 6.11). Only a single neonatal jaw was recovered from the earliest phase with a further three neonates and an immature individual in the latest phase. In the

neonates the dP4 was not fully in wear indicating animals that died at less than one month old. A single shed dP4 was recovered from context 44.

The presence of neonatal jaws and long bones suggests that whole young animals were present on site. The absence of adult jaws suggests that they were slaughtered and butchered elsewhere.

The early death for most cattle is even more pronounced than for sheep. The presence of neonates suggests a breeding population, but for cattle the evidence for adults is scarce and a trade in calves may have occurred. The predominance of what appears to be prime meat bones has to be reassessed in the light of the age structure of the population. The paucity of fused bone suggests these elements must derive from younger animals. This could support the notion of trade in calves, with young animals killed elsewhere and only the most useful parts of the skeleton imported. Alternatively, the limb extremities of such young animals may have been preferentially destroyed by taphonomic processes.

Articulated bone groups. There was a group of neonatal bone recovered from context 6. This mainly comprised of fragmentary bones of the left fore and

Table 6.9 Site PY10: sheep: butchery by element.

	1st–3rd		2nd–4th		6th–9th	
	Cut	Chop	Cut	Chop	Cut	Chop
Horncore	1	4			1	1
Premaxilla	1					
Mandible	5		2		2	
Scapula	2				3	
Humerus	5				5	1
Radius	4		1		3	
Ulna	3		1			
Metacarpal	3	1				
Pelvis	1	2		1	2	1
Femur	6	2			1	
Tibia	2					1
Astragulus	5					
Calcaneum			1			
Nav. Cuboid	2				2	
Metatarsal	3					
VC01	4	1				4
VC02		2				
VC	12	10			3	6
VT	1	6				10
VL	2	1				1
V. Caud.		1				
Vert. Frag.						2
Sacrum	1	2				
Rib	19	5			16	3
1st Phalanx	1					
Total	83	37	5	1	38	30
% butchered		10%		17%		10%

hind limbs and may constitute a partial skeleton. The astragalus showed disarticulation butchery, while two femurs, one of the few elements present in pairs, were snapped midshaft. The only other bone groups noticed were two pairs of cattle radii in context 45. Their state of fusion indicates the animals were neonates when they died. Eleven other neonatal cattle bones were present but only as single elements with no obvious articulations. Again, these are likely to represent partial burials, but this cannot be confirmed.

Butchery. Around 10–20% of bone was butchered, with the highest proportion of butchered bone in the small 2nd–4th century sample. As for sheep, most recorded butchery marks were knife cuts. A mandible showed evidence of tongue removal, whilst a hyoid showed knife cuts associated with cutting of the throat. Head removal was indicated by chop marks on a cervical vertebra. Disarticulation marks and defleshing marks were noted on some of the long bones. Adult and neonates both bore butchery marks; a neonatal humerus and astragalus were cut and a neonatal third phalanx chopped. Two neonatal femurs were snapped midshaft (see above), probably to extract the marrow.

Pig

Pig bones were few and made up 1% or less of the NISP in each phase. Unlike the wild species the MNI

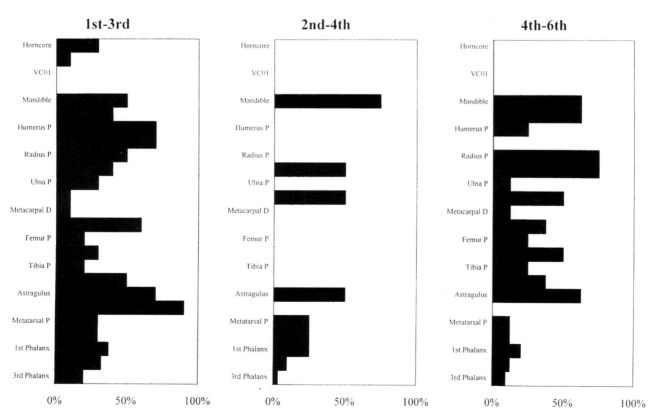

Figure 6.24 PY10: cattle: percentage survival by anatomical element.

Table 6.10 Site PY10: cattle: fusion data.

	1st–3rd				2nd–4th				6th–9th			
	Unfused	Neonate	Fused	% Unfused	Unfused	Neonate	Fused	% Unfused	Unfused	Neonate	Fused	% Unfused
Scapula	3	1	2						3	1		
Pelvis	4	1	1		1				3			
<1 year	7	2	3	75	1		0	100	6	1	0	100
Humerus D.	4				1		1		1			
Radius P.		1	4						2	4		
<2 years	4	1	4	56	1		1	50	3	4	0	100
Tibia D.	1	1	1									
Metacarpal D.		1			2						1	
Metatarsal D.	1	1	2		1				1		1	
Calcaneum	7	0	2							1		
<3 years	9	3	5	71	0	3	0	100	1	1	2	50
Femur P.	1	1								1		
Humerus P.	2	1									1	
Radius D.	2								1	4		
Ulna P.	2											
Femur D.		2							2		1	
Tibia P.	1	1							1			
<4 years	8	5	0	100					3	5	2	80

	Neonates	Total	% Neonates		Neonates	Total	% Neonates		Neonates	Total	% Neonates
	11	51	22		3	6	50		11	28	39

Table 6.11 Site PY10: cattle: mandibular wear stage.

Stage	Age	1st–3rd	2nd–4th	6th–9th	Total	Cumulative Mortality (%)
A	0–1 month			1	1	17
A/B	1 month	1		3	4	83
B	1–8 months					83
C	8–18 months			1	1	100
		1	0	5	6	

for pig is two for the earliest and latest phases. Elements present include parts of the skull, mandible, upper and lower limbs and vertebra.

A high percentage of pig long bones were unfused and neonatal (Table 6.13) indicating an early death. This is common for pigs, their only utility is in meat production, and with large litter sizes many of the piglets are killed when young. The presence of neonates suggests on site breeding. However, as for cattle, the very small number of individuals present could suggest a trade in piglets rather than the presence of breeding sows and boars.

A single lower canine was present, context 44. This was a large left adult male canine of a size comparable to wild boar. The only other recorded incidence of wild boar was at the Neolithic site of Northton (Finlay 1984). The presence of this adult element, in a small assemblage dominated by juveniles, with no other bone of a comparable size, suggests the tusk was traded independently. A humerus, a pelvis and a split vertebrae were the only butchered bones present. No articulated bone groups were identified.

Red deer

Only a single red deer long bone was present in each phase (Tables 6.4–6.6). These were a fragment of radius, an unfused femur and a metatarsal joint surface. Four antler tips were recorded, while a number of other antler fragments were noted. Red deer are present at most sites in small quantities, and in most cases antler fragments predominate (Mulville 1999). At Pabbay the antler all showed signs of working; two

Table 6.12 Site PY10: cattle: butchery by element.

| | 1st–3rd | | 2nd–4th | | 6th–9th | |
	Cut	Chop	Cut	Chop	Cut	Chop
Mandible	1		1		2	
Hyoid	1					
Humerus	1					
Pelvis		1	1			
Femur					1	
Tibia	1					
Astragulus	2		1			
Calcaneum	1					
Hyoid	1					
Metapodial	1					
Nav. Cuboid			3			
Metatarsal	1				1	
VC02				1		
VC	1	2				
Vert. Frag.		2				1
Rib					3	1
1st Phalanx	2					
3rd Phalanx		1				
Total	13	6	6	1	7	2
% butchered		10		23		8

pegs, a handle and working waste was recorded. The paucity of long bones and the use of antler in tool production does not suggest a breeding population on the island, but probably indicates a trade in antler and possibly venison. If this is the case the presence of the fragment of metatarsal is of interest; these bones bear little meat, but their long straight shaft does make them ideal for working. The nearest known breeding population of red deer existed on South Uist (Mulville 1999) and it is possible that animals were traded from there. Even at Dun Vulan, deer did not form a significant part of the assemblage, leading to the suggestion that deer bones do not enter the main assemblage (Mulville 1999).

Otter

Otter bones were only recovered from the later phases (Tables 6.4–6.6) and comprised of two partial otter skeletons (contexts 18 and 52) in addition to two individual bones. There is the possibility that the skeletons are from intrusive animals. The majority of otter bone was unfused indicating immature individuals, although the partial skeleton in context 18 came from an adult. Context 19 contained an otter kitten scapula, and context 18 most of a juvenile otter skeleton. All the otter bones came from interior contexts. At Dun Vulan butchery indicated the use of otter fur, and here a possible cut mark was noticed on the pelvis of the skeleton in context 52.

Otters are found on several other sites in small quantities (Mulville 1999). Pabbay has a relatively large number of otter bones; only 16 were recovered from the much larger assemblage at Dun Vulan. This is due to the presence of possible intrusive individuals represented by partial skeletons.

Common seal

Groups of bones were recovered from a number of contexts, in the earliest and latest phases (Tables 6.4–6.6). Few bones were found in isolation and although not buried in articulation they may represent the processed remains of a single animal. The metapodials and phalanxes could indicate the processing of seal skins with flippers still attached, while the presence of small fragments of meat bones indicates utilization of the flesh.

All of the long bones are unfused and derive from juveniles; a complete unfused femur appears to be from a neonate. Two of the bones bear knife cuts; there are filleting marks on the neonatal femur and disarticulation cuts on the astragalus. Radius and femur distal epiphyses were also recorded. These are unlikely to have been imported without the accompanying

Table 6.13 Site PY10: pig: fusion data.

| | Fused | 1st–3rd | | 2nd–4th | 4th–6th | | |
		Unfused	Neonate	Unfused	Fused	Unfused	Neonate
Scapula			1				
Humerus P		1	1				1
Humerus D	1						1
Radius P			1				
Radius D			1				
Ulna						1	
Pelvis					1		
Tibia P		1					
Tibia D		1		1			
Metapodials	2	1					
Phalanges	3				1		
Total	6	4	4	1	2	1	2
% Unfused		57		100		60	
% Neonate		29				40	

long bone and their presence highlights the loss of material.

The number of common seal bones outnumbers those of the Atlantic seal. The latter is easier to capture as they come ashore to breed (Corbett and Harris 1991), however, the predominance of common seals suggests that at least some individuals were taken at sea.

Atlantic seal
The Atlantic seal shows a similar distribution of elements (Tables 6.4–6.6). The groups of metapodials and phalanxes are likely to represent the remnants of seal skins. The majority of bones are from immature animals with only evidence for skeletally mature animals a fused calcaneum and phalanxes. As for the common seal the proximal epiphysis of a radius was recovered, which suggests that the entire bone was present at site but not recovered. As noted above, Atlantic seals are easily captured during breeding and the uninhabited islands of the Outer Hebrides are important breeding grounds for them today.

A small number of seal vertebrae could not be identified to species.

The number of seal bones recovered are quite high; the larger assemblage of Dun Vulan only produced a NISP of 55. At Dun Vulan the majority of seals were adults, while at Pabbay nearly all bone was unfused. This could indicate a difference in strategy, the adult animals would have provided more meat but possibly infants of both species were easier to catch.

Cetaceans: whales and dolphins
Worked fragments of cetacean bone were recovered from the site (Tables 6.4–6.6). The most complete element is a sperm whale vertebral epiphyseal plate, shaped into a lid. These artifacts are relatively common on Atlantic Scotland Iron Age sites (Mulville, forthcoming). The remaining cetacean material is also likely to derive from whales but has been reduced through working into unidentifiable fragments.

Fish

Species representation. Cod family fish (Gadidae) and sea bream are the dominant fish families, comprising 40% and 39% respectively of the identifiable assemblage (Table 6.3). The majority of sea bream were identified as red sea bream, and these are the most numerous species. Saithe are the most numerous of the gadids. Ballan wrasse are also well represented. Conger eel is represented by 35 fragments and the remaining species by only a few fragments each.

Table 6.14 Gadidae: body part representation.

	Pollack		Saithe			Large Gadid		
	1st–3rd	6th–9th	1st–3rd	2nd–4th	6th–9th	1st–3rd	2nd–4th	6th–9th
Vomer					2	2		2
Post Temporal		2	3	1	2			2
Parasphenoid				1	9	1	1	5
Upper Pharyngeal								2
Lower Pharyngeal								5
Premaxilla	2	3	4		11	2		2
Maxilla	1	2	2	3	13	2		1
Palatine					2			1
Dentary	2	3	14	4	29	1		2
Articular		2	8	2	22	4		2
Quadrate		1	1		5			
Cerotohyale						9	2	20
Epihyale								4
Hyomandibular	1		2		10			3
Operculum			1		10	1		2
Preoperculum						1		11
Suboperculum					1			
Precaudal vert.	3	11	4	1	17	6		2
Total head	9	24	39	12	133	29	3	66
Caudal Vert.	8	8	2		8	1		1
Ectopterygoid								2
Frontal			2	2	11			1
Interoperculum					1			1
Cleithrum			1			3		7
Supracleithrum	1							1
Total body	9	8	5	2	20	4	0	13
Total	18	32	44	14	153	33	3	79

Table 6.15 Red sea bream and ballan wrasse: body part representation.

	Red Sea Bream			Balan Wrasse		
	1st–3rd	2nd–4th	6th–9th	1st–3rd	2nd–4th	6th–9th
Neurocranium				1		
Vomer		1		1		2
Lachrymal				1		
Post temporal			4			
Basioccipital		1	2			
Parasphenoid	1	2	3			
Upper Pharyngeal			2	8		5
Lower Pharyngeal			6	10		10
Premaxilla	1		10	7		3
Maxilla	3		4	2	1	1
Palatine	2		7			1
Dentary	4	2	8	7		1
Articular	2	2	3	3		1
Quadrate	1	1	5	2		
Cerotohyale	3		1	2		
Epihyale	1		1			
Hyomandibular	5		7	2		
Operculum	2		3	4	1	3
Preoperculum			4	2	1	
Suboperculum	1	1		1		
Urohyale			1			
Precaudal Vert.	23	5	58	11	1	5
Total head	49	15	129	64	4	32
Caudal Vert.	22	8	58	6		4
Basipterygium			2			1
Cleithrum	5	7	4	3		6
Coracoid		3				
Postcleithrum						1
Scapula		1	1	1		
Supracleithrum	5		2	2		4
Total body	32	19	67	12	0	16
Total	81	34	196	76	4	48

Body part frequency. Saithe and large gadids display an overrepresentation of head parts compared to body parts (Table 6.14). This is not surprising due to the large number of elements pertaining to the head and the robustness of the mouth parts, however, caudal vertebrae are also under-represented in comparison to pre-caudal vertebrae. In addition, both caudal vertebrae and cleithrum are robust elements and therefore it is unlikely that this is the result of differential preservation alone. In contrast, although head parts dominate the remains of red sea bream and ballan wrasse, both precaudal and caudal vertebrae are well represented (Table 6.15).

Context. The largest concentration of fish bones was recovered from context 8, which contained about 25% of the identifiable assemblage (Table 6.16). Both saithe and red sea bream were well represented. Significant concentrations were also recovered from contexts 10, 37, 41, 44, 45 and 60. Red sea bream dominated context 44, representing half of the fragments from this deposit.

Taphonomy. The assemblage is well preserved as exemplified by the wide range of elements represented. Vertebrae and mouth parts are the most numerous elements and also the most robust, indicating that the assemblage has been affected by differential preservation. However, in the absence of sieved samples this may also be a reflection of biased recovery in favour of large, easily recognized elements. Two caudal (contexts 9 and 44) and one precaudal (context 9) vertebrae belonging to red sea bream were partially charred.

Size. The size of the saithe were calculated using measurements taken on the dentaries and compared with those taken on specimens of known length (Table 6.17). Almost three-quarters belonged to fish approximately 480 mm in length and therefore estimated at approximately four years old (Wheeler 1968). Fewer measurements were available for pollack, and therefore size and age were estimated using measurements taken on a range of elements, which suggested a wider age distribution (Table 6.18). Four

Table 6.16 Site PY10: contexts containing significant quantities of fish bones.

| | 1st–3rd | | | 6th–9th | | | |
	37	41	44	8	10	45	60
Tope	1						
Common Eel	1					1	
Conger Eel	2	5	1	3	2		
Pollack			7	1	3	3	11
Saithe	7	6	5	88	11	3	30
Cod			5	14		2	
Ling			4	6	2	4	1
Large Gadid	8		7	34	8	6	16
Small Gadid	2	5	4	3		2	1
Scad		2	1	2		1	
Red Sea Bream	4	2	54	101	15	21	21
Sea Bream	1	6	1	16	13	3	16
Balan Wrasse	13	38	9	11	8	23	1
Wrasse	6				1	1	
Mullet?							2
Sea Scorpion				2			
Flatfish	5		1	1			
Total	50	64	99	282	63	70	99

Table 6.17 Site PY10: saithe: approximate size and age calculated from dentaries.

Approximate Length (mm)	Estimated Age	n
< 480	under 4 years	5
480	4 years	2
480–700	4–7 years	3
700	7 years	1

Table 6.18 Site PY10: pollack: approximate size and age calculated from all elements.

Approximate Length (mm)	Estimated Age	n
< 570	under 5 years	3
570–660	over 5 years	3
660	over 5 years	1
660–800	over 5 years	2
800	over 5 years	1

measurements were obtained from conger eel, all of which suggest a size greater than 1,150 mm.

Ecology and environment. All of the fish species represented can be found in the inshore zone. The preferred habitat of young saithe, pollack, sea bream, ballan wrasse and conger eel, rockling and John Dory (Wheeler 1968) is close to the shore over rough ground or rocky areas. Both tope and scad can be found close inshore during the warmer months but migrate to deeper water in winter.

Discussion. There is no evidence on the bones themselves to suggest that the fish remains were deposited by natural agencies, such as otters or sea birds. As almost all of the species recovered make good eating fish there is little doubt that they were

deliberately caught and introduced to the site by the inhabitants. Scad, weever and scorpion fish are not considered of economic importance today, however, it is possible that they were consumed in the past, especially if caught by chance.

In the absence of sieved samples any interpretation should be treated with caution, however, the considerable quantity of fish remains recovered from Pabbay suggests that fish were considered an important resource. The assemblage is dominated by inshore species, particularly saithe, red sea bream and ballan wrasse, which are known to take bait readily (Wheeler 1968). This suggests that the inhabitants of Pabbay were practising a low-risk fishing strategy in order to meet their fish requirements. This would probably have involved exploitation of the inshore waters from the shore or small boats using lines and nets.

As previously mentioned, saithe and members of the large gadid category are noticeably underrepresented by such body parts as caudal vertebrae and cleithrum, which is unlikely to be caused solely by differential preservation. These elements often remain in the body after decapitation and processing in order to add rigidity to the fillets. This may account for their low numbers, especially if processed fillets were being traded away from the site. This pattern is not apparent for either red sea bream or ballan wrasse, which suggests that whole fish were being consumed at the site. The presence of a cut mark on a red sea bream precaudal vertebra may be the result of such food preparation techniques as gutting and filleting.

Evidence from contemporary sites
The small size of the island is likely to have had a bearing on what domestic animals were kept and how they were farmed. At 83% the predominance of sheep among the main food animals is higher than that seen at any other Iron Age Hebridean site, while the low proportion of pig is lower than that at other brochs (Mulville 1999). At Dun Vulan, for example, pig made up about 30–50% of the major domesticates. Other differences between Pabbay and Dun Vulan exist in the wild fauna. At Dun Vulan the impoverished natural fauna was supplemented by the importation of non-native species: pine marten, hare, badger and roe deer. At Pabbay none of these exotics were recorded. The low proportion of pig and the lack of exotics make Pabbay more similar to wheelhouses. These differences probably indicate less access to resources and the problems with living on such a small island. The mammal assemblage is only a third the size of Dun Vulan, but at over 2000 fragments should not be affected by bias of small sample size.

The slaughter pattern for sheep at Pabbay is similar to that at Dun Vulan and other sites across the islands, with two slaughter peaks identified from the mandibular data (Mulville 1999). At Pabbay, however, the animals are killed earlier, with peaks at 2–6 months and 2–3 years rather than the 6–12 months and 3–4 years seen at Dun Vulan. Both sites have a paucity of adults and a relatively low proportion of neonatal bone, 4–7% at Pabbay and 13% at Dun Vulan.

For cattle the proportion of neonatal bone is extremely high (20–50%) and exceeds that at Dun Vulan. However, Dun Vulan mandibular data indicates that half of the cattle jaws aged were neonates. It is interesting to note the highest proportion of neonates at Dun Vulan were found adjacent to the broch in a similar location to the excavated deposits at Pabbay. While the proportion of neonates are similar at both sites, Dun Vulan had a larger adult population that would have provided secondary products and some prime meat. The lack of adults at Pabbay could be related to disposal practices, with larger and older animals disposed of away from the excavated area.

The majority of Iron Age Hebridean sites have a high proportion of neonatal cattle. A number of reasons for this have been put forward: feeding constraints, dairying and poor husbandry (Mulville 1999). At Pabbay the earlier age of slaughter for sheep suggests some problems with feed provision. However, as the proportion of cattle neonates is similar to that at Dun Vulan, it is unlikely that conditions particular to Pabbay are affecting when these animals die. As suggested for Dun Vulan, the calves may have been killed to free milk for human consumption, however, the virtual absence of adults at Pabbay makes it hard to argue for a sustainable cattle or pig population. Either adults are missing from the assemblage or calves are imported; the former may allow milk production but the latter would not, although trade in dairy produce as well as meat may have occurred.

No dog bones were recorded from Pabbay, although a small quantity of gnawed bones attests to their presence. They are generally present in small numbers on Iron Age sites (Mulville 1999). The absence of dog skeletal remains suggests that dogs may have been disposed of away from the settlement.

Shed deciduous teeth have been recovered from Dun Vulan (Mulville 1999), Hornish Point and Baleshare (Halstead, in press). Halstead considers the presence of shed teeth, particularly in midden deposits, to indicate some sort of containment of young animals. It is possible that stock were afforded shelter within, and kept close to, the settlement.

Owing to the small number of bones, it is difficult to define any temporal changes in species other than sheep. There is a slight shift in emphasis towards more prime meat bones and less fragmentation in the later phase for sheep. Ageing information shows little patterning though fusion suggests more animals survive their first year in the later phase. Cattle show a slightly higher level of neonatal and first-year slaughter during the 6th–9th century, and a greater emphasis on prime meat bones. Wild species are equally rare throughout.

This information suggests a slight change from the earliest to the latest phase with more prime meat bones, sheep surviving longer and an increase in calf slaughter. This could suggest a more successful farming community, confident in their ability to overwinter more sheep, allowing them to sacrifice more calves. The increase in meat bones may suggest trade, and indicate a society with surplus to exchange for meat.

At the present time, few fish assemblages from Hebridean sites have been analysed with the exception of Dun Vulan (Cerón-Carrasco and Parker Pearson 1999), Hornish Point and Baleshare (Jones 1987). In addition, small amounts of fish bone were recovered from the nearby sites of Mingulay and Sandray (this volume).

The geographical proximity and retrieval methods used on the assemblages from Mingulay and Sandray render them useful for comparison. However, the small size of both assemblages suggests that fishing was of less importance than it was at Pabbay. Although the species lists are similar, both Mingulay and Sandray were dominated by large gadids, whereas at Pabbay red sea bream were exploited in equal quantities. The predominance of inshore species at all three sites indicates a similar low-risk strategy with exploitation of the inshore zone.

At Dun Vulan the fish bone assemblage was composed predominately of members of the Gadidae family, including saithe, cod and pollack. Here, the evidence of cut marks and the underrepresentation of head parts suggests that the fish were processed elsewhere and that the assemblage represents food waste. The author also suggests that in rocky surroundings the local fish population was exploited from crag seats, while the presence of a sandy beach and sand bar allowed safe offshore fishing using hand lines. On North Uist, hake (*Merluccius merluccius*) was the dominant species recovered from Hornish Point followed by cod, while at Baleshare cod outnumbered hake. The absence of small species was attributed to preservation and retrieval bias.

In the Orkney Islands, large quantities of immature saithe were recovered from St Boniface. In its later phase this was interpreted as a large-scale fish-processing site (Cerón-Carrasco 1994). At Scalloway, Shetland, again the commonest taxa was Gadidae, particularly cod and saithe, and there is also evidence for on-site processing in the later phase (Cerón-Carrasco 1994).

Conclusion

The assemblage at Pabbay indicates a reliance on sheep husbandry identical to that at many other Hebridean sites. Sheep were killed for meat, with many slaughtered before the first winter. Cattle may have been used to produce milk and storable dairy products, with all calves excess to breeding requirements slaughtered once lactation was established. Pigs were used exclusively for meat. The presence of a breeding population of any species other than sheep is unproven, though likely. Butchery points to extensive use of the entire carcass. Animals had their throats cut and were skinned. Their heads were removed and split for brain extraction. Horns were chopped off, probably to make use of the horn sheath. The carcass was sometimes split prior to butchery and use was made of the marrow. Even very young animals were eaten, with neonatal calves demonstrating evidence of butchery. Entire animals and part burials were deposited at the site, suggesting a ritual aspect to these deposits and possible feasting. Animals were offered shelter close to the settlement, perhaps from the winter winds. The animal bones suggest a slight change over time; circumstances may have improved with sheep dying older, more prime meat bone and a possible increased emphasis on dairying.

Wild species provided only a small amount of meat, and deer seem to be prized for their antlers, seals for their skins and cetacea for bone to work. Otter played an unknown role, though it may have provided fur. The procurement of some of the seals at sea is likely given the reliance on seafaring for trade and communication. Red deer and possibly other animals were traded either between sites, or, for the former, mostly probably between islands.

Comparison with other Iron Age Hebridean sites, particularly Dun Vulan, reveals an impoverished site. The earlier death and paucity of adult domestic animals, the low proportion of pig, the few wild species and the emphasis on the harder to capture common seal suggest a community with sustainability problems. It was probably hard to keep many domestic animals in such a small area, and the only wild mammals available would have been those in the sea.

Fishing would have been essential to the community. Evidence from contemporary sites on the Scottish islands leaves little doubt that fishing activities were generally focused on members of the cod family. The relative abundance of the different gadids is variable and probably reflects local conditions and fish populations, however, it appears that young saithe were commonly exploited. The large numbers of red sea bream recovered from Pabbay is unusual, but is probably a simple reflection of the presence of a local fish population and possibly dietary preference. All of the species recovered could easily have been caught from the shore or close inshore using small boats, lines and nets. Therefore, it appears that during the Iron Age, the inhabitants of the Scottish islands were practising a fishing strategy requiring little risk and low technology. There is evidence for the processing of young saithe at contemporary sites on the Orkney islands and possibly on a smaller scale at Sandray. Therefore, it is likely at least some of the saithe caught at Pabbay were being processed and stored for later consumption or trade.

Worked Bone and Antler

Emma Gowans and Andrew Hammon

A wide range of worked bone artifacts was recovered from the excavations at Dùnan Ruadh (Fig. 6.25). The majority of the objects, where species could be identified, were manufactured from either deer antler or sheep bone. While the worked bone assemblage is a great deal smaller than those from Sollas, Dun Vulan, Dun Cuier and À Cheardach Mhor, only a small proportion of the site was preserved *in situ*. The types of artifact recovered are not uncommon, nor are the species from which the bone is obtained, with one exception—whalebone. All of the bone objects from À Cheardach Mhor were manufactured from whalebone, and similarly whalebone artifacts accounted for just under one-third of the pieces of worked bone from Dun Vulan. Only one piece of whalebone, an unworked vertebra derived from the deposits associated with phase 1c of the interior, was recovered during the course of excavations at Dùnan Ruadh. Although the assemblage is dominated by functional objects, such as knife handles, a single bone pin was recovered from the site. This simple undecorated pin, while undiagnostic, is comparable to others found at Dun Vulan (Parker Pearson, Giles and Sharples 1999c: 220, object 1346).

Interior

Phase 1a

24 context 25. A bone plate measuring 134 × 38 mm with a thickness of 9 mm. A rectangular plate with squared ends and bevelled edges. The bevelled edges, running parallel to the long axis of the plate, invade the surface of the plate prescribing a shallow arc. One of the bevelled edges is cut by a series of diagonal notches. This plate could be an unfinished blank for a bone comb.

25 context 25. A bone point or awl, measuring 123 mm in length, manufactured from a split long bone. The tip of the point has been carefully shaped and rounded and shows polish through use.

26 context 25. An antler wedge, measuring 110 × 31 mm, with carefully trimmed edges. One end of the wedge has been trimmed to a bevelled point that has been polished through use.

29 context 31. A bone point, measuring 121 mm in length, manufactured from a cattle mandible (deer?). The tip of the point has been deliberately rounded and is polished through use.

30 context 31. A bone handle, measuring 136 mm long, manufactured from a left metatarsal of an adult sheep. One end of the handle is cut flat and hollowed out to receive the tang of a utensil or implement.

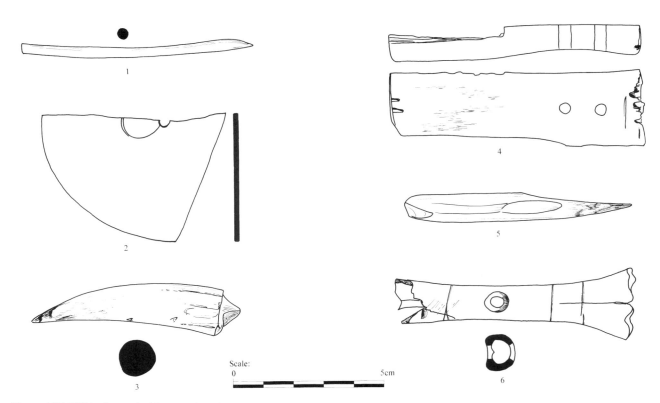

Figure 6.25 PY10: the worked bone and antler.

31 context 32. A bone point/handle, measuring 74 mm long, manufactured from the distal end of a metatarsal of an adult sheep/roe deer. One end of the handle is cut flat and hollowed out to receive the tang of an implement, while the other end is pointed and shows polish through wear.

32 context 33. A broken fragment of a perforated circular bone plate, measuring 79 mm in diameter and with a thickness of 1.5 mm (Fig. 6.25.2). A hole, 3 mm in diameter, has been drilled through the midpoint of the plate. One of the broken edges is heavily polished through use.

33 context 35. A bone point, measuring 75 × 11 mm, manufactured from the split shaft of a long bone, trimmed to a point at the end (Fig. 6.25.5). The tip of the point is highly polished from use.

Phase 1b

22 context 24. A chisel, measuring 160 mm in length with a diameter of 40 mm, manufactured from the antler of a red deer. While the tip of the chisel is heavily abraded, the butt of the chisel is unworn and is scored by 'fresh' saw marks.

23 context 24. A perforated bone toggle, measuring 79 mm in length, manufactured from a right metacarpal of a juvenile sheep (Fig. 6.25.6). A hole, 4.5 mm in diameter, has been drilled through the midpoint of the bone toggle. One of the surfaces, presumably the

upper surface, has been incised with two parallel lines one either side of the perforation.

27 context 26. A fragment of antler measuring 32 × 17 mm with an average thickness of 3.1 mm.

Phase 1c

21 context 21. A bone spoon measuring 55 mm long. It has a subrectangular bowl measuring 33 × 26 mm. The handle and one edge of the bowl are missing.

Phase 2

17 context 19. A perforated bone plate measuring 49 × 47 mm. All four edges of the plate have been broken. A subrectangular hole, 9 mm in diameter, has been cut into the surface of the plate.

Phase 3

9 context 8. A bone knife handle, measuring 83 × 25 mm, manufactured from the shaft of a long bone (Fig. 6.25.4). Two holes, 3 mm in diameter, have been drilled through one end of the plate. The plate would have formed part of a composite knife handle.

10 context 8. An antler point, measuring 69 mm in length, manufactured from a smoothed tine (Fig. 6.25.3). The butt of the point has been crudely shaped.

11 context 9. A bone point, measuring 109 mm in length, manufactured from the shaft of a tibia of a juvenile sheep. The tip of the point has been carefully trimmed and subsequently fire hardened.

266

12 context 9. A bone pin measuring 77 mm in length with a diameter of 4 mm (Fig. 6.25.1). The pin, with a trimmed point and parallel sides, has a simple rounded head.

13 context 9. A fragment of notched antler measuring 86 × 34 mm. An irregular wedge of antler with a well-rounded notch on one surface.

14 context 15. A fragment of antler measuring 100 × 51 mm. The end of the antler has been trimmed with cut marks, indicating where the tine has been removed.

42 context 52. A bone point measuring 55 mm in length. One end of the piece of bone has been trimmed to a point and subsequently fire hardened. The other end has been crudely trimmed and may have been inserted into a handle.

43 context 60. A crudely trimmed piece of antler, measuring 29 mm in length and approximately 13 mm in diameter. One end of the piece of antler has been heavily battered, while the other has been finely cut to create a flat surface. A second cut mark runs parallel to the flat end of the piece of antler.

44 context 10W. A bone point, measuring 69 mm in length, manufactured from the shaft of a sheep metatarsal. The tip of the bone point has become polished through use.

Chamber A
38 context 45. A perforated fragment of bone, measuring 39 × 26 mm with an average thickness of 4.8 mm. A broken triangular piece of bone with a drilled hole, 5 mm in diameter.

39 context 45. A bone toggle measuring 54 mm long with a diameter of 16 mm. The toggle has been manufactured from a crudely trimmed piece of bone, one end of which is rounded whilst the other is snapped. The perforation, tapering from 6 mm to 3 mm in diameter, is slightly off centre and is positioned close to one of the long edges of the toggle.

Chamber B
35 context 44. A bone spatula/shovel manufactured from a scapula. Although the implement has been broken, the blade survives intact. The leading edge of the blade, measuring 150 × 14 mm, is worn and the corners have been deliberately rounded. There are scratch marks along both sides of the leading edge.

Unstratified
1 context 1. A bone point, measuring 80 mm in length, manufactured from the shaft of a juvenile tibia (species unknown). The tip of the point has been deliberately rounded and is slightly abraded.

2 context 1. An antler point measuring 55 mm in length with a diameter of approximately 13 mm. The

tip of the point has been crudely trimmed and possibly hardened by fire.

7 context 1. A polished and shaped fragment of bone measuring 33 mm by 13 mm.

Environmental Sampling

Pat Wagner

Approximately 1 litre of residual material from the occupational deposit (context 52) within the temporary shelter constructed within the upper levels of the site was extracted and washed out over a 500 pm sieve. This sample yielded an abundance of molluscan shells, a large number of mammal, avian, and fish bones and several charred barley grains (Table 6.19). The molluscan shells are derived from at least two very different habitats and may have been transported intentionally or accidentally by humans. The shells are dominated by the seashore species *Littorina saxatilis* or rough periwinkle. This small, coiled mollusc inhabits the upper and top of middle shores and is widely distributed. Another marine mollusc recovered from this sample is the flat periwinkle, *Littorina littoralis*, which lives on the middle and top of lower shores, especially on the wrack seaweeds (*Fucus*). The single specimen of the estuarine dweller *Hydrobia ulvae* was burnt and, as the name suggests, this very small snail lives mainly on sea lettuce. The subassemblage of land snails included the rupestral species *Clausilia bidentata*, *Discus rotundatus* and *Aegopinella nitidula* that live in damp shady rocky places, but also a significant number of *Helicella itala*, which is normally associated with dry grassland or dune habitats. The marine and estuarine species may have been brought on to the site with seaweed. The common zone for both species of periwinkle is the middle shore, where wracks and other robust seaweeds are abundant. However, the lack of burning evidence on the marine shells may indicate direct collection as a food source, or the use of seaweed for animal fodder. Only the *Hydrobia* shows

Table 6.19 PY10: summary of the species present within the environmental sample taken from context 52.

Mollusca	*Littorina saxatilis*	71
	Littorina littorea	7
	Hydrobea ulvae	1 (burnt)
	Spirobis sp	1
	Cochlicopa lubrica	3
	Helicella itala	25
	Aegopinella nitidula	37
	Discus rotundatus	8
	Leiostyla angelica	5
	Cochlicella acuta	16
	Clausillia bitenta	38
Charred Seeds	Hulled Barley	8
	Barley (indeterminate)	13

evidence of burning, though the use of the finely fronded sea lettuce as a fuel source is improbable.

Bird bones from Pabbay PY10, Mingulay MY384 and Sandray SY14

Judith Cartledge

A range of bird species have been identified from Pabbay PY10. These are mainly sea birds and include shag, cormorant, Manx shearwater, gannet, several species of auk, including one bone from the now extinct great auk, and gulls. There is also a scatter of bones from waders, raven and thrush species throughout the site. There is no evidence for any domesticated species.

Most species occur in small numbers. The vast majority of bones belong to a single species, shag, which form over two-thirds of the identified bones. It occurs in similar proportions at both the Mingulay sites and out of the four bird bones identified from Sandray, two come from shag. The shag is a large bird, related to the cormorant. It is exclusively marine and nests on rocky coasts (Heinzel, Fitter and Parslow 1974). Many of the bones come from very young birds. There is evidence of butchery and it seems clear that this bird was being harvested to be eaten. F.S. Beveridge, writing in 1918 of the birds of North Uist, describes the shag as more common than the cormorant and that it 'is held in great esteem by the natives, who

make soup out of it—if properly made it is very like the best hare soup' (Cunningham, 1983: 40).

The other species that occurs frequently is the Manx shearwater, more so at the Mingulay sites, where the range of species is small, than at Pabbay PY10. At the Mingulay site, Manx shearwater represents over 20% of the identified bones. The Manx shearwater is a medium-sized, long-winged sea bird, related to the albatross. It is exclusively pelagic and only comes to land to breed on marine islands (Heinzel, Fitter and Parslow 1974).

The frequency of shag from these sites provides an interesting contrast to the bird bone assemblage from Dun Vulan. There, there is less emphasis on a single species, with a range of sea birds, the auk family, gannet and cormorant and shag all occurring frequently (Cartledge and Grimbley in Parker Pearson and Sharples 1999).

Worked stone

Caroline Wickham-Jones and Patrick Foster

Sixteen pieces of worked stone were recovered during the course of excavations at Dùnan Ruadh, namely 2 irregular chunks of flint, 13 cobble tools and a broken fragment of a perforated? stone axe (Fig. 6.26). The two pieces of 'worked' flint, perhaps debitage from tool manufacture, were unstratified. In the absence of further evidence of flint knapping, their interpretation must remain subject to doubt. A range of cobble tools was identified within the assemblage of worked stone, including 6 hammer stones, 5 biface grinders and 2 stone rubbers. The majority of the cobble tools were derived from the interior of the site, however, a hammer stone was recovered from the displaced stonework derived from the collapse of the corbelled roof of chamber A (context 45). A number of the cobble tools had been reused for a different purpose. One of the biface grinders had been reutilized as a hammer stone and another had been reused as a stone rubber. The range of cobbled tools found at Dùnan Ruadh is less than that from the aisled roundhouse at Alt Chrisal (p. 183). This disparity can perhaps be attributed to the relative proportions of each site excavated and preserved *in situ*. Finally, the broken fragment of the stone axe was found within the fill (context 18) of one of the drainage channels associated with the phase 2 occupation of the site. It was manufactured from a fine-grained metamorphic rock containing a moderate frequency of pyroxene inclusions up to 3.5 mm across. Only the blade of the axe remains, the butt is missing. The blade of the axe is 46 mm long and curves slightly towards the base. The lower face of the axe has been heavily worn and is crossed by a series of fine parallel striations associated with this abrasion. This possible Bronze Age perforated axe was most likely found elsewhere on the island and was broken through misuse as a hammer.

Table 6.20 PY10, MY384 and SY14: identified bird bones.

Species	Pabbay PY10	Mingulay MY384	Sandray SY14
Goose sp.	1		
Duck sp.	1	1	
Manx Shearwater	18	20	
Gannet	3		1
Shag	265	64	2
Cormorant	5	2	
cf. Corncrake	1		
Golden Plover	2		
Lapwing	1		
cf. Knot	1		
Snipe	4		
Gull sp.	18		
Great Black Backed Gull		1	
cf. Kittiwake	1		
Great Auk	1		
Little Auk	4		
Razorbill/Guillemot	5		1
Puffin/Black Guillemot	15		
cf. Skylark	1		
Thrush sp.	3		
cf. Song Thrush	1		
Starling	4		
Raven	5		
Total Number	360	26	4

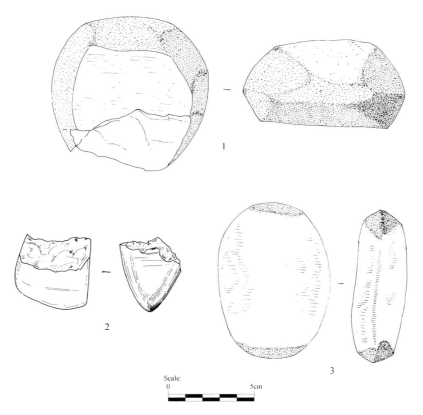

Figure 6.26 PY10: worked stone.

Copper alloy 'hand pin'

Emma Gowans

A copper alloy 'hand pin', 71 mm long (Fig. 6.27), was recovered from context (45). This was a dump of refuse, containing much fish bone, on top of the wall at the aperture leading to chamber A spilling on top of collapsed roof corbel stones. The shaft of this pin, measuring 67 mm in length, has straight parallel sides, with a diameter of 2.1 mm, tapering only at the tip. The head of the pin consists of a semicircular 'palm', approximately 6.8 mm in diameter, to which three 'fingers', 6.1 mm long and 2 mm in diameter, are attached in a straight row. The fingers, the palm and the shaft have all been cast separately and attached at a later date. The top of the shaft bends at a right angle, formed by a mitred joint, so that the head is projecting outwards away from the shaft.

Pins from the Scottish Atlantic Iron Age are classified and dated on the basis of the material from which the pin is made and the forms of the shaft and head (Foster 1990). Copper alloy was used in the manufacture of pins from the Middle Iron Age until the Norse period. Shorter metal pins (<69 mm in length), such as that from Dùnan Ruadh, are generally regarded as earlier than longer ones and are thought to date from the Late Iron Age onwards. The pin cannot be dated from the shaft, as only swollen and hipped shaft pins bear any chronological significance. However, the head of the pin does give an indication of the date of the Pabbay pin. The 'hand pin' developed from a form of cast, projecting, ring-headed pin produced at Traprain Law in the 3rd and 4th centuries AD. The semirosette—a pin with three to six beads on the upper section and a lower semicircular plate—was manufactured at Traprain Law between the 2nd and 3rd centuries AD (Kilbride-Jones 1980). From the 3rd century onwards the number of beads were reduced to five, then four, and finally to three, thus developing the 'proto-hand pin' (Kilbride-Jones 1980). From this emerged the hand pin—the row of beads developing into a straight row of 'fingers'—the earliest example of which dates to the late 4th century AD. The majority of 'hand pins' date to the late 5th or 6th centuries AD, continuing into the 8th and 9th centuries in an altered form (Foster 1990).

A pin mould found at Scalloway, Shetland, appears to belong to a pin similar to the one found on Pabbay (Campbell 1998b: 171 and Fig. 103). It is part of the valve of a two-piece mould, that had three fingers in a horizontal line. Only the rear of the mould, that associated the back of the pin, survives. However, the surviving fragment of the mould would suggest that the fingers were separate from the palm, and that the fingers had been cast at the same time as the shaft and possibly the palm. While no mould was found at Pabbay, it is likely that the pin may have been cast in

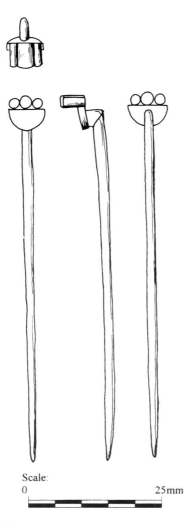

Scale:

0   25mm

Figure 6.27 PY10: the Pabbay pin.

the same manner—it is clear that the three components of the pin are separate as in the case of the Scalloway mould.

The hand pin, possibly dating to the 5th or 6th century AD, suggests occupation at the site after the abandonment of the Dun, with later material being incorporated into the deposits associated with the collapse of the wall circuit. A second 'hand pin' was recovered from midden deposits to the east of the cemetery (PY55) at Bàgh Bàn at the turn of the century: 'One of the islanders produced a bronze pin about six inches in length which had been found there. Many old things he said had been got and sold to Jew peddlers at Castlebay' (Wedderspoon 1915: 326). This second pin, an enamelled 'hand pin' measuring 146 mm in length, has been dated to the late 7th century AD (Stevenson 1955).

Technological materials

Catherine Mortimer

Nine finds related to high-temperature processes were recovered during the course of excavations at Dùnan

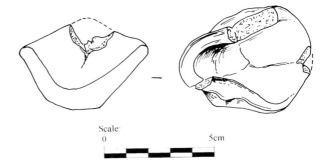

Scale:

0   5cm

Figure 6.28 PY10: the crucible.

Ruadh. The most distinctive item found at the site is a small crucible from context 8 (Fig. 6.28). The crucible is rather shallow (c. 35 mm deep) and has a roughly triangular mouth. The walls are quite thick relative to the overall size of the artifact, ranging from 5 mm towards the edge to 15 mm at the base. The crucible was heated from below, where some vitrification has taken place on the outside, extending in one area over the edge into the inside of the vessel. The heat has also caused some bloating within the walls. The fabric is gritty with visible sand particles. Although this find is from the upper deposits, which are disturbed, it is quite similar to other Iron Age examples. Such crucibles would be used to melt small amounts of non-ferrous metals, such as bronze, brass or silver, prior to casting. In this example, the vitrification is black and there are no metallic deposits visible whose colour might indicate the type of material being worked (e.g. green deposits denoting copper-rich metals). XRF analysis of the surface of the crucible detected very small traces of copper, zinc and lead. This confirms that a copper alloy was melted in the crucible, but it is impossible to determine the precise type of alloy from this type of analysis.

Four of the other pieces originate from ironworking, three being small pieces of ironworking slag and the fourth a piece of ironworking slag attached to vitrified clay. It is not clear what processes these slags come from—iron smelting (extraction from ores) or iron smithing (working ready-formed metal). The density of the slags suggests smelting is a possibility, but the small amount of material means it is impossible to be sure, since small amounts of dense slag might be formed during iron smithing. Three finds are vitrified clay, two of the heavily vitrified pieces might also be fuel ash slag (the product of the reaction of fuel ashes at high temperatures). These may come from either ironworking or non-ferrous working, or possibly from other high-temperature processes, such as pottery firing or domestic fires. Finally, a small piece of pottery has vitrification on its inside and outside surfaces, culminating in a glassy lump at one end. The sherd is coarse with large inclusions, and is from a large vessel with a shallow curvature. It is unlikely to be directly related to metalworking but may have gained the vitrification by accident (due to proximity to metalworking) or in any of a number of other high-temperature processes.

At least some evidence for ironworking is found at nearly every archaeological site, from the Iron Age onwards. It is easy to imagine that small-scale manufacture or repair of such items as tools would have taken place at sites like Pabbay, although smelting would be more unexpected (local resources of bog iron could be investigated in this respect). Evidence for non-ferrous metalworking is less frequently found, and it is interesting that this was taking place on such a small island within what was presumably a rather isolated community. Small crucibles, such as that found at Pabbay, could have been used to cast small artifacts like dress ornaments, for example, brooches or pins. Specific stone-built roundhouse sites with crucible finds include Midhowe, Orkney, but triangular crucibles are found throughout Britain during the Iron Age and later (e.g. Mortimer and Starley 1995).

Spindle whorls

Three complete spindle whorls were recovered during the course of excavation. First, a clay spindle whorl, 46 mm in diameter with a thickness of 11 mm, was recovered from context (44) within chamber B. It is manufactured from a pottery sherd with evidence of sooting on one surface. Secondly, a shell sand conglomerate spindle whorl, 41 mm in diameter with a thickness of 10 mm, was found within the fill (context 28) of the stone-lined drain associated with the phase 1b occupation of the interior. Thirdly, a shell sand conglomerate spindle whorl, 49 mm in diameter with a thickness of 16 mm, was recovered from the re-worked phase 1 deposits (context 48) towards the northern extent of the site. The spindle whorls are larger than those found at Alt Chrisal T17.

Discussion

John Pouncett

The Atlantic roundhouse at Dùnan Rudah has largely been destroyed by the action of the sea, rendering detailed interpretation of the site impossible. Analysis of the structural and stratigraphic sequences recorded during the course of excavation suggests three distinct phases of occupation. These phases can be correlated with ceramic typologies to provide a chronological framework for the development of the site:

Phase 1 (1st–3rd century AD): the primary occupation of the Atlantic roundhouse.
Phase 2 (2nd–4th century AD): the secondary occupation of the Atlantic roundhouse.

Phase 3 (6th–9th century AD): the intermittent reuse of the site after abandonment.

As with many similar sites, the Atlantic roundhouse at Dùnan Ruadh has been reused and modified on a number of occasions. Furthermore, the site continued to be used after the abandonment of the Atlantic roundhouse, with the construction of a cellular building within the interior of the wall circuit.

While the architectural elaboration of the wall circuit of the Pabbay roundhouse is characteristic of an Atlantic roundhouse, the site shares a number of affinities with wheelhouses or aisled roundhouses. First, there is evidence for formalised organization of the use of space within the interior of the building. The stone settings and uprights identified within the interior of the site are suggestive of the radial piers that are characteristic of wheelhouses. Secondly, discrete burials of articulated animal bone were identified within the wall circuit and beneath the floor of the roundhouse. These deliberate burials are comparable to the 'ritual' deposits identified at a number of wheelhouses or aisled roundhouses in the Outer Hebrides. Finally, the absence of exotic species and the low incidence of pig within the faunal assemblage are also characteristic of a wheelhouse rather than an Atlantic roundhouse.

Comparison of the artifact assemblages from Dùnan Ruadh with those from other recently excavated Iron Age sites, namely Alt Chrisal T17, Mingulay MY384 and Sandray SY14, reveals considerable similarities. Differences in both pottery and animal bone assemblages can largely be attributed to the availability of resources in a given locality. Preliminary analysis of the stone structures and associated occupation deposits at these sites would suggest a high degree of homogeneity within the southern islands of the Outer Hebrides.

The Bàgh Bàn Earth House (PY56) Excavations 1997–98

Pabbay PY56 (National Grid Reference NL60768758) is one of a number of stone-built sites located in an area of sand dunes and machair that have formed in the valley bottom and on the hillside at the northern end of the bay area behind a range of coastal foredunes (Fig. 6.29 and 6.30). Apart from the coastal foredunes this landscape has been stable for a very long time and there is no evidence for mobility, accumulation or erosion. Any archaeological sites found on the surface may therefore be either recent or prehistoric in date. However any exposed subsurface structure would soon become infilled and levelled up to the local ground level with wind-blown sand. This, as we found, was the fate of PY56.

Most of the dune sites are largely destructured, usually appearing as collections of disorganized stone

Figure 6.29 PY56: the Bàgh Bàn earth-house, facing south.

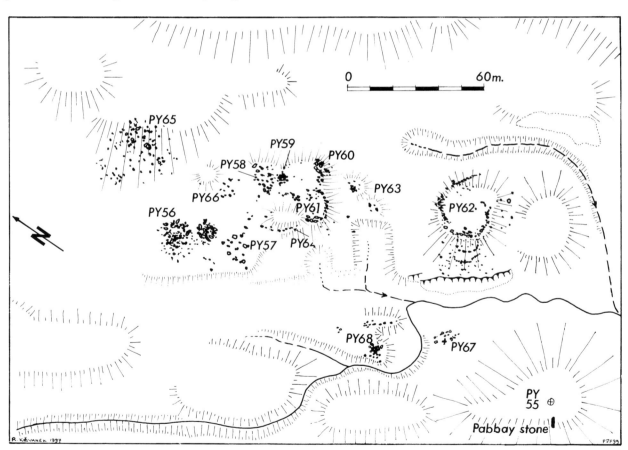

Figure 6.30 PY56: stone structures within the limits of dune encroachment at Bàgh Bàn.

rubble, which most likely results from the common practice of stone robbing, possibly to construct the nearby enclosure walls. The stonework of PY56, although displaying a similar degree of displacement, was exceptional in that almost all of the exposed mate-

rial was composed of massive slabs of monumental proportions (context 3). Most may have been considered too massive to haul away during the construction of the early modern settlement, although some of the buildings did possess a number of large slabs, often

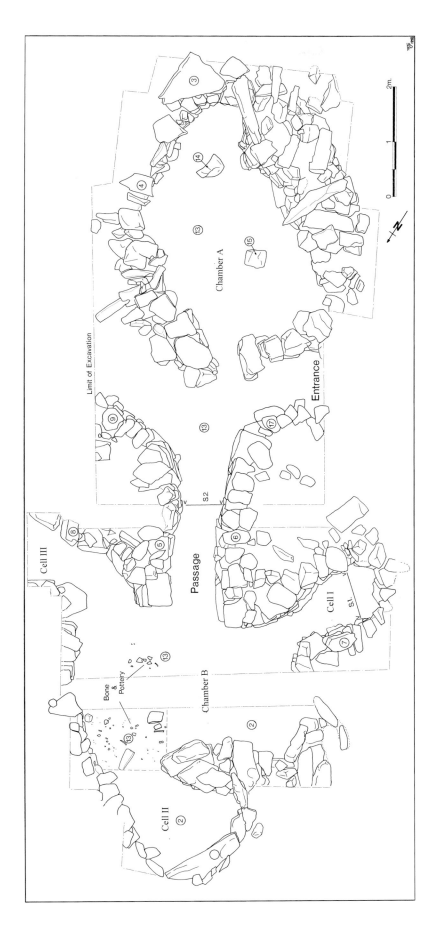

Figure 6.31 PY56: the Bàgh Bàn earth-house.

the door lintels, that may have originated from PY56. The desirability to investigate a site that was more likely to be prehistoric, as the unusually large stones suggested, led us to undertake excavations over a period of two seasons. The work was supervised by Linda Čihakova, recording was elegantly performed by Linda, Roman Křivanek and Gill Johnstone.

The excavation

After planning and photographing the surface stonework, clearly displaced material was removed and an area incorporating the perceived *in situ* stonework was de-turfed revealing the outline of a stone-built structure, aligned north-west to south-east (Fig. 6.31). This stonework proved to be the upper courses of drystone walling that continued down deep into the dune, forming a complex range of subterranean chambers and small cells. The initial excavation, which accounted for approximately three-quarters of the observable site mainly concerned the removal of wind-blown sand (context 2, 12 and 17) from the internal space. That many of the roofing slabs were, although displaced, still resting upon the surface of this sand indicates that the infilling of the subterranean elements of the structure was completed while the roof was still in place and no doubt commenced as soon as the site was abandoned. Other collapsed walling and roof stone was encountered at various levels indicating a continuous process of infilling and decay, but at a depth varying between 1.25 m and 1.60 m a grey-stained sand paleosoil (context 11) (context 16 is similar, but less significant) indicating a period of environmental stability was found occupying almost all of the internal space excavated. Resting on and within this paleosoil was a quantity of displaced stonework showing that the decay of the structural stonework continued unabated. The internal walling however continued down below this level as did the wind-blown sand for a further 0.20 m where another, reddened ginger-stained, paleosoil (context 13) was reached. Careful probing with a survey pin showed that the internal walls also terminated at this level and an environmental column box sample, that included the whole of the paleosoil and the sand below and above it, which was removed from the terminal section at the north-eastern end of the excavation, both indicate that this paleosoil represents the occupation floor level of the complex. The whole of the excavation area was reduced to the surface of this floor level, but since the site is not at present threatened this floor paleosoil of approximately 0.03 m thickness was left intact and the excavation terminated leaving this important material for future investigation.

The structure and its architecture

The site as a whole was most likely planned in a single operation using a building technique which simply entailed excavating a large shaped hole in the dune and lining it with a skin of drystone walling up to the surface level. Additional internal walling was added to form the shape of the chambers. Extra height may have been gained by mounding up the sides slightly with sand reinforced with embedded stones. The floor does not appear to have received any special treatment, but a detailed analysis of context 13 may shown that turf was laid to stabilize the surface of the sand.

Figure 6.32 PY56: chamber A, facing south-east.

Entrance into the complex is through an opening at surface level on the south-western flank of the site that leads, via a short gently downward sloping passage angled to the north-east, into an entrance area. Another short passage angled in from the east could be another entrance, but since it continues beyond the excavated area it may also be the way into another deep chamber. The wall (context 9) of this passage appears to have been rebuilt, possibly after a collapse, which is easy to imagine in such a sandy soil, and is the only part of the complex to show more than one period of construction. This arrangement of passages appears to act as a funnel into the main passage that descends to the north-west opening out into an ante-chamber (B), from which three other small chambers or cells (I to III) radiate. At the opposite end of the complex another, relatively large and deep chamber (A) is entered from the south-east side of the entrance area. The entrance area is quite shallow compared to the main passage and chambers and it is unlikely therefore to have been roofed with stone being either open or perhaps roofed with timber.

Figure 6.33 PY56: the stone arcade within chamber A, facing south.

Figure 6.34 PY56: displaced stone lintels within the rubble fill of chamber A, facing west.

Chamber A (Fig. 6.32) is a sub-rectangular room 3.20 m × 2.50 m, with a lobed annex at the rear adding a further 1.20 m. The floor level is steeply inclined down into the chamber immediately within the door threshold to a depth of 1.30 m. The stone slab roof of chamber A was supported by two central columnar, vertically set, 1 m high orthostats (contexts 14 and 15), which were found standing *in situ* within the chamber. The drystone wall skin along the eastern and western sides is built with an inward curve that is supported by arcades of upright orthostats set inside the line of the wall within the room by 0.10 m (Fig. 6.33). This technique was only used in chamber A. A collapse of roof slabs was found in the western corner of the chamber (Fig. 6.34) associated with a deposit of reddish ginger-stained sand, which is most likely derived from an original surface turf covering that has fallen in with the collapsed stonework. The architecture and building technique employed here is reminiscent of the southern chamber of the megalithic dolmen Le Château Bû at Saint Just, Brittany (personal observation).

The passage (Fig. 6.35) is 3.60 m × 0.60 m leading from the entrance area down 1.20 m into the ante-chamber B. The drystone walling is finished at the eastern corner with a single vertically set columnar orthostat.

The ante-chamber B is a sub-rectangular room 4.20 m × 2.5 m, larger than chamber A, but there was no evidence for roof support orthostats, inwardly curved walls or numerous roof slabs on the surface to give any indication that this chamber possessed a stone roof. If the passage and chamber was roofed at all, and their considerable depth suggests that they were, then the evidence has been either robbed or the roof was of timber construction. Three small cells (I, II and III) radiate from the northern, western and eastern sides of the chamber.

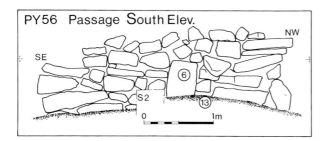

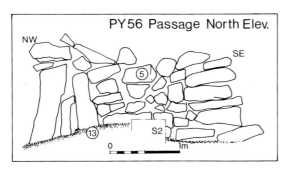

Figure 6.35 PY56: north and south elevations of the passage.

Cell I has a 2 m × 1 m tear-drop shape in plan, angled to the south-west, which could easily have been roofed with stone slabs without any extra support.

Cell II was only excavated to a depth of 0.50 m due to lack of time, however that did revealed a subcircular, 2 m diameter chamber, which was entered from the northern side of chamber B. The wall skin appears to be of regular drystone walling, but at a level just above that of the present ground surface the wall begins to become corbelled and at least one long (1.30 m) orthostat is balanced across the wall edge and there were several other similar orthostats displaced nearby.

Cell III was only proven to exist by expanding the area of the excavation slightly, but was not fully revealed. However its entrance was angled back to the east mirroring that of cell I and giving the passage a funnel appearance reflecting that found in the southern entrance area.

The finds and dating

Over the two seasons a greater part of the floor surface (context 13) was revealed which although left intact did provide some cultural material. Of the excavated area chamber A; the entrance area; the main passage; cell I; the entrance to cell II and about 25% of chamber B were completely devoid of any sort of material find—the floor was totally clean. Only in the area of chamber B before the entrance to cell II did 'domestic' refuse appear consisting of handmade pottery fragments and animal bone along with small pieces and flecks of charcoal. Unfortunately a box shaft that was excavated specifically to gain more material from the floor surface during 1998 did not extend further into cell II and it is therefore not known whether the floor inside that particular cell is 'dirty'. However enough material was gathered from the floor surface to provide C14 and thermoluminescence dating in the future if desired. A sherd of 19th century porcelain was found, along with numerous periwinkle shells, at the junction of walls 5 and 9 in an area that appeared to show some stone robbing at a sub-surface level.

The coarseware pottery

John Pouncett and Patrick Foster

Fifty-nine sherds of pottery (396 g) were recovered from the surface of the floor (context 13) in Chamber B close to the entrance to cell II. The fabric is extremely friable and would not survive under even moderate degrading conditions. Although little success was achieved joining sherds it is considered that only two vessels may be represented and the assemblage is therefore divided into two groups. Group A: sherds with a body thickness of 8 mm, quite robust, with a fine texture derived from a fabric containing abundant flecks of biotite mica and whose igneous inclusions do not exceed 3 mm. Colouring is a reddish-brown outer face, very dark grey inner face and black core. Group B: very thick-walled, 16 mm, coarsely textured and very friable with a similar fabric to Group A, but some of the igneous grits measure over 10 mm. Colour is generally a grey to grey-brown throughout. There is a single rim sherd is of a simple rounded out-turned profile and a single sherd decorated with two parallel incised lines. Many sherds from both groups have deposits of soot on the outer face. This assemblage is comparable to that found at Cladh Hallan, which is tentatively dated to the Late Bronze Age or Earl Iron Age (personal communication, Mike Parker Pearson).

The faunal remains

Andrew Hammon

A small assemblage of 32 animal bones (110 g) was collected from the surface of context 13 in the same area as the pottery. The identifiable fragments are one bovine horncore; a sheep mandible, right P2 and P3 present (adult); two sheep femur shafts; a sheep distal metacarpal with unfused shaft (juvenile); a sheep molar, M1/2 (adult) and a sheep axis.

Interpretation and discussion

Parallels for this complex can be drawn from the Bronze Age structures excavated at Cladh Hallan, South Uist (J. Mullville and M.P. Pearson n.d.) and Kirkwell, Orkney (M.P. Pearson, personal communication). Architecturally there is some resemblance to the Bronze Age ritual site at Saint Just mentioned above, but whether PY56 is a ritual or purely domestic site is difficult to determine at present and the answer may reside within the composition of the floor soil—context 13. The apparent absence of a hearth at any position in the floor area exposed and the almost antiseptic cleanliness of most of the excavated area possibly rules against the site being purely domestic, but lack of floor deposit accumulations, soils or cultural refuse, may only be due to a short occupation period or very careful regular cleaning. Conversely the presence of charcoal, pottery and animal bone so neatly concentrated in chamber B could be the evidence of ritual activity—ritual meals or deliberate dumping. The orientation of the building range may also prove to be of interest. The sophistication of construction and economic effort that is represented in this building complex is also noteworthy. A supply of large stone slabs and columnar orthostats, shapes that are not usually available in quantity in the local landscape was required to construct this building complex and unless a certain minimal amount of quarrying and crude shaping is contemplated, this material may have necessitated transportation from all over the island. Whether domestic or ritual, this site leaves little doubt that at a period during the Late Bronze Age and Early Iron Age these islands were not considered insignificant.

7.   Sampling Excavations on Sandray and Mingulay, 1995–1996

Patrick Foster and John Pouncett

Sheader, Sandray (SY14)

Excavation at Sandray SY14 was undertaken by the Department of Archaeology and Prehistory at the University of Sheffield, on behalf of Historic Scotland. Two exploratory trenches were excavated in the vicinity of the 'modern' village of Sheader during June 1995. Within recent years heavy seas have breached the site, destabilizing the surface vegetation. A series of archaeological deposits have been exposed beneath the late 19th- or early 20th-century village. Excavation was initiated to assess the nature and extent of these deposits, and to determine the character and time depth of activity/occupation they represent.

The site is centred upon National Grid Reference NL63129199. It is located on the southern margin of the beach within the bay at Sheader. The site lies within a shallow valley between the rocky eastern coast of Sandray and the Galtar massif. This valley follows the line of a dyke running the length of the island. To the east of the village a shallow stream flows along the valley bottom. Nearby, a series of intermittent springs outcrop along the eastern margin of Sheader Point (*Rubha Sheader*). A series of black-

houses and attendant buildings were recorded at Sandray SY14. These structures are traditionally associated with the village of Sheader, occupied between 1908 and 1911 (Buxton 1995). Recent field survey, however, has shown that the 'modern' village has a much more complex history than hitherto recognized.

The northern extent of the settlement is defined by an irregular rubble bank. This bank has been modified and extended on a number of occasions. Marked changes in direction along its length suggest that it may have been built to respect buildings no longer visible above ground level. The nucleus of the village is comprised of a row of blackhouses (houses 2, 4 and 5) running from east to west. Two of these black-houses (houses 2 and 4) overlie the vestiges of an earlier building (house 3). A single skin structure immediately to the east of house 2 has been interpreted as a byre. To the north of this byre, an additional blackhouse (house 1) is set forward from the other buildings. A rectilinear enclosure, subdivided by an ephemeral rubble wall or bank, extends along the valley to the south of the village. The northernmost parcel of land contains a series of outbuildings.

Figure 7.1 SY14: Sheader, facing south.

278

The village itself is built towards the rear of a substantial mound comprised of occupational debris, displaced stonework, and windblown sand (Fig. 7.1). Towards the eastern extent of the site, an irregular curvilinear wall or bank is exposed within the eroded surface of the mound. This feature almost certainly predates the 'modern' village, representing part of a boundary or enclosure associated with earlier usage of the site.

Archaeological background

A sketch plan of the village and associated mound, along with a description of the landscape setting of the site, was produced as part of the SEARCH survey of the islands south of Barra. During the course of field survey, a number of sherds of Iron Age pottery were recovered from the surface of the mound. A sample of limpet shell was also taken from the shell middens exposed at the base of the mound for the purposes of radiocarbon dating. This sample yielded an uncalibrated date of 3540 ± 50 BP (GU-3857). Sheader lies approximately 500 m to the south-east of the Iron Age dun at Cairn Galtar. It has been suggested that the 'modern' village is built upon the site of an earlier settlement or dwelling associated with the Dun (p. 73). The antiquity of settlement at this site is suggested by place-name evidence. Sheader, or *Siadar* in Gaelic, is thought to be derived from the Old Norse term *Sitr* meaning 'dwelling place' (Buxton 1995). The unstratified material collected from the surface of the mound suggests an even greater time depth to the occupation of the site.

Excavations 1995

A 5 m wide section was established to the south of house 1 (Fig. 7.2). This section incorporated a substantial erosion scar at the southern extent of the site. The strip of land between the section and the base of the mound was deturfed. Once all displaced material had been removed, the trench was cleaned and excavated down to subsoil. The site was excavated in plan, removing each deposit in reverse order of deposition. Structural elements were planned and recorded before being removed to allow further excavation. Owing to the sandy nature of the site, the trench had to be stepped twice in order to prevent collapse of the section. As a result of extensive burrowing towards the southern margin of the site, the second step of the trench was extended 5 m to the west. A section through the mound was achieved at the full excavation (Fig. 7.3).

The structural and stratigraphic sequences

Sandray SY14 lies within the limits of dune encroachment at Sheader, that is, within the machair. The site itself appears to have been established upon the stabilised surface of the sand dune (context 27).

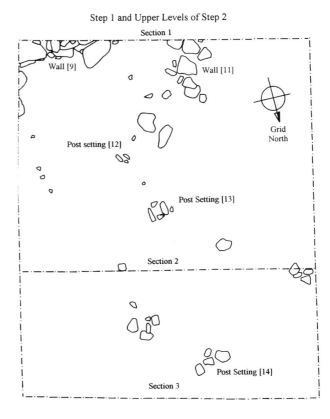

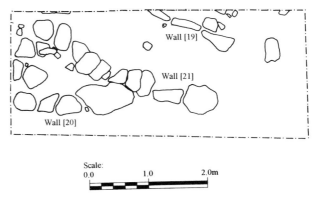

Figure 7.2 SY14: plan of the structural elements identified within the excavated area.

An iron-rich sandy loam (context 26) at the interface with the subsoil has tentatively been interpreted as a mineralized soil. Excavations on the islands to the south of Sandray have shown that a comparable site, that at Mingulay MY384, was constructed upon a cultivated land surface (p. 000).

An orange-brown sandy loam (context 23) overlies the mineralized soil exposed at the base of the mound. Two shell middens (contexts 24 and 25) were formed during the accumulation of this deposit. Although badly disturbed by recent burrowing and collapse, these poorly sorted dumps of limpet shell appear to represent discrete midden deposits. Comparable deposits, often associated with ceramic and lithic materials, are recorded elsewhere in the Outer Hebrides (Wedderspoon 1915). Context 23 is exposed

279

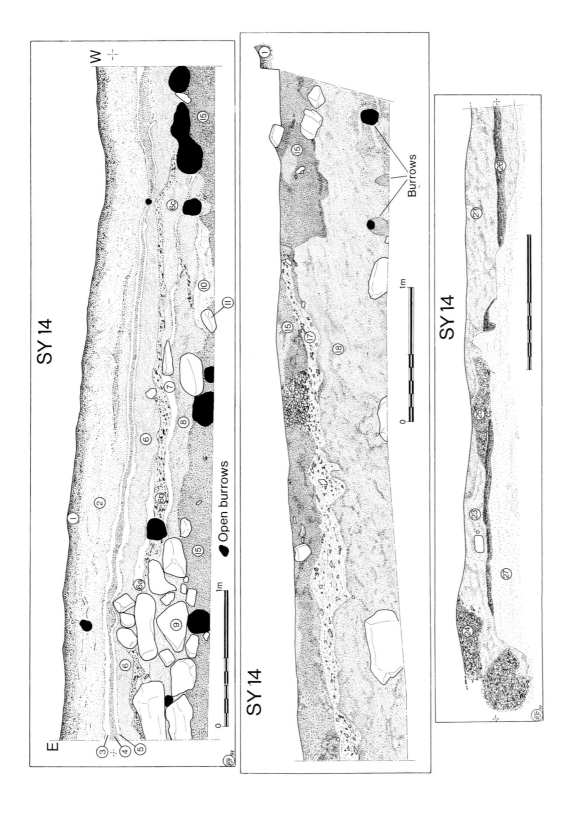

Figure 7.3 SY14: section excavated through the depositional sequence at Sheader.

within the eroded surface of the mound and has been heavily disturbed by recent burrowing and collapse. The subtle difference in colour between this deposit and those at the base of the second step can be attributed to differential weathering.

Context 23 is overlain by an accumulation of sandy loam (contexts 18 and 15). These deposits are separated by a discrete layer of limpet shells (context 17; Fig. 7.4). While this agglomeration of limpet shells is more dispersed than the discrete mounds described above, context 17 can also be interpreted as a shell midden. The cumulative thickness of contexts 18 and 15 would suggest that they represent a considerable time depth, however, similarities in their colour and composition indicate that depositional conditions at the site remained constant. Each deposit is associated with a series of structural elements (Figs. 7.5 and 7.6). Two distinct structural phases were identified, the first within the lower levels of context 18 (walls 21, 19 and 20), the second within the upper levels of context 15 (walls 9 and 11).

Wall 21 is located at the base of the second step within the lower levels of context 18. It is constructed from a series of irregular schist blocks, which survive to a height of up to two courses. The wall extends northwards from the base of the section, arcing gently to the west. It can be traced for a distance of approximately 3.8 m. The northern extent of the wall is exposed within the eroded surface of the mound, and may have been truncated by later disturbance. A short section of walling, wall 19, runs parallel to this wall. Although there is no direct relationship between these two walls, their common alignment would suggest

that they are part of the same structure. Wall 19 is constructed from a series of schist boulders laid end to end. Only a single course of masonry survives, however, a cluster of stone in the vicinity of the wall appears to have been displaced from a higher level.

Wall 20 is situated towards the eastern extent of the second step within the lower levels of context 18. Only a single course of stonework survives, however, the fabric of this wall appears to be comparable to that of wall 21. The short length of wall exposed within the trench runs from east to west, terminating where it intersects wall 21. Wall 20 lies at the same level as the walls described above, and its relationship with wall 21 suggests that it is either contemporary with, or postdates, that structure. An agglomeration of schist blocks to the north of wall 20, against the eastern section of the trench, may represent the start of a second wall on the same alignment. Alternatively, it may represent stonework displaced from the upper levels of wall 21.

Wall 9 is exposed at the base of the first step, within the upper levels of context 15. It is a substantial structure, surviving to a height of up to three courses, constructed from unhewn schist blocks. The short length of the wall exposed within the trench appears to run from north-east to south-west. To the east of wall 9 an ephemeral rubble wall extends northwards from the southern edge of the trench. This wall, wall 11, is constructed from a series of irregular boulders. It proscribes a gentle arc that runs at a tangent to wall 9. Although the base of this wall appears to lie at a slightly lower level, the relationship between walls 9 and 11 is uncertain.

Figure 7.4 SY14: shell midden (context 17), facing south.

Figure 7.5 SY14: walls 21, 19 and 20 within the lower levels of context 18, facing south-west.

A series of stone settings, associated with the later structural elements (walls 9 and 11), were identified at the base of the first step. Post-settings 12 and 13 are associated with well-defined post sockets, however post-setting 14 has been heavily disturbed. The position of this stone setting is marked by a discrete group of stones exposed within the eroded surface of the mound. A similar cluster of stone at a slightly lower level possibly represents the remains of a fourth stone

setting, post-setting 16. Post-settings 12, 13 and 14 form part of a post alignment, running from south-east to north-west. Although the posts seem to be spaced at regular intervals, there would appear to be a gap between post settings 13 and 14.

A dark-brown sandy loam (context 8) is deposited across the site following the construction of the structural elements within the upper levels of context 15. A discontinuous layer of windblown sand (context 10)

Figure 7.6 SY14: walls 9 and 11 within the upper levels of context 15, facing south-east.

is deposited at the interface between contexts 8 and 15. This deposit represents a drift of sand against the north-western face of wall 11. Although context 10 may be indicative of abandonment of the site, its restricted spatial distribution would suggest that this structure was still in use. Discrete lenses of limpet shells within context 8 indicate continued occupation at the site. However, the nature and extent of this occupation are uncertain.

The continuous layer of windblown sand (context 7) sealing context 8 marks the watershed between pre-historic and 'modern' occupation at Sandray SY14. This sand deposit is overlain by an accumulation of sandy loam (context 6) containing an abundance of coal. This deposit, interspersed with lenses of wind-blown sand, has provisionally been interpreted as midden material derived from the extant blackhouses. The depth of this deposit would suggest that it accu-mulated over a protracted period of time. Following the abandonment of the settlement at Sheader, the site is reclaimed by the sand dunes. Context 6 is overlain by a sequence of deposits comprising alternate layers of windblown sand and organic sandy loam, contexts 5 through to 2 respectively. The dune surface has subsequently stabilized and a layer of turf (context 1) has been established across much of the site.

The Pottery

Jane Timby

The excavations at Sandray S14 yielded some 1,285 sherds of pottery with a total weight of 7,003 g. Sherds were associated with just 5 of the 17 contexts iden-tified, with the largest group of material, some 938 sherds (73%), being derived from unstratified collec-tions. The assemblage was sorted macroscopically into broad fabric types based on the density and size of the inclusions present. Details of decoration and surface finish were noted along with any evidence of use. The assemblage was quantified by sherd count and weight for each recorded context. A selection of decorated or other featured sherds have been illustrated (Fig. 7.7).

Fabric types

Although a moderately small group of wares at least ten fabrics could be discriminated. Descriptive terms are based on those recommended in the prehistoric Ceramics Research Group guidelines (PCRG 1997).

S1: A fairly compact sandy-textured ware of medium to coarse character. The paste contains a moderate to com-mon frequency of ill-sorted rock inclusions, the larger fragments up to 2.5 mm in size. Surface colour varies from orange-brown to grey. A distinction is made of particularly thick-walled sherds (S1b).

S2: Fabric as S1 but finer with smoother surfaces and less coarse rock fragments. Some sherds are quite thin-walled (S2b).

S3: A relatively smooth ware with mainly orange surfaces often showing surface cracking. The fired clay has a slight linear fracture. The paste contains a sparse to moderate frequency of ill-sorted inclusions, the larger fragments up to 4 mm across.

S4: An orange-brown or grey fabric containing a sparse scatter of very coarse fine-grained grey igneous rock inclusions up to 12 mm across.

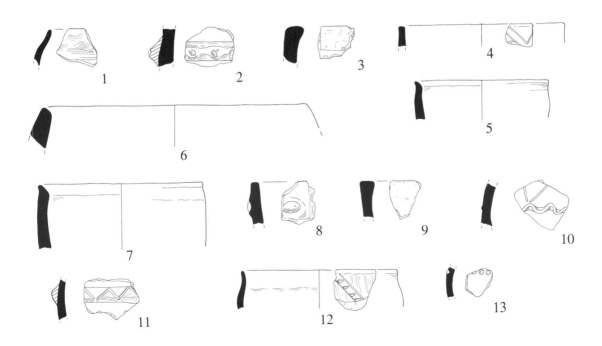

Figure 7.7 SY14: the pottery.

S5: A grey or brown ware containing a sparse to moderate frequency of ill-sorted rock inclusions up to 2–3 mm in size. The main distinguishing characteristic is the presence of a moderate to common frequency of fine organic matter (?dung) visible both on the surfaces and in the body of the pot.

S6: A very coarse fabric with a dense frequency of ill-sorted crystalline rock inclusions up to 8 mm in size.

S7: A very fine fabric with pale orange-brown surfaces and a light blue-grey inner core. The surfaces have a very fine silky feel and the paste shows no macroscopically visible inclusions.

S8: A very fine, slightly powdery fabric with a sparse frequency of rock inclusions occasionally with coarse fragments 2–3 mm in size.

S9: A fine fabric containing white specks of shell.

S10: A grey or brown ware with a hard sandy texture. The paste contains a moderate to common frequency of well-sorted sand and rock inclusions.

Vessel form

Featured sherds were quite rare and many of the rims quite fragmentary. The typology developed for Pabbay, based on the shape of the rim, was used for the Sandray assemblage, with a few additional types. Most of the rims are of simple shape, either simple vertical types (rim type C) with squared (rim type C1), rounded (rim type C2) or internally bevelled (rim type C4) profiles. Also present are rounded expanded rims (rim type A), curving types (rim type D), globular-bodied vessels with short everted rims (rim type E), or rounded rims (rim type F) and simple inward-pointing forms (rim type G).

Stratified material

Pottery was only associated with three 'prehistoric' deposits (contexts 18, 15, and 8), while a few sherds came from the fabric of wall 19 and the 19th-century loam (context 6) yielded a single small prehistoric sherd. The lowest horizon in the excavated sequence to yield pottery was context (18), an orange-brown sandy loam. This produced 118 sherds, 890 g dominated by sherds of fabric type S1. Small numbers of fabric types S3, S4, S6 are also present. Forms include vessel rim types C2, C4 and F all typical early Iron Age shapes (cf. Fig. 7.7.6-7). The only decoration noted is a vessel (fabric type S3) with two parallel, incised horizontal lines below the bevelled rim Several sherds are externally blackened or sooted.

The fabric of wall 19 yielded 14 plain body sherds of fabric type S1. The brown loam layer (context 15) above this contained a good assemblage of some 149 sherds (1,166 g). Although the group is again dominated by sherds of fabric type S1 there is slightly more diversity, with examples of fabric types S2, S3, S4, S6, S8 and S10 represented. Only seven rims were present with types C1, C2, C4 and D present (cf. Fig. 7.7.5). Decoration is limited to a single body sherd (fabric type S1) with finger-depressions. A lower proportion of the vessels show evidence of use in the form of sooting compared to context 18.

Context 8 produced 65 sherds (727 g), mainly fabric type S1 with a few sherds of fabric type S2. Decorated wares are more conspicuously present compared with the earlier layers, with one example of an applied wavy-line cordon, 1 sherd with an applied horizontal cordon with stab marks (Fig. 7.7.2), 1 sherd decorated with impressed dots and 1 sherd with incised vertical lines. Only 1 rim sherd was present (rim type F) (Fig. 7.7.1).

Although the sample is relatively small, the sequence appears to show typical early Iron Age material from the lower parts of the mound in context 18. Context 15 shows similar material but is distinguished both by having a slightly greater diversity of wares and an example of a vessel with finger depressions possibly more typical of the earlier part of the middle Iron Age. The upper horizon (context 8) has an assemblage containing decorative elements more typical of the middle Iron Age.

Unstratified material

A significant proportion of the assemblage came from surface collection comprising a mixture of prehistoric, mediaeval, post-mediaeval and modern sherds. The disturbed nature of the collection is reflected in the much lower average sherd size of just 4.4 g. Examples of all the fabrics associated with the mound were present with many featured sherds typical of the Iron Age. A thin-walled bowl in fabric type S2 (Fig. 7.7.12), decorated with a diagonal slashed cordon, is typical of the earlier middle Iron Age. It is likely that material visually classified as fabric type S1-2 is in fact later in date, but the fragmentary nature of the sherds precluded meaningful division. The dot-impressed sherd (Fig. 7.7.13) is typical of the late mediaeval or post-mediaeval ceramics of the region. Some of the harder fired sherds with orange-brown exteriors and grey-brown interiors are typical of the 13th–14th century (Mike Parker Pearson, personal communication). Three additional fabrics were recorded that not noted among the mound or blackhouse assemblages: fabric types S5, S7 and S9. Fabric type S7 may be of earlier prehistoric date, whilst fabric types S5 and S9 could be mediaeval or later, although it should be noted that organic-tempered material, similar to type S5, featured amongst the Iron Age assemblage from Pabbay (p. 167).

Discussion

Although a much smaller assemblage than those recovered from the other islands (Barra, Mingulay, and Pabbay), the assemblage from Sandray is much more diverse in character with some very distinctive fabric types. The material from the excavation into the mound has an average sherd size of 8.4 g; the sherds are quite broken up with no reconstructable profiles.

The faunal remains (excluding birds)

Jacqui Mulville (mammals) and C. Ingrem (fish)

(For methods see Chapter 6, p. 250).

The site at Sandray produced only a very small assemblage dated to the Iron Age, with 145 mammal and 251 fish bones identified (Table 7.1). The majority of bone came from two sandy loam layers, contexts 15 and 18.

Mammals were dominated by cattle and sheep with few bones of other species: pig, seal and cetacea. A single loose horse incisor was also noted. Although teeth are not included in the suite of recorded elements, bones of otherwise underrepresented species are recorded. Ten species of fish were represented: conger eel (*Conger conger*), pollack (*Pollachius pollachius*), saithe (*Pollachius virens*), haddock (*Melanogrammus aeglefinus*), ling (*Molva molva*), John Dory (*Zeus faber*), sea bream (Sparidae), cuckoo wrasse (*Labrus mixtus*), ballan wrasse (*Labrus bergylta*) and flatfish.

The small size of the mammal assemblage hampers analysis and some of the differences between Sandray and other sites may be a function of this. The NISP and MNI calculations indicate a mammalian assemblage dominated by sheep (Table 7.1) as at other Iron Age sites (Mulville 1999). These results differ slightly in that sheep appear to be relatively more abundant using from MNI calculation compared to the NISP, the reverse of the pattern found at other sites.

The identified fish assemblage is dominated by large Gadidae species (cod family) (Table 7.1). Saithe compose almost half of the Gadidae fragments with only a few fragments of pollack and ling identified. Haddock was represented by an otolith. The remainder could be identified only as either large or small gadid. There were 11 fragments of conger eel with the remaining species represented by only 1 or 2 fragments.

Taphonomy

The mammal bone had suffered little post-mortem damage, with only 3% gnawed, 5% burnt and 9% butchered. A single fish bone had been butchered, and there was no evidence of gnawing or burning.

Mammals

Sheep. A range of skeletal elements was found (Table 7.2). The assemblage is dominated by limb bones, with the fragile skull bones and small foot bones only present in small numbers. Sheep-sized vertebrae and ribs represent only a small proportion of those expected from the minimum of six individuals.

Only two mandibles and a single deciduous premolar provided dental wear information. The two jaws came from animals aged 6–12 months and 2–3 years. The single tooth could not be accurately aged.

Fusion evidence was also sparse, and indicates a low mortality in the first year that rises during the second but does not increase during the third (Table 7.3). Of the bone with fusion information 18% was neonatal.

Knife cuts were recorded on the vertebrae, humerus, radius, pelvis and astragalus. An atlas had cuts associated with head removal, with a cervical and a lumber vertebra chopped in half. The latter suggests the carcass was hung and split into sides of meat. Cuts at the joints of the humerus, tibia and across the astragalus are consistent with division of the carcass.

Two articulated bone groups were recovered. Context 8 contained an articulating right neonatal humerus and radius in association with a range of other fore and hind limb bones. In context 15 there was an articulating left unfused femur and tibia, again found in association with a range of other bone. In these contexts the large number of similarly aged immature bones made it difficult to assign material to a particular skeleton. No paired elements were noted but a minimum of five immature individuals were represented.

Cattle. The elements of cattle showed a more even distribution, although the assemblage was dominated by limb bone fragments (Table 7.2). Loose teeth and a hyoid were recovered, indicating the presence of cattle

Table 7.1 Site SY14: number of identified specimens.

Mammals	NISP	%	MNI	%
Sheep	87	60	6	55
Cattle	53	37	3	27
Pig	4	3	1	9
Atlantic Seal	1	1	1	9
Total	145		11	
Horse	Present			
Whale	3			
Cattle-sized	4			
Sheep-sized	9			
Total	16			
Fish				
Conger Eel	11	4		
Pollack	11	4		
Saithe	109	43		
Haddock	1	<1		
Ling	3	1		
Large Gadid	10	4		
Small Gadid	98	39		
John Dory	2	1		
Sea Bream	2	1		
Cuckoo Wrasse	2	1		
Ballam Wrasse	1	<1		
Flatfish	1	<1		
Total	251			

ISP = number of identified specimens.
MNI = minimum number of individuals.

285

Table 7.2 Site SY14: abundance of elements.

	Cattle	Pig	Sheep	Seal	Whale	Cattle-Sized	Sheep-Sized
dP4	2		1				
LM3	1						
Nasal			2				
Hyoid	1						
Mandible	8	1	4				
Scapula	6		1				
Humerus	4		7	1			
Ulna	2		3				
Radius	5		11				
Magnum			1				
Metacarpal	3	3	2				
Femur	4		9				
Tibia	4		5				
Pelvis	3		4				
Astragalus	2		5				
Calcaneum	1		5		1		
Metatarsal	2		7				
Metapodial	1		3				
Nav. Cuboid			2				
Phalanx 1			5				
Phalanx 2	1		1				
Phalanx 3	1		2				
VC01	1		2				
VC02	1						
VC			2			1	
VT			2				1
VL			1				
Vert. Frag.							1
Rib						3	7
Unid					2		
Total	53	4	87	1	3	4	9

skulls at the site. The number of foot bones, cattle-size vertebra and ribs recovered was low.

Dental ageing was only possible on three loose teeth and a mandible. Two dP4s were at wear stage A indicating animals in their first few weeks of life. A third dP4 was shed from an adult, while a single third molar was at wear stage H. The third molar had the third pillar absent.

The small amount of fusion data provides no evidence of animals older than two years. The proportion of neonatal bone is 38%. A single shed deciduous premolar may suggest the stalling of cattle (Halstead, in press).

Butchery was recorded on the hyoid, scapula, femur, metatarsal and axis. All except the latter were cut marks. Two scapulae had knife cuts across the blade, indicating filleting to remove the flesh from these prime meat-bearing bones. Cut marks were left on a hyoid as the animal's throat was cut, and a heavy-bladed tool left marks on an axis consisted with removal of the head. Finally, cut marks on the distal femur indicate disarticulation of the skeleton.

Few articulated bones were recovered with only a humerus and metacarpal found in association in context 15. The metacarpal was laterally unfused, indicating a foetal individual.

Pig. Four pig bones were recorded from context 8 a mandible fragment and three metacarpals. One complete metacarpal is from a neonate, whilst the others are fragments from older animals.

Horse. The single horse incisor was also recovered from context 8. This tooth was deciduous and had been shed, which indicates the presence of a young horse. The recovery of this tooth suggests that the animal was stalled within the area of the site.

Atlantic seal. A single fragment of unfused distal humerus shaft was recovered. This would have come from an animal under two to three years old (Storå 1994). The fragment bore cut marks consistent with filleting of meat, suggesting use of this individual for food.

Cetacea. Three fragments of bone identified as belonging to cetacea were recorded. One of these was burnt. Whale bone has often been recorded as burnt and ethnographic evidence suggests the use of this oily bone as fuel (Mulville 1999). A second piece of cetacea showed signs of working, although no finished object could be identified.

Table 7.3 Site SY14: fusion data.

	Sheep			
	Unfused	Neonate	Fused	%
Humerus D	2		3	
Radius P		1	2	
Scapula			1	
Pelvis	1		1	
<1 year	3	0	7	30
Tibia D	2	2	2	
Metatarsal D				
Metacarpal D				
<2 year	2	2	2	67
Calcaneum	3			
Femur P	3	1	2	
Humerus P		1	1	
Radius D				
Ulna P		1		
Femur D	2	2		
Tibia P	1	1		
<3.5 years	9	4	3	81

	Neonates	Total	% Neonates
	6	32	19

	Cattle			
	Unfused	Neonate	Fused	%
Scapula		1	4	
Pelvis		1	1	
<1 year	0	2	5	*29*
Humerus D	1		3	
Radius P		1		
<2 years	1	1	3	*40*
Tibia D				
Metacarpal D		2		
Metatarsal D	1			
Calcaneum				
<3 years	1	2	0	*100*
Femur P		1	2	
Humerus P				
Radius D		2	1	
Ulna P				
Femur D				
Tibia P				
<4 years	0	3	3	*50*

	Neonates	Total	% Neonates
	8	21	*38*

Fish

Body part representation. Table 7.4 shows body part representation for members of the Gadidae family. It is apparent that the assemblage is composed pre-dominately of vertebrae; a few other elements, mainly derived from saithe, are also present. Pollack and saithe are well represented by both precaudal and caudal vertebrae. In contrast, large gadid precaudal

Table 7.4 Site SY14: Gadidae: body part representation.

	Pollack	Saithe	Haddock	Ling	Large Gadid	Small Gadid
Otolith			1			
Parasphenoid		2		1	1	1
Premaxilla		2				
Dentary		4			1	5
Articular		3			2	
Quadrate					1	
Ceratohyale					1	1
Hyomandibular		4				
Opercular					1	1
Preopercular		1				1
Precaudal Vert.	4	46		2	2	10
Total head	4	62	1	3	9	19
Caudal vert.	7	47			1	71
Total body	7	47	0	0	1	71
Total	11	109	1	3	10	90

vertebrae are overrepresented while those belonging to the small gadids are underrepresented.

More than half of the fish bones were derived from context 15, where all of the species, with the exceptions of pollack and ballan wrasse, were represented (Table 7.5). Contexts 18 and 19 also contained a significant number of fragments and both were dominated by saithe and small gadid. In addition, context 19 contained several pollack bones.

Preservation and recovery. The predominance of the more robust elements, such as vertebrae, and virtual absence of fragile bones, such as opercula, coupled with the unidentifiable nature of many of the Gadidae vertebrae, indicates poor preservation. However, as the material was recovered by hand collection this may be the result of retrieval bias, vertebrae being relatively large and easily recognizable elements. The absence of sieved samples renders it unlikely that this

assemblage is representative of the species, body part representation or size of the fish originally present.

Butchery. A transverse chop mark on the dorsal face of the centrum was noted on a precaudal vertebra belonging to a large ling (context 15).

Size. Measurements could only be obtained from two elements. However, relative size was noted in comparison with the reference material. This allowed an estimation of approximate length and hence age (Table 7.6). The majority of saithe were below 50 cm in length although a few were between 50 and 70 cm (Table 7.6). This suggests that the majority were young, probably under four years. In addition, at least one conger eel was larger than 115 cm; two of the ling bones were noted as large and the parasphenoid indicates a length over 116 cm. The precaudal vertebrae from a John Dory suggest a length of approximately 24 cm.

Ecology and environment. According to Wheeler (1968) conger eel, pollack, young saithe, John Dory, sea bream and ballan wrasse are all found close to the shore over rough ground or rocky areas. Older saithe

Table 7.5 Site SY14: fish: distribution according to context.

	Context				
	8	15	18	19	Total
Conger Eel		6	5		11
Pollack				11	11
Saithe	6	45	36	23	110
Haddock		1			1
Ling	1	1	1		3
Large Gadid	1	72	6	1	80
Small Gadid		8	10	11	29
John Dory		2			2
Sea Bream		1	1		2
Cuckoo Wrasse		1	1		2
Ballan Wrasse			1		1
Wrasse		2			2
Flatfish			1		1
Total	8	139	62	46	255

Table 7.6 Site SY14: saithe: estimated length and age.

Element	Approximate Length (mm)	Estimated Age	N
Articular	<500 mm	<4 years	3
Caudal Vert.	<500 mm	<4 years	2
Hyomandibular	<500 mm	<4 years	1
Parasphenoid	<500 mm	<4 years	2
Precaudal Vert.	<500 mm	<4 years	2
Preopercular	<500 mm	<4 years	1
Dentary	500–700 mm	4–6 years	3
Premaxilla	500–700 mm	4–6 years	1

tend to be found further offshore in deeper water. The cuckoo wrasse generally prefers deeper water but is frequently found in rocky areas during the summer. Ling is generally a deep-water fish, however, mature individuals can be found close to the shore.

Discussion. There is no evidence on the bones themselves to suggest that the fish remains were deposited by natural agencies, such as otters or sea birds. As all of the species recovered are good eating fish there is little doubt that these were deliberately caught and introduced to the site by the inhabitants.

In the absence of sieved samples any interpretation should be treated with caution. The small quantity of fish remains recovered from Sandray suggests that fishing was only practised on a small scale. The assemblage is dominated by young saithe, which, like the other species recovered, are all found in the inshore zone and are known to take bait readily (Wheeler 1968). This suggests that the inhabitants of Sandray were practising a low-risk fishing strategy in order to meet their fish requirements. This would probably have involved exploitation of the inshore waters from the shore or small boats using lines and nets.

As a considerable proportion of the small gadid remains are likely to be derived from saithe, body part representation suggests that some fish may have been processed for storage and later consumption or trade (Fig. 7.1). The overrepresentation of saithe and large gadid head bones suggests that they were bought to the site whole, beheaded and processed for storage or trade. The presence of a chopped ling vertebra may also be the result of food preparation techniques, such as beheading, gutting and filleting. The large number of small gadid caudal vertebrae indicates that not all fish were processed in this manner.

Evidence from contemporary sites
The assemblage from Sandray is small and any comparisons made with other sites must consider this. The proportions of the three main food animals are within the range found at other Hebridean sites (Mulville 1999). Sandray is more similar to wheelhouses than to brochs, in that there was only a small amount of pig recovered. The presence of a butchered meat-bearing seal bone indicates the active exploitation of seals. Cetacean bone could be recovered from stranded or hunted animals (Mulville, in press) and with only unidentified fragments no further conclusions can be drawn.

The age profile of the domestic livestock is also comparable to other sites (Mulville 1999). From the sparse information it appears that sheep die in their first few years, and this pattern is similar to that at Dun Vulan. However, the proportion of neonatal sheep bone is higher. Cattle show the typical pattern of high infant mortality reported at so many other sites. The lack of adult cattle at Sandray raises issues

about the representative nature of the sample and the sustainability of the herd.

There is a predominance of limb bones present for both sheep and cattle. This could suggest a consumer site supplied with prepared carcasses. Alternatively, preservation and recovery factors could be affecting the assemblage.

Pig is found in only one context, and at least two individuals are present, a neonate and an older animal. The presence of metacarpal and mandible fragments, bones of lower meat-bearing value, suggest that for this species the prime joints of meat were removed elsewhere. It is impossible to know whether this was to another part of the site or further afield.

As at Dun Vulan, the high infant mortality of cattle, and at Sandray for sheep, raises questions about feed provision, poor husbandry and milk production. Unfortunately, in such a small assemblage it is hard to find answers. Any or all three of these factors may have produced this pattern. The ubiquity of the high levels of infant mortality across the Hebrides suggests that this is a deliberate herd management strategy (Mulville 1999). This strategy is probably related to a paucity of fodder and an emphasis on milk production in cattle and meat production in sheep.

Finally, it must be borne in mind that this assemblage constitutes only part of the site. Fragments of bones from older animals and larger species may have been deposited elsewhere. The presence of a horse tooth and canid gnawing, but no other evidence of these species, highlights the absence of some animals from the recovered material.

To date, few fish assemblages from Hebridean sites have been analysed, with the exception of Dun Vulan (Cerón-Carrasco and Parker Pearson 1999), Hornish Point and Baleshare (Jones 1987). In addition, there is the fish bone recovered from nearby Pabbay and Mingulay. The proximity, retrieval methods and size of the assemblage from Mingulay renders it particularly useful for comparison. Here, the small size of the assemblage and the predominance of inshore species, especially gadids, similarly indicates relatively small-scale exploitation of the inshore zone. However, the abundance of mature pollack and the presence of tope suggest that fishing may have been primarily a summer occupation focused on mature pollack.

At Dun Vulan the fish bone assemblage was retrieved by sieving, which probably accounts for the greater range of species. However, it was similarly composed predominantly of members of the Gadidae family, including saithe, cod and pollack. Here, the evidence of cut marks and the underrepresentation of head parts suggests that the fish were processed elsewhere and that the assemblage represents food waste. The author also suggests that in rocky surroundings the local fish population was exploited from crag seats, while the presence of a sandy beach and sand bar allowed safe offshore fishing using hand lines.

On North Uist, hake (*Merluccius merluccius*) was the dominant species recovered from Hornish Point followed by cod, while at Baleshare cod outnumbered hake. The absence of small species was attributed to preservation and retrieval bias.

In the Orkney Islands, large quantities of immature saithe were recovered from St Boniface. In its later phases this was interpreted as a large-scale fish processing site (Cerón-Carrasco 1994). At Scalloway, Shetland, again the commonest taxa were Gadidae, particularly cod and saithe, and there is evidence for on-site processing in the later phase (Cerón-Carrasco 1994).

Conclusion

The small assemblage at Sandray reflects many of the larger assemblages found across the Hebrides. Farming concentrated on sheep, killing them young for their meat. Calves were killed very young, probably to release milk, and subsequently eaten. The small number of pigs and wild species suggest a site without a wide access to resources and a lack of trade. Some use was made of the local marine fauna, with seal and whale present, but the low numbers of these species suggest a community that focused on farming supplemented by fishing.

Evidence from contemporary sites on the Scottish islands leaves little doubt that fishing activities were focused on members of the cod family. Although the relative abundance of the different species is variable and is likely to reflect local conditions and fish populations, it does seem that young saithe were commonly exploited. Fishing appears to have involved little risk and low technology; the species recovered from Iron Age sites could easily have been caught from the shore or close inshore using small boats, lines and nets. There is evidence for the processing of young saithe at contemporary sites on the Orkney islands, and it would therefore not be unusual if this occurred on Sandray, albeit on a small scale.

The bird bones

Judith Cartledge

See the report for PY10 in Chapter 6 above and Table 6.20. Species identified with numbers of bones were gannet (1), shag (2), razorbill/guillemot (1).

The worked stone

Caroline Wickham-Jones

Twenty-one pieces, all of flint, were recovered from the midden at Sheader. The majority of the assemblage is unstratified (Table 7.7). Only 4 pieces of worked stone came from secure contexts. The assemblage is based on pebble flint, and there was one pebble in the collection, though it is very small and unlikely to have had much potential for knapping. There is 1 bipolar core, which is also retouched. A few of the flakes show signs of bipolar knapping, but there is too little material for any detail of the knapping techniques to be inferred. There is a general lack of debitage, but this is probably due to the fact that most of the assemblage was recovered from an eroding midden section. Six retouched pieces, all quite different, were identified within the assemblage. The core has been retouched along one side to make an edge-retouched piece. There are 2 scrapers: a tiny thumbnail scraper on an inner flake; and a larger, coarse, end-scraper on a primary flake. The remainder of the retouched pieces include a small broken flake with a length of microlithic retouch, and 2 other broken retouched fragments from which it is impossible to deduce the original tool. The assemblage is too small to offer any detail of the activities with which it was associated. Likewise, it does not offer any precise data as to date. The edge-retouched piece and the scrapers are all general tool forms that were common throughout prehistory. The lithics from the midden at Sheader confirm that activity on site dates back into prehistory, but they throw little light on this.

Cobble tools

Two biface grinders were recovered from the mound at Sheader, one of which had been reused as a hammer stone. One of the cobble tools was derived from an accumulation of sandy loam (context 15), and the other came from the fabric of wall 19. Both were derived from the deposits associated with the 'prehistoric' use of the site.

Worked bone

One piece of worked bone, a point measuring 49×4 mm with a thickness of 3mm, was recovered

Table 7.7 SY14: distribution of worked stone.

	Context 8	Context 18	Context 19	Unstratified	Total
Pebbles	—	—	—	1	1
Chunks	—	1	—	2	3
Flakes	1	—	1	9	11
Retouched Pieces	—	—	1	5	6
Total	1	1	2	17	21

from the site at Sheader. It is manufactured from a splinter of bone that has been trimmed to a point, the tip of which is polished through wear. The bone point was recovered from context 8 a deposit that postdates the Iron Age structures at Sheader.

Mingulay (MY384)

Excavation at Mingulay MY384 was undertaken by the Department of Archaeology and Prehistory at the University of Sheffield, on behalf of Historic Scotland. The western extent of the mound was excavated during late June and early August 1996. Excavation was initiated in response to the rapid deflation of the sand dunes in which the site was situated. It constituted one of a series of 'rescue' excavations carried out at similar Iron Age sites in the Outer Hebrides. The site (National Grid Reference NL565834) is situated on the western margin of the sand dunes at Mingulay Bay (Fig. 7.8). It is located towards the eastern extent of the former village of Mingulay, close to the late 19th-century Chapel House. The site lies on uneven ground, immediately to the east of a shallow gully on the line of an intermittent stream. Mingulay MY384 consists of a low mound measuring approximately 10.5 m from north to south. Whilst the eastern extent of the mound is elevated above the surface of the dunes, the western extent of the site lies within the limits of dune encroachment. Where the mound is exposed, it survives to a height of up to 1.2 m. The western extent of the mound has been subject to intensive erosion. Deflation of the sand dunes in the vicinity of the site has resulted in the exposure of the underlying subsoil and bedrock. Denudation of the site itself has been exacerbated by rabbit infestation. A series of structures and distinct archaeological deposits have been exposed in the eroded surface of the mound.

Archaeological background

Buxton (1981) and Phillips (n.d.) describe the site as an Iron Age midden. A series of such archaeological features is recorded in and around Mingulay village. Although later settlement has encroached upon the area of dunes within which Mingulay MY384 lies, a number of other prehistoric sites have been identified close to the site. Two circular enclosures, two cairns, a possible cist and a number of ephemeral walls have been recorded in the vicinity of the mound (Buxton 1981). A shell midden was also noted during the late nineteenth century (Wedderspoon 1915). However, this has since been covered by drifting sand.

A small assemblage of unstratified Iron Age pottery was recovered from the deflated surface of the mound in 1959. This material, held by the National Museum of Antiquities (Accession No. HR1212–14), was probably exposed by heavy storms during the previous winter. Subsequent examination of the site in 1971 identified a series of archaeological deposits from which further material was obtained (Phillips n.d.). Two distinct 'midden' deposits, interspersed with lenses of windblown sand, were exposed in an erosion scar at the western extent of the site. A test pit, 2 × 1.5 m, was cut into the 'midden' deposit. Two geotechnic pits, each measuring 1.5 × 0.8 m, were also

Figure 7.8 MY384: the Iron Age midden at Mingulay Bay, facing south-east.

excavated close to the site. These excavations yielded a small quantity of ox and sheep bone, and a few sherds of pottery.

In excess of 200 sherds of pottery were collected from the surface of the mound (Phillips n.d.). A sample of animal bone, shell and pottery was also recovered from the erosion scar at the western extent of the site (Buxton 1981). The faunal assemblage was dominated by ox, sheep and limpet; however, seal, cormorant, pollack, limpet and scallop were also present. Although unstratified, the pottery assemblage seems to consist of two distinct components. First, 'fine', cordoned vessels characteristic of Clettraval Ware (Young 1966). Secondly, coarse, undecorated vessels with crude, upright rims. These components are thought to be derived respectively from the upper and lower 'midden' deposits. As a whole, the assemblage is comparable to those from Dun Cuier, Barra (Young 1955), A' Cheardach Mhor, South Uist (Young and Richardson 1959), and Udal, North Uist (Crawford 1977).

Excavations, 1996

A section, approximately 10.50 m long, was established along the exposed axis of the mound (Fig. 7.9). It incorporated the erosion scars at the western extent of the site. The eroded face of the mound was cleaned and any displaced material was removed. Once planned, the site was excavated down to subsoil. Deposits were removed in reverse order of deposition, and the site planned after the removal of each deposit. Any structural elements were recorded and removed

when excavated. A profile across the mound was achieved at the full extent of excavation. The site was subsequently backfilled and the excavated face consolidated.

The structural and stratigraphic sequences

The deposits and structures recorded during excavation represent a clearly defined stratigraphic sequence (Fig. 7.10). Mingulay MY384 rests directly upon a ploughed, or cultivated, land surface. Remnants of the palaeosoils (contexts 37, 40, 39, 36 and 38) associated with this land surface are preserved in plough marks etched into the surface of the subsoil (Fig. 7.11). The fabric of the mound is composed of a series of sandy silt and clay deposits interspersed with layers of wind-blown sand (contexts 16, 12 and 2). These aeolian deposits can be interpreted either as periods of abandonment or as episodes of intensified sand drifting. They may provide a useful basis for phasing the site. The intermediate layers of sandy silt are associated with a series of structural elements and excavated features (Fig. 7.12).

A series of walls, perhaps part of the same structure, were identified in the lower levels of the mound. A substantial wall (context 4) was constructed at the southern extent of the site. This wall was built upon or sunk into the surface of context 32. It runs parallel to another section of walling (context 22) at the same level. Wall 22 is constructed from a series of unhewn, medium-sized boulders. Another short section of walling (context 26) is defined by two flat stones at the western extent of the site. Although these overlie

Figure 7.9 MY384: section excavated through the mound, facing north-east.

292

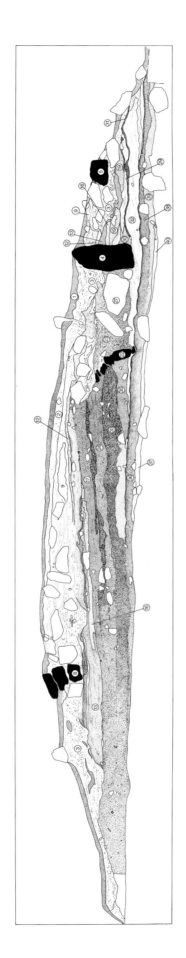

Figure 7.10 MY384: section excavated through the depositional sequence at Mingulay Bay.

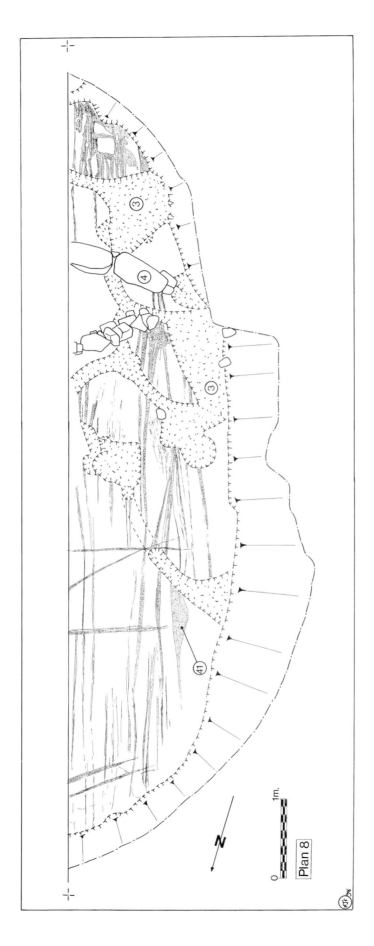

Figure 7.11 MY384: plough marks etched into the subsoil at the base of the mound, facing north-east.

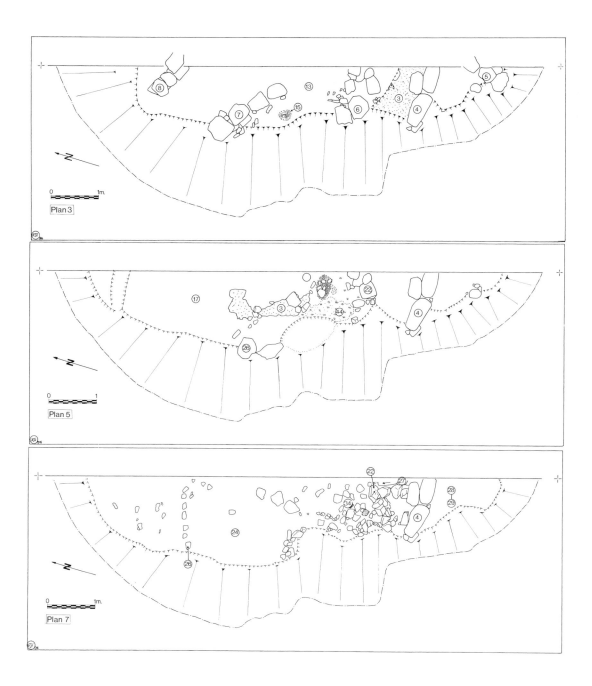

Figure 7.12 MY384: the structural elements identified within the excavated area.

context 24 they have been displaced and may possibly represent a continuation of wall 22. The cavity between walls 4 and 22 is filled by an agglomeration of medium to large stones (context 27). These stones appear to have formed part of an internal connecting wall. Alternatively they may constitute the rubble core of a more substantial double-thickness wall formed by walls 4 and 22. The walls identified within the lower levels of the mound are exposed within the erosion scars at the south-western extent of the site. They have been subject to heavy erosion and will almost

certainly have been 'robbed' to procure stone for the construction of later structures.

Further structures were identified within the upper levels of the mound. Two walls (contexts 6 and 7) were built upon the upper surface of context 17. Both were constructed from flat stone slabs, the cavities between which were packed with smaller stones. The relationship between walls 6 and 7 is uncertain. At a higher level, two substantial drystone walls (contexts 5 and 8) were built upon the surface of context 13. Wall 5 at the south-western extent of the site, was constructed from a series of flat stone slabs. Only one course of stone work survives *in situ*, however, displaced stone work in the vicinity is almost certainly derived from the collapse of the upper courses of this wall. Wall 8 at the northern extent of the site, consists of a short length of drystone walling, surviving to a height of up to three courses. Walls 5 and 8 perhaps form part of the same structure. They are probably associated with the later settlement that encroached upon the sand dunes within which Mingulay MY384 lies.

In addition to the structural elements described above, a number of excavated features were identified within the upper levels of the mound. A shallow scoop was cut into the surface of context 17. This pit was filled by a charcoal-rich clay (context 43) and was lined by a compact layer of burnt clay (context 44). It contained an abundance of mussel shell softened by heat. The scoop can be interpreted as a fire pit or temporary hearth. It is possibly associated with walls 6 and 7. During the accumulation of context 13, a sheep burial was inserted into the surface of the mound. A shallow hollow cut into the surface of the deposit contained the articulated but disturbed skeleton of a sheep (context 15). The sheep burial was probably related to the structure associated with walls 5 and 8. At the northern extent of the site, a vertical cut corresponds to the edge of the trench excavated by Phillips in 1971. The fill of this trench (context 46) is derived from contexts 17 and 33. Accordingly, these deposits can be correlated with the upper and lower midden deposits described by Phillips (n.d.) and Buxton (1981).

The pottery

Jane Timby

The pottery assemblage recovered from MY384 amounted to some 1,616 sherds weighing 17,500 g. The pottery was sorted macroscopically into broad fabric groups and quantified by sherd number and count. Details of decoration, surface finish and use wear were noted where relevant. A representative selection of the featured sherds have been illustrated (Fig. 7.13).

Fabric types

Macroscopic examination of the sherds failed to show many clear cut differences between the sherds, with most of the material comprising fairly coarse, locally made rock-tempered wares similar to those found throughout the Hebrides. Four minor fabric variants were noted:

> Fabric M1: The commonest fabric group. A fairly coarse ware with a 'sandy' texture and containing a moderate to common scatter of coarse ill-sorted, angular inclusions of rock derived from the local Lewisian Gneiss. Although the category is quite wide it did not seem valid to try and

separate the minor variances. Occasionally sherds showed some vegetative impressions on the vessel surfaces.

> Fabric M2: A distinctively finer variant of M1. A finely micaceous ware with no visible coarse rock components. Dense hard fabric with a slightly harsh feel.

> Fabric M1/M2: A variant of the above occurs where the paste is generally that of M2, finely micaceous with a smoother feel but with sparse, coarse inclusions.

> Fabric M3: Distinguished from M1 on the basis of the inclusion of a small amount of organic material within the body of the pot as well as surface impressions. The use of organic tempering has been noted elsewhere, and the use of dung has been suggested in some cases (Campbell 1991: 150). The material present in the Mingulay examples is quite sparse and perhaps slightly coarser than might be expected from dung that is usually quite finely comminuted.

> Fabric M4: Distinguished on the basis of a particularly marked presence of mica on the vessel surfaces.

Vessel forms

The fragmentary nature of most of the sherds and the small sample size precluded a meaningful analysis of vessel shape. The majority of the rims are of the simple undifferentiated type suggestive of plain bucket-shaped vessels. A range of sizes is evident with some large examples (Fig. 7.13.3, 6 and 14), down to smaller, finer examples (Fig. 7.13.2, 7 8, 10, 21 and 27). It was observed that similar large bucket-shaped vessels from Sollas, North Uist, were never decorated. One of the vessels from Mingulay with joining sherds from contexts 40 and 39 (Fig. 7.13.3) has incised lines on the upper rim surface. One variant (Fig. 7.13.20 and 24) has a slightly pinched rim with slack walls.

Slightly out-curving rims (Fig. 7.13.5) are rare. Simple everted S-shaped rims suggestive of more globular bodies (e.g. Fig. 7.13.22) are present across the site. Other rare types include vessels with expanded rims (Figs. 7.13.1 and 17) and a unique vessel with an expanded rim internally bevelled (Fig. 7.13.9). Similar rim forms are present amongst material from A' Cheardach Mhor, South Uist (Young 1960: Fig. 6.33) and Dun Cul Bhuirg, Iona (Topping 1985: Ill. 2, 132). Slightly beaded types (Fig. 7.13.28) came from the upper levels of the site. Other unusual examples include a curved simple rim with finger-tipping on the upper surface (Fig. 7.13.18), a more bowl-like vessel with finger depressions below the rim (Fig. 7.13.13) and a squared expanded rim decorated with fingernail and stab marks (Fig. 7.13.4).

Decorative Styles

In addition to the decorated rims noted above a small number of sherds exhibited other forms of decoration. It may be of some significance that apart from eight rims (two vessels) from the lower levels of the site, all the following sherds came from the upper levels of the site or from disturbed horizons. There are eight sherds with some form of applied cordon, ranging from very heavy, thumbed examples (Fig. 7.13.15, 25 and 26) to slighter horizontal examples with slashed lines (Fig. 7.13.16). One sherd has a zone of incised vertical

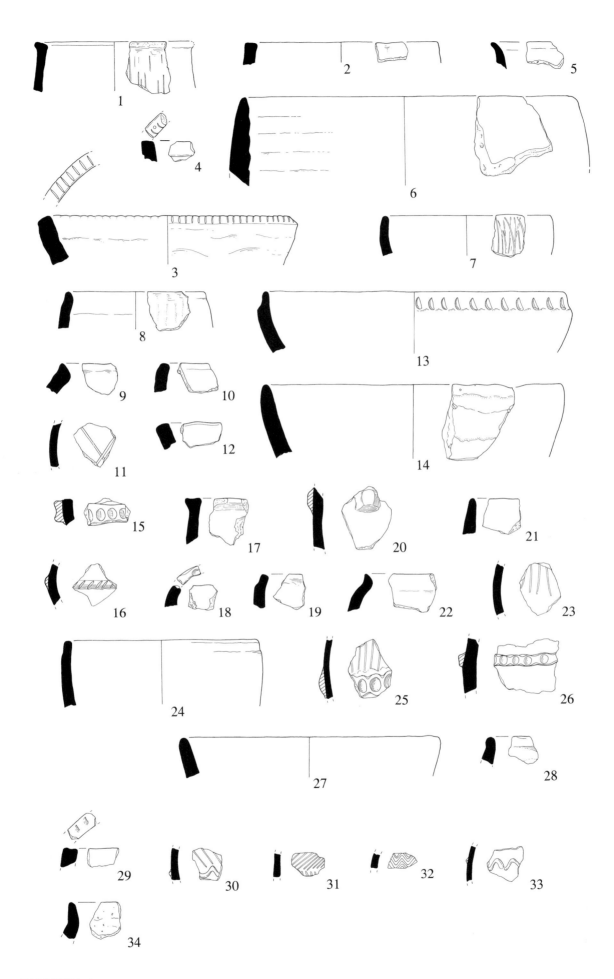

Figure 7.13 MY384: the pottery.

lines above the cordon (Fig. 7.13.25). Three other sherds show incised decoration, two sherds with vertical lines (e.g. Fig. 7.13.23) and one with an incised lattice (Fig. 7.13.11). One sherd has an applied boss/lug (Fig. 7.13.20). Raised bosses feature on the material from A' Cheardach Mhor (Young and Richardson 1959: Fig. 5.17), although these are not quite as prominent as this example. One base sherd from context 17 in the upper midden has pronounced random finger depressions on the interior surface, a feature noted elsewhere in the Hebrides, for example, Sollas, North Uist (Campbell 1991:154), A' Cheardach Mhor, South Uist (Young and Richardson 1959: Fig. 6), Dun Mor Vaul, Tiree (Mackie 1974: Fig. 11.31) and Dun Cul Bhuirg, Iona (Topping 1985:204). Examples also feature amongst the recent material from T17, Barra (p. 169).

Surface treatment
Two distinct types of surface finish were observed. The first is a coarse wet slurry/slipped type of finish possibly from the lower part of the vessel, with two examples of such sherds from the lower levels of the site. The second, noted on nine sherds, is irregular vertical scoring on the exterior surface where the vessel has been smoothed off with coarse grass or light brushwood.

Distribution
Pottery was recovered from 18 separate contexts. No sherds were recovered from the old ground surface at the bottom of the sequence, or from the early cultivation horizon (context 41) immediately above this. The earliest assemblage comes from contexts 40, 39, 36/38 and 32, within the lower levels of the site. In total some 515 sherds (5,732 g) came from this sequence. The largest assemblage, recovered from the upper levels of the site, comprised some 931 sherds (10,360 g). Levels allocated to the early modern phase were aceramic but a further 81 sherds (868 g) were collected from the modern rabbit disturbance and 87 sherds from unstratified collections.

Discussion
Although the overall average sherd size at 15 g seems quite high, the fabric is very dense and the vessels quite thick-walled so that in reality most of the sherds were quite fragmentary and very friable. The material from both the lower and the upper levels of the site is very similar in terms of preservation, with an average sherd size of 11 g, which can be contrasted with the disturbed material where the average sherd size is just 8 g. There were no reconstructable profiles. From the assemblage as a whole there were 89 rim sherds (of which 10 were decorated), 48 base sherds and 12 featured body sherds. In total decorated sherds account for less than 1% of the assemblage. The remaining sherds were plain. A high proportion of

the sherds was heavily burnt with sooty deposits, presumably the result of cooking over a peat-fuelled fire. Alternatively the blackening may result from the primitive firing of the vessels prior to use.

Handmade pottery has a very long history on the Hebrides and the raw materials exploited and technology employed show very little change over several millennia. It is thus important to have diag-nostic material with decorative features of distinctive forms. Although the Mingulay group is quite large by most Hebridean standards, it is generally poorly preserved and has a relatively limited range of diagnostic material. There are no associated artifacts to assist in dating and any conclusions must be regarded as tentative. The chronological sequence of Hebridean pottery developed by Young (1966) has been strongly challenged by Topping (1987) and Lane (1990). More recent work has highlighted not only the complexity of pottery development in the Western Isles, but the necessity for independent dating and the excavation and study of well stratified sequences. Differences in the composition of assemblages may reflect social and functional distinctions rather than chronological factors.

The Mingulay assemblage is largely homogenous, and there are no overriding differences perceivable in terms of the fabrics—the minor fabrics being too rare to have any significance. However, there are some observable trends in terms of the presence/absence of decorative features. The traditional view is that deco-rated Iron Age pottery first appears in the last few centuries BC or the early 1st century AD (Lane and Cowie 1997). Within the lower levels of the site, deco-ration is restricted to rims with examples of incised lines (Fig. 7.13.3) and a combination of impressed fingernail and punch marks (Fig. 7.13.4). Surface finishes include vertically striated exteriors. The rims present are mainly plain undifferentiated types and include a number of large bucket-shaped vessels (e.g. Fig. 7.13.3 and 6), but also include expanded thickened rims (Fig. 7.13.1) and a thinner-walled, smoothly everted rim vessel (Fig. 7.13.5). The presence of decoration on top of the rims is an unusual feature with no immediate parallel (Mike Parker Pearson, personal communication). A single stray find of a notched rim is illustrated from Dun Cuier, on the Isle of Barra (Young 1955: Fig. 2.8). On the basis of the thickness of the vessels and the texture of the fabrics, it is suggested that the deposits associated with the lower levels of the site belong to the later part of the early Iron Age. It was noted above that all the cordoned sherds were derived from the upper levels of the site. Unstratified material collected by Buxton (1981), also thought to derive from the upper midden layer, similarly included several cordoned sherds. Although relatively limited, such material can generally be regarded as typical of the middle Iron Age.

Radiocarbon dating at Sollas, North Uist, suggested that the introduction of sharply everted rim vessels together with finger channelled decoration, the so-called Clettraval ware, dates to the 1st–2nd century AD, coinciding with the construction of the wheelhouse (Campbell 1991). Neither trait is evident in the present group of pottery from Mingulay, although an everted rim vessel with a cordon featured amongst unstratified material discussed by Buxton (1981). There were also no examples of the ring-pin stamped wares commonly found on other sites in the Hebrides. Other features, such as the use of organic tempering and the presence of cordons, were not considered to be chronologically sensitive traits at Sollas (cf. Campbell 1991: 152). Linear decoration is a characteristic feature of wheelhouse pottery, and at Sollas the presence of cordoned and incised vessels was particularly marked in the later phases relating to the construction and use of the wheelhouse (Campbell 1991). Designs appear to be more complex in the later material, another trait not evident in the Mingulay group. It could perhaps be suggested, therefore, that

the upper midden deposits broadly date to around the 1st century BC/AD.

The faunal remains (excluding birds)
Jacqui Mulville (mammals) and C. Ingrem (fish)

(For methods see above, Chapter 6, p. 250).

The Iron Age assemblage at Mingulay was small, comprising only 547 fragments in total (Fig. 7.14). Mammals dominated, making up nearly 90% of the assemblage. The majority of bone was recovered from contexts 17 and 24, occupational deposits within the mound.

Taphonomy and recovery
The mammal bone was generally in good condition, only 2% of bone was gnawed and 3% burnt to any degree. Butchery was recorded on 8% of bone. There was no evidence for butchery, gnawing or burning on the fish bone.

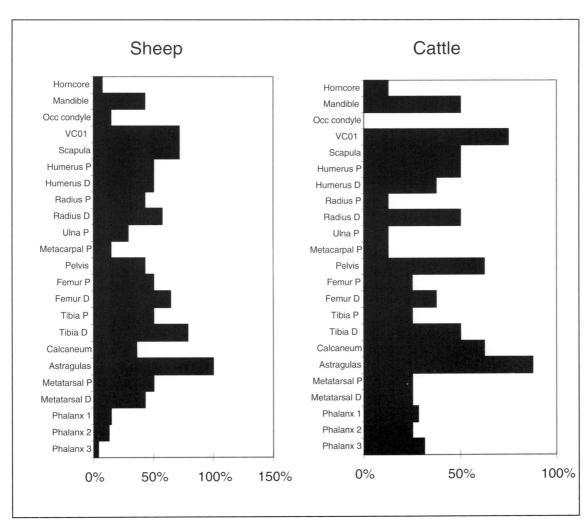

Figure 7.14 MY384: percentage survival by anatomical element for sheep and cattle bones.

Table 7.8 Site MY384: mammals and fish present by species.

Mammals	NISP	%	MNI	%
Cattle	163	39	4	31
Sheep/Goat	249	60	7	54
Pig	2	< 1	1	8
Red Deer	1	< 1	1	8
Total	415		13	
Cow Size	15			
Sheep Size	41			
Fish				
Tope	2	3		
Conger Eel	1	1		
Pollack	26	37		
Saithe	13	18		
Cod	18	25		
Ling	1	1		
Large Gadid	8	11		
Sea Bream	1	1		
Ballam Wrasse	1	1		
Total	71			

NISP = number of identified specimens.
MNI = minimum number of individuals.

Species present

There was a restricted range of mammals present: cattle, sheep, red deer, Atlantic seal, common seal and cetacea (Table 7.8). The tiny fish assemblage of 72 fragments comprised eight species of fish: tope (*Galeorhinus galeus*), conger eel (*Conger conger*), pollack (*Pollachius pollachius*), saithe (*Pollachius virens*), ling (*Molva molva*), sea bream (Sparidae) and ballan wrasse (*Labrus bergylta*).

Sheep were the most abundant mammals in terms of NISP, although cattle made up a large proportion of the assemblage (Table 7.8). Pig, deer, seal and cetacea were represented by a few fragments of bone. Using the MNI calculation sheep remain dominant, although to a slightly lesser degree. All the rarer species are represented by a single individual, although if the state of fusion of bone is taken into consideration, it is possible that more than one Atlantic seal was present.

The fish remains comprised mainly of members of the Gadidae (cod family), which make up three quarters of the identified fragments (Table 7.8). Pollack are the most numerous although saithe and cod are also well represented. Other species were present only as a couple of fragments.

The main food mammals

Sheep. A wide range of elements was recorded, suggesting that whole animals were present at the site (Table 7.9). Figure 7.14 uses the minimum number of elements (MNE) to demonstrate the relative abundance of sheep elements (after Brain 1981). Bones of the skull are poorly represented, as are the small bones of the foot. There are few metacarpals, but apart from their absence most long bones are present in similar amounts. The small, but robust, astragalus and the robust early fusing distal tibia predominate. The latter is commonly an abundant element, but this quantity of the small astragalus is of interest. In a population with many neonates (see below), the astragalus, complete from birth may survive better than other neonatal bone. This pattern of relative abundance suggests the breaking up of the skull, poor recovery of the small foot bones and destruction of the metacarpals through marrow extraction or possible preferential use in tool production.

Ageing information available from long-bone fusion suggests an early death for many of the sheep (Table 7.10). The proportion of unfused bone is high from the earliest age group, and the percentage of neonatal bone is also very high, 63%. This is at odds with the information from the dental wear (Table 7.11). There is only one very young jaw and most animals die in the latter part of their first year or in their second or third years. There are also older individuals. This discrepancy between the fusion and mandibular ageing is interesting. There is a predominance of neonatal bone within these deposits, but also on site are the jaws of older animals. The older animals would be necessary as breeding stock. The absence of the long bone associated with these individuals could indicate trade or different disposal patterns for these older individuals.

Butchery. The recorded butchery marks are summarized in Table 7.12. Cut marks predominate over chop marks, and both appear on a range of bones. Butchery was noted on neonates as well as older animals. A zygomatic and a couple of hyoids, one neonatal, were the only parts of the head cut. The hyoid is likely to have been marked as the throat was cut. The atlas and axis show evidence of butchery to remove the head, although none of the few other vertebra present showed evidence of butchery. The limb bones showed evidence of skinning, with cuts on the metapodials, disarticulation at the hock and elbow joints and filleting on the humerus. The presence of disarticulation and filleting butchery on neonatal bone suggests an intensive use of the lambs, with them treated in a similar manner to older individuals.

Articulated bone groups. A number of pairs of neonatal sheep bones were recorded. These probably represent partial burials of neonates that became mixed during deposition or excavation. Context 17 contained a pair of radii, a femur and a tibia that may have come from a single burial. A number of foetal bones were also present that may have come from a second individual. Other contexts contained large

Table 7.9 Site MY384: abundance of elements.

	Cattle	Sheep/Goat	Pig	Red Deer	Cow Size	Sheep Size	
Horn Core	3	2					
Nasal	2	1					
Occ. Condyle		2					
Zygomatic		6					
Lower Decid. Premolar	7						
Lower 3rd Molar	4	4					
Mandible	6	11	1				
Hyoid	4	3					
Atlas	4	5				3	
Axis		4					
Scapula	4	12					
Humerus	8	13					
Radius	6	16					
Ulna	1	5					
Magnum	1	1					
Metacarpal	1	3					
Pelvis	8	14					
Femur	9	27		1			
Patella	1	1					
Tibia	6	25					
Astragalus	7	18					
Calcaneum	7	6					
Nav.-Cuboid	5	1					
Metatarsal	2	10					
Metapodial	15	16					
1st Phalanx	13	12					
2nd Phalanx	10	9					
3rd Phalanx	14	2					
Cervical Vert.	6	5	1				
Thoracic Vert.	1	2				2	
Caudal Vert.	3						
Lumbar Vert.		2				1	
Vert. Frag.	5	5			12	15	
Sacrum		1					
Rib		5			3	20	
Total	163	249	2	1	15	41	471

quantities of neonatal bone, and while individual pairs of elements were recognized no other potential burials were noted, although they may have been present.

Cattle. As for sheep a wide range of elements were recovered (Table 7.9). When the minimum number of elements are compared to those expected from the MNI (after Brain 1981) many bones are under-represented (Fig. 7.8). Few bones of the skull were recovered, while the numbers of proximal radius and ulna, femur and metapodials was low. Phalanxes were poorly represented, and it is unlikely that they were not recovered, as these are relatively large elements in cattle. As for sheep, the most abundant element was the astragalus. The site has neither a pattern of exportation, with lesser meat bones left behind, nor importation with an abundance of prime meat bones. This pattern, with small amounts of both long bones and phalanxes, may suggest the destruction of much of the assemblage during marrow

extraction. This process would result in small fragments of bone that were not recovered through hand collection.

The sparse fusion information available for cattle reveals a population with a very high mortality rate (Table 7.10). Few bones are fused and the proportion of neonates is extremely high, with 80% of all long bone with fusing information coming from animals in the first few weeks of life.

Unlike sheep, most of the cattle mandibles with recordable wear came from very young neonatal animals, with only a few older animals present (Table 7.11). This is in agreement with the long-bone information, and indicates that little adult bone was deposited at the site.

A couple of shed teeth were recovered, a dP3, context 17, and a dP4 from context 24. These suggest possible containment or stalling of cattle (Halstead, in press), keeping the young animals at the site where their shed teeth become incorporated into deposits.

Table 7.10 Site M384: fusion data.

	Sheep			
	Unfused	Neonate	Fused	*% Unfused*
Humerus D		2	4	
Radius P	0	4	0	
Scapula	1	5	2	
Pelvis		9	0	
<1 year	1	14	6	*71*
Tibia D	1	6	2	
Metatarsal D				
Metacarpal D	1	1	1	
<2 years	2	7	3	*75*
Calcaneum	4	1	1	
Femur P	1	5	0	
Humerus P	1	6		
Radius D	1	7	3	
Ulna P	1	5		
Femur D		11		
Tibia P	0	4	0	
<3.5 years	8	20	4	*88*
	Neonates	Total	*% Neonates*	
	41	65	*63*	

	Cattle			
	Unfused	Neonate	Fused	*% Unfused*
Scapula	1	3		
Pelvis	1	4		
<1 year	2	7	0	*100*
Humerus D	0	1	1	
Radius P	0	2	0	
<2 years	0	3	1	*75*
Tibia D	1	1	1	
Metacarpal D	0	0	0	
Metatarsal D	0	1	0	
Calcaneum	0	4	0	
<3 years	1	6	1	*88*
Femur P	0	2	0	
Humerus P	0	2	0	
Radius D	0	1	0	
Ulna P				
Femur D	0	1	1	
Tibia P	0	2	0	
<4 years	0	8	1	*89*
	Neonates	Total	*% Neonates*	
	24	30	*80*	

Butchery. A lower proportion of cattle bones are butchered compared to sheep (Table 7.12). Two hyoids show evidence of the throat being cut, and there are skinning marks found on two fragments of skull. Evidence of disarticulation is noted at the elbow and hock joints, a humerus and tibia are chopped and two astragali show knife cuts. A vertebra and a rib are also butchered. Cut marks on a third phalanx could

Table 7.11 Site MY384: mandibular wear stage.

	Sheep		Cattle	
Stage	Age	N	Age	N
A	0–2 months	0	0–1 month	2
A/B	2 months	1	1 month	5
B	2–6 months	0	1–8 months	0
C	6–12 months	3	8–18 months	1 > C
D	1–2 years	4	18–30 months	1 > D
E	2–3 years	4	30–36 months	1
F	3–4 years	0	Young adult	0
G	4–6 years	1	Adult	10
H	6–8 years	1		
Total		14		11

relate to removal of the hoof for processing. Four of the 14 butchered bones are neonatal. Finally, two first phalanx from context 40 were split, although no butchery marks are evident, to extract the marrow.

Articulated bone groups. The only cattle bone noted as articulating are four neonatal toes from a single foot in context 40. The range of neonatal bone found in other large contexts suggests partial burial in these contexts as well.

Pig. Only two fragments of pig were recovered. The ramus of a right pig mandible (context 24) and a cervical vertebra (context 21). The vertebra was unfused, indicating it came from an immature individual, and butchered, suggesting it had been consumed.

Table 7.12 Site MY384: butchery by element.

	Sheep		Cattle	
	Cut	Chop	Cut	Chop
Zygomatic	1			
Nasal			1	
Hyoid	2		2	
Atlas	1			
Axis	1	1		
Scapula	1			
Humerus	2			2
Femur	3	1	1	
Tibia	1		1	1
Astragalus	3	1	1	
Metapodial	2			2
Calcaneum	1			
1st Phalanx	2		1	
2nd Phalanx	1			
3rd Phalanx			1	
Cervical Vert.	1	1		
Sacrum		1		
Vert. Frag.		1		1
Total	22	6	8	6
% butchered		*11*		*9*

Wild mammals

Red deer. A fragment of red deer femur was recovered from the context 22. This was a femoral head, removed from the shaft by chopping. Fusion evidence indicates it came from a mature individual.

Atlantic seal. Four fragments of Atlantic seal were recovered from context 17: a humerus, tibia, astragalus and a phalanx. The fusion evidence suggests that these are likely to represent the remains of more than one individual with both mature fully fused bones (a humerus and phalanx) and immature unfused bone (a tibia) present. No butchery was visible on the bones.

Common seal. Two Iron Age contexts contained common seal bone. A metapodial was identified from context 24 and a scapula from context 33. Both came from immature individuals; in particular the scapula appeared to be from a very young seal. As for the Atlantic seal, no butchery marks were noted.

Fish

The fish remains are generally well preserved, as is exemplified by the recovery of two vertebrae belonging to the catilaginous tope. The greater frequency of the more robust elements, such as vertebrae and mouth parts, is indicative of density related survival. However, in the absence of sieved samples the fish remains are unlikely to provide a representative sample of the species, body part representation or size of the fish originally present. In addition to their robustness, the mouth parts and vertebrae are the elements most easily recognized and their abundance may be the result of retrieval bias. This may also account for the absence of young gadids and very small species, such as herring.

Individual elements derived from the large gadids are shown in Table 7.13. These have been divided into head and body parts and it is apparent for pollack and cod that both head and body elements are well represented. In contrast, only elements derived from the heads of saithe were recovered.

Ling was represented by a single precaudal vertebra. Two caudal vertebrae were identified as tope. Conger eel is represented by a dentary, sea bream by a caudal vertebra and ballam wrasse by a supracleithrum.

Size. An estimation of size has been obtained by the comparison of measurements with those taken on comparative specimens of known weight or size. This has allowed an approximate age to be obtained (Table 7.14). It is apparent that all of the elements from which measurements could be obtained belonged to mature fish.

Ecology and environment. All species, with the exception of ling, are commonly found close inshore. Ling,

Table 7.13 Site MY384: Gadidae: body part representation.

	Pollack	Saithe	Cod	Ling	Large Gadid
Neurocranium	0	0	2	0	0
Frontal	0	2	0	0	0
Parasphenoid	0	1	0	0	1
Premaxilla	1	1	2	0	0
Maxilla	1	0	0	0	0
Dentary	1	4	0	0	0
Articular	1	2	1	0	1
Ceratohyale	0	0	0	0	2
Epihyale	1	0	0	0	1
Hyomandibular	0	1	0	0	0
Preopercular	0	1	0	0	0
Precaudal Vert.	4	1	6	1	0
Total Head	9	13	11	1	5
Caudal Vert.	13	0	7	0	0
Cleithrum	0	0	0	0	2
Total body	13	0	7	0	2
Total	22	13	18	1	7

although deep-water fish, are occasionally found inshore. Tope migrate offshore during the winter, as do mature pollack, but move inshore during the summer months. Conger eel, pollack, saithe, cod, sea bream and ballan wrasse all display a preference for rocky shores or rough ground. All of the species recovered can be caught using lines from the shore. Pollack, saithe, cod, sea bream and ballan wrasse are known for either their readiness to take bait or as good angling fish (Wheeler 1968).

Discussion

The mammal and fish bones can only give a brief outline of life at this particular site. The farming focused on sheep, supplemented by cattle and only occasionally on other species. The predominance of sheep is similar to that found at other Iron Age sites, such as Dun Vulan (Mulville 1999), Baleshare and Hornish Point (Halstead, in press), while the few pig bones indicate more similarities with assemblages

recovered from wheelhouses rather than brochs (Mulville 1999).

This site is unusual in its extremely high level of neonatal sheep and cattle. These levels are far in excess of those recorded at other Hebridean sites. Dun Vulan has about 50% neonatal cattle compared to 80% at Mingulay and only 13% neonatal sheep compared with 63% at Mingulay. The predominance of neonates in the assemblage suggests either unusual deposits or an unusual site. If these animals represented the entire cull from a herd, the high level of slaughter would soon result in a diminishing population. Alternatively, this sample is only part of the culled population. It is possible that larger older animals were deposited elsewhere and that only part of the herd was recovered. Whatever the reason we can state that very young animals were being slaughtered and consumed and the remains deposited at the site. In some cases these represent partial burials, which suggests their immediate consumption and burial. The small size of neonatal carcasses means that a smaller

Table 7.14 Site MY384: Gadidae: approximate age and size.

Species	Element	Approx. Size	Approx. Age
Cod	Premaxilla	Slightly > 914 mm	Adult
Pollack	Premaxilla	Slightly < 500 mm	4 years
Pollack	Articular	c. 660 mm	Adult
Saithe	Dentary	c. 480 mm	3–4 years
Saithe	Dentary	c. 700 mm	Adult
Saithe	Dentary	c. 700 mm	Adult
Saithe	Dentary	Slightly > 700 mm	Adult
Saithe	Premaxilla	Slightly < 700 mm	Adult
Saithe	Hydromandibular	Slightly < 700 mm	Adult

number of people would be fed by a single beast. The lack of elements of the lower limb suggests that primary butchery, marrow extraction or taphonomy is affecting the relative abundance of elements.

Sheep and cattle were used in meat production; with such a high neonatal population represented it is hard to describe any other use for these animals. Adults would have been needed as breeding stock and their absence may indicate a failing herd. It is possible that milk was procured from the mothers of these young, however, it is also possible that a trade in such young animals existed and milk production did not occur at this site.

The few pig and deer bones at Mingulay can only indicate the consumption of these animals. The few seal bones present reflect other Iron Age sites in the preponderance of Atlantic seal. It is interesting to note that adult and juvenile Atlantic seal are recorded but only immature common seal. This may be linked to the ease of capture of the Atlantic seal at the breeding grounds and the difficulty in procuring common seal from the sea. It is possible that juvenile seals are an easier target in the sea. Unlike most other Hebridean sites there is no evidence for cetacean bone.

There is no evidence on the bones themselves to suggest that the fish remains were deposited by such natural agencies as otters or sea birds. In the absence of sieved samples any interpretation should be treated with caution, however, the small quantity of fish remains recovered from Mingulay suggests that fishing was only practised on a small scale. The predominance of large gadids may be a reflection of recovery, although it is highly likely that these relatively large, good-eating fish were deliberately targeted by the Iron Age inhabitants. The predominance of inshore species along with adult pollack and tope suggest that fishing may have been practised during the summer when larger pollack can be found in areas close to the shore.

The absence of caudal vertebrae or other elements that generally remain in the body after the head is removed may indicate that saithe were being processed for later consumption or trade. However, no evidence for butchery was visible and the pattern may simply reflect survival and retrieval bias. In contrast, the frequency of elements derived from both the head and body indicates that pollack and cod were caught and consumed at the same location.

The predominance of inshore species indicates that a low-risk fishing strategy, involving little risk or technology, was being practised. All of the species recovered could have been exploited from the shore or small boats, using lines or nets.

At the present time, few fish assemblages from Hebridean sites have been analysed with the exception of Dun Vulan (Cerón-Carrasco and Parker Pearson 1999), Hornish Point and Baleshare (Jones 1987).

In addition, fish bone were recovered from the nearby sites of Pabbay and Sandray. At Dun Vulan the fish bone assemblage was retrieved by sieving through 10 mm and 1 mm mesh, which probably accounts for the greater range of species recovered. Like Mingulay the assemblage was composed predominately of members of the Gadidae family including saithe, cod and pollack. The absence of immature gadids, particularly saithe, evidence of cut marks and the underrepresentation of head parts suggests that the fish were processed elsewhere and that the assemblage represents food waste. The author also suggests that in rocky surroundings the local fish population was exploited from crag seats, while the presence of a sandy beach and sand bar allowed safe offshore fishing using hand lines. On North Uist, hake (*Merluccius merluccius*) was the dominant species recovered from Hornish Point followed by cod, while at Baleshare cod outnumbered hake. The absence of small species was attributed to preservation and retrieval bias.

In the Orkney Islands, large quantities of immature saithe were recovered from St Boniface, which, in its later phases was interpreted as a large-scale fish processing site (Cerón-Carrasco 1994). At Scalloway, Shetland again the commonest taxa were Gadidae, particularly cod and saithe, and there is evidence for on-site processing in the later phase (Cerón-Carrasco 1994).

Conclusion

Mingulay is a very unusual site. The very early death of most cattle and sheep animals is perplexing and while butchery evidence suggests the consumption of these animals there is no evidence of a sustainable farming community. The use of other species for food is suggested by the few butchered pig, seal and deer bones, but they are present in very small quantities. The absence of cetacea is also atypical. From this assemblage, the site at Mingulay can only be describe as a failing farming community, supplemented to a very minor degree by wild species.

Evidence from contemporary sites on the Scottish islands leaves little doubt that fishing activities were generally focused on members of the cod family. The relative abundance of the different gadids is variable and probably reflects local conditions and fish populations. The species represented suggest that fishing involved low risk and simple technology during this period and was probably carried out using lines and nets from the shore or close inshore with the aid of small boats. The evidence for fish-processing activities at several contemporary sites add weight to the possibility that saithe were being processed for storage and later consumption at Mingulay. The small sample size suggests that fishing was practised on a small scale, in order to supplement the diet, and was not of major importance in the economy of the inhabitants of Mingulay during the Iron Age.

The bird bones

Judith Cartledge

See the report for PY10 in Chapter 6, p. 268, and Table 6.20, p. 268. The species identified and number of bones were: duck sp. (1), Manx shearwater (20), shag (64), cormorant (2), great black-backed gull (1).

The worked stone

Caroline Wickham-Jones

Thirty-two pieces, all of flaked flint, were recovered during survey work in the dune area of Mingulay Bay. The majority of these were regular flakes, but there were also some chunks and four retouched pieces. Most of the material is highly polished and abraded. The assemblage is so small that there is little detail to be drawn from it, but a few points are worth note. The cortex indicates that pebble nodules were used as a source of raw material, and this is common on west coast sites. There are no cores, but the flakes indicate that both bipolar and platform reduction were used, and again this is in line with other local material. The flakes are quite large and with the exception of the chunks there is no debitage in the assemblage.

The four retouched artifacts are all different. First, two scrapers, namely an end scraper and a small thumbnail scraper. Both have very convex scraping edges and have visible edge damage undercutting the scraping edge. Secondly, a large flake with fine retouch along the left side and around the distal end and part of the right side. Traditionally, it would be classified as a plano-convex knife, though it is not worked fully over the dorsal surface. In effect it is impossible to say how it was used and so it is better to avoid the word knife. There is some visible edge damage at the butt end, perhaps resulting from insertion into a haft. Finally, a much smaller edge-retouched tool, clearly of a very different type to the previous piece. It is generally triangular in shape and has steep edge retouch along the left and right sides, which converge to form a blunt point at the distal end. It is broken across the proximal end and the whole piece is very abraded so that it is difficult to know whether it was originally longer.

It is very unusual for a lithic assemblage not to contain some small debitage pieces, and the lack of this element here may be due to the collection of the material from the surface. Larger pieces tend to collect on the surface of a site, while smaller pieces have been shown to migrate downwards. At the same time, larger pieces are easier to recognize and collect during survey work. This means that the composition of the assemblage today may not reflect its original state so that no detailed conclusions as to tool use and manufacture may be drawn. The abraded condition of the material is also a reflection of its origin. It is likely to be a result of wind gloss, where flints have spent time lying on the surface and in a silica-rich environment.

The retouched pieces provide some hints as to the affinities of the site, but these are vague, coming as they do from single artifacts. Scrapers like those from the dunes were in use throughout prehistory, though both are of types that tend to be more common on later Neolithic sites when small thumbnail scrapers and stubbier end scrapers were popular. The abraded tool is not of any use chronologically, but the plano-convex edge tool is of a type that was common elsewhere through the later Neolithic and Early Bronze Age.

The assemblage is small and clearly reflects its origin as a surface collection from a dune area. The artifacts offer little to the interpretation of the human history of the dunes, and of course they may well have come from several different sites, but they do confirm that human activity has taken place here in prehistory, probably at least in the later Neolithic and Early Bronze Age. These early islanders had access to a supply of pebble flint, probably on local beaches, from which they made tools, including regular flakes, scrapers and edge-retouched pieces.

Cobble tools

Five cobble tools were recovered during the course of excavations at Mingulay MY384, including two biface grinders, a hammer stone and a stone rubber. One of the cobble tools, derived from context 36 within the lower levels of the site, had a carefully maintained working surface (Fig. 7.15).

Shell

One piece of worked shell, measuring 47×35 mm with a thickness of 6 mm, was found at Mingulay MY384. The shell, roughly triangular in shape, had been trimmed along the two shorter edges. It was recovered from the clay loam (context 40) pushed into the plough marks etched into the cultivated land surface at the base of the site.

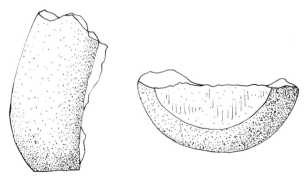

Figure 7.15 MY384: a cobble tool.

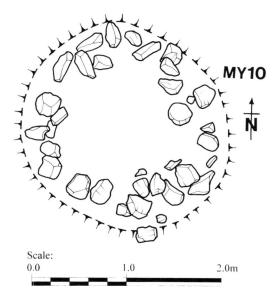

Scale:
0.0   1.0   2.0m

Figure 7.16 Site MY10.

Mingulay (MY10, 11 and 12)

During the initial coastal erosion field survey three small cairns MY10, 11 and 12 were located in the floor of the dyke between Tom O'Reihden and Macphee's Hill at its eastern end. All three monuments were either already suffering from severe peat deflation and erosion or were immanently threatened with it. In the face of this threat excavations were initiated on all three cairns to record and, if possible, to obtain some dateable material from them before their natural destruction from erosion occurred.

MY10 (Fig. 7.16) was a flat, raised, 4 m diameter disc of peat soil around the upper edge of which a number stones had been carelessly placed with no apparent structural order. On excavation it was found that the stones did not continue with depth and that the mound itself was composed of a bland mass of peat soil. There were no material finds.

MY 11 was in a state of advanced destruction with only a small proportion of its structure still in place. Severe deflation of the peat soils that make up the local natural soil cover and the bulk of the monument's mass had resulted in the disappearance of the soils completely, spilling the stone element of the structure out on to denuded bedrock. Although in a deranged state the mass of stonework, some 2 m in diameter, still retained some element of its original form, which suggested a small circular cairn of piled stones, possibly with a stone-free central zone. No material evidence was found.

MY12, in contrast to the other cairns, was a 1.5 × 1 m oval of carefully placed stones resting on the surface of the peat topsoil. However, in accordance with MY10 and 11, no material finds were recovered.

Mingulay (MY346)

In the southern coastal valley of Skipisdale, on the island of Mingulay, two complex, drystone walled settlements (MY345 and 346) occupy the central valley floor on either side of a major stream that drains the valley into the sea. Both settlements appear to consist of a large circular roundhouse, approximately 10 m in diameter, obscured to a great extent by

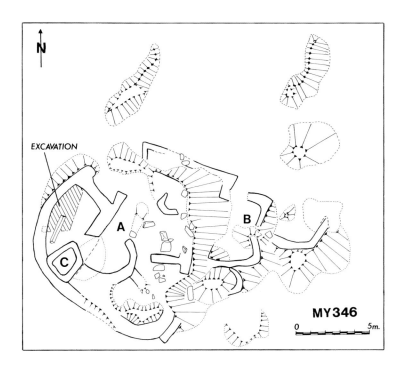

Figure 7.17 Site MY346.

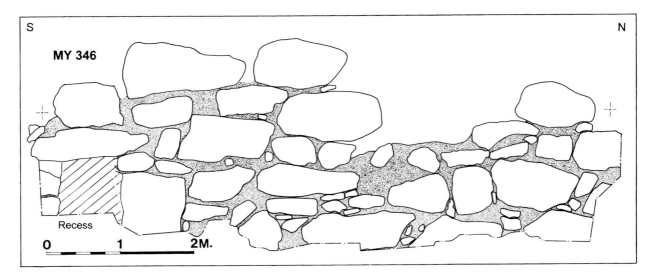

Figure 7.18 MY346: elevation against internal wall of putative wheelhouse.

later buildings that have been built over and around this early core structure. A sherd of possible Iron Age pottery was recovered from a rabbit burrow dug into the lower outer levels of MY346 and, in an attempt to gain further and more stratigraphically secure dateable material, a small sondage was opened within the bounds of the roundhouse at MY346.

Before the excavations commenced a measured survey of the exposed stonework was made which showed that at least three separate building phases could be distinguished (Fig. 7.17):

> Phase 1: the large circular building A.
> Phase 2: a number of subrectangular buildings (B) constructed over and away from the eastern side of building A.
> Phase 3: a relatively modern shieling hut (C) built over the south-west corner of building A.

The excavation of an area against the west wall of building A revealed detail of the construction of the superstructure, which still survived to a height of six or seven courses of drystone walling facing an earthen core (Fig. 7.18), which in turn was presumably faced with a turf outer skin since no stonework was found in place there. An internal division wall, knitted into the main wall, suggests that if the roundhouse structure is of Iron Age date it may be of wheelhouse type. Located at a low level in the inner wall a recess had been built into the stone face, possibly to provide some form of cupboard.

The upper soil deposit within the excavation area consisted almost entirely of loose peat soil thoroughly mixed and displaced by the action of rabbit burrowing, which was still active as the excavation proceeded. Lying on and within this deposit, a massive 2 m long lintel stone had obviously fallen from the upper wall levels. The sheer size and shape of this stone was not in keeping with the general blockiness of the other building stone in use and suggests that it

may have been robbed from some other local, earlier monument, such as the possible Neolithic chamber tomb MY347 (below).

The disturbed peat soil gave way after approximately 0.2 m to a stone-paved surface without providing a single dateable sherd of pottery. The only feature was a thin ash deposit above the floor level that may represent a small camp fire connected with the recent shieling hut (C). Not wishing to disturb stratified archaeological structures within this important site, the excavation work was terminated at this point.

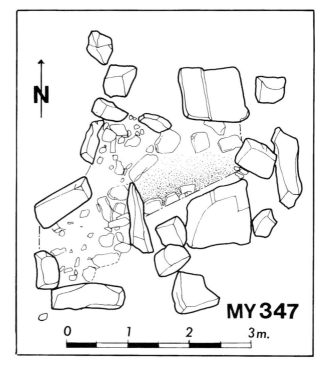

Figure 7.19 Site MY347.

While not producing the information hoped for, the excavation did allow a small insight into the construction methods used in building the round-house and has added something to our understanding of the structural sequence and form of the settlement.

Mingulay (MY347)

MY347 is located in the Skipisdale valley, on a low prominence close to the coastline, to the south of the large settlement sites that occupy the central valley floor area. The monument is considered to be a Neolithic chamber tomb, possibly with a double rectangular chamber, constructed from very large slabs of local gneiss set on edge. In plan the chamber area measures 4.5 m by, approximately, 2.5 m. However, the superstructure appears to have suffered from considerable stone robbing and general disturbance. Many of the 1 m plus stone slabs have been overthrown and have become displaced so that determining the exact form and overall dimensions is not readily accomplished. Since the site is not threatened with further destruction at present, the excavator, Linda Cihakova, restricted her investigation to only removing any recent peat soil overburden down to any surviving archaeologically sensitive level from a section across the inner chamber area (Fig. 7.19). A surface of burnt peat soil was encountered at a depth not exceeding 0.1 m, at which point the excavation was terminated, and after recording the sondage was refilled. No artifacts were recovered, but the opportunity to obtain a C14 date from the burnt material in the future may be a possibility.

8.   The Vegetational History of Barra

Kevin Edwards and Barbara Brayshay

Abstract

Pollen-analytical evidence is presented for the Post-glacial vegetational history of parts of Barra. Like the Inner Hebrides and the other islands of the Outer Hebrides, it is clear that woodland was a feature of some sites. Birch and hazel were the most abundant arboreal components with lesser amounts of Scots pine, oak, elm, alder and ash. Woodland reduction was a result of climatic, pedological and perhaps anthropogenic pressures on plants at the northern and western extremes of their ranges. Grass-sedge-heathland characterized all areas, especially from mid-Postglacial times onwards.

Introduction

The analysis of fossil pollen and plant remains from the Outer Hebrides have provided archaeologists with a wealth of information on the environmental history of the islands since the end of the last (Devensian) glaciation c. 10,000 years ago. A substantial number of records are radiocarbon dated and therefore referable to the settlement history of the islands (Birks and Madsen 1979; Bohncke 1988; Bennett *et al.* 1990; Edwards 1990, 1996; Brayshay 1992; Edwards, Whittington and Hirons 1995; Brayshay and Edwards 1996; Fossitt 1996; Lomax 1997; Mulder 1999).

The present-day vegetation of Barra is typical of the Outer Hebrides. The central upland core of the island has a cover of heath communities together with rare arctic-alpine subcommunities at the summit of Heaval (383 m) (Fig. 8.1; Weaver *et al.* 1996). Acid grasslands are widespread on the better-drained slopes. A number of valleys radiate from the uplands towards the fringing west coast dunes and machair grasslands. The transitional 'blacklands' zone between the peatlands and the machair constitutes the most productive agricultural land (Caird 1979). Natural woodland is virtually absent, but surviving plantation woods at Northbay (Gearey and Gilbertson 1997) demonstrate that Barra is not outside the present limits of tree growth.

Palaeoecological evidence for past woodland on the Outer Hebrides is considerable, although we have little notion, as yet, of the density of the arboreal component in the landscape. The fossil remains of wood buried beneath peat were recorded by early travellers to the islands (e.g. Martin 1994; Lewis

1906, 1907; Beveridge 1911). More recent studies of subfossil wood (Wilkins 1984; Fossitt 1996) clearly demonstrate the presence of *Pinus sylvestris* (pine), *Betula* (birch), *Alnus glutinosa* (alder) and *Salix* (willow) through much of the Holocene (Postglacial). Barra has not been investigated comprehensively, but *in situ* remains of birch were found at Port Caol (Brayshay and Edwards 1996), the Borve Valley (Ashmore *et al.* 1999) and Lochan nam Faoileann (Blackburn 1946). Detailed analyses of Holocene pollen records demonstrate the variable nature of woodland cover on these islands (Birks and Madsen 1979; Bohncke 1988; Bennett *et al.* 1990; Edwards, Whittington and Hirons 1995; Brayshay and Edwards 1996; Fossitt 1996; Ashmore *et al.* 1999; Mulder 1999).

This chapter presents evidence for the Late- and Post-glacial vegetation history of Barra, drawn principally from pollen and spore analysis. It will demonstrate that this small island at the southern tip of the island chain was as diverse vegetationally as the rest of the Outer Hebrides, and that natural processes and human activity have played a part in landscape change.

The Sites and Field Sampling

Four principal sites are referred to in this account (Fig. 8.1):

Port Caol (NGR NF647021)

This intertidal peat deposit is located on the north-facing side of Borve Point. The site fills a rock basin that extends beneath a machair-backed storm beach. A small stump of birch was rooted in the exposed peat. A total of 1.58 m of sediment was recovered.

Borve Valley cairn (NGR NF677016)

A 30 cm section of peat was sampled beneath a small cobble and boulder cairn (~0.6 long and 0.3 m high) on the side of the upper Borve Valley. The peat overlay a degraded mineral soil and the profile included the soil-peat interface.

Borve Valley, Barra (NGR NF677015)

The Borve Valley is exposed and west-facing, the sampling site consists of a 5 m core from a basin peat

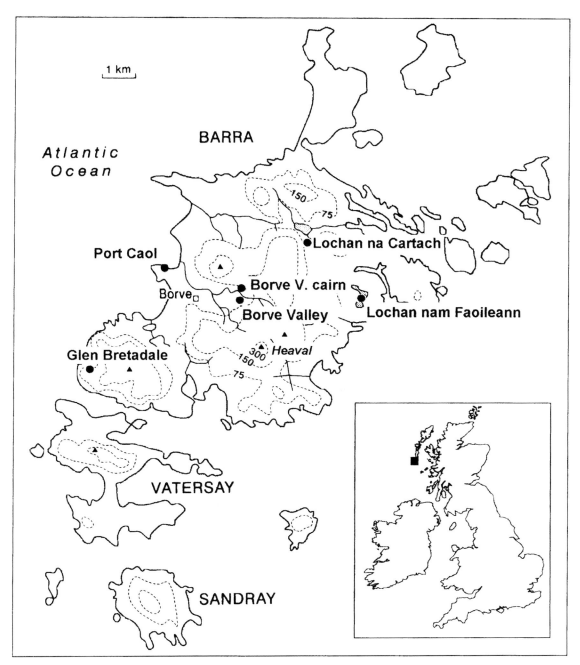

Figure 8.1 The location of pollen sites on Barra (contours in metres).

located at 65 m OD in the upper valley mire (Pratt 1992; Grattan, Gilbertson and Pyatt 1996; Ashmore *et al.* 1999). The Borve Valley is archaeologically rich, with sites dating from the Neolithic onwards (Branigan 1988–97; Branigan and Foster 1995).

Lochan na Cartach, Barra (NGR NF695027)

This small lochan is situated in a sheltered valley (altitude 30 m OD) to the north-east of the hill Grianan. The depth of deposit retrieved from the deepest point of the infilled loch margin was 5.25 m. The nearest visible archaeological feature is the dun in Loch nic Ruaidhe.

Laboratory Methods and Presentation of Results

All samples received standard pretreatments (see Brayshay and Edwards 1996). Microscopic charcoal was recorded as numbers of fragments $>10\,\mu m$ and expressed as % TLP. The computation and construction of pollen diagrams (Figs. 8.2–8.5) were achieved with the computer programs TILIA and TILIA-GRAPH (Grimm 1991). Core lithology and available radiocarbon dates are shown at the side of the pollen diagrams. The radiocarbon sequences from the Borve Valley and Lochan na Cartach cores are anomalous in parts as a consequence of their sediment accumulation

311

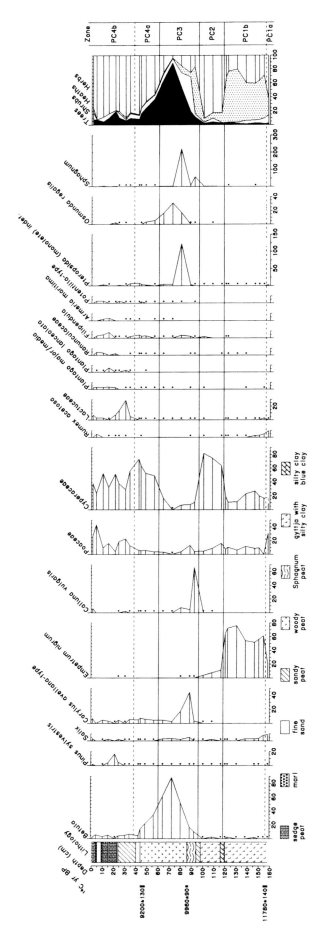

Figure 8.2 Selected pollen and spore diagram from Port Caol.

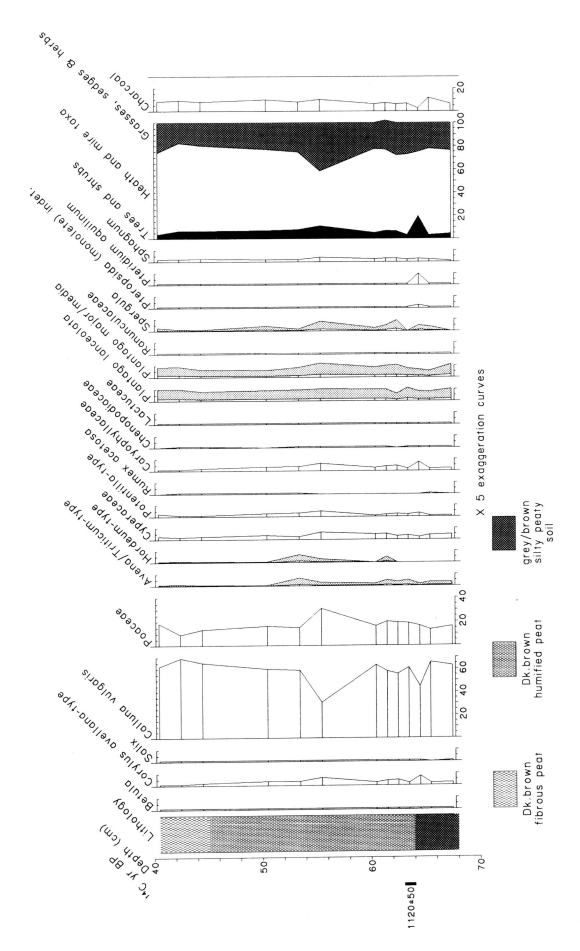

Figure 8.3 Selected pollen and spore diagram from the Borve valley cairn.

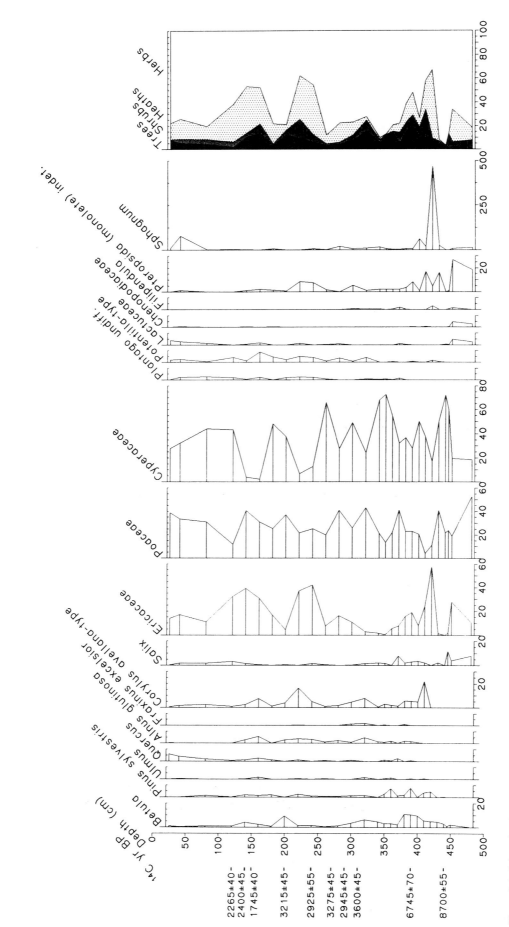

Figure 8.4 Selected pollen and spore diagram from the Borve valley mire.

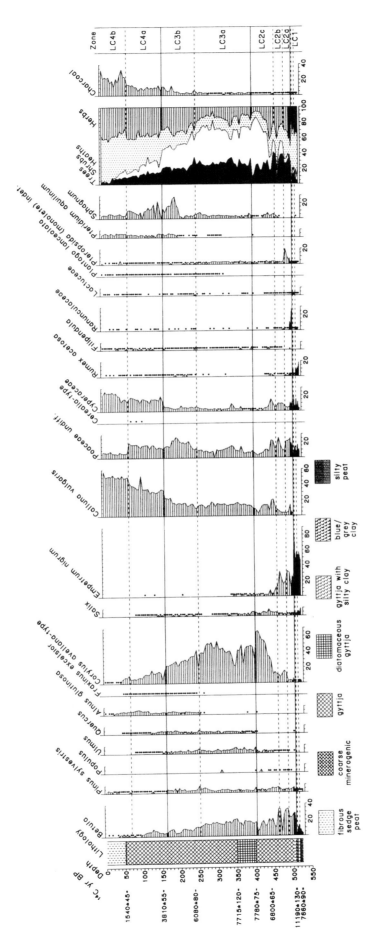

Figure 8.5 Selected pollen and spore diagram from Lochan Na Cartach.

315

histories. This is discussed elsewhere (Brayshay 1992; Ashmore *et al.* 1999). All dates are expressed as uncalibrated radiocarbon years before present (BP). Pollen and plant nomenclature follows Bennett (1994) and Stace (1997) respectively.

The Early Holocene Vegetational Record

The climatic amelioration at the start of the Holocene is clearly signalled in the sedimentary and palynological data from Port Caol and Lochan na Cartach. The onset of organic sedimentation occurred at c. 10,270 BP at Port Caol and c. 10,210 BP at Lochan na Cartach (Brayshay 1992; Brayshay and Edwards 1996). *Empetrum nigrum* (crowberry)-dominated heaths and open grasslands of the Lateglacial were gradually replaced by woodland, tall-herbs, grassland, and *Calluna vulgaris* (heather)-rich heath and blanket bog communities. The high percentage frequencies of birch and hazel pollen in the Port Caol and Lochan na Cartach records for this period (Figs. 8.2 and 8.5) are similar to those of many other sites from the Outer Hebrides and are striking given the present-day absence of trees on the islands. The adjacent Borve Valley appears to have been more sparsely wooded, and here tree and shrub percentage values attained maximum levels of only about 20% TLP, even though fossil wood fragments in the deposits demonstrated the local presence of *Betula*. Tree and shrub pollen values in the Borve Valley diagram are comparable with those found at the exposed west-facing sites of Little Loch Roag, Lewis (Birks and Madsen 1979) and Reineval, South Uist (Edwards, Whittington and Hirons 1995; Brayshay and Edwards 1996). Ashmore *et al.* (1999) have suggested that the arboreal pollen values at the Borve Valley mire may be suppressed by the overrepresentation of local mire taxa, or low pollen productivity for trees and shrubs responding to excessive exposure to powerful and continuous salt-laden westerly winds, rather than a scarcity of woodland. However, comparison with the pollen data from Lochan na Cartach, where the high tree and shrub values were calculated using the same pollen sum (i.e. including mire taxa), indicates that woodland in the Borve Valley was more open and scattered than at Lochan na Cartach. At the latter site, other minor woody taxa present in the early birch-hazel woods included *Populus tremula* (aspen), *Sorbus*-type (cf. *rowan*), *Salix* spp. (willow), *Lonicera periclymenum* (honeysuckle) and *Hedera helix* (ivy). The woodland communities of Barra remained dominated by birch and hazel, despite the arrival of other more slowly-migrating canopy-forming taxa, such as *Ulmus* (elm) and *Quercus* (oak), which arrived at approximately 7,780 BP and 7,730 BP at Lochan na Cartach and at c. 7,723 and 6,745 BP respectively in the upper Borve Valley. Later migrants, particularly *Alnus glutinosa* at

c. 6,330 BP and *Fraxinus excelsior* (ash) at around 6,260 BP also remained minor woodland components. The charcoal and arboreal pollen data from Lochan na Cartach and Port Caol reveal no evidence of the possible Mesolithic burning seen at South Uist sites (Edwards 1996).

Pollen spectra from this period also contain pollen and spores characteristic of heath and mire communities. *Calluna*, *Potentilla*-type (cf. tormentil), *Sphagnum* (bog-moss) and species of Poaceae (grass family) and Cyperaceae (sedge family) were present from the early Holocene.

The site of Port Caol furnishes evidence for the degree of vegetational and environmental variability in Barra in the first millennium of the Holocene. From c. 9,200 BP, increasing quantities of sand were recruited into the sediments as a result of the onshore movement of sands consequent upon rising Postglacial sea levels. Tree pollen values declined dramatically at this time, and the premarine transgression vegetation of fern-rich birch-hazel woodland observed in zone PC3 (Fig. 8.2) was replaced by grassland and mire taxa. The pollen spectra of subzone PC4b include a suite of taxa that are typical of present-day coastal machair and machair loch-edge plant communities (Gimingham 1964; Kent *et al.* 1994), for example, Poaceae, Cyperaceae, *Rumex acetosa* (common sorrel), *Plantago major/media* (cf. greater plantain), *Plantago lanceolata* (ribwort plantain), *Filipendula* (meadowsweet), *Armeria maritima* (thrift) *Potentilla*-type (cf. silverweed), species of Ranunculaceae (buttercup family) and Lactuceae (dandelion family). Unfortunately, the fossil record does not extend beyond an estimated date of 8,345 BP, making it impossible to assess continuity between the ingress of sand at Port Caol and the developed machair dunes and plain so much in evidence in the area today (cf. Ritchie 1979; Whittington and Ritchie 1988; Whittington and Edwards 1997; Gilbertson *et al.* 1999).

The Mid to Late Holocene Vegetational Record

Broad patterns

The early woodland decline at Port Caol is likely to have been a function of environmental influences arising from its coastal location. Elsewhere, the earliest signs of woodland decline in Barra are most evident in the pollen diagram from Lochan na Cartach from c. 6,330 BP, when the previously stable woodland phase (subzone LC3a) gave way to grass (LC3b) and then sedge and heath (LC4a). Birch and hazel are reduced initially and other less abundant trees, such as pine, oak and alder, appear unaffected until the start of subzone LC4a (4140 BP). The gradual increase in *Calluna vulgaris* and microscopic charcoal mirrors the pattern of arboreal reductions and there is also a marked increase in the representation of *Sphagnum* in the upper part of subzone LC3b. A reduced woodland cover possibly resulted in increased run-off into water-receiving sites and a resultant expansion of waterlogged and loch-edge habitats.

In the exposed, upland Borve Valley, woodland was less developed and woodland demise is less easily detectable from the pollen data. The site shows strong evidence for peat erosion and the incorporation of peat of different ages, leading to a nonsequential series of radiocarbon determinations. If any estimated date can be said to attach to the reduction in arboreal pollen seen in the summary diagram from which local mire species have been excluded (Fig. 8.4), then c. 3,400 BP might be suggested. However, the woodland pollen, other than some of the *Betula*, may derive from lowland sources (cf. Edwards and Whittington 1997).

There are no radiocarbon dates from Lochan nam Faoileann. By comparison with Lochan na Cartach, samples from the lower part of Blackburn's site may date from around 6,000 BP. The diagram is dominated by grasses, Ericaceae (heather family) and *Sphagnum*. In fact, the blanket mire and rough pasture dominated landscapes of inland areas of Barra seen at the present day have essentially typified the pollen records of the last few millennia from all sites discussed here and this would also include the coastal records from the undated site of Glen Bretadale on the Tangaval Peninsula (Gilbertson *et al.* 1995).

Environmental and anthropogenic interpretations

The gradual nature of the initial phase of woodland loss between about 6,330 BP and 4,000 BP might be taken to suggest a progressive deterioration in soils and climate such as to hinder tree and shrub regeneration and to favour plant communities tolerant of wetter or more acid conditions. Inferences concerning a general climatic downturn in more marginal areas of north-western Europe at around 4000 BP are certainly to be found (Bennett 1984; Anderson 1998). Although human influence cannot be excluded, there is no strong support for this, and cultural pollen indicators (e.g. expansions in agricultural weeds or the presence of cereal pollen) and charcoal frequencies remained relatively low compared with after c. 4,000 BP. The onset of woodland decline in Barra predates the available archaeological evidence for Neolithic settlement by perhaps 1,000 years or more (Branigan and Foster 1995). This situation runs counter to that apparent in pollen records from other parts of the Outer Hebrides, such as Loch Olabhat, North Uist (Mulder 1999).

Major changes in vegetation are associated temporally with the later Neolithic and the early Bronze Age. Archaeological remains in the Borve Valley confirm settlement during this period (Branigan, pp. 27–33). At Lochan na Cartach the increasing *Calluna* and charcoal frequencies from c. 4,000 BP possibly reflect fire management of heathland aimed at maintaining browse for grazing (Gimingham 1972; Legg, Maltby and Procter 1992; Stevenson and Thompson 1993). The sporadic indications of cereal-type pollen from Lochan na Cartach range from the late Bronze Age (2,790 BP) to the Iron Age (2,110 BP). Similarly, in the upper Borve Valley, increased land use pressure from the mid Bronze Age to the local late Iron Age may have contributed to peat erosion between c. 3,000 and 1,750 BP.

Plant Macrofossil and Pollen Evidence from Archaeological Contexts

Analysis of charcoal and plant macrofossils from Neolithic and Beaker/early Bronze Age archaeological contexts at Alt Chrisal on the Tangaval Peninsula (Foster 1995; Boardman 1995) have contributed some interesting details of human activity not apparent in the pollen records. Excavation at the site revealed a possible farmstead with associated industrial areas. Radiocarbon dates from three samples of birch charcoal ranged from 4,820 ± 60 to 4,470 ± 60 BP. Charcoal and cereal-rich samples contained burnt fragments of *Alnus*, *Betula*, *Corylus*, *Pinus*, *Prunus spinosa*-type (blackthorn) and other species of Pomoideae. Boardman (1995) concluded that the wood was probably local in origin as there was no evidence of the non-native species common in driftwood on the western Atlantic coast (Dickson 1992). Indicators of cultivated fields included *Hordeum vulgare* var. *nudum* (naked six-row barley) and a range of weed taxa, including *Persicaria maculosa* (redshank), *Spergula arvensis* (corn spurrey), and species of Chenopodiaceae (goosefoot family) and Brassicaceae (cabbage family). *Carex* spp. (sedges), Poaceae and Ericaceae were frequent. The overall picture is one of arable fields, damp fields and heathland, all of which may have been exploited for animal grazing and fodder. Wood rather than peat was being used in domestic fires.

The pollen-analytical study of the material sealed beneath the Borve Valley clearance cairn produced soil and peat pollen spectra that allow a glimpse of land use history during the mediaeval period (basal peat overlying the soil produced a date of 1,120 ± 50 BP). The pollen record contains arable and pastoral indicators, including *Avena/Triticum*-type (cf. oats), *Hordeum*-type (barley) and weed taxa, such as Chenopodiaceae, *Spergula*, *Plantago lanceolata*, *Plantago major/mediam.*, *Rumex acetosa* and species of Lactuceae, Caryophyllaceae (pink family) and Ranunculaceae.

Conclusions

The Holocene vegetation record from Barra is limited. Of the four sites discussed at length here and analysed in recent times, only three provide records covering a prolonged period and one of these, Port Caol, only permits an early Postglacial glimpse of what was to become the culturally important coastal zone. The greater part of the Holocene is reliant upon very disparate sites—Lochan na Cartach, located in a sheltered but possibly relatively unimportant part of the island, and the Borve Valley mire, an upland basin site that is distant from major lowland occupation to the west. Sites can only be examined where they exist, and although able to furnish important environmental evidence, including variability of woodland and erosional processes, the long profiles are not optimally located for the discernment of all forms of human activity.

The pollen profiles do, however, reflect the existence of pastoral and arable activity against a back-drop of environmental change that favoured woodland reduction, peat expansion and, at best, mixed agriculture dominated by pastoralism. Fire, if involved in land use management, may only have become a characteristic tool during later Neolithic times. The Bronze Age saw cereal growing in the pollen catchment area of Lochan na Cartach and upland peat instability above the Borve Valley. There was an increased incidence of charcoal dispersal from c. 1,940 BP at Lochan na Cartach, while the later mediaeval period witnessed land clearance of stones and cereal cultivation in part of the Borve Valley.

The charcoal from the excavations at Alt Chrisal—if the material was gathered locally—confirms the palynological evidence for the growth of local woodland elements during the Neolithic. In addition, the plant macrofossils, although restricted to a single site, augment the nonspecific identifications yielded by the pollen analyses.

Acknowledgments

Radiocarbon dating at Lochan na Cartach and Port Caol was carried out at the NERC Radiocarbon Dating Laboratory, East Kilbride under the direction of Dr Douglas Harkness; the Borve profile was dated at the University of Glasgow Radiocarbon Laboratory under the direction of Gordon Cook with funding from Historic Scotland and the encouragement of Patrick Ashmore. All are thanked for their assistance.

9.   The Earlier Prehistory of Barra and Vatersay

Keith Branigan

This and the following chapter attempt to draw together the evidence of the field survey and excavations presented in the earlier chapters of this volume and to present an overview of the prehistory of Barra and Vatersay. Although there is inevitably some reference to prehistoric settlement and sites elsewhere in the Western Isles, a discussion of how the evidence from all the southern isles, from Barra to Berneray, fits into the wider picture of the prehistory of western Scotland is left to the final chapter.

In attempting to produce an overview of the islands' prehistory, we obviously have to rely to a considerable degree on the evidence of field survey. Our excavations have been carefully selected to examine a wide range of site types, and particularly those whose date and purpose is not yet well established. But we have only been able to sample about 3% of the sites recorded in field survey, and with a few notable exceptions most sites have yielded only small amounts of material culture (or none!) to assist in both their dating and their functional interpretation. Of the remaining 97% of sites, some can be ascribed to a period and function without difficulty.

Among prehistoric monuments this would include Neolithic passage graves, Bronze Age kerbed cairns, and thick-walled Iron Age roundhouses. But other monuments are more difficult to ascribe to a period or function. The circular stone and turf hut is notorious for its longevity in the Western Isles, probably stretching over a period in excess of four millennia, while the 'enclosures' formed by circular and oval settings of stones may have fulfilled a variety of functions and date to a variety of periods. In the discussion that follows, we explain why we have attributed certain sites and monuments to a particular period and/or function, but we recognize that most attributions have a degree of uncertainty, and that some are likely to be wrong.

A Mesolithic Colonization?

To date, Barra and Vatersay have yielded no artifactual evidence at all for the occupation of the islands by postglacial hunters, fishers and gatherers who neither farmed nor knew the technology of pottery making; nor have any of the other islands in the Outer Hebrides, despite some efforts in recent years to target likely locations. On Barra we undertook a sampling excavation on the platform outside the cave below Dun Scurrival to test the hypothesis that this would have been an obvious base from which to exploit both

the shell-fish and offshore fishing of Eoligarry during the Mesolithic. But as reported above no evidence for such early use of the cave (or at least, the platform outside it) was recovered. In view of the complete absence of Mesolithic artifacts from the Outer Hebrides, it would be reasonable to conclude that there was no Mesolithic occupation of the islands. Yet all recent researchers who have considered this problem have agreed that a Mesolithic colonization of the Outer Hebrides took place.

Armit (1996: 34), Barber (1985: 21), and Edwards (1996: 36) have all committed themselves to this position, and we are firmly of this opinion too. With Mesolithic occupation of the west coast of Scotland facing the Outer Hebrides well documented, and prolific evidence from the islands of Colonsay and Islay, it has long been difficult to imagine that for three thousand years no one made the short voyage to the Western Isles. Now that the Mesolithic settlement of the islands of Skye and Rhum is confirmed, in the case of Rhum from before 7000 BC, it is really inconceivable that none of the Mesolithic inhabitants of these islands, from which Barra and Uist are clearly visible, crossed the Minches to explore new territories. Edwards (1996) has argued a convincing case that the postglacial pollen and charcoal record now emerging from recent research may reflect human impact in the Mesolithic.

The reasons why no artifactual evidence has yet been forthcoming have been well rehearsed and can be very briefly summarized here. The most suitable area for Mesolithic occupation of the Western Isles was the west coast of the islands, where waters were shallow. But we know that since the end of the Ice Age, the west coast has been gradually sinking. Mesolithic sites that were on the coast when they were in use might now be submerged up to a mile offshore. The development of the machair may equally have covered Mesolithic sites that were set back from the coast. Inland, any sites used for seasonal hunting would now be covered by blanket peat. The prospects for discovering Mesolithic sites are therefore not good, yet we are confident that in due course firm evidence of a Mesolithic occupation of the Western Isles, including Barra and Vatersay, will emerge.

Neolithic Settlement (Figs. 9.1, 9.4)

But for the fortuitous discovery of an extensive area of Neolithic occupation beneath and around the black-house at Alt Chrisal on the north coast of the Sound

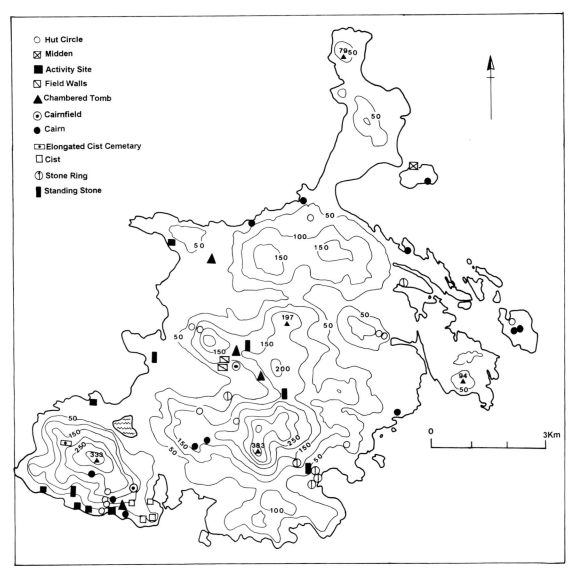

Figure 9.1 Earlier prehistoric sites on Barra.

of Vatersay, we would be hard-pressed to say much about the Neolithic settlement of the two islands. Apart from the cluster of Neolithic and Beaker structures at Alt Chrisal (T15, 18, 19, 25/26) we tentatively identify five other Neolithic or Beaker occupation sites: E4, VN43, BM8 (all middens), T70 (rock shelter), 8 (pits and hearth).

A near-basal deposit at Alt Chrisal produced an uncalibrated C14 date of 4,820 ± 60 BP, and a hearth/firing clamp in the third phase of occupation yielded a determination of 4,700 ± 100 BP (Foster 1995: 81, 88). On the calibrated chronology we can therefore confidently place the appearance of pottery-using Neolithic settlers on Barra at some time before 3500 BC. Carbon-dated external parallels for undecorated bowls, Unstan ware and incised pottery from the site support this conclusion (Gibson 1995: 114–15).

The site at Alt Chrisal was described in detail in the first SEARCH volume (Foster 1995: 64–99),

but its nature and its economy were only briefly discussed (Foster 1995: 97–98; Branigan 1995: 199–201). A more extended discussion is now needed. The first occupants at Alt Chrisal went to the trouble of levelling the hillslope by constructing a rough revetment and infilling behind it with earth and small boulders over an area of 12 × 4 m. On this levelled-up area and the slope behind it, a total area of about 12 × 15 m was occupied and used in the earlier Neolithic, later expanding a further 3 m upslope.

No certain structural traces of habitations were found on the site. The lower part of the area had been levelled for the building and occupation of the overlying blackhouse so that any structures here would have been completely removed. On the upper area, however, gullies, post pits, hearths and stone alignments were found. The earliest such features reveal no obvious patterns at all, but in phase 1b an arc of post pits (features 615, 625, 603, 604, 605, 590,

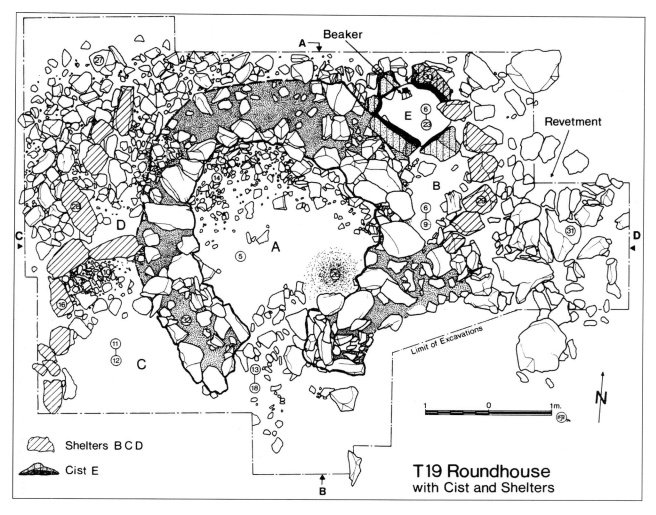

Figure 9.2 The Late Neolithic hut T19, at Alt Chrisal.

586) could be interpreted as the remains of a circular timber-framed hut about 4 m in diameter, with one or two hearths (features 596 and 597) on the south side. Timber was still naturally available, though in declining quantities in the earlier 4th millennium BC on Barra (Gilbertson *et al* 1995: 24–26), so that an initial phase of timber construction is possible. Later phases of the Neolithic occupation reveal no post pits at all, and by phases 3 and 4 circular stone and turf huts stood higher up the slope, overlooking the still-utilized platform area.

From phase 2 onwards there are increasing signs that the platform area was being used for a variety of activities that, while essentially domestic, were not taking place in the living house. The purpose of the neatly built rectangular hearth (feature 535) is uncertain, but in phase 3 it was replaced by a second built hearth that directly overlay it and measured 3 × 1.3 m, which seems unlikely to have been a purely domestic cooking place. Furthermore, by phase 3 there were several clay and turf features around it that were almost certainly small clamps for firing pots. Similarly, the platform reveals evidence for both the manufacture and use of a variety of flint tools at this

time (Wickham-Jones 1995: 124–26) and most of the 45 grinders and hammer stones belong in the later Neolithic phases too. The common occurrence of scrapers (over a hundred from the platform area) suggests perhaps some relatively specialized skin processing activity. Finally the 4 × 3 m area of paving at the east end of the area, with no trace of a structure around it and no domestic occupation material lying on it, is best explained as a specialized activity area of some sort.

To see what domestic huts contemporary with this later Neolithic working area were like, we can turn to site T19 about 150 m north and upslope from the platform area. This hut had stone-faced foundations with an earth core, making a wall up to 1 m wide (Fig. 9.2). It enclosed an area about 3 m in diameter, to which access was gained by a 0.8 m doorway on the south side, looking straight down the valley to the activity site below. A small fireplace was situated just to the right of the door.

From the debris on the floor and from the floor sweepings thrown down the slope outside the door over 250 pieces of flint were recovered and the remains of at least 28 pottery vessels were identified. The flint

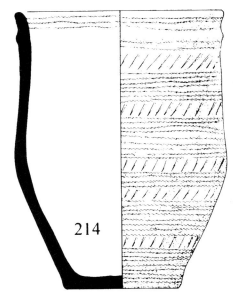

214

Figure 9.3 The beaker found in the cist at the back of hut T19.

material 'resulted from the use and maintenance of tools rather than their manufacture' (Wickham-Jones 1995: 122). Most of the pottery was from undecorated wares, but along with incised and impressed sherds there were beakers too, and most important of all a stylistically early almost complete beaker was found in the cist built on to the back of the hut (Fig. 9.3). We believe the hut was built and in use at the same time as phases 3 and 4 on the platform below.

A second circular hut (T18), only 20 m downslope from T19, yielded no pottery but only 22 pieces of flint. Its date is therefore uncertain, but it seems most likely to be a contemporary of T19 and perhaps to have served as a store for the household, being only about 1.8 m diameter inside. Its wall was built almost entirely of stone. A third even smaller hut (T15) was found across the stream to the west of the platform area, but apart from two pieces of flint in the overlying level no artifact material was found. This hut, with an interior diameter of little more than 1.2 m and a wall mostly of stone, may have fulfilled a similar storage function to that of T18 but its function and date are unclear.

The economic basis of life in the Neolithic settlement at Alt Chrisal is poorly documented. In particular, like so many sites on Barra, Alt Chrisal yielded no preserved faunal material so we can say nothing about the exploitation of sheep and cattle for meat, dairy produce or skins and wool. Nine soil samples from a variety of Neolithic and Beaker deposits all yielded six-row barley, which was clearly the dominant, if not the only, cereal crop. Weeds associated with prehistoric cultivated fields were also found in these samples (Boardman 1995) and there is little doubt that the barley was being grown by the site's occupants. There is limited evidence for the

gathering of hazelnuts, brambles and strawberry to vary and supplement the diet. We assume that marine food sources, which even today remain relatively abundant, must have provided an important element in the diet, but in the absence of faunal material this is impossible to demonstrate. We believe that some of the pumice collected and utilized by the inhabitants was used for net floats, however (Branigan, Newton and Dugmore 1995: 145, Fig. 4.49), and we wonder if the many scrapers found on the platform area were made and used for cleaning the skins of seals rather than those of sheep or cattle.

We have discussed the evidence from Alt Chrisal at some length because it is not just the only excavated evidence for a Neolithic occupation site on Barra and Vatersay but because it is one of the few such sites in the Western Isles. There were no doubt other similar sites on the two islands, and the two small huts situated just above a stream and 200 m from the shore at A127 strongly recall the location and character of huts T15, 18 and 19 at Alt Chrisal, but we can only point to one other occupation site with confidence. This is the midden on the offshore island of Biruaslam (BM8), which fortunately yielded the rim of a decorated bowl along with a handful of other sherds and flints. Other sites we believe to belong in the Neolithic include another midden to the north of Biruaslam in Traigh Varlish (VN43) from which came a small 'thumb-nail' scraper, and a third, with collapsing stone structures associated with it, on the island of Orosay at the north end of Barra (E4). This is potentially an important site, as the midden and structures form a mound over 30 m across, but the only indication of its date at present are five small sherds that, on the basis of their fabric, are thought to be Beaker. Finally we might note the rock shelter at T70, in which a windbreak had been constructed. Seven pieces of flint and a single sherd of probably Neolithic pottery were recovered and the site was interpreted as a temporary shelter used in the Neolithic by occasional hunter/fishers exploiting the resources in the Sound of Vatersay. At present, the only certain or probable Neolithic occupation sites known to us on the two islands are all on the edge of the sea, but whether that reflects the 'visibility' created by coastal erosion (three of the above sites have been exposed in this way) or whether there was a strong preference amongst Neolithic settlers for sites from which marine resources could be easily exploited is uncertain.

Neolithic Burials (Figs. 9.1, 9.4)

The meagre settlement evidence for the earlier Neolithic is supplemented by three circular chambered cairns of passage grave type, and three other megalithic structures we believe to be Neolithic burial monuments. These sites are B1, B3, VN157, T55, G93 and BM5.

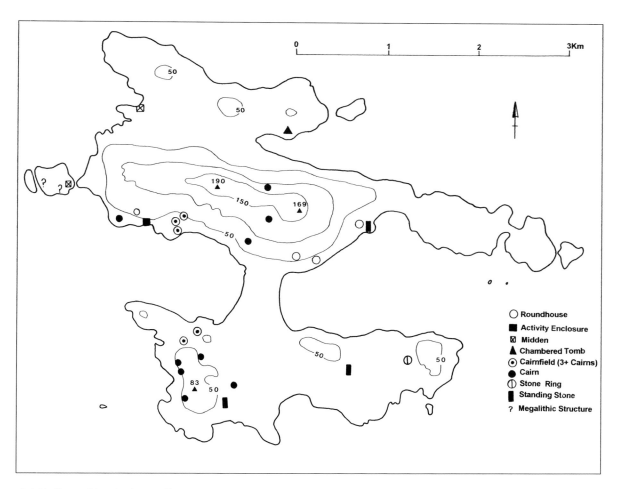

Figure 9.4 Earlier prehistoric sites on Vatersay.

Two of the chambered cairns are within 800 m of each other on the north side of the Borve Valley. Dun Bharpa (B1) is extremely well preserved and is a prominent landmark on the skyline from much of the valley. An incomplete ring of 15 standing mono-liths, many between 2 m and 3 m high, runs around the circumference of the cairn. Cairn material presently extends 1.5–4 m beyond the standing stones, but whether this is entirely collapsed cairn material or whether the stones were always set within rather than beyond the edge of the cairn is uncertain. Our impression is that the stones may have been deliberately set within the cairn material. Although it is likely that stones have been removed from the ring of monoliths, so we cannot be sure how many there were originally, a run of 4 on the south-east arc of the cairn appear to be in their original positions and show considerable variations in spacing (between 0.5 m and 3 m). This might support our conjecture that the stones were not all put in place at the time of the cairns' construction—in which case we might expect regular spacing of a known number of stones—but that they were added to the monument at various times in its history. If that were the case, might they each represent an ancestor buried in the tomb, not

necessarily every ancestor, but more likely a person of status, such as the head of family?

Balnacraig (B3) was identified by Henshall (1972: 498) as a long cairn, but we are convinced that it was a passage grave in a circular cairn, a view shared by the RCAHMS (1928: 135, No. 458). It was almost certainly somewhat smaller than Dun Bharpa in diameter, and although the site's long history of reuse and remodelling means that little apart from some of the megaliths in the chamber are still even broadly *in situ*, there is nothing to suggest that this tomb was similarly surrounded by a ring of standing stones. We must assume that the two tombs were at least partly coeval, and, given the prominent location of Dun Bharpa, its size and its impressive ring of stones, it is difficult to avoid the conclusion that it was not only the more significant of the two tombs but that it must have been a monument of sociopolitical importance for the entire island. We might expect the social group who were buried here to occupy land in the valley over which the tomb held such visual dominance, but at present we have no evidence for Neolithic settlement in the Borve valley.

The third passage grave (VN157), in Cornaig Bay on north Vatersay, somehow escaped attention until

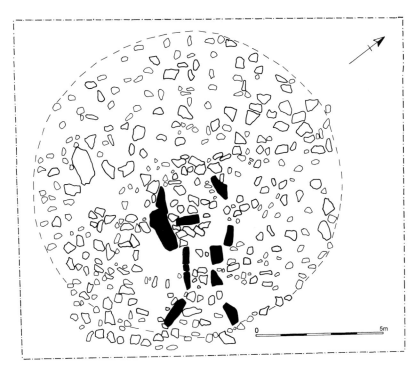

Figure 9.5 Measured plan of the passage grave at VN157, Ben Orosay, Vatersay.

found by Patrick Foster in 1989 (Fig. 9.5). Although the cairn has mostly been removed, it is still visible, and both the chamber and the passage are still marked out by the standing monoliths that formed their walls. It is a considerably smaller monument than either Dun Bharpa or Balnacraig, unless the cairn originally spread much further than its now denuded remains suggest, and its location is very different to the two tombs in the Borve valley. Whereas they are perched high on the hill-slopes, over 2 km from the sea, VN157 is only 20 m OD and 100 m from the water. The settlement it served is presumably somewhere nearby, although the nearest known probable Neolithic occupation site is VN43 1.5 km to the west at Traigh Varlish. Much nearer is the site of VN32 by the head of Cornaig Bay, about 700 m from the passage grave. This is a low mound with very heavily embedded stone foundations apparently belonging to an oval hut about 6 × 4.5 m. A small flint blade and three handmade sherds, one with traces of impressed decoration, were recovered from the site. We have ascribed this site to the Iron Age on the basis of the pottery fabric and the shape and size of the hut compared to excavated Neolithic huts (T19, 18) and an Iron Age one (B54), but it could be Neolithic, or indeed Bronze Age.

The creators of the midden with the decorated bowl on Biruaslam (BM8) might also have had their own megalithic tomb, at site BM5, which, although perhaps modified for use as a shelter in more recent times, has the suggestion of a megalithic ancestry, incorporating five upright stones, the largest of which was over

1 m high. There is, however, no suggestion of a cairn or a passage to the putative burial chamber, and there is of course no dating evidence for the structure.

We assume on the basis of the admittedly sparse finds from excavated Hebridean passage graves that the tombs on Barra and Vatersay were erected in the late 4th or earlier 3rd millennium, and may have seen their last burials in the later 3rd millennium to judge from Beaker sherds found in a few tombs. They would thus have been broadly contemporary with the site at Alt Chrisal, but at present there is no reason to associate either the Borve valley or Cornaig Bay tombs with the inhabitants of Alt Chrisal.

Only 500 m east of Alt Chrisal there is one monument that might be the burial place of the some of the last occupants of the settlement, and that is the structure excavated at T55 (Branigan 1995: 163–55). As it survived this featured an oblong 'chamber' 3.5 m × 1.25 m constructed of small megaliths to about 1 m in height. Around the chamber were the remains of a narrow U-shaped cairn 5 m long and 4 m wide, with a low kerb. Nothing whatever was found in the peaty infill of the chamber, so that the purpose and date of the structure are uncertain. We believe it is a small chambered tomb, however, related to either the heeled-cairns of Shetland or the Irish 'wedge-shaped' tombs. The latter at least seem to belong at the end of the Neolithic.

We realize the interpretation of this monument is speculative and even controversial, but since it was proposed another megalithic tomb has been discovered on Barra that provides some support for the proposal that the island's funerary monuments were open to influence from the Northern Isles. Site G93 at Grean is badly damaged but enough survives to reveal its basic form. It is a D-shaped cairn with stones set on edge along its flat side and traces of a small rectangular stone setting behind the centre of this 'facade'. There is little doubt that it is a heeled-cairn similar to those found almost exclusively in Shetland; the identification was supported by the then inspector for the area, Dr N. Fojut, who saw the site within a day of its discovery. The dating of cairns of this sort is still not well documented, partly because excavated examples prove to contain little or no artifact material (like T55), but they were still in use in the later Neolithic. There are no known or suspected Neolithic occupation sites in the valley, which runs down through Grean to the sea, but it is an area of light soils and machair and the D-shaped cairn sits on a local eminence that overlooks the lower valley without in any sense dominating it. There can be little doubt that it was built and used by a group of people who exploited this favoured landscape.

Neolithic Ritual (Figs. 9.1, 9.4)

If tombs were to some extent territorial markers as well as cemeteries for the dead, then there were probably other contemporary monuments in the 3rd millennium that also served to commemorate the dead and/or lay claim to landscapes. The recognition of standing stones is often open to doubt, even when the stones are still standing, unless they are particularly impressive specimens or they are associated with other ritual monuments. Once a standing stone has fallen, it is difficult to be sure (without excavation) whether it ever stood. A further problem on Barra is that there are very few natural stones that provide the required form—long, reasonably regular shape, and relatively thin. Nevertheless, the standing stones built into Dun Bharpa certainly provide a vivid demonstration that the idea of selecting long stones to be stood upright as part of a ritual monument was adopted in Barra during the Neolithic. We have identified up to ten possible standing stones on Barra and Vatersay, of which only three are still standing: S19(2), B4(2), B31, B39, T145, VS32, VS64, VN140.

The most confident identification is the stone at Brevig (S19), 2.8 m high, which is accompanied by a second fallen stone that in 1915 was recorded as being 3.2 m long (RCHAMS 136, No. 460), though it has since been broken into smaller pieces. The pair of stones recorded on Borve headland (B4), though less impressive at 2.9 m and 1.7 m long, provide a matching pair on the west side of the island, again with the larger stone now fallen and broken up (RCHAMS 136, No. 461). The third standing example is that on south Vatersay (VS32), which is 1.8 m high and 0.65 m wide, also recorded by RCHAMS (136, No. 462).

It actually forms one side of the entrance to a small enclosure that is almost certainly of relatively recent date. Whether the enclosure was constructed around the standing stone, or the stone was moved here to use in the enclosure is not clear, but the location is certainly not a dominant one.

Of the fallen stones, the most convincing are those overlooking the Borve valley. The stone at B31 on the watershed between Borve and Cuier is only 100 m from Dun Bharpa, and with a height of 3 m might be a robbed stone from the ring around the cairn. But it is notably narrower than those stones and on balance we believe it was probably not robbed from the tomb. A second stone lies almost at the head of the Pass of the Mouth (B39), from where, if it was standing, it would command almost the whole valley. This is the tallest stone we have seen on Barra, 5.8 m long, and its shape may have been artificially enhanced by 'pecking' to produce a rounded tip. Given the position of these two stones, one on the northern and one of the eastern limit of the Borve valley, we looked hard for a third stone on the western watershed on Beinn na Moine, but none was found.

On the western slope overlooking the Goirtein valley, a regularly shaped monolith 2.4 m long and 1.5 m wide was found with traces of a setting of smaller stones just downslope from it (T145). Large regularly shaped monoliths are scarce on Barra and Vatersay and so we record this as a possible standing stone. The same criteria are applied to two stones on Vatersay. That on south Vatersay (VS64) is 2.15 m long and 1.1 m wide and very regularly shaped. It lies in the gap between the northern and southern stretches of a broad bank that runs across southern Vatersay just east of Ben Cuier. The bank is clearly a major land division but completely undated. Finding this stone lying between the two stretches of this boundary strengthens its claim to be a territorial marker, but whether it goes with the bank, or the bank follows an earlier boundary on which this stone stood, is unknown. A second fallen stone, close to the water's edge on north Vatersay (VN140) is much smaller, 1.7 m long and 0.55 m wide, but its regularity again draws attention to it. Of all the stones discussed, however, this seems the least likely to have a prehistoric pedigree, if only because it is the smallest and the only stone found so close to the sea.

Just as the standing stones in Dun Bharpa confirm the erection of monoliths in Neolithic Barra, so it might be argued their circular arrangement provides an example if not a prototype of the stone circle. The Old Statistical Account (MacQueen 1794) appears to confirm the existence of stone circles on the island: '[H]ere also are several Druidical temples, none of them remarkable for extent or structure'. It is difficult to believe, particularly in an 18th-century source, that 'druidical temples' refers to anything other than stone circles. Having said that, apart from the stones incorporated into Dun Bharpa, our survey has revealed no monument that we would like to dignify with the term 'stone circle'. Instead we have eight sites that, with varying degrees of confidence, we identify as 'stone rings'. These are circular or oval spaced settings of moderately large stones (0.5–1.5 m tall), usually set upright. The rings vary from 6 m to 23 m diam., and the estimated number of original stones from 8 to 25. The eight sites are: B55, A121, S28, S20, S25, S26, K16, VS58.

Site B55 in the Borve valley is situated on a knoll that projects into the centre of the valley at the point where the ground begins to rise quite steeply from the low pastures and arable. It is almost directly due south of Dun Bharpa and the two monuments are clearly intervisible. The stones are set in a ring 17 × 13 m and, of eight stones believed to be more or less *in situ*, the largest is 1.2 m tall. We estimate that

four further stones may be moved, and excavation (p. 191) revealed what appear to be the settings of two such stones. On the north an arc forms a 'cove'.

Site A121 is situated on a plateau overlooking the waters of Bagh Hirivagh. Ten stones survive marking out a ring about 23 m in diameter. The largest stone is 1.3 m long. There are two nearby stones that may have been part of the monument originally, and it is estimated that the ring originally consisted of 12–14 stones.

Site S28 is on a small low plateau flanked by two streams at Brevig. The monument has been very much altered and robbed but the remains of an original ring about 14 m in diameter is indicated by 6 stones *in situ* and 8 slightly displaced. Another 15 stones all over 0.8 m (and 5 over 1m) long were found incorporated into a series of small cairns immediately around the ring, so that we believe the original ring may have had

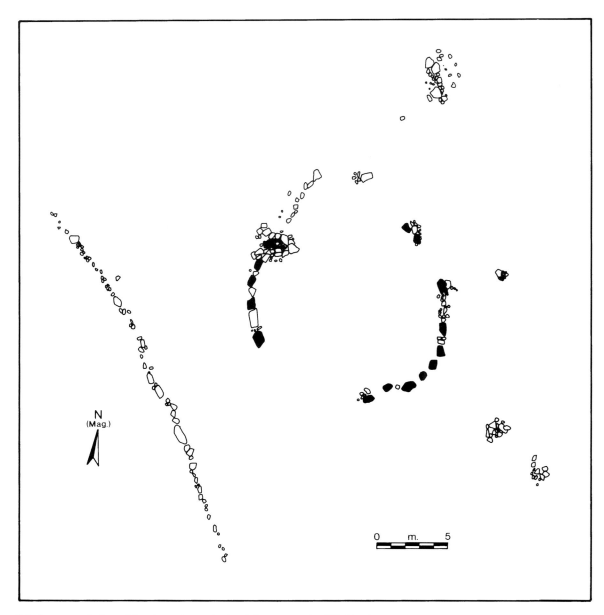

Figure 9.6 A measured plan of the stone ring and related features at site S28, Brevig.

about 30 stones. This site is overlooked by the 2 standing stones (S19).

These three are the most convincing of our 'stone rings' and we feel reasonably confident in ascribing them to a Neolithic ritual function. They are nicely spread to act as foci for the north, east and west of the island but whether they really were contemporary ceremonial places for a localized group of communities we cannot say.

The remaining sites are less impressive monuments, but they are all potentially of interest. It may be significant that no less than three of them are found at Brevig (Fig. 9.6), so that within 300 m of the standing stones we have four potential stone rings. Site S20 stands on a low rise around which a stream runs to the east. It has a diameter of about 11 m, 6 stones *in situ*, 3 displaced, and a further 3 shifted into a heap nearby, but the largest is only 0.75 m long. Situated at 120 m OD it is the highest of our rings, and is 300 m upslope from the standing stones. S25 and 26 are close to one another and on low ground about 150 m from the sea. The smaller is S26, only about 10 m in diameter, with 9 of an estimated 12 stones *in situ*, the largest of which is only 0.7 m tall. Site 25 is the only one of our rings that is a real oval, 21 m × 1 m, with 11 stones *in situ* and possibly as many removed. The largest stone is again only 0.7 m long. None of these sites is impressive, even by the standards of the other Barra stone rings, but each is very well-embedded and difficult to explain in terms of any of our more recent monument types. The possibility that at Brevig there is a concentration of early ritual monuments is obviously an intrig.uing one that deserves further attention in the future.

The remaining sites are the smallest of the group, and only tentative identifications. Site K16 survives as only one-third of an oval about 6.5 m × 5 m with five stones *in situ*; a boundary of seven spaced 'megaliths' (K15) runs past about 30 m upslope. On south Vatersay VS58 stands on a levelled area near the foot of Am Meall, looking out over Eorisdale. It is probably only 6 m in diameter, with five stones in place, a sixth moved, and an estimated two missing. Two stones are a little over 1 m tall.

Bronze Age Settlement (Figs. 9.1, 9.4)

With the exception of two sites that are in use at the very end of the Bronze Age, it must be said at once that we have no certain, or even probable Bronze Age occupation sites yet identified on Barra and Vatersay. Hebridean Bronze Age pottery, particularly when it is weathered sherds from surface collections, is still difficult to recognize, but in any case the vast majority of sites found in survey yield no surface finds at all. The significance of a barbed flint arrowhead of EBA type found together with half a dozen other pieces of flint during the excavation of a blackhouse by Loch Obe (site L8) may be revealed during further excavations on the blackhouse settlement.

The sites that we tentatively identify as possible Bronze Age houses are all circular or almost circular, between 4 m and 5 m overall diameter, with stone and turf walls 0.6–0.8 m wide where measurable, and all are very heavily embedded. They are therefore slightly smaller and slightly less well-walled than the Beaker hut excavated at T19. They are smaller than excavated examples of Iron Age huts, which have thicker walls (usually upwards of 1 m wide) and a few are slightly oval with a maximum dimension of 4–5 m. Thin-walled oval huts in the range 5–6 m long are also found on Barra and are presently undated by excavated examples, but they generally seem much less embedded than the small circular huts described here and we believe they are either later Iron Age or mediaeval. In essence then, our tentative identification of Bronze Age houses rests upon a combination of their degree of embedding, which in every case suggests they are prehistoric rather than mediaeval or later, and their difference in form and size to Iron Age huts, and their similarity to the Beaker hut at T19. We recognize this is not compelling evidence, and that some sites may be later in date, and some earlier. Equally, there are other similar sites that on balance we have decided not to include in our tentative list that might prove to be Bronze Age on excavation. Although it played no part in our deliberations, it may be noted that several of the sites identified as possible Bronze Age houses are found in areas where there are also cairns, more certainly of Bronze Age date, to be found. This might be thought slightly to strengthen our case.

The sites that we identify as possible Bronze Age huts are tabulated in Table 9.1.

There is no uniformity or pattern in their location. The three sites on Vatersay are all on low-lying land near the sea, in contrast to the two Borve valley huts at around 150 m and 190 m OD, and that on Tangaval at about 220 m OD. The remaining huts are situated between 50 m and 100 m OD at varying distances from the sea. All are near the course of streams or burns, but on a wet island like Barra that is to be expected. If these huts are indeed broadly contemporary with each other—that is, Bronze Age—then the variety of their locations would suggest that the Bronze Age inhabitants of Barra and Vatersay had a variety of subsistence strategies. The Tangaval and Borve sites seem best located for sheep pastures, but Brevig, Benn Mhartainn and Ben Vaslain sit on the edge of sheep pasture, overlooking land suitable for small-scale crop production. The Vatersay huts are so close to the sea that a marine contribution to their diet seems highly likely. There is the possibility in the Borve valley that we have glimpsed Bronze Age field walls suggestive of arable farming on the lower slopes of Benn Mhartainn at about 80 m OD. Sites B11 and

Table 9.1 Possible Bronze Age huts on Barra and Vatersay.

Area	Site Code	Ext. Diam.	Door to	Nearest Cairn
Ben Vaslain	G21	4.3 × 3.7 m	N	300 m NW
Fuiay	AF6	4 m	E	300 m SW (2)
Beinn Mhartainn	C45	4 m	SW	1 km SE (3)
Beinn Mhartainn	C46	4 m	E?	1 km SE (3)
Borve Valley	B47	4 m	?	1.3 km N (3)
Borve Valley	B65	4 m	E	1.4 km N (3)
Brevig	S39	4 m	?	none
Garrygall	S55	5 × 4 m	SW	none
Tangaval	T212	3.5 m	SW	100 m E (3)
Tresivick	VN113	3.6 m	?	200 m SW
Heishival Beag	VN120	5 × 4 m	E?	500 m NW
Heishival Beag	VN122	5 m	?	350 m NW
Heishival Beag	VN141	4 m	?	1 km W

B12, exposed in modern drain cutting revealed what appeared to be two wall foundations about 1 m wide and about 50 m apart, buried beneath the peat. There was no trace of occupation material associated with these structures, so they seem more likely to be field walls than house walls, sealed as they are by the peat blanket they are probably pre-Iron Age.

Only at the very end of the Bronze Age do we have occupation sites to which we can put a date. The site B54 in the Borve valley is discussed in detail in the following chapter, since the best-preserved phase of occupation is Early Iron Age, but as described above (p. 000) the first phase of occupation on site is associated with Late Bronze Age pottery with flat-topped rims. Although a lined drain, a well-cobbled surface, and a well-worn path of stone slabs belong in this LBA phase, no traces of a contemporary house were noted. Nevertheless a LBA occupation of the lower slopes of the Borve valley seems clear.

Broadly contemporary with B54, but dated by C14 rather than pottery, site T169 on the Tangaval peninsula is of a different sort altogether. A roughly arranged ring of boulders 7.5 m × 6 m, within which there are traces of a turf or peat windbreak and a hearth, looks altogether more ephemeral and impermanent than the rammed-in cobbles and well-trodden path of B54 (Branigan 1995a: 170–76). Furthermore, at T169 not a single scrap of pottery was found; only 360 pieces of flint. However, a C14 determination for an early phase of use of the site produces a calibrated date of 793–522 BC (Branigan 1995a: 174). Situated almost on the high-water mark, with a specialized material culture (only flint debris and two stone pounders) we identified this structure as an 'activity site', that is, a temporary enclosure with a windbreak, which was used for nondomestic activities, most probably associated with marine resources. Another enclosure marked out by a ring of stones was found in a very similar situation, just above the high-water mark, on the north coast of the island (E11). This ring is larger, 14 × 12 m, and the stones are set closer together, with two tall stones set 0.5 m apart on the west side apparently flanking a narrow entrance. Rescue excavation of the northern half of the enclosure is described above (p. 231) and the interpretation offered is that the enclosure had a turf wall for which the stone ring acted as a basal revetment. Again, no pottery was found, but equally there was only a handful of pieces of quartz from the excavated area. However, these included primary and secondary flakes and presumably indicate prehistoric use of the enclosure. We tentatively identify this site as a second 'activity site' associated with exploitation of marine resources. Two other similar enclosures in similar situations on the edge of the sea might be worth future investigation, at Grean (G1) and west of Tresivick on Vatersay (VN107). It is possible that we have identified a 'site type' in these small coastal enclosures but their date and function may vary widely.

Bronze Age Funerary Monuments: Cists (Figs. 9.1, 9.4)

Some of the most intriguing structures found on Barra are the elongated cists found only on a single ridge above Bretadale, in the remote south-west corner of the island (sites T180, 181, 182, 183, 185, 187, 231, 232). These have previously been discussed at length (Branigan 1994: 6–12; 1995: 176–83) so we shall summarize their principal features and our interpretation of their use. The enlarged cists consist of oblong enclosures marked out by stones set on edge, closed at one end by usually the largest stones in the structure, and open at the other end (Fig. 9.7). The four apparently complete structures measure between 7.1 × 1.2 m and 9.2 × 2.8 m; the widths of the four partly destroyed cists suggest that they would have been in the range 8–9 m in length. There is no evidence of their ever having been covered by a cairn or barrow. Excavation of one example (T180) showed that it had been constructed on bare rock, and that peat had accumulated inside it at some time after, presumably when it was no longer in use and

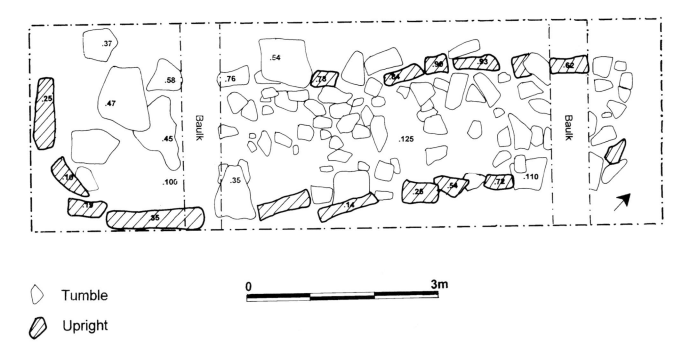

◇ Tumble

⬭ Upright

0   3m

Figure 9.7 The elongated cist at T180 after excavation.

abandoned. No material of any kind was found in the cist, and, although the absence of bone is to be expected in this soil, the complete absence of any pottery and lithic material is best explained by assuming it was never there in the first place.

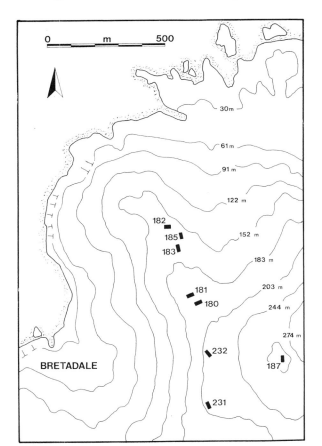

Figure 9.8 The location of the elongated cists on a ridge overlooking Bretadale.

Two C14 determinations were obtained for the early formation of peat within the structure after it had gone out of use, and the calibrated results were 1938–1776 BC and 1608–1462 BC, suggesting perhaps that the cist had been abandoned sometime in or before the 18th–16th centuries BC. Taking into account the bleak location of these structures, their design, and the absence of any artifactual material within them, we came to the conclusion that these enlarged cists are best interpreted as mortuary enclosures in which the dead were exposed. After defleshing the bones were removed for cremation or burial elsewhere.

We do not know whether all eight cists were entirely or partly contemporary, or were successive. If they were successive then they could have served a single social group, be it a nuclear family, an extended family or a small community. On the other hand as contemporary monuments they could have served seven or eight nuclear families. However, the elongated cists found only on the ridge overlooking Bretadale (Fig. 9.8) are unparalleled amongst the 975 other sites and monuments found on Barra and there remains the possibility that they served the entire island community in the early 2nd millennium BC (Branigan 1994).

On the Tangaval peninsula the obvious repositories for bones removed from the enlarged cists are the small rectangular cists represented by five examples, all found in the south-east corner of the peninsula (T34, 66, 85, 89, 221). An early 2nd millennium BC date (i.e. contemporaries of T180 enlarged cist) would not be out of line for small cists of this kind, but only one example (T66) has been excavated, and this proved completely empty. A possible formal link between the two groups of monuments is therefore entirely speculative. An alternative relationship for the small cists would be with the final Beaker phase of occupation at Alt Chrisal, perhaps replacing the small chambered tomb at T55 as the settlement's cemetery.

Bronze Age Cairns (Figs 9.1, 9.4)

Immediately above Alt Chrisal there is another monument that can plausibly be interpreted as the burial place of the Beaker phase inhabitants. This is the cairn (T214) for which we used the term 'paved cairn', situated at 150 m OD overlooking the Beaker huts and the activity platform (Branigan 1995: 185). It was a roughly built monument with a crude 'kerb' of irregular stone blocks, and a spread of further stone blocks and small slabs laid flat across the inside of the enclosed area. In the south-east quadrant there was a cist 1.5 × 0.6 m with a paved floor; two flat slabs 2 m away may well have been its cover slabs. Nothing was found in the cist, or indeed elsewhere in the monument but for a small flint chunk. We assume the monument is part of the Bronze Age cairn tradition, and one peculiarity of the structure suggests it might not be far removed from Neolithic burial practice. On the south-east side, the circular perimeter of the cairn flattened and there was a suggestion of an inturned entrance 'passage' 0.5 m wide. Immediately before this was a fallen monolith a metre long that appears to have stood in the entrance to this passage. That is, the cairn, on its south-eastern side, took on some of the features of a Neolithic passage grave.

A second possible example of a similar monument (G35) was found on another elevated position on a cliff-top north-east of Cleat. This circular structure had certainly been modified in the recent past, but its original structure included a kerb 4.3 m in diameter with a 0.75 m wide entrance on the south side, flanked by two upright monoliths about 0.8 m high. Immediately inside these a third, recumbent, stone of similar height but slimmer appears to be a fallen blocking or standing stone. There is a good deal of stone inside the ring, but due to later interference we cannot be sure if this monument was originally 'paved' like T214. If this is a burial cairn, then it too appears to reflect some aspects of the Neolithic megalithic funerary tradition.

The remaining cairns on Barra and Vatersay are all circular structures without any visible megalithic attributes (but for one example revealed by excavation and discussed further below). Altogether we have identified a further 54 sites as burial cairns, and we divide these into two groups, kerbed and bordered. The kerbed cairns have well-constructed kerbs of regular stone blocks and in many cases a distinctive profile, with a flat berm inside the kerb and a central raised cairn. The bordered cairns appear to be much less carefully built, with a ring of irregular stones used to retain the base of a cairn that rises immediately inside the perimeter. They also tend to be less regular in shape, and we include in our group at least three cairns that are clearly intentionally oval rather than circular. Where cairns have been partly robbed or where they are overgrown, attribution to one group or the other is not easy, but we classify our 54 sites as follows:

Bordered cairns: E3, E21, T62, T129, T234, T235, B7, G14, VN57, VN69, VN76, VN117, VS13, VS15, VS34

Kerbed cairns: EF1, EF2, A77, AF15, AF16, L35, K51, K72, B2, B6, VN80, VN81, VN82, VN83, VN84A, VN84B, VN87, VN88, VN89, VN90, VN93, VN85A-I, VS4A-D, VS6, VS7, VS16, VS29, VS34.

The bordered cairns are found scattered widely on Barra, though with a clear bias to the west side of the island. On Vatersay they occur only on Heishival Mhor (4) and Ben Rulibreck (3). None have been found on the east side of the island. They are mostly found as isolated structures except for a pair above Crubisdale (T234 and 235) and a pair on Ben Rulibreck (VS13 and 15). In size the bordered cairns range from 2.5 m to 8 m in diameter, but with an average of 4.7 m they are mostly relatively unimpressive monuments. None of the bordered cairns have been excavated, and how they relate chronologically to the kerbed cairns is unknown. They could be identified as primitive prototypes, contemporary poor relations, or late degenerate imitations of kerbed cairns. What can be said with some confidence is that they do represent significantly lower energy expenditure in their construction, and significantly lower social significance in their location.

The kerbed cairns are, on the whole, larger than the bordered cairns, with an average diameter of 6.2 m, although the range—2.8–8.8 m—is similar to that of the bordered cairns. The kerbstones appear to have been selected and placed with care, the shape of the cairns is usually close to a true circle and the cairn material has been carefully placed to produce the distinctive profile—kerb, berm, cairn. From the excavated examples at VS4B and VS7 we also know that the kerbed cairns represent complex and carefully structured monuments (pp. 192–216). Overall, the kerbed cairns form a more uniform group of monuments than the bordered cairns.

Their structural uniformity is mirrored by their communality. It is rare to find a kerbed cairn in isolation. On the island of Fuday, off the north coast of Barra, a pair of impressive cairns is hidden in the tall grass that now covers this island. On Fuiay, off the coast at Bruernish, two kerbed cairns (AF15, 16) sit within 20 m of each other on the highest point on the island. On Barra kerbed cairns occur in pairs at K51 and K72, and B2 and B6. It is tempting to see the latter, 250 m downslope from the passage grave at Dun Bharpa, as representing the continuity of a burial tradition on this south-facing slope overlooking the Borve valley. However, there is probably a substantial chronological gap between the last use of Dun Bharpa and the construction of the kerbed cairns. Furthermore, none of the other megalithic tombs on Barra or Vatersay have kerbed or bordered cairns located nearby.

On south Vatersay a cemetery of 4, possibly 5, cairns are tightly grouped on the headland below Dun Vatersay, and a pair (or possibly a trio) are 300 m to the south on the next headland. The most dramatic grouping, however, is found in the valley west of Tresivick, on the south coast of north Vatersay (Fig. 9.9). In an area only 250 m square, at least 18, and possibly 19 kerbed cairns are found. They form subclusters within this larger group, with 2 close to the shore (VN80, 81), 4 just below the rock face that forms the east side of the valley (VN82, 83, 84A and B), and 3 or 4 (VN87, 88, 89 and possibly 90) on a shelf at the north-east corner of the valley. Finally, on a low hillock, near the stream that bisects the valley are no less than 9 kerbed cairns (VN85), the largest almost 9 m in diameter and the smallest just 2.8 m (Fig. 9.10). Although there are other, probably Iron

Age monuments, on the western side of this valley, the concentration of all the kerbed cairns east of the stream that bisects the valley must surely reflect a conscious decision to create a cemetery area here in the Bronze Age. In view of the evidence from the excavated cairns at VS4B and VS7 that each cairn contained only a single cremated burial, it is tempting to see this cemetery as a family necropolis representing either several generations, if all adults were provided with their own cairn, or the burial place of the head of the family perhaps representing a considerably longer time span. In that case we might also wonder whether our interpretation of the settlement mounds in the western half of the valley is wrong, and they are actually the living houses of the family that used the cemetery.

On balance, however, we think this interpretation is less likely than another. First, we should note that the 18 or 19 cairns in this cemetery are the only kerbed cairns found on north Vatersay. This raises the possibility that the cemetery was the burial ground for the population of the entire northern half of the island. This interpretation is perhaps supported by the clustering of the cairns into four distinct groups, suggesting perhaps the burial places of at least four families rather than one. Finally, the suggested juxtaposition of family cemetery and settlement is not supported by the other kerbed cairn clusters. The

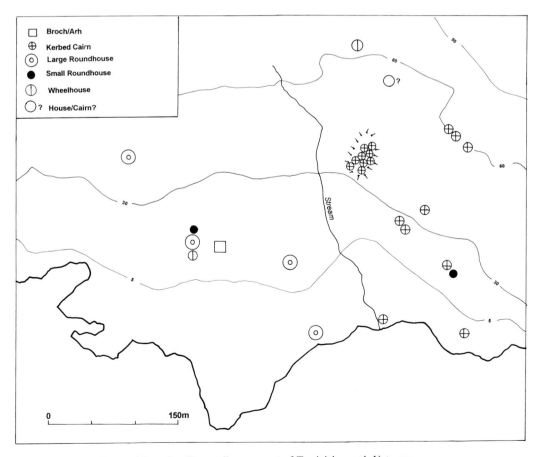

Figure 9.9 Bronze Age kerbed cairns and Iron Age(?) roundhouses west of Tresivick, north Vatersay.

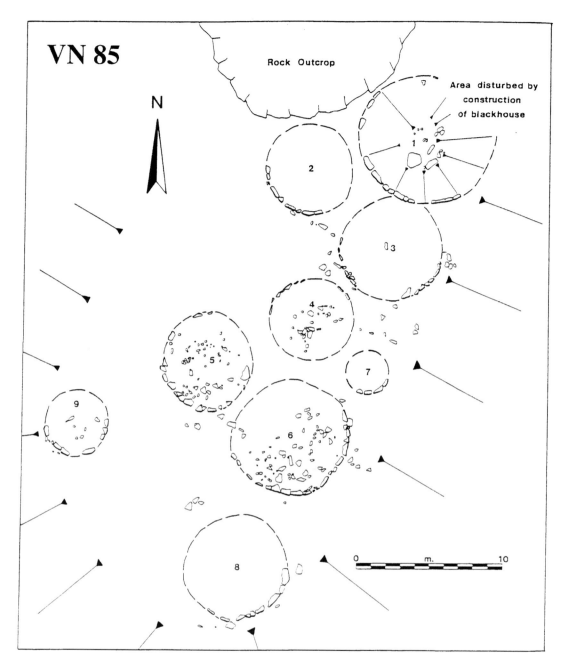

Figure 9.10 Measured plan of the kerbed cairn cemetery at VN85.

two clusters on south Vatersay are both on exposed headlands on which we have found no trace of settlement (at any time), and the pair on Fuiay are in the most exposed position possible, totally unsuited for, and with no evidence of, a contemporary settlement close by.

If the kerbed cairn cemeteries served a group of families or settlements, then unless they were the products of a very short-lived fashion, they must surely represent the burial of selected individuals rather than the entire population or even the entire adult population. Whether these would be the head of family or persons selected by reason of some other status or role we can only speculate. It might be

argued that the dearth of grave goods in the two excavated cairns is hardly indicative of people of wealth or high status. But even setting aside the long-standing debate about the extent to which poverty in death reflects poverty in life, this would be a simplistic judgment. Throughout the prehistory of the Western Isles there is little sign of wealth as expressed by material goods of metal, clay or stone. Relative wealth was more probably expressed in terms of the size of one's herd or flock, the amount of land that one controlled and exploited, or perhaps one's general level of food surplus above subsistence level. As for status, that was almost certainly determined principally in terms of kin-relationships. None of these things need find any material expression in grave-goods, though we might note that VS4B yielded some indications of a link with arable farming.

The chronology of the kerbed cairns is still uncertain. The OSL dates from VS4B and VS7 have large error margins, although they both confirm a Bronze Age date. The later of the two dates is for VS4B, from the cairn material of which was recovered the bronze terminal of a LBA cloak-fastener. This provides a *terminus ante quem* for the construction of the cairn, but it is impossible to estimate the gap that occurred between cairn construction and the loss of the bronze fastener. Carbon-dated kerb cairns and cremations further north in the Western Isles fall in the early to mid 2nd millennium BC and this sort of date is not out of line with the limited evidence from our two cairns on Vatersay.

One final observation must be made about the kerbed cairns. We have discovered a total of 39 such cairns, of which 20 are on north Vatersay, 9 on south Vatersay, 2 on each of the offshore islands of Fuday and Fuiay and just 6 possible examples on Barra (A77, L35, K51, K72, B2, T62). On Vatersay kerbed cairns make up 60% of all earlier prehistoric sites identified, on Barra the 6 possible examples represent just 10% of earlier prehistoric monuments. This is, by any standards, a very skewed distribution. Even allowing for the possible misidentification of one or two heavily overgrown Barra cairns as bordered, we have no reason to doubt that the figures broadly represent the Bronze Age reality. Kerbed cairns really were numerous on Vatersay and scarce on Barra. At present we can suggest no plausible explanation for this phenomenon.

10. The Later Prehistory of Barra and Vatersay

Keith Branigan

Later prehistory in the Western Isles extends from the beginning of the Iron Age to the beginnings of Norse settlement, broadly from the 5th century BC to the 9th century AD. In southern Britain the greater part of this period, from the 1st century AD, would be involved with the complex interaction first between the Roman conquerors and the native population, and then between the Britons and the Saxons. But Romans and Saxons do not impinge on the history of human settlement in the Western Isles, save for a handful of Roman trinkets and scraps of pottery. Iron Age traditions of architecture and material culture continue and evolve throughout this period, and even the emergence of the Pictish kingdom(s) in the middle of the 1st millennium AD has little visible impact in the Outer Hebrides.

In attempting to provide an overview of developments on Barra and Vatersay in this period we are just as dependent on field survey data as we were in discussing earlier prehistory. Again we have the problem of identifying potential Iron Age sites from surface indications alone, although the big thick-walled stone houses usually called brochs can be identified and placed in this period with confidence. Circular and oval hut sites, as we noted in the previous chapter, are far more difficult to ascribe to even broad chronological periods. This is particularly true in the Outer Hebrides, where, in addition to the long currency of their usage, very few of them have been subjected to any sort of agricultural disturbance that might bring characteristic pottery to the surface. Even where cultural material is exposed (usually by rabbits), it cannot always be dated with any degree of certainty and even less frequently with any measure of accuracy. This makes it difficult to ascribe sites with certainty to the Iron Age and to place them in the early, middle or later Iron Age even more hazardous.

There is, however, a fabric that has been found on excavated sites like B54, T166, E16 and L8, where it is unquestionably part of an IA assemblage, and in disturbed deposits by site survey at IA sites, such as Dun Caolis (VN150), Dun Vatersay (VS1), Dun Clieff (G9) and Dun na Cille (B5). This fabric is gritty in a sandy brownish-red matrix and comes from relatively thin-walled vessels. It is a variant within fabric A as described in the excavation of sites B54 and E16 (pp. 221, 226). It appears to be undecorated. It is unlike anything from the Neolithic deposits at Alt Chrisal, and is significantly thinner and grittier than Bronze Age pottery from the Vatersay cairns and from sites excavated by the SEARCH team on South Uist. While we cannot be sure that the fabric is not still in use in the mediaeval period, it is not found in mediaeval assemblages from sites B88 and L15. We believe this fabric is essentially an Iron Age fabric. It appears in context 8 at B54, which is probably LBA/EIA transitional, but its appearance at several broch and ARH sites suggests it continued into at least the middle, and quite possibly the late, Iron Age too. The appearance of this fabric at a small number of circular house or hut sites is one of the reasons why we have suggested they are probably of Iron Age date.

In the discussion which follows we explain why we have ascribed sites to a particular period, based on comparative evidence from excavated sites on Barra and Vatersay, and on supporting evidence from excavations elsewhere in the Western Isles, as well as the very limited artifactual evidence. Again we must remind the reader that most attributions are uncertain, and that some are probably wrong. In general, however, we are more confident of our attributions of houses and huts to the Iron Age than to the Bronze Age.

Thick-Walled Round and Oval Houses (Figs. 10.1, 10.3)

We include in this group houses with diameters estimated between 8 m and 12 m and with walls 1–1.5 m wide. Estimated internal areas are between 30 m^2 and 65 m^2. Of the 32 examples identified 16 are oval, the remainder circular. Although there is usually a quantity of stone blocks in the material that makes up the mound on most of these sites, and the perimeter foundation can sometimes be clearly seen, these house sites are not associated with prominent mounds of collapsed masonry. We believe their walls had stone foundations but may have been completed in turf. The sites we place in this category are as follows: A78, L16, K9, K36, K136, T118, T160, T164, T166, T233, B89, C4, C5, C26, C32, C43, G22, G39, G63, G74, G92, VN51, VN68 (B, F), VN93, VN94, VN99, VN104, VN112, VN119, VN121. In addition the partial remains of a house about 12 m diam. with a wall about 0.8 m wide was found under the wheelhouse at T17 (p. 150) and A93 may well be a similar structure, although its exact size is uncertain.

Site T166 had a sampling trench excavated through it (Branigan 1995: 168–70) and yielded two dozen small pieces of handmade pottery and four flints. The pottery includes the reddish-brown fabric described above, and one rim of Roman Iron Age date.

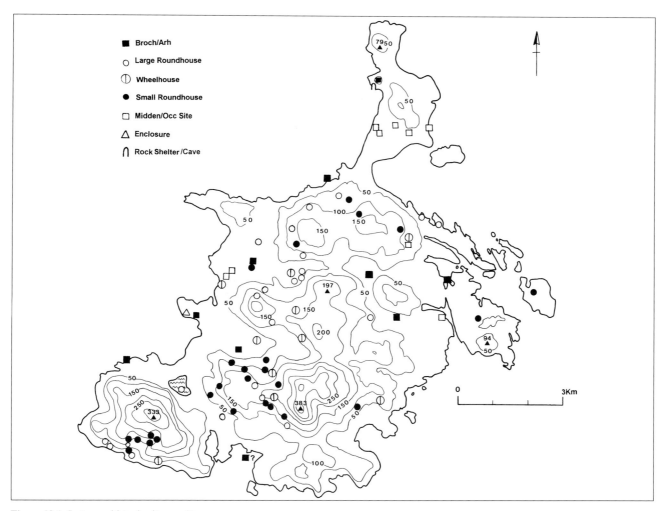

Figure 10.1 Later prehistoric sites on Barra.

Two sherds of the same gritty red-brown fabric and a flint flake were recovered from rabbit disturbance at the house at C5, which also had an associated shell midden.

On the Scottish mainland houses of this size are often ascribed to a Bronze Age date, and of course it is possible that some of the houses we have in this group are pre-Iron Age. However, there are now sufficient early Iron Age houses of similar type from other parts of western and northern Scotland (Skye, Sutherland, Orkney) to give us some confidence in taking the admittedly limited evidence of the pottery from T166 and C5 at face value and ascribing our examples of the type to an early or middle Iron Age date. The discovery of the remains of a large circular stone-founded structure beneath the wheelhouse (T17) at Alt Chrisal (p. 150) provides further and firmer evidence for an earlier Iron Age dating for these large houses.

The location of the houses in this category is somewhat varied and somewhat surprising (Fig. 10.1). There are several close to the sea, mostly close to small but usable areas of potential arable and cattle grazing as well as marine food sources. But half of the houses are over 50 m OD, and seven are above the 100 m contour. Some, like K36, G39, G62, C43 and VN51,

are in exposed locations with little visible subsistence resource but for rough sheep pasture. These locations are surprising if we are right in ascribing them to the early Iron Age, and if orthodox opinion is correct in believing that the environment had become colder and wetter and blanket peat was spreading across the hillslopes by this time. In these conditions one might expect a retreat from the higher ground, and the location of these houses might be thought to argue for a Bronze Age date for them. It is of course possible that houses of this type and size were built and used from the later Bronze Age through into the Iron Age, and there is certainly no reason to suppose that all the houses of this type were contemporaneous. Given that the only roundhouse sites to produce pottery in our 'Iron Age' fabric are both on low ground, it is even possible to postulate that roundhouses on the high ground were built in the later Bronze Age and, as environmental decline took hold, were abandoned and new houses built on lower, less exposed areas. On this hypothesis one could see K36 abandoned for K9, G63 for G92, G89, C43 and C26 for C4, C5, and C32, T160 for T164 or T166, and VN51 for VN94.

An alternative view might challenge the proposition that there was significant environmental decline in the Late Bronze Age. The most recent review of the evidence (Whittington and Edwards 1997) has both questioned the assumptions that have been made in previous interpretations of the vegetational record, and also summarized the results of new research that do not support the recognition of a wet and cold early 1st millennium BC. Indeed isotope analysis by Dubois and Ferguson (1985) has suggested that wet episodes occurred around 5200–4700 BC, 2900–2300 BC, and AD 700–the 1st millennium BC has so far revealed no such episodes.

The environmental debate will no doubt continue for years to come but there is certainly no reason to allow the hypothesis of environmental decline in the 1st millennium BC to constrain our interpretation of the settlement pattern in the earlier Iron Age. While we may reasonably assume that not all of the larger roundhouses were contemporaneous, we cannot assume that those on high ground were abandoned and replaced by those on the coasts and in the valleys. Alternative interpretations would include the possibility that upland and lowland houses played their part in a seasonal movement of people and animals, so that the suggested pairings of upland and lowland houses mentioned above could be seen as the product of a subsistence strategy rather than environmental change. Another scenario would see the upland houses as the permanent home of upland pastoralists, and those on the lowlands as the focus of more mixed economies involving crops and marine resources as well as livestock. In considering any of these alternatives, the chronological and spatial relationship of the large roundhouses to other domestic buildings has to be taken into account.

The Smaller Roundhouses (Figs. 10.1, 10.3)

It has to be said at once that the distinction between these structures and those discussed in the preceding section is drawn entirely on the basis of size. Overall diameters range from 5 m to 7 m, walls are 0.75–1.5 m thick, and estimated internal areas range from 8 m² to 25 m². Our decision to draw the line between 7 m and 8 m diameters, and 25 m² and 30 m² estimated internal space, is not entirely arbitrary. As can be seen in Figure 10.2, there does seem to be a clear division of the roundhouses into two groups. We also note a more clearly marked tendency to the oval house among the smaller structures. This is reflected not so much in the prevalence of oval houses (25 of the 33 smaller houses are oval) as in the degree of ovalness, as indicated by the excess of length over width. Whereas only 2 of the 16 oval large houses have lengths that exceed their width by more than 50%, and an average excess of length over width of 26%, 9 of the 23 oval small houses have an excess of over 50% and the average excess is 40%. Whether there is

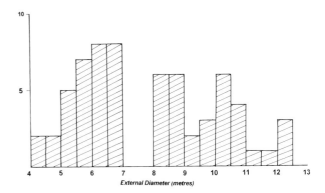

Figure 10.2 Histogram showing the external diameters of round-houses on Barra and Vatersay.

any social or chronological significance in this preference for an oval form is at present a matter for speculation. The sites that we identify as falling into the small roundhouse group are: A102, A110, AF7, S32, K24, K31, K33, K126, K134, K142, T123, T132, T134, T139, T158, B43, B54, B62, B64, B70, B72, G26, G58, VN24, VN32, VN56, VN57, VN68 (G, H), VN101, VN123, VS19, VS41.

All of these sites are very heavily embedded and are of considerable antiquity, but the principal evidence for placing them in the Iron Age comes from the excavated example at B54. This site revealed three stratified phases of prehistoric activity, beginning in the transitional LBA/IA and ending with the construction of a roundhouse with an external size of 6.5 × 5.75 m, and walls 1.25 m wide. Although this had been extensively damaged by later lazy-bedding, we think it likely that the stone foundations never stood more than four or five courses (1–1.5 m?) high, and that the superstructure was completed in turf. This structure was associated with pottery of early Iron Age type, as well as a small lithic assemblage.

In size, shape and restricted quantity of stone material, this hut is similar to the unexcavated examples in our list. Although we recognize that not all huts can be assumed to be broadly contemporary (i.e. Iron Age) on this basis, taking into account the degree of embedding of the sites listed, we think it likely that most of these houses are of Iron Age date. The only other site to have yielded material (from site survey) is VN32, which produced two sherds of our 'Iron Age' fabric and a flint blade.

Despite its damaged condition, the site at B54 does provide some limited insights into both the development of a farmstead site of this type, and the main features of the house itself. Beneath the house were found two successive phases of occupation, the first associated with a cobbled area and a well-worn path of stone slabs, and the second marked by the construction of a slab-lined drain across the path and the burning of a peat stack. Unimpressive as these remains were, they seem to attest to an occupation and domestic use of the site for some time preceding the erection of the roundhouse. There may well have been an earlier house associated with one or both of these phases close by on the same hillock.

The roundhouse itself provided about 15 m² of internal space. The location of its door is uncertain, although it was not on the west/north-west or on the north-east. Against the western arc of wall the remains of a hearth survived, and immediately south of it an insubstantial but clear and apparently nonrandom alignment of small stones suggested the position of some sort of internal partition. The house was big enough for no more than a nuclear family, and we cannot be certain that it was occupied throughout the year rather than seasonally. The presence of five further examples of the type less than 800 m upslope to the south might perhaps suggest a grouping of seasonal houses situated to exploit the higher pastures, although B54 is at a lower altitude than any of the others.

Certainly, many of these smaller houses are found at relatively high altitude. Seven (20%) are at over 150 m OD, and 50% are found above the 100 m contour. There is no point in repeating the discussion above concerning the relationship between the altitude of these houses and the contemporary environment and what this might mean in terms of their chronology and/or function. Being less substantial constructions than the large roundhouses, however, they may be more open to interpretation as seasonal homes for summer pastures.

Wheelhouses (Figs. 10.1, 10.3)

We here use the term wheelhouse to include circular houses with radial piers, whether the piers are free-standing or joined to the circuit wall. Without excavation it is impossible to distinguish between the two. Further, as the excavation at T17 confirmed, a house may be built with free-standing piers that are later extended to meet the circuit wall.

The wheelhouse excavated by Alison Young (1952) at Tigh Talamhanta, Allasdale (C2) was one of the few well-known prehistoric monuments on Barra prior to SEARCH. It attracted some attention by reason both of its adjacent outbuildings and its rarity as a free-standing wheelhouse. The vast majority of the wheelhouses in the Western Isles were essentially subterranean, sunk into pits in the sand dunes, their walls a single skin of stone set against the side of the pit. By definition such structures are distributed close to the west coast, on the machair. The Allasdale wheelhouse, however, was built above the 100 m contour and over 2 km from the coast (even as the crow flies). A second free-standing wheelhouse is now known on Barra, at Alt Chrisal (T17), the excavation report of which appears earlier in this volume. Although this house is only 70 m above the high-water mark it is built on a steep and rocky hillside so that its location

left no opportunity at all for a subterranean structure.

Barra and Vatersay have much less machair than the islands to the north, and although there may well be wheelhouses to be found here in the machair, it is equally likely that Allasdale and Alt Chrisal may represent something nearer the norm for Barra and Vatersay. These two wheelhouses, after excavation, proved to be 11 m and 9 m respectively in overall diameter. But before excavation they represented substantially larger mounds. Allasdale was reported by the RCHAMS (136, No. 459) to be about 20 m in diameter and 3 m high, and was sufficiently full of stone to be identified as a cairn covering a megalithic burial chamber. Alt Chrisal was measured by Armit at 16.5 m (1992: 163, A.B14) and again formed a cairn of stone rather than a grass-covered mound.

We believe there are a number of sites that we have identified in field survey that present a similar appearance to both Allasdale and Alt Chrisal before excavation and are likely to be free-standing wheelhouses rather than large roundhouses. The sites we put into this category range in visible diameter from 12 m to 25 m, and all are prominent mounds 2 m or more in height with large quantities of building stone (Fig. 10.3). The only exception to the latter criterion is site VN100, mostly grassed over; this could be a large roundhouse, but it stands out as a larger, more prominent mound in a group that seems to consist of other roundhouses. All of the sites we list here are identified on the basis of these surface indications. The only artifactual evidence to support a probably Iron Age date for these sites are five sherds in our 'Iron Age' fabric from VN29. The sites we suggest are wheelhouses are A93, S41, K34, T17, B3, B44, B130, C2, C9, C60, VN29, VN62, VN91, VN 100, VN118.

We have seen no traces of wheelhouse-like structures in the machair, although we think it highly likely that such houses exist, particularly in Eoligarry and on south Vatersay. The site of E4 was first identified as a probable subterranean wheelhouse but was later tentatively reclassified as a Beaker settlement on the evidence of the fabric of five small sherds found in the midden. Although the site is a grass-covered mound, the eroding edge reveals large amounts of stone from a built structure or structures, and identification of the site as a wheelhouse can still not be discounted. More sherd material is needed but its very scarcity in a thick and eroding midden is somewhat surprising if the site is Iron Age. Possible machair wheelhouse sites are recorded in the NMR on Borve headland (NF65190167) and in the dunes just north of Borve (NF65630285). In each case a short arc of walling with possible traces of a radial pier were seen. Despite intensive survey we have yet to see any traces of such structures, but the dune systems shift constantly, and we have no doubt that stone structures were seen here. Records of Iron Age pottery and other material in the dunes just north of Borve (C52) very close to the

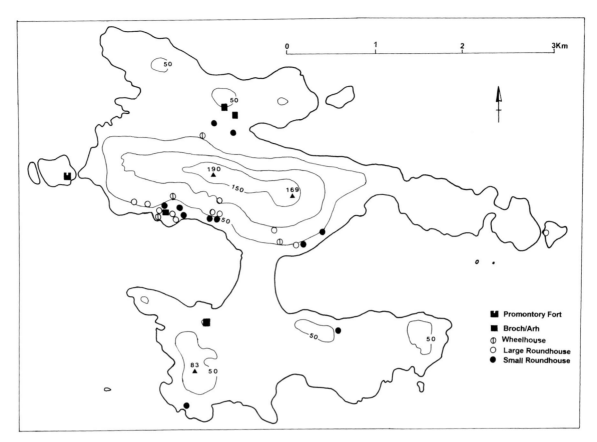

Figure 10.3 Later prehistoric sites on Vatersay.

reported stone structure lend support to its proposed identification as a wheelhouse, and we therefore include site C60 in our list of wheelhouse sites.

If we are right in our identifications of sites K34, B3 and B44 then we have wheelhouses at 200 m, 100 m and 160 m OD, and the excavated wheelhouse at Allasdale stands at 120 m OD. Since no one suggests that wheelhouses were built as seasonal homes to be occupied only when summer pastures were in use, these houses perhaps support the interpretation of the large roundhouses found on high rough grazing as permanent settlement sites. Other wheelhouses, such as B130 and C9, appear to be located to exploit mainly the lower inland pastures and arable plots of the Borve and Grean valleys, while T17, C60 and VN101 are all within 70 m of the sea with limited arable or quality pasture nearby. As far as we can tell from their topographic locations, the wheelhouses of Barra and Vatersay were supported by a variety of subsistence strategies. Sadly, the soil conditions at both Allasdale and Alt Chrisal robbed us of any insights into animal husbandry and meat consumption, and neither produced much evidence for grain production or processing.

The dominant features of both the two excavated wheelhouses, and indeed of most excavated wheelhouses elsewhere in the Western Isles are the huge central hearths and the piers that divide the perimeter space into separate cells. The size of the central

hearths is such that they must be seen as a social focus as well as a cooking place. At Alt Chrisal, given the size of the fire and the heat it must have generated, it is difficult to see how the occupants could have sat anywhere but in the cells between the piers. It is still not clear whether different cells were for different functions or were allocated to a specific person or persons. The highly formalized plan of the wheelhouses, however, certainly suggests a structured use of the internal space and a society in which social relationships were important and controlled.

The social and spatial relationships with other Iron Age households is something we shall need to return to below. As for the chronological position of the wheelhouses, neither Allasdale nor Alt Chrisal offer much reliable evidence. Three beads from Allasdale might suggest occupation either side of the start of the Christian era, which would not be out of line with orthodox dating for wheelhouses in general. But some recent C14 dates suggest that Hebridean wheelhouses may appear two or three centuries earlier (Armit 1996: 145–47) so it is possible that the wheelhouses and roundhouses may have been at least partial contemporaries.

Brochs, Duns and Forts (Figs. 10.1, 10.3)

There has been endless debate about the differences between, and the classification of, brochs, galleried duns, and island duns. Armit (1991) attempted to solve the problem by using the term Atlantic round-house to include all of these monuments. But just as there remain a distinctive group of structures within the ARH classification that can be called 'broch towers' or 'true brochs', so there are other monuments often labelled as 'duns' that do not easily fit into the notion of the 'roundhouse'. Here we discuss a group of 15 monuments found on Barra and Vatersay of which we confidently identify 6 as broch towers or true brochs. For some of the others we have too little infor-mation to allow detailed classification. Some appear to be monumental circular or oval structures but probably broch towers, and one is a promontory fort. The sites included in this discussion are:

Broch towers: A38, L32, B5, C59, T226, VN150
Other ARHs: E15, L33, B136, G9, VS1
Promontory forts: BM7
Other possible ARHs: K4, VN25, VN98

The six sites we identify as broch towers include the excavated site of Dun Cueir (C59), the reasonably well-known sites of Dun Ban (T226) and Dun Caolis (VN150), and the less well-known monuments in North Bay (A38), on Loch nic Ruiadhe (L32) and on Borve headland (B5). The unexcavated sites, with the exception of B5, survive sufficiently well to allow their inner and outer wall structures and intramural gallery to be seen and their overall size to be established. Dun Cueir, with external dimensions of 22.5 × 21 m, is the largest, followed by the North Bay broch at 19.8 ×

17.1 m. Dun Ban has a diameter of 18 m, Dun Caolis is 16 × 14 m and Dun Loch nic Ruiadhe is 15 × 14 m. The remaining site, B5, is mostly covered by the modern cemetery on Borve headland, so that only part of its outer wall face survives. This is very well built, with a distinct batter, still stands 1.7 m high, and has a narrow door low at the visible base of the wall on the east side (Fig. 10.4). Inside the cemetery, the mound formed by the collapsed masonry is prominent and suggests a total surviving height of between 4 m and 5 m. We have no hesitation in identifying this as the remains of a broch tower.

The interior diameters of these monuments are of course much smaller than their overall size due to the double wall and gallery basal structure. Dun Ban and the North Bay broch have interiors about 10 m in diameter, and Dun Caolis (Fig. 10.5) and Dun Cuier are about 9 m across inside. The interiors are thus rather more standardized in size than the exteriors, and they are no larger in size than the living areas of the largest of the roundhouses. On the other hand, they possessed galleries and chambers in the walls that added to the total space available to the occupants. In three cases we have also detected traces of an apparently contemporary extramural enclosed space. At B5 the enclosure is marked by a low bank that runs from close to the east side of the broch in an arc southwards and then swings westwards and returns to disappear under the modern cemetery wall about 15 m beyond the broch. At both Dun Caolis and North Bay the enclosed area is much smaller and can only be reached from the broch itself. In each case a

Figure 10.4 The door in the base of the broch wall on Borve headland (B5).

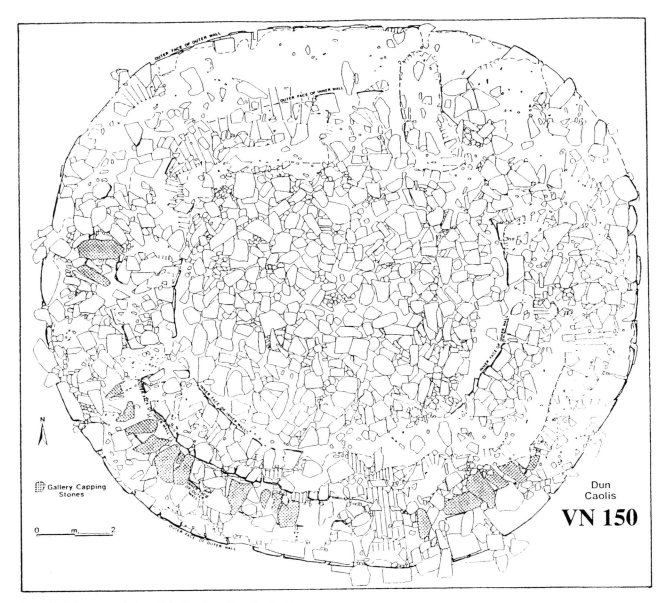

Figure 10.5 A measured plan of the broch at Dun Caolis, Vatersay.

flat semicircular yard area occupies the space between the broch and a natural rock face that protects the approach to the broch from that direction.

The topographic location of these six broch towers could scarcely be more varied. Dun Cueir (C59) stands on a hill, only 40 m OD but steep-sided and rocky, overlooking the machair of the Grean valley to the north, the sheltered valley of Allasdale to the south and machair and dunes of Seal Bay to the west. Dun Ban (T226) is at 10 m OD on a small exposed headland surrounded by sea on three sides, and overlooked by the northern slopes of Ben Tangaval. Dun na Kille (B5) is on the machair of Borve headland at 5 m OD and is flanked on the east side by a steep-sided inlet that forms a very protected harbourage with a small beach, although the approach to it is difficult. Beyond the machair of the headland to the east, the broch has a view right up the Borve valley. North Bay

(A38) is on a rocky islet in a sea loch and is approached by a substantial built causeway, while Dun Loch nic Ruiadhe is in a freshwater loch. Dun Caolis (VN150) stands at 40 m OD on a low rocky hill overlooking the Sound of Vatersay to the north and Cornaig Bay, which would provide a sheltered harbourage to the east. When the tower stood to its full height, Traigh Varlish and the machair around it were probably visible from the top of the broch.

Only Dun Cueir and North Bay stand in a reasonably defensive location, the one defended by the steep slopes of its hill, the other by the tidal waters around it. One could argue that Dun Cuier's location is as much dominant as defensive, with its command of machair and pasture to north and south, and shellfish, seal and fish resources to the west. Equally, one can interpret Dun na Kille as dominating not only the headland on which it stands but the whole of the

340

valley behind it, and the shell-fish and sea birds of the headland. Dun Caolis similarly dominates the pasture and arable of Ben Orosay and the machair to the west, but also the passage through the Sound of Vatersay with its fish resources. In contrast Dun Ban seems to dominate nothing; it is surrounded by steep, rocky, poor-quality land and has no immediate safe access to the sea. If one was looking for a broch in this area, one would naturally look a kilometre to the east overlooking Halaman Bay. North Bay too can scarcely be said to be in a dominant position. It has only poor-quality land in its immediate vicinity, and if it were located to dominate the waters of North Bay, one would expect it to be built either on the Bruernish headland or one of the islets just off its rocky shore. Instead the North Bay broch is tucked away in a small side channel, as if it were seeking to avoid attention.

Some of the structures that we classify as 'other ARHs' may well have been broch towers but for various reasons we are not yet convinced that this was the case. The most obvious candidates, partly due to their locations, are Dun Scurrival (E15) and Dun Vatersay (VS1). Dun Scurrival stands at 60 m OD on a steep-sided hill overlooking both Traigh Eias (to the south) and the machair of Eoligarry to the north and east (Fig. 10.6). The site has a mass of collapsed masonry and there is no doubt that a massive structure stood here. The problem is to define its shape, and in doing so to decide whether it could have been constructed as a 'true broch'. The RCHAMS (132, No. 449) describe it as pear-shaped, roughly 16 × 12 m. Armit (1992: 161) gives dimensions of 17 × 13 m but notes an external wall that 'may be contemporary' and a possible 'secondary extension'. Our first survey

team recorded the structure as 'roughly triangular' 21 × 14 m. An EDM survey subsequently recorded a structure somewhere between oval and oblong, with overall dimensions of 24 × 16 m (Fig. 2.4). What these varying descriptions tell us is that this site, on the surface, is little more than a huge mass of stone building blocks with tantalizing glimpses of possible wall faces. There are certainly secondary (probably much later) structures built into it to complicate the picture. We agree with RCAHMS that traces of a gallery and inner and outer walls are visible at one point. The structure seems to fall within Armit's ARH definition, but because of the considerable uncertainty about its shape we are not convinced it is a true broch. We have reservations about Dun Vatersay for exactly the opposite reasons. Virtually nothing survives on top of the steep-sided 50 m OD hill-top on which it stands. The position is certainly dominant, overlooking both the east and west beaches, the machair to the east and the headland to the west. Remains of the structure itself include some large stone blocks up to 1 m in length and enough can be seen to suggest a building about 13 × 10.3 m overall. This structure would have occupied the entire hill-top—there is no room for anything of greater diameter. However we could see no trace of an inner wall, and, given the minimum overall width of a double wall and gallery, it is difficult to see how one could have been constructed to leave a central space more than c. 7 m × 4.5 m at best. It might be noted, however, that at this site too there are traces of an appended semicircular yard.

Dun Clieff (G9) is on a rocky tidal promontory or island, much damaged by winter storms (Fig. 10.7). The structure on the summit is a rather flimsy

Figure 10.6 Dun Scurrival (E15) perched at 60 m OD on the summit of a steep hill.

Figure 10.7 Dun Clieff (G9) on a tidal islet on the west coast of Barra.

secondary feature, sitting inside the collapsed ruins of a more impressive monument built of larger blocks of stone. The perimeter wall of this monument seems to follow the contours of the top of the promontory/ island closely, and delineates a structure about 20 m long and 10 m wide that may be a flattened oval. There is no clear sign of a double wall at basal level, and again given the assumed thickness of such a wall we cannot see how a 'true broch' could be constructed here. The two remaining ARH identifications are not identified as brochs because we have too little information to go on. Dun an t'Sleibh, standing on a low hillock in the Borve valley, has a thick enough basal wall to have been carried up to a considerable height, but the topography of the site and the curve of the length of surviving wall all suggest a markedly oval structure that does not suggest a 'true broch' stood here. The RCAHMS description of Loch an Duin, on an islet in a fresh-water loch, suggests this may have been a 'true broch' with a diameter of about 16 m, a wall a little over a metre wide, traces of a basal gallery and a causeway linking the islet to the loch shore. Unfortunately the site was extensively robbed for the construction of a dam, and the site then totally submerged by the raised water level of the loch. It is thus impossible to confirm or expand upon the RCHAMS description.

Of the three possible ARH sites we list, the site of K4, Kiessimul Castle is included only because much coarse handmade pottery, thought to be prehistoric, was found during the excavations in the castle court-yard by Robert Lister Mcneil. The most likely, but not the only, explanation of this material would be that a substantial structure, such as an ARH, occupied this rocky islet in Castlebay and was obliterated by the building of the castle.

The two remaining sites are better documented, by field survey, and potentially of great interest. The site of VN98, standing 70 m from the sea in the valley west of Tresivick is a steep-sided grassed-over mound about 15 × 12 m and about 4 m high. Much building stone lies around the mound or protrudes through the turf. There is clearly a substantial building within this mound. Although the site is associated with the Bish-opric of the Isles (Wilson and Hurst 1966), the only material recovered from the site appears to be IA, and a later prehistoric structure is a probability. The size, height and steep-sidedness of the mound suggest to us a broch, but we cannot be certain because of the turf obscuring the details of the masonry. Site VN25, on the opposite (north) side of Heishival Mor, is 250 m west of Dun Caolis. Heaps of massive stone blocks, many between 1 m and 2 m in length, are piled here, alongside an arc of laid foundations 1.9 m wide (Fig. 10.8). Indications suggest a structure about 16m × 11.5 m was laid out here, but we are convinced that the building was never erected. A building this size with such massive masonry and foundations is likely to have been an ARH and we are tempted to think that this site was initially chosen for the erection of the Dun Caolis broch but for some reason the site was then moved eastwards. There is of course no way of confirming this hypothesis.

Finally, we need to briefly discuss the promontory fort on the island of Biruaslum (BM7). This represents a massive input of energy to collect the stone and build

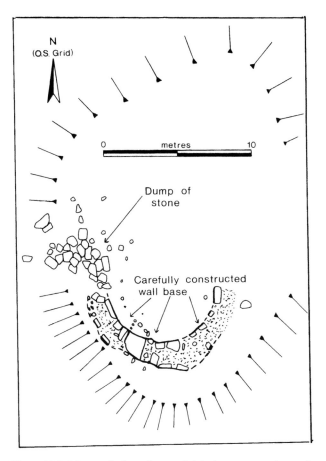

Figure 10.8 Measured plan of an unfinished monumental round-house at VN25.

a defence wall, which is at least 100 m long, 2 m wide and still stands to 3 m in height. The size and nature of the wall are suggestive of the monumental tradition of architecture associated with the Iron Age in northern and western Britain, and the arc of walling to shut off an area that backs on to a vertical cliff is very reminiscent of some Irish 1st millennium AD forts. The builders of the fort clearly felt well-protected by the sea-dyke that separates Biruaslum from the mainland of Vatersay, and felt the only threat would come from the west, storm-battered, side of Biruaslum itself. There is not a scrap of structural or artifactual evidence for Iron Age occupation inside the defended area, although there is a thick Neolithic midden (and presumably therefore an occupation site) in the southeast corner. Nevertheless, it is difficult to envisage this fort belonging to any era other than the Iron Age on the basis of similar sites elsewhere.

The dating of the other sites discussed in this section is fixed with varying degrees of precision. Dun Cuier is not as well dated as it should be for an excavated monument, but its mixed pottery corpus includes E/MIA material as well as much that is later, through into the 7th century AD. Sherds found in the midden adjacent to the Borve headland broch include one with an impressed cordon of E/MIA date, most

probably 1st century BC to 2nd century AD. Other sherds here include the widespread 'Iron Age' fabric discussed earlier, and sherds of the same fabric were recovered from rabbit disturbance at Dun Caolis, Dun Clief, Dun Scurrival and Dun Vatersay.

Other Iron Age Sites (Figs. 10.1, 10.3)

In addition to all the sites discussed and classified above, there are 11 other locations on Barra and one on Vatersay where we identify evidence of IA occupation. These sites are E6, E9, E16, E18, E24, L8, C52, C53, T119, B85, VN133.

Five of these are on the machair and in the shifting dunes of Eoligarry. Some were clearly middens with no trace of any associated structures. They may have been the sites of temporary seasonal camps to exploit the famous cockle beach. Others, like E6, yield midden debris from rabbit disturbance of a substantial mound that could cover a roundhouse or wheelhouse. All four sites have yielded sherds of the 'Iron Age' fabric. Two finds of Iron Age pottery and other material in the dunes north of Borve (C52, 53) may be associated with the possible wheelhouse sighted here (C60), although C53 seems too far distant to be immediately related and may be the midden of another roundhouse. The blackhouse settlement at Goirtein (T119) is partly sited on a low but large mound from which a handful of 'Iron Age' fabric sherds have been recovered. We suspect a roundhouse or wheelhouse here but have no structural evidence. Another blackhouse settlement with Iron Age material beneath it is that on the edge of Loch Obe at Balnabodach (L8). There was sufficient pottery (241 sherds) together with four pieces of flint and a pumice net float to identify this as an occupation site of MIA date, although the overlying blackhouse had destroyed any trace of a structure.

There remain two unusual sites on Barra. The occupation on the platform outside the cave below Dun Scurrival (E16) presumably relates to use of the cave as a shelter but whether on a seasonal or more permanent basis is unclear. The heavy saucer-quern perhaps implies a reasonably prolonged occupation of the site rather than the occasional visit. It may be that this site precedes the building of the ARH on the hilltop above. The second site is the curious triangular enclosure with embanked monoliths on Borve headland. There is no artifactual evidence for the date of this enclosure but we ascribe it to the Iron Age on two grounds. First, because it is linked to a bank that can be traced across the headland running directly towards the broch (B5) at the point where it passes under the cemetery wall. Second, because the combination of earth embankment and spaced stone blocks embedded in the top of it is repeated in the vicinity of Dun Caolis and Dun Scurrival. All three examples are much reduced and residual. At Dun Caolis, the land boundaries of this type can be traced in an arc around the south and south-west of the broch and about 60–70 m distant from it. Three 'radial' lengths of walling link the hill on which the broch stands to the encircling arc. These boundaries are clearly laid out using the broch as a focal point, and they are clearly of considerable antiquity, as in two places the encircling arc disappears beneath a bog to emerge again 30–40 m further on. Probing confirms the boundary continues beneath the bog. There is therefore some reason to suspect this may be an Iron Age form of boundary on Barra and Vatersay. An example in the Borve valley proved, on excavation, to predate an early modern hut (site B60 excavation report in volume 6), but otherwise there is no other evidence for their date. If the enclosure is indeed Iron Age its purpose may as well have been economic as ritual. The remaining site, on the tidal islet of Uinessan at the eastern tip of north Vatersay, is a low mound from which sherds of 'Iron Age' fabric have been recovered. It is overlain by the remains of Cille Bhrianain (VN133). The chapel is probably built on the site of an earlier Iron Age roundhouse.

A Crowded Iron Age Landscape?

It is not surprising that we appear to have more surviving Iron Age sites than earlier prehistoric ones. It is not just that they have not had to survive as many millennia as earlier monuments, but many of the Iron Age structures were more monumentally built than their Neolithic and Bronze Age counterparts. Nevertheless, the far greater number of Iron Age occupation sites might seem to be clustered both chronologically and spatially. The majority of our proposed Iron Age sites would traditionally be placed in the period between the 2nd century BC and the 3rd century AD for their construction. However, we have noted above the evidence that both the smaller roundhouses and the larger thick-walled roundhouses are found in the LBA/EIA, and we think it likely that on Barra and Vatersay many of these structures represent earlier Iron Age occupation. Whether they were effectively replaced by wheelhouses and brochs/ARHs or whether the various structures were all in use alongside one another in the MIA is not yet clear. If, however, Armit (1996: 112–20), Parker Pearson and Sharples (1999, 364–66) and others are right in seeing brochs and wheelhouses as indigenous developments (as we believe they are) then presumably the descendants of at least some of the thick-walled roundhouse families were responsible for their construction.

The geographical clustering of Iron Age sites still demands attention, however. First we have the clusters of smaller roundhouses like those on the south side of the Borve valley or above Gortien, where five or six of these houses are found within a square kilometre. Clusters like these, mostly well above the 100 m contour, might be interpreted as seasonal sites associated with upland grazing. In a similar cluster west of Tresivick on Vatersay, however, all the huts are found below the 50 m contour and close to the sea. There are similar clusters of larger thick-walled roundhouses in Allasdale, in and west of Gortien, and again both north and west of Tresivick, all of which are on lower ground either side of the 50 m contour. If we are right in thinking that these larger thick-walled structures were permanent rather than seasonal homes, then these clusters must either represent successive buildings that replaced one another over the course of centuries, or real contemporary clusters of households. We favour the latter interpretation because there is little to suggest the robbing of one house to build an adjacent one. Most houses in these clusters look to be in similar degrees of collapse, degradation and embedding.

Thus we would have three large roundhouses within 400 m below the western slope of Ben Verrisey in Allasdale, four within 700 m at Gortien, five within 500 m west of Tresivick, and three within 200 m north of Tresivick. Given that these clusters are in each case surround by substantial tracts of land in which few or no other traces of IA occupation are found, they apparently reflect a deliberate decision of the households involved to live in close proximity. The reason for this is uncertain, but the clusters are not sited in defensive locations, nor are they tight enough to offer significant mutual security. We believe that these clusters are essentially social clusters, perhaps of extended families or kingroups.

The picture is, however, more complicated than this because we do not simply have clusters of smaller roundhouses and clusters of larger roundhouses. There are also clusters, often tighter or closer, that include both types of structure, and in some cases wheelhouses and ARHs too (Fig. 10.3). Above the school and hall overlooking Vatersay Bay, for example, we identify a possible wheelhouse, a large roundhouse and a small roundhouse all sitting on or around the 50 m contour within 250 m of each other. About 100 m away further upslope is a second possible wheelhouse. Along the south-west slope of Heaval on Barra, there is a wheelhouse, a large roundhouse and two smaller roundhouses within 200 m of each other. The most remarkable cluster is in the valley west of Tresivick (Fig. 9.9). Near the sea are one small and one large roundhouse, a possible wheelhouse and mound that is so substantial we believe it must hide a broch. A hundred metres to the east and south-east are two further large roundhouses, and another is 100 m to the northwest. The questions inevitably arise, does each cluster represent a succession of houses or were all the buildings in each cluster in contemporary occupation, and if so what was their relationship to one another? Given that our evidence for the nature and date of all these sites is derived solely from field survey, it would be pointless to speculate, but when we come to try and place our discoveries in the southern isles of the Outer Hebrides in their wider context in our final chapter, any similar clusters elsewhere in Western Scotland will deserve brief consideration.

11. Barra and its Islands in the Prehistory of Northern Britain

Keith Branigan

So far in this report we have largely avoided drawing comparisons or contrasts between the prehistoric archaeology of the islands on which we have worked and those that make up the rest of the Western Isles or the Outer Hebrides. Nor have we attempted to relate our discoveries to those made in other regions of the Atlantic province of north Britain—Ireland, the Inner Hebrides, Argyll and the north-west of Scotland, and the Northern Isles of Orkney and Shetland. Our concern in the chapters that precede this has been two-fold—to present a record of what we have discovered, and to present a locally focused interpretation of those discoveries. Having done that we must now attempt to place the prehistory of our islands in its broader context.

Variability and Island Identities

Before we can do this, however, we need first briefly to consider to what extent the discoveries we have made reveal a prehistoric landscape and society that is common to all six of the larger islands in our study area. The logistics of our fieldwork have moulded the logistics of compiling this report, and the field survey and excavations conducted on the various islands have been presented for the most part in a series of self-contained packages that may have masked both similarities and differences in the evidence which each island has yielded. There is certainly a modern perception that Barra and the islands to the south form one of three 'natural' units in the Outer Hebrides, the others being the great landmass of Lewis and Harris, and the long island made up of North Uist, Benbecula and South Uist with their linking causeways. The perceived unity of Barra, Vatersay, Sandray, Pabbay, Mingulay and Berneray is enhanced and given historical depth by the fact that the islands together comprise the Parish of Barra. And because the Royal Commission published their reports by county and parish, that unity is archaeologically enshrined in the RCAHMS report of 1928, where all the monuments from Eoligarry to Barra Head are listed under the heading BARRA. We ourselves contribute to this picture with the title of this chapter.

But this is a title of convenience rather than conviction, and all of us who have worked on these islands believe each island has its own distinctive

character that is sometimes reflected in its archaeology. The brief descriptions of each island that we have given earlier (Chapters 2 and 3), and particularly the elegant images conveyed by Patrick Foster, underline the message that each island has a different shape and topography, even a different orientation, and these differences partly explain the considerable variations in the balance of sand beaches, rock shelves, machair, moorlands, bogs and high plateaux, and in the fauna and flora of the islands. And in the same way that animals, birds and plants reflect the topographic and geomorphological variations from one island to another, so does human behaviour as reflected by the archaeological remains.

In earlier prehistory (Neolithic and Bronze Age), settlement evidence is so sparse, and often so very tentatively dated, that it is difficult to draw any useful comparisons between one island and another. Burial evidence is more prolific and more securely dated, however, and some variations in funerary architecture can be identified. The four chamber tombs found on Barra include two circular cairns with megalithic chambers approached by a passage (B1 and B3), and two smaller, probably later tombs that appear to be local adaptations of the heeled cairn found mostly in Shetland. The single tomb on Vatersay is a third passage grave, but unlike both B1 and B3 it clearly has a small V-shaped entrance court set into the front of the cairn, the closest parallels to which are found on the Uists and Skye. Megalithic tombs on the southern islands do not take such well-known forms, and are inevitably therefore less firmly identified, but they appear to represent local variations on the megalithic tradition. The examples on Sandray (SY16 and 71) have chambers large enough to match those of other Scottish passage graves, but little evidence for substantial covering cairns. The same is true of the two most convincing Mingulay examples (MY347 and 389), the former possibly having a segmented chamber and the latter possibly a wedge-shaped chamber, both with straight rather than curving walls, like those of B1, B3 and VN157. Berneray stands out immediately by reason of the number of suggested megalithic tomb structures—nine—particularly on such a small island, which might raise the possibility that it was used as a cemetery for a Neolithic population living on Mingulay. Some of the proposed tombs are certainly capable

346

of other interpretations and the total number may therefore be misleading but at least half a dozen of the sites cannot be lightly dismissed. These are notable for falling into two groups one of which is not represented elsewhere in our islands. These are small square or oblong chambers (they could equally well be called cists) with an area not exceeding about 2 m^2 set in small circular or oval mounds. The remaining two sites (BY68 and 84) sit inside larger circular mounds (around 7 m diam.) and may be similar to B3 or possibly even VN157. Pabbay has produced no evidence for megalithic chamber tombs.

Neolithic or earlier Bronze Age ritual sites are even more scarce on the southern islands than on Barra. Barra has the six tallest standing stones, Vatersay has the next three tallest. Sandray also has three stones, the tallest of which matches the shortest on Vatersay and Barra. Mingulay has a single example, and only one of the three possible examples on Berneray is convincing (though Martin noted a stone 2 m plus in height in 1695). A similar picture emerges from an overview of stone rings. The six largest examples are all on Barra, Vatersay has one small and tentative example, Mingulay the same, and Sandray, Berneray and Pabbay no convincing examples at all. Taking into consideration the much smaller areas of the southern islands, it might be argued that the Neolithic populations of Mingulay and Berneray were as well or better provided with a Neolithic ritual focus (standing stone) as Barra or Vatersay. But it is difficult to say the same for the possibly later (earlier Bronze Age?) foci provided by stone rings. Here, Barra seems clearly different to all the other islands. And in terms of 'quality', as expressed in the size of the stones used, as opposed to quantity, the southern islands seem badly provided for in both standing stones and rings. It may be argued that Barra provided the ritual focus for the whole group of islands, and there is the possibility that the area around Brevig had a particular ritual role.

Turning to Bronze Age funerary architecture, Barra has two small groups of monuments, both with a very tightly clustered distribution, that do not appear on other islands in the group. These are the elongated cists above Bretadale and the small rectangular cists of south-east Tangaval. Vatersay in contrast is notable for its kerbed cairns. Although they are found in small numbers (and often in pairs) elsewhere, Vatersay's 29 examples, including several clusters of 3 or 4 and one of 9, establish the kerbed cairn as particularly favoured on Vatersay. In the southern islands kerbed and bordered cairns make rare appearances, the former perhaps at SY37b and PY1, and the latter at SY121 and MY75A, but there are only a handful of other cairns that are even large enough to be likely examples of either type. Mingulay, however, has a mass of small cairns among which we believe there are probably some prehistoric burial cairns. They are not in areas

suitable for, or with any evidence of, cultivation. Neither are they in areas where they might be considered clearance cairns for pastoral land (Edwards and Whittington 1998: 16). Rather they are located in many cases on the very highest points of the island, and often in clusters. These cairns are usually only 1–2.5 m diam., with varying amounts of visible stonework. We believe they may well represent a distinctive localized prehistoric burial tradition on Mingulay. Two examples occur also on Berneray.

In the Iron Age the archaeological record is heavily biased away from funerary monuments to settlement sites. Although some of these sites are easily identified in field survey for what they are, simple roundhouses are not easily ascribed a date and sometimes a roundhouse and a wheelhouse can be confused if a site is heavily grassed over. With that caveat in mind, we have nevertheless identified two groups of simple roundhouses on Barra and Vatersay, the first with overall diameters in the 8–10 m range, and the second in the 5–7 m range, which we believe are Iron Age. On both Barra and Vatersay these monuments share the Iron Age landscape with both wheelhouses and brochs/galleried duns (complex ARHs). Vatersay, which is about a sixth the size of Barra, is the more densely populated landscape in terms of each and every one of these settlement types. We do not of course believe that all the buildings were in contemporary occupation, and on Barra one example of each of the simple roundhouse types (T17 and B54) is firmly placed in the earlier Iron Age. Nevertheless, the overall pattern and shape of settlement on the two islands seems broadly the same. This might be said of Sandray too, where all four types of monument are found, the only difference being that small roundhouses appear to be notably more numerous than the large ones (SY22a, 43, 58a, 62, 115, and 150 as against 32A). South of Sandray the picture seems very different. Pabbay again displays a shortage of sites, the broch of Dunan Ruadhe sharing the Iron Age landscape with no more than a possible small roundhouse at PY89. Mingulay, by far the biggest of the four southern islands, is the only one without a broch or galleried dun. We can recognize no small roundhouses either, but there are five large roundhouses, two of which are very probably wheelhouses (MY344A and 346) and the others (MY194A, 345 and 384) of the large simple roundhouse group. Finally, Berneray repeats the picture from Pabbay, with a single dominant site (the galleried dun on Barra Head) and perhaps one small roundhouse (BY66). One site type is also common to Vatersay (Biruaslum), Mingulay and Berneray and that is the promontory fort found on the west coast of each, although none of the three examples has produced any evidence for their date, which is often thought to be in the later Iron Age. Other than these sites, evidence for Late Iron Age (Pictish) occupation is difficult to identify—even on some excavated sites where it is suspected but poorly documented by dateable finds. Pabbay, with its cemetery mound, 7th-century stone, and bronze and bone Pictish pins is a welcome light in a dark corner. It is possible that Sandray too provides a brief glimpse of the Pictish occupation. Sites SY79 and SY80, flat, almost square cairns, at least one with stones laid across the top, could be Pictish burial cairns.

This brief overview of the prehistoric monuments found on Barra and the islands to the south has, we hope, demonstrated that there are some notable variations in the type of monuments found on each island, and also that the balance between the various types may change from one island to another. Such variations appear to reflect highly localized adaptations that were developed partly in response to equally localized variations in topography and geomorphology, and partly perhaps as statements of identity by small close-knit communities. Although it is outside the scope of this volume, we believe similar variations can be seen in the more recent archaeological monuments of the islands and this is something we may return to in SEARCH volume 6.

Nevertheless, important as these variations may be, there is of course much that unites all the islands in our study area, not only to each other but also to other islands further north in the Outer Hebrides.

The Western Isles

The absence of any direct artifactual evidence for a Mesolithic population is as marked in the rest of the Outer Hebrides as it is in our islands. Reductions in tree pollen from Mesolithic age levels at Loch an t-Sil (Edwards 1996) may reflect human activity, an interpretation encouraged by similar reductions in samples taken within 300 m of the broadly contemporary Mesolithic occupation site at Kinloch on Rhum (Hirons and Edwards 1990). There is a general consensus amongst prehistorians of the Hebrides that the outer islands were exploited by Mesolithic hunter-gatherers just as we now know the inner ones to have been. With the submergence of the most suitable habitats on the west coast, however, the direct evidence is proving hard to find.

On Barra, there is a reduction in tree pollen in the mid 5th millennium BC, about a thousand years earlier than the C14 date for an early (but not the earliest) phase of occupation at Alt Chrisal. Although it is tempting to associate this with a Mesolithic colonization of the island, present indications are that climatic rather than anthropogenic factors are involved (Edwards and Brayshay, above p. 311). Nevertheless this does suggest some differences from the pattern of vegetation development seen further north in the Outer Hebrides, and there is some evidence for a north–south variation in vegetation in early prehistory (Boardman 1995: 149).

On the C14 evidence presently available Barra at least seems to have been occupied by the first farmers as early as any of the other islands in the Western Isles. The settlement at Alt Chrisal seems in many respects similar to that at Carinish on North Uist, which had few traces of building structures but a variety of hearths, stake holes, post holes and spreads of ash. A similar site on North Uist may also have been sampled recently at Screvan (Downes and Badcock 1998), where the main feature excavated was a wide but shallow pit full of pottery, lenses of charcoal, part-fired pottery, etc. Armit has suggested (1996: 56–57) that such sites may be 'more transient or seasonal activity areas', and that permanent bases were mainly located on islet settlements, such as Eilean Domhnuill and Eilean an Tighe (Scott 1950). At present we have no indication of islet settlements of this sort at the southern end of the island chain, although the islet in Loch Tangusdale has become a possible candidate, since reconnaisance in 1999 revealed no evidence for a complex ARH but remains of a smaller, simpler structure.

The earliest circular hut on Barra on present evidence is that with Beaker pottery (T19), with which probably belong huts T15 and T18 on the same site. These can be compared to the Beaker-period oval house at Northton on Harris (Simpson 1976), the oval and circular huts at Dalmore, Lewis (Sharples 1984), and the U-shaped house at Rosinish, Benbecula (Shepherd and Tuckwell 1977). There seems to be the widespread appearance of the single oval or circular hut alongside the adoption of Beaker-style pottery, although we suspect that huts of this sort appeared earlier than this in the Western Isles. Interestingly, whilst the Dalmore and Northton huts were essentially lined pits in the sand, those at Alt Chrisal were free-standing built structures, a difference that repeats itself, more vividly, in the Iron Age.

There is nothing in the general run of pottery, lithic assemblage, pumice and heavy stone tools from Alt Chrisal, either in the earlier Neolithic or the Beaker-using phase that would be out of place in contemporary settlements on the islands to the north. Only the richness of both the ceramic and the lithic assemblage on a single site is unusual, but that may be explained by the particular role of the 'platform' at Alt Chrisal for much of its long life as an area devoted to a variety of activities—pottery manufacture, stone tool making, preparation of animal and possibly seal skins and cooking.

The three major chambered tombs on our islands (Dun Bharpa, Balnacraig and Caolis [VN157]) also fit comfortably into the Outer Hebridean repertoire. Dun Bharpa, the most impressive of the three, with its ring of tall monoliths set in the perimeter of its cairn, is matched by similar monuments at Leacach an Tighe Chloiche and Gula na h-Imrich on North Uist (RCHAMS: 76, 78, Figs. 136, 138), although neither can match Dun Bharpa for size or for the number of stones (surviving at least) in the circle. The nearby tomb at Balnacraig is not set in a long cairn (*pace* Henshall), but despite its much robbed and damaged condition may be compared to other Hebridean chambered tombs which have an apparently isolated chamber set in a circular cairn, like Frobost (South Uist), Oban nam Fiadh and perhaps South Clettraval (North Uist). Caolis is different again, with its V-shaped entrance court, but can be matched with Glac Hukarvat, Loch a'Bharp (South Uist) and Marrogh (North Uist).

Nowhere in our southern islands do we appear to have long cairns covering chamber tombs of the Clyde type, but since these occur only on North Uist in the Outer Hebrides their absence from Barra and its islands is neither surprising nor significant.

It is much more difficult to assess the significance, both numerical and visual, of the standing stones. In the southern islands we have listed 17 possible examples, only 5 of which are listed by the RCHAMS. Our list certainly includes 'fallen' stones, which by reason of their distinctive shape and size we believe once stood erect either as important markers in the landscape or as a focus for ritual activity. It also includes upright stones that the RCHAMS were either unaware of or decided were unlikely to be ancient monuments. Assuming the Commission employed the same criteria on the islands further north, then it is obviously difficult to compare *their* list of standing stones for say the Uists, with *ours* for the southern islands. Even on the basis of their lists, however, South Uist and Benbecula appear to have a distinct deficit of standing stones. Well over five times the land area of Barra, South Uist has just 3 stones to Barra's 4, while Benbecula, which is about 40% larger than Barra, has none. North Uist, on the other hand has a broadly comparable density to Barra, with 15 stones recorded in an area about five times the size of Barra. Pairs of stones are also favoured on both islands, with four recorded pairs on North Uist and two on Barra. In terms of size, the stones of North Uist and Barra are also similar, with all of those on North Uist and eight of the ten Barra stones being less than 3 m tall. The stone at the Pass of the Mouth in the Borve valley at 5.8 m is the tallest (though now recumbent) south of the Sound of Harris. Further north, the standing stone tradition seems stronger and is of course dominated by the stones of Callinish on Lewis.

The same might be said for the stone circles, and again the circle at Callinish is the focus of interest with its superb ring of 13 tall, thin standing stones, surrounded by further arrangements of standing monoliths. But this was obviously a major ritual centre of regional importance and it is not typical of the stone circles of the Western Isles. Aubrey Burl (1976: 140–41) describes them, collectively, as 'mostly small', emphasizes their diversity, and notes that 'the true

circle becomes rare in these islands'. This description certainly befits the stone rings identified in our survey. Burl's catalogue of sites again demonstrates the relative richness of North Uist, with 5 circles, compared to 11 in the seven-times larger landmass of Lewis and Harris. There are two further circles in Benbecula, but none in South Uist. Neither, of course, does Burl list any in Barra and its islands. This may well reflect both the small size of the southern stone rings, and the even less impressive dimensions of the stones used to build them. Only two of our rings exceed 15 m in diameter, whereas the smallest of the North Uist and Benbecula circles is over 18 m. The Lewis circles are mostly smaller (even Callanish is under 15m) but their stones are much larger than those employed in the southern islands, so they remain impressive monuments. Our stone rings are undoubtedly poor relations of those further north in the island chain, but their existence confirms that broadly the same ritual traditions and practices were followed throughout the Outer Hebrides during the Neolithic and earlier Bronze Age.

Whether the same may be said of both burial ritual and funerary architecture in the Bronze Age is less certain. The handful of cists, which we believe are burial sites, found on the Tangaval peninsula on Barra are similar to others found further north in the island chain (Armit 1996: 96), which belong mainly in the first half of the 2nd millennium BC.

There is no evidence from our islands, however, for the corbelled cists found at Cnip, Rosinish and Northton (Armit 1996: 98), although it may be that such monuments can only be recognized if they are excavated. Cairns ringed by a continuous setting of stones and commonly labelled kerb cairns occur sporadically north of Barra. One was recently partly excavated at Otternish on North Uist (Downes and Badcock 1998: 49–50) and in size, 8–9 m diam., would be at the top end of the range in our islands. Unfortunately, the presumed central burial area was not excavated so that we cannot usefully compare this cairn with those we excavated on Vatersay. Two excavated examples on Lewis, however, do provide a basis for comparison. At Cnip (Armit 1996: 98) a 6 m diam. kerb of boulders enclosed the cairn, at the centre of which was a small 3 m cairn of small stones with its own kerb of boulders. Cremated bone was found scattered amongst the small stones of the inner cairn. At Olcote, Callanish, a cairn 8 m in diameter was surrounded by a kerb of stones that the excavator notes were 'laid flat, not set on end' (Neighbour 1996: 112). An inner kerb of smaller stones had a maximum diameter of about 6 m. At the centre of the cairn was a cist of three orthostats, inside which was an urn containing cremated bone. The cairn itself was mostly of redeposited peat, including much burnt material thought to be the remains of the cremation pyre. Since there appears to be no evidence for the pyre or burning beneath the cairn itself, this material was presumably brought from elsewhere. Although there are some significant differences to our two Vatersay cairns, notably a central cist containing an urn, there are also many similarities. An inner cairn with its own boulder kerb, a single central cremation, evidence for pyre material brought to the site from elsewhere, even a cultivated land surface underneath the cairn and many small field stones in the area between the inner and outer kerb. The *flat* kerbstones are also significant, for, as the excavator says, most 'kerb cairns' have stones set on end. The Olcote cairn falls happily into our definition of a kerbed cairn, whereas both the Cnip and Otternish cairns appear to be examples of what we have called 'bordered cairns' in the southern islands (with the 'kerb' stones set on end). Both types of cairn, then, appear to be represented further north in the Western Isles, although the kerbed cairn (in our terms) seems very scarce indeed. What is not so clearly established is that the funerary ritual in North Uist and Lewis was as complex as that on Vatersay. On the evidence published to date, none of the three cairns described above revealed anything like the complexity of the depositional sequence seen in VS4B and to a lesser degree in VS7.

Armit has suggested (1996: 107) that the closure of the chamber tombs, apparently while Beaker pottery was in fashion, and the adoption of cists and cairns for burial may reveal a new emphasis on the individual ancestor rather than collective ancestry. That is probably true, but the remarkable concentration of kerbed cairns west of Tresivick on Vatersay, and the lesser cluster of four or five below Dun Vatersay, equally reflect an ongoing communality in burial practice here. Taken together with several examples of pairs and trios of cairns that we have identified, this clustering of kerbed cairns on Barra, Vatersay, Fuiay and Fuday is a feature not yet paralleled elsewhere in the Western Isles.

The dearth of excavated, and therefore dated and structurally clarified domestic buildings of the later Bronze Age in the Outer Hebrides makes any comparative discussion of Bronze Age housing difficult. Recent excavations at Cladh Hallan on South Uist, however, provide an insight into Late Bronze Age housing (Parker Pearson, personal communication). A row of three circular houses with internal diameters of about 8 m was built in the machair, their interior walls basically lining a shallow flat-bottomed pit. The walls were about 1.2 m wide, so that the houses were about 10.5 m diam. in total. Nearby were two figure-of-eight houses built in a similar manner. Pottery associated with the earlier floor levels in the roundhouses was of LBA type and was accompanied by many bone points, as well as antler picks and shoulder-blade shovels. They were modified and continued in use into the EIA, so that in their later phases they were contemporary with the incompletely preserved earliest

structures at Sollas (site A) on North Uist. These too were roundhouses of about 9–10 m diam., built in a similar manner to those at Clad Hallan and associated with EIA pottery (Campbell 1991: 122–25). The 8–10 m roundhouse can therefore be identified as an element in the LBA/EIA landscape of the Uists.

Whether the three dozen large roundhouses found in our surveys can be placed alongside these houses is uncertain. Sampling excavations at T166 produced a small quantity of pottery of MIA date (Branigan 1995a, 169–70), and the house of about 12 m diam. underneath the wheelhouse at Alt Chrisal (p. 150) is also associated with pottery that is Iron Age rather than Bronze Age. The roundhouse excavated in the Borve valley (B54) dates to the very beginning of the EIA, and follows on immediately from LBA occupation. Although it is considerably smaller than the Uist houses, it confirms that roundhouses with walls in excess of a metre wide, and diameters in excess of 6 m, appear on Barra not later than the mid-1st millennium BC. In all probability the large roundhouse was part of the landscape on Barra and Vatersay for centuries from that time onwards. Because the known examples on our islands are not from the limited areas of machair, they do not share the sunken floors of the Uist examples, neither do we have any examples of a row of three like those at Clad Hallan, but there are several locations where they are found in pairs. Although both the large and smaller roundhouses are not common in the islands south of Vatersay, they occur in appreciable number on Barra and Vatersay, with over 30 examples of each identified. We believe the roundhouse was a common feature of the Iron Age landscape of these islands. Until the excavations at Sollas and Clad Hallan, one would have believed that here there was a complete contrast between the southern islands and the Uists. Now we cannot be so sure, although the numbers on Barra and Vatersay still look very impressive for such small islands. To be comparable, for example, South Uist would have to yield about 175 examples in field survey. Nevertheless, Parker Pearson and Sharples (1999: 364) report 20 LBA/EIA settlement mounds on the Uist machair, which probably hide more roundhouses, and there are scattered examples of medium-sized roundhouses known from opportunistic finds in the peatlands and hills to the east (RCAHMS 1928: 115–8). The LBA/EIA roundhouse was probably more common on the Uists than their previous invisibility has suggested.

In the Middle Iron Age, the Western Isles are the home of the wheelhouse, an architectural form scarcely found outside of the island chain. Our islands adopt the type with as much enthusiasm as the islands to the north, with about 20 examples identified in our survey. This includes the two excavated wheelhouses in Allasdale and at Alt Chrisal. These are both free-standing structures, and all the examples we have identified in survey appear to be the same. This of course is in

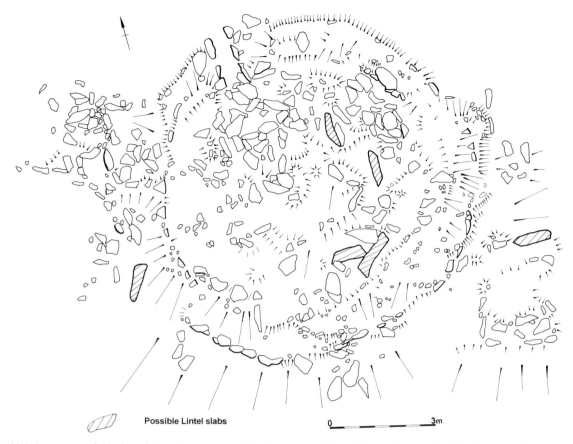

Possible Lintel slabs

0   3m

Figure 11.1 A measured field plan of the wheelhouse at K34, sited at over 200 m OD on a high rock shelf, facing south.

marked contrast to the situation north of the Sound of Barra, where almost all the excavated and surveyed sites are subterranean structures sunk into the machair. We think it likely that such subterranean structures exist on Barra and Vatersay, and possibly Sandray, but the restricted areas of machair on all of our islands means that the number of such houses must have been limited. There is no doubt that on our islands, the free-standing wheelhouse was the dominant type. Furthermore, our wheelhouses are not only found on rocky ground close to the coast (such as Alt Chrisal), and not only in low-lying valleys close to areas of machair. Some are well inland and at elevated locations with no likely arable land within easy reach. Site K34 is the extreme example, situated on a high shelf at 200 m OD, surrounded by rough pasture and overlooking a bog. Such sites confirm Armit's cautionary words about the machair-dominated distribution of wheelhouses (1992: 125) and support his suggestion that some wheelhouses may been supported by an economy associated with stock-rearing.

In terms of size and internal layout and complexity, the excavated wheelhouses at Allasdale and Alt Chrisal, suggest that the free-standing wheelhouses of Barra and the islands to the south were similar to those of the Uists. Nevertheless one essential difference should be noted, and that is the amount of energy expended in their construction. Whilst the free-

standing wheelhouse did not require the excavation of a circular pit in the sand, this was more than offset by the requirement to collect and move to the site large quantities of stone to construct the ring-wall. The walls at Alt Chrisal, for example, averaging almost 2 m in width, probably required five to six times the amount of stone that a subterranean house of the same internal diameter would require. Some of these stones were very large blocks indeed, particularly when the house was built on a slope, and would have required both considerable numbers of people and some expertise to move them. We believe it unlikely that the majority of wheelhouses in the southern islands could have been constructed by a single nuclear family working alone.

The same must surely be true of the broch towers, although recent discussions of the social-economic nature and significance of the brochs have ignored the question of how many people, in what sort of social configuration, were responsible for the construction of an individual broch. The brochs and related structures found in our islands share with those found in the Uists and Lewis and Harris a marked preference for defensive locations—on peaks, promontories, and in lochs. Only the two structures at Borve do not follow this pattern, B5 being on machair and B136 just above the valley floor. Otherwise, in terms of location, size and architecture, the brochs

351

and complex ARHs of the southern islands appear to fit easily into the general picture from the Western Isles. Even their distribution is somewhat similar to that on the Uists, allowing for the marked topographical differences between the two island groups, with a string of seven brochs/ARHs spaced about every 3 km along the west side of Barra and Vatersay.

Although controversy still rages over the date at which brochs and wheelhouses appeared in the Hebridean landscape (Armit 1991: 189; MacKie 1997; Parker Pearson and Sharples 1999: 355–59) there seems to be a consensus that brochs and wheelhouses shared that landscape for at least some centuries in the MIA. This obviously raises the problem of the socio-economic relationship between them. Parker Pearson and Sharples (1999: 363–34) have made an attractive case that the two forms are 'mutually reliant opposites', with the sunken wheelhouses sitting in settlement clusters in the machair concerned principally with arable cultivation, and the towering brochs occupying marginal locations close to territorial boundaries and focused mainly on stock-rearing. While this is a plausible interpretation of the evidence on the Uists, on Barra it does not fit so well, in particular with respect to wheelhouse location. Many Barra wheelhouses are found in relatively high situations associated with pastoral land rather than arable. Barra's different topography appears to have modified its socioeconomic exploitation. In one respect, however, the MIA settlement pattern of Barra and Vatersay is similar to the Uists. The clustering of households into settlement groups to which we drew attention at the close of Chapter 10 is a marked feature of the pattern on South Uist (Parker Pearson and Sharples 1999: 364–36).

The remodelling and continued reoccupation of both wheelhouses and brochs in the LIA seems to be a widespread phenomenon in the Outer Hebrides. The evidence from Dun Cuier (Young 1955; Armit 1992: 34–38) is now joined by that from T17 at Alt Chrisal, so that Barra has excavated examples of both a broch and a wheelhouse that support this view. Survey evidence from several other sites suggests remodelling and reuse were common, but without excavation these episodes cannot be dated. Whether promontory forts like those on Berneray, Mingulay and Vatersay should be placed alongside the remodelled brochs and wheelhouses is uncertain, but often proposed.

The material from Dun Cueir shows that its late occupation certainly fell within the period of the Pictish kingdom on northern Scotland, but evidence of Pictish cultural and political affiliations is scarce and difficult to interpret. The Pabbay stone, however, belonging to Class I of the Pictish symbol stones (and one of only two found in the Western Isles) is a significant testimony to such connections. 'Pictish' pins from the Pabbay broch and from the cemetery area support this view. Patrick Foster suggests (personal communication) that other cobble-covered enclosed cemetery mounds on Berneray and Mingulay might have begun as Pictish burial places too. The two square 'flat' cairns on Sandray (SY79 and 80) may also belong in the Pictish era, and demonstrate that the southern islands were still in step with developments further north in the island chain. A similar 'Pictish' cairn was excavated at Kilpheder on South Uist in 1998 (M. Parker Pearson, personal communication), and another discovered and cleaned (but not excavated) on the northern island of Berneray (off North Uist) in the same year (Badcock 1998). Nevertheless, it is clear that the whole of the Western Isles were very much on the fringes of the Pictish kingdom, whose focus lay much further east and to whom the Outer Hebrides must have been no more than a remote and probably loosely controlled outlier.

The Atlantic Province

Even today, when there is a daily air and sea link to Barra, the Uists and Lewis and Harris, the Western Isles are still regarded as somewhat remote, a world of their own, separated from that of the mainland by the waters of The Minches and battered along its entire western seaboard by the Atlantic. Yet archaeologists have long recognized that the seas provided not only a barrier but also a corridor between the various islands and coastlines of north-west Britain, from Ireland to the Northern Isles. Along this corridor moved people, products and ideas. For the most part such movements were sporadic, small-scale, opportunistic and undirected.

This is presumably how the first farmers who grew barley and raised sheep arrived in the Outer Hebrides. They may have come from the mainland, perhaps via Skye and Rhum, or by a longer voyage from the north coast of Ireland; they probably came from both directions. They had arrived on North Uist and Barra by 3500 BC, but certainly the people who settled at Alt Chrisal were not first-generation immigrants. From the first, their pottery belongs to a recognizable tradition of Hebridean pottery, which must have been developed over a period of some centuries somewhere within the island chain. If we are right in interpreting the lowest structural remains at Alt Chrisal as the remains of a circular hut erected on a timber frame, then the ultimate origins of the settlers at Alt Chrisal may have been in south-west Scotland where sub-circular huts of similar size and date have been excavated at Ardnadam, rather than in Ireland where early Neolithic houses are predominantly rectangular structures.

Wherever their origins lay, the people living at Alt Chrisal maintained sporadic and probably indirect links with the islands of the Inner Hebrides and with northern Ireland. This is demonstrated by the occasional use of Rum bloodstone, Arran pitchstone, Eigg pitchstone and banded mudstone from Skye for chipped stone implements, and the acquisition of at least one stone axe from the Tievebulliagh/Rathlin Island 'factory'. Contacts northwards, beyond the island chain, are suggested not only by the Unstan bowls, adopted into the Hebridean tradition but named after one of many sites in Orkney where they are also found, but also by occasional 'exotic' vessels that are of Orcadian inspiration—like a bowl decorated with circular stab decoration, best paralleled at Isbister (Gibson 1995:110, Fig. 43.5, No. 146). The most remarkable testimony to links with the Northern Isles during the Neolithic, however, is the heel-shaped cairn at Grean (G93), if our identification of this damaged monument is correct. Heel-shaped cairns are found only in Shetland, but for a single outlier in Caithness, so that the example at Grean is both surprising and controversial, but if confirmed it is important. It is difficult to imagine how such a monument could come to be built on Barra other than by someone who had seen the heel-shaped cairns of Shetland.

The discovery of this cairn in 1998 provides a possible local antecedent, albeit of a 'foreign' kind, for the curious chambered cairn, site T55, excavated on Tangaval in 1989. At the time we suggested that this tomb 'may be related to the tradition of either the small, heel-shaped cairns of Caithness and Shetland, or to the so-called wedge-shaped gallery graves of Ireland' (Branigan 1995a: 165) and that it was probably of late Neolithic or EBA date. The discovery of a middle–late Neolithic heel-shaped cairn of authentic Shetland type at Grean makes that identification a little more plausible. However, there are features of T55 that are certainly at variance with the Shetland cairns. The most obvious is the fact that the cairn is longer than it is wide and that the sides of the cairn run parallel to the chamber for much of their distance. The chamber opens directly on to the facade too, with no intervening passage. It is precisely these features that first drew our attention to the Irish 'wedge tombs' as a possible source of inspiration for our cairn at T55. O'Riordain (1979: 127) notes that a frequent feature of the wedge tombs is that an outer wall runs parallel to the walls of the chamber, and sometimes curves around the back of the chamber to make an elongated U-shape. That, of course, exactly describes T55's chamber and surrounding kerb. The general form and proportions of tombs like Boviel in Co. Derry, Culdaly in Co. Sligo and Island in Co. Cork are similar to those of T55, and, although T55 is on the small side, smaller chambers are found in Irish wedge tombs like that at Eanty Beg in Co. Clare (O'Riordain 1979: 124–28, Fig. 10). Where T55 differs significantly from the wedge tombs is that it had—on the surviving evidence—only a small cairn built over and around the chamber, whereas many wedge tombs have circular cairns that cover the chamber and any surrounding inner wall. Wedge tombs with D-shaped cairns,

however, are found in northern Ireland, and, although these cairns are still far more substantial than that around T55, they could provide a possible prototype for it.

Some of the modified megalithic chambers found on Berneray, Mingulay and Biruaslam could originally have been similar monuments to T55—that is, simple megalithic chambers set in small cairns. There is sometimes evidence of a cairn, but never enough to determine its original shape and size. Other examples may have had no cairn at all. At present there are no known similar sites in the Western Isles, and if they are not an entirely indigenous development at the very southern end of the island chain, they may have been inspired by a 2nd millennium fashion for the simple megalithic tomb in Argyll (Ritchie 1997b: 84–87), examples of which are found on Coll and Tiree, the nearest of all the inner islands to Mingulay and Berneray.

Given the isolation of the stone rings of Barra and Vatersay from the nearest examples elsewhere in the Western Isles (60–70 km to the north, in North Uist), and their notably smaller scale (both in terms of their diameters and the stones employed), we should perhaps consider whether here too the southern islands looked to traditions established in Argyll and the Inner Hebrides. There are not large numbers of stone circles or rings recorded in this region, but their size range (from about 5 m to 20 m) is similar to that of our examples and they often employ stones no more than a metre tall. The stone circles of Arran are particularly reminiscent of our rings, not only because they are of similar size and use stones of modest dimensions (e.g. Haggerty 1991) but also because as Burl notes (1976: 144) oval rings are common on Arran as they are on Barra and Vatersay (three of our seven rings).

Carbon dates from stone circles in Wales, Ireland and Scotland confirm that some circles were probably not erected until the mid 2nd millennium BC, and at Machrie Moor on Arran one of the small circles proved on excavation to overlie a sequence of earlier and later Neolithic and Beaker features and structures (Haggerty 1991). They are thus contemporaries of the kerb cairns found in some numbers in Argyll, and we may envisage both in Argyll and our islands, a second millennium landscape where small stone circles and stone-bordered cairns formed complementary ritual foci. Excavations of the kerb cairns of Argyll, however, have emphasized the differences rather than the similarities between them and the kerbed cairns of Barra and Vatersay. There is not only the difference in the form of the kerb—with our stones laid flat to form a continuous flat-topped kerb, and those of Argyll set upright and forming a serrated surface. Some Argyll cairns appear to have traces of the cremation taking place on site, many of the cairns are very low and flat, some have the cremations placed in cists, and some cover multiple cremations (Ritchie 1997b: 89–90). These practices seem at variance with those seen in our two excavated cairns. Kerb cairns have also been excavated on Orkney (Ovrevik 1985: 134–36), but covering cremations mostly placed in cists and covered by low mounds surrounded by kerbs of upright stones. The most recently excavated examples at Rendall (Downes 1999) reveal some similar practices to those seen on Vatersay (e.g. pyre material brought from elsewhere and deposited in the cairn) and have kerbs that are flat by reason of being low drystone walls, but multiple cremations in cists and pits confirm that the Orkney kerb cairns are closer in construction and usage to those of Argyll than Barra and Vatersay. As for the kerb cairn excavated at Scord of Brouster in Shetland (Whittle 1986), it was built in two quite separate episodes, possibly up to two millennia apart, and there is no evidence that it ever served as a burial monument. Only the stone ard tip found on the kerb of Vatersay 4B hints at a connection between the kerbed cairns of our islands and the contemporary kerb cairns of the Northern Isles. Stone ard tips were of course commonplace in the Northern Isles, whereas they have no place in the Hebridean assemblage. However, on present evidence the kerbed cairn, as we define it, appears to be a distinctive local variation on a 2nd millennium theme, developed and used almost exclusively in the southern islands of the Outer Hebrides.

With the Iron Age, the Atlantic Province becomes more visible as brochs and related forms of complex Atlantic roundhouses appear throughout the Western Isles, in the Inner Hebrides, in south-west Scotland, sporadically along the coast of Caithness and Sutherland, and then in impressive numbers in Orkney and Shetland. No matter where the broch originated, it was an architectural form that seems to have been quickly adopted by peoples living alongside and in the Atlantic corridor, throughout its length. Whether its

adoption over such a widespread region implies a similar social structure was in place throughout this area is more uncertain. Armit has noted, for example (1996, 122), that the brochs of the Western Isles did not spawn 'broch villages' as happened at some sites in the Northern Isles.

Similarly, the much more restricted distribution of the wheelhouse may reflect differences in social structure as much as in topography, building materials and environment. The wheelhouse, on present evidence, is essentially a feature of the MIA landscapes of the Uists and the islands to the south. It is rare in Lewis and Harris, and unknown in Caithness and Sutherland and the Orkney Islands, although related radially divided roundhouses do appear in these areas. Yet strangely, the wheelhouse appears in Shetland, apparently reflecting an episode of close links with the southern end of the Outer Hebrides that are difficult to explain, and that have only been hinted at in earlier periods.

The overall impression that emerges from a discussion of the prehistoric archaeology of Barra and its islands is perhaps best described as three-dimensional. In the background are the other regions of the Atlantic Province, which seen from Barra and its islands seem to move in and out of focus at different times. The middle ground is occupied by the islands immediately to the north of Barra—the Uists and Benbecula—where patterns of settlement may differ in a very different topographical setting, but architectural forms, mobile material culture and many common traditions seem to be shared with the southern islands. Finally, in the foreground, are Barra, Vatersay, Sandray, Pabbay, Mingulay and Berneray, where we can observe sometimes highly localized idiosyncrasies and variations on common themes, partly resulting from local topographical and environmental variability, so that each island can to some extent claim a prehistory of its own.

Bibliography

Allardyce, K., and E.M. Hood
  1986 *At Scotland's Edge: A Celebration of Two Hundred Years of the Lighthouse Service in Scotland and the Isle of Man* (Glasgow: Collins).

Allen, J., and J. Anderson
  1993 *The Early Christian Monuments of Scotland* (Balnavies, Angus: Pinkfoot Press, reprint of 1903 ed.).

Anderson, D.E.
  1998 'A reconstruction of Holocene climatic changes from peat bogs in north-west Scotland', *Boreas* 27: 208–24.

Anderson, J.
  1893 'Notice of Dun Stron, Bernera, Barra Head', *Proceedings of the Society of Antiquaries of Scotland* 27: 341–46.
  1897 'Notes on some recently discovered inscribed and sculptured stones', *Proceedings of the Society of Antiquaries of Scotland* 31: 299–300.

Armit, I.
  1988 'Broch landscapes in the Western Isles', *Scottish Archaeological Review* 5: 78–86.
  1988a 'Excavations at Cnip, West Lewis' (unpublished report, Department of Archaeology, University of Edinburgh).
  1990 'Brochs and beyond in the Western Isles', in Armit 1990a: 41–70.
  1990a 'Broch building in northern Scotland: the context of innovation', *World Archaeology* 21.3: 434–45.
  1991 'The Atlantic Scottish Iron Age: five levels of chronology', *Proceedings of the Society of Antiquaries of Scotland* 121: 181–214.
  1991a 'Loch Olabhat', *Current Archaeology* 127: 284–87.
  1992 *The Later Prehistory of the Western Isles of Scotland* (Oxford: British Archaeological Reports [British Series], 221).
  1996 *The Archaeology of the Western Isles and Skye* (Edinburgh: Edinburgh University Press).

Armit, I. (ed.)
  1990 *Beyond the Brochs: Changing Perspectives on the Atlantic Scottish Iron Age* (Edinburgh: Edinburgh University Press).

Ashmore, P.J.
  1996 *Neolithic and Bronze Age Scotland* (London: Batsford).

Ashmore, P.J., B.A. Brayshay, K.L. Edwards, D.D. Gilbertson, J.P. Grattan, M. Kent, K.M. Pratt and R.E. Weaver
  1999 'Allochthonous and autochthonous mire deposits in relation to slope instability: palaeoenvironmental investigations in the Borve Valley, Barra, Outer Hebrides, Scotland', *The Holocene*, in press.

Badcock, A.
  1998 *Archaeological Watching Brief at Aird na-Ruibhe, Berneray, North Uist* (ARCUS Report 231d/e; Sheffield: ARCUS).

Baldwin, J.R.
  1996 'Heaps, humps and hollows on the Foula Skattald', in D. Waugh (ed.), *Shetlands Northern Links: Language and History* (Edinburgh: Scottish Society Northern Studies).

Barber, J.
  1985 *Insegall: The Western Isles* (Edinburgh: Donald).

Barber, J., P. Halstead, H. James and F. Lee
  1989 'An unusual Iron Age burial at Hornish Point, South Uist', *Antiquity* 63: 773–78.

Bennett, K.
  1994 *Annotated Catalogue of Pollen and Pteridophyte Spore Types of the British Isles* (http://www.kv.geo.uu.se/pc-intro.html).

Bennett, K., J. Fossitt, M. Sharp and V. Switsur
  1990 'Holocene vegetational and environmental history at Loch Lang, South Uist, Scotland', *New Phytologist* 114: 281–98.

Bennett, K.D.
  1984 'The Post-Glacial history of *Pinus sylvestris* in the British Isles', *Quaternary Science Reviews* 3: 133–56.

Beveridge, E.
  1911 *North Uist: Its Archaeology and Topography with Notes upon the Early History of the Outer Hebrides* (Edinburgh: Wiliam Brown).

Beveridge, E., and J.G. Callander
  1931 'Excavation of an earth house at Foshigarry and a fort, Dun Thomaidh, in North Uist', *Proceedings of the Society of Antiquaries of Scotland* 65: 299–357.

Bird, I.
  1866 'Pen and pencil sketches among the Outer Hebrides', *Leisure Hour* 15: 646–50, 668–69.

Birks, H.J.B., and B.J. Madsen
  1979 'Flandrian vegetational history of Little Loch Roag, Isle of Lewis, Scotland', *Journal of Ecology* 67: 825–842.

Blackburn, K.B.
  1946 'On a peat from the island of Barra, Outer Hebrides: data for the study of post-glacial history', *New Phytologist* 45: 44–49.

Boardman, S.
  1995 'Charcoal and charred plant macrofossils', in Branigan and Foster 1995: 149–57.

Boardman, S., and G. Jones
  1990 'Experiments on the effects of charring on cereal plant components', *Journal of Archaeological Science* 17: 1–11.

Boessneck, J.
  1969 'Osteological differences between sheep (*Ovies aries* Linne) and goat (*Capra capra* Linne)', in D. Brothwell and Higgs E. (eds.), *Science in Archaeology* (London: Thames & Hudson, 2nd edn): 331–58.

Bohnke, S.J.P.
  1988 'Vegetation and habitation history at the Callanish area, Isle of Lewis, Scotland', in H.H. Birks, H.J. Birks, B.P.E. Kaland and D. Moe (eds.), *The Cultural Landscape: Past, Present, Future* (Cambridge: Cambridge University Press): 445–61.

Bonsall, C.
  1997 'Coastal adaptation in the Mesolithic of Argyll', in Ritchie 1995: 25–37.

Boyd, J.M.
  1979 'The natural environment of the Outer Hebrides', *Proceedings of the Royal Society of Edinburgh* 77B: 3–19.

Boyd, J.M., and I.L. Boyd
  1990 *The Hebrides* (London: Collins).

Brain, C.K.
  1981 *The Hunters or the Hunted? An Introduction to African Cave Taphonomy* (Chicago: University of Chicago Press).

Bibliography

Branigan, K.
1994   'The giant cists of Glen Bretadale, Barra, Outer Hebrides', *Armchair Anthropologist* 1.1: 6–12.
1995   'The archaeological survey of the Tangaval peninsula', in Branigan and Foster 1995: 31-48.
1995a 'Sampling excavations on the Tangaval peninsula', in Branigan and Foster 1995: 161–86.
1995b 'Human settlement on the Tangaval peninsula', in Branigan and Foster 1995: 199–207.

Branigan, K., and P. Foster (eds.)
1995   *Barra: Archaeology on Ben Tangaval* (Sheffield: Sheffield Academic Press).

Branigan, K., and J. Grattan
1998   *Coastal Assessment Survey: Barra and Vatersay*, vols. I and II (Sheffield: Historic Scotland and University of Sheffield [archive report]).

Branigan, K., A. Newton and A. Dugmore
1995   'Pumice', in Branigan and Foster 1995: 144–48.

Brayshay, B.A.
1992   'The vegetation and the vegetational history of South Uist and Barra in the Outer Hebrides' (unpublished Ph.D thesis, University of Sheffield).

Brayshay, B., and K.J. Edwards
1996   'Late glacial and holocene vegetational history of South Uist and Barra', in Gilbertson *et al.* 1996: 13–26.

Bruck, J.
1995   'A place for the dead: the role of human remains in late Bronze Age Britain', *Proceedings of the Prehistoric Society* 61: 245–78.

Burl, A.
1976   *The Stone Circles of the British Isles* (London: Yale University Press).

Buxton, C.B.
1981   'The Archaeology of Mingulay Bay, Mingulay, Outer Hebrides' (unpublished BA dissertation, University of Durham).
1995   *Mingulay: An Island and its People* (Edinburgh: Birlinn).

Caird, J.B.
1979   'Land use in the Uists since 1800', *Proceedings of the Royal Society of Edinburgh* 77B: 505–26.

Campbell, E.
1991   'Excavation of a wheelhouse and other Iron Age structures at Sollas, North Uist, by R.J.C. Atkinson in 1957', *Proceedings of the Society of Antiquaries of Scotland* 121: 117–73.
1998a 'Spearhead', in N. Sharples, *Scalloway: A Broch, Late Iron Age Settlement and Medieval Cemetery in Shetland* (Cardiff Studies in Archaeology/Oxbow Monograph, 82; Oxford: Oxbow Books): 159.
1998b 'Metal pins', in N. Sharples, *Scalloway: A Broch, Late Iron Age Settlement and Medieval Cemetery in Shetland* (Cardiff Studies in Archaeology/Oxbow Monograph, 82; Oxford: Oxbow Books): 168–72.

Campbell, E., and J. Finlay
1991   'Ritual pit deposits of period B', in Campbell 1991: 141–47.

Cerón-Carrasco, R.
1994   'The investigation of fish remains from an Orkney farm mound', in W. Van Neer (ed.), *Fish Exploitation in the Past: Proceedings of the 7th Meeting of the ICAZ Fish Remains Working Group* (Tervuren: Annales du Musée Royall de l'Afrique Centrale, Sciences Zoologiques, No. 274).

Cerón-Carrasco, R., and M. Parker Pearson
1999   'The fish bones', in Parker Pearson and Sharples 1999: 274–82.

Chambers, W.
1866 'My holiday', *Chambers Journal* 1866: 632–33.

Clapham, A.R., T.G. Tutin and D.M. Moore
1989   *Flora of the British Isles* (Cambridge: Cambridge University Press, 3rd edn).

Clarke, A.
1989   'The skaill knife as a butchery tool', *Lithics* 10: 16–27.

Corbett, G.B., and S. Harris
1991   *The Handbook of British Mammals* (Oxford: Blackwell Science).

Crawford, B.
1987 *Scandinavian Scotland* (Leicester: Leicester University Press).

Crawford, I.A.
1977   *Excavation and Research at Coileagan An Udail, North Uist* Interim Report (Cambridge: Cambridge University).

Crone, A.
1993   'Excavation and survey of sub-peat features of Neolithic, Bronze Age and Iron Age date at Bharpa Carinish, North Uist, Scotland', *Proceedings of the Prehistoric Society* 59: 361–82.

Cunningham, P
1983   *Birds of the Outer Hebrides* (Perth: Melven).

Davidson, A. and I. Simpson
1994   'Soils and landscape history: case studies from the Northern Isles of Scotland', in S. Foster and T. Smout (eds.), *The History of Soils and Field Systems* (Aberdeen: Scottish Cultural Press): 66–74.

Davis, S.
1992   *A Rapid Method for Recording Information about Mammal Bones from Archaeological Sites* (London: English Heritage Ancient Monuments Laboratory Report 19/92).

Dey, J.
1991   *Out Skerries: An Island Community* (Lerwick: Shetland Times).

Dickens, A.
n.d. 'A study of the lithic assemblage from Alt Chrisal, Barra, Outer Hebrides' (unpublished dissertation, University of Sheffield).

Dickson, J.H.
1992   'North American driftwood, especially *Picea* (spruce) from archaeological sites in the Hebrides and Northern Isles of Scotland', *Review of Palaeobotany and Palynology* 73: 49–56.

Dimbleby, G.W.
1985   *The Palynology of Archaeological Sites* (London: Academic Press).

Downes, J.
1999   *Orkney Barrow Project Stage 3: Fieldwork and Education* (ARCUS Report 245c.1; Sheffield: Historic Scotland).

Downes, J., and A. Badcock
1998   *Archaeological Watching Brief and Excavations at the Screvan Quarry Site and Otternish, North Uist* (ARCUS Report 231c; Sheffield: ARCUS).

Driesch, A. von den
1976   *A Guide to the Measurement of Animal Bones from Archaeological Sites* (Boston, MA: Peabody Museum Bulletin 1).

Dubois, A., and D. Ferguson
1985   'The climatic history of pine in the Cairngorms based on radiocarbon dates and stable isotope analyses, with an account of the events leading up to its colonisation', *Review of Palaeobotany and Palynology* 46: 55–80.

Edwards, K.J.
1990   'Fire and the Scottish Mesolithic: evidence from microscopic charcoal', in P.M. Vermeersh and P. Van Peers (eds.), *Contributions to the Mesolithic in Europe* (Leuven: Leuven University Press): 71–79.

1996 'A Mesolithic of the Western and Northern Isles of Scotland? Evidence from pollen and charcoal', in Pollard, T. and A. Morrison (eds.), *The Early Prehistory of Scotland* (Edinburgh: Edinburgh University Press): 23–38.

Edwards, K.J., and G. Whittington
1997 'Vegetation history', in K.J. Edwards and I.B.M. Ralston (eds.), *Scotland: Environment and Archaeology, 8000 BC–AD 1000* (Chichester: John Wiley): 63–82.

1998 'Landscape and environment in prehistoric west mainland Shetland', *Landscape History* 20: 5–17.

Edwards, K.J., G. Whittington and K. Hirons
1995 'The relationship between fire and long-term wet heath development in South Uist, Outer Hebrides, Scotland', in D.B.A. Thompson, A. Hester and M.B. Usher (eds.), *Heaths and Moorlands: Cultural Landscapes* (Edinburgh: HMSO): 240–48.

Faegri, K., and J. Iversen
1989 *Textbook of Pollen Analysis* (Chichester: John Wiley, 4th edn).

Fairhurst, H.
1971 'The wheelhouse site at A' Cheardach Bheag on Drimore Machair, South Uist', *Glasgow Archaeological Journal* 2: 72–106.

Feacham, R.
1963 *A Guide to Prehistoric Scotland* (London: Batsford).

Finlay, J.
1984 'Faunal evidence for prehistoric economy and settlement in the Outer Hebrides to c. 400 AD' (unpublished PhD thesis, University of Edinburgh).

1991 'The animal bone', in Campbell 1991: fiche 1: D-3F10.

Fossitt, J.A.
1996 'The Quaternary vegetation of the Western Isles, Scotland', *New Phytologist* 132: 185–95.

Foster, P.
1995 'Excavations at Alt Chrisal 1989–94', in Branigan and Foster 1995: 49–160.

Foster, P., and R. Krivanek
1993 'The Anglo-Czech survey of the island of Berneray in the Outer Hebrides, Scotland', *Archeologicke Rozhledy* 45.3: 418–28.

Foster, S.
1990 'Pins, Combs and the Chronology of Later Atlantic Iron Age Settlement', in Armit, I. 1990a: 143–74.

Gearey, B., and D.D. Gilbertson
1997 'Pollen taphonomy of trees in a windy climate: Northbay Plantation, Barra, Outer Hebrides', *Scottish Geographical Magazine* 113: 113–20.

Gelling, P.
1985 'Excavations at Skaill, Deerness', in Renfrew, C. (ed.), *The Prehistory of Orkney* (Edinburgh: Edinburgh University Press): 176–82.

Getty, R.
1975 *Sisson and Grossman's The Anatomy of Domestic Animals* (Philadelphia, PA: W.B. Saunders Company, 5th edn).

Gibson, A.
1995 'The Neolithic pottery from Alt Chrisal', in Branigan, K. and P. Foster 1995: 100–15.

Gilbertson, D., and J. Grattan
1995 'The environment of the Tangaval Peninsula: physiography and the erosional status of cultural sites at the coast', in Branigan and Foster 1995: 5–15.

Gilbertson, D., J. Grattan and B. Pyatt
1996 'A reconnaisance of the potential coastal-erosion archaeological hazard on the islands of Barra, Vatersay, Sandray and Mingulay', in Gilbertson, Kent and Grattan 1996: 103–22.

Gilbertson, D., M. Kent and J. Grattan (eds.)
1996 *The Outer Hebrides: The Last 14,000 Years* (Sheffield: Sheffield Academic Press).

Gilbertson, D. *et al.*
1995 'The vegetation of the Tanagaval Peninsula: past and present', in Branigan and Foster 1995: 15–30.

Gilbertson, D.D., J.P. Grattan, B. Pyatt and J-L. Schwenninger
1996 'The Quaternary geology of the coasts of the islands of the Southern Outer Hebrides', in Gilbertson, Kent and Grattan 1996: 59–101.

Gilbertson, D.D., M. Kent, R.E. Weaver, P. Wathern, Y.L. Mulder, B.A. Brayshay and W.J. Gill
1995. 'The vegetation of the Tangaval Peninsula: present and past', in K. Branigan and P. Foster, *Barra. Archaeological Research on Ben Tangaval* (Sheffield: Sheffield Acadaemic Press): 15–30.

Gilbertson, D.D., J-L. Schwenninger, R.A. Kemp and E.J. Rhodes
1999 'Sand-drift and soil formation along an exposed north Atlantic coastline: 14,000 years of diverse geomorphological, climatic and human impacts', *Journal of Archaeological Science* 26: 439–69.

Giles, M., and M. Parker Pearson
1999 'Learning to live in the Iron Age', in B. Bevan (ed.), *Northern Exposures: Interpretative Evolution in the Iron Ages in Britain* (Leicester: School of Archaeological Studies): 217–232.

Gimingham, C.H.
1964 'Maritime and sub-maritime communities', in J.H. Burnett (ed.), *The Vegetation of Scotland* (Edinburgh: Oliver & Boyd).

1972 *Ecology of Heathlands* (London: Chapman & Hall).

Godwin, H.
1975 *History of the British Flora* (Cambridge: Cambridge University Press).

Grant, A.
1982 'The use of tooth wear as a guide to the age of domestic ungulates', in R. Wilson, C. Grigson and S. Payne (eds.), *Ageing and Sexing Animal Bones from Archaeological Sites* (Oxford: British Archaeological Reports [British Series], 109): 91–108.

Grant, J.W.
1979 'Cereal and grass production in Lewis and the Uists', *Proceedings of the Royal Society of Edinburgh* 77B: 567–75.

Grattan, J.P, D.D. Gilbertson and F.B. Pyatt
1996 'Geochemical investigations of environmental change in the Outer Hebrides', in D.D. Gilbertson, M. Kent and J.P. Grattan (eds.), *The Outer Hebrides: The Last 14,000 years* (Sheffield: Sheffield Academic Press): 27–43.

Grimm, E.C.
1991 *TILIA and TILIA-GRAPH* (Springfield: Illinois State Museum).

Haggerty, A.
1991 'Macrie Moor, Arran: recent excavations at two stone circles', *Proceedings of the Society of Antiquaries of Scotland* 121: 51-94.

Hall, A.
1996 'Quaternary geomorphology of the Outer Hebrides', in Gilbertson, D., M. Kent and J. Grattan 1996: 5–12.

Halstead, P.J.
1985 'A study of mandibular teeth from Romano-British contexts at Maxey', in F. Pryor and C. French (eds.), *Archaeology and Environment of the Lower Welland Valley*, vol. I (Norwich: East Anglian Archaeology 27): 219–24.

in press 'The mammal bones', in J. Barber *Bronze Age Farms and Iron Age Farm Mounds of the Outer Hebrides* (Edinburgh: Scottish Trust for Archaeological Research Monograph, 4).

Harman, M.
1997　*An Island Called Hirte: A History and Culture of St. Kilda to 1930* (Skye: Maclean Press).

Harvie-Brown, J., and T. Buckley
1888　*A Vertebrate Fauna of the Outer Hebrides* (Edinburgh: Douglas).

Hedges, J.W.
1987　*Bu, Guerness and the Brochs of Orkney*, vols. I–III (Oxford: British Archaeological Reports [British Series], 163–65).

Heinzel, H, R. Fitter and R. Parslow
1974　*The Birds of Britain and Europe* (London: Collins, 3rd edn).

Henshall, A.
1963　*The Chambered Tombs of Scotland*, vol. I (Edinburgh: Edinburgh University Press).
1972　*The Chambered Tombs of Scotland*, vol. II (Edinburgh: Edinburgh University Press).

Hill, J.D.
1995　*Ritual and Rubbish in the Iron Age of Wessex: A Study on the Formation of a Specific Archaeological Record* (Oxford: British Archaeological Reports [British Series], 242).

Hill, M.O.
1979　*DECORANA-A FORTRAN Program for Detrended Correspondance Analysis and Reciprocal Averaging* (Ithaca, NY: Cornell University).

Hillman, G.
1981　'Reconstructing crop husbandry practices from charred remains of crops', in R. Mercer (ed.), *Framing Practice in British Prehistory* (Edinburgh: Edinburgh University Press): 123–62.

Hingley, R.
1992　'Society in Scotland from 700 BC to AD 200', *Proceedings of the Society of Antiquaries of Scotland* 122: 17–63.

Hirons, K., and K.J. Edwards
1990　'Pollen and related studies at Kinloch, Isle of Rhum, Scotland, with particular reference to early human impacts on vegetation', *New Phytologist* 116: 715–27.

Historic Scotland
1999　*Burrowing Animals and Archaeology* (Technical Advice Note 16; Edinburgh: Historic Scotland).

Hodges, R.
1991　*Wall to Wall History* (London: Duckworth).

Hunter, J.
1991　'The multi-period landscape', in W. Hanson and E. Slater (eds.), *Scottish Archaeology: New Perspectives* (Aberdeen: Aberdeen University Press): 178–95.
1995　*The Making of the Crofting Community* (Edinburgh: John Donald).

Jolly, W.
1883　'The nearer St. Kilda: impressions of the island of Mingulay', *Good Words* 1883: 716–20.

Jones, A.K.G.
1987　*The Fish Bones from Baleshare and Hornish Point, North Uist* (unpublished report).

Jones, G.
in press　'Charred plant remains from Iron Age deposits at Baleshare and Hornish Point, Uist', in J. Barber, *Bronze Age Farms and Iron Age Farm Mounds of the Outer Hebrides* (Edinburgh: Scottish Trust for Archaeological Research Monograph, 4).

Jones, M.K.
1988　'The arable field: a botanical battleground', in M.K. Jones (ed.), *Archaeology and the Flora of the British Isles* (Oxford: Oxford University Committee for Archaeology Monograph, 14): 86–92.

Kent, M., B.A. Brayshay, D.D. Gilbertson, P. Wathern and R. Weaver
1994　'A biogeographical study of plant communities and environmental gradients on South Uist, Outer Hebrides, Scotland', *Scottish Geographical Magazine* 110: 85–99.

Kenward, H.E., A.R. Hall and A.K.G. Jones
1980　'A tested set of techniques for the extraction of plant and animal macrofossils from waterlogged deposits', *Science in Archaeology* 22: 3–15.

Kilbride-Jones, H.E.
1980　*Celtic Craftsmanship in Bronze* (London: Croom Helm).

Laing, L.
1974　*Orkney and Shetland: An Archaeological Guide* (Newton Abbot: David & Charles).

Lane, A.
1990　'Hebridean pottery: problems of definition, chronology, presence and absence', in Armit 1990: 108–30.

Lane, A., and T. Cowie
1997　'The pottery collections', in J. Crawford, 'Archaeological collections from sandhill sites in the Isle of Coll, Argyll and Bute', *Proceedings of the Society of Antiquaries of Scotland* 127: 467–511.

Last, J.
1998　'The residue of yesterday's existence: settlement space and discard at Miskovice and Bylany', in I. Pavlu (ed.), *Bylany: Varia 1* (Prague: Archeologicky Ustav Praha): 17–46.

LaTrobe-Bateman, E.
1999　'The Pottery', in Parker Pearson and Sharples 1999: 211–217.

Legg, C.J., E. Maltby and M.C.E. Proctor
1992　'The ecology of severe moorland fire on the North York Moors: seed distribution and seedling restablishment of *Calluna vulgaris*', *Journal of Ecology* 80: 737–52.

Lethbridge, T.
1952　'Excavations at Kilpheder, S. Uist and the problem of brochs and wheelhouses', *Proceedings of the Prehistoric Society* 18: 176–93.

Lewis, F.J.
1906　'The plant remains in the Scottish peat mosses II. The Scottish Highlands', *Transactions of the Royal Society of Edinburgh* 45: 335–60.
1907　'The plant remains in the Scottish peat mosses III. The Scottish Highlands and the Shetland Islands', *Transactions of the Royal Society of Edinburgh* 46: 33–70.

Lomax, T.M.
1997　'Holocene vegetation history and human impact in western Lewis, Scotland' (unpublished PhD thesis, University of Birmingham).

Mack, A.
1997　*Field Guide to the Pictish Symbol Stones* (Angus: Balgavies).

McDonald, R.A.
1997　*The Kingdom of the Isles* (Scottish Historical Revue Monograph No. 4; Edinburgh: Tuckwell Press).

McKay, M. (ed.)
1980　*The Reverend John Walker's Report on the Hebrides of 1764 and 1771* (Edinburgh: John Donald).

MacKie, E.W.
1965　'The origins and development of the broch and wheelhouse building cultures of the Scottish Iron Age', *Proceedings of the Prehistoric Society* 30: 93–146.
1974　*Dun Mhor Vaul: An Iron Age Broch on Tiree* (Glasgow: University of Glasgow).
1997　'Dun Mor Vaul revisited: fact and theory in the reappraisal of the Scottish Atlantic Iron Age', in Ritchie 1997: 141–80.

MacQueen, E.
1794 'Parish of Barray', in Sir John Sinclair (ed.), *The Old Statistical Account of Scotland*: XIII, 326–42.

Martin, M.
1994 *A Description of the Western Isles of Scotland* (Edinburgh: Birlinn [London, 1703]).

Mercer, R.
1972 'Micolithic and Bronze Age camps, 75–26 ft OD, North Carn, Isle of Jura', *Proceedings of the Society of Antiquaries of Scotland* 104: 1–22.

Morales, A., and K. Rosenlund
1979 *Fish Bone Measurements: An Attempt to Standardize the Measuring of Fish Bones from Archaeological Sites* (Copenhagen: Steenstrupia).

Mortimer, C., and D. Starley
1995 'Ferrous and non-ferrous metalworking', in J. Coles and S. Minnitt, *The Glastonbury Lake Village* (Exeter: Somerset Levels Project and Somerset County Council Museums Service): 138–41.

Muir, T
1885 *Ecclesiological Notes on Some of the Islands of Scotland* (Edinburgh: Douglas).

Mulder, Y.
1999 *Aspects of Vegetation and Settlement History in the Outer Hebrides, Scotland* (unpublished PhD thesis, University of Sheffield).

Mulville, J.
1999 'The mammal bones', in Parker Pearson and Sharples 1999: 234–74.
in press 'The role of Cetacea in prehistoric and historic Atlantic Scotland', *International Journal of Osteoarchaeology*.

Mulville, J., and M. Parker Pearson
n.d. 'The Late Bronze Age/earliest Iron Age house at Cladh Hallan, South Uist: excavations in 1995' (unpublished Report: University of Sheffield).

Munro, D.
1994 *A Description of the Western Isles of Scotland Called The Hybrides: An Account of 1549* (Edinburgh: Birlinn [1774]).
1994 'A Description of the Western Isles of Scotland', in M. Martin, *A Description of the Western Isles of Scotland* (Edinburgh: Birlinn, reprint of 1775 ed.): 481–526.

Munro, R.W.
1979 *Scottish Lighthouses* (Stornoway: Acair).

Neighbour, T.
1996 'Olcote, Breasclete Park, Callanish', *Discovery and Excavation in Scotland* 1996: 112–13.

Neustupný, E. (ed.)
1998 *Space in Prehistoric Bohemia* (Prague: Institute of Archaeology, Academy of Sciences of the Czech Republic).

O'Connor, T.P.
1988 'Bones from the General Accident site', in V.E. Black (ed.), *Archaeology of York* (London: Council for British Archaeology).

O'Kelly, M.
1958 'A wedge-shaped gallery grave at Island, Co. Cork', *Journal of the Royal Society of Antiquaries of Ireland* 88: 1–23.

O'Riordain, S.
1979 *Antiquities of the Irish Countryside* (London: Methuen).

O'Riordain, S., and G. O'Iceadha
1955 'Lough Gur excavations. The megalithic tomb', *Journal of the Royal Society of Antiquaries of Ireland* 85: 34f.

Ovrevik, S.
1985 'The second millennium BC and after', in C. Renfrew, (ed.), *The Prehistory of Orkney* (Edinburgh: Edinburgh University Press): 131–49.

Pankhurst, R.
1991 'The vegetation of the Outer Hebrides', in R. Pankhurst and M. Mullins (eds.), *Flora of the Outer Hebrides* (London: Natural History Museum): 38–48.

Pankhurst, R.J. and J.M. Mullin
1991 *Flora of the Outer Hebrides* (London: Natural History Museum Publications).

Parker Pearson, M., and N. Sharples
1999 *Between Land and Sea: Excavations at Dun Vulan, South Uist* (Sheffield: Sheffield Academic Press).

Parker Pearson, M., M. Giles and N. Sharples
1999 'The composition of the midden layers', in Parker Pearson and Sharples 1999: 104–6.

Parker Pearson, M., A. Brossler, P. Collins and A. Royles
1999 'The worked bone and antler assemblage', in Parker Pearson and Sharples 1999: 217–28.

Parker Pearson, M., N. Sharples, J. Mattes and A. Royles
1999a 'The stone tools', in Parker Pearson and Sharples 1999: 230–32.

Payne, S.
1969 'A metrical distinction between sheep and goat metacarpals', in P.J. Ucko and G.W. Dimbleby (eds.), *The Domestication and Exploitation of Plants and Animals* (London: Duckworth).
1973 'Kill off patterns in sheep and goats: the mandibles from Asvan Kale', *Anatolian Studies* 23: 281–303.

Peacock, J.D.
1984 'Quaternary geology of the Outer Hebrides', *Report of the British Geological Survey* 16: 1–26.
1991 'Glacial deposits of the Hebridean region', in J. Ehlers, P.L. Gibbard and J. Rose (eds.), *Glacial Deposits in Great Britain and Ireland* (Rotterdam: Balkema): 109–20.

PCRG (Prehistoric Ceramics Research Group)
1997 *The Study of Later Prehistoric Pottery: Guidelines for Analysis and Publication* (PCRG Occasional Paper, 2 (1995 revised 1997).

Phillips, A.M.
n.d. 'Iron Age site (NL56558345)' (unpublished Report, University College London).

Pratt, K.
1992 'Vegetational history of the upper Borve Valley, Barra, Outer Hebrides' (unpublished MSc dissertation, University of Sheffield).

RCHAMS
1928 *The Outer Hebrides, Skye and the Small Isles* (Edinburgh: HMSO).

Rees, S.
1979 *Agricultural Implements in Prehistoric and Roman Britain* (Oxford: British Archaeological Reports [British Series], 69).

Reid, M.
1989 'A room with a view: an examination of roundhouses with particular reference to northern Britain', *Oxford Journal of Archaeology* 8.1: 1–39.

Renfrew, C.
1974 *Investigations in Orkney* (London: Society of Antiquaries).

Ritchie, G. (ed.)
1997 *The Archaeology of Argyll* (Edinburgh: Edinburgh University Press).
1997 'Early settlement in Argyll', in Ritchie 1997: 38–60.
1997 'Monuments associated with burial and ritual in Argyll', in Ritchie, (Prehistoric Ceramics Research Group) 1997: 67–94.

Ritchie, W.
1979 'Machair development and chronology in the Uists and adjacent islands', *Proceedings of the Royal Society of Edinburgh* 77B: 107–22.

Rose, F.
1981   *The Wild Flower Key* (London: Warne).
Saville, A., and R. Miket
1994   'An Corran, Staffin, Skye', *Discovery and Excavation in Scotland* 1994: 40–41.
Scott, W.
1947   'The problem of the brochs', *Proceedings of the Prehistoric Society* 13: 1–37.
1948   'Gallo-British colonies: the aisled roundhouse culture in the North', *Proceedings of the Prehistoric Society* 14: 46–125.
1950   'Eliean an Tighe: a pottery workshop of the second millennium BC', *Proceedings of the Society of Antiquaries of Scotland* 85: 1–37.
Serjeantson, D.
1991   '"Rid grasse of bones": a taphonomic study of the bones from midden deposits at the Neolithic and Bronze Age site of Runneymede, Surrey', *International Journal of Osteoarchaeology* 1: 73–89.
1998   'Birds: a seasonal resource', *Environmental Archaeology* 3: 23–34.
Sharples, N.
1984   'Dalmore', *Current Archaeology* 91: 235.
Shepherd, I., and A. Tuckwell
1977   'Traces of Beaker period cultivation at Rosinish, Benbecula', *Proceedings of the Society of Antiquaries of Scotland* 108: 108–13.
Simpson, D.
1976   'The later Neolithic and Beaker settlement at Northton, Isle of Harris', in C. Burgess and R. Miket (eds.), *Settlement and Economy in the 3rd and 2nd Millenia BC* (Oxford: British Archaeological Reports, 33): 209–20.
Smith, H
1994   'Middening in the Outer Hebrides: an ethnoarchaeological investigation' (unpublished PhD thesis, University of Sheffield).
1996   'An investiagtion of site formation processes on a traditional Hebridean farmstead using environmental and geoarchaeological techniques', in Gilbertson, Kent and Gratton 1996: 195–206.
1999   'The plant remains', in Parker Pearson and Sharples 1999: 297–336.
Stace, C.
1997   *New Flora of the British Isles* (Cambridge: Cambridge University Press, 2nd edn).
Stevenson, A.C., and D.B.A. Thompson
1993   'Long term changes in heather moorland in upland Britain and Ireland: palaeoecological evidence for the importance of grazing', *The Holocene* 3: 70–76.
Stevenson, J.
1984   'The excavation of a hut circle at Cul a'Bhaile, Jura', *Proceedings of the Society of Antiquaries of Scotland* 114: 127–60.
Stevenson, R.B.K.
1955   'Pins and the chronology of brochs', *Proceedings of the Prehistoric Society* 21: 282–94.
Storå, J.
1994   'Åldersbedömning av Salben: En Relativ Fusioneringssekvens för Grönlandssal *Pagophilus groenlandicus* samt en Analys av Åldersstrkturen for Benmaterialet från Jettböle Stenåldersboplats på Åland' (unpublished undergraduate dissertation, Stockholm University).
Swanton, M.J.
1973   *The Spearheads of the Anglo-Saxon Settlements* (London: Royal Archaeological Institute).
Tabraham, C.
1977   'Excavations at Dun Carloway broch, Isle of Lewis', *Proceedings of the Society of Antiquaries of Scotland* 108: 156–67.

Thom, A.
1976   *Megalithic Sites in Britain* (Oxford: Clarendon Press).
Thomas, F.
1890   'On the duns of the Outer Hebrides', *Archaeology Scotica* 5.3: 365–415.
Topping, P.G.
1985   'Later prehistoric pottery from Dun Cul Bhuirg, Iona, Argyll', *Proceedings of the Society of Antiquaries of Scotland* 115: 199–209.
1987   'Typology and chronology in the later prehistoric pottery assemblages of the Western Isles', *Proceedings of the Society of Antiquaries of Scotland* 117: 67–84.
Turner, V.
1998   *Ancient Shetland* (London: Batsford).
Tylecote, R.
1986   *The Prehistory of Metallurgy in the British Isles* (London: Institute of Metals).
ul Haq, S.
1989   'Remains of mammalian fauna from Kildonan, South Uist, Outer Hebrides' (unpublished report, University of Sheffield).
Valamoti, T.
1989   'The plant remains from Kildonan Midden III: excavation season June 1989' (unpublished report, University of Sheffield).
Van der. Veen, M.
1987   *Crop Husbandry Regimes: An Archaeological Study of Farming in Northern England* (Sheffield: J.R. Collis Publications).
Weaver, R., M. Kent, D. Gilbertson, P. Wathern and B.A. Brayshay
1996   'The acidic and upland vegetation of the southern Outer Hebrides', in Gilbertson, Kent and Grattan 1996: 147–62.
Wedderspoon, J.
1915   'The shell middens of the Outer Hebrides', *Transactions of the Inverness Scientific Society and Field Club* 7 (1906–12): 322.
Wheeler, A.
1968   *The Fishes of the British Isles and North-West Europe* (London: Macmillan).
Whittington, G., and K.J. Edwards
1993   'Vegetation change on Papa Stour, Shetland, Scotland: a response to coastal evolution and human interference?', *The Holocene* 3: 54–62.
1997   'Evolution of a machair landscape: pollen and related studies from Benbecula, Outer Hebrides, Scotland', *Transactions of the Royal Society of Edinburgh Earth Sciences* 87: 515–31.
Whittington, G., and W. Ritchie
1988   *Flandrian Environmental Evolution of North-East Benbecula and Southern Grimsay, Outer Hebrides, Scotland* (Aberdeen: OÒDell Memorial Monograph, Department of Geography, University of Aberdeen).
Whittle, A.
1986   *Scourd of Brouster: an Early Agricultural Settlement in Shetland* (Oxford: Oxbow).
Wickham-Jones, C.J.
1990   *Rhum: Mesolithic and Later Sites at Kinloch, Excavations 1984–86* (Edinburgh: Society of Antiquaries of Scotland Monograph, 7).
1995   'Flaked stone tools', in Branigan and Foster 1995: 120–37.
Wilkins, D.A.
1984   'The Flandrian woods of Lewis (Scotland)', *Journal of Ecology* 72: 251–58.
Wilson, D., and D.G. Hurst
1966   'Medieval Britain in 1976', *Medieval Archaeology* 10: 168–214.

360

Wilson, D.G.

1984   'The carbonization of weed seeds and their repre-
        sentation in macrofossil assemblages', in W. van Zeist
        and W.A. Casparie (eds.), *Plants and Ancient Man:
        Studies in Palaeoethnobotany* (Rotterdam: Balkema):
        201–6.

Young, A.

1952   'An aisled farmhouse at the Allasdale, Isle of Barra',
        Proceedings of the Society of Antiquaries of Scotland
        87: 80–106.

1955   'Excavations at Dun Cuier, Isle of Barra, Outer
        Hebrides', *Proceedings of the Society of Antiquaries of
        Scotland* 89: 290–328.

1961   'Brochs and Duns', *Proceedings of the Society of
        Antiquaries of Scotland* 95: 171–99.

1966   'The sequence of Hebridean pottery', in A.L. Rivet
        (ed.), *The Iron Age in Northern Britain* (Edinburgh:
        Edinburgh University Press): 45–58.

Young, A., and K.M. Richardson

1959   'À Cheardach Mhor, Drimore, South Uist', *Proceedings
        of the Society of Antiquaries of Scotland* 93: 135–73.

Abbreviations

ARH	Atlantic Roundhouse
IA	Iron Age
NGR	National Grid Reference
NMS	National Museum of Scotland
OS	Ordnance Survey
RCAHMS	Royal Commission on the Ancient and Historical Monuments of Scotland